29th Italian Symposium on Advanced Database Systems (SEBD 2021)

Pizzo, Italy
5 - 9 September 2021

ISBN: 978-1-7138-3890-6

Printed from e-media with permission by:

Curran Associates, Inc.
57 Morehouse Lane
Red Hook, NY 12571

Some format issues inherent in the e-media version may also appear in this print version.

Printed by Curran Associates, Inc. (2022)

Edited by:
Sergio Greco
Maurizio Lenzerini
Elio Masciari
Andrea Tagarelli

Additional copies of this publication are available from:

Curran Associates, Inc.
57 Morehouse Lane
Red Hook, NY 12571 USA
Phone: 845-758-0400
Fax: 845-758-2633
Email: curran@proceedings.com
Web: www.proceedings.com

TABLE OF CONTENTS

REGULAR PAPERS

Preface of the 29th Italian Symposium on Advanced Database Systems

The twenty-ninth edition of the *Italian Symposium on Advanced Database Systems* (SEBD - Sistemi Evoluti per Basi di Dati) was organized by Università della Calabria, and held in Pizzo Calabro (Italy) from the 5th of September to the 9th of September 2021.

The symposium is the major annual event of the Italian database research community at large, as it is thought of as a gathering forum to meet, discuss and exchange experiences among all those, both in the academy and industry, who are interested in database systems and in all their broad range of applications.

The topics of SEBD 2021 covered the theoretical foundations, technology development, and real-world applications associated with database systems and related fields, including data integration, data inconsistency, NoSQL databases, knowledge management and ontologies, data mining, machine and deep learning, network analysis, cybersecurity.

The programme of SEBD 2021 was organized into 18 sessions of oral presentations of 61 papers accepted at the end of a peer-reviewed process, and authored by researchers from 28 Italian universities and research institutes, 8 Italian companies, and 16 foreign universities and companies. The programme also included 2 invited tutorials, 3 keynote speeches by Stefano Ceri (Politecnico di Milano), Phokion G. Kolaitis (University of California at Santa Cruz and IBM Research), and Carlo Zaniolo (University of California at Los Angeles), and a panel discussion on "The Past and the Future of Computer Science Theory" with the participation of four distinguished computer science theorists (Ronald Fagin, Georg Gottlob, Christos Papadimitriou and Moshe Vardi), who were interviewed by Giorgio Ausiello, Maurizio Lenzerini, Luigi Palopoli, Domenico Saccà, and Francesco Scarcello.

A joint seminar on "*Reminiscence of TIDB 1981*" was also held on the 9th of September, and organized in mixed online/in-presence sessions of invited lectures. Forty years ago, on September 13-19 of 1981, Gran Hotel San Michele hosted the progenitor of ICDT: the Advanced Seminar on Theoretical Issues in Databases (TIDB).

We would like to thank all the contributing speakers for making SEBD 2021 a great event, and we are grateful to the members of our Steering, Technical Program, and Local Organization Committees, as well as ICT-SUD and Calabriatour.net for timely providing their support in all of the organizational and technical aspects.

September 2021

Sergio Greco,
Maurizio Lenzerini,
Elio Masciari,
Andrea Tagarelli

SEBD 2021: The 29th Italian Symposium on Advanced Database Systems, September 5-9, 2021, Pizzo Calabro (VV), Italy

Keynote Speech: Storing and analyzing viral sequences through data-driven Genomic Computing – Abstract

Stefano Ceri[1]

[1]*Politecnico di Milano, P. Leonardo Da Vinci 32, 20133 Milano, Italy*

Abstract

The first part of the talk illustrates, in simple and data-inspired terms, what is a viral sequence, what are mutations, how mutated sequences become organized forming a "variant", what are the effects of individual mutations and of variants, how viral sequences are deposited to public repositories (GenBank, COGUK, GISAID). The second part of the talk presents the systems that were developed within my group, thanks to ERC and EIT funding. Specifically, I will illustrate (i) *ViruSurf*, a search system enabling free meta-data driven search over the integrated and curated databases, now hitting about 3 million SARS-CoV-2 sequences, continuously updated from the above repositories; (ii) *VirusViz*, a data visualization tool for comparatively analyzing query results; (iii) *VirusLab*, a tool for exploring user-provided viral sequences; (iv) *EpiSurf*, a tool for intersecting viral sequences with epitopes - used in vaccine design. I will also hint at ongoing projects for viral surveillance and for exploring a knowledge base of viral resources.

Keywords

viral sequences, SARS-CoV-2 viral genome, genomic computing

SEBD 2021: The 29th Italian Symposium on Advanced Database Systems, September 5-9, 2021, Pizzo Calabro (VV), Italy

stefano.ceri@polimi.it (S. Ceri)

Keynote Speech: Computational Social Choice and Incomplete Information – Abstract

Phokion G. Kolaitis[1]

[1]University of California Santa Cruz and IBM Research, Santa Cruz, CA 95064, USA

Abstract

Computational social choice is an interdisciplinary field that studies collective decision-making from an algorithmic perspective. Determining the winners under various voting rules is a mainstream area of research in computational social choice. Such rules assume that the voters provide complete information about their preferences, an assumption that is often unrealistic because typically only partial preference information is available. This state of affairs has motivated the study of the notions of the necessary winners and the possible winners with respect to a variety of voting rules.

In the first part of the talk, we will present an overview of results about the complexity of winner determination under incomplete information. In the second part of the talk, we will discuss the framework of election databases, a new framework that aims to create bridges between the computational social choice and the data management communities. An election database contains incomplete information about the preferences of voters (in the form of partial orders), alongside with standard database relations that provide contextual information. The availability of relational context enables the formulation of sophisticated queries about voting rules, candidates, winners, issues, and positions on issues. We will introduce the semantics of queries on election databases and explore their computational complexity.

Keywords

voting rules, complexity of winner determination under incomplete information, queries on election databases

SEBD 2021: The 29th Italian Symposium on Advanced Database Systems, September 5-9, 2021, Pizzo Calabro (VV), Italy

kolaitis@ucsc.edu (P. G. Kolaitis)

Keynote Speech: Scalable Algorithms and Big-Data Applications by Recursive SQL Queries with Aggregates: a Datalog-enabled approach – Abstract

Carlo Zaniolo[1]

[1]*University of California, Los Angeles, CA 90095, USA*

Abstract

The use of basic SQL aggregates in recursive queries enables programmers to employ query languages to develop complete big-data applications, including graph, machine learning and data mining applications. To achieve this goal, programmers must make sure that their SQL queries can be converted into equivalent Datalog programs that combine rigorous declarative semantics with very efficient and highly scalable fixpoint based semantics. Thus, our approach provides methods and tools to verify that (i) queries with recursive aggregate have Stable Model Semantics (SMS) and (ii) such SMS can be represented via a fixpoint-based computation that is conducive to bulk-synchronous and stale-synchronous parallelism. We also provide techniques to restructure queries that satisfy (i) but not (ii) into queries that satisfy both.

Keywords

Datalog programs, Recursive SQL queries, Stable Model Semantics (SMS)

SEBD 2021: The 29th Italian Symposium on Advanced Database Systems, September 5-9, 2021, Pizzo Calabro (VV), Italy

zaniolo@cs.ucla.edu (C. Zaniolo)

Tutorial: Machine and Deep Learning for Earth Observation: Advanced Approaches and Practical Use Cases – Abstract

Dino Ienco[1,3], Roberto Interdonato[2,3]

[1] *INRAE, TETIS, Montpellier, France*
[2] *Cirad, TETIS, Montpellier, France*
[3] *TETIS, Univ. of Montpellier, APT, Cirad, CNRS, INRAE, Montpellier, France*

Abstract

Nowadays, modern space missions continuously collect information about the earth surface that corresponds to massive amounts of data. The multitude of Earth Observation (EO) systems allows the acquisition of data via different sensors (e.g., optical, radar, LiDAR) at different spatial and temporal resolutions, with diverse spectral characteristics. This huge and diverse volume of information opens up new opportunities to better understand and monitor agricultural, natural and anthropized spaces at different scales.

In this context, data-intensive methodologies such as machine and deep learning approaches are demonstrating their value, as they already did in several domains dealing with signal data. Multiple data science challenges were already addressed using satellite imagery (e.g., building footprints, road networks, iceberg detection) but crucial open questions remain unsolved (e.g., biodiversity monitoring, urban mapping, deforestation tracking and food risk prevention, triaging disaster zones). We are at the beginning of a new era for the analysis of Earth Observation data (EOD) where one of the main questions is how to leverage the complementarity and the diversity of the information collected by the different available observation systems, in order to answer important societal challenges and monitor changes on the Earth Surface.

The MDL4EO team (Machine and Deep Learning for Earth Observation) at the UMR TETIS (Montpellier, France) has the objective to scientifically contribute to this new era providing AI methods and algorithms able to extract valuable knowledge from massive heterogeneous Earth Observation Data.

In this tutorial, we will discuss in detail the main research questions addressed by the MDL4EO team: How to exploit data streams of satellite Images (Satellite image Time Series) in order to characterize natural and agricultural areas? How to effectively combine multi-sensor and multi-scale information? How to transfer knowledge between different geographical areas?

It's time to fill the gap between Remote Sensing and AI. To this end, MDL4EO is working in that direction bringing together different expertises: Data Science, Computer Vision, Machine Learning, Remote Sensing and Geoinformatics. In this tutorial we will give an overview on how such interdisciplinary dynamics can be successfully exploited in an applied research context.

Keywords

Remote Sensing, Earth Observation Data, Deep Learning, Land Cover Classification

SEBD 2021: The 29th Italian Symposium on Advanced Database Systems, September 5-9, 2021, Pizzo Calabro (VV), Italy
dino.ienco@inrae.fr (D. Ienco); roberto.interdonato@cirad.fr (R. Interdonato)

Tutorial: Fairness and Neural Networks – Abstract

Roberto Esposito[1]

[1]Department of Computer Science, Università di Torino, Corso Svizzera 185, 10149, Torino, Italy

Abstract

Recent years have witnessed a Cambrian explosion of tools and techniques able to tackle problems that were only solvable by humans up to a few years ago; deep learning in particular is accumulating astounding successes at a breakneck pace in both research and applications: from helping in recovering photos by their descriptions on devices used by billions of people, to providing tools for investigating the depths of the visible universe. It is then unfortunate that these very models are utterly inscrutable and inaccessible to human understanding.

While in many cases the difficulty of understanding these models does not matter, in some very specific contexts it creates problems that are important and hard to solve. Big and small companies are, in fact, investing in these technologies and deploying them in contexts that directly impact human well-being such as loan applications, candidate selection for job offers, and evaluating the chance of re-offending for people who committed crimes. In all these cases using inscrutable models poses difficult ethical issues related to the risk of discrimination of people belonging to protected groups.

In absence of techniques allowing to solve the problem by explaining the decisions of these models, the fair ML literature focused on approaches based on the construction of non-discriminating models. In this context, neural networks provide both challenges and opportunities. In this tutorial I will contextualize the problem, show how there exists many different (and contrasting) definitions of fairness, and introduce some of the state-of-the-art approaches in this field. I will focus in particular on methods targeting neural networks, specifically on methods that constrain the representation learnt by the network to be fairer with respect to given sensible attributes.

Keywords

Fairness, Neural Networks, Representation Learning

SEBD 2021: The 29th Italian Symposium on Advanced Database Systems, September 5-9, 2021, Pizzo Calabro (VV), Italy

roberto.esposito@unito.it (R. Esposito)

Efficient Validation of Functional Dependencies during Incremental Discovery

Loredana Caruccio, Stefano Cirillo, Vincenzo Deufemia and Giuseppe Polese

Department of Computer Science, University of Salerno, via Giovanni Paolo II n.132, 84084 Fisciano (SA), Italy

Abstract

The discovery of functional dependencies (FDs) from data is facing novel challenges also due to the necessity of monitoring datasets that evolves over time. In these scenarios, incremental FD discovery algorithms have to efficiently verify which of the previously discovered FDs still hold on the updated dataset, and also infer new valid FDs. This requires the definition of search strategies and validation methods able to analyze only the portion of the dataset affected by new changes. In this paper we propose a new validation method, which can be used in combination with different search strategies, that exploits regular expressions and compressed data structures to efficiently verify whether a candidate FD holds on an updated version of the input dataset. Experimental results demonstrate the effectiveness of the proposed method on real-world datasets adapted for incremental scenarios, also compared with a baseline incremental FD discovery algorithm.

Keywords

Data Profiling, Functional Dependency, Incremental Discovery

1. Introduction

The usefulness of functional dependencies (FDs) has been widely demonstrated due to their application in several contexts, such as for cleaning data [1], evaluating the feasibility of classification models [2], and so forth. Although in the last decades many algorithms have been proposed for the automatic discovery of FDs from data, e.g., [3, 4, 5], they lack the capability of managing dynamic data. In this context, the set of discovered FDs should be kept consistent with the possible data changes over the time, e.g., by means of insert, update, and delete operations. As a consequence, incremental FD discovery algorithms have to adopt discovery strategies that limit the search of candidate FDs to specific parts of the search space according to previously discovered FDs.

Most of the incremental FD discovery algorithms existing in literature extend traditional FD search strategies with mechanisms that exploit the knowledge generated by the previous executions [6, 7]. However, none of these algorithms introduce optimizations in their validation methods aiming to consider data changes only.

SEBD 2021: The 29th Italian Symposium on Advanced Database Systems, September 5-9, 2021, Pizzo Calabro (VV), Italy
lcaruccio@unisa.it (L. Caruccio); scirillo@unisa.it (S. Cirillo); deufemia@unisa.it (V. Deufemia); gpolese@unisa.it (G. Polese)
0000-0002-6711-3590 (L. Caruccio); 0000-0003-0201-2753 (S. Cirillo); 0000-0002-6711-3590 (V. Deufemia); 0000-0002-8496-2658 (G. Polese)

Traditional validation methods, such as the partition-based ones, exploit the possibility to organize data into partitions according to attribute candidate sets, which will consistently be redefined by following a level-by-level search strategy. In this way, the validation can be performed by testing properties of partitions involved in each candidate FD [5]. Instead, row-based discovery algorithms directly derive candidate FDs by comparing attribute values for all possible combinations of tuples pairs, so implicitly inferring the validation of the FDs [4, 8].

In this paper, we propose an FD incremental discovery algorithm, named REXY (RegeX-based incremental discoverY), which includes a new validation method exploiting regular expressions (RegExs) to extract the subset of data affecting discovery results. It employs a compressed data representation, which limits the memory load and optimizes the data analysis. The incremental search strategy of REXY is based on an upward/downward candidate generation method based on the set of previously holding FDs without the need of exploring the complete search space. We experimentally evaluated REXY on 22 real-world datasets. In particular, we evaluated the effectiveness of the algorithm in its incremental identification of FDs using as performance benchmark the incremental algorithm described in [9]. The results demonstrate that REXY improves the time performances of a baseline algorithm of several orders of magnitude.

The remainder of the paper is organized as follows. Section 2 reviews the main discovery strategies and algorithms existing in the literature. Section 3 introduces the incremental discovery problem. Section 4 describes the proposed validation method and its integration in an incremental search strategy, whereas the whole discovery algorithm is reported in Section 5. Experimental results are discussed in Section 6, and conclusions are included in Section 7.

2. Related Work

In the literature several algorithms for the discovery of FDs from data have been defined. They are mainly devoted to the analysis of data from scratch, yielding specific methodologies to explore and prune the search space. In particular, column-based and row-based represent the two main strategies they follow.

Column-based strategies model the search space as an attribute lattice, which permits to consider candidate dependencies at each level in terms of lattice's edges, enabling the representation of the Left-Hand-Side (LHS) and the Right-Hand-Side (RHS) of an FD. After the generation of FD candidates at each level, it is necessary to validate each of them, entailing the evaluation of combination values or making the FD representations efficient, such as data partitions [3, 5, 10]. By following a level-by-level search strategy, column-based strategies exploit the possibility to progressively organize data, and to test the validation of a candidate FD by considering how data are collected into partitions. On the contrary, row-based strategies directly derive candidate FDs by analyzing all possible combinations of tuples pairs, aiming to derive two attribute subsets in terms of *agree-sets* or *difference-sets*, and entailing the automatic derivation of all holding FDs [4, 8]. In this case, the validation of an FD is implicitly inferred by the overall analysis over the set of data. Finally, in order to improve the efficiency of discovery algorithms, hybrid strategies have also been proposed [11, 12]. The latter calculate FDs on a randomly selected small subset of records (row-based), and validates the discovered FDs on the entire dataset, by focusing on a small subset of the search space determined by FD candidates and validation results (column-based).

In literature, there exist several FD discovery algorithms for incremental scenarios. In particular, one of the first algorithms exploits the concepts of tuple partitions and monotonicity of FDs to avoid the re-scanning of the database [7]. Another proposal is based on the concept of functional *independency*, through which the algorithm maintains the set of FDs updated over time [13]. Finally, the DynFD algorithm is able to discover and maintain FDs in dynamic datasets [6]. In particular, it extends an aforementioned hybrid strategy, by continuously adapting the FD validation structures according to a batch of insert, update, and delete data operations. With respect to these incremental approaches, REXY uses a new validation method that focuses the verification of candidate FDs only on the subset of data affected by the data changes. This can improve the efficiency of FD discovery in incremental scenarios.

3. Incremental discovery of Functional Dependencies

Functional Dependencies (FDs) express relationships between attributes of a database relation. An FD $X \rightarrow Y$ states that the values of an attribute set Y are uniquely determined by the values of X. More Formally, given a relation schema R, an FD over R is a statement $X \rightarrow Y$ (X determines Y), with $X, Y \subseteq attr(R)$, such that, given an instance r over R, $X \rightarrow Y$ is satisfied in r if and only if for every pair of tuples (t_1, t_2) in r, whenever $t_1[X] = t_2[X]$, then $t_1[Y] = t_2[Y]$. X and Y are also named Left-Hand-Side (LHS) and Right-Hand-Side (RHS) of an FD, respectively. The latter is said to be *non-trivial* if and only if $X \supseteq Y$, and *minimal* if and only if there is no attribute $B \in X$ such that $X \backslash B \rightarrow Y$ is also an FD holding on r. For sake of simplicity and w.l.o.g, in the rest of the paper we assume that Y consists of a single attribute.

In general, the FD discovery problem aims at finding a set of all *minimal* FDs holding on a relation instance r. It entails searching for a partition of tuples sharing the same values on RHS attributes whenever they share the same value on LHS attributes [14]. To do this, it is possible to first generate FD candidates, and then verifying their validity and minimality, yielding a column-based strategy.

Column-based strategies model the search space as a graph representation of a lattice, which contains a collection of attribute sets, where *Level 0* maps the empty set, *Level 1* singleton sets, one for each attribute, *Level 2* the pair sets, one for each possible combination of two attributes, and so forth. Finally, the last level, namely *Level M*, will contain a single set of all the attributes from R. It permits to consider candidate FDs at each level in terms of edges. For instance, the edge highlighted in blue in Figure 1 defines the candidate FD $B \rightarrow D$.

The validation process of column-based strategies performs simple computations on the cardinalities of the partitions calculated over attribute combinations, which correspond to the lattice nodes. This process is particularly efficient when it is possible to follow a level-by-level search strategy from *Level 1* to *Level M*, and to gradually construct partitions over ever-increasing attribute set sizes. This could not be guaranteed when it is necessary to explore the search space with different starting points, such as a set of FDs.

Incremental scenarios require to update a set of minimal FDs Σ_τ discovered over data collected until time τ according to the set of tuple modifications $D_{\tau+1}$ at time $\tau+1$. This yields the necessity to (re)-consider all FDs in Σ_τ, and possibly generates new FD candidates according to validation

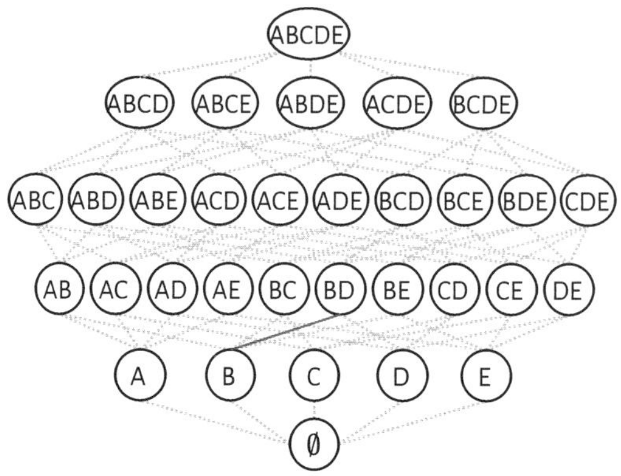

Figure 1: The lattice search space representation for the attribute set {A,B,C,D,E}.

results. In fact, the addition of a new tuple can entail the *invalidation* of a previously holding FD, whereas the deletion of a tuple can entail to a previously holding FD be no longer *minimal*. More formally, let $X \rightarrow A$ be an FD holding at time τ, and t a tuple yielding a dataset modification, then we need to consider the following effects:

- **Invalidation**: when a tuple t is added, it could produce the invalidation of $X \rightarrow A$ at time $\tau + 1$. Consequently, one or more FD candidates on the next lattice level having the same RHS and a superset of its LHS could be validated. Thus, it is necessary to consider all possible FD candidates $XB \rightarrow A$ such that $B \notin X$ and $B \neq A$.
- **Minimality**: when a tuple t is removed, $X \rightarrow A$ could be no longer minimal at time $\tau + 1$. Consequently, one or more FD candidates on the previous lattice level having the same RHS and a subset of its LHS could be validated, yielding a minimal FD. Thus, it is necessary to consider all possible FD candidates $X \setminus B \rightarrow A$ such that $B \in X$.

Notice that, a tuple update can always be managed as the deletion of the stored tuple and the subsequent addition of the tuple containing the modified values.

Invalidation and minimality checks determine how FD candidate should be generated and managed throughout the search space according to previously holding FDs and validation results. This entails moving the focus on different parts of the search space, by focusing the attention on a subset of data characterized by specific candidate FDs under analysis. Thus, we propose a new validation method based on RegExs, which checks how modified data entail some violations, and/or verifies the minimality of a candidate FD.

4. The RegEx-based validation method

In this section, we first describe the compressed data structures used to optimize the time and space usage of the discovery algorithm. Then, we introduce the new RegEx-based validation method, and how it can be adopted within an incremental FD discovery process.

	Identif (A)	River (B)	Location (C)	Erected (D)	Purpose (E)	Length (F)	Lanes (G)	Clear-G (H)	T-Or-D (I)	Material (J)	Span (K)	Rel-L (L)	Type (M)
t_1	E22	A	24	1876	Highway	1200	4	G	Through	Wood	Short	S	Wood
t_2	E26	M	12	1883	RR	1150	2	G	Through	Steel	Medium	S	Simple-T
t_3	E28	M	3	1884	Highway	1000	2	G	Through	Steel	Medium	S	Arch
t_4	E31	M	8	1887	RR	1161	2	G	Through	Steel	Medium	S	Simple-T
t_5	E34	O	41	1888	RR	4558	2	G	Through	Steel	Long	F	Simple-T
t_6	E35	A	27	1890	Highway	1000	2	G	Through	Steel	Medium	F	Simple-T

(a) Before the mapping step.

	Identif (A)	River (B)	Location (C)	Erected (D)	Purpose (E)	Length (F)	Lanes (G)	Clear-G (H)	T-Or-D (I)	Material (J)	Span (K)	Rel-L (L)	Type (M)
t_1	1	1	1	1	1	1	1	1	1	1	1	1	1
t_2	2	2	2	2	2	2	2	1	1	2	2	1	2
t_3	3	2	3	3	1	3	2	1	1	2	2	1	3
t_4	4	2	4	4	2	4	2	1	1	2	2	1	2
t_5	5	3	5	5	2	5	2	1	1	2	3	2	2
t_6	6	1	6	6	1	3	2	1	1	2	2	2	2

(b) After the mapping step.

Table 1: Snippet of *Bridges* to illustrate validation and discovery strategies.

4.1. Compressed data structures

Before introducing the new validation method, it is necessary to provide details about its data structures. In particular, in order to minimize the memory load, we represent a dataset by using lightweight references to its tuples without losing significance. To do this, we map each attribute data to a unique numeric value, which allows to efficiently identify data changes. In particular, whenever new tuples are added to the dataset, their values are mapped into their corresponding numerical values. This representation leads to a fast tuple comparison during the FD discovery process, and permits to create RegExs in a simple way, avoiding character encoding issues.

Example 1. Let us consider the snippet of the *Bridges* dataset in Table 1(a) containing 13 attributes. As shown in Table 1(b), after the mapping phase, each value has been mapped to a unique ID for each attribute. Let us now consider the insertion of the following two tuples in the *Bridges* dataset:

t_7	E37	M	18	1891	RR	1350	2	G	Through	Steel	Medium	S	Simple-T
t_8	E34	O	41	1888	RR	4558	2	G	Through	Steel	Long	F	Simple-T

then each of these values is parsed according to the previous values of the dataset, and mapped to the following two tuples:

t_7	7	2	7	7	2	6	2	1	1	2	2	1	2
t_8	5	3	5	5	2	5	2	1	1	2	3	2	2

Although this data representation allows us to quickly retrieve information, it is necessary to define a new structure to support the validation step of candidate FDs. To this end, we exploit a hashmap, namely RegExHashMap, whose keys are unique ID combinations, whereas the associated values correspond to the number of their occurrences in the dataset. In this way, it is possible to avoid duplicate entries and to quickly perform insertion and/or removal operations.

Example 2. Let us consider Example 1, where the mapped tuples t_7 and t_8 should be inserted in Table 1(b). Thus, for t_7 the ID "7, 2, 7, 7, 2, 6, 2, 1, 1, 2, 2, 1, 2" is inserted into the RegExHashMap as key, whose associated value is set to 1, since no other tuples in Table 1(b) contains the same values of t_7. Instead, for t_8 the key "5, 3, 5, 5, 2, 5, 2, 1, 1, 2, 3, 2, 2" is already included into the RegExHashMap, then the associated value is set to 2, since tuple t_8 is equal to t_5, yielding to two occurrences of the same key.

4.2. Validation approach

An efficient discovery methodology should permit to quickly validate candidate FDs on the set of data under analysis, and ensure high adaptability to possible data changes. The proposed validation method relies on RegExs and exploits the RegExHashMap for fast retrieval operations. In particular, let $\varphi : X \rightarrow A$ a candidate FD over a dataset D. The proposed approach aims to create a RegEx ρ to validate φ over D. For sake of clarity, we describe the creation of ρ by considering a new tuple t. However, this strategy could be easily adapted to consider a large number of new tuples by chaining different RegExs.

The validation algorithm considers the projection of attributes in X and A onto the tuple t to select value combinations that must be considered into the validation process. More specifically, to validate φ, it is necessary to create a RegEx for the attribute set $X = X_1, X_2, \ldots, X_k$ by considering $t[X_1], t[X_2], \ldots, t[X_k]$, in the following way:

$$\rho_{LHS} = \texttt{t[}B_1\texttt{][,]([0-9]}^*\texttt{[,])}^*\texttt{t[}B_2\texttt{][,]([0-9]}^*\texttt{[,])}^*\ldots\texttt{([0-9]}^*\texttt{[,])}^*\texttt{t[}B_k\texttt{]}$$
$$\rho_{RHS} = \texttt{(?!.}^*\texttt{t[}A\texttt{]).+}$$
$$\rho_\varphi = \texttt{([0-9]}^*\texttt{[,])}^*\rho_{LHS}\texttt{([,][0-9]}^*\texttt{)}^*\rho_{RHS}\texttt{([,][0-9]}^*\texttt{)}^*$$

We can notice that ρ_{LHS} contains comma character as separator, whereas each value could be followed from zero or more numeric characters, i.e., $[0-9]^*$, representing all the possible IDs for the attributes that are not in φ. In fact, one of the strengths of this approach is to avoid considering specific values for attributes that must not be considered during the validation step. Similarly to the LHS, it is necessary to define a RegEx for the RHS, i.e., ρ_{RHS}. To this end, we can define ρ_{RHS} as the negative look ahead of $t[A]$ (i.e., all values not equal to $t[A]$), so enabling to consider only the tuples in which $t[A]$ does not appear. The combination of ρ_{LHS} and ρ_{RHS} allows us to define a new RegEx ρ_φ to validate the candidate φ after the insertion of t. In this way, it is possible to verify if there exists at least one key in the RegExHashMap satisfying ρ_φ.

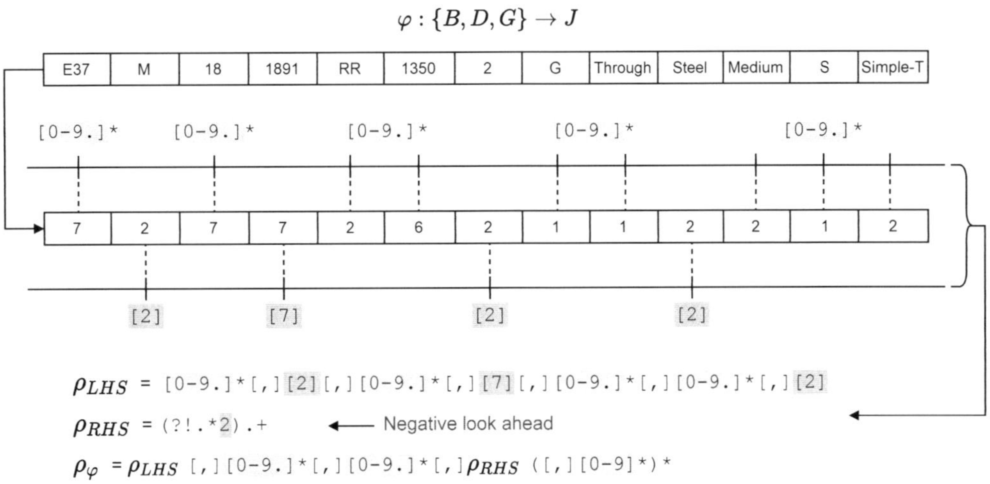

Figure 2: An example of RegEx creation for *Bridges* dataset.

Example 3. Let us consider the snippet dataset in Table 1(b), a candidate FD $\varphi : \{B, D, G\} \rightarrow J$, and the new tuple t_7 defined in Example 1. The validation algorithm should verify if this new tuple leads to the invalidation of φ, according to the strategy defined above. To this end, it is necessary to define the RegEx ρ_φ to validate φ shown in Figure 2. We can observe that the validation approach permits to consider the new value $t_7[B]$, $t_7[D]$, and $t_7[G]$ for the attributes B, D, and G, while it considers a generic numeric value (i.e., $[0-9]^*$) for the remaining attributes. As a consequence, the regex ρ_{LHS} has been defined as shown in Figure 2. We can notice that ρ_{LHS} allows the validation strategy to check if already exists at least one tuple in the dataset with the same value for the attributes B, D, and G. However, it is necessary to define the regex ρ_{RHS} for the attribute J by exploiting the negative look ahead of $t_7[J]$, in order to check if exist at least one key in the RegExHashMap with the same value for the attributes B, D, and G, but a different value for J.

4.3. An incremental search strategy

The proposed validation method can be used in any discovering strategy that, by working incrementally, can properly define FD candidates to be validated. In particular, the algorithm REXY uses a version of the algorithm described in [15], adapted for incrementally managing any kind of data changes. In particular, given a dataset D at time τ, REXY considers the set of FDs holding at time τ, denoted as Σ_τ, as starting points, and collect them in a hash map ordered by LHS cardinality [15]. Then, it follows a bottom-up search strategy by considering Σ_τ as the set of candidate FDs, and by validating each of them according to the validation method described above. Consequently, given a candidate FD φ, REXY performs a *downward* discovery step when a tuple is removed or φ is a novel candidate (i.e., $\varphi \notin \Sigma_\tau$). It consists in the generalization of the candidate φ performed by iteratively removing one attribute on its LHS, until REXY meets a valid FD in the lower levels. Conversely, when a new tuple is added and φ is not valid, an *upward* discovery step is accomplished in order to find the possible new holding FDs. It consists in the specialization of φ performed by adding a new attribute on its LHS.

The usage of an ordered hash map into a bottom-up search strategy permits to reuse the analysis performed at the previous levels, and forward the validation of newly generated candidate FDs to the next level, yielding an optimization in the pruning of the search space.

5. The REXY Algorithm

The main procedure of REXY is shown in Algorithm 1. Given a set of minimal FDs Σ_τ valid at time τ, the set of tuples $D_{\tau+1}$ updating D at time $\tau + 1$, and an instance of the RegExHashMap Λ_τ at time τ, the main procedure of REXY starts the discovery process by considering Σ_τ as the set of candidate FDs. In particular, REXY performs a discovery step in ascending order by the LHS cardinalities of Σ_τ (line 3) and extracts all the candidate FDs from Σ_τ with a specific LHS cardinality (line 4). Then, for each of them, it checks if the candidate $\varphi : X \rightarrow A$ is still valid after the updating of the dataset according to the validation approach defined in Section 4.2 (line 6). If the analyzed FD is not valid at time $\tau + 1$, the procedure first removes it from the set of the analyzed candidates (line 7), and then generates new candidate FDs at a higher lattice level (line 8), by discarding those that can be inferred from other FDs already validated at time $\tau + 1$ (lines 9-10). On the other hand, if the analyzed FD is still valid at time $\tau + 1$, REXY tries to find if there exist other FDs at a lower lattice level (line 12) that have been validated after update operations (lines 13-18). At the end of each iteration, the procedure removes all the FDs that are not minimal at time $\tau + 1$ w.r.t. the FDs already validated in the previous iterations (line 19). Finally, RegExHashMap is updated with the new tuples (line 20), and the procedure returns a new set of minimal and valid FDs at time $\tau + 1$ (line 21).

The validation procedure of REXY is shown at the bottom of Algorithm 1. Given a candidate FD $\varphi : X \rightarrow A$ at time $\tau + 1$, an instance of the RegExHashMap Σ_τ at time τ, and the set of the new tuples $D_{\tau+1}$ at time $\tau + 1$, the procedure creates a new RegEx for each new tuple in $D_{\tau+1}$, in order to check the validation of the candidates on the updated dataset. In particular, the procedure starts by analyzing each new tuple in $D_{\tau+1}$ (line 24). Then, for each of them, REXY defines a new RegEx according to the approach defined in Section 4.2. More specifically, for each attribute B in *attr*(R), if B does not belong to the attributes of φ, the procedure adds to ρ_φ a generic value (lines 28-30). On the other hand, if B belongs to the attributes on the LHS, then the procedures add to the final RegEx ρ_φ the corresponding value for the analyzed tuple $t[B]$ (line 32). Otherwise, if none of the previous cases is verified, the attribute B belongs to the RHS, so the procedure adds to ρ_φ the negative look ahead of this value (line 33). After the creation of the RegEx ρ_φ, REXY checks if exists at least a tuple in the RegExHashMap that matches this RegEx. If true, it means that φ is not valid on the dataset at time $\tau + 1$, since there exists at least one pair of tuples that invalidate φ (line 35). Otherwise, if the previous case is never verified for any other tuple, it means that the candidate is valid at time $\tau + 1$ (line 36).

It is worth notice that, while the implementation of REXY considers several code optimizations and takes advantage of the defined data structures, for sake of clarity, the pseudo-codes of Algorithm 1 do not show such optimizations. They mainly guarantee that each possible candidate FD is validated at most once.

Algorithm 1: Main Procedures of REXY

Input: A set Σ_τ of minimal FDs at time τ; Updated tuples $D_{\tau+1}$ for the dataset D at time $\tau + 1$; An instance of the RegExHashMap Γ_τ at time τ

Output: The set of new minimal FDs at time $\tau + 1$, i.e., $\Sigma_{\tau+1}$

Function MAIN_PROCEDURE:
    $\Sigma_{\tau+1} \leftarrow \emptyset$
    for c **in** $[\ 1, \dots, |attr(R)|\ ]$ **do**
        $\Sigma_c \leftarrow \Sigma_\tau$.CARDINALITY_FILTER($c$)
        for ***each*** $X \rightarrow A \in \Sigma_c$ **do**
            if *VALIDATION_REGEX*($X \rightarrow A, \Gamma_\tau, D_{\tau+1}$) ***is False*** **then**
                $\Sigma_c \leftarrow \Sigma_c \backslash X \rightarrow A$
                $\Sigma_s \leftarrow$ SPECIALIZE_CANDIDATE($X \rightarrow A$)
                for ***each*** $\{Z \rightarrow A\} \in \Sigma_s$ **do**
                    if *IS_MINIMAL*($\{Z \rightarrow A\}, \Sigma_\tau$) ***is True*** **then**
                        $\Sigma_\tau \leftarrow \Sigma_\tau \cup \{Z \rightarrow A\}$
            else
                $\Sigma_g \leftarrow$ GENERALIZE_CANDIDATE($X \rightarrow A$)
                for ***each*** $\{W \rightarrow A\} \in \Sigma_g$ **do**
                    if *VALIDATION_REGEX*($\{W \rightarrow A\}, \Gamma_\tau, D_{\tau+1}$) ***is False*** **then**
                        $\Sigma_g \leftarrow \Sigma_g \backslash \{W \rightarrow A\}$
                    $\Sigma_g \leftarrow \Sigma_g \cup$ GENERALIZE_CANDIDATE($\{W \rightarrow A\}$)
                $\Sigma_c \leftarrow \Sigma_c \cup \Sigma_g$
        if $|\Sigma_c| > 0$ **then** $\Sigma_{\tau+1} \leftarrow \Sigma_{\tau+1} \cup$ MINIMALITY_CHECK($\Sigma_{\tau+1}, \Sigma_c$)
    $\Gamma_{\tau+1} \leftarrow \Gamma_{\tau+1} \cup D_{\tau+1}$ // Updating of the RegExHashMap
    return $\Sigma_{\tau+1}$

Function VALIDATION_REGEX($X \rightarrow A, \Gamma_\tau, D_{\tau+1}$):
    $\rho_\varphi \leftarrow \emptyset$
    for ***each*** $t \in D_{\tau+1}$ **do**
        ATTRS $\leftarrow attr(R)$
        for c **in** $[\ 1, \dots, |attr(R)| - 1\ ]$ **do**
            $B \leftarrow$ATTRS$[i]$
            if $B \notin X \wedge B \neq A$ **then**
                if $i == 0$ **then** $\rho_\varphi \leftarrow \rho_\varphi \cup ([0-9]^*[,])^*$
                else $\rho_\varphi \leftarrow \rho_\varphi \cup ([,][0-9]^*)^*$
            else
                if $B \in X$ **then** $\rho_\varphi \leftarrow \rho_\varphi \cup t[B]$
                else if $B \in A$ **then** $\rho_\varphi \leftarrow \rho_\varphi \cup (?!.^*t[B]).+$
                if $i < |ATTRS| - 1$ **then** $\rho_\varphi \leftarrow \rho_\varphi \cup [,]$
            if Γ_τ.*EXIST_MATCHING*(ρ_φ) ***is True*** **then return False**
    return True

6. Experimental results

REXY has been developed in Java 15. The execution tests have been performed on an iMac with an Intel Xeon processor at 3.40 GHz, 36-core, and 128GB of RAM. Furthermore, in order

#	Dataset	Cols [#]	Rows [#]	FDs [#]	Exec (Avg) [ms]	Validations [#]	Validations (Min) [ms]	Validations (Max) [ms]	Validations (Avg) [ms]	Memory [MB]
1	Iris	5	150	4	1	766	11	12	12	95
2	Balance-scale	5	625	1	1	1330	8	38	13	100
3	Bupa	6	345	16	18	6979	11	36	14	120
4	Appendicitis	7	107	72	39	7890	9	37	23	116
5	Chess	7	2000	6	2	17142	13	13	13	39
6	Abalone	9	4148	137	335	705498	12	33	18	114
7	Nursey	9	12960	1	82	59137	5	18	16	121
8	Tic-tac-toe	9	958	9	28	14613	5	6	5	122
9	Glass	10	214	123	140	28138	14	21	18	117
10	Cmc	10	1473	1	13	17832	20	31	24	138
11	Yeast	10	1484	50	12	95531	11	11	11	46
12	Breast-cancer	11	699	46	175	56269	8	15	11	66
13	Fraud-detection	11	28000	48	1482	1723242	5	230	207	414
14	Poker-hand	11	264000	1	19	2401240	9	12	10	156
15	Echocardiogram	13	132	538	160	65932	8	13	8	59
16	Bridges	13	108	142	153	34017	11	31	11	94
17	Australian	14	690	535	374	501588	10	26	12	124
18	Adult	15	32560	60	281	3747386	8	23	12	803
19	Tax	15	6848	310	7038	2378734	10	532	287	202
20	Lymphography	19	147	2730	71844	5156312	14	34	20	4921
21	Hepatitis	20	155	8250	194553	4528681	11	170	126	48878
22	Parkinson	24	195	1724	524195	874789	16	16470	10492	127

Table 2: Details of the considered real-world datasets and REXY performances.

to ensure proper executions of REXY on the considered datasets, the Java memory heap size allocation has been set to 100GB.

Table 2 summarizes the time performances of REXY on 22 real-world datasets varying in the number of rows and columns[1]. In our experimental session, we simulate a scenario of continuous insertions of tuples by considering one tuple at a time. This allowed us to deeply analyze the performances of the validation process on each candidate FD. More specifically, Table 2 reports the minimum, the maximum, and the average times of the validation process for each dataset. We also report the number of resulting FDs and the number of validations performed at the end of the last execution of REXY on each dataset.

The results highlight that the average execution time is almost always less than 10 seconds, except for the *Lymphography*, *Hepatitis*, and *Parkinsons* datasets. This is probably due to the large number of FD invalidated during the discovery process, possibly leading to a larger number of new candidates to be validated. Concerning the validation process, the average time of this process is almost always less than 25 milliseconds per FD, and the maximum time almost never exceeds 40 milliseconds, except for the *Fraud-detection*, *Tax*, *Hepatitis*, and *Parkinsons* datasets. Despite these time peaks, the average times demonstrate that such values can be considered as outliers. In general, although execution times increase when the number of attributes increases, on average they remain low for validating each candidate FD.

We performed a comparative evaluation of REXY with respect to the incremental FD discovery algorithm presented in [9] (baseline). In particular, both the algorithms follow the same search strategy, but differ on how they organize data, also yielding to completely different validation methods. Thus, the comparison allowed us to highlight the improvements in terms of execution times of the proposed validation strategy with respect to the traditional partition-based used in

[1]The datasets are available on: https://github.com/DastLab/TestDataset

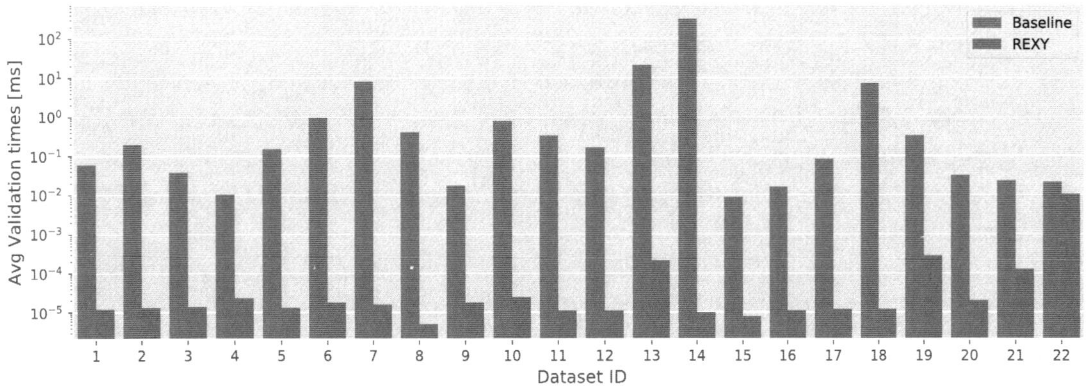

Figure 3: Validation times of REXY and the baseline algorithm proposed in [9].

[9]. Figure 3 shows time performances on average of both algorithms on the 22 datasets. We can notice that, REXY outperforms the baseline algorithm with several orders of magnitude, ranging from 2 to 7, except for the *Parkinson* dataset for which the baseline takes advantage from a caching strategy that allows to reuse the computation performed in the previous iterations.

In general, partition-based validation strategies, such as the one included in [9], are particularly efficient when a complete discovery process has to be performed, since partitions can be incrementally computed following a level-by-level bottom-up search strategy. However, the incremental scenario requires the discovery process to browse the search space starting from the previously holding FDs (i.e., not all FD candidates have to be considered in each level). Thus, the proposed validation method is able to perform the verification without having the necessity to compute sparse partitions, yielding faster execution times as can be noted in the discussed experimental results.

7. Conclusion

In this paper we presented REXY, an incremental algorithm for FD discovery. It exploits a new Regex-based validation method to efficiently select tuples affected by dataset updates. REXY follows an incremental strategy to explore the search space based on the previously holding FDs. Experimental results over real-world datasets show that REXY can efficiently update the set of holding FDs, without having the necessity to execute algorithms from scratch. In the future, we would like to include REXY in a visual monitoring tool [16], and extend it for updating Relaxed Functional Dependencies [17] in incremental scenarios.

References

[1] X. Chu, I. F. Ilyas, P. Papotti, Holistic data cleaning: Putting violations into context, in: Proc. of IEEE International Conference on Data Engineering, 2013, pp. 458–469.
[2] M. Le Guilly, J.-M. Petit, V.-M. Scuturici, Evaluating classification feasibility using func-

tional dependencies, in: Transactions on Large-Scale Data-and Knowledge-Centered Systems XLIV, Springer, 2020, pp. 132–159.
[3] Z. Abedjan, P. Schulze, F. Naumann, DFD: Efficient functional dependency discovery, in: Proc. of the 23rd ACM International Conference on Information and Knowledge Management, 2014, pp. 949–958.
[4] P. A. Flach, I. Savnik, Database dependency discovery: A machine learning approach, AI communications 12 (1999) 139–160.
[5] Y. Huhtala, J. Kärkkäinen, P. Porkka, H. Toivonen, TANE: An efficient algorithm for discovering functional and approximate dependencies, The Computer Journal 42 (1999) 100–111.
[6] P. Schirmer, T. Papenbrock, S. Kruse, D. Hempfing, T. Meyer, D. Neuschäfer-Rube, F. Naumann, DynFD: Functional dependency discovery in dynamic datasets., in: Proc. of 22nd International Conference on Extending Database Technology, 2019, pp. 253–264.
[7] S.-L. Wang, J.-W. Shen, T.-P. Hong, Incremental discovery of functional dependencies using partitions, in: Proc. of Joint 9th IFSA World Congress and 20th NAFIPS International Conference, volume 3, 2001, pp. 1322–1326.
[8] C. Wyss, C. Giannella, E. Robertson, FastFDs: A heuristic-driven, depth-first algorithm for mining functional dependencies from relation instances, in: Proc. of International Conference on Data Warehousing and Knowledge Discovery, 2001, pp. 101–110.
[9] L. Caruccio, S. Cirillo, V. Deufemia, G. Polese, Incremental discovery of functional dependencies with a bit-vector algorithm, in: M. Mecella, G. Amato, C. Gennaro (Eds.), Proceedings of the 27th Italian Symposium on Advanced Database Systems, volume 2400 of *CEUR Workshop Proceedings*, CEUR-WS.org, 2019.
[10] H. Yao, H. J. Hamilton, C. J. Butz, FD_Mine: Discovering functional dependencies in a database using equivalences, in: Proc. of IEEE International Conference on Data Mining, 2002, pp. 729–732.
[11] T. Papenbrock, F. Naumann, A hybrid approach to functional dependency discovery, in: Proc. of the 2016 International Conference on Management of Data, 2016, pp. 821–833.
[12] Z. Wei, S. Link, Discovery and ranking of functional dependencies, in: Proc. of IEEE 35th International Conference on Data Engineering, IEEE, 2019, pp. 1526–1537.
[13] S. Bell, Discovery and maintenance of functional dependencies by independencies, in: Proc. of the 1st International Conference on Knowledge Discovery and Data Mining, 1995, pp. 27–32.
[14] L. Caruccio, V. Deufemia, G. Polese, Mining relaxed functional dependencies from data, Data Mining and Knowledge Discovery 34 (2020) 443–477.
[15] L. Caruccio, S. Cirillo, Incremental discovery of imprecise functional dependencies, J. Data and Information Quality 12 (2020).
[16] B. Breve, L. Caruccio, S. Cirillo, V. Deufemia, G. Polese, Visualizing dependencies during incremental discovery processes, in: A. Poulovassilis et al. (Ed.), Proceedings of the Workshops of the EDBT/ICDT 2020 Joint Conference, volume 2578 of *CEUR Workshop Proceedings*, CEUR-WS.org, 2020.
[17] L. Caruccio, V. Deufemia, F. Naumann, G. Polese, Discovering relaxed functional dependencies based on multi-attribute dominance, IEEE Transactions on Knowledge and Data Engineering (2021) To appear.

Non-Linear Analytic Prediction of IP Addresses for Supporting Cyber Attack Detection and Analysis

Alfredo Cuzzocrea[1], Enzo Mumolo[2], Edoardo Fadda[3], Selim Soufargi[4] and Carson K. Leung[5]

[1]*iDEA Lab, University of Calabria, Rende, Italy*
[2]*University of Trieste, Trieste, Italy*
[3]*Politecnico di Torino & ISIRES, Torino, Italy*
[4]*iDEA Lab, University of Calabria, Rende, Italy*
[5]*University of Manitoba, Winnipeg, MB, Canada*

Abstract

Computer network systems are often subject to several types of attacks. For example the distributed Denial of Service (DDoS) attack introduces an excessive traffic load to a web server to make it unusable. A popular method for detecting attacks is to use the sequence of source IP addresses to detect possible anomalies. With the aim of predicting the next IP address, the Probability Density Function of the IP address sequence is estimated. Prediction of source IP address in the future access to the server is meant to detect anomalous requests. In this paper we consider the sequence of IP addresses as a numerical sequence and develop the nonlinear analysis of the numerical sequence. We used nonlinear analysis based on Volterra's Kernels and Hammerstein's models. The experiments carried out with datasets of source IP address sequences show that the prediction errors obtained with Hammerstein models are smaller than those obtained both with the Volterra Kernels and with the sequence clustering by means of the K-Means algorithm.

Keywords

Cyber Attack, Distributed Denial of Service, Hammerstein Models

1. Introduction

User modeling is an important task for web applications dealing with large traffic flows. They can be used for a variety of applications such as to predict future situations or classify current states. Furthermore, user modeling can improve detection or mitigation of Distributed Denial of Service (DDoS) attack [1, 2, 3], improve the quality of service (QoS) [4], individuate click fraud detection and optimize traffic management. In peer-to-peer (P2P) overlay networks, IP models can also be used for optimizing request routing [5]. Those techniques are used by severs for deciding how to manage the actual traffic. In this context, also outlier detection methods are often used if only one class is known. If, for example, an Intrusion Prevention System wants to mitigate DDoS attacks, it usually has only seen the normal traffic class before and it has to

SEBD 2021: The 29th Italian Symposium on Advanced Database Systems, September 5-9, 2021, Pizzo Calabro (VV), Italy
alfredo.cuzzocrea@unical.it (A. Cuzzocrea); mumolo@units.it (E. Mumolo); edorardo.fadda@polito.it (E. Fadda); selim.soufargi@unical.it (S. Soufargi); kleung@cs.umanitoba.ca (C. K. Leung)

detect the outlier class by its different behavior. In this paper we deal with the management of DDos because nowadays it has become a major threat in the internet. Those attacks are done by using a large scaled networks of infected PCs (bots or zombies) that combine their bandwidth and computational power in order to overload a publicly available service and denial it for legal users. Due to the open structure of the internet, all public servers are vulnerable to DDoS attacks. The bots are usually acquired automatically by hackers who use software tools to scan through the network, detecting vulnerabilities and exploiting the target machine. Furthermore, there is also a strong need to mitigate DDoS attacks near the target, which seems to be the only solution to the problem in the current internet infrastructure. The aim of such a protection system is to limit their destabilizing effect on the server through identifying malicious requests. There are multiple strategies with dealing with DDoS attacks. The most effective ones are the near-target filtering solutions. They estimates normal user behavior based on IP packet header information. Then, during an attack the access of outliers is denied. One parameter that all methods have in common is the source IP address of the users. It is the main discriminant for DDoS traffic classification. However, the methods of storing IP addresses and estimating their density in the huge IP address space, are different. In this paper, we present a novel approach based on system identification techniques and, in particular, on the Hammerstein models.

2. Non-Linear Analytic Prediction of IP Addresses

Data driven identification of mathematical models of physical systems (i.e. nonlinear) starts with representing the systems as a black box. In other terms, while we may have access to the inputs and outputs, the internal mechanisms are totally unknown to us. Once a model type is chosen to represent the system, its parameters are estimated through an optimization algorithm so that eventually the model mimics at a certain level of fidelity the inner mechanism of the nonlinear system or process using its inputs and outputs. These approach is, for instance, widely used in the related *big data analytics* area (e.g., [6, 7, 8, 9, 10, 11, 12, 13, 14])

In this work, we consider a particular sub-class of nonlinear predictors: the Linear-in-the-parameters (LIP) predictors. LIP predictors are characterized by a linear dependence of the predictor output on the predictor coefficients. Such predictors are inherently stable, and that they can converge to a globally minimum solution (in contrast to other types of nonlinear filters whose cost function may exhibit many local minima) avoiding the undesired possibility of getting stuck in a local minimum. Let us consider a causal, time-invariant, finite-memory,continuous nonlinear predictor as described in (1).

$$\hat{s}(n) = f[s(n-1), \ldots, s(n-N)] \tag{1}$$

where $f[\cdot]$ is a continuous function, $s(n)$ is the input signal and $\hat{s}(n)$ is the predicted sample. We can expand $f[\cdot]$ with a series of basis functions $f_i(n)$, as shown in (2).

$$\hat{s}(n) = \sum_{i=1}^{\infty} h(i) f_i[s(n-i)] \tag{2}$$

where $h(i)$ a re proper coefficients. To make (2) realizable we truncate the series to the first N

terms, thus we obtain

$$\hat{s}(n) = \sum_{i=1}^{N} h(i) f_i[s(n-i)] \tag{3}$$

In the general case, a linear-in-the-parameters nonlinear predictor is described by the input-output relationship reported in (4).

$$\hat{s}(n) = \vec{H}^T \vec{X}(n) \tag{4}$$

where $\vec{H}^T$ is a row vector containing predictor coefficients and $\vec{X}(n)$ is the corresponding column vector whose elements are nonlinear combinations and/or expansions of the input samples.

2.1. Linear Predictor

Linear prediction is a well known technique with a long history [15]. Given a time series $\vec{X}$, linear prediction is the optimum approximation of sample $x(n)$ with a linear combination of the N most recent samples. That means that the linear predictor is described as eq. (5).

$$\hat{s}(n) = \sum_{i=1}^{N} h_1(i) s(n-i) \tag{5}$$

or in matrix form as

$$\hat{s}(n) = \vec{H}^T \vec{X}(n) \tag{6}$$

where the coefficient and input vectors are reported in (7) and (8).

$$\vec{H}^T = \begin{bmatrix} h_1(1) & h_1(2) & \dots & h_1(N) \end{bmatrix} \tag{7}$$

$$\vec{X}^T = \begin{bmatrix} s(n-1) & s(n-2) & \dots & s(n-N) \end{bmatrix} \tag{8}$$

2.2. Non-Linear Predictor based on Volterra Series

As well as Linear Prediction, Non Linear Prediction is the optimum approximation of sample $x(n)$ with a non linear combination of the N most recent samples. Popular nonlinear predictors are based on Volterra series [16]. A Volterra predictor based on a Volterra series truncated to the second term is reported in (9).

$$\hat{x}(n) = \sum_{i=1}^{N_1} h_1(i) x(n-i) + \sum_{i=1}^{N_2} \sum_{j=i}^{N_2} h_2(i,j) x(n-i) x(n-j) \tag{9}$$

where the symmetry of the Volterra kernel (the h coefficients) is considered. In matrix terms, the Volterra predictor is represented in (10).

$$\hat{s}(n) = \vec{H}^T \vec{X}(n) \tag{10}$$

where the coefficient and input vectors are reported in (12) and (12).

$$\vec{H}^T = \begin{bmatrix} h_1(1) & h_1(2) \ldots h_1(N) \\ h_2(1,1) & h_2(1,2) \ldots h_2(N_2,N_2) \end{bmatrix} \tag{11}$$

$$\vec{X}^T = \begin{bmatrix} s(n-1) & s(n-2) \ldots s(n-N_1) \\ s^2(n-1) & s(n-1)s(n-2) \ldots s^2(n-N_2) \end{bmatrix} \tag{12}$$

2.3. Non-Linear Predictor based on Functional Link Artificial Neural Networks (FLANN)

FLANN is a single layer neural network without hidden layer. The nonlinear relationships between input and output are captured through function expansion of the input signal exploiting suitable orthogonal polynomials. Many authors used for examples trigonometric, Legendre and Chebyshev polynomials. However, the most frequently used basis function used in FLANN for function expansion are trigonometric polynomials [17]. The FLANN predictor can be represented by eq.(13).

$$\hat{s}(n) = \sum_{i=1}^{N} h_1(i)s(n-i) + \sum_{i=1}^{N}\sum_{j=1}^{N} h_2(i,j)\cos[i\pi s(n-j)] + \sum_{i=1}^{N}\sum_{j=1}^{N} h_2(i,j)\sin[i\pi s(n-j)] \tag{13}$$

Also in this case the Flann predictor can be represented using the matrix form reported in (10).

$$\hat{s}(n) = \vec{H}^T \vec{X}(n) \tag{14}$$

where the coefficient and input vectors of FLANN predictors are reported in (22) and (23).

$$\vec{H}^T = \begin{bmatrix} h_1(1) & h_1(2) \ldots h_1(N) \\ h_2(1,1) & h_2(1,2) \ldots h_2(N_2,N_2) \\ h_3(1,1) & h_3(1,2) \ldots h_3(N_2,N_2) \end{bmatrix} \tag{15}$$

$$\vec{X}^T = \begin{bmatrix} s(n-1) & s(n-2) & \ldots & s(n-N) & \\ \cos[\pi s(n-1)] & \cos[\pi s(n-2)] & \ldots & \ldots & \cos[N_2\pi s(n-N_2)] \\ \sin[\pi s(n-1)] & \sin[\pi s(n-2)] & \ldots & \ldots & \sin[N_2\pi x(s-N_2)] \end{bmatrix} \tag{16}$$

2.4. Non-Linear Predictors based on Hammerstein Models

Previous research [18] shown that many real nonlinear systems, spanning from electromechanical systems to audio systems, can be modeled using a static non-linearity. These terms capture the system nonlinearities, in series with a linear function, which capture the system dynamics as shown in Figure 1.

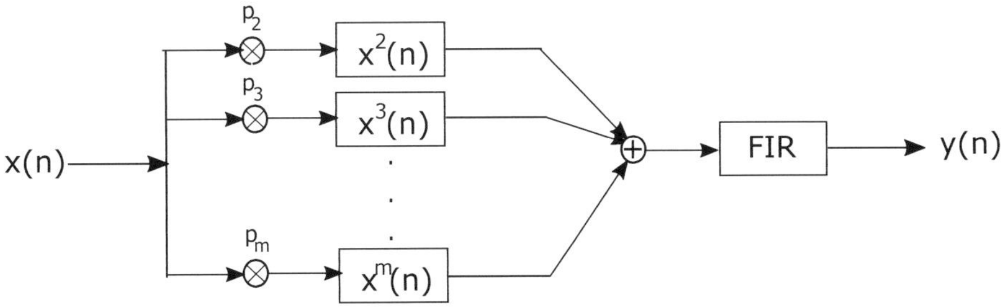

Figure 1: Representation of the Hammerstein Models

Indeed, the front-end of the so called Hammerstein Model is formed by a nonlinear function whose input is the system input. Of course the type of non-linearity depends on the actual physical system to be modeled. The output of the nonlinear function is hidden and is fed as input of the linear function. In the following, we assume that the non-linearity is a finite polynomial expansion, and the linear dynamic is realized with a Finite Impulse Response (FIR) filter. Furthermore, in contrast with [18], we assume a mean error analysis and we postpone the analysis in the robust framework in future work. In other word,

$$z(n) \quad = \quad p(2)x^2(n) \ + \ p(3)x^3(n) \ + \ \dots p(m)x^m(n) \quad = \quad \sum_{i=2}^{M} p(i)x^i(n) \tag{17}$$

On the other hand, the output of the FIR filter is:

$$\begin{aligned} y(n) = h_0(1)z(n-1) + h_0(2)z(n-2) + \dots + h_0(N)z(n-N) = \\ = \sum_{j=1}^{N} h_0(j)z(n-j) \end{aligned} \tag{18}$$

Substituting (17) in (20) we have:

$$\begin{aligned} y(n) = \sum_{i=1}^{N} h_0(i)z(n-i) = \sum_{j=1}^{N} h_0(j) \sum_{i=2}^{M} p(i)x^i(n-j) = \\ \sum_{i=2}^{M}\sum_{j=1}^{N} h_0(j)p(i)x^i(n-j) \end{aligned} \tag{19}$$

Setting $c(i,j) = h_0(j)p(i)$ we write

$$y(n) = \sum_{i=2}^{M}\sum_{j=1}^{N} c(i,j)x^i(n-j) \tag{20}$$

This equation can be written in matrix form as

$$\hat{s}(n) = \vec{H}^T \vec{X}(n) \tag{21}$$

where

$$\vec{H}^T = \begin{bmatrix} c(2,1) & c(2,2)\dots c(2,N_2) \\ c(3,1) & c(3,2)\dots c(3,N_2) \\ \dots c(M,1) & C(M,2)\dots C(M,N) \end{bmatrix} \quad (22)$$

$$\vec{X}^T = \begin{bmatrix} s^2(n-2) & s^2(n-3)\dots s^2(n-N) & \\ s^3(n-2) & s^3(n-3)\dots s^3(n-N) & \\ s^M(n-2) & s^M(n-3)\dots s^M(n-1) & s^M(n-3)\dots s^M(n-N) \end{bmatrix} \quad (23)$$

3. Predictor Parameters Estimation

So far we saw that all the predictors can be expressed, at time instant n, as

$$\hat{s}(n) = \vec{H}^T \vec{X}(n) \quad (24)$$

with different definitions of the input, $\vec{X}(n)$, end parameters vectors $\vec{H}^T$. There are two well known possibilities for estimating the optimal parameter vector.

3.1. Block-based Approach

The Minimum Mean Square estimation is based on the minimization of the mathematical expectation of the squared prediction error $e(n) = s(n) - \hat{s}(n)$

$$E[e^2] = E[(s(n) - \hat{s}(n))^2] = E[(s(n) - \vec{H}^T \vec{X}(n))^2] \quad (25)$$

The minimization of (25) is obtain by setting to zero the Laplacian of the mathematical expectation of the squared prediction error:

$$\nabla_H E[e^2] = E[\nabla_H e^2] = E[2e(n)\nabla_H e] = 0 \quad (26)$$

which leads to the well known unique solution

$$\vec{H}_{opt} = \vec{R}_{xx}^{-1} \vec{R}_{sx} \quad (27)$$

where

$$\vec{R}_{xx}(n) = E[\vec{X}(n)\vec{X}^T(n)] \quad (28)$$

is the statistical auto-correlation matrix of the input vector $\vec{X}(n)$ and

$$\vec{R}_{sx}(n) = E[s(n)\vec{X}(n)] \quad (29)$$

is the statistical cross-correlation vector between the signal $s(n)$ and the input vector $\vec{X}(n)$. The mathematical expectations of the auto and cross correlation are estimated using

$$\vec{R}_{xx}(n) = \frac{\sum_{k=1}^{n} \vec{X}(n)\vec{X}^T(n)}{n} \quad (30)$$

is the statistical auto-correlation matrix of the input vector $\vec{X}(n)$ and

$$\vec{R}_{sx}(n) = \frac{\sum_{k=1}^{n} s(k)(n)\vec{X}(n)}{n} \quad (31)$$

3.2. Adaptive Approach

Let us consider a general second order terms of a Volterra predictor

$$y(n)=\sum_{k=0}^{N-1}\sum_{r=0}^{N-1}h_2(k,r)x(n-k)x(n-r) \tag{32}$$

It can be generalized for higher order term as

$$\sum_{k_1=1}^{N}\cdots\sum_{k_p=1}^{N}c_{k_1}\cdots c_{k_p}H_p\left\{x_{k_1}(n),\cdots x_{k_p}(n)\right\} \tag{33}$$

where

$$\sum_{k=1}^{N}c_kx_k(n). \tag{34}$$

For the sake of simplicity and without loss of generality, we consider a Volterra predictor based on a Volterra series truncated to the second term

$$\hat{r}(n)=\sum_{i=1}^{N_1}h_1(i)r(n-i)+\sum_{i=1}^{N_2}\sum_{j=i}^{N_2}h_2(i,j)r(n-i)r(n-j) \tag{35}$$

By defining

$$H^T(n)=|h_1(1),\cdots,h_1(N_1),h_2(1,1),\cdots,h_2(N_2,N_2)| \tag{36}$$

and

$$\begin{aligned}X^T(n)=\big|r(n-1),\cdots,r(n-N_1),r^2(n-1)\\ r(n-1)r(n-2),\cdots,r^2(n-N_2)\big|\end{aligned} \tag{37}$$

Eq (35) can be rewritten as follows

$$\hat{r}(n)=H^T(n)X(n). \tag{38}$$

In order to estimate the best parameters H, we consider the following loss function

$$J_n(H)=\sum_{k=0}^{n}\lambda^{n-k}\left[\hat{r}(k)-H^T(n)X(k)\right]^2 \tag{39}$$

where λ^{n-k} weights the relative importance of each squared error. In order to find the H that minimizes the convex function (39) it is enough to impose its gradient to zero, i.e.,

$$\nabla_HJ_n(H)=0 \tag{40}$$

That is equivalent to

$$R_{XX}(n)H(n)=R_{rX}(n) \tag{41}$$

where

$$\begin{array}{c} R_{XX}(n) = \sum_{k=0}^{n} \lambda^{n-k} X(k) X^T(k) \\ R_{rX}(n) = \sum_{k=0}^{n} \lambda^{n-k} r(k) X(k) \end{array} \tag{42}$$

It follows that the best H can be computed by

$$H(n) = R_{XX}^{-1}(n) R_{rX}(n) \tag{43}$$

Since

$$R_{XX}(n) = \lambda R_{XX}(n-1) + X(n) X^T(n) \tag{44}$$

it follows that

$$R_{XX}^{-1}(n) = \frac{1}{\lambda}\left[R_{XX}^{-1}(n-1) - k(n) X^T(n) R_{XX}^{-1}(n-1)\right] \tag{45}$$

where $k(n)$ is equal to

$$k(n) = \frac{R_{XX}^{-1}(n-1) X(n)}{\lambda + X^T(n) R_{XX}^{-1}(n-1) X(n)} \tag{46}$$

Instead, matrix $R_{rX}(n)$ in (43) can be written as

$$R_{rX}(n) = \lambda R_{rX}(n-1) + r(n) X(n) \tag{47}$$

Thus, inserting Eq (47) and Eq (45)in Eq (43) and rearranging the terms, we obtain

$$H(n) = H(n-1) + R_{XX}^{-1}(n) X(n) \epsilon(n) \tag{48}$$

where

$$\epsilon = \hat{r}(n) - H^T(n-1) X(n) \tag{49}$$

By recalling Eq. (46), we can write Eq. (48) as

$$H(n) = H(n-1) + \epsilon(n) k(n) \tag{50}$$

By introducing, the new notation,

$$F(n) = S^T(n-1) X(n) \tag{51}$$

The previous equations can be resumed by the following system

$$\begin{cases} L(n) = S(n-1) F(n) \\ \beta(n) = \lambda + F^T(n) F(n) \\ \alpha(n) = \frac{1}{\beta(n) + \sqrt{\lambda \beta(n)}} \\ S(n) = \frac{1}{\sqrt{\lambda}}\left[S(n-1) - \alpha(n) L(n) F^T(n)\right] \\ \epsilon(n) = \hat{r}(n-1) - \alpha(n) L(n) F^T(n) \\ \epsilon(n) = H(n-1) + L(n) \frac{\epsilon(n)}{\beta(n)} \end{cases} \tag{52}$$

It should be noted that by using Eq (52) the estimation adapts in each step in order to decrease the error. Thus, the system structure is somehow similar to the Kalman filter.

Finally, we define the estimation error as

$$e(n) = r(n) - H^T(n) X(n) \tag{53}$$

It is worth noting that the computation of the predicted value from Eq. (38) requires $6N_{\text{tot}} + 2N_{\text{tot}}^2$ operations, where $N_{\text{tot}} = N_1 + N_2 (N_2 + 1)/2$.

4. Experiments

In order to prove the effectiveness of the proposed approach, in this section we present our experimental results for a real dataset. Specifically, we consider the requests made to the 1998 World Cup Web site between April 30, 1998 and July 26, 1998 [1]. During this period of time the site received 1,352,804,107 requests. The fields of the request structure contain the following information: (*i*) *timestamp* the time of the request, stored as the number of seconds since the Epoch. The timestamp has been converted to GMT to allow for portability. During the World Cup the local time was 2 hours ahead of GMT (+0200). In order to determine the local time, each timestamp must be adjusted by this amount; (*ii*) *clientID* a unique integer identifier for the client that issued the request; due to privacy concerns these mappings cannot be released; note that each *clientID* maps to exactly one IP address, and the mappings are preserved across the entire data set - that is if IP address 0.0.0.0 mapped to *clientID* X on day Y then any request in any of the data sets containing *clientID* X also came from IP address 0.0.0.0; (*iii*) *objectID* a unique integer identifier for the requested URL; these mappings are also 1-to-1 and are preserved across the entire data set; (*iv*) *size* the number of bytes in the response; (*v*) *method* the method contained in the client's request (e.g., GET); (*vi*) *status* this field contains two pieces of information; the 2 highest order bits contain the HTTP version indicated in the client's request (e.g., HTTP/1.0); the remaining 6 bits indicate the response status code (e.g., 200 OK); (*vii*) *type* the type of file requested, generally based on the file extension (.html), or the presence of a parameter list; (*viii*) *server* indicates which server handled the request. The upper 3 bits indicate which region the server was at; the remaining bits indicate which server at the site handled the request.

In the dataset, 87 days are reported. We use the first one in order to initialise the estimator in (35) and we use the others as test set by using a rolling horizon method (as in [18]). Particularly, for each day t we compute the estimation by using all the IP observations in the previous days $[0, t-1]$. The results are reported in Figure 2. The increase of errors in June is due to the sudden

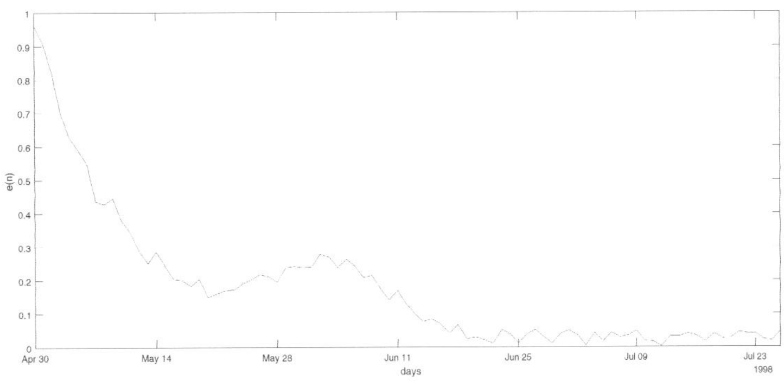

Figure 2: Estimation error for each day of activity of the website.

increment of different IP accessing the website due to the start of the competition (see [19]). It should be noted that the estimation error decrease exponentially despite dealing with several millions of IPs.

[1] ftp://ita.ee.lbl.gov/html/contrib/WorldCup.html

Since the computation of the optimal coefficient $H(n)$ may require some time, we measure the percentage of available data that our approach needs in order to provide good results. Particularly, in this experiment we consider the average estimation error done by the model at time t by considering a subset of the IPs observed in interval $[0, t-1]$. The experimental results on real data cubes are depicted in Figure 3.

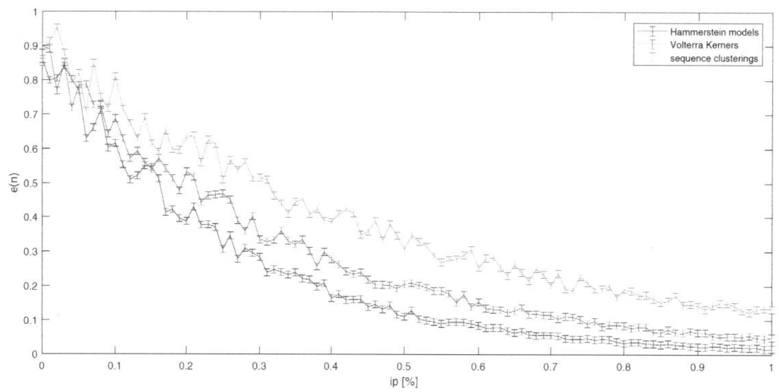

Figure 3: Estimation error vs. percentage size of the training set

It should be noted that the Hammerstain model outperform the results by the Volterra's kernel as well as the clustering techniques. In more detail, the clustering techniques are the one less performing. This is due to the nature of the clustering techniques that exploit the geometric information of the data more than their time dependency. We highlight that despite the calculation of $H(n)$ is computational intensive, this does not effect the real time applicability of the method. In fact, the access decision is taken by considering the estimator $\hat{r}(n)$ that is computed once per day. Thus the computation of $H(n)$ does not need to be fast.

5. Conclusions and Future Work

In this paper, we presented a new way to deal with cyber attack by using Hammerstein models. Experimental results clearly confirm the effectiveness of the proposed techniques for a real data set, outperforming other well-known techniques. Future work will have two objectives. First, we want to consider the problem in a stochastic optimization settings, as for example in [20]. Second, we want to test the approach on other case studies, by also exploiting *knowledge management methodologies* (e.g., [21, 22]).

Acknowledgements

This work is partially supported by NSERC (Canada) and University of Manitoba.

References

[1] M. Goldstein, C. Lampert, M. Reif, A. Stahl, T. Breuel, Bayes optimal ddos mitigation by adaptive history-based ip filtering, in: Seventh International Conference on Networking (icn 2008), 2008, pp. 174–179.

[2] H.-X. Tan, W. Seah, Framework for statistical filtering against ddos attacks in manets, 2006, pp. 8 pp.–. doi:10.1109/ICESS.2005.57.
[3] G. Pack, J. Yoon, E. Collins, C. Estan, On filtering of ddos attacks based on source address prefixes, 2006, pp. 1–12. doi:10.1109/SECCOMW.2006.359537.
[4] Y. Yang, C.-H. Lung, The role of traffic forecasting in qos routing - a case study of time-dependent routing, 2005, pp. 224 – 228 Vol. 1. doi:10.1109/ICC.2005.1494351.
[5] A. Agrawal, H. Casanova, Clustering hosts in p2p and global computing platforms, 2003, pp. 367– 373. doi:10.1109/CCGRID.2003.1199389.
[6] A. Cuzzocrea, R. Moussa, G. Xu, Olap*: Effectively and efficiently supporting parallel OLAP over big data, in: Model and Data Engineering - Third International Conference, MEDI 2013, Amantea, Italy, September 25-27, 2013. Proceedings, 2013, pp. 38–49.
[7] G. Chatzimilioudis, A. Cuzzocrea, D. Gunopulos, N. Mamoulis, A novel distributed framework for optimizing query routing trees in wireless sensor networks via optimal operator placement, J. Comput. Syst. Sci. 79 (2013) 349–368.
[8] A. Cuzzocrea, E. Bertino, Privacy preserving OLAP over distributed XML data: A theoretically-sound secure-multiparty-computation approach, J. Comput. Syst. Sci. 77 (2011) 965–987.
[9] A. Cuzzocrea, V. Russo, Privacy preserving OLAP and OLAP security, in: Encyclopedia of Data Warehousing and Mining, Second Edition (4 Volumes), 2009, pp. 1575–1581.
[10] A. Bonifati, A. Cuzzocrea, Storing and retrieving xpath fragments in structured P2P networks, Data Knowl. Eng. 59 (2006) 247–269.
[11] R. C. Camara, A. Cuzzocrea, G. M. Grasso, C. K. Leung, S. B. Powell, J. Souza, B. Tang, Fuzzy logic-based data analytics on predicting the effect of hurricanes on the stock market, in: 2018 IEEE International Conference on Fuzzy Systems, FUZZ-IEEE 2018, Rio de Janeiro, Brazil, July 8-13, 2018, IEEE, 2018, pp. 1–8.
[12] P. Braun, A. Cuzzocrea, C. K. Leung, A. G. M. Pazdor, S. K. Tanbeer, G. M. Grasso, An innovative framework for supporting frequent pattern mining problems in iot environments, in: O. Gervasi, B. Murgante, S. Misra, E. N. Stankova, C. M. Torre, A. M. A. C. Rocha, D. Taniar, B. O. Apduhan, E. Tarantino, Y. Ryu (Eds.), Computational Science and Its Applications - ICCSA 2018 - 18th International Conference, Melbourne, VIC, Australia, July 2-5, 2018, Proceedings, Part V, volume 10964 of *Lecture Notes in Computer Science*, Springer, 2018, pp. 642–657.
[13] A. Cuzzocrea, C. Mastroianni, G. M. Grasso, Private databases on the cloud: Models, issues and research perspectives, in: J. Joshi, G. Karypis, L. Liu, X. Hu, R. Ak, Y. Xia, W. Xu, A. Sato, S. Rachuri, L. H. Ungar, P. S. Yu, R. Govindaraju, T. Suzumura (Eds.), 2016 IEEE International Conference on Big Data, BigData 2016, Washington DC, USA, December 5-8, 2016, IEEE Computer Society, 2016, pp. 3656–3661.
[14] A. Cuzzocrea, Accuracy control in compressed multidimensional data cubes for quality of answer-based OLAP tools, in: 18th International Conference on Scientific and Statistical Database Management, SSDBM 2006, 3-5 July 2006, Vienna, Austria, Proceedings, IEEE Computer Society, 2006, pp. 301–310.
[15] J. Makhoul, Linear prediction: A tutorial review, Proceedings of the IEEE 63 (1975) 561–580.
[16] Z. Peng, C. Changming, Volterra series theory: A state-of-the-art review, Chinese Science Bulletin (Chinese Version) 60 (2015) 1874. doi:10.1360/N972014-01056.
[17] H. Zhao, J. Zhang, Adaptively combined fir and functional link artificial neural network equalizer for nonlinear communication channel, IEEE Transactions on Neural Networks 20 (2009) 665–674.
[18] V. Cerone, E. Fadda, D. Regruto, A robust optimization approach to kernel-based nonparametric error-in-variables identification in the presence of bounded noise, in: 2017 American Control Conference (ACC), IEEE, 2017. doi:10.23919/acc.2017.7963056.
[19] M. Arlitt, T. Jin, H. packard Laboratories, A workload characterization study of the 7998 world cup web site, ????
[20] E. Fadda, G. Perboli, R. Tadei, Customized multi-period stochastic assignment problem for social engagement and opportunistic iot, Computers & Operations Research 93 (2018) 41–50.
[21] A. Cuzzocrea, Combining multidimensional user models and knowledge representation and management techniques for making web services knowledge-aware, Web Intelligence and Agent Systems 4 (2006) 289–312.
[22] M. Cannataro, A. Cuzzocrea, C. Mastroianni, R. Ortale, A. Pugliese, Modeling adaptive hypermedia with an object-oriented approach and XML, in: M. Levene, A. Poulovassilis (Eds.), Proceedings of the Second International Workshop on Web Dynamics, WebDyn@WWW 2002, Honululu, HW, USA, May 7, 2002, volume 702 of *CEUR Workshop Proceedings*, CEUR-WS.org, 2002, pp. 35–44.

From Digital to Computational Humanities: The VAST Project Vision

Silvana Castano[1], Alfio Ferrara[1], Stefano Montanelli[1] and Francesco Periti[1]

[1]*Università degli Studi di Milano*
Department of Computer Science
Via Celoria, 18 - 20133 Milano, Italy

Abstract

In the shift from Digital to Computational Humanities, the role of artificial intelligence, data science and digital technologies is fundamental to achieve advances and results. As a concrete example of *Computational Humanities Research*, we present the vision of the EU H2020 VAST project (*Values Across Space and Time*) recently started, where cutting edge digital technologies and knowledge modeling tools are in place to study how the meaning of European moral values has been expressed, transformed, and appropriated throughout time, going back to the stories that helped to shape part of the European culture.

Keywords

Computational Humanities, Knowledge Modeling, Ontology-based data management

1. Introduction

In the field of the Humanities, Social Sciences, and Cultural Heritage, the demand is increasing for semantic text-analysis techniques as well as for intelligent discovery, linking, querying, and visualization of massive volumes of data [1]. On the one side, this leads to large-scale digitization projects and tools for producing, curating, and exploiting humanities and social-science data, by relying on text analysis techniques and new hybrid methodologies derived from the intersection/intertwining of the involved research communities [2]. On the other side, the need to keep humans "in-the-loop" leads to crowdsourcing solutions, to help in large-scale, human-intensive processes such as text tagging, commenting, rating, and reviewing, as well as in the creation and upload of content in a methodical, task-based fashion. Furthermore, the rapid development and diffusion of artificial intelligence techniques and data science approaches, enable research in the field of humanities and social sciences to become more and more computational. For example, various studies are devoted to exploit AI techniques to analyze literary texts, historic productions, or public opinions about political events for knowledge extraction and/or classification/analytics purposes. As a consequence, we are assisting to a shift from *Digital Humanities* (DH) to the so-called *Computational Humanities* (CH) research, where the

SEBD 2021: The 29th Italian Symposium on Advanced Database Systems, September 5-9, 2021, Pizzo Calabro (VV), Italy
silvana.castano@unimi.it (S. Castano); alfio.ferrara@unimi.it (A. Ferrara); stefano.montanelli@unimi.it (S. Montanelli); francesco.periti@unimi.it (F. Periti)

role of artificial intelligence, data science and cutting edge digital technologies is fundamental to achieve research advances and results [3].

In this paper, we present the EU H2020 VAST project (*Values Across Space and Time*), a concrete example of Computational Humanities Research (CHR). Going beyond analysing the transformation of moral values in the past, the VAST project will study how moral values are communicated and perceived today, by collecting, digitising, and analysing narratives and experiences of both communicators of moral values, like for example artists, directors, culture and creative industry institutions, museum curators, storytellers, educators, and the respective audiences, like spectators, museum visitors, students, and pupils. Within VAST, an interdisciplinary consortium of scholars from both humanities and computer science has been created. VAST aims to study the transformation of moral values across space and time, with particular emphasis on the core European Values, such as freedom, democracy, equality, rule of law, tolerance, dialogue, and dignity, that are widely recognized as the essential pillars to constitute a society in which inclusion, tolerance, justice, solidarity, and non-discrimination prevail [4].

The project envisions to bring European Values to the forefront by using cutting edge technologies to create a digital platform and a knowledge base by including narratives from three main areas: i) *theater*, focusing on ancient Greek Drama, ii) *science*, focusing on Scientific Revolution and natural-philosophy documents of the 17th century, and iii) *folklore*, focusing on folktales and fairy-tales. Through advanced techniques and digital tools, the research teams in the project are going to study how the meaning of specific values has been expressed, transformed, and appropriated throughout time, going back to the stories that helped to shape part of the European culture. VAST will examine narratives and user experiences that represent significant moments of European culture and history such as the classical period, and the Scientific Revolution of the 17th century, when the conceptual, methodological and institutional foundations of modern science were first established, to the modern era. In this respect, the main VAST issues about knowledge modeling and architectural design are discussed in the paper both from methodological and technical point of view.

The paper is organized as follows. Section 2 provides an overview of the VAST goals and features. In Section 3, the architectural design of the VAST platform is presented. Details about the VAST ontology meta-model are discussed in Section 4. In Section 5 and 6, related work and concluding remarks are finally provided.

2. The VAST project overview

The aim of the VAST project is to investigate how the values at the basis of the European Union have been transformed over the ages. Across time, from antiquity to modernity, a value represents a message that is communicated through different mediums (e.g., text, visual art, drama, oral narration) and this message can change when the context and the society where citizens live change. As a first goal, VAST aims at representing values and associated messages as they are extracted from sources of the past, such as for example literature texts and theatrical performances. As a further goal, VAST aims at collecting and digitizing the today messages associated with values as they are perceived by the general audience in the present days. To this end, the activities of the project are organized in three pilots that are characterized by i) different significant moments of the European history and ii) different types of sources that are exploited for extraction of the value messages. In particular, we focus on studying the transformations of values from ancient Greek tragedies to modern theatrical plays (i.e., *Pilot 1: Ancient Greek Drama*), from seventeenth century works of natural philosophy to science museum exhibits (i.e., *Pilot 2: Scientific Revolution Texts*), and from traditional European fairy tales to different types of storytelling (i.e., *Pilot 3: European Folktales*). The pilot features are summarized in Table 1 and they are described in the following.

Table 1
The VAST pilot properties

Pilot	Pilot 1	Pilot 2	Pilot 3
General Context	Arts	Science	Folklore
Type of Narrative	Greek Tragedies	17th Century Texts	European Folktales
Time	Antiquity Present	Early Modern Present	Modern Present
Space	Western Europe	Western Europe	Western Europe
Communication Medium	Theatre	Museum Exhibitions, Educational Activities	Museum Exhibitions, Educational Activities
Theoretical background-Methodology	Philosophical, Philological, Theatrological	Philosophical, Pedagogical, History & Communication of Science	Philosophical, Pedagogical Psychological
Communicators	Artists, Culture/Creative Industry Institutions	Curators	Curators, artists, storytellers
User Engagement	Theatrical Plays	Exhibitions, Educational Programs, Special Events	Exhibitions, Educational Programs, Special Events
Target Audiences	Spectators	Visitors, Students, Pupils	Visitors, Students, Pupils
Studied Values	Freedom, democracy, equality, tolerance, dialogue, human dignity, the rule of law		

Pilot 1: Ancient Greek Drama. The Pilot 1 of VAST is related to values in ancient Greek tragedies and how they are perceived by contemporary theatrical plays and general audiences. It is mainly focused on Greek tragedies and their adaptations across Europe and the World along time. The goal is to analyze how the values of the antiquity, that are recognized to be discussed in specific tragedies (e.g., *Lysistrata*, Comedy, 411 BC), are revisited in the present through modern artistic reproductions, such as acting, music, and voice. The pilot aims at inspiring ideas and debates on what people find important in their own life and in their life with the others, like for example human rights, the right of political asylum, expansionism, genocide, the conflict between East and West, and the concept of the "other".

Pilot 2: Scientific Revolution Texts. The Pilot 2 of VAST is related to values in texts of 17th century about natural philosophy and how they are perceived by experts in science museums and museum visitors like students and pupils. It is mainly focused on the early-modern era, the period known as the *Scientific Revolution* featured by great discoveries and inventions. The texts considered in the project are mostly about imaginary travel stories or fictional communities of ideal perfection in which the new intellectual achievements were embedded in an imaginary narrative context (e.g., *The Man in the Moone*, Francis Godwin, 1638). The goal is to analyze the shift in the message communicated by values concerned with the science of the past and the those concerned with the modern science. The pilot aims at promoting the organization of educational programs for museum visitors, focused events, such as talks and debates, where visitors are encouraged to share their experiences and visions about science-related values (e.g., freedom of research, science for public good).

Pilot 3: European Folktales. The Pilot 3 of VAST is related to values in folktales throughout the History of Europe and how they are perceived by storytelling experts in fairytale museums and museum visitors. Though fictitious, folktales are important simulations of the reality. Moreover, the variability of tales makes them the ideal case study for cross-cultural comparisons on social dynamics, including cooperation, competition, or decision making. The pilot is mainly focused on archetypical stories (e.g., the *Grimms' Fairy Tales*, 1812) and it includes texts from several European countries (i.e., Portugal, Italy, Slovenia, Greece, Cyprus). Folktale narratives are central to the construction of the self, embodied with memories, emotions, appetites, and culture-based values. The goal is to analyze the value dichotomies that are typically addressed in folktales, such as for example good/evil, right/wrong, punishment/reward, moral/immoral, trust/distrust, and male/female. The pilot aims at promoting events where a given folktale with a number of associated national adaptations are presented and the museum visitors can provide their feedback and emotions in the form of comments and/or storytelling with respect to the received value(s).

3. The VAST architecture

The VAST architecture describes the modules and the tools that are employed to enforce the project activities and the pilot development (Figure 1). In particular, the VAST architecture is

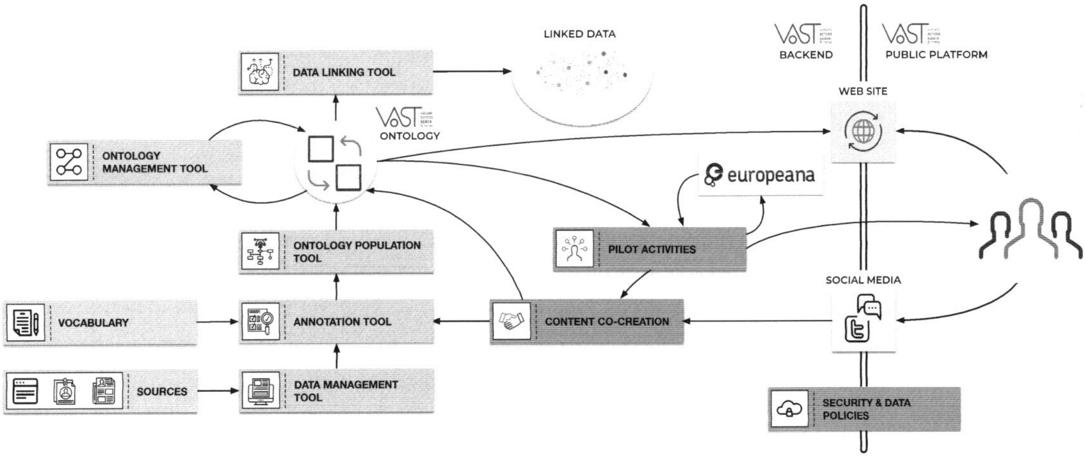

Figure 1: The VAST architecture

designed to support a computational-oriented approach focused on three main targets described in the following.

Historical content digitization. The VAST pilots require the acquisition of a number of heterogeneous historical sources that are selected to provide either explicit and implicit references to messages/interpretations associated with values. Document annotation modules and tools are designed in the VAST architecture to support historians and humanity scholars in the extraction of value-related knowledge from sources. A crucial aspect for annotation task is the specification of a reference vocabulary to support the work of human annotators and to avoid undisciplined proliferation of keywords. The idea is to go beyond conventional annotation approaches and to investigate the adoption of semi-automated solutions to the progressive enrichment of the reference vocabulary based on machine learning techniques (see for example [5]).

Multi-dimensional knowledge modelling and visualization. A key aspect in the VAST project is about the use of space and time as dimensions of analysis for observing the transformation of values throughout the considered historical sources. As a further issue, it is possible that a certain value is associated with multiple, different interpretations provided by distinct individuals in the same historical period. As a result, the VAST ontology meta-model needs to be defined not only around the specification of concepts featuring the values, but also around the association of each value with the keywords (i.e., the tags) used by individuals to denote the meaning of that value. In addition to the knowledge extracted from the historical sources through annotation, it is important to note that the VAST ontology has to contain the value interpretations provided by the final users (e.g., museum visitors, educators, students) as a feedback to the activities/events proposed within the pilots (see Section 4 for further details). The ontology-related modules and tools of the VAST architecture are designed to enforce modeling, population, and linking functionalities over the knowledge acquired through annotation. The VAST ontology aims at supporting i) dissemination tasks to the general audience through the VAST website, and ii) content creation activities to the final users involved in the pilots. In both scenarios the idea is to go beyond conventional visualization tools of the ontology contents and to provide interactive dashboards characterized by topic-driven organization of values aimed at highlighting the available value interpretations collected across space and time from sources and users (see [6] for a possible solution in this direction).

Collaborative content creation. Each VAST pilot aims at promoting focused events and activities to engage different target audiences on the project ambitions. The idea is to design interactive experiences where the final users are exposed to the value messages and interpretations coming from the Past, so that they can realize how these values have been transformed and differently perceived in the Present. The users involved in the pilot activities are encouraged to share their feelings according to modalities and mediums that are being defined within the project. A first modality is called *immediate* and it is based on the "syncronous" collection of user feedback during and/or at the end of the event/activity. In this modality, we expect to rely on interviews and questionnaires to enforce the user contributions. A further modality is called *remote* and it is based on the "asyncronous" collection of the user feedback some days/weeks after the participation to the event/activity. In this modality, social media channels represent a spontaneous medium that a user can exploit to share her personal feedback. As a further option, we plan to develop content-creation mechanisms where users are involved in collaborative writing experiences. The idea is to define a human-in-the-loop approach to *participatory storytelling* where users can contribute to the definition of a value interpretation by providing personal considerations as well as like/dislike reactions to the proposals of the other users (see for example [7]).

4. The VAST ontology meta-model

The VAST ontology is based on three main notions, namely i) *VAST annotation*, ii) *VAST interpretation* and iii) *VAST concept*, as highlighted in Figure 2. A **VAST annotation** represents an

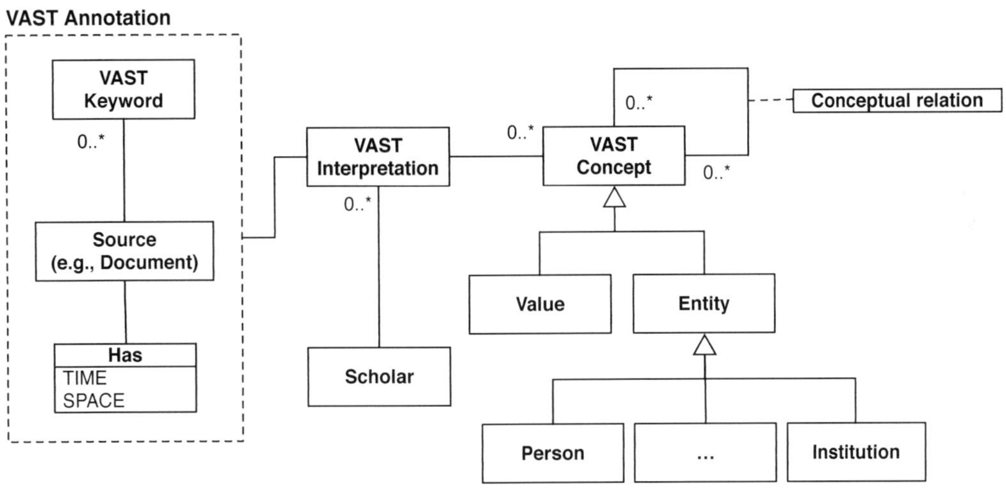

Figure 2: The VAST ontology meta-model

association between a source document, either a whole document or a small part of it, and one or more VAST keywords taken from a controlled vocabulary. Annotations are performed by scholars and expert of the source documents under examination. One of the main goals of annotation is to tag and select the specific portions of document that may be relevant for the understanding of values in time and space. In fact, each document in VAST is a historical source of information that is associated with a temporal dimension, typically the date of the document, and a spatial dimension, typically the country or the geo-political entity where the document has been historically written and published. VAST keywords are mainly tags that have been defined by domain experts with the goal of providing a first level of abstraction over the document contents but that still do not represent a conceptualization of the document contents. So, the goal of the VAST keywords is mainly related to the fact of overcoming the linguistic differences among documents (to this purpose all the VAST keywords are English words or short English sentences) and of providing a reference terminology that can be associated with document portions that are similar in terms of content but different in style and lexicon. The step of conceptualizing the document content with respect to the VAST values of interest is represented by interpretation.

A **VAST concept** is the ontology representation of an entity, like a person or an institution, or a value considered in VAST, like freedom, democracy, and equality. The VAST concepts are interconnected by conceptual relations. In particular, a binary relationship among a pair of concepts can be specified to denote a semantic relation holding between them.

A **VAST interpretation** is a relation between an annotation, that means a textual portion with time and space metadata and with VAST keywords associated, and a VAST concept. The association of concepts about entities with annotations is usually straightforward because such entities are mentioned directly in the source document or because there is a historical or philological evidence supporting that annotation. In case of values, the association of the concept representing the value and the document annotation is less straightforward because it derives from a specific interpretation that a scholar gives of the text at hand. For this reason, the design choice of the VAST ontology is to reify the notion of interpretation as a class of spatial ontology entities that represent the relation between a VAST concept, an annotation, and the scholars who propose or support that interpretation. Thanks to this design, the VAST ontology can model the existence of multiple interpretations of the same annotation. Moreover, we implicitly introduce a notion of consensus concerning interpretations because different, and potentially controversial, interpretations might be supported by more or less scholars. This flexibility of design is motivated by the need of supporting different views of the VAST values across time and space. In fact, by selecting a specific time and space frame we can easily select the interpretations involved and - through those - the keywords that are associated with a value in that interpretations in order to study how the definition of values in terms of keywords and documents vary in the temporal and spatial dimensions.

Example. As an example of how the VAST ontology is used in the project, in Figure 3 we present a portion of the concrete instance that describes the Galileo *Sidereus Nuncius*, published in the Republic of Venice on March 13, 1610. The source document is associated with several metadata, including the date of publication and the spatial reference to the Republic of Venice. This last reference is also linked to the corresponding entity in Wikidata. From the text, we take the example of a text snippet (TS1) that has been annotated with the keywords K1 ("for the people") and K2 ("democratic"). This association between keywords and text is represented in the VAST ontology by the annotation A1. Note that keywords may be used for multiple annotations as for the keyword K1 and the annotation A2. Then a scholar, omitted in the example just for the sake of readability, provides an interpretation of the fact that keywords K1 and K2 have been used to annotate TS1. Her interpretation is that the portion of the document annotated by A1 is related to both the value of democracy, represented by the concept C1, and the topic of science revolution, represented by the VAST concept C2. By providing her interpretation, the scholar generates an instance of VAST interpretation I1 that is linked to both A1 and C1 and C2, which are in turn related by a conceptual relation the one to the other. Although not shown in this example, I1 will also be associated with the scholar who proposed the interpretation and could be associated further with all the other scholar who will support this interpretation. Assuming that a second scholar wants to argue against this interpretation by claiming that TS1 is actually related to science revolution but not to the value of democracy, the second scholar may create a different interpretation linking A1 to C2 only. This way, multiple interpretations of the same text

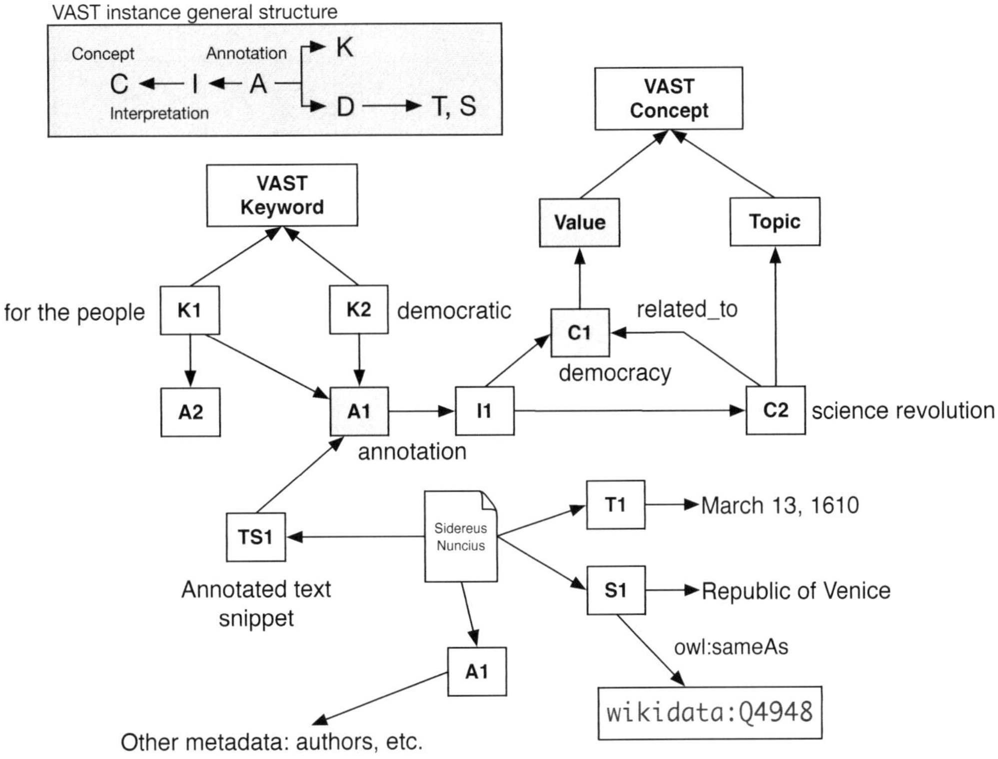

Figure 3: Example of a VAST ontology instance

may co-exists in the VAST ontology. At the same time, a given value (e.g., C1) can be associated with different interpretations and also with different texts and keywords. As an example of retrieval, consider the query Find democracy in the XVII century and the corresponding answer extracted from the VAST ontology:

```
{
   Value: democracy,
   Time: March 13, 1610,
   Space: Republic of Venice,
   Snippet: "Neque porro quisquam ...",
   Source: Sidereus Nuncius,
   Keyword: democratic
}
{
   Value: democracy,
   Time: March 13, 1610,
```

```
    Space: Republic of Venice,
    Snippet: "Neque porro quisquam ...",
    Source: Sidereus Nuncius,
    Keyword: for the people
}
```

The example shows how a value can be associated with a set of space locations (i.e., the Republic of Venice) and keywords (i.e., "democratic", "for the people") given a temporal constraint. By shifting the temporal reference along history trough other queries we can support a study on how the spatial reference and the keywords associated with values change.

VAST ontology implementation. For implementation of the VAST ontology meta-model, we rely on the CIDOC Conceptual Reference Model, (also referred to as CRM) [8]. CRM is a formal ontology specifically designed to support the integration, mediation, and interchange of heterogeneous cultural heritage information. It is developed by the ICOM/CIDOC group and it has been accepted as ISO standard (ISO21127:2006) since 2006[1]. In CRM, basic classes and properties are specified aimed at representing documentation of cultural heritage and scientific activities. The ontology is complemented by a number of modular extensions of the basic model. These extensions are designed to support different types of specialized research questions (e.g., representation of bibliographic data, geographical and archaeological data, data about social phenomena) and they are harmonized with the base ontology.

The choice of CRM for implementing the VAST meta-model is based on multiple motivations. First, CRM is a standard that aims to offer a complete and relatively off-the-shelf solution that is readily applicable. In VAST, we need to represent both temporal and spatial data, and CRM provides specific constructs to this end. For instance, a document to annotate has a creation/publication date and this feature can be represented by exploiting the class E52-Time-Span and the property P160-has temporal projection. As a further example, the class E53-Place and the property P161-has spatial projection are defined in CRM to represent geo-referenced data about documents. Furthermore, CRM supports an *event-oriented modeling* of knowledge, meaning that fact representation is articulated in a set of event-based relationships. As an example, a value interpretation that we aim to model in the VAST ontology can be implemented as an instance of the class E5-Event to represent a specific association between a document text snippet, a keyword, and a scholar, thus providing an explicit description of a document annotation. Moreover, CRM can be integrated with the CRMdig extension about representation of provenance metadata [9]. This extension provides formal constructs for annotation representation like the class D30 Annotation Event and the property L43 annotates (is annotated by).

5. Related work

In this section, we focus on available solutions about knowledge modeling and representation in the framework of Digital and Computational Humanities research. A main issue regarding knowledge modeling in the DH/CH is that metadata from different institutions (e.g., museums,

[1]The current standard is the one renewed and updated in 2014 (ISO 21127:2014)

archives, libraries) are heterogeneous and need to be integrated to offer a complete view of information about any period, geographic location, and aspect of human activity in the past. In [10], the use of metadata schemas like for example Dublin Core, MPEG7, and METS standards, is discouraged due to the fact that the available metadata are usually insufficient to represent all the real-world feature that need to be described. In this direction, the use of a common conceptualization model is recommended for ensuring interoperability of repositories, uniform access to data, and querying functionalities.

A number of conceptualization models exist that are already employed also in the field of cultural heritage, humanities, and social sciences [11]. A brief overview is available in [12] and [11]. An additional survey on this topic is provided in [13]. As an example, DOLCE [14] is a large Descriptive first-order Ontology for Linguistic and Cognitive Engineering. According to [12], the rigorous DOLCE's logical formulation makes difficult for domain experts to understand and use it. Moreover, as a difference with CRM, a modular organization of the ontology specifications is not supported in DOLCE. For instance, this means that the design of space and time data is represented as properties of concepts and not as concepts existing per sé. A further example is the PROTON (PROTo ONtology) [15]. This is an upper-level ontology characterized by a hierarchy of classes and properties without any restriction on the meaning. As a difference with CRM, PROTON does not provide specific constructs for conceptualization of space and time data.

In the context of DH/CH, CHARM [16] (Cultural Heritage Abstract Reference Model) represents an alternative to the CRM. The are three major differences between CHARM and CRM: i) the CHARM ontology is wider in scope than CRM, and this could be a matter of confusion for ontology designers with focused domain target and limited experience; ii) CHARM provides an abstract model that needs to be extended to fit a specific organisation need; iii) CHARM is expressed in ConML, a well-defined conceptual modelling language, while CRM is a conceptual model that is compatible with implementation through different formalization languages (e.g., RDF).

Finally, we note that the modular extensions of the CIDOC CRM also constitute an additional option for ontology representation of specific types of data. In particular, we mention i) CRMtex [17] for supporting knowledge representation of ancient documents, and ii) CRMsci [18] for archaeological excavations, scientific observations, and measurements.

6. Ongoing and future work

In this paper we have presented the vision of the VAST project in the context of the transition from digital to computational humanities. One of the main drivers of this transition is the need of methods and techniques capable of adding value to the historical collections of documents held by museums, archives and other cultural institutions. The vision of VAST is summarized by the principles that inspired the VAST architecture which is designed to support multidimensional modeling and visualization of knowledge extracted from the source documents and from the contents created by final users. Ongoing activities are about the following issues.

Document annotation. The VAST scholars already defined the first version of the common vocabulary to employ for document annotation. The VAST keywords are integrated within the annotation tool and they have been associated with a set of shared annotation guidelines.

Ontology design and implementation. The VAST ontology meta-model presented in Section 4 is going to be implemented through the CIDOC Conceptual Reference Model. Details about modeling of the VAST entities through the CRM constructs are going to be investigated.

Our future work will be focused on defining the methodology and the techniques for **ontology population and exploitation**. The idea is to support a semi-automated ontology population process, where text analysis and data linking techniques are exploited to aggregate keywords and contents, and to define mapping with the VAST ontology concepts in order to suggest possible interpretations to the scholars and experts. Moreover, we will also study how to integrate the knowledge extracted from documents, concerning the Past of values, with activities and user feedback and experiences, concerning the Present of values.

Acknowledgments

This project has received funding from the European Union's Horizon 2020 research and innovation programme under grant agreement No 101004949. This document reflects only the author's view and the European Commission is not responsible for any use that may be made of the information it contains.
This paper is partially funded by the RECON project within the UNIMI-SEED research programme.

References

[1] F. Karsdorp, B. McGillivray, A. Nerghes, M. Wevers (Eds.), Computational Humanities Research 2020, volume 2723, Amsterdam, the Netherlands, 2020.
[2] C. Biemann, G. Crane, C. Fellbaum, A. Mehler, Computational Humanities - Bridging the Gap between Computer Science and Digital Humanities (Dagstuhl Seminar 14301), Dagstuhl Reports 4 (2014) 80–111.
[3] G. Michael, Agent-Based Modeling and Historical Simulation, DHQ: Digital Humanities Quarterly 8 (2014).
[4] The EU values, The EU values, 2020. URL: https://ec.europa.eu/component-library/eu/about/eu-values/.
[5] S. Castano, M. Falduti, A. Ferrara, S. Montanelli, The LATO Knowledge Model for Automated Knowledge Extraction and Enrichment from Court Decisions Corpora, in: Proc. of the 1st Int. Workshop "CAiSE for Legal Documents" (COUrT 2020), Grenoble, France, 2020, pp. 15–26.
[6] S. Castano, A. Ferrara, S. Montanelli, Topic Summary Views for Exploration of Large Scholarly Datasets, Journal on Data Semantics (JoDS) 7 (2018) 155–170.
[7] S. Castano, A. Ferrara, S. Montanelli, Crowdsourcing task assignment with online profile learning, in: Proc. of the 26th Int. Conference on Cooperative Information Systems (CoopIS 2018), La Valletta, Malta, 2018.
[8] M. Doerr, The CIDOC conceptual Reference Module: an Ontological Approach to Semantic Interoperability of Metadata, AI magazine 24 (2003) 75–75.

[9] M. Doerr, M. Theodoridou, CRMdig-An extension of CIDOC-CRM to support provenance metadata, Technical Report, ICS-FORTH, 2014.
[10] G. Bruseker, N. Carboni, A. Guillem, Cultural Heritage Data Management: the Role of Formal Ontology and CIDOC CRM, Heritage and Archaeology in the Digital Age (2017) 93–131.
[11] V. Mascardi, V. Cordì, P. Rosso, A Comparison of Upper Ontologies, Technical Report, Dipartimento di Informatica e Scienze dell'Informazione (DISI), Università degli Studi di Genova, 2007.
[12] M. Doerr, Ontologies for Cultural Heritage, Springer, 2009, pp. 463–486.
[13] C. Partridge, A. Mitchell, A. Cook, J. Sullivan, M. West, A Survey of Top-Level Ontologies-to Inform the Ontological Choices for a Foundation Data Model, Technical Report, Cambridge University, 2020.
[14] J. Lehmann, S. Borgo, C. Masolo, A. Gangemi, Causality and causation in DOLCE, in: Proc. of the Int. Conference FOIS-Formal ontology in information systems, 2004, pp. 273–284.
[15] I. Terziev, A. Kiryakov, D. Manov, et al., Base Upper-Level Ontology (BULO) Guidance, Technical Report, Ontotext Lab, Sirma Group, 2005.
[16] C. Gonzalez-Perez, An Ontology for Cultural Heritage, Springer, 2018, pp. 195–215.
[17] F. Murano, A. Felicetti, CRMtex-An Ontological Model for Ancient Textual Entities, in: Decimo convegno annuale dell'Associazione per l'Informatica Umanistica e la Cultura Digitale, Pisa, 2021.
[18] M. Doerr, A. Kritsotaki, Y. Rousakis, G. Hiebel, M. Theodoridou, CRMsci: The Scientific Observation Model-An Extension of CIDOC-CRM to Support Scientific Observation, Technical Report, FORTH, 2014.

From Data Quality to Big Data Quality: A Data Integration Scenario

Carlo Batini[1], Anisa Rula[2]

[1]University of Milano-Bicocca
[2]University of Brescia

Abstract

Big data has made its appearance in many fields, including scientific research, business, public administration and so on. Although, it is acknowledged that there exist different aspects (e.g., acquisition of data, extraction, pre-processing, analysis modelling and functionality, interpretation, etc.) that might affect the benefit of such data, several authors identify *data quality* as the most decisive one. More recently, a variety of data types have arisen from linguistic and visual information, used and diffused through social networks, Internet of things, enterprise and public sector information systems as well as the Web. The big data phenomenon has deeply impacted on the diversity of types of data. In our previous work, we provided a deep investigation on how data quality concepts can be extended to such vast set of data types, encompassing, e.g., semi-structured texts, maps, images and linked data. In this work, we focus on Linked Data, a type of data that can be viewed as big data and study the effect of data quality in a data integration scenario.

Keywords

Data Quality, Semantic Annotations, Tabular Data

1. Introduction

Big data has made its appearance in many fields such as scientific research, business and public administration. There are different definitions provided for the concept of big data [1]. According to Gartner, "Big data is high-volume, high-velocity and/or high-variety information assets that demands cost-effective, innovative forms of information processing that enable enhanced insight, decision making, and process automation."[1]. In other words, big data goes beyond large amount of data by exceeding the capabilities of traditional computing environments [2]. Although it is acknowledged that there exist different aspects (e.g., acquisition of data, extraction, pre-processing, analysis modelling and functionality, interpretation, etc.) that might affect the benefit of such data [3], several authors identify *data quality* as the most decisive one [2]. Consequently, using data with adequate levels of data quality is paramount to obtain the maximum benefit.

There exist many methodologies proposed in the information system and database communities to identify and manage the quality of the published data, all addressing different aspects of

SEBD 2021: The 29th Italian Symposium on Advanced Database Systems, September 5-9, 2021, Pizzo Calabro (VV), Italy
carlo.batini@unimib.it (C. Batini); anisa.rula@unibs.it (A. Rula)

[1]http://www.gartner.com/it-glossary/big-data/

quality assessment by proposing appropriate dimensions, measures and tools [4, 5, 6, 7]. More recently, a variety of data types have arisen from linguistic and visual information, used and diffused through social networks, Internet of things, enterprise and public sector information systems as well as the Web. The big data phenomenon has deeply impacted on the diversity of types of data. In this work, we focus on linked data, a type of data that can be viewed as big data [8]. In recent years, the linked data paradigm has emerged as a simple mechanism for employing the Web as a medium for data and knowledge integration where both documents and data are linked. Linked data essentially refers to a set of best practices for publishing and connecting structured data on the Web, which allows publishing and exchanging information in an interoperable and reusable fashion [9]. Many different communities on the Internet such as geographic, media, life sciences and government communities have already adopted these linked data principles. This is confirmed by the dramatically growing linked data Web, where currently more than 150 billion facts are represented[2].

Modelling and constructing linked data poses different challenges with respect to the three coordinates: *volume*, *variety* and *velocity*. First, the increasing diffusion of the linked data paradigm as a standard way to share knowledge on the Web allows consumers to fully exploit vast amount of open structured data that were not available in the past (high *volume* of data). Second, linked data refers to a Web-scale knowledge base consisting of interlinked published data from a multitude of *autonomous* information providers[3]. Although it is suggested to reuse as much as possible existing vocabularies, still there exist a lot of heterogeneous datasets (*variety* of data). Third, linked data can be considered as a dynamic environment where information can change rapidly and cannot be assumed to be static (*velocity* of data) [10]. In addition to the aforementioned three characteristics, there exists a fourth characteristic named *veracity*. Transforming data into linked data does not necessarily require the definition of a schema thus following a schema-last approach that first publishes the data and subsequently (and optionally) creates the schema. Therefore, the veracity of data should be checked since linked data does not intrinsically prevent to add incorrect or inconsistent information to the datasets.

Quality dimensions and metrics are important for measuring quality of linked data. However, an important question is "How do data quality dimensions and metrics evolve in the transformation process from tabular to linked data?" To answer this question, we need to study the evolution of quality dimensions from traditional databases to linked data based on the differences of the structural characteristics of both data models. A study of the evolution between quality dimensions of relational data and linked data according to the differences in their structural characteristics, enables us managing the huge variability of methods and techniques needed to manage data quality in linked data. In this paper, we provide a data integration use case to show that data integration over semantically enriched datasets provides a higher quality result than integrating two relational datasets. In other words, we would like to answer to the following question: *How data quality drives the data integration process?*

Running Example Throughout this manuscript, we consider a data integration use case study having two relation tables (see Figure 1). The two tables contain information about Tourist

[2]http://lod-cloud.net/state/

[3]linked data is different from centralized databases that are designed and built by a (single) database administrator.

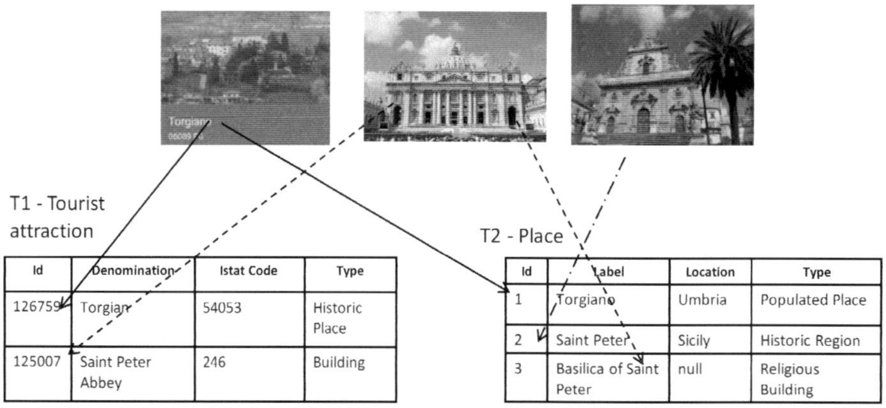

Figure 1: Two relational datasets to be used in the running example.

Attraction (hereafter called T1) and Place (hereafter called T2). T2 contains three instances of place of interest, consisting of the Torgian locallity, the Basilica of Saint Peter, seen as a religious building and the Saint Peter in Modica in Sicily, seen as a place of interest in the historic region (Historic Region). Figure 1 shows the correspondences between the objects of the real world (the observables) and the records of the two tables. We consider the integration process by keeping in mind the quality of the sources and how it will influence the final integration.

Organizational Structure This paper is organized as follows. Section 2 presents related work on the mapping of relational databases to linked data and the quality assessment of the RDF mappings. Section 3 presents the differences and similarities of structural characteristics as well as other important differences between the two data models. In Section 4, we analyse the evolution of quality metrics according to the classification model defined in the previous section. Section 5 presents a use case implementing our methodology. Finally, we conclude in Section 6.

2. Related Work

In this section we provide details about the state of the art regarding the relational model to linked data mapping problem and the quality of the mappings. This section is divided into two subsections. Section 2.1 compares the characteristics of the relational and linked data and describes the mapping approaches. Section 2.2 describes the quality assessment approaches.

2.1. Relational model and linked data

The survey in [11] analyses approaches that tackle the problem from database to ontology mappings. The authors use different criteria for analysing the approaches such as mapping languages or software availability. Before proposing the classification of the approaches, the authors first analyse the characteristics of the data models from Extended Entity Relationship (EER) model to relational model and finally to RDF model.

In addition, the authors in [11] propose other characteristics related to the RDF data model and RDFS as follows: i) classes of individual resources, ii) properties, connecting two resources, iii) hierarchies of classes, iv) hierarchies of properties, and v) domain and range constraints on properties. In this work, we provide both characteristics at instance and schema level. In addition, at instance level we include the position of the elements in a triple e.g. subjects vs objects. The work in [12] identifies 25 structural characteristics separately for the ontology and the relational model. These characteristics were collected as a summary of answers to the following questions (used to understand the differences and similarities): What is it for?, What does it look like? How do you build one? How is it implemented and used? and Where are the semantics? The author in [13] studies the differences between the Semantic Web and the Relationl Databases. In particular, he studies the mapping languages. There exists a group on W3C named RDB2RDF[4] that worked on two language mappings standards. The two proposed standards are named Direct Mapping[5] and R2RML[6].

2.2. Quality Assessment of the Mappings

The database community has deeply investigated the problem of data quality by proposing different methodologies and frameworks [4, 5, 6, 7]. Most of these works have focused on data in relational models, traditionally adopted in Data Base Management Systems [4]. Nevertheless, a variety of data types such as semi-structured texts and linked data, produced over social networks and the Web resulted in an investigation on how data quality concepts can be extended. In [14], we started to investigate the evolution and the adoption of quality metrics according to the structural characteristics of linked data, while in this work we study how the adoption of quality metrics support the data integration process.

Different approaches have been proposed to assess the quality of linked data. These approaches can be distinguished in those applied to the quality assessment of datasets [15, 16] and mapping definitions [17] which can be classified as i) manual, ii) semi–automatic and iii) automatic.

In particular, the work in [15] focuses on the definitions and formalization of quality assessment metrics for linked data. In a more recent work, [16] proposes the formalization of quality metrics from the practical and implementation point of view. In [18], the authors evaluate the quality assessment of crawled datasets containing around 12M RDF triples. The aim was to discuss common problems found in RDF datasets, and possible solutions. More specifically, the work aimed at uncovering errors related to accessibility, reasoning, syntactical and non-authoritative contributions. The authors also provided suggestions on how publishers can improve their data, so that the consumers can find "high quality" datasets. However, all these approaches focus on the quality assessment of the dataset and do not study the evolution of quality metrics; furthermore, they do not provide any evidence about the model adopted for the generation of new quality metrics for linked data based on existing metrics for relational databases.

Whereas [19] and [20] derive actual quality checks from the dataset under assessment, a

[4] https://www.w3.org/2001/sw/rdb2rdf/

[5] https://www.w3.org/TR/rdb-direct-mapping/

[6] https://www.w3.org/TR/r2rml/

mapping quality assessment method should take the transformation process into account. Only a few works provide attempts for the quality assessment of RDF mappings [21, 17, 22]. Dimou, et. al. [22] demonstrate that assessing an RDF dataset requires a considerable measure of time, therefore it cannot be often executed, and when that happens, the violations' root is not detected. Despite what might be expected, specifically assessing RDF mappings requires essentially less effort, while the violations' root is detected. In [17], they assess mappings from semi-structured data to RDF by proposing incremental, iterative and uniform validation workflow where violation might derive from incorrect usage of schemas; in addition, they suggest mapping refinements based on the results of these quality assessments. Similar to our work, they focus on three quality dimensions that are completeness, accuracy and consistency. A more recent work in [21] proposes a predicting algorithm to detect incorrect mappings which is applied to the DBpedia dataset. The corresponding discussions do not include any quality metric preservation. So, while there are metrics dedicated to other domains that could be re-used for the RDF quality assessment mapping, there is (to the best of our knowledge) no study to support guiding the generation of RDF mappings based on a quality evaluation of these transformations. Moreover, we could not find an existing method or methodology whose target is the improvement of the quality of RDF integration results through the quality assessment and improvements of mappings.

3. Structural Characteristics of Linked Data

A common classification framework characterized by several quality dimensions, allows us to compare dimensions across different data types. The framework is based on a classification in clusters of dimensions proposed in Batini et al. (2012) where dimensions are included in the same cluster according to their similarity.

We consider three main types of data that can be viewed as BD (i) maps, (ii) semi-structured texts and (iii) linked data. Each one of these data types has inherently associated several structural characteristics, which are relevant for the investigation of quality dimensions defined in the literature. In this section we discuss in detail the structural characteristics for linked data.

Linked Data. The Web has been in the last years an extraordinary vehicle of production, diffusion, and exchange of information. Data as the lowest level of abstraction, from which information is derived, can be provided on the Web as open data under the open data initiative. Open data is mainly provided in different domains including economy, science, employment, environment and education. Open data gain popularity with the rise of the Internet and World Wide Web especially, with the launch of open-data government initiatives. The philosophy behind open data has been long established in public bodies, while the term "open data" itself is recent. Open data is data that can be freely used, reused and redistributed by anyone - subject only, at most, to the requirement to attribute and sharealike. Open data become open linked data when, according to Tim Berners-Lee (2006):

- Information is available on the Web (any format) under an open license.
- Information is available as structured data (e.g. an Excel sheet instead of an image scan of a table).
- Non-proprietary formats are used (e.g. CSV instead of MS Excel).

- URI identification is used so that people can point at individual data.
- Data is linked to other data to provide context.

Linked data enables publishers to link and publish structured data by generating semantic connections among data sets. Linked data exhibits structural characteristics referring to the issues discussed in [14].

4. Evolution of quality dimensions in Linked Data

We have studied the evolution of quality dimensions and metrics in [14]. As to linked data, we report here the evolution of one quality dimension named accessibility to show how the structural characteristics from one data model to the other influence the way quality is measured. **Accessibility in relational data.** Accessibility measures the ability of the user to access data from his or her own culture, physical status/functions, and technologies available. Several guidelines are provided by international and national bodies to govern the production of data, applications, services, and Web sites in order to guarantee accessibility, with specific concern on accessibility for disabled persons. Guidelines referring to relational tables in Web sites are provided by the World Wide Web Consortium in (WWWC); guidelines identify the characteristics of the HTML representation of tables to be made accessible by means of assistive technologies, for example: for all data tables, identify row and column headers; for data tables that have two or more logical levels of row or column headers, use markup to associate data cells and header cells; for data tables elements, label elements with the "scope", "headers", and "axis" attributes, so that future browsers and assistive technologies will be able to select data from a table by filtering on categories. **Accessibility in linked data.** Public bodies, for reasons of transparency and accessibility, have progressively published public data in order to enable citizens to access data for their own purposes and interests. To make the data accessible in a standard way, the first step is that to release the format of data from proprietary formats to open formats (i.e. RDF), which are not only understood by humans, but also by machines. The format issue is considered in several structural characteristics discussed for linked data in the previous section, corresponding to several possible mechanisms that can be adopted to improve accessibility. In Figure 2 we classify the relevant quality dimensions according to such mechanisms. One mechanism can be the use of HTTP URI, a combination of globally unique identification (through URIs) and a retrieval mechanism (through HTTP), which enables the identification of objects and abstract concepts and their descriptions; in this case the accessibility dimension refers to dereferencability, or resource accessibility. To make datasets available through SPARQL endpoints, the user should indicate the URI of the dataset and the location of the corresponding SPARQL endpoint and should check whether the server responds to a SPARQL query; in this case we refer to dataset accessibility. A further mechanism to access a dataset is by making an RDF dump available for download; in this way the location of the RDF dump can be exploited, and we refer to browsing accessibility.

In order to specify the connection between real world objects, a mechanism of interlinking has been proposed based on the RDF links. Interlinking refers to the degree to which objects are linked to each other, be it within or between two or more data sources. It represents a relevant dimension for accessibility in linked data, since the process of data integration is made

	Structural characteristics				
	Dereferenceable Resource	*SPARQL Endpoint*	*RDF dumps*	*Interlinking*	*Licensing*
Quality dimension	*Quality sub-dimension*				
Accessibility	Resource accessibility	Dataset accessibility	Browsing accessibility	Integration accessibility	Reuse accessibility

Figure 2: Quality dimensions of linked data classified by linked data structural characteristics.

possible through the links created between various data sets. In this case the accessibility dimension corresponds to integration accessibility, since RDF links describe the relationship between objects and enables discovering new data through integration. Previous approaches to accessibility have evolved to investigate the new juridical licensing aspects of data. Licensing is a new quality dimension not considered for relational databases but mandatory in an open data world. Providing licensing information is an indication of how much data is accessible to be potentially re-used, based on the specification of legal rights and allowances; in this case the accessibility dimension corresponds to reuse accessibility.

As envisioned by this section the evolution of data quality dimensions according to the research coordinates that are relevant in Big Data, such as the variety of data types, is important to be studied to have an understanding of data quality assessment in a new settings of information. In Section 5 we study two additional quality dimensions: the accuracy and the completeness. Our aim is to study the advantage/disadvantage in terms of data quality of the data integration process according to traditional techniques and the "new" techniques applied in linked data.

5. Use Case

This section presents a practical data integration use case that shows how the transformations can affect the overall quality of single and integrated datasets. We show a data integration process on two datasets performed according to two different workflows. In Section 5.1, the first workflow considers the integration of the two tabular datasets based on traditional techniques and after the transformation of the integrated dataset into linked data. In Section 5.2, the second workflow considers the transformation in linked data of the two datasets and after their integration. In both workflows the two datasets of Tourist attraction (T1) and Place (T2) of the running example introduced in Section 1 are used. We simplified the schema information by using the same names for the same attributes when possible since we are not interested in schema matching but in instance matching.

Instance Matching. Given two records r1 and r2 which represent two distinct observables in the universe, an integration process must allow us to decide whether:

- r1 and r2 refer to the same observable, in this case there exists a match between the two objects.
- r1 and r2 do not refer to the same observable, in this case there is no match between the two objects.

In the first case, we refer to either *true positives*, or to *false positives*. In the second case, we refer either to true negatives or to false negatives. The quality of the distance measurement should be an indication of minimizing false positives or false negatives. In the following, we discuss the two workflows.

5.1. Integration vs Transformation

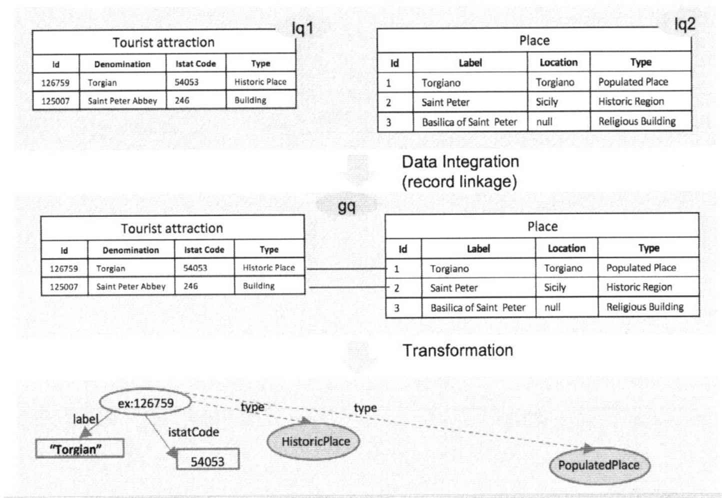

Figure 3: First workflow: data integration first and then transformation.

In the first workflow (see Figure 3), the integration of the two datasets is performed first by using traditional techniques such as record linkage followed by the transformation into RDF and enrichment with external knowledge bases.

- We measure the distance between the first record of T1 (*Torgian*) and the first record of T2 (*Torgiano*) on `Denomination` and `Label` attributes respectively, see Figure 3. The edit distance returns 1, thus there is a **match**.
- We measure the distance between the second record of T1 (*Saint Peter Abbey*) and the second record of T2 (*Saint Peter*) `Denomination` and `Label` attributes respectively. Jaccard distance function returns 0.33, thus there is a **match**.
- We measure the distance between the second record of T1 (*Saint Peter Abbey*) and the third record of T2 (*Basilica of Saint Peter*) `Denomination` and `Label` attributes respectively. The Jaccard distance function returns 0.60, thus there is a **non-match**.

The final result compared with the "true" matches are: a true positive (R11 and R21 records), a false positive (R12 and R22 records), a false negative (R12 records and R23 records).

5.2. Transformation vs Integration

In the second workflow, the integration of the datasets is performed after the transformation and enrichment steps, see Figure 4. In the semantic transformation and enrichment steps, the datasets are transformed into a semantically richer model, the RDF model, which, by the virtue of its graph structure, it can exploit semantic resources and techniques available on the Web. For example, we can connect some of the data present in the two graphs to a taxonomy or ontology, so that it is possible to compare the data not only by means of distances measured between strings, but exploiting their meaning provided by the taxonomies.

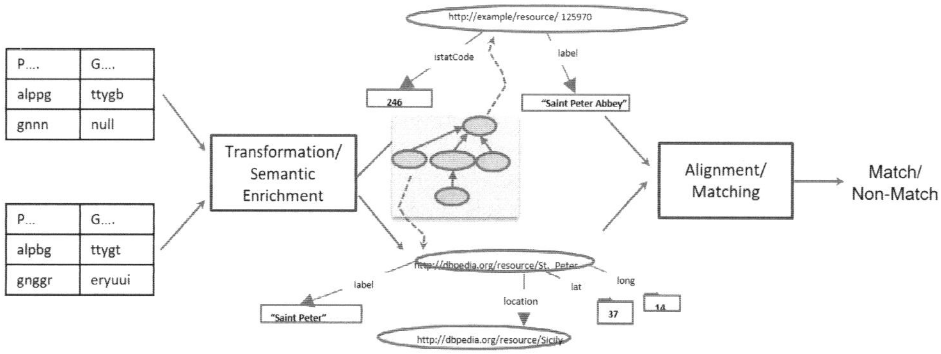

Figure 4: Second workflow: transformation first and then integration.

First, we transform the tables from the relational model into the RDF model; Figure 5 shows the RDF graph relating to the first records of the two tables (R11 and R21) and then those relating to the second record of the Tourist attraction table (R21) and to the second and third records of the Place table (R22 and R23).

Tourist attraction

Id	Denomination	Istat Code	Type
126759	Torgian	54053	Historic Place
125007	Saint Peter Abbey	246	Building

Place

Id	Label	Location	Type
1	Torgiano	Umbria	Populated Place
2	Saint Peter	Sicily	Historic Region
3	Basilica of Saint Peter	null	Religious Building

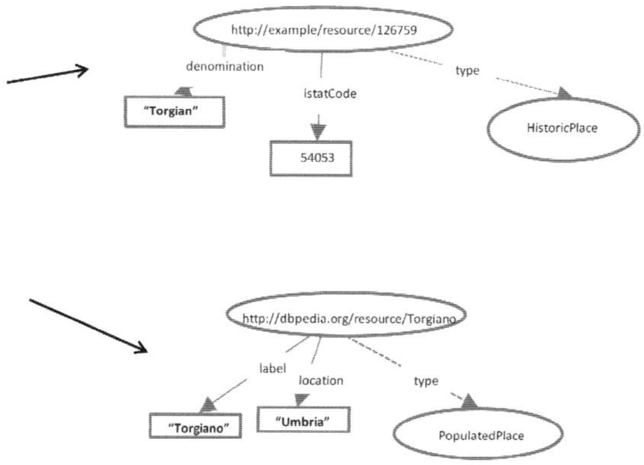

Figure 5: Second workflow: transformation into RDF of the records R11, R21.

After finishing with the transformation we can compare the values in the triples, i.e., *Torgiano* and *Torgian*. A similarity metric based on the edit distance between the two values is applied. The result obtained is 1 meaning that the two records represent the same observable object. We achieved the same result in the first workflow too. To further enrich our tabular data, we use the DBpedia ontology, available in the Linked Open Data Cloud (https://wiki.dbpedia.org/).

At this point, we can compare the similarity of the entities not only on similarity metrics based on the edit distances between two strings but based on the meaning of the two entities

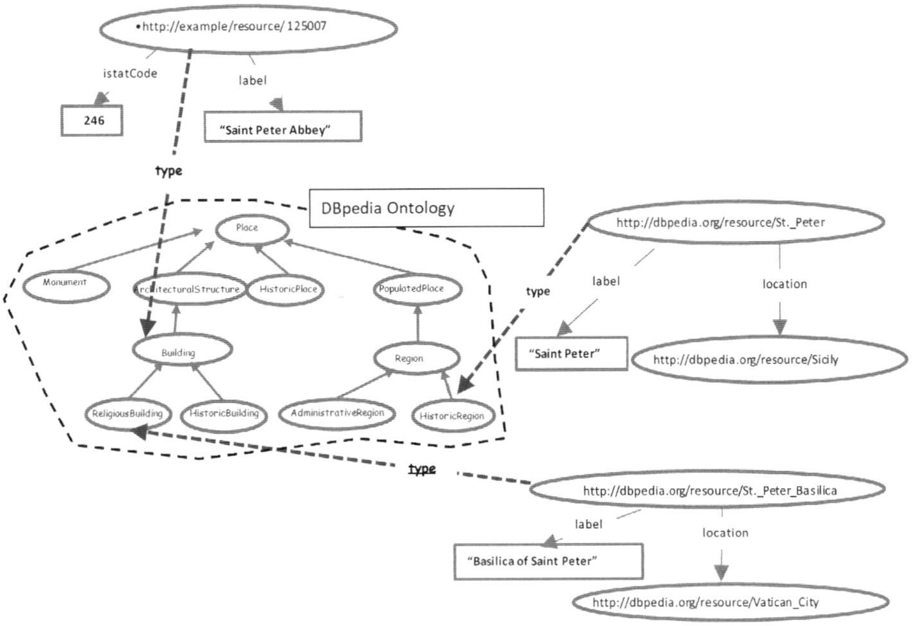

Figure 6: Second Workflow: distances in the DBpedia ontology.

which is measured based on the distance between concepts in a hierarchy. By measuring the distances between the DBpedia concepts of the R12 record and the concepts of the R22 and R23 records, we can deduce that *Saint Peter Abbey* actually corresponds to *Basilica of Saint Peter* (distance in the tree equal to 1), and not to *Saint Peter* (distance equal to 5).

Now suppose we produce another transformation and a semantic enrichment in which we are less precise; in this way we introduce the problem of semantic accuracy known as imprecise annotation or classification. Suppose we classify all instances to be of type *Place* instead of classifying them with a more specific type such as *HistoricalPlace* or *Building*. Further, we apply the matching to the last transformation (see Figure 7) and we obtain distances all equal to 0, thus producing a qualitative result worse than before, because we introduced a false positive. This is due to the fact that the classification of the ontology is not exploited, and the attribution of meaning remains at a high level of abstraction which does not help to exploit the ontological classification. This example has shown that during the transformation process there can be quality problems, and a *degradation* of the meaning of the concepts represented can occur. So the overall quality, in our case of integration, can improve if semantic enrichment is exploited, but at the same time, we should be careful during transformation process since noisy data can be inserted and thus worsening the precision with which they represent the reality.

The final outcome of the second workflow is given as follows: 2 pairs true positive and 1 pair true negative In conclusion, the initial example demonstrated the superiority of the process where first a transformation of the model from relational to RDF is performed and then a semantic enrichment (creation of correspondences with DBpedia) is applied.

Our model shows through this use case that generated the two datasets according to the two different workflows, through the quality metrics we can evaluate which of the two workflows

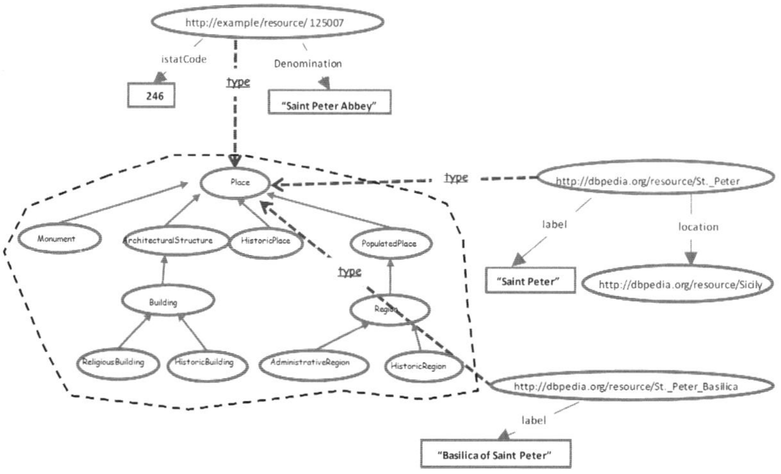

Figure 7: Second Workflow: distances in the DBpedia ontology for records R12, R21, R22.

generated the dataset with the highest quality. As we can see from this results, the best workflow with the highest quality is the one that takes as input the two datasets that are first transformed and then aligned to existing vocabularies when possible and finally enriched with additional data from other datasets.

6. Conclusions

This work demonstrate the importance of integration in the data life cycle. Data integration is inherent to the data modelling of the datasets. To evaluate whether a data transformation from one data model to the other is appropriate we should ask whether the quality of the transformed dataset has increased meaning that the resources available on the Linked Data cloud provide additional information on the accuracy and the completeness of the initial dataset. Moreover, we should check if we can take advantage of this transformation in the data integration process so that available techniques of matching based on hierarchy of the concepts can be applied. The lesson learnt from this use case is that it is better to do first integration followed by transformation if no domain knowledge is needed. Otherwise, transformation followed by alignment is better when: i) aligning attributes to existing vocabularies; ii) identification of the distance between concepts is defined; iii) enriching the dataset with the missing values.

References

[1] C. P. Chen, C.-Y. Zhang, Data-intensive applications, challenges, techniques and technologies: A survey on big data, Information Sciences 275 (2014) 314 – 347.

[2] D. Loshin, Big Data Analytics: From Strategic Planning to Enterprise Integration with Tools, Techniques, NoSQL, and Graph, Morgan Kaufmann, Amsterdam, 2013.

[3] A. Gandomi, M. Haider, Beyond the hype: Big data concepts, methods, and analytics, International Journal of Information Management 35 (2015) 137–144.

[4] C. Batini, M. Scannapieco, Data and Information Quality: Dimensions, Principles and Techniques, Springer, 2016.

[5] Y. W. Lee, D. M. Strong, B. K. Kahn, R. Y. Wang, AIMQ: a methodology for information quality assessment, Information Management 40 (2002) 133 – 146.

[6] L. L. Pipino, Y. W. Lee, R. Y. Wang, Data quality assessment, Communications of the ACM 45 (2002) 211–218.

[7] R. Y. Wang, A product perspective on total data quality management, Communications of the ACM 41 (1998) 58 – 65.

[8] P. Hitzler, K. Janowicz, Linked data, big data, and the 4th paradigm., Semantic Web 4 (2013) 233–235.

[9] T. Heath, C. Bizer, Linked data: Evolving the web into a global data space, volume 1, Morgan & Claypool Publishers, 2011.

[10] T. Käfer, A. Abdelrahman, J. Umbrich, P. O'Byrne, A. Hogan, Observing linked data dynamics, in: ESWC, volume 7882, Springer, 2013, pp. 213–227.

[11] D. Spanos, P. Stavrou, N. Mitrou, Bringing relational databases into the semantic web: A survey, Semantic Web 3 (2012) 169–209.

[12] M. Uschold, Ontology and database schema: What's the difference?, Applied Ontology 10 (2015) 243–258. URL: https://doi.org/10.3233/AO-150158. doi:10.3233/AO-150158.

[13] J. F. Sequeda, Integrating relational databases with the semantic web: A reflection, in: Reasoning Web. Semantic Interoperability on the Web, 2017, pp. 68–120.

[14] C. Batini, A. Rula, M. Scannapieco, G. Viscusi, From data quality to big data quality, J. Database Manag. 26 (2015) 60–82.

[15] A. Zaveri, A. Rula, A. Maurino, R. Pietrobon, J. Lehmann, S. Auer, Quality assessment for linked data: A survey, Semantic Web 7 (2016) 63–93. URL: http://dx.doi.org/10.3233/SW-150175. doi:10.3233/SW-150175.

[16] J. Debattista, C. Lange, S. Auer, D. Cortis, Evaluating the quality of the LOD cloud: An empirical investigation, Semantic Web 9 (2018) 859–901.

[17] A. Dimou, D. Kontokostas, M. Freudenberg, R. Verborgh, J. Lehmann, E. Mannens, S. Hellmann, R. Van de Walle, Assessing and refining mappingsto rdf to improve dataset quality, in: ISWC, Springer, 2015, pp. 133–149.

[18] A. Hogan, J. Umbrich, A. Harth, R. Cyganiak, A. Polleres, S. Decker, An empirical survey of linked data conformance, JWS 14 (2012) 14–44.

[19] C. Fürber, M. Hepp, Swiqa - a semantic web information quality assessment framework, in: 19th ECIS, 2011, p. 76.

[20] D. Kontokostas, P. Westphal, S. Auer, S. Hellmann, J. Lehmann, R. Cornelissen, A. Zaveri, Test-driven evaluation of linked data quality, in: Proceedings of the 23rd international conference on World Wide Web, ACM, 2014, pp. 747–758.

[21] M. Rico, N. Mihindukulasooriya, D. Kontokostas, H. Paulheim, S. Hellmann, A. Gómez-Pérez, Predicting incorrect mappings: A data-driven approach applied to dbpedia, in: 33rd ACM SAC, 2018, pp. 323–330.

[22] A. Dimou, D. Kontokostas, M. Freudenberg, R. Verborgh, J. Lehmann, E. Mannens, S. Hellman, R. Van de Walle, Dbpedia mappings quality assessment, in: ISWC, 2016, pp. 1–4.

snpStorage: a database to store and share experimental SNPs data sets

Giuseppe Agapito[1,3], Mario Cannataro[2,3]

[1]*Dep. of Legal, Economic and Social Sciences, University Magna Græcia,Catanzaro, 88100, Italy*
[2]*Dep. of Medical and Surgical Sciences, University Magna Græcia, Catanzaro, 88100, Italy*
[3]*Data Analytics Research Center, University Magna Græcia, Catanzaro, 88100, Italy*

Abstract

The last years have seen a continuous improvement in sequencing and genotyping technologies. These improvements have spawned a rapid advancement in bioinformatics databases and software relating to the collection and analysis of genetic data. Genetic data holds several types of variations such as: *indels, microsatellites, copy number variants (CNV),* and *Single Nucleotide Polymorphisms (SNPs).* SNPs are the most abundant type of genetic variation and are now the principals raw material underlying most genetic studies and databases. SNPs can be used as potential biomarkers to investigate cancer growth or progression, and planning more effective treatment regimens. To make data quickly accessible to the users, e.g., to face the burden related to the relation of several experiments and to allow an easy and controlled sharing of genotyping data among different labs, the need for specialized SNP databases arises. For these reasons, we developed *snpStorage* (and related querying service), a database to collect experimental SNPs data integrated with clinical data if available. *snpStorage* collects experimental SNPs data in pharmacogenomics studies, obtained by using DMET (*Drug Metabolism Enzymes and Transporters*) platform and subsequently enriched with clinical data. The main contributions of snpStorage are *i)* automatic translation, normalization and integration of SNP data sets with clinical data and mapping in relational schema. *ii)* A repository where research laboratories can store data (anonymously), merge and handle SNP data sets for more specific analysis; *iii)* To provide medical professionals a software instrument to facilitate clinical decisions based on the individual's genome, and tailoring health care services to the patient's genotype.

Keywords

Databases, Single Nucleotide Polymorphisms (SNPs), SQL, NoSQL, Genomics, Integrative Bioinformatics

1. Introduction

The last years have seen exponential growth in the investigation of genetic and genomic variations as more genomes have been sequenced, corresponding with the continuous improvement in sequencing and genotyping technologies.

These improvements have spawned a rapidly advanced in bioinformatics databases and softwares relating to the collection, management, and analysis of genomics data.

Genomics data include the variations that are very common and useful in genomics studies,

SEBD 2021: The 29th Italian Symposium on Advanced Database Systems, September 5-9, 2021, Pizzo Calabro (VV), Italy
agapito@unicz.it (G. Agapito); cannataro@unicz.it (M. Cannataro)
https://kmitd.github.io/ilaria/ (M. Cannataro)
0000-0002-0877-7063 (G. Agapito); 0000-0001-7116-9338 (M. Cannataro)

CEUR Workshop Proceedings (CEUR-WS.org)

including *indels, microsatellites, copy number variants (CNV)*, and Single Nucleotide Polymorphisms (*SNPs*). SNPs are the most abundant type of genetic variations, and are now the principal raw material underlying most genetic studies. SNPs are common mutations in the population; the most common and frequent SNP type is the substitution of a single DNA's bases. The DNA's bases are Adenine, Cytosine, Guanine, and Thymine (while Thymine is replaced from the Uracil into the RNA) in short the nucleotides are $(A, C, G, \{T/U\})$. Among the other types of variations SNPs are mainly the easiest to observe and the most useful and widely applied markers in genetic and epigenetic studies. The continue development and improvement of the high-throughput assays such as Next Generation Sequencing (*NGS*), gene-expression and SNP microarrays, enable the production of massive quantities of data that have to be opportunely stored to perform further analysis, such as discriminative statistical analysis [1], or data mining by using association rules [2, 3, 4] to find multiple correlations among SNPs.

Thus, researchers and clinician-researchers need databases able to store, and retrieve SNPs data. In addition, the integration of SNP data sets with clinical data, can be used for assessing disease risks, predict susceptibility, early diagnosing, and planning treatment regimens. Data collection, arrangement and storage are essential steps in the execution of daily activities ranging from the individual research level as well as in research areas. Hence, it is mandatory to permanently store and make data quickly accessible to the users through the employment of apposite containers such as databases. A database is a collection of data, used to manage and store information for any domain of interest.

Currently, genomics studies results are stored in flat textual files (not structured), and memorized locally into the research storage-system. The use of flat text files put some limitations such as: it makes difficult to integrate data referring to the same genomic study, to share data among researchers and research laboratories, excluding or making challenging the production of bigger and more informative datasets obtained by sharing and merging multiple SNP data sets. Thus, the need to represent not structured experimental genomics data in structured format arises. Goal that can be accomplished by mapping the experimental genomics information contained into the flat files in a structured model by means of a relational databases management system (*RDBMS*).

Thus, in this scenario where the data to handle are of different types, alongside the classic relational database management systems (RDBMS) [5], have been developed several different kinds of database management systems (*DBMS*) known as *NoSQL* (No Structured Query Language) [6]. *RDBMS* are relational data management systems based primarily on tables and use the *SQL* (Structured Query Language) language for data manipulation. Conversely, NoSQL databases are not relational data management systems, they are not based on tables to represent the association among data, and do not use SQL for data manipulation. Examples of NoSQL databases are graph databases, employed to handle data coming from social networks, biological networks (proteins interaction networks and biological pathways), where data do not require a relational model to be handled.

Databases have become essential for genetics, proteomics and interactomics studies.

The available public online SNP databases are a source of information from which researchers can readily retrieve and use data to design in silico studies. In silico studies allow researchers to improve the way to perform wet-lab experiments. Because, in silico studies make it possible to obtain in advance the most likely genomic regions affected by the SNPs to investigate. For example, the knowledge of the genomic region to investigate avoids to the researchers to proceed by attempts saving in this way time and money, since a wet lab experiment may cost thousands of dollars.

There are different databases that provide information on SNPs data such as dbSNP [7], HGBASE [8], GBD [9], OMIM [10], and HapMap [11]. All the listed SNP databases represent a comprehensive, general and reliable catalogue of human SNPs, from which browsing and searching the core human genome SNP data. The listed databases contain relevant information for coding regions, including transcription structure, genome maps, bibliography, protein data, sequences, and the links to the supporting data, to facilitate large-scale studies in association genetics, pharmaco-genomics etc. On the other hand, the listed databases lack in the capability to handle experimental SNPs data obtained from clinical studies and enriched with clinical data. In this paper we present *snpStorage* a database able to collect experimental SNPs data obtained by using DMET (Drug Metabolism Enzymes and Transporters) [12] platform and enriched with clinical information. With respect to the above listed databases, snpStorage is not a comprehensive catalog of SNPs, but it is an attempt to produce a SNPs repository where research laboratories can store data (anonymously), merge and handle them, with which to yield more accurate SNP data sets annotated with clinical data when available, to perform more in-depth analysis. The goal pursuit by snpStorage is to make the analysis of integrated multiple SNP datasets more accurate w.r.t small SNP datasets, allowing users to extend and collect all their data in an unique repository. Current DMET SNPs outputs are arranged in a tabular form with 1931 rows (probes) and a number of column related to the number of patients enrolled in the study (commonly, in a number less than 100). Thus, snpStorage allows researchers of a research center or from different research centers, to store and query SNP data sets as well as, to merge together outcomes from several studies, making it possible to extend a small experimental study in a more informative one. Enlarging the size of an experimental study, allows to produce more informative data sets, providing a more accurate description of the study under-investigation, than analyzing data sets individually.

The rest of the paper is arranged as follows. Section 2 describes the major popular SNP databases, Section 3 describes the requirements analysis of snpStorage along with the input data. Section 4 illustrates how snpStorage has been implemented, highlighting the efficiency in store and retrieve information. Finally, Section 5 outlines the future directions of snpStorage and concludes the paper.

2. Related Work

Over the years, many public and private data repositories have been developed to facilitate the researcher's studies by freely collecting and sharing curated and inferred SNP data worldwide. Below, we report the list of some popular SNP databases.

- dbSNP [1] [7] is a comprehensive and reliable catalogue of human SNP variability with an efficient system to cross-reference multiple submissions of the same SNPs from centers outside NCB.

[1]https://www.ncbi.nlm.nih.gov/projects/SNP/

- The Human Gene Mutation Database (HGMD)[2] [13] is a catalog of disease-associated mutation. In particular, HGMD comprises the following information: SNPs in coding regions, regulatory and splicing of relevant regions in human, insertions/deletions, invariant regions and complex rearrangements.
- The Human Genic Bi-Allelic SEquences (HGBASE)[3] database [8] collects information about SNPs along with the connection among SNP and the affected gene. Data in HGBASE are obtained by collecting data from all the available public sources.
- The Genome Database (GDB)[4] [9] is a public data repository and catalogue of human's SNPs, genes and clones. GDB's data are obtained from the scientific literature and collecting submissions from genotyping centers.
- GenBank[5] [14] is a nucleotide sequence database available in NCBI. GenBank is a collection of sequences obtained from several different species updated daily. GenBank can provide to the users interested in SNP analysis specific context sequence of nucleotides to design a genotyping study.
- HapMap[6] [15] provides a wide range of data, but it is focused on SNPs data. HapMap allows users to graphically browse the genome to visualize the SNP variability currently available. Finally, SNPs characterized by HapMap are linked to their public databases from which retrieve more insight related to the specific entry.

All the listed databases pursue the goal of providing an online catalog containing all the identified genetic variations, which can be used to guide research in genomics, pharmacogenomics studies with information about the association of genetic variations and phenotypic traits. Conversely, from the listed database, snpStorage is not only a human SNP catalog. It provides users with a sandbox where they can store his/her data in an anonymous and secure place, encouraging collaboration among researchers who belong to the same research centers and affiliates to different research centers.

snpStorage's primary mission is to provide a collection of intuitive procedures that can automatize complex tasks like data harmonization, integration, and annotation, responsible for the difficulties encountered by the researcher in sharing their data to start new collaborations. In addition, to make it even more straightforward, using snpStorage for users unfamiliar with query languages, e.g., SQL, for data querying, and performing complex tasks such as harmonization, integration, and annotation, snpStorage will provide all these features interactively through a customized Graphical User Interface (GUI). In this manner, snpStorage could serve as a valuable resource for creating more accurate and helpful models to investigate complex conditions from a broader perspective, contributing to gain more knowledge than analyzing a single data set at the time.

Briefly, snpStorage is more than a repository where researchers can only store their experimental SNPs data sets obtained using genomics platforms (i.e., DMET microarrays). Still, it provides an automatic panel of graphical operations to quickly and intuitively enrich SNP with

[2]http://www.hgmd.cf.ac.uk/ac/index.php
[3]http://hgbase.cgr.ki.se
[4]http://www.gdb.org
[5]https://www.ncbi.nlm.nih.gov/genbank/
[6]https://www.genome.gov/10001688/international-hapmap-project

clinical information, joining several experimental SNP data sets, store the newly built data models, query new data set as well as old data sets, encouraging data sharing.

3. Requirement Analysis

Experimental SNPs data obtained from pharmacogenomics studies using DMET microarrays are arranged in a tabular format and saved as flat textual files (without a structure).

The current analysis practice poses some limitations, w.r.t. the possibility to increase the size of an experiment by merging more files regarding equivalent pharmacogenomics studies. Moreover, this merging operation has to be done manually by the researchers limiting at the same time the possibility to share data to obtain more informative data sets. Indeed, statistical analysis and machine learning techniques produce more accurate and relevant results when dealing with a huge amount of data than smaller ones. The current DMET outcomes are arranged in the form of a textual table saved in flat text files. In a generic DMET SNP data set, each row represents a probe (a well-defined genomic region known as chromosome containing several genes). In the current version of DMET microarray, there are 1931 probes able to investigate 233 genes involved in pharmacogenomics ADME (Absorption, Distribution, Metabolism, and Excretion). Instead, the number of columns is variable. The columns represent the number of patients enrolled in the experiments, the (*i-th*, *j-th*) cell contains the SNP detected in the *i-th* probes belonging to the *j-th* subject. Also, the subjects are memorized into the table using generic labels, making it impossible to harm the subjects' privacy. An example of DMET SNP dataset is depicted in Figure 1.

The possible operations that can be carried out on flat textual files are limited and complex because, researchers have to know how the data are related among them into the file to manually extract the information of interest to perform the next analysis. To figure out how the SNPs are distributed in a specific gene, for example the gene `CYP7B1` that consists of the following probes: `'AM_15053', 'AM_15085', 'AM_15086', and 'AM_15090'`, researchers have to extract for each subject the values related to those probes, to figure out the presence/absence of a specific SNP could be used as biomarkers for the condition under investigation. Gene extraction is not an easy operation due to the flat data representation of the DMET SNP data sets, so it must be performed manually. In addition, clinical data are stored in different formats and into separate flat text files, for which it is a not trivial operation to merge properly clinical and SNP data sets. The current structure and organization of SNP and clinical data sets highlights many limitations: *i)* do not allow to represent relationships among data; *ii)* make it challenging to share data among researchers into the same research center, as well among different research center; *iii)* limit the investigation power of the analysis. Mapping SNP data sets in a relational database system allows to overcome the actual limitation of flat files representation in particular: *i)* it makes it convenient to store and merge more experimental SNP and clinical data sets; *ii)* it promotes file sharing and consequently data integration; *iii)* it allows to perform further analysis other than classic case/control studies, such as it will enable to discriminate SNPs and clinical data in all the population. *iv)* Finally, it allows the extraction of complex relations among SNPs, diseases, and clinical condition quickly through queries.

4. snpStorage

To promote storing, merging, and sharing of experimental SNPs data sets with the possibility to integrate SNP data using clinical information, we implemented and developed snpStorage, a database using the relational database management systems (RDBMS) [5] MySQL server 8.0.13. snpStorage allows handling SNP data sets obtained by performing experimental investigation using the DMET microarray platform, and to integrate SNP data with clinical information if available. All the information related to subjects enrolled in a pharmacogenomics case-control

A	B	C	D	E	F	G	H
Probe Set ID	CEU_1	CEU_2	CEU_3	CEU_4	CEU_5	CEU_6	CEU_7
AM_10001	C/C	C/C	C/C	C/C	C/C	C/C	C/C
AM_10002	G/G	G/G	G/G	G/G	G/G	G/G	G/G
AM_10003	C/C	C/C	C/C	C/C	C/C	C/C	C/C
AM_10004	A/G	A/G	A/G	A/G	A/G	A/G	A/G
AM_10005	C/C	C/C	C/C	C/C	C/C	C/C	C/C
AM_10006	T/T	T/T	T/T	T/T	T/T	T/T	T/T
AM_10008	A/A	A/A	A/A	A/A	A/A	A/A	A/A
AM_10010	C/C	C/C	C/C	C/C	C/C	C/C	C/C
AM_10011	A/A	A/A	A/A	A/A	A/A	A/A	A/A
AM_10012	AG	G/G	G/G	G/G	G/G	G/G	G/G
AM_10013	A/A	A/A	A/A	A/A	A/A	A/A	A/A
AM_10014	C/C	C/C	C/C	C/C	C/C	C/C	C/C
AM_10016	T/T	T/T	T/T	T/T	T/T	T/T	T/T
AM_10017	G/G	G/G	G/G	G/G	G/G	G/G	G/G
AM_10019	A/A	A/A	A/A	A/A	A/A	A/A	A/A
AM_10020	T/T	C/T	C/T	C/T	C/T	C/T	C/T
AM_10021	A/A	A/A	A/A	A/A	A/A	A/A	A/A
AM_10022	G/G	G/G	G/G	G/G	G/G	G/G	G/G
AM_10023	T/T	T/T	T/T	T/T	T/T	T/T	T/T
AM_10024	A/A	A/A	A/A	A/A	A/A	A/A	A/A
AM_10025	G/G	G/G	G/G	G/G	G/G	G/G	G/G
AM_10028	C/C	C/C	C/C	C/C	C/C	C/C	C/C
AM_10030	C/C	C/C	C/C	C/C	C/C	C/C	C/C
AM_10031	G/G	G/G	G/G	G/G	G/G	G/G	G/G
AM_10033	G/G	G/G	G/G	G/G	G/G	G/G	G/G
AM_10034	C/C	C/C	C/C	C/C	C/C	C/C	C/C
AM_10035	G/G	G/G	G/G	G/G	G/G	G/G	G/G
AM_10039	A/T	A/T	T/T	T/T	T/T	T/T	T/T

Figure 1: Illustration of the outcomes obtained form a DMET microarray analysis.

study and stored in snpStorage are anonymized, making it impossible to harm patients' privacy. This is possible because snpStorage does not store sensitive information such as name, surname, address, etc., that could provide some clues on the identity of the subjects.

Analyzing Figure 1 it is worthy to note that the columns are named using generic labels, i.e., "CEU_1, CEU_2 ..." making it challenging to associate them with a real subject (except the data owner).

To store the SNP data sets permanently and to make it possible and convenient to extend the stored SNP data sets, it is necessary to map the flat textual SNP data sets into a database management system, along with all the additional, i.e., clinical information. In this way, we make it convenient and quick investigate, integrate, and share multiple SNP data sets. The tables used in snpStorage to map SNP data sets are: *Subjects* table contains the essential information necessary to link a subject with the healthcare center of belonging, the pathology under investigation, the detected SNPs, and the collected clinical data. *HealthcareCenters* table stores information about the center, the performed experiments, and the enrolled subjects in every study. *ClinicalInformation* table contains the clinical data, the pathology under investigation, and the information to link clinical data with the subject to which they belong. The pathology is stored and identified using the International Classification of Disease[7] (ICD). To overcome

[7]https://www.who.int/standards/classifications/classification-of-diseases

the main limitation imposed from the textual files, it is not enough to map the SNP data sets into the DBMS. It is necessary to relate the relationships between SNPs, diseases, subjects and laboratories to support complex queries. A possible solution is to group the 1931 probes using the genes and to link each gene to the *Subjects* table (let see Figure 2 gene table "*PPP*"). To accomplish the mapping task we used the annotations information provided by DMET microarray vendor Affymetrix [8]. As a result, we obtained 233 genes table (i.e., one table for each supported ADME gene from DMET platform), linking all the gene tables to the *Subject* table. Finally, the *ProbesGenesMapping* table contains the mapping between the probes and the gene of belonging, in the current version it contains only the DMET microarray mapping. Figure 2 shows the Entity-Relation schema (E/R) implemented to store and collect experimental DMET data enriched with clinical information. It is worthy to note that it is a simplified schema because we visualized 1 gene table (e.g., the PPP gene table) to simplify the visualization and readability of the diagram.

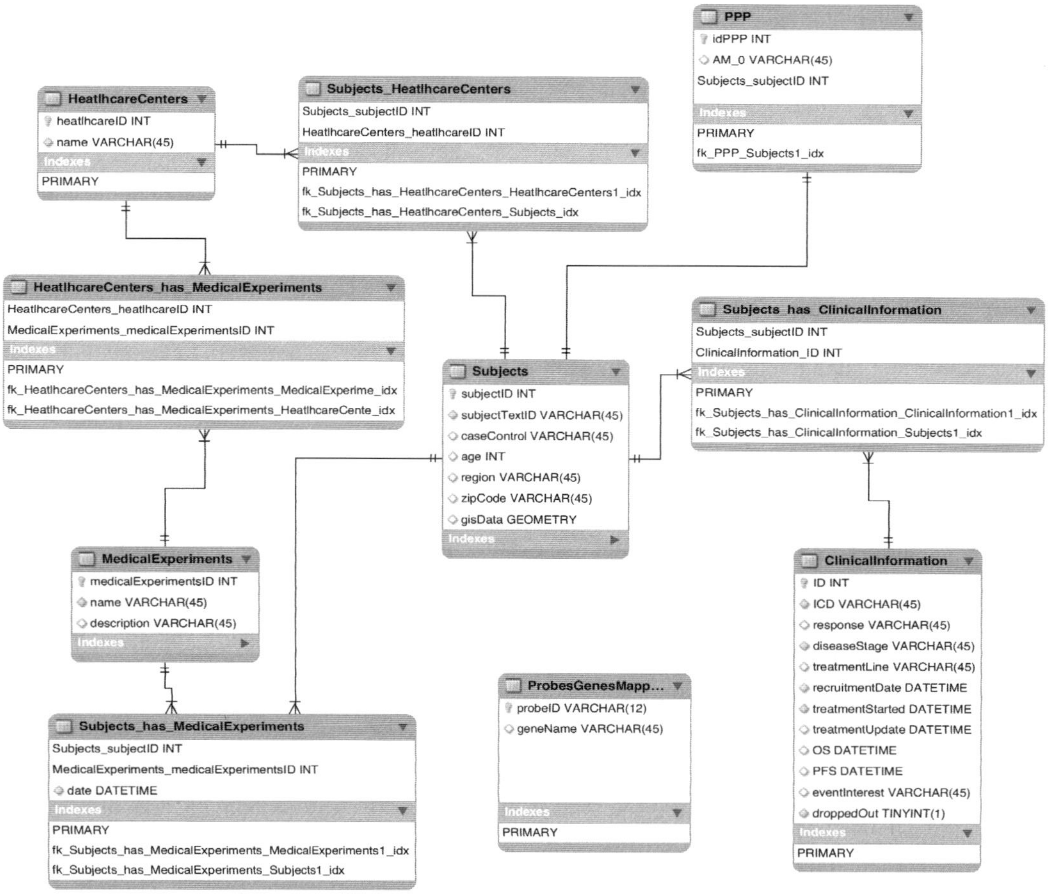

Figure 2: The E/R schema used to implement the data representation model.

snpStorage stores and efficiently handles SNPs and clinical information. Thus, it can help

[8] http://www.Affymetrix.com/support/technical/byproduct.affx?product=dmet_2

researchers to quickly share and integrate data from experimental pharmacogenomics SNP data sets possibly integrated with clinical data. Also, the integration of multiple SNP data sets, contribute to increasetypes of analysis to be performed, as well as the accuracy of the results. More data allow to describe the problem under investigation more accurately, opening new perspective not reachable by analyzing single small SNP data sets individually.

4.1. Performance evaluation

snpStorage is a relational database composed of 243 small tables. This design choice is due to the necessity to relate all the SNPs data with the correct probes, the diseases under investigation, the subjects and the laboratory/ies to which they belong. The relation schema allows obtaining narrow tables, with the advantage that they fit into the main memory. Thus the querying operation is faster than retrieving data from the secondary memory. Moreover, the SQL's operations such as *count, avg, sum* as well as *group by, order*, and so on, are available and can be computed easily through join operations among tables. The only limitation of this solution could be that join operations are CPU and RAM-intensive tasks. However, it is worthy to note that selecting some columns from specific tables does not require all the 243 sub-tables to be joined. Indeed, we will join only the sub-tables columns referenced in a given query.

An alternative solution to the multiple small tables could be the use of object-values columns. The object column type memorizes objects as values, allowing to obtain an enormous number of virtual columns into a single table. The object-value solution will enable tables to benefit from the compactness of regular columns while still allowing huge tables to exist, albeit less efficiently. Object columns require an extra layer of elaboration. The retrieved data have to be converted into the native data type, introducing extra CPU work to parse the object in the native type object. The object approach's advantage is that joining operations among tables is unnecessary since whole data can be held into a single table.

To compare the two possible implementations, we created small and object tables, evaluating the query's average response time by simulating multiple parallel queries using multiple parallel threads. Both tables contain the same number of tuples equals to $1,000$. The average response times refer to the time necessary to perform the queries on both implementation the small and object tables, respectively. As a benchmark, we used two queries, a simple *Select* query and a *Count* query, monitoring even if the number of simultaneously performed queries influences the average query time. The *select* queries are: `SELECT * FROM Subjects_smallTable` and `SELECT * FROM Subjects_objectColumn`. The *count* queries are: `SELECT COUNT(Allele) FROM Subjects_smallTable WHERE Allele = "A/A";` and `SELECT * FROM Subjects_objectColumn`. To count in the objectColumn table we need to select all the value and after convert the object in the native domain and counting it by using the additional computational layer. The query times on both representation are reported in Table 1 and Table 2. Analyzing Figure 3 we can see that until the queries retrieve values without being necessary to manipulate it, the trend querying between small and object tables is quite similar. Running a simple *count* query on both models, we can see a slight increase in the response query time in small table querying (since it added a little extra work-load due to the count function). Conversely, the response query's time increase in some order of magnitude when necessary to use the additional layer of computation to extract the further essential information that returns the count value of the submitted query.

In conclusion, snpStorage allows to convert unstrutured SNP data sets in structured data sets, as well as to take advantage of the native SQL functions to handle the stored data. In this way, further complex data analysis can be performed faster and in a shorter time since it can handle directly relevant data without using an additional computational layer to extract the necessary information.

Table 1
The measured average time in second necessary to perform the *Select* and *Count* query on the database containing small tables implementation, varying the number of threads used.

	#Th=1	#Th=5	#Th=10	#Th=15	#Th=20
Select	4.218	6.36	6.571	8.24	8.105
Count	4.383	5.957	6.29	8.009	9.751

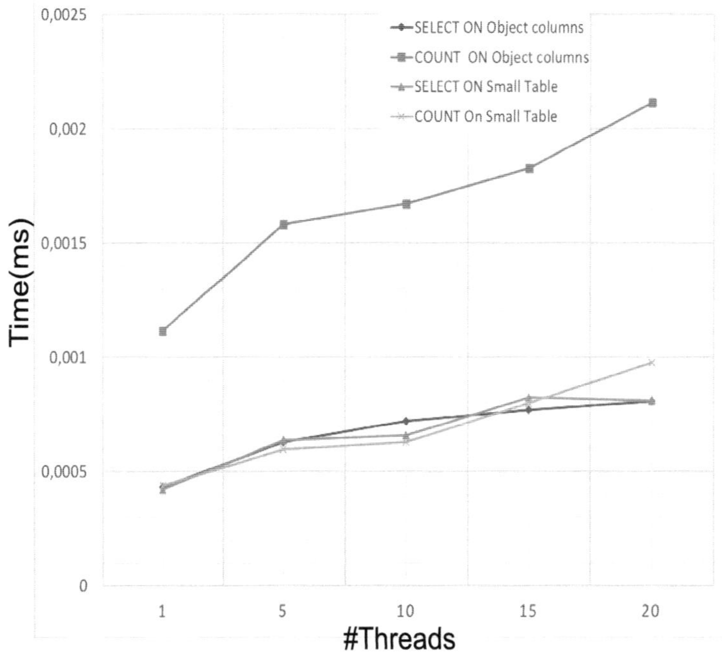

Figure 3: Average times of multiple *Select* and *Count* queries.

Table 2
The measured average time in second necessary to perform the *Select* and *Count* query on the database based on object column tables implementation, varying the number of threads used.

	#Th=1	#Th=5	#Th=10	#Th=15	#Th=20
Select	4.319	6.277	7.203	8.070	7.477
Count	11.147	15.809	16.721	18.259	21.1344

5. Conclusion

SNPs are a relevant source of information spanning from genomics to pharmacogenomics and personalized medicine. Linking SNP information with clinical data allows spurring light on the possible hidden relation between the healthy/diseased status of subjects and the arrangement of the patient's genome. In this way, SNPs may help scientists assume better the susceptibility of an individual to a disease or the adverse drug reaction. Since snpStorage stores and efficiently handles SNPs and clinical information, it can help researchers to quickly discriminate information among SNPs and clinical data into the population under investigation through simple queries. Future works will be focused on developing and implementing the web interface of snpStorage, through which analysis pipelines will be made available to help researchers quickly analyze their data stored into snpStorage without being necessary to use additional software tools. snpStorage pursues the target to provide an environment where researchers can perform queries built in a graphical way, without to be necessary to use SQL, on specific genes a group of genes, or consider detailed clinical information. Thus, the unification of the SNPs and clinical data represents a step toward defining individual and personalized treatments of complex diseases such as psychiatric disorders, diabetes, hypertension, and cancer.

Finally, snpStorage is more than a repository where researchers can only store their experimental SNPs data sets obtained using genomics platforms (i.e., DMET microarrays). Still, it provides an automatic panel of graphical operations to quickly and intuitively enrich SNP with clinical information, joining several experimental SNP data sets, store the newly built data models, query new data set as well as old data sets, encouraging data sharing.

References

[1] P. H. Guzzi, G. Agapito, M. T. Di Martino, M. Arbitrio, P. Tassone, P. Tagliaferri, M. Cannataro, Dmet-analyzer: automatic analysis of affymetrix dmet data, BMC Bioinformatics 13 (2012) 258. URL: https://doi.org/10.1186/1471-2105-13-258. doi:10.1186/1471-2105-13-258.

[2] G. Agapito, P. H. Guzzi, M. Cannataro, Dmet-miner: Efficient discovery of association rules from pharmacogenomic data, Journal of Biomedical Informatics 56 (2015) 273 – 283. URL: http://www.sciencedirect.com/science/article/pii/S153204641500115X. doi:https://doi.org/10.1016/j.jbi.2015.06.005.

[3] G. Agapito, P. H. Guzzi, M. Cannataro, Parallel extraction of association rules from genomics data, Applied Mathematics and Computation 350 (2019) 434–446.

[4] G. Agapito, P. H. Guzzi, M. Cannataro, Parallel and distributed association rule mining in life science: A novel parallel algorithm to mine genomics data, Information Sciences (2018).

[5] P. G. Selinger, M. M. Astrahan, D. D. Chamberlin, R. A. Lorie, T. G. Price, Access path selection in a relational database management system, in: Proceedings of the 1979 ACM SIGMOD International Conference on Management of Data, SIGMOD '79, ACM, New York, NY, USA, 1979, pp. 23–34. URL: http://doi.acm.org/10.1145/582095.582099. doi:10.1145/582095.582099.

[6] J. Han, H. E, G. Le, J. Du, Survey on nosql database, in: 2011 6th International Conference

on Pervasive Computing and Applications, 2011, pp. 363–366. doi:10.1109/ICPCA.2011.6106531.

[7] S. T. Sherry, M.-H. Ward, M. Kholodov, J. Baker, L. Phan, E. M. Smigielski, K. Sirotkin, dbsnp: the ncbi database of genetic variation, Nucleic Acids Research 29 (2001) 308–311. URL: http://dx.doi.org/10.1093/nar/29.1.308. doi:10.1093/nar/29.1.308.

[8] A. J. Brookes, H. Lehväslaiho, M. Siegfried, J. G. Boehm, Y. P. Yuan, C. M. Sarkar, P. Bork, F. Ortigao, Hgbase: a database of snps and other variations in and around human genes, Nucleic Acids Research 28 (2000) 356–360. URL: http://dx.doi.org/10.1093/nar/28.1.356. doi:10.1093/nar/28.1.356.

[9] S. I. Letovsky, R. W. Cottingham, C. J. Porter, P. W. D. Li, Gdb: The human genome database, Nucleic Acids Research 26 (1998) 94–99. URL: http://dx.doi.org/10.1093/nar/26.1.94. doi:10.1093/nar/26.1.94.

[10] A. Hamosh, A. F. Scott, J. S. Amberger, C. A. Bocchini, V. A. McKusick, Online mendelian inheritance in man (omim), a knowledgebase of human genes and genetic disorders, Nucleic Acids Research 33 (2005) D514–D517. URL: http://dx.doi.org/10.1093/nar/gki033. doi:10.1093/nar/gki033.

[11] G. A. Thorisson, A. V. Smith, L. Krishnan, L. D. Stein, The international hapmap project web site, Genome Research 15 (2005) 1592–1593. URL: http://genome.cshlp.org/content/15/11/1592.abstract. doi:10.1101/gr.4413105. arXiv:http://genome.cshlp.org/content/15/11/1592.full.pdf+html.

[12] M. Arbitrio, M. T. Di Martino, F. Scionti, G. Agapito, P. H. Guzzi, M. Cannataro, P. Tassone, P. Tagliaferri, Dmet™(drug metabolism enzymes and transporters): a pharmacogenomic platform for precision medicine, Oncotarget 7 (2016) 54028–54050. URL: https://www.ncbi.nlm.nih.gov/pubmed/27304055. doi:10.18632/oncotarget.9927.

[13] P. D. Stenson, M. Mort, E. V. Ball, K. Howells, A. D. Phillips, N. S. Thomas, D. N. Cooper, The human gene mutation database: 2008 update, Genome Medicine 1 (2009) 13. URL: https://doi.org/10.1186/gm13. doi:10.1186/gm13.

[14] D. A. Benson, M. Cavanaugh, K. Clark, I. Karsch-Mizrachi, D. J. Lipman, J. Ostell, E. W. Sayers, GenBank, Nucleic Acids Research 41 (2012) D36–D42. URL: https://doi.org/10.1093/nar/gks1195. doi:10.1093/nar/gks1195. arXiv:https://academic.oup.com/nar/article-pdf/41/D1/D36/3680750/gks1195.pdf.

[15] I. H. Consortium, et al., A second generation human haplotype map of over 3.1 million snps, Nature 449 (2007) 851.

The Document Chain: a Delta CRDT framework for arbitrary JSON data

Amos Brocco[1]

[1]*Department of Innovative Technologies, SUPSI, Lugano, Switzerland*

Abstract

In this paper we present a generic δ-CRDT framework for arbitrary JSON data called the Document Chain. In contrast to similar approaches based on explicit update operations, the proposed solution is able to automatically determine changesets for nested data structures. Data can be stored on different backends, and replication can be performed without locking and with non-destructive conflict resolution. The Document Chain is meant to support the development of collaborative applications by exploiting existing communication and storage solutions, such as shared folders or file sharing platforms in the cloud. An evaluation of the performance in terms of storage overhead, replication cost and computation time indicates that the proposed framework compares favorably with other solutions, and is therefore suitable for implementing collaboration features into existing applications.

Keywords

JSON, CRDT, Data Synchronization

1. Introduction

Many collaborative applications enable users to concurrently create and modify content on the web. Some applications provide real-time collaboration and continuous synchronization of the users' activity within a live environment, where each user sees changes made by other users. An alternative approach employs asynchronous replication, which allows for implementing offline-first (or local-first) solutions that can operate even without network connectivity. In order to replicate updates made while offline, when the system is online the application will connect to a server or to another instance, submit updates made to its local replica and possibly retrieve remote changes made on other replicas. The synchronization process itself would normally be performed in a synchronous manner: both the local system and the remote one need to be online at the same time. Furthermore, the synchronization logic must deal with conflicts that arise when the same data is concurrently modified by different users while offline: in this regard, applications not only need to store all the updates and changes made by the user, but must also implement algorithms to safely integrate third-party changes into the data model.

An interesting approach to this problem is provided by conflict-free replicated data types (CRDTs) [1, 2]: these data structures can be replicated between multiple participants in a network, and each participant can update the data independently and concurrently without coordination between the replicas. The logic behind CRDTs ensures that it is always possible to

SEBD 2021: The 29th Italian Symposium on Advanced Database Systems, September 5-9, 2021, Pizzo Calabro (VV), Italy
amos.brocco@supsi.ch (A. Brocco)

resolve conflicts that might arise from those concurrent updates and prevent inconsistencies. Although these technologies solve the problem of data replication, the problem of having an adequate infrastructure for exchanging data between the participants remains. Alongside with the client application, both in the synchronous and the asynchronous approaches, a suitable data exchange infrastructure must also be offered and maintained: such an infrastructure is typically created for the specific needs of the application and might pose some risks concerning security and privacy. To ease the burden of implementing such a complex architecture, we propose a generic framework called Document Chain which enables the use of existing file sharing and communication solutions to provide asynchronous conflict-free replication of JSON data and support the development of non-realtime collaboration features. By exploiting existing platforms (for example, a shared folder or a cloud-based file sharing service), which might already be in use by the end-user, we can reduce the overall maintenance costs for the developer while ensuring that data is stored according to the end-user requirements. The following sections will discuss some of the related work in the field of CRDTs, the architecture and technical details of the proposed solution and an evaluation of its performance.

2. Related work

In [1] the authors provide a definition for conflict-free replicated data types which entails two fundamental properties: first, any replica should be modifiable without any coordination with another replica, second, when any two replica receive the same set of updates they reach the same state. There exist different types of CRDTs: operation-based, state-based and delta. Operation based solutions only record update operations and use specific strategies to merge contents generated on different systems (such as [3]). Operation based CRDTs are suited for high-frequency updates, such as within real-time collaborative text editors. To support those applications, and in particular the ones which rely on JSON data, specific libraries have been developed. An example which is worth mentioning is called *json-crdt* [4], which is based on the *automerge* [5] library. The authors provide several example use cases and applications that exploit the realtime replication capabilities of the library to synchronize several instances of a collaborative online editor. The system performs as intended, but as pointed out by the authors themselves, the very same nature of operation-based CRDTs results in a very large history of change records, and it is almost impossible to remove unneeded historical data (pruning), because if a client comes back online later in time it might require that information to successfully merge its changes. Moreover, some concurrent operations, such as modification and deletion, might produce unexpected results and objects with partially missing data fields. State-based CRDTs [6] always store the full state of the data, and are therefore more suitable in situations with low-frequency updates or where single operations are not commutative. Another advantage of state-based replication is the fact that it is easier to verify the correctness of the data in a particular point in time. State-based CRDTs can be implemented by means of a distributed database such as *CouchDB* [7] or one of its variants (such as [8]). The main drawback of state-based CRDTs is that the storage required to save all states can become very large [9]. To overcome this issue delta-based solutions which rely on disseminating updates (changesets) called delta mutations (referred to as delta CRDT or δ-CRDT) have been proposed

[9]. An important property of such updates is that they are idempotent, which means that they can be applied possibly several times to an existing state without compromising its consistency.

In this paper we present an approach based on deltas called Document Chain, which can be used on JSON documents: delta updates are determined by comparing full states, and are subsequently grouped into blocks which are linked together as a chain. The chain structure keeps changes ordered and ensures consistency. Document Chains are useful as an alternative to state-based CRDTs for arbitrary JSON documents because they reduce the storage requirements for each update while allowing arbitrarily complex documents to be synchronized. As with any CRDT, users can update a Document Chain independently, without the need for locks or any explicit conflict management mechanism. Document Chains follow an eventual consistency model: each sequence of blocks can be used to reconstruct a specific version of the document. Conflicts are dealt with in a non destructive manner by keeping all versions inside the Document Chain and by electing a winning version using a deterministic algorithm. Document Chains can be stored on a filesystem, on a cloud storage, inside a database or just kept in memory: changes can be merged irrespective of the underlying storage technology.

This works improves and extends the one presented in [10] as follows: first, it allows for creating JSON documents which can be concurrently modified by several users without the need for locks and other synchronization mechanisms; furthermore, it introduces commit points which can be used to validate changes and to navigate through the history of the document. Last, it is designed to work not only in-memory but with multiple storage backends, such as shared folders in a local network or file-sharing platforms in the cloud. In contrast to the aforementioned operation-based approaches, the solution discussed in this paper does not require that the client application keeps track of the changes made to its data model in order to update the CRDT accordingly, and thanks to non-destructive conflict resolution it avoids issues such as partially missing data fields when processing concurrent updates and deletions. Compared to existing state-based solutions such as CouchDB, our approach can be easily embedded into an application and does not require an explicit mapping between the the data model of the client application and the internal organization of the database (typically a collection of JSON objects).

3. Technical overview

The implementation of the Document Chain comprises two key elements: a suitable CRDT data model and a high-level API for accessing the document chain and enabling the use of different types of storage backends. In this section both elements will be presented and discussed.

3.1. CRDT for arbitrary JSON documents

At the lowest level the CRDT employed in our solution improves on the work presented in [10], and allows for an arbitrary JSON document (referred to as the client application's own document) to be processed as input data. In contrast to operation-based CRDTs, the client application is not required to provide an explicit list of editing operations.

The framework implements a two-step difference detection algorithm to determine the changes between the input data (an arbirary JSON document) and the latest available state of the CRDT. In the first step (called flattening [10]), the input document is processed to destructure nested objects: each one of those objects is assigned a unique identifier (according to some user-specified rules) and is stored in an output collection. Since the flattening procedure needs to be reversible, during flattening nested objects are replaced with string references. In contrast to [10], we've been able to significantly reduce the storage space generated by changes made to nested arrays by storing only differential updates to ordering documents. In the second step, each object that has been placed in the output collection is compared with the latest version found in the chain, in order to determine the correct update operation (creation, deletion or update). Each operation is subsequently recorded as a transition between two revisions of an object, alongside with the contents of new revisions. Revision strings are comprised of a numerical index and the hash value of the object. To support CRDT operations, the contents (user data) and revision information are separated into two different structures, namely *data packs* and *revision update records blocks*.

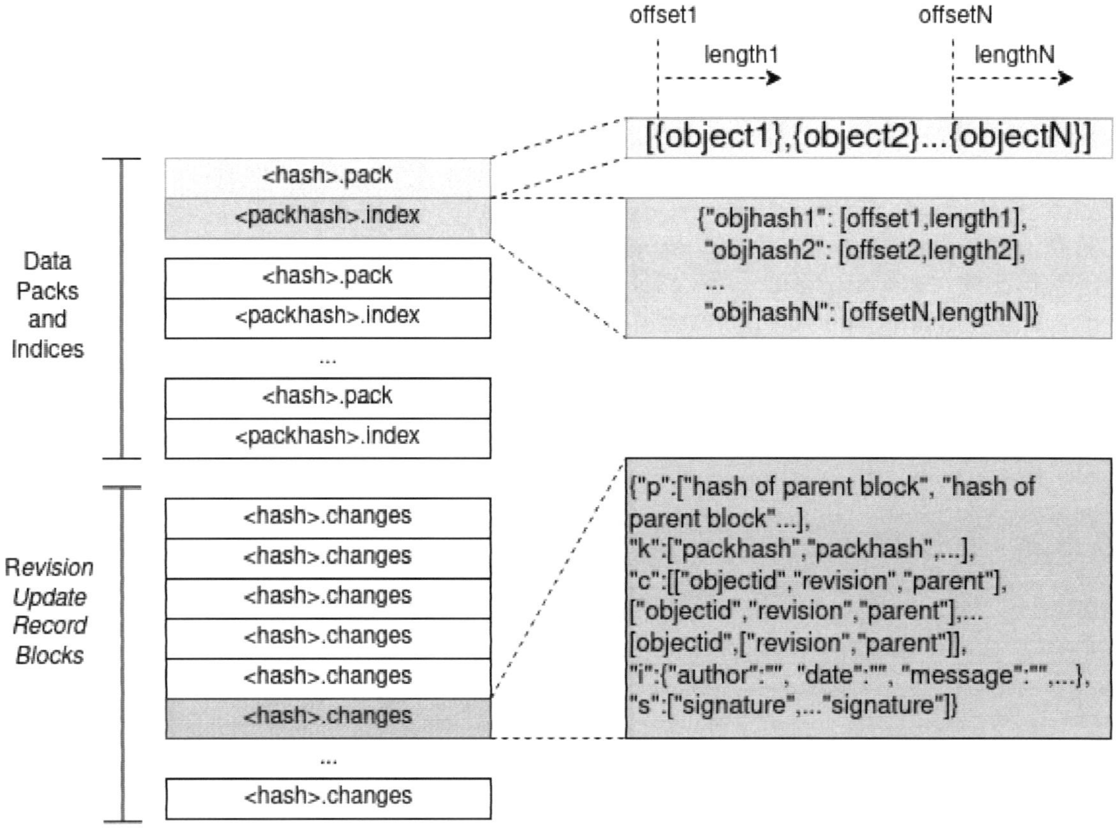

Figure 1: The Document Chain - Data Structures: : Revision Update Record Blocks are denoted using the *.changes* suffix, Data Packs use the *.pack* suffix and Data Pack Indices use the *.index* suffix; the *[offset,length]* tuples inside indices refer to a byte range within the corresponding pack.

3.1.1. Data packs

Objects extracted during the flattening procedure are stored within pack files: each object is uniquely identified by the hash value of its contents to avoid duplicates. To efficiently enumerate the objects contained in a pack file and retrieve their content, a corresponding index file is also generated. The index maps the hash value of an object to a position inside the pack file. Pack files and the corresponding indices share the same stem (the name of the file without the extension), which is generated by hashing the contents of the pack file. For redundancy purposes, pack files can also be parsed as collections of JSON documents (since they represents a JSON array), therefore the corresponding indices can be recovered if necessary. Indices also provide an advantage in a distributed environment, since they are smaller in size than the corresponding packs, can be cached locally (since they are immutable) and allow for determining the available content without the need for downloading the data packs.

3.1.2. Revision update record blocks

Revision update records store a log of all changes made to a particular object: more specifically, they record a transition between the previous and the next revision of one or more objects. Since revision strings contain the hash value of the contents of an object, it is trivial to recover the actual data by fetching the corresponding pack file. Records are grouped inside blocks, which correspond to a specific commit point made to the application data. Blocks also store the identifier of all related pack files created for the same commit point, and optional metadata such as the author and date of the update or digital signatures to prove the authenticity of the block. Blocks are identified by a key obtained by computing the hash value of their content. To keep track of dependencies between subsequent commit points and determine the order in which blocks need to be processed, each block also stores references to one or more previous blocks (referred to as *anchors*). If concurrent edits happen, multiple blocks might reference the same *anchors*: this situation won't affect the consistency of the chain, because conflicts are dealt with by a deterministic algorithm.

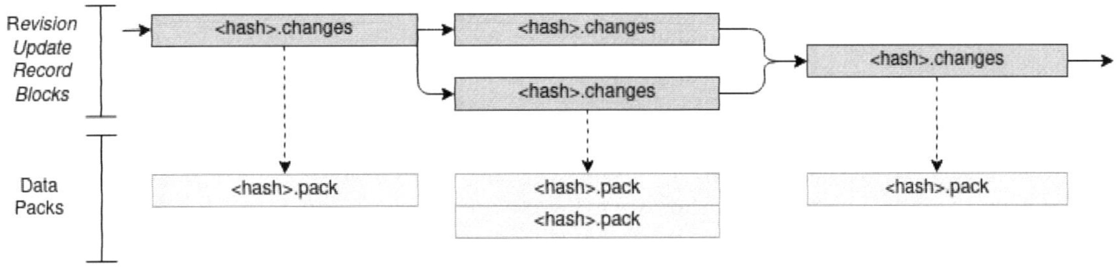

Figure 2: The Document Chain - Logical overview: Revision Update Record Blocks are denoted using the *.changes* suffix, whereas Data Packs use the *.pack* suffix; arrows represent *hash references* between elements in the chain.

3.1.3. Document chain

The history of all changes made to the application's own JSON document, as recognized by the library, is stored as a collection of linked revision update blocks and data packs called Document Chain (as shown in Figure 2). To obtain the latest version of the client's data, the changes recorded in all update record blocks are replayed and data packs are read to source the required revisions for each object. The unflattening procedure [10] is subsequently executed on the resulting collection of JSON objects to reconstruct the full state of the JSON document. Since each block in the Document Chain represents a separate commit point, it is possible to navigate through the history of all committed changes and retrieve a specific version of the JSON document.

Figure 1 illustrates the data structures used inside a Document Chain (data packs, indices and revision update record blocks). It should be noted that those structures can reside on different kinds of storage, such as the local filesystems, shared folders in a company's intranet, databases or cloud platforms, and can be updated independently by each participant without locking.

3.1.4. Conflict-free modification and replication

The Document Chain supports lock free concurrent modifications as long as the backend storage (which will be discussed in the forthcoming section) allows for concurrent appending of new data. The replication process can also be performed without any locking mechanism: chains can be replicated by simply merging two or more collections of blocks, packs and indices together. For example, if blocks and packs are stored as files inside a directory, replication to a target chain is achieved by simply copying files between the two locations. Because files are named after the hash value of their content, files that already exist in the target directory can be ignored. At any time, the integrity of the chain can be verified: thanks to hash references inside blocks it is possible to determine wheter the chain is complete or not, and identify the missing or corrupted blocks or packs. If digital signatures are employed, the authenticity of the data can also be verified.

3.2. Document chain API

The functionalities of the underlying CRDT are exposed through a high-level API which implements methods to read and update data, navigate the underlying Document Chain (to retrieve previous versions, or states), fork new chain or merge the current state into another chain. In order to provide a flexible way of storing data on different backends, the low-level task of reading or writing the elements of the chain is fulfilled by pluggable adapters, which can interface with several backends. We are currently experimenting with a filesystem adapter (which stores blocks and packs as files), adapters for cloud sharing services (such as Dropbox and Nextcloud), a database adapter (for storing data inside relational databases such as MariaDB or SQLite), and an in-memory adapter.

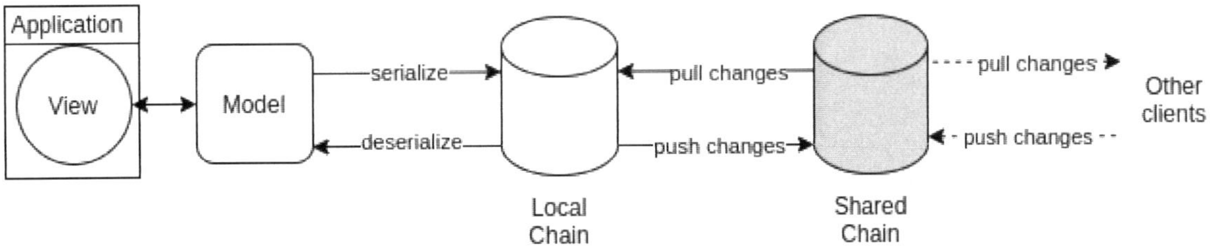

Figure 3: The Document Chain - Collaborative Application Architecture

3.2.1. Collaborative application design

Using the Document Chain a single-user application can be seamlessly converted into a collaborative application by implementing some additional operations to serialize and deserialize the existing data model into a JSON document. As shown in Figure 3, it is possible to employ different Document Chains (in the example, a *shared* one and *local* ones) to exchange modifications made by different users. The serialized data from the model is compared against the local chain in order to determine the changeset which is subsequently committed to the local chain. The *push changes* operation merges changes from the local Document Chain into the shared one, whereas the *pull changes* operation merges changes from the shared chain into the local one. Finally, the local chain can be read and deserialized in order to obtain an updated model.

As replication does not enforce any specific communication channel, a particularly cost-effective way to exchange updates between multiple clients/participants is through cloud-based file sharing platforms. As discussed in the introduction, the use of such infrastructure can reduce the overall maintenance costs for the developer while ensuring that data is stored according to the end-user requirements. Since Document Chains are based on immutable elements (which are identified by the hash value of their contents) it is easy to implement a caching mechanism to reduce network traffic in remote replication.

4. Evaluation

To evaluate the Document Chain solution we present an experiment derived from [10], in order to determine the storage overhead, the changeset size, the maximum resident set size, and the time required to reconstruct the full state from all changesets. We compare the obtained results with *automerge* [5], which was chosen because it is a well-known CRDT which natively supports JSON data and exhibits some commonality with our solution. We simulate subsequent edits to a JSON document which contains an array of financial transactions: the first version (denoted as V_1) is listed in Listing 1. The root object contains a *data* field, which corresponds to a sub-object containing an array of *transactions*. Each transaction is defined by an identifier (the *_id* field), a string representing a *currency*, a numerical value, and two strings which stand for the sender and recipient accounts. Furthermore, the root object also contains a filed named *info* which maps to an object with a transaction counter (associated with the *txcount* key).

```
{"data": { "transactions":[ {" _id ":"391...32",
        "currency": "EUR", "value": 22412,
        "from": "13465 -45566", "to": "34655 -67554"
```

```
}]}, "info": {"txcount ": 1}}
```

Listing 1: Sample JSON document V_1

The evaluation is comprised of 1000 steps, each comprising several edits to the data structure. More specifically, document version V_N is modified to produce a new version (denoted as V_{N+1}) by performing the following changes: first, a new object is added to the *transactions* array, and second, the value of the *currency* field of two existing objects is replaced with new data (specifically with the "EUR" or "USD" string). Moreover the value of the field *txcount* is updated to reflect the size (number of elements) of the *transactions* array. With *automerge*, new versions of the document are generated by passing the required update operations to the *change* method (since it is an operation-based CRDT): each changeset in then saved to a separate file; on the contrary, with the Document Chain the new version of the whole document is processed by the update logic, which will automatically devise the corresponding changeset. Moreover, each step entails a commit of the chain, which relies on the filesystem adapter to produce three files: a revision update record block, a data pack and the corresponding index. To evaluate the impact of the hashing function used to generate revision strings and block/pack names inside the chain, we consider both SHA256 (with a 256 bit digest) and xxHash (with a 64 bit digest). To keep the evaluation scenario as simple as possible, digital signatures are omitted. All tests are performed on an AMD Phenom^{TM} II X4 965 processor with 16 GiB of RAM running Ubuntu 20.10. For *automerge*, version 0.14.2 running on *Node.js* version 12.18.2 is used.

4.1. Storage overhead

The first measurement concerns the overhead due to the additional information required for maintaining a history of all updates made to the data structure. Concerning the Document Chain we consider the total size of the data, which comprises pack files, the corresponding indices and the revision update blocks; for *automerge* we compute the cumulative size of all changesets obtained using the *getChanges* method (which returns an array of operations to be applied to version V_N in order to obtain V_{N+1}).

As shown in Figure 4 the Document Chain approach results in an overhead comparable to *automerge*, nonetheless depending on the hashing algorithm used for generating revision strings, a slight difference is observable. It should be noted that *automerge* records changes made to single fields whereas the Document Chain stores full JSON objects for each revision: the former might therefore produce better results for small changes in large objects, whereas the latter ensures the inner consistency of each object. The size of the input document is reported as *Full state*: since both CRDTs record and enable access to the whole history of the document, we report both the size of a single version of the full state as well as the cumulative size including all previous states. In this regard, both CRDTs allow for maintaining the full history of a document with considerably less storage overhead.

4.2. Size of the changeset

Changesets group a series of updates that need to be applied to version V_N in order to obtain version V_{N+1}. In a distributed scenario the size of a changeset determines the amount of data

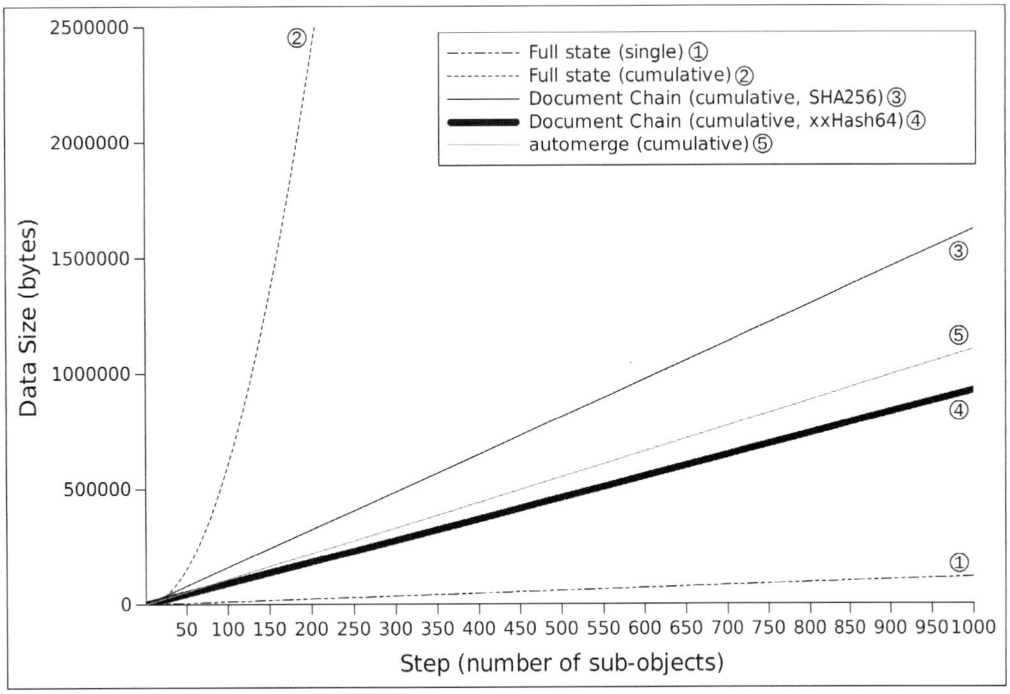

Figure 4: Storage Overhead

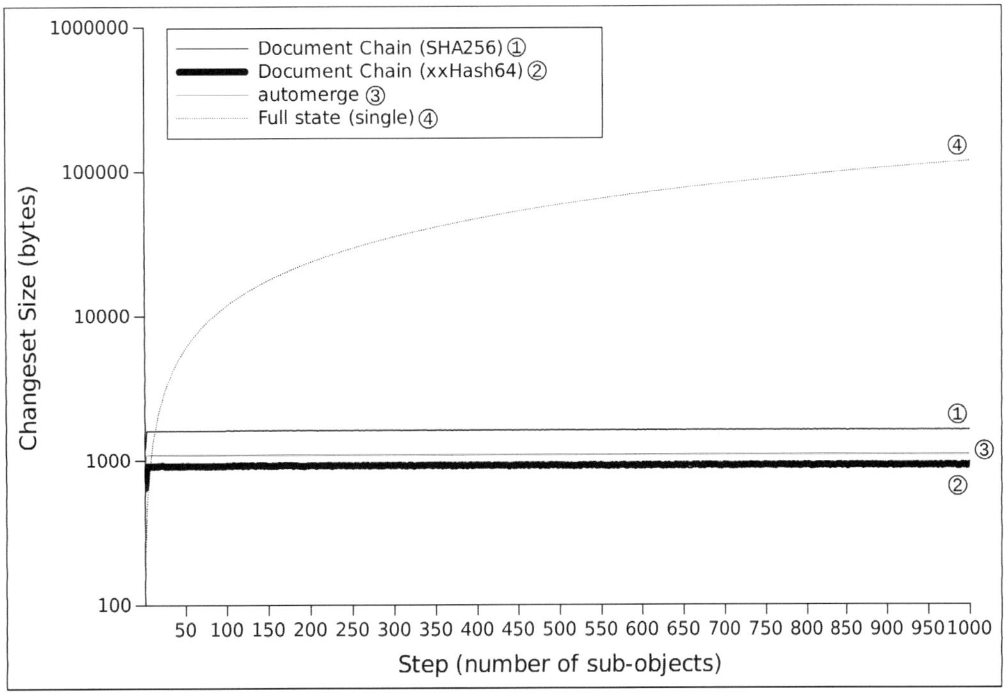

Figure 5: Size of the changeset

that needs to be exchanged between participants in order to update their current state. As can be observed in Figure 5, both CRDTs provide an efficient way of replicating changes, with a resulting cost which is orders of magnitude less than transmitting the full state at each update.

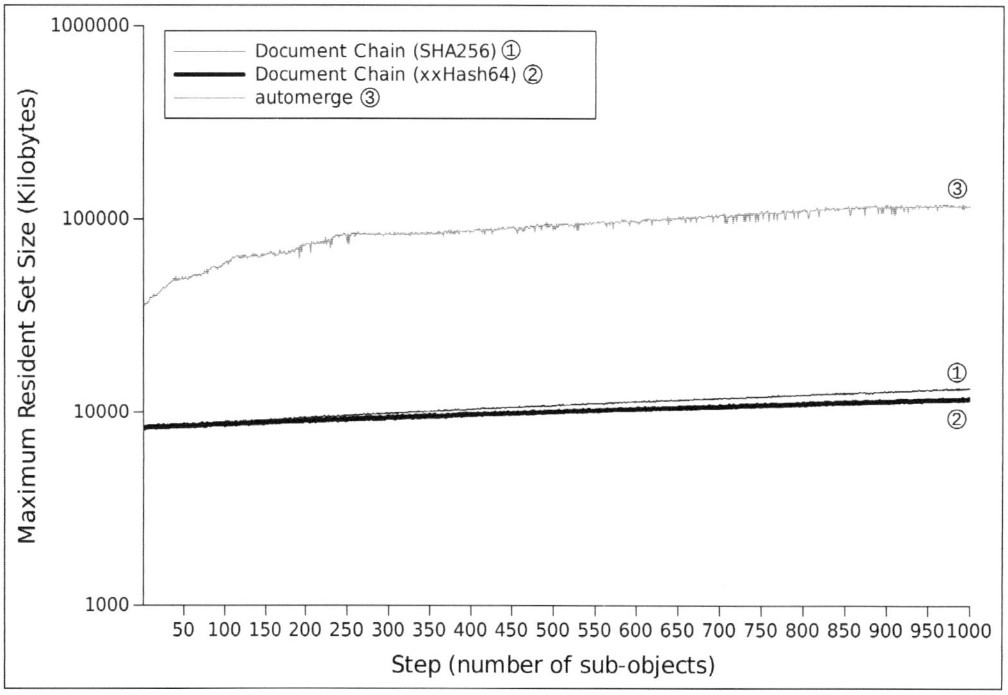

Figure 6: Maximum resident set size (RSS)

4.3. Maximum resident set size (RSS) for full state reconstruction

Manipulating large JSON data structures can be expensive in terms of memory, in particular on resource constrained devices. Accordingly we measure the maximum resident set size (RSS) during each experiment to evaluate the memory used by the CRDTs while reconstructing the full state based on the changesets available at each step. For the Document Chain, measurements have been obtained using the *time* command, whereas for *automerge* we employ the built-in *process.memoryUsage().rss*. As shown in Figure 6, *automerge* requires more memory than the Document Chain. This difference can be explained by the fact that all changesets produced and replayed by *automerge* need to be loaded in memory (those also contain the edited values), whereas the *Document Chain* keeps data inside packs which remain solely on disk until they are needed during the reconstruction process. Furthermore, *automerge* is a Javascript library which depends on the garbage collector of *Node.js*, whereas the Document Chain is a native library written in C/C++ which performs manual memory management.

4.4. Full state reconstruction time

Reconstructing the full state requires replaying all changesets. For the Document Chain, we evaluate the time required by this operation using the *time* command, whereas for *automerge* we employ *Date.now()* to obtain the time before and after the process (therefore the initialization time of the Node.js runtime is ignored). As shown in Figure 7, *automerge* takes considerably more time compared to Document Chain (either using the SHA256 algorithm or xxHash). In this regard, an important contributing factor is that with the former all changesets need to be loaded and replayed, whereas with the latter only revision update record blocks and indices need to be fully processed, as only the relevant packs (those that contain referenced objects) need to be subsequently read.

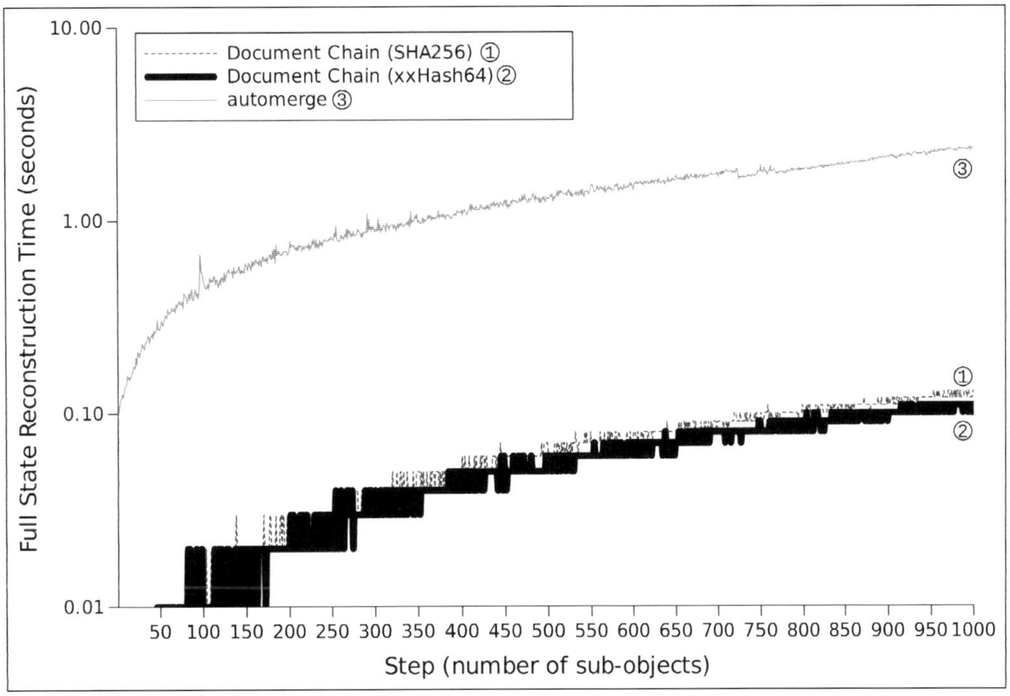

Figure 7: Full state reconstruction time

5. Conclusion

In this paper, we presented the concept of Document Chain, which implements a δ-CRDT framework for arbitrary JSON data. The proposed solution supports the development of collaborative applications by exploiting existing communication and storage solutions, such as shared folders or cloud services. The chain can be replicated and independently modified by multiple users: the replication process is efficient and ensures non-destructive conflict management. Moreover, since the full history of all the changes made to the document is recorded into the chain, it is possible to retrieve previous versions with ease. The Document Chain compares favorably with similar CRDTs, such as *automerge*, while offering a simpler interface which does not require explicit updates to the document to determine state changes. Future work includes the integration of an adapter for the SOLID infrastructure [11], in order to store data inside a private pod.

Acknowledgments

This work has been financially supported by the Swiss Innovation Agency, Project nr. 42832.1 IP-ICT and by Banana.ch SA.

References

[1] N. M. Preguiça, C. Baquero, M. Shapiro, Conflict-free replicated data types (crdts), CoRR abs/1805.06358 (2018).

[2] M. Letia, N. Preguiça, M. Shapiro, Consistency without concurrency control in large, dynamic systems, SIGOPS Oper. Syst. Rev. 44 (2010) 29–34.

[3] C. Baquero, P. S. Almeida, A. Shoker, Making operation-based crdts operation-based, in: Proceedings of the First Workshop on Principles and Practice of Eventual Consistency, PaPEC '14, Association for Computing Machinery, New York, NY, USA, 2014.

[4] P. Grosch, R. Krafft, M. Wölki, A. Bieniusa, Autocouch: A json crdt framework, in: Proceedings of the 7th Workshop on Principles and Practice of Consistency for Distributed Data, PaPoC '20, Association for Computing Machinery, New York, NY, USA, 2020.

[5] M. Kleppmann, A. R. Beresford, A conflict-free replicated json datatype, IEEE Transactions on Parallel and Distributed Systems 28 (2017) 2733–2746.

[6] M. Shapiro, N. Preguiça, C. Baquero, M. Zawirski, A comprehensive study of Convergent and Commutative Replicated Data Types, Research Report RR-7506, Inria – Centre Paris-Rocquencourt ; INRIA, 2011.

[7] Couchdb 2.0 reference manual, 2015.

[8] pouchdb, the javascript database that syncs!. accessed apr. 23, 2021, 2020. URL: https://pouchdb.com.

[9] P. S. Almeida, A. Shoker, C. Baquero, Delta state replicated data types, Journal of Parallel and Distributed Computing 111 (2018) 162–173.

[10] A. Brocco, P. Ceppi, L. Sinigaglia, libjots: JSON that syncs!, in: M. Agosti, M. Atzori, P. Ciaccia, L. Tanca (Eds.), Proceedings of the 28th Italian Symposium on Advanced Database Systems, Villasimius, Sud Sardegna, Italy (virtual due to Covid-19 pandemic), June 21-24, 2020, volume 2646 of *CEUR Workshop Proceedings*, CEUR-WS.org, 2020, pp. 116–127.

[11] Solid technical reports. accessed apr. 23, 2021, 2020. URL: https://solidproject.org/TR/.

Federated Recommender Systems with Learning to Rank

Vito Walter Anelli[1], Yashar Deldjoo[1], Tommaso Di Noia[1], Antonio Ferrara[1] and Fedelucio Narducci[1]

[1]*Politecnico di Bari, Via E. Orabona, 4, 70126 Bari, Italy*

Abstract

Recommendation services are extensively adopted in several user-centered applications as a tool to alleviate the information overload problem and help users in orienteering in a vast space of possible choices. In such scenarios, data ownership is a crucial concern since users may not be willing to share their *sensitive* preferences (e.g., visited locations, read books, bought items) with a central server. Unfortunately, data harvesting and collection is at the basis of modern, state-of-the-art approaches to recommendation. To address this issue, we extend Federated Pair-wise Learning (FPL), an architecture in which users collaborate in training a central factorization model while controlling the amount of sensitive data leaving their devices. The proposed approach implements pair-wise learning-to-rank optimization by following the *Federated Learning* principles, conceived originally to mitigate the privacy risks of traditional machine learning.

Keywords

Federated Learning, Recommender Systems, Information Retrieval, Learning to Rank

1. Introduction

Collaborative filtering (CF) models have been mainstream research in the recommender system (RS) community over the last two decades thanks to their performance accuracy [1, 2]. Among them, a prominent class uses the matrix factorization (MF) approach as the inference model. The MF model's main aim is to uncover user and item latent representations whose linear interaction explains observed feedback. To date, the majority of existing MF models are trained in a *centralized* fashion causing several concerns about the privacy of user data.

The consequent data scarcity dilemma can thereby jeopardize the training of MF models. Training high-quality MF models strongly relies on sufficient in-domain interaction data to ensure that enough co-occurrence information exists to shape similar behavioral/preference patterns in a user community. Although cross-domain recommendation approaches allow combating the issue of data scarcity, their applicability largely depends upon the availability of data providers that can collect/supply cross-domain in their platform (e.g., Amazon). However,

SEBD 2021: The 29th Italian Symposium on Advanced Database Systems, September 5-9, 2021, Pizzo Calabro (VV), Italy

vitowalter.anelli@poliba.it (V. W. Anelli); yashar.deldjoo@poliba.it (Y. Deldjoo); tommaso.dinoia@poliba.it (T. D. Noia); antonio.ferrara@poliba.it (A. Ferrara); fedelucio.narducci@poliba.it (F. Narducci)

these approaches remain out of focus in this work. In recent years, federated learning (FL) was proposed by Google as a mean to offer a *privacy-by-design* solution [3, 4, 5] for machine-learned models. Federated learning aims to meet ML privacy shortcomings by horizontally distributing the model's training over user devices; thus, clients exploit private data without sharing them [5]. Despite its original formulation, the FL concept is extended to a more comprehensive idea of privacy-preserving, decentralized, collaborative ML techniques [6] where different data partitions share the same feature space (horizontal federation) or not (vertical federation). Weiss *et al.* [7] state that privacy can be preserved by limiting data collection, which is one of the main privacy concerns [8]. Indeed, the accuracy of RS based on the CF paradigm is strictly dependent on the amount of user preferences available.

Our idea is to put users in control of their sensitive data by allowing them to choose the amount of information to share with the server. Hence, if data collection from the server side is reduced, other threats related to retention, sales, and unauthorized data browsing are limited. The proposed system extends FPL [9, 10] (short for Federated Pair-wise Learning), is a *federated* factorization model for collaborative recommendation[1]. It extends state-of-the-art factorization approaches to build a RS that puts users in control of their sensitive data. Users participating in the federation process can decide *if* and *to which extent* they are willing to disclose their *sensitive* private data (i.e., what they liked/consumed). FPL mainly leverages not-sensitive information (e.g., places the user has not visited) – which can be large and non-sensitive – to reach a competitive accuracy and, at the same time, respect a satisfactory balance between accuracy and privacy. We have carried out extensive experiments on real-world datasets [11] in the Point of Interest (PoI) domain by considering the accuracy of recommendation and diversity metrics. The experimental evaluation shows that FPL can provide high-quality recommendations, putting the user in control of the amount of sensitive data to share.

2. Approach

In this section, after a brief introduction of background technologies, we extend FPL [9, 10] (depicted in Fig. 1). To the best of our knowledge, FPL is the first attempt to put pair-wise optimization in federated recommender systems and give the users the possibility to select the trade-off between data disclosure and the recommendation utility.

2.1. Background Technologies

Federated Learning. Federated learning (FL) is a paradigm initially envisioned by Google [3, 12, 5] to train a machine-learning model from data distributed among a loose federation of users' devices (e.g., personal mobile phones). The rationale is to face the increasing issues of ownership and locality of data to mitigate the privacy risks (and leaks) resulting from centralized machine learning [13, 14]. In particular, given Θ denoting the parameters of a machine learning model, we consider a learning scenario where the objective is to minimize a generic loss function $G(\Theta)$. FL is a learning paradigm in which the users $u \in \mathcal{U}$ of a federation collaborate to solve the learning problem under the coordination of a central server S without sharing or exchanging

[1] A public implementation of FPL is available at https://github.com/sisinflab/FedBPR/.

their raw data with S. From an algorithmic point of view, we start with S sharing Θ with the federation of devices. Then, specific methods solve a local optimization problem on the single device, i.e., using its data, and exploiting Θ. Afterwards, the client shares the parameters of its local model with S. The parameters provided by the clients are used to update Θ, which is sent back to the devices in a new iteration step.

Factorization Models and Pair-Wise Recommendation A recommendation problem over a set of users $\mathcal{U}$ and a set of items $\mathcal{I}$ is defined as the activity of finding for each user $u \in \mathcal{U}$ an item $i \in \mathcal{I}$ that maximizes a utility function $g : \mathcal{U} \times \mathcal{I} \rightarrow \mathbb{R}$. In this context, $\mathbf{X} \in \mathbb{R}^{|\mathcal{U}| \times |\mathcal{I}|}$ is the user-item matrix containing for each x_{ui} an explicit or implicit feedback (e.g., rating or check-in, respectively) of user $u \in \mathcal{U}$ for item $i \in \mathcal{I}$. In the work at hand, an implicit feedback scenario is considered – i.e., feedback is, e.g., purchases, visits, clicks, views, check-ins –, with $\mathbf{X}$ containing binary values. Therefore, $x_{ui} = 1$ and $x_{ui} = 0$ denote either user u has consumed or not item i, respectively.

In FPL, the underlying data model is a Factorization model, inspired by MF [15], a recommendation model that became popular in the last decade thanks to its state-of-the-art recommendation accuracy [16]. This technique aims to build a model Θ in which each user u and each item i is represented by the embedding vectors $\mathbf{p}_u$ and $\mathbf{q}_i$, respectively, in the shared latent space $\mathbb{R}^F$. The algorithm relies on the assumption that $\mathbf{X}$ can be factorized such that the dot product between $\mathbf{p}_u$ and $\mathbf{q}_i$ can explain any observed user-item interaction x_{ui}, and that any non-observed interaction can be estimated as $\hat{x}_{ui}(\Theta) = b_i(\Theta) + \mathbf{p}_u^T(\Theta) \cdot \mathbf{q}_i(\Theta)$ where b_i is a term denoting the bias of the item i. Among pair-wise approaches for learning-to-rank the items of a catalog, Bayesian Personalized Ranking (BPR) [17] is one of the most broadly adopted, thanks to its capabilities to correctly rank with *acceptable* computational complexity. In detail, given a training set defined by $\mathcal{K} = \{(u, i, j) \mid x_{ui} = 1 \wedge x_{uj} = 0\}$, BPR solves the optimization problem via the criterion $\max_{\Theta} \sum_{(u,i,j)\in\mathcal{K}} \ln \sigma(\hat{x}_{uij}(\Theta)) - \lambda \|\Theta\|^2$, where $\hat{x}_{uij}(\Theta) = \hat{x}_{ui}(\Theta) - \hat{x}_{uj}(\Theta)$ is a real value modeling the relation between user u, item i and item j, $\sigma(\cdot)$ is the sigmoid function, and λ is a model-specific regularization parameter to prevent overfitting.

Pair-wise optimization can be applied to a wide range of recommendation models, included factorization. Hereafter, we denote the model $\Theta = \langle \mathbf{P}, \mathbf{Q}, \mathbf{b} \rangle$, where $\mathbf{P} \in \mathbb{R}^{|\mathcal{U}| \times F}$ is a matrix whose u-th row corresponds to the vector $\mathbf{p}_u$, and $\mathbf{Q} \in \mathbb{R}^{|\mathcal{I}| \times F}$ is a matrix in which the i-th row corresponds to the vector $\mathbf{q}_i$. Finally, $\mathbf{b} \in \mathbb{R}^{|\mathcal{I}|}$ is a vector whose i-th element corresponds to the value b_i.

2.2. FPL: Federated Pair-wise Learning for Recommendation

Following the aforementioned federated learning principles, let us assume that users in $\mathcal{U}$ consume items from a catalog $\mathcal{I}$ and give feedback about them. S is aware of the whole catalog $\mathcal{I}$, while only user u knows her own set of consumed items. Given these conditions, the classic BPR-MF learning procedure [17] for model training can not be applied to the federated learning scheme [5]. Instead, we propose a novel learning paradigm (depicted in Figure 1) that is executed for a number E of epochs and works by rounds of communication that envisages **Distribution→Computation→Transmission→Aggregation** sequences between the server and the clients.

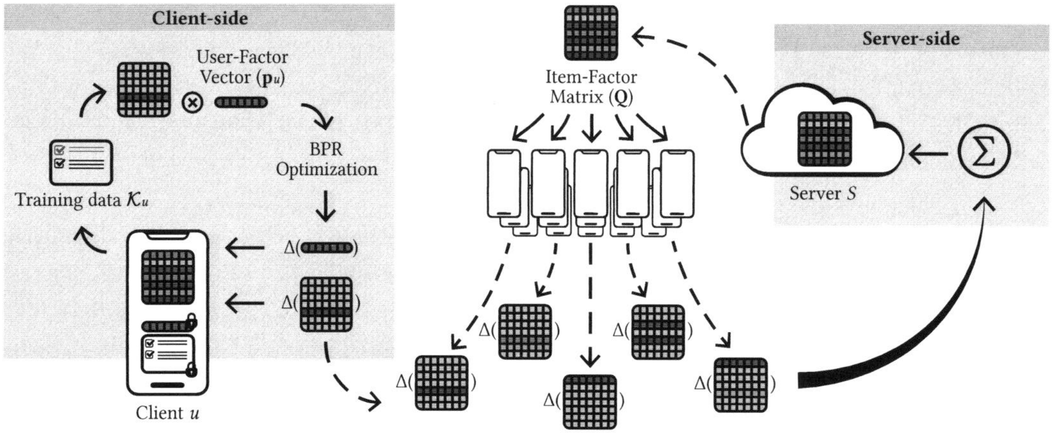

Figure 1: Item-Factor Matrix (center) is sent by the server to the federation of devices (left side) which perform the local training phase. Local outputs are sent to the server which aggregates them (right side).

In the FPL setting, a global model Θ_S is built on S such that $\Theta_S = \langle \mathbf{Q}, \mathbf{b} \rangle$, where $\mathbf{Q} \in \mathbb{R}^{|\mathcal{I}| \times F}$ and $\mathbf{b} \in \mathbb{R}^{|\mathcal{I}|}$ are the item-factor matrix and the bias vector (introduced in Section 2.1). On the other hand, on each device in the federation, FPL builds a model $\Theta_u = \langle \mathbf{p}_u \rangle$, which corresponds to the representation of user u in a latent space of dimensionality F. It is noteworthy that, in FPL, only user u holds the embedding vector $\mathbf{p}_u$; therefore, each user u autonomously computes her personalized item ranking, by combining the global model Θ_S, sent by S to the devices in the federation, with her local model Θ_u. In such a setting, each user u holds her own private feedback dataset $\mathbf{x}_u \in \mathbb{R}^{\mathcal{I}}$, which – compared with a centralized recommender system – corresponds to the u-th row of matrix $\mathbf{X}$. Each FPL client u hosts a user-specific training set $\mathcal{K}_u : \mathcal{U} \times \mathcal{I} \times \mathcal{I}$ defined by $\mathcal{K}_u = \{(u, i, j) \mid x_{ui} = 1 \wedge x_{uj} = 0\}$, where x_{ui} represents the i-th element of x_u. Please note that, in the following, we refer to $X^+ = \sum_{u \in \mathcal{U}} |\{x_{ui} \mid x_{ui} = 1\}|$ as the number of positive interactions.
The number of rounds of communication performed in each learning epoch is a parameter denoted by the symbol *rpe* (*round-per-epoch*). Each round of communication is envisioned as a four-step **protocol**, described in the following.

1. **Distribution.** S randomly selects a subset of users $\mathcal{U}^- \subseteq \mathcal{U}$ and delivers them the model Θ_S.

2. **Computation.** Each user u generates T triples (u, i, j) from her dataset $\mathcal{K}_u$ and for each of them performs BPR stochastic optimization to compute the updates for the local $\mathbf{p}_u$

vector of Θ_u, and for $\mathbf{p}_i$, b_i, $\mathbf{p}_j$, and b_j of the received Θ_S, following:

$$\Delta\theta = \frac{e^{-\hat{x}_{uij}}}{1+e^{-\hat{x}_{uij}}} \cdot \frac{\partial}{\partial\theta}\hat{x}_{uij} - \lambda\theta, \qquad \text{with} \quad \frac{\partial}{\partial\theta}\hat{x}_{uij} = \begin{cases} (\mathbf{q}_i - \mathbf{q}_j) & \text{if } \theta = \mathbf{p}_u, \\ \mathbf{p}_u & \text{if } \theta = \mathbf{q}_i, \\ -\mathbf{p}_u & \text{if } \theta = \mathbf{q}_j, \\ 1 & \text{if } \theta = b_i, \\ -1 & \text{if } \theta = b_j. \end{cases} \tag{1}$$

It is worth noticing that Rendle [17] suggests, in a centralized scenario, to adopt a uniform distribution (over $\mathcal{K}$) to choose the training triples randomly. The purpose is to avoid data is traversed item-wise or user-wise, since this may lead to slow convergence. Conversely, in a federated approach, we required to train the model user-wise since the training of each round of communication is performed separately on each client u knowing only data in $\mathcal{K}_u$. This is the reason why, in FPL, the designer can control of the number of triples T used for training, to tune the degree of local computation – i.e., how much the sampling is user-wise traversing.

3. **Transmission.** The clients in $\mathcal{U}^-$ send back to S a portion of the updates for the computed item factor vector and item bias. More in detail, since the training output of a triple (u, i, j) in BPR lets the server distinguish the consumed item i from the non-consumed one j (for example just by analyzing the positive and the negative sign of Δb_i and Δb_j), while they show the same absolute value, we argue that sending all the updates computed by u may allow S to reconstruct $\mathcal{K}_u$ thus raising a privacy issue. Since our primary goal is to put users in control of their data, FPL proposes a solution to overcome this vulnerability. By sending the sole update $(\Delta\mathbf{q}_j, \Delta b_j)$ of each training triples (u, i, j), user u would share with S indistinguishably negative or missing values, which are assumed to be *non-sensitive* data. Furthermore, in FPL we introduce the parameter π, which allows users to control of the number of consumed items to share with the central server S. The parameter π works as a probability that clients send also a specific positive item update $(\Delta\mathbf{q}_i, \Delta b_i)$ in addition to $(\Delta\mathbf{q}_j, \Delta b_j)$.
4. **Global aggregation.** S aggregates all the received updates in $\mathbf{Q}$ and $\mathbf{b}$ to build the new model $\Theta_S \leftarrow \Theta_S + \alpha \sum_{u \in \mathcal{U}^-} \Delta\Theta_u$, with α being the learning rate (each row of the matrix $\mathbf{Q}$ and each element of $\mathbf{b}$ is updated by summing up the contribution of all clients in $\mathcal{U}^-$ for the corresponding item).

3. Experimental Setup

In this section, we introduce the experimental setting designed to analyze the performance of FPL. To this extent, we introduce the choice of the datasets with a brief analysis of their characteristics. Then, we describe the state-of-the-art algorithms we have involved. For the sake of reproducibility, for each method, we report the explored hyper-parameters in a specific section. Lastly, we present the evaluation protocol, and the metrics considered in the study.

Table 1
Characteristics of the evaluation datasets used in the offline experiment: $|\mathcal{U}|$ is the number of users, $|\mathcal{I}|$ the number of items, X^+ the number of records.

Dataset	$\|\mathcal{U}\|$	$\|\mathcal{I}\|$	X^+	$\frac{X^+}{\|\mathcal{U}\|}$	$\frac{X^+}{\|\mathcal{I}\|}$	$\frac{X^+}{\|\mathcal{I}\|\cdot\|\mathcal{U}\|}\%$
Brazil	17,473	47,270	599,958	34.34	12.69	0.00073%
Canada	1,340	29,518	63,514	47.40	2.15	0.00161%
Italy	1,353	25,522	54,088	39.98	2.20	0.00157%

3.1. Datasets

The evaluation of FPL needs to meet some particular constraints: the availability of transaction data to obtain a reliable experimental setting and a domain that guarantees the presence of data the user may prefer to protect. In our view, the optimal domain would be that of the Point-of-Interest (PoI), which concerns data that users usually perceive as sensitive. Among the many available datasets, we think that a very good candidate is the *Foursquare* dataset [11]. Indeed, it is often considered as a reference for evaluating PoI recommendation models.

To mimic a federation of devices in a single country, we have extracted check-ins for three countries, namely Brazil, Canada, and Italy. Since our only constraint was to obtain datasets with different size/sparsity characteristics, we took the liberty of choosing three countries of recent RecSys conference venues. To fairly evaluate FPL against the baselines, we have kept users with more than 20 interactions[2]. Moreover, we have split the datasets by adopting a realistic temporal hold-out 80-20 splitting on a per-user basis [18, 19]. Table 1 shows the characteristics of the resulting training sets.

3.2. Baselines

To evaluate the efficacy of FPL, we have conducted the experiments by considering non-personalized methods (random and most popular recommendation), and different recommendation approaches, including the centralized **BPR-MF** implementation [17], **VAE** [20], and **FCF** [21], which is, to date, the only federated recommendation approach based on MF (since no source code is available, we reimplemented and considered it in the reader's interest). To evaluate the impact of feedback deprivation on recommendation accuracy, we have evaluated different values of π in the range $[0.0, 1.0]$. We remember that $\pi = 0.0$ means u is not sharing any update $(\Delta \mathbf{q}_i, \Delta b_i)$ with S regarding her positive items feedback, while $\pi = 1.0$ means u is sharing the updates on all positive items. Hence, we have considered four different configurations regarding computation and communication:

- ***s*FPL**: it aims to reproduce the stochastic learning approach of centralized factorization model with pair-wise learning, where the central model is updated sequentially; therefore, we set $|\mathcal{U}^-| = 1$ to involve just one random client per round, and it extracts solely one triple (u, i, j) from its dataset ($T = 1$) for the training phase;

[2]The limitations of the Collaborative Filtering in a cold-start user setting are well-known in the literature.

- **sFPL+**: we increase client local computation by raising to $\frac{X^+}{|\mathcal{U}|}$ the number of triples T extracted from $\mathcal{K}_u$ by each client involved in the round of communication;
- ***p*FPL**: we enable parallelism by involving all clients in each round of communication ($\mathcal{U}^- = \mathcal{U}$); we keep $T = 1$;
- ***p*FPL+**: we extend *p*FPL by letting each client sample $T = \frac{X^+}{|\mathcal{U}|}$ triples from $\mathcal{K}_u$; the rationale is that the overall training samples are exactly X^+, as in centralized BPR-MF.

In Rendle *et al.* [17], authors suggest to set the number of triples in one epoch of BPR to X^+, which corresponds to the number of optimizations steps. A particular choice is to randomly sampling $T = \frac{C^+}{|\mathcal{U}|}$ triples per user. To make a federated training epoch of FPL comparable to BPR and among different configurations, we set *rpe* to obtain always the same number of interactions ρ between clients and server in one epoch. This value is equal to the overall number of optimization steps in one epoch of the centralized pair-wise learning. In detail, we set $\rho = X^+$ and then $rpe = \rho \cdot |\mathcal{U}^-|$ which results in $rpe = X^+$ for *s*FPL, and $rpe = \frac{X^+}{|\mathcal{U}^-|}$ for *p*FPL.

3.3. Reproducibility

For the splitting strategy, we have adopted a **temporal hold-out** 80/20 to separate our datasets in training and test set. Moreover, to find the most promising learning rate α, we have further split the training set, adopting a temporal hold-out 80/20 strategy on a user basis to extract her validation set. **VAE** has been trained by considering three autoencoder topologies, with the following number of neurons per layer: 200-100-200, 300-100-300, 600-200-600. We have chosen candidate models by considering the best models after training for 50, 100, and 200 epochs, respectively. For the **factorization models**, we have performed a grid search in BPR-MF for $\alpha \in \{0.005, 0.05, 0.5\}$ varying the number of latent factors in $\{10, 20, 50\}$. Then, to ensure a fair comparison, we have exploited the same learning rate and number of latent factors to train FPL and **FCF**, and we explored the models in the range of $\{10, \ldots, 50\}$ iterations. We have set *user-* and *positive item*-regularization parameter to $\frac{1}{20}$ of the learning rate. The *negative item*-regularization parameter is $\frac{1}{200}$ of the learning rate, as suggested in *mymedialite*[3] implementation as well as by Anelli *et al.* [22].

3.4. Evaluation Metrics

We have evaluated the performance of FPL under the accuracy and diversity perspective. The accuracy of the models is measured by exploiting Precision ($P@N$) and Recall ($R@N$). They respectively represent, for each user, the proportion of relevant recommended items in the recommendation list, and the fraction of relevant items that have been altogether suggested. We have assessed the statistical significance of results by adopting Student's paired T-test considering p-values < 0.05[4]. The results are in general statistically significant but the differences among BPR-MF, *s*FPL, and *p*FPL, which is a very important result. To measure the diversity of recommendations, we have measured the Item Coverage ($IC@N$), and the Gini

[3]http://www.mymedialite.net/

[4]The complete results are available at https://github.com/sisinflab/fpl-results/.

Table 2

Results of accuracy and beyond-accuracy metrics for baselines and FPL on the three datasets. For each configuration of FPL and for each dataset, the experiment with the best π is shown (see the bottom part for details). For all metrics, the greater the better.

	Brazil				Canada				Italy			
	PR	RE	IC	Gini	PR	RE	IC	Gini	PR	RE	IC	Gini
Random	0.00013	0.00015	**46120**	**0.709455**	0.00030	0.00035	**10815**	**0.26809**	0.00030	0.00029	**10478**	**0.28914**
Top-Pop	0.01909	0.02375	19	0.000203	0.04239	0.04679	18	0.00030	0.04634	0.05506	19	0.00035
VAE *	0.10320	0.13153	5503	0.02117	0.06060	0.06317	1044	0.00652	0.10421	0.21324	165	0.02336
BPR-MF	0.07702	0.09494	2552	0.00756	0.03694	0.03650	1216	0.00998	0.04560	0.05458	19	0.00036
FCF	0.03089	0.03749	911	0.00095	0.03724	0.03836	504	0.00174	0.03126	0.03708	403	0.00158
***s*FPL**	0.07757	0.09581	1581	0.00561	0.04515	0.04550	451	0.00243	0.04701	0.05600	18	0.00036
***s*FPL+**	0.08682	0.11004	5200	0.01449	0.05701	0.05665	1510	0.01259	0.05595	0.06229	932	0.00789
***p*FPL**	0.07771	0.09582	2114	0.00638	0.04582	0.04637	425	0.00213	0.04642	0.05465	96	0.00056
***p*FPL+**	0.08733	0.11085	3820	0.01106	0.05761	0.05755	1214	0.00981	0.05565	0.06291	936	0.00725

Best π obtained for each the proposed FPL variations for Brazil, Canada, and Italy are: *s*FPL = (0.5, 0.1, 0.4), *p*FPL = (0.8, 0.1, 1)
* VAE does not always produce recommendations for all the users. For Italy, the reported results cover the 14% of the users. For this reason, it is not marked with **bold** in the table.

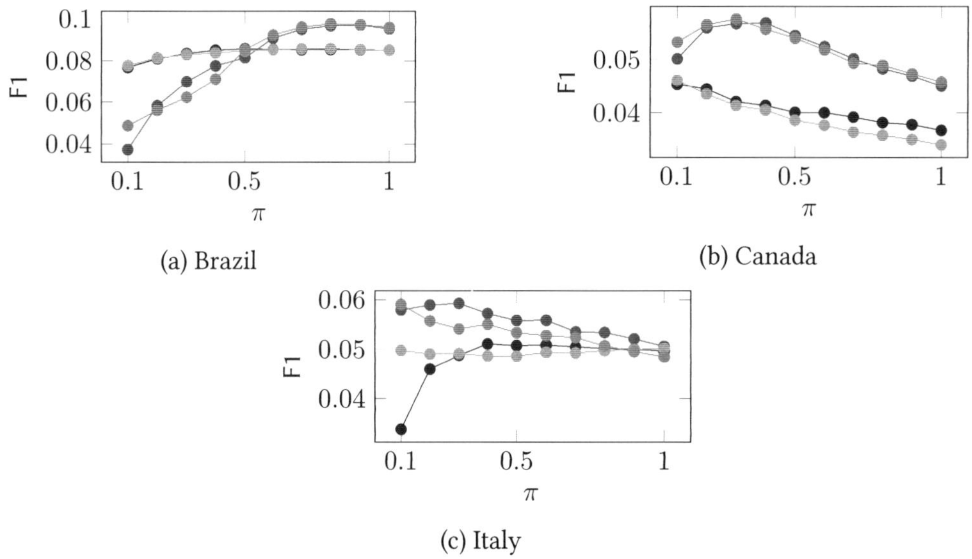

Figure 2: F1 performance at different values of π in the range $[0.1, 1]$. Dark blue is *s*FPL, dark green is *s*FPL+, light blue is *p*FPL, light green is *p*FPL+.

Index ($Gini@N$). IC provides the number of diverse items recommended to users. It also conveys the sense of the degree of personalization [23]. $Gini$ measures distributional inequality, i.e., how unequally different items a RS provides users with [24]. A higher value of $Gini$ [18] corresponds to higher personalization.

4. Discussion

The main goal of the experiments is assessing whether it is possible to obtain a recommendation performance comparable to a centralized pair-wise learning approach while allowing the users to control their data. In this respect, Table 2 shows the accuracy and diversity results of the comparison between the state-of-the-art baselines and the four configurations of FPL presented in Section 3. By focusing on accuracy metrics, we may notice that User-kNN outperforms the other approaches in the three datasets, while the performance of Item-kNN and BPR-MF approximately settle in the same range of values. This is possibly due to the user-item ratio [25], that favors the user-based schemes (see Table 1). On the other hand, it is important to investigate the differences of FPL with respect to BPR-MF, which is a pair-wise centralized approach, being FPL the first federated pair-wise recommender based on a factorization model. The performance of BPR-MF against FPL, in the configuration *s*FPL, shows how precision and recall in *s*FPL are slightly outperforming BPR-MF for the three datasets. This result is surprising since the two methods share the sequential training, but *s*FPL exploits a π reduced to 0.5, 0.1, and 0.4, respectively, for Brazil, Canada, and Italy. This behavior is more evident in Figure 2, where the harmonic mean between Precision and Recall (F1) is plotted for different values of π. If we look at the dark blue line, we may observe how the best result does not correspond to $\pi = 1$. In the last three rows of Table 2, we explore an increasing of the local computation (*s*FPL+), or an increased parallelism (*p*FPL), or a combination of both (*p*FPL+). In detail, we observe that *s*FPL+ takes advantage of the increased local computation, and FPL significantly outperforms BPR-MF for the three datasets; for instance, for Canada, we observe an interesting increase in precision. Instead, when comparing *p*FPL with *s*FPL, we observe that the increased parallelism does not affect the performance significantly. Even then, the increased local computation boosts the Precision and Recall performance, up to 24% for precision in the Italy dataset. The results confirm that *the proposed system can generate recommendations with a quality that is comparable with the centralized pair-wise learning approach. Moreover, the increased local computation causes a considerable improvement in the accuracy of recommendation. On the other side, the training parallelism does not significantly affects results. Finally, when the* ***local computation*** *is combined with* ***parallelism****, the results show a further improvement.*

Afterwards, we varied π in the range $\{0.1, \ldots, 1.0\}$ to assess how removal of the updates for consumed items affects the final recommendation accuracy, and we plotted the accuracy performance by considering F1 in Figure 2. As previously observed, the best performance rarely corresponds to $\pi = 1$. On the contrary, a general trend can be observed: the training reaches a peak for a certain value of π — depending on the dataset —, and then the system performance decays in accuracy when increasing the amount of shared positive updates. In rare cases, e.g., *s*FPL, and *p*FPL for Brazil dataset, the decay is absent, but results that are very close for different values of π. The general behavior suggests that the system learning exploits the updates of positive items to absorb information about popularity. This consideration is coherent with the mathematical formulation of the learning procedure, and it is also supported by the observation that for Canada and Italy FPL reaches the peak before with respect to Brazil. Indeed, Canada and Italy datasets are less sparse than Brazil, and the increase of information about positive items may lead to push up too much the popular items (this is a characteristic of pair-wise learning), while the same behavior in Brazil can be observed for values of π very close to 1.

The same mathematical background, for *s*FPL+ and *p*FPL+ with Brazil dataset, which is very sparse, explains the higher value of π needed to reach good performance. Here, the lack of positive information with a vast catalog of items, confuses the training that cannot exploit item popularity. Now, we can positively assert that *user can receive high-quality recommendations also when decides to disclose a small amount of her sensitive data. However, it should be noted that the more the dataset is sparse, the more the amount of sensitive data should be large.*

5. Conclusion and Future Work

Inspired by the potential ubiquity of the federated learning paradigm, we extend FPL, a novel federated learning framework that exploits pair-wise learning for factorization models. To this purpose, we have designed a model to leave the user-specific information of the original factorization model in the clients' devices. With FPL, a user may be completely in control of her sensitive data and could share no positive feedback with the centralized server. The framework can be envisioned as a general factorization model in which clients can tune the amount of information shared among devices. We have conducted an exploratory, but extensive, experimental evaluation to analyze the degree of accuracy, the diversity of the recommendation results, the trade-off between accuracy, and amount of shared transactions. We have assessed that the proposed model shows performance comparable with several state-of-the-art baselines and the classic centralized factorization model with pair-wise learning. The evaluation shows that clients may share a small portion of their data with the server and still receive high-performance recommendations. We believe that the proposed privacy-oriented paradigm may open the doors to a new class of ubiquitous recommendation engines.

References

[1] B. McFee, L. Barrington, G. R. G. Lanckriet, Learning content similarity for music recommendation, IEEE Trans. Audio, Speech & Language Processing 20 (2012) 2207–2218.

[2] J. Yuan, W. Shalaby, M. Korayem, D. Lin, K. AlJadda, J. Luo, Solving cold-start problem in large-scale recommendation engines: A deep learning approach, in: 2016 IEEE Int. Conf. on Big Data, BigData 2016, Washington DC, USA, December 5-8, 2016, IEEE Computer Society, 2016, pp. 1901–1910.

[3] J. Konecný, B. McMahan, D. Ramage, Federated optimization: Distributed optimization beyond the datacenter, CoRR abs/1511.03575 (2015). arXiv:1511.03575.

[4] V. W. Anelli, Y. Deldjoo, T. Di Noia, A. Ferrara, Towards effective device-aware federated learning, in: International Conference of the Italian Association for Artificial Intelligence, Springer, 2019, pp. 477–491.

[5] H. B. McMahan, E. Moore, D. Ramage, S. Hampson, et al., Communication-efficient learning of deep networks from decentralized data, arXiv preprint arXiv:1602.05629 (2016).

[6] Q. Yang, Y. Liu, T. Chen, Y. Tong, Federated machine learning: Concept and applications, ACM TIST 10 (2019) 12:1–12:19.

[7] S. Weiss, The need for a paradigm shift in addressing privacy risks in social networking

applications, in: IFIP International Summer School on the Future of Identity in the Information Society, Springer, 2007, pp. 161–171.

[8] A. J. P. Jeckmans, M. Beye, Z. Erkin, P. H. Hartel, R. L. Lagendijk, Q. Tang, Privacy in recommender systems, in: N. Ramzan, R. van Zwol, J. Lee, K. Clüver, X. Hua (Eds.), Social Media Retrieval, Computer Communications and Networks, Springer, 2013, pp. 263–281.

[9] V. W. Anelli, Y. Deldjoo, T. Di Noia, A. Ferrara, F. Narducci, How to put users in control of their data in federated top-n recommendation with learning to rank, in: Proceedings of the 36th Annual ACM Symposium on Applied Computing, SAC '21, Association for Computing Machinery, New York, NY, USA, 2021, p. 1359–1362. URL: https://doi.org/10.1145/3412841.3442010. doi:10.1145/3412841.3442010.

[10] V. W. Anelli, Y. Deldjoo, T. D. Noia, A. Ferrara, F. Narducci, Federank: User controlled feedback with federated recommender systems, in: D. Hiemstra, M. Moens, J. Mothe, R. Perego, M. Potthast, F. Sebastiani (Eds.), Advances in Information Retrieval - 43rd European Conference on IR Research, ECIR 2021, Virtual Event, March 28 - April 1, 2021, Proceedings, Part I, volume 12656 of *Lecture Notes in Computer Science*, Springer, 2021, pp. 32–47. URL: https://doi.org/10.1007/978-3-030-72113-8_3. doi:10.1007/978-3-030-72113-8_3.

[11] D. Yang, D. Zhang, B. Qu, Participatory cultural mapping based on collective behavior data in location-based social networks, ACM TIST 7 (2016) 30:1–30:23.

[12] J. Konecný, H. B. McMahan, D. Ramage, P. Richtárik, Federated optimization: Distributed machine learning for on-device intelligence, CoRR abs/1610.02527 (2016). arXiv:1610.02527.

[13] K. Bonawitz, H. Eichner, W. Grieskamp, D. Huba, A. Ingerman, V. Ivanov, C. Kiddon, J. Konecný, S. Mazzocchi, H. B. McMahan, T. V. Overveldt, D. Petrou, D. Ramage, J. Roselander, Towards federated learning at scale: System design, CoRR abs/1902.01046 (2019). arXiv:1902.01046.

[14] P. Kairouz, H. B. McMahan, B. Avent, A. Bellet, M. Bennis, A. N. Bhagoji, K. Bonawitz, Z. Charles, G. Cormode, R. Cummings, et al., Advances and open problems in federated learning, arXiv preprint arXiv:1912.04977 (2019).

[15] Y. Koren, R. M. Bell, C. Volinsky, Matrix factorization techniques for recommender systems, IEEE Computer 42 (2009) 30–37.

[16] D. kumar Bokde, S. Girase, D. Mukhopadhyay, Role of matrix factorization model in collaborative filtering algorithm: A survey, CoRR abs/1503.07475 (2015). arXiv:1503.07475.

[17] S. Rendle, C. Freudenthaler, Z. Gantner, L. Schmidt-Thieme, BPR: bayesian personalized ranking from implicit feedback, in: J. A. Bilmes, A. Y. Ng (Eds.), UAI 2009, Proc. of the Twenty-Fifth Conf. on Uncertainty in Artificial Intelligence, Montreal, QC, Canada, June 18-21, 2009, AUAI Press, 2009, pp. 452–461.

[18] A. Gunawardana, G. Shani, Evaluating recommender systems, in: F. Ricci, L. Rokach, B. Shapira (Eds.), Recommender Systems Handbook, Springer, 2015, pp. 265–308.

[19] V. W. Anelli, T. D. Noia, E. D. Sciascio, A. Ragone, J. Trotta, Local popularity and time in top-n recommendation, in: European Conf. on Information Retrieval, volume 11437, Springer, 2019, pp. 861–868.

[20] D. Liang, R. G. Krishnan, M. D. Hoffman, T. Jebara, Variational autoencoders for collaborative filtering, in: Proceedings of the 2018 World Wide Web Conference, 2018, pp. 689–698.

[21] M. Ammad-ud-din, E. Ivannikova, S. A. Khan, W. Oyomno, Q. Fu, K. E. Tan, A. Flanagan, Federated collaborative filtering for privacy-preserving personalized recommendation system, CoRR abs/1901.09888 (2019). arXiv:1901.09888.

[22] V. W. Anelli, T. D. Noia, E. D. Sciascio, C. Pomo, A. Ragone, On the discriminative power of hyper-parameters in cross-validation and how to choose them, in: Proc. of the 13th ACM Conf. on Recommender Systems, ACM, 2019, pp. 447–451.

[23] G. Adomavicius, Y. Kwon, Improving aggregate recommendation diversity using ranking-based techniques, IEEE Trans. Knowl. Data Eng. 24 (2012) 896–911.

[24] P. Castells, N. J. Hurley, S. Vargas, Novelty and diversity in recommender systems, in: F. Ricci, L. Rokach, B. Shapira (Eds.), Recommender Systems Handbook, Springer, 2015, pp. 881–918.

[25] G. Adomavicius, J. Zhang, Impact of data characteristics on recommender systems performance, ACM Trans. Management Inf. Syst. 3 (2012) 3:1–3:17. URL: https://doi.org/10.1145/2151163.2151166. doi:10.1145/2151163.2151166.

A neural network strategy for supervised classification via the Learning Under Privileged Information paradigm

Ludovica Sacco[1], Dino Ienco[2,4] and Roberto Interdonato[3,4]

[1]*DIMES - University of Calabria, P. Bucci 41C, 87036 Rende (CS), Italy*
[2]*INRAE, UMR TETIS, Univ. Montpellier, Montpellier, France*
[3]*CIRAD, UMR TETIS, Montpellier*
[4]*TETIS, Univ. of Montpellier, APT, Cirad, CNRS, INRAE, Montpellier, France*

Abstract

Devising new methodologies to handle and analyse Big Data has become a fundamental task in our increasingly service-oriented and interconnected society. One of the problems arising while handling such data is that, for a given set of entities, not all the entities may be described at the same level of detail, i.e., the number of features describing each entity may vary. In general cases, in order to apply classic data science methods, it is necessary to have a common features set over a data set. This will then correspond to the maximum number of common features among the entities, resulting in a loss of information for the entities for which additional information may be available. In order to exploit such additional information, the Learning Using Privileged Information (LUPI) paradigm has been proposed, based on the use of the teacher role in the learning process. In this schema the teacher acquires a strategic position, by exploiting at the training stage some additional privileged information about the entities, which will not be available at the test stage. In this work, we apply this paradigm in the context of neural networks, by proposing a LUPI based deep learning architecture able to exploit a larger set of attributes at training time, with the aim to improve classification performances on a set of entities associated to a reduced attribute set. Experimental results show how the proposed approach improves upon the ones applying the same schema to classic machine learning methods (e.g., SVM).

Keywords

Big Data, LUPI paradigm, Neural Networks

1. Introduction

The developments achieved in recent years in machine learning, due both to theoretical studies and to the constant increase of computational power of the processors, have led to several advancements on the traditional learning techniques. Moreover, these years have also seen a sudden increase in the quantity of available data. Massive quantities of information are produced, collected and digitally stored everyday, in contexts that touch different domains

SEBD 2021: The 29th Italian Symposium on Advanced Database Systems, September 5-9, 2021, Pizzo Calabro (VV), Italy
l.sacco@dimes.unical.it (L. Sacco); dino.ienco@inrae.fr (D. Ienco); roberto.interdonato@cirad.fr (R. Interdonato)
0000-0003-0235-6273 (L. Sacco); 0000-0002-8736-3132 (D. Ienco); 0000-0002-0536-6277 (R. Interdonato)

and aspects of human life (human health and behavior, agriculture, biology, and so on). The availability of these so called *big data*, together with that of machines that can handle higher volumes of data than ever before, have also led to an increase in the use of supervised learning techniques, i.e., techniques that rely on labeled data in order to train a machine learning model. However, in practical contexts, these data are generally noisy, and may include a diversity of features that are not always easy to exploit for computational analyses. A typical scenario is that in which entities of the same type are associated to a non homogeneous set of attributes that describe them. When using traditional machine learning methods, this would require the need to reduce the set of the attributes exploited to learn the model to just the common ones, thus resulting in a significant loss of information.

One of the solutions that have been proposed in order to overcome this problem, and allow the use of such diverse set of attributes, is the Learning Using Privileged Information paradigm (LUPI) paradigm [1]. The idea behind LUPI is to introduce a teacher-student model in the learning process, that allows to train a model on a larger set of attributes than that available at testing time. More specifically, the idea is to select a subset of entities for which a larger set of attributes is available (i.e., the *privileged information*), and then to train a model that can use such information to discern among entities that are associated to a reduced set of attributes (i.e., entities for which the priviliged information is not available, but just a limited set of *regular* attributes). The original implementations of the LUPI paradigm where introduced on classic machine learning techniques, e.g., Support Vector Machines (SVM) [1]. However, this paradigm can also be integrated in more advanced frameworks, such as the ones based on deep learning architectures [2], that are nowadays the state of the art in several domains.

In this paper, we present a LUPI based deep learning approach based on a three-branch architecture where a first model (M1) is trained on the full set of attributes (regular and privileged information), a second one (M2) exploits the representation learnt by M1 in order to stretch the representation learnt from regular attributes towards the one obtained from privileged ones, and a third model (M3) is optimized on the regular attributes only. The final feature set is then obtained by combining the otput of M2 and M3. While the proposed architecture is implemented by using a classic Multi-Layer Perceptron to instantiate the three models, it is general enough to be extended to different neural network models (e.g., Convolutional Neural Networks and Recurrent Neural Networks), and to be effectively applied to data coming from different domains. Experimental evaluation on six real world dataset show how the proposed methodology improves upon a competitor that applies the LUPI paradigm to an SVM approach (SVM+). The paper is organized as follows: Section 2 discusses the related work, section 3 introduces the proposed architecture, Section 4 discusses experimental results, while Section 5 concludes the work.

2. Related Work

The first algorithm that implements the LUPI paradigm is an extension of the classic SVM algorithm, known as SVM+ [1, 3]. SVM+ proposes a modified formulation of SVM in order to evaluate the misclassification of the training example through a function that learns from the privileged information as slack variables. Successively, different improvements and alternatives have found place into supervised learning problems. In [4] it has been remarked that the LUPI paradigm has always been implemented with the L-2 support vector machine, with the result of the number of the tuning parameters doubled and a consequent increase of the computational cost. So the decision to employ the L-1 norm, widely used for feature and variable selection [5], brought to the creation of L-1 SVM and its use in LUPI. Some amelioration to the optimization problem of the SVM+ is provided with the presentation of two new SMO-style algorithms [6]: `aSMO` and `gSMO`. When large training sets are used, both show to be more efficient in terms of generalization error/running treade-off than the generic optimizer LOQO, based on the interior point optimizers. Further similar algorithms can be found in [7], with some comparison between `aSMO` and `caSMO`. Considerations on differentiating easy examples from the difficult ones are discussed and formalized in [8], where a new approach in choosing weights associated with every training example is presented. More recent works [9, 10] discuss the importance of the knowledge transfer concept into SVM+ and neural networks to improve their convergence properties and therefore accelerating the speed of Student's learning.

Privileged information plays an important role in domains like computer vision, where several studies have successfully introduced the LUPI paradigm [11, 12]. Other applications are based on the use of bounding-boxes, image captions and descriptions as additional information and combine it with the Rank Transfer techniques to overcome the limitations of the SVM+ [13]. In recent years, other studied use the privileged information often associated to neural networks and exploited to solve various tasks. Classifying fine-grained images or recognizing images from a data set containing annotation noise is possible thanks to the DeepLUPI framework [14]. In [15] a two-stream fully convolutional network, named MIML-FCN+, is proposed to solve the multi-instance multi-label problem by using privileged bags of labels. A LUPI framework for CNNs and RNNs is offered in [16], where a heteroscedastic dropout is used and the privileged information is represented by the variance of the dropout. In this work, while we exploit a simple Multi-Layer Perceptron to instantiate the models at the base of our architecture, we propose a deep learning framework that is general enough to be extended to different neural network models (e.g., Convolutional Neural Networks and Recurrent Neural Networks), and to be effectively applied to data coming from different domains.

3. The LUPI Architecture

3.1. Learning Using Privileged Information Paradigm

In the classic machine learning paradigm, the role of a teacher in the human learning process has been underestimated. The supervised learning task considers a simple strategy. Given a set of pairs $(x_1, y_1), ..., (x_l, y_l), x_i \in X, y_i \in \{-1, 1\}$, where the vector $x_i \in X$ is the description of the example and y_i its classification, finding the function $y = f(x, \alpha^*)$ that minimizes the probability of incorrect classifications. In the LUPI paradigm the goal is exactly the same, but it contemplates the knowledge provided by the teacher at the training stage, the so called Privileged Information. So triplets $(x_1, x_1^*, y_1), ..., (x_l, x_l^* y_l), x_i \in X, x_i^* \in X^*, y_i \in \{-1, 1\}$ are now considered instead of pairs and each one is independently generated by some underlying unknown distribution $P(x, x^*, y)$.

3.2. Implementation

The proposed LUPI based deep learning architecture (Figure 1) is an end-to-end framework consisting of three neural networks (e.g. multi-layer perceptron) that process the input data to produce the final classification.

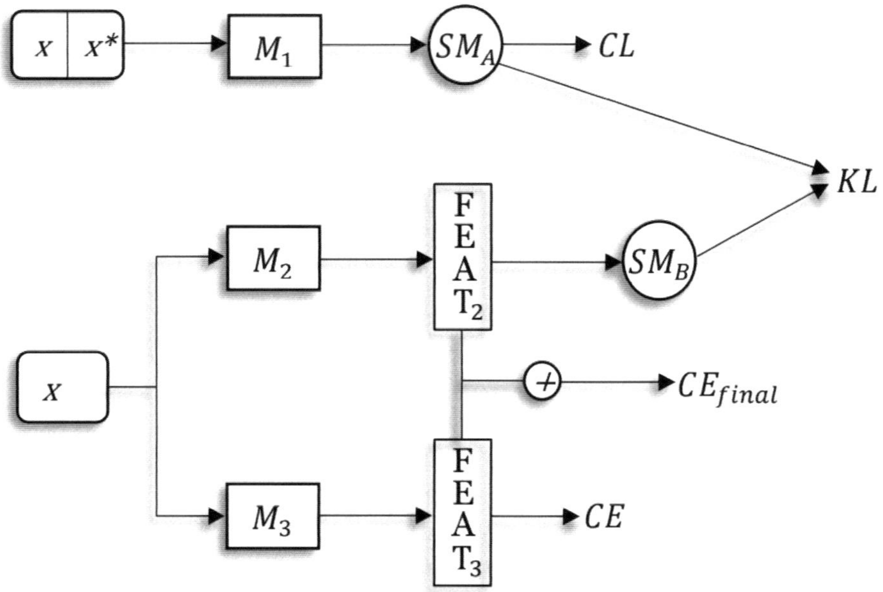

Figure 1: The general overview of the proposed LUPI based architecture. The privileged information is identified by X^* and the regular training example by X. The architecture has three different streams, two of which (M2 and M3) run in parallel, and their outputs are combined to get the final classification.

The first stream analyzes the training examples X (i.e., the entity with the associated regular information) with the addition of the privileged information X^*, while the other two streams work only on the training example X. This choice allows to exploit the knowledge acquired when the privileged information is available. In particular, the distribution of the labels got as an output from the execution of the first model (M1) is channeled into the second neural network. From this configuration, the second model (M2) uses as input a set of pairs (x_i, y_p) where $x_i \in X$ and $y_p \in \{-1, 1\}$ and y_p corresponds to the output obtained from M1. Moreover, to train the second neural network we choose the Kullback Leibler divergence [17] to let M2 behaves as similar as possible to M1. Finally, the third stream manages the training examples without any additional information to help during the classification. It should be noted that the M1 model is executed separately from the other two, and that M2 and M3 are run in parallel, as part of a single multi-output neural network.

Regarding the loss function the Categorical Cross Entropy has been used, except for M2, where the Kullback Leibler divergence is employed with the aim to mimic the behavior of the M1 model trained with the privileged information.

4. Experiments

This section reports the experimental setup, the results achieved and the data used to evaluate our architecture. To evaluate the proposed LUPI architecture, we carried out the experiments on six dataset, from different domains. We describe how we preprocessed them for the utilization in the experimental phase. We introduce setup details for both our implementation and competitors, specifying the metrics adopted for the comparison. Finally we discuss the results, aiming to validate our architecture.

4.1. Datasets

Six well-known datataset were used in the experiments :

- COIL20 [18]: image dataset including 20 different objects. For each of them 72 images are included in the size 128x128. The background has been discarded.
- HAR [19]: sensors data, built through a smartphone, from the recording of 30 subjects, performing various activities of daily living and containing six different activities: walking, walking upstairs, walking downstairs, sitting, standing and laying.
- Isolet [20]: 150 subjects spoke the name of each letter of the alphabet twice. Hence, there are 52 training examples from each speaker.
- landsat [21]: dataset of agricultural land images in Australia to classify seven different soil classes constituting dissimilar soil types.
- USPS [22]: 9298 images belonging to 10 different classes with size 16x16.
- waveform [23]: generator generating 3 classes of waves. Each class is generated from a combination of 2 to 3 base waves.

Structural characteristics of these datasets are summarized in Table 1.

Table 1
Datasets used to perform the experiments.

	# Features	# Objects	# Classes	Type
COIL20	1024	1440	20	Image
HAR	561	10299	6	Sensor
Isolet	617	1560	26	Speech
landsat	36	2859	7	Image
USPS	256	9298	10	Image
waveform	40	5000	3	Numbers

4.2. Setup

In order to evaluate the significance of the proposed approach, we provide an experimental evaluation including tests on different percentages of privileged information and a comparison with the performance of the SVM+ algorithm [1, 3]. For training and evaluation purposes, the datasets were divided into three parts: training, validation and test set, respectively representing the 50%, the 20% and the 30% of the instances (i.e., *rows* of the dataset). In line with recent deep learning literature, the model obtaining the best performance on the validation set has been used for the evaluation on the test set. The privileged information is provided by selecting a portion of the available features for each dataset, i.e., a certain number of *columns*. In detail, indices are randomly shuffled and then 9 different percentages of attributes are taken into account: 5%, 10%, 25%, 30%, 50%, 60%, 70%, 80%, 90%. The indices are selected in an incremental fashion, so that the higher percentages contain the indices included in the lower ones. Bear in mind that the percentage of privileged and "regular" information are complementary, so that for a certain percentage x of privileged information, the number of attributes available at testing time will be the $(100 - x)\%$ of total attributes. In our setting, this means that higher percentages of privileged information will correspond to harder test stages, because lower quantities of information will be available at testing time. Obviously this assumption is only related to our need to "artificially" partition the available attributes in privileged and regular, and does not hold in real world cases, where higher quantities of privileged information should correspond to better performances.

In order to avoid the bias induced by this selection process, these operations are executed 10 times, in order to get 10 different configurations of privileged indices for each considered percentage of privileged information. In relation to the deep learning parameters, the number of epochs is set to 100 and the learning rate of the Adam optimizer is equal to 1×10^{-4} [24]. While the metrics identified to evaluate our architecture are *Accuracy* and *F-measure*.

Regarding the internal structure of the LUPI architecture, the three models, M1, M2 and M3 are built using a multi-layer perceptron neural network (MLP). Each MLP has an input, three internal layers and an output layer, with respectively 256, 192, 128, 64 neural units and the number of classes of each dataset as the units for the output layer. As the activation function, the Rectified Linear Unit (ReLU) is employed for each layer, a part from the output one which utilized the SoftMax function to normalize the output vector values so that their sum is equal to 1. The experiments are run 30 times for each configuration of the different privileged indices, then mean and standard deviation are taken into account to evaluate the results. The reported experiments are carried out on the following platform: Intel(R) Core(TM) i5-7300U CPU @ 2.60GHz 2.71 GHz with 8,00 GB of RAM. The LUPI based deep learning architecture is implemented in Python Tensorflow 2.0 library. The source code for SVM+ is written in C and it is available online [1].

4.3. Experimental Results

Table 2 and table 3 report the average result in term of Accuracy and F-Measure for the 6 different datasets. It can be noted that the proposed approach has better performances for percentages of privileged information lower or equal to 30%. This result is actually not surprising since, as explained in Section 4.2, higher percentages of privileged information correspond to harder test stages (i.e., lower quantities of information are available at testing time). For higher percentages of privileged information, performances are slightly lower, but still comparable for most datasets, showing the robustness of the proposed approach even in the cases when only 10% of the total attributes are available at testing time (i.e., 90% of privileged information).

[1] https://github.com/cypw/svm-plus

Table 2
Average and standard deviation accuracy performance of the proposed LUPI based architecture as the percentage of privileged information in the dataset (columns in the table) increases.

	5%	10%	25%	30%	50%	60%	70%	80%	90%
COIL20	98.17 ± 0.44	98.19 ± 0.44	98.18 ± 0.50	**98.21** ± 0.43	98.19 ± 0.49	98.14 ± 0.45	98.05 ± 0.48	98.06 ± 0.49	97.31 ± 0.46
HAR	**94.15** ± 0.87	94.08 ± 0.86	93.74 ± 0.89	93.65 ± 0.70	93.23 ± 0.71	92.66 ± 0.83	92.21 ± 0.79	91.05 ± 0.79	86.44 ± 0.87
Isolet	**91.60** ± 0.86	91.51 ± 0.80	91.08 ± 0.75	91.02 ± 0.82	90.11 ± 0.84	89.43 ± 0.87	88.30 ± 0.92	86.81 ± 0.93	81.01 ± 1.21
landsat	**88.82** ± 0.94	88.60 ± 0.93	88.14 ± 0.90	88.02 ± 0.95	86.97 ± 0.97	86.41 ± 0.96	85.57 ± 1.01	84.78 ± 0.96	79.34 ± 0.85
USPS	96.49 ± 0.26	**96.52** ± 0.23	96.44 ± 0.20	96.42 ± 0.23	96.34 ± 0.19	96.21 ± 0.23	95.87 ± 0.21	94.79 ± 0.26	91.72 ± 0.34
waveform	**85.66** ± 0.65	85.36 ± 0.63	83.54 ± 0.63	82.95 ± 0.64	79.85 ± 0.63	76.95 ± 0.55	73.94 ± 0.57	68.91 ± 0.53	54.50 ± 0.65

Table 3
Average and standard deviation F-Measure performance of the proposed LUPI based architecture as the percentage of privileged information in the dataset (columns in the table) increases.

	5%	10%	25%	30%	50%	60%	70%	80%	90%
COIL20	98.22 ± 0.49	98.26 ± 0.49	98.22 ± 0.55	**98.27** ± 0.50	98.25 ± 0.53	98.19 ± 0.50	98.14 ± 0.52	98.13 ± 0.53	97.39 ± 0.53
HAR	**94.02** ± 0.95	93.97 ± 0.92	93.65 ± 0.95	93.54 ± 0.77	93.08 ± 0.78	92.57 ± 0.88	92.09 ± 0.85	90.95 ± 0.89	86.37 ± 0.95
Isolet	**91.90** ± 0.92	91.83 ± 0.82	91.40 ± 0.81	91.35 ± 0.85	90.45 ± 0.94	89.82 ± 0.92	88.67 ± 1.00	87.10 ± 0.96	81.34 ± 1.27
landsat	**86.51** ± 1.48	86.15 ± 1.52	85.56 ± 1.45	85.37 ± 1.58	83.79 ± 1.63	82.99 ± 1.65	81.63 ± 1.88	80.29 ± 1.91	73.70 ± 1.56
USPS	96.04 ± 0.31	**96.08** ± 0.31	96.02 ± 0.18	96.03 ± 0.22	95.92 ± 0.22	95.88 ± 0.24	95.54 ± 0.36	94.32 ± 0.33	90.89 ± 0.44
waveform	**85.63** ± 0.70	85.34 ± 0.68	83.48 ± 0.67	82.91 ± 0.70	79.77 ± 0.65	76.83 ± 0.60	73.64 ± 0.70	67.63 ± 0.87	51.07 ± 1.61

Actually, the only dataset showing a significance degradation in performances for higher percentages of privileged information is *waveform*, which is also the one corresponding to the lowest performances for all configuration. A reason for this behavior may be found in its synthetic nature. On the contrary, the dataset who produces the best results is *COIL20*, which is the dataset including the highest number of features, also corresponding to a relatively low number of objects. This probably allows to obtain a better classification, thanks to the large amount of available information at the training time over a relatively small numbers of tuples. As a general observation, all the other datasets show good Accuracy and F-Measure results, confirming the effectiveness of the proposed approach on datasets coming from different application domains.

Table 4 shows the average Accuracy results for the SVM+ algorithm. It can be noted how in most cases the performances begin to degrade already for a *PI* around the 10%, making SVM+

Table 4
Average accuracy performance of the SVM+ as the percentage of privileged information in the dataset (columns in the table) increases.

	5%	10%	25%	30%	50%	60%	70%	80%	90%
COIL20	**96.70**	96.17	96.16	96.14	96.23	96.28	96.33	95.80	95.03
HAR	**94.15**	93.55	92.97	92.58	91.65	90.86	90.27	88.43	81.63
Isolet	**91.30**	90.79	90.45	90.30	89.72	89.02	88.18	86.71	81.13
landsat	**85.73**	85.19	84.65	84.92	84.74	84.02	83.61	81.42	73.27
USPS	**96.38**	96.25	96.07	96.01	95.81	95.67	95.26	93.90	89.71
waveform	**82.96**	82.95	81.97	81.40	77.81	72.77	69.97	63.79	48.81

significantly less robust to our approach. To ease the comparison between the two approaches, in Figure 2 we present a visual comparison between our architecture and SVM+ in terms of Accuracy. It is evident how the LUPI architecture dominates the scene, clearly outperforming SVM+ in most datasets. The only two datasets in which the performances are not clearly superior (remain still comparable) are USPS and Isolet.

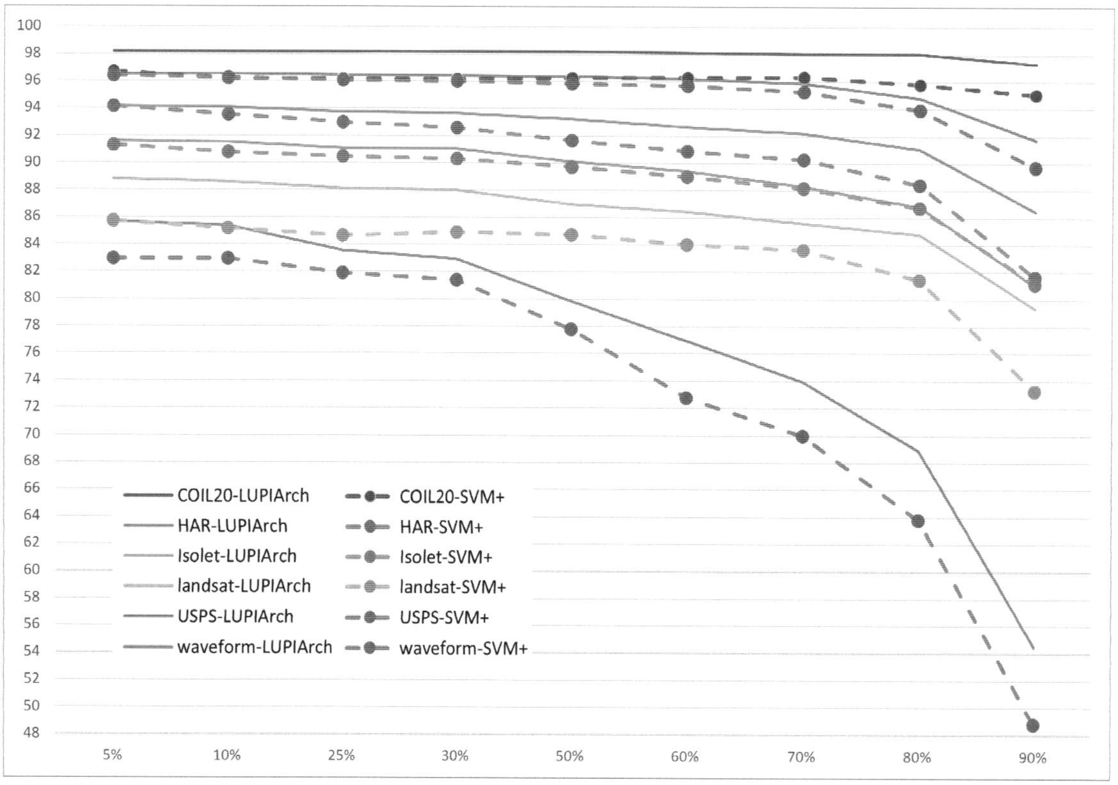

Figure 2: Accuracy comparison between our LUPI architecture and the SVM+ algorithm

The scenario described so far reflects the reality, regarding the Teacher-Student metaphor on which the LUPI paradigm is based. Too high percentages of *PI* would not allow the student to develop such skills to adequately face the testing phase. While percentages of up to 30% represent the right measure to develop one's own method and acquire such knowledge as to be able to build precise classification models. Our architecture proves to be able to fully perform this task, providing a valid structure for an optimal learning up to 30% of *PI*, also allowing to improve the performance in terms of Accuracy compared to the SVM+ algorithm.

5. Conclusions

In this work, we introduced a new deep learning architecture based on the Learning Using Privileged Information (LUPI) paradigm. The LUPI paradigm allows to exploit extra information that may be available only for a subset of the total objects in a dataset, i.e., the so called *privileged* information. More specifically, a model is trained by exploiting such privileged information, which is then able to classify test examples associated only to regular one. Experimental performances on six well-known datasets show the significance of our approach, proving its robustness to different available quantities of privileged and regular information. Experimental results also showed how the proposed deep learning architecture outperforms a competitor integrating the LUPI paradigm on a classic machine learning method (SVM+).

While in this work, in order to test the significance of our approach, we resorted to an artificial partitioning of the available information between privileged and regular one, in the future we plan to test the architecture on real-world case studies, corresponding to specific application domains. A first example can be that of remote sensing, when the availability of different sensors on specific areas may be exploited as privileged information (e.g., exploiting drone images associated to a limited geographical area, associated to satellite images available on larger portions of the scene). From a methodological point of view, we also plan to extend our approach by instantiating the three models included in the architectures with different neural networks (e.g., Recurrent and Convolutional ones).

6. Acknowledgments

This work was supported by the Regione Calabria, as part of the Ph.D scolarship of Ludovica Sacco.

References

[1] V. Vapnik, A. Vashist, A new learning paradigm: Learning using privileged information, Neural Networks 22 (2009) 544–557. doi:10.1016/j.neunet.2009.06.042.

[2] Y. LeCun, Y. Bengio, G. E. Hinton, Deep learning, Nat. 521 (2015) 436–444. URL: https://doi.org/10.1038/nature14539. doi:10.1038/nature14539.

[3] V. Vapnik, A. Vashist, N. Pavlovitch, Learning using hidden information (learning with teacher), in: Proceedings of the 2009 International Joint Conference on Neural Networks, IJCNN'09, IEEE Press, 2009, p. 1252–1259.

[4] L. Niu, Y. Shi, J. Wu, Learning using privileged information with l-1 support vector machine, in: 2012 IEEE/WIC/ACM International Conferences on Web Intelligence and Intelligent Agent Technology, IEEE, 2012. doi:10.1109/wi-iat.2012.52.

[5] T. Hastie, R. Tibshirani, J. Friedman, The Elements of Statistical Learning, Springer New York, 2009. doi:10.1007/978-0-387-84858-7.

[6] D. Pechyony, R. Izmailov, A. Vashist, V. Vapnik, Smo-style algorithms for learning using privileged information., 2010, pp. 235–241.

[7] D. Pechyony, V. Vapnik, Fast Optimization Algorithms for Solving SVM+, 2011, pp. 27–42. doi:10.1201/b11429-5.

[8] M. Lapin, M. Hein, B. Schiele, Learning using privileged information: SVM and weighted SVM, Neural Networks 53 (2014) 95–108. doi:10.1016/j.neunet.2014.02.002.

[9] V. Vapnik, R. Izmailov, Learning using privileged information: Similarity control and knowledge transfer, Journal of Machine Learning Research 16 (2015) 2023–2049. URL: http://jmlr.org/papers/v16/vapnik15b.html.

[10] V. Vapnik, R. Izmailov, Knowledge transfer in SVM and neural networks, Annals of Mathematics and Artificial Intelligence 81 (2017) 3–19. doi:10.1007/s10472-017-9538-x.

[11] J. Feyereisl, S. Kwak, J. Son, B. Han, Object localization based on structural svm using privileged information, in: Z. Ghahramani, M. Welling, C. Cortes, N. Lawrence, K. Q. Weinberger (Eds.), Advances in Neural Information Processing Systems, volume 27, Curran Associates, Inc., 2014. URL: https://proceedings.neurips.cc/paper/2014/file/6c4b761a28b734fe93831e3fb400ce87-Paper.pdf.

[12] W. Li, L. Niu, D. Xu, Exploiting privileged information from web data for image categorization, in: Computer Vision – ECCV 2014, Springer International Publishing, 2014, pp. 437–452. doi:10.1007/978-3-319-10602-1_29.

[13] V. Sharmanska, N. Quadrianto, C. H. Lampert, Learning to rank using privileged information, in: 2013 IEEE International Conference on Computer Vision, IEEE, 2013. doi:10.1109/iccv.2013.107.

[14] M. Chevalier, N. Thome, G. Hénaff, M. Cord, Classifying low-resolution images by integrating privileged information in deep CNNs, Pattern Recognition Letters 116 (2018) 29–35. doi:10.1016/j.patrec.2018.09.007.

[15] H. Yang, J. Zhou, J. Cai, Y. Ong, Miml-fcn+: Multi-instance multi-label learning via fully convolutional networks with privileged information, 2017, pp. 5996–6004. doi:10.1109/CVPR.2017.635.

[16] J. Lambert, O. Sener, S. Savarese, Deep learning under privileged information using heteroscedastic dropout (2018). arXiv:1805.11614.

[17] S. Kullback, R. A. Leibler, On information and sufficiency, The Annals of Mathematical Statistics 22 (1951) 79–86. doi:10.1214/aoms/1177729694.

[18] S. A. Nene, S. K. Nayar, H. Murase, Columbia university image library (coil-20) (1996). URL: http://www.cs.columbia.edu/CAVE/software/softlib/coil-20.php.

[19] J. L. Reyes-Ortiz, D. Anguita, A. Ghio, L. Oneto, X. Parra, A public domain dataset for human activity recognition using smartphones, 21th European Symposium on Artificial Neural Networks, Computational Intelligence and Machine Learning (2013).

[20] R. Cole, M. Fanty, Spoken letter recognition, n Advancesin Neural Information Processing Systems (1991) 220–226.

[21] Statlog landsat satellite data set: Machine learning repository, Univ. California, Irvine, Irvine, CA, USA (1993).

[22] J. Hull, A database for handwritten text recognition research, IEEE Transactions on Pattern Analysis and Machine Intelligence 16 (1994) 550–554. doi:10.1109/34.291440.

[23] L. Breiman, J. Friedman, R. Olshen, C. Stone, Classification and regression trees (1984) 49–55.

[24] D. P. Kingma, J. Ba, Adam: A method for stochastic optimization, 2017. arXiv:1412.6980.

From Low-Level-Event-Logs to High-Level-Business-Process-Model-Activities: An Advanced Framework based on Machine Learning and Flexible BPMN Model Translation

Alfredo Cuzzocrea[1], Ernesto Damiani[2], Hamda Al-Ali[3], Rabeb Mizouni[4], Ghalia Tello[5] and Edoardo Fadda[6]

[1]*iDEA Lab, University of Calabria, Rende, Italy*
[2]*Khalifa University & EBTIC, Abu Dhabi, UAE*
[3]*Khalifa University, Abu Dhabi, UAE*
[4]*Khalifa University, Abu Dhabi, UAE*
[5]*Khalifa University, Abu Dhabi, UAE*
[6]*Politecnico di Torino & ISIRES, Torino, Italy*

Abstract

Process mining is an emerging discipline that aims to analyze business processes using event data logged by IT systems. In process mining, the focus is on how to effectively and efficiently predict the next process/trace to be activated among all the possible processes/traces that are available in the process schema (usually modeled as a graph). Most of the existing process mining techniques assume that there is a one-to-one mapping between process model activities and the events that are recorded during process execution. However, event logs and process model activities are at different level of granularity. In this paper, we present a machine learning-based approach to map low-level event logs to high-level activities. With this work, we can bridge the abstraction levels when the high-level labels of the low-level events are not available. The proposed approach consists of two main phases: automatic labeling and machine learning-based classification. In automatic labeling a modified k- prototypes clustering approach has been used in order to obtain the labeled examples. Then, in the second phase, we trained different ML classifiers using the obtained labeled examples. Since, in real-life applications and systems, business processes are expressed according to the Business Process Model and Notation (BPMN) format, we improve our proposed framework by means of an innovative, flexible BPMN model translation methodology that acts at the first phase.

Keywords

Business process management, Business process mining, BPMN model translation

1. Introduction

With the advent of Information technology (IT), companies and organizations adopt IT services to model and execute their business processes. A shift from data orientation to process orienta-

SEBD 2021: The 29th Italian Symposium on Advanced Database Systems, September 5-9, 2021, Pizzo Calabro (VV), Italy
alfredo.cuzzocrea@unical.it (A. Cuzzocrea); ernesto.damiani@kustar.ac.ae (E. Damiani); 100035242@kustar.ac.ae (H. Al-Ali); rabeb.mizouni@kustar.ac.ae (R. Mizouni); ghalia.tello@kustar.ac.ae (G. Tello); edoardo.fadda@polito.it (E. Fadda)

tion has been witnessed by the last decades [1]. A business process intends to break up a certain job into sequence of activities, where different individuals can be responsible for different activities. Managing these business processes in an accurate, efficient, and well-organized way has a vast influence on the organization output and so its success. Accordingly, Business Process Management (BPM) became a vital discipline to organizations in order to model, discover, analyze and improve their business processes. Process mining is an emerging research area in the field of process management, which focuses on extracting process related information using event data logged by the IT systems. Process mining techniques can automatically discover process models, check the conformance of process execution to model specification, and enhance existing process models [2, 3].

Recently, an interesting synergy between business processes and emerging *big data management and processing* (e.g., [4, 5, 6, 7, 8, 9, 10, 11]) has been highlighted by several studies, among which noticeable ones are: [12, 13, 14, 15]. Looking at the actual literature, there are several initiatives about on how to shape the process mining framework, particularly for what regards the mapping between event log database and the sovereign process model. First, we focus on one-to-one mapping approaches. Most of these approaches assume that there is a one-to-one mapping between events in the log and process model activities. One-to-one mapping can be achieved by simple string substitution of the event names with activities names. However, event logs and process model activities are at different level of granularity [16]. Specifically, events in the log are finer grained than activities in process models. Therefore, an efficient algorithm for mapping low-level events to high-level activities is required in order to enable process mining techniques such as conformance checking and model enhancement. Moreover, this mapping is important for process discovery algorithms in order to discover more representative and interpretable process models. Without this mapping, the discovered models might be too complicated with too specific and non-meaningful activity names. On the other hand, many-to-many mapping approaches try to recover the activity life-cycle from a set of correlated event in the trace of the log. This model better capture real-life systems. Our proposed framework, indeed, fits well right in the direction of hybrid approaches, where the goal is, as mentioned, bridging the gap between activity logs and business process management.

In this paper, we design and implement an artificial intelligence model that is able to learn the mapping between low-level event logs and process model activities. This model comprises two main phases. The first phase is an automatic labeling approach. The goal of this phase is to automatically assign sequences of low-level events with high-level target labels. This phase is crucial since the labels for log traces are usually unavailable, and manual labeling might be infeasible, time consuming or too expensive. In the second phase, a supervised Machine Learning (ML) classifier is used to learn the mapping between low-level event logs and model activities. The labeled examples generated by the first phase are used to train the supervised ML classifier of the second phase. Since, in real-life applications and systems, business processes are expressed according to the Business Process Model and Notation (BPMN) format, we improve our proposed framework by means of an innovative, flexible BPMN model translation methodology that acts at the first phase. In particular, the need to supporting BPMN translation to BP rules is necessary as we need to "reduce" the complex BPMN models to lower-level rules to be included in the machine learning phase directly. With this work, we can automatically and accurately bridge the abstraction levels when target labels are not available. Moreover, most of the existing abstraction approaches aim to support model discovery techniques in order to discover more interpretable process models. However, we aim to enable conformance checking techniques by getting a high accuracy of mapping event logs to existing activities in the process model.

Under a broader umbrella, our framework is focused to support conformance checking of business processes. Indeed, the final goal of our framework is to support the mapping between low-level event logs and high-level business processes model activities, thus implementing the conformance checking between the two components of any arbitrary business process system. It should be noted that this requirement is extremely important in a wide range of actual application scenarios, ranging from traditional banking/assurance systems to emerging industry 4.0 settings. Conformance checking falls under the umbrella of *anomaly detection* because it provides information about mismatches (often called *violations*) between logs and process models and helps process owners to understand the causes. Business rules define constrains or guidelines that apply to an organization. Organizations use business rules to enforce policy, comply with legal obligations, communicate between various parties and perform process analysis.

In particular, we deal with process-specific rules, i.e. rules that constrain the behavior of a business process in order to achieve a specific goal. These rules can be hidden in source code, inside use cases or in workflow descriptions [17]. In this work, we use a simple language to extract logic constraints directly from BPMN models and then translate them into business rules. Using the language, any user can extract the rules easily since they are simple and tool-independent. We build a prototype to extract the logic rules automatically using the XML schema of the BPMN model. Our approach builds on previous work proposed by [18]. In their paper, the authors introduced a mechanism to translate BPMN models to Business Process Execution Language (BPEL), our technique, instead, focuses on the translation of BPMN model to business rules[1].

2. Overview on the Proposed Framework

The proposed framework is summarized in Fig. 1. The overall approach can be subdivided into two phases. The first phase is an automatic labeling task. The high-level target labels should be available in order to learn the mapping between low-level events and high- level activities. Manual labeling is time consuming or even infeasible [19]. Therefore, the automatic labeling module is used to create labeled examples. These labeled examples are refined by taking only a subset of examples that contribute to the goodness of the labeling task. With the aim of improving the effectiveness and the quality of the proposed framework, since, in real-life applications and systems, business processes are usually expressed in terms of BPMN models, we include an innovative, flexible BPMN model translation methodology that allows us to translate such models in suitable BP rules. Indeed, as highlighted in Section 1, the need to supporting BPMN translation to BP rules is necessary as we need to "reduce" the complex BPMN models to lower-level rules to be included in the machine learning phase directly. In the second phase, the labeled examples are used to train a machine learning classifier. The classifier will learn the mapping between low-level sequences and high-level activities. After learning the

[1]Some definitions used in our work are taken verbatim from their paper.

mapping, the classifier will be able to map a new set of unlabeled low-level sequences of events to the corresponding high-level activities. Hence, a high-level activity log can be created.

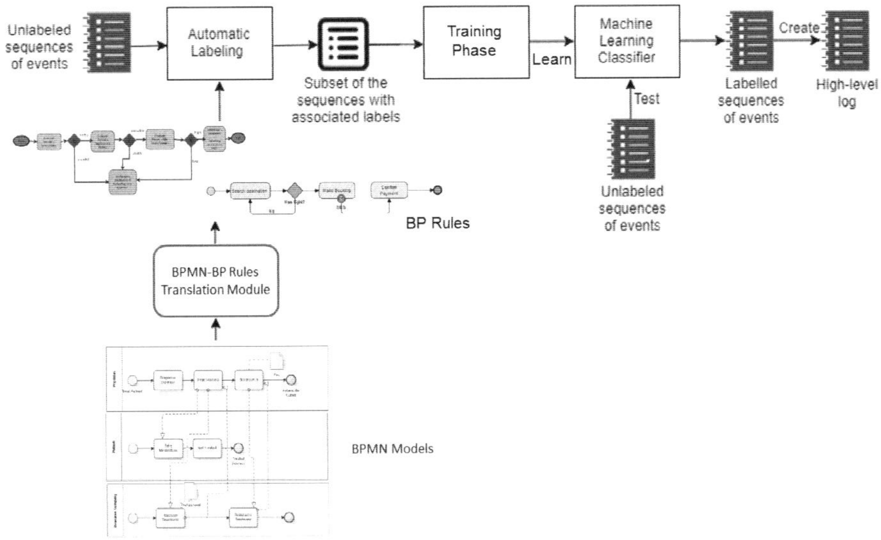

Figure 1: Overview of the proposed framework

As shown in Fig. 1, the proposed framework is composed by the following entities and (software) modules:

- *Unlabeled sequences of events* – these are low-level events from which the framework finally extracts the high-level business process activities;
- *BPMN Models* – these are the BPMN models of the reference BPMN; they are exploited by our translation module in order to improve the overall effectiveness and the quality of the proposed framework;
- *BPMN-BP Rules Translation Module* – it is the module for supporting the translation from BPMN models to BP rules, in a flexible manner;
- *Automatic Labeling* – it is the module that is in charge of supporting the creation of labeled examples to be provided as input to the supervised machine learning classification phase;
- *Subset of the sequences with associated labels* – these are the sequences extracted from the automatic labeling phase, which embed associated labels;
- *Unlabeled sequences of events* – similarly to the main input, these are low-level events that are processed by the machine learning classification phase;
- *Machine Learning Classifier* – it is the main component where the machine learning classification phase is performed in order to finally extract the high-level business process activities;
- *Labeled sequences of events* – these are the output of the machine learning classification phase; (classification) labels are used to finally build the desired high-level business process activities;

- *High-level logs* – these are the final output of the proposed framework: high-level business process activities constructed from the low-level events directly.

3. Translating BPMN to Business Process Rules

In the BPMN-BP rules translation phase, we introduce a simple, human-readable rule language based on a fragment of First-Order Logic (FOL) and show how compliance rules can be generated directly from BPMN models. We focus on control flow aspects of BPMN models by (1) transforming the model to obtain a uniform representation of task activation (2) dividing the model into sets of components and (3) using our proposed language to generate compliance rules for each component. We show that these rules can be used in the analysis of the business process execution log using British Telecom's Aperture business process analysis tool.

We start by extracting FOL constraints directly from BPMN models. Our constraints will be translated later into business rules. We rely on an initial graph transformation to achieve an implicit uniform task activation semantics; then, we apply the basic definitions given in [18] with some minor variations [2].

3.1. Graph Transformation

We start by translating the BPMN model into a fully synchronous workflow. In BPMN, activity are by default performed synchronously in relation to the invoking process flow, i.e. the process waits for an activity to complete before the process can proceed. However, BPMN syntax allows specifying asynchronous activity execution, e.g. requiring an external event to take place for enabling the execution of an activity. Using asynchronous events (rather than the completion of a previous activity) to enable execution of activities provides a general way to express different enabling semantics. The gist of our transformation is to avoid this complexity by treating synchronization events as special case of ordinary activities, and always use activity enabling by-compilation (of previous activity). In other words, before any analysis, all intermediate events in a BPMN model are transformed to special tasks with double borders to distinguish them. While such transformation may decrease the expressive power of the language, it has the advantage of decreasing the complexity of the model. For the exclusive gateway (XOR), we exclude the default statement, which leads to nothing. The WHILE component will be replaced with REAPEAT to avoid null activity. Summarizing, we perform the following transformations of the BPMN model:

1. ***step 1.*** *Conversion of events into activities*;
2. ***step 2.*** *Elimination of DEFAULT in XOR component*;
3. ***step 3.*** *Substitution of WHILE with REPEAT component.*

As shown in Fig. 2, the intermediate event e_1 is transformed to a task t_2. The DEFAULT sequence flow in the switch component is removed. At the end, the WHILE component is substituted with REPEAT component.

[2]The full definitions can be found in [18]

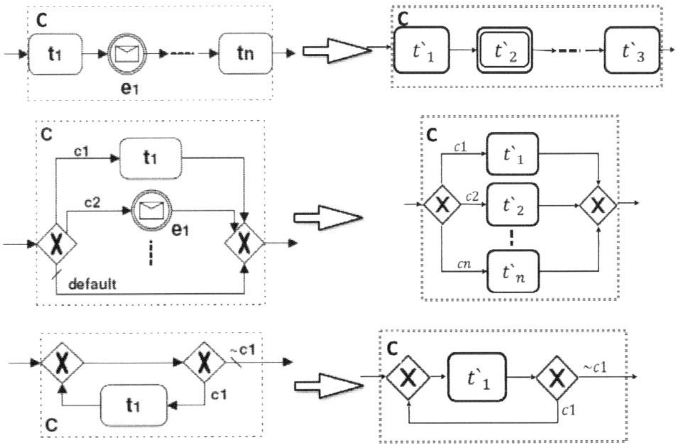

Figure 2: Intermediate event, elimination of DEFAULT and substitution of WHILE transformation

3.2. Business Process Diagram (BPD)

Business processes are expressed graphically using BPMN elements in a BPD. The model is composed of a set of different tasks, events and gateways referred as objects. A task is a single activity in the model while events can represent the start, intermediate, end, and termination of the process (graph transformation will exclude intermediate events), While the gateway represents parallel and XOR forks and joins. Fig. 3 shows the graphical representation of some BPMN elements in a core BPD which is composed of set of objects that can be partitioned into disjoint sets of tasks $\mathcal{T}$, events $\mathcal{E}$ and gateways $\mathcal{G}$ [18].

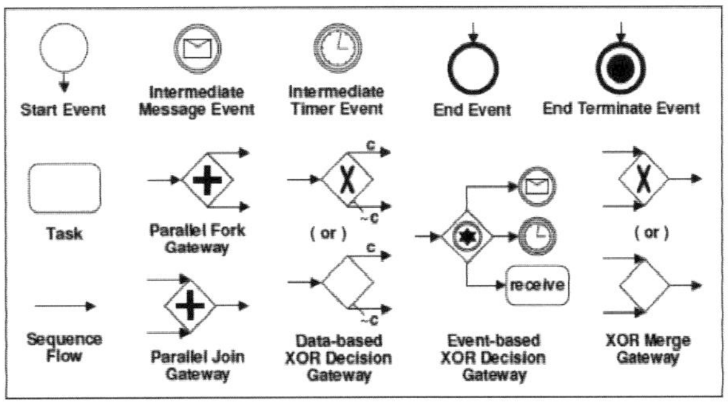

Figure 3: A core subset of BPMN elements [18]

In the remainder of the paper, we only consider well-formed core $\mathcal{BPD}$s as defined in [18]. Moreover, without losing generality we assume that both $\mathcal{E}^{\mathcal{S}}$*and* $\mathcal{E}^{\mathcal{E}}$ *are singletons, i.e.* $\mathcal{E}^{\mathcal{S}} = \{s\}$ *and* $\mathcal{E}^{\mathcal{E}} = \{e\}$.

3.3. Decomposing a BPD into Components

The notion of component is used to transform a graph structure into set of business rules. To facilitate this transformation, the BPD is decomposed into different components. Again according to [18] "A component is a subset of the BPD that has one entry and one exit point". Each component will be mapped into a single logic rule. Each component should include a minimum number of two different objects (source and sink). A BPD with no component which only contain a single task between the start and end events is called a *trivial* BPD. Whenever we reach a *trivial* BPD, no rule can be extracted and therefore we stop the translation. Breaking down the BPD into set of components helps to define an iterative method to transform BPD into rules. A function **Fold** is defined in [18] which substitutes a component with single task. **Fold** function can be utilized to reduce the BPD iteratively until we reach a *trivial* BPD.

3.4. Structured Activity-Based Translation

In our approach, different components are mapped into a subset of FOL rules including AND, XOR and sequence operations. Paper [18] defines seven forms of well-structured components. Fig. 4 represents the mapping of each component into the corresponding FOL rules [18].

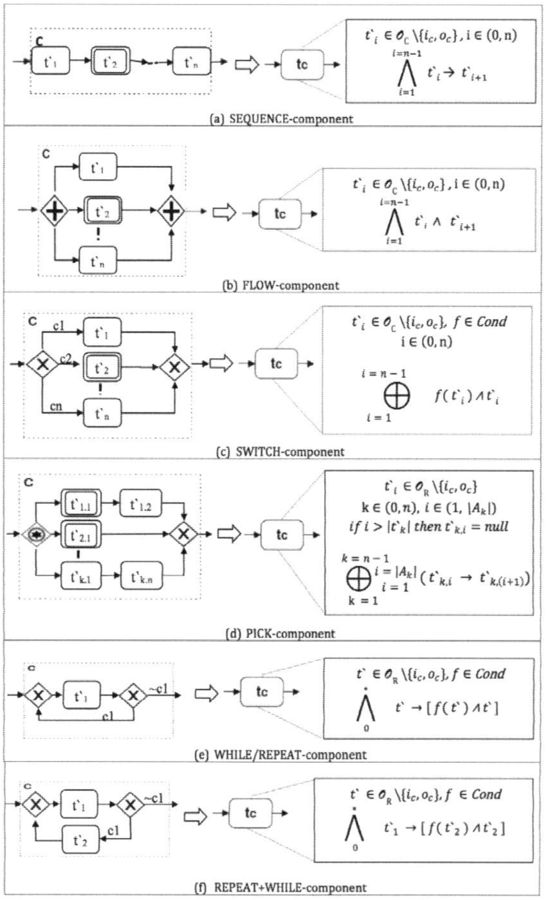

Figure 4: Folding a well-structured component $\mathscr{C}$ into single task object t_c attached with the corresponding FOL rule translation of $\mathscr{C}$ [18]

Each rule corresponds to a specific position in the BPD. The position information can be utilized in different ways in the conformance checking process and introduces two different types of dependencies: sequential and hierarchical dependencies. Sequential order means rules extracted from earlier components should be checked before rules from later components. It should be noted that sequential order is the most "natural" way to derive the corresponding BP rules, as it completely adheres to the the FOL that is at the basis of the entire process. Indeed, at a practical level, this is also more convergent to the "intuitive" folding of structural components (i.e., components that are composed by a collection of basic components), which is the most convenient approach for real-life complex business process management systems.

On the other hand, this technique presents the notion of hierarchy of constraints, which to the best of our knowledge, is not well found in the literature. One or more rules can depend on another rule and therefore executing high-level constraints plays critical role in the execution of other low-level constraints. It should be noted that the hierarchical order is instead prone to capture even more complex real life settings where BPMN schema model emerging applications like e-government or e-procurement procedures (e.g., [20, 21, 22]). In fact, in such settings, it is easy to recognize a hierarchical structure of components into sub-components, which demand for different folding strategies.

3.5. Translation Algorithm

After mapping each component to the corresponding rule, we introduce the algorithm used to translation a well-formed core BPD into FOL rule which is similar to the algorithm introduced in [18] with some modifications. The algorithm includes three different steps, selecting a well-structured component then providing its FOL rule and finally fold the component. This is done repeatedly until we reach a *trivial* BPD.

[**Algorithm 1**[18]]

Let $\mathcal{BPD} = (\mathcal{O}, \mathcal{F}, Cond)$ be a well-formed core $\mathcal{BPD}$ with one start event and one end event. $[X]_c$ is the set of components of BPD$[X]$.

1. $X := \mathcal{BPD}$
2. if $[X]_c = \emptyset$ (i.e., X is initially a *trivial*$\mathcal{BPD}$), stop.
3. while $[X]_c \neq \emptyset$ (i.e., X is a non-trivial $\mathcal{BPD}$)
    a) if there is a maximal SEQUENCE component $\mathcal{C} \in [X]_c$, select it and goto (3-c).
    b) if there is a well-structured (non-sequence) component $\mathcal{C} \in [X]_c$, select and goto (3-c).
    c) Attach logic rule translation of $\mathcal{C}$ to task object t_c.
    d) $X :=$ **Fold**$(X, \mathcal{C}, t_c)$ and return to (3).
4. Output the logic rule attached to the task object t_c.

4. Automatic Labeling

The goal of this phase is to create labeled examples to feed the supervised machine learning classifier of the next phase. In the process mining field, the execution of processes is reflected by event logs. The eXtensible Event Stream (XES) defines a standard for recording information system's events. Typically, an event in the log is defined as $e = (c, n, r, t)$, representing the occurrence of an event n, in a case c, using the resource r , at time-stamp t [23]. Additional attributes for the events can be included such as price, originator, location, etc. As highlighted in Section 2, the automatic labeling phase takes advantages from the BPMN-BP Rules Translation Module, in order to discover useful business rules hidden in BPMN models.

In the automatic labeling module, we followed a clustering approach to cluster the multivariate time series log sequences with numerical and categorical attributes. Different clustering algorithms can be followed to achieve this task. In the following, we specifically focus on such clustering tools.

When implementing automatic labeling based on clustering approaches, the general architecture of the proposed framework depicted in Fig. 1, such architecture specifies as reported in Fig. 5. The overall approach can be subdivided into two phases. The first phase is a clustering-based labeling approach. Our framework is not strictly constrained to a particular clustering algorithm. Indeed, in this phase different clustering algorithms can be used, depending on the particular application setting considered (in fact, we later discuss the specific clustering algorithm selected in our implementation). The "orthogonality" of the clustering algorithm should be intended as another amenity of our proposed framework. The high-level target labels should be available in order to learn the mapping between low-level events and high- level activities. Manual labeling is time consuming or even infeasible [19]. Therefore, the labeling module is used to create labeled examples. For every activity, a cluster of sequences of events should be formed. And then, all samples will be labeled with same labels as their corresponding clusters. After that, these labeled examples are refined by taking only a subset of examples that contribute to the goodness of the labeling task. In the second phase, the labeled examples are used to train a machine learning classifier. The classifier will learn the mapping between low-level event sequences and high-level activities. After learning the mapping, the classifier will be able to map a new set of unlabeled low-level sequences of events to the corresponding high-level activities. Hence, a high-level activity log can be created.

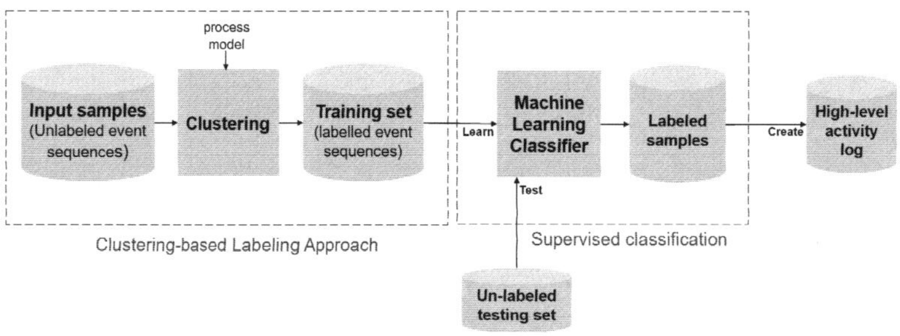

Figure 5: Overview of the proposed framework when implementing automatic labeling based on clustering approaches

4.1. Clustering-Based Labeling Approach

The first phase is the clustering-based labeling approach, which is illustrated in Fig. 6. The goal of this phase is to create labeled examples to feed the supervised machine learning classifier of the next phase.

The input samples of this phase are unlabeled event sequences. Each sample is a set of

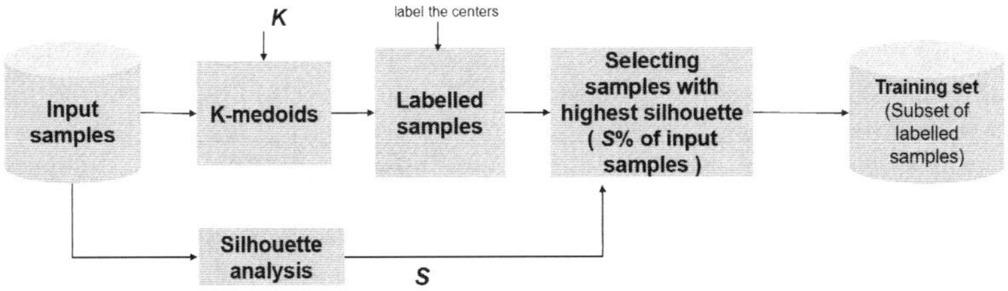

Figure 6: Clustering-based Labeling approach being K the number of high-level activities from the high-level process model, and S the percentage of samples with highest silhouette

low-level events. In order to provide labels for these samples, we will cluster them into different clusters, where each cluster represents a high-level activity. Different clustering algorithms can be followed to achieve this task. As discussed in Section 4, the specific clustering algorithm is orthogonal to the proposed framework. In our implementation, we selected k-medoids (e.g., [24]) as main clustering algorithm.

In particular, we use two clustering algorithms based on the attribute types of the input samples. Specifically, k-prototypes is utilized to cluster multivariate time series log sequences with numerical and categorical attributes, while k-medoids is applied to cluster samples with categorical attributes. Furthermore, clustering-based approach can know from the high-level process model the number of high-level activities in the process, which accordingly represents the number of clusters that should be formed. Each sample within one cluster will be labeled with its cluster label. In fact, in order to label the clusters, the domain expert should label only the cluster centers, and then each cluster label will be the same as the label of it's center.

In the process mining field, the execution of processes is reflected by event logs. The eXtensible Event Stream (XES) defines a standard for recording information system's events. Typically, an event in the log is defined as $e = (n, c, r, s, t)$, representing the occurrence of an event n, in a case c, using the resource r, having a status $s \in$ {start, complete}, at time-stamp t [23]. Additional attributes for the events can be included such as price, originator, location, etc.

5. Conclusions and Future Work

In this paper, we proposed a ML-based approach to bridge the gap between low-level event logs and high-level activities when high-level labels of the low-level events are not available. Our proposed method consists of two main phases: clustering-based labeling approach and supervised ML-based classification. Since, in real-life applications and systems, business processes are expressed according to the BPMN format, we improved our proposed framework by means of an innovative, flexible BPMN model translation methodology that acts at the first phase. Future work is oriented towards embedding adaptive metaphors to our proposed framework, even inherited by different-but-related contexts (e.g., [25]).

References

[1] M. Dumas, W. M. Van der Aalst, A. H. Ter Hofstede, Process-aware information systems: bridging people and software through process technology, John Wiley & Sons, 2005.

[2] W. M. P. van der Aalst, Process Mining - Discovery, Conformance and Enhancement of Business Processes, Springer, 2011.

[3] A. Augusto, R. Conforti, M. Dumas, M. L. Rosa, F. M. Maggi, A. Marrella, M. Mecella, A. Soo, Automated discovery of process models from event logs: Review and benchmark, IEEE Trans. Knowl. Data Eng. 31 (2019) 686–705.

[4] A. Cuzzocrea, Improving range-sum query evaluation on data cubes via polynomial approximation, Data Knowl. Eng. 56 (2006) 85–121.

[5] P. Braun, J. J. Cameron, A. Cuzzocrea, F. Jiang, C. K. Leung, Effectively and efficiently mining frequent patterns from dense graph streams on disk, in: KES, volume 35 of *Procedia Computer Science*, Elsevier, 2014, pp. 338–347.

[6] C. Yang, J. Liu, C. Hsu, W. Chou, On improvement of cloud virtual machine availability with virtualization fault tolerance mechanism, The Journal of Supercomputing 69 (2014) 1103–1122.

[7] K. Li, H. Jiang, L. T. Yang, A. Cuzzocrea (Eds.), Big Data - Algorithms, Analytics, and Applications, Chapman and Hall/CRC, 2015.

[8] A. Cuzzocrea, E. Bertino, Privacy preserving OLAP over distributed XML data: A theoretically-sound secure-multiparty-computation approach, J. Comput. Syst. Sci. 77 (2011) 965–987.

[9] A. Cuzzocrea, V. Russo, Privacy preserving OLAP and OLAP security, in: Encyclopedia of Data Warehousing and Mining, IGI Global, 2009, pp. 1575–1581.

[10] A. Cuzzocrea, R. Moussa, G. Xu, Olap*: Effectively and efficiently supporting parallel OLAP over big data, in: MEDI, volume 8216 of *Lecture Notes in Computer Science*, Springer, 2013, pp. 38–49.

[11] A. Campan, A. Cuzzocrea, T. M. Truta, Fighting fake news spread in online social networks: Actual trends and future research directions, in: 2017 IEEE International Conference on Big Data, BigData 2017, Boston, MA, USA, December 11-14, 2017, IEEE Computer Society, 2017, pp. 4453–4457.

[12] L. Dezi, G. Santoro, H. Gabteni, A. C. Pellicelli, The role of big data in shaping ambidextrous business process management: Case studies from the service industry, Business Proc. Manag. Journal 24 (2018) 1163–1175.

[13] G. Festa, I. Safraou, M. T. Cuomo, L. Solima, Big data for big pharma: Harmonizing business process management to enhance ambidexterity, Business Proc. Manag. Journal 24 (2018) 1110–1123.

[14] R. Rialti, G. Marzi, M. Silic, C. Ciappei, Ambidextrous organization and agility in big data era: The role of business process management systems, Business Proc. Manag. Journal 24 (2018) 1091–1109.

[15] S. F. Wamba, Big data analytics and business process innovation, Business Proc. Manag. Journal 23 (2017) 470–476.

[16] T. Baier, J. Mendling, Bridging abstraction layers in process mining: Event to activity mapping, in: Enterprise, Business-Process and Information Systems Modeling, Springer, 2013, pp. 109–123.

[17] B. von Halie, L. Goldberg (Eds.), The Business Rule Revolution, Happy About, 2006.

[18] C. Ouyang, W. M. van der Aalst, M. Dumas, A. H. ter Hofstede, Translating bpmn to bpel, 2006.

[19] N. Tax, N. Sidorova, R. Haakma, W. M. van der Aalst, Event abstraction for process mining using supervised learning techniques, in: Proceedings of SAI Intelligent Systems Conference, Springer, 2016, pp. 251–269.

[20] A. A. Kalenkova, A. A. Ageev, I. A. Lomazova, W. M. P. van der Aalst, E-government services: Comparing real and expected user behavior, in: Business Process Management Workshops - BPM 2017 International Workshops, Barcelona, Spain, September 10-11, 2017, Revised Papers, 2017, pp. 484–496.

[21] S. Alfadhel, S. Liu, F. O. Oderanti, Business process modelling and visualisation to support e-government decision making: Business/is alignment, in: Third International Conference, ICDSST 2017, Namur, Belgium, May 29-31, 2017, Proceedings, 2017, pp. 45–57.

[22] R. Costa, O. Garcia, M. J. Nuñez, P. M. N. Maló, R. Jardim-Gonçalves, Integrated solution to support enterprise interoperability at the business process level on e-procurement, in: Proceedings of the 3th International Conference on Interoperability for Enterprise Software and Applications, IESA 2007, March 27-30, 2007, Funchal, Madeira Island, Portugal, 2007, pp. 89–100.

[23] P. Ceravolo, E. Damiani, M. Torabi, S. Barbon, Toward a new generation of log pre-processing methods for process mining, in: International Conference on Business Process Management, Springer, 2017, pp. 55–70.

[24] H. Park, C. Jun, A simple and fast algorithm for k-medoids clustering, Expert Syst. Appl. 36 (2009) 3336–3341.

[25] M. Cannataro, A. Cuzzocrea, C. Mastroianni, R. Ortale, A. Pugliese, Modeling adaptive hypermedia with an object-oriented approach and XML, in: Proceedings of the Second International Workshop on Web Dynamics, WebDyn@WWW 2002, Honululu, HW, USA, May 7, 2002, volume 702 of *CEUR Workshop Proceedings*, CEUR-WS.org, 2002, pp. 35–44.

Development of a decision tree model to improve case detection via information extraction from veterinary Electronic Medical Records

Oscar Tamburis [1], Elio Masciari [2] and Gerardo Fatone [1]

[1] *Federico II University, Dept. of Veterinary Medicine and Animal Productions, Naples 80137, ITALY*
[2] *Federico II University, Dept. of Computer Science and Electrical Engineering, Naples 80125, ITALY*

Abstract
The increasing importance of Veterinary Informatics is currently witnessed, among the other things, also from the very good results achieved by data mining techniques for what concerns computer aided disease diagnosis and exploration of risk factors and their relations to diseases. To such purpose, the present work describes the analysis conducted on the diagnoses made during the general physical examinations in the decade 2010–2020, starting from the database of the Electronic Medical Record previously implemented in the University Veterinary Teaching Hospital at Federico II University of Naples. A decision tree algorithm was then implemented to work out a predictive model for an effective recognition of neoplastic diseases and zoonoses for cats and dogs from Campania Region, in order to figure out, according to the One (Digital) Health perspective specifics, the connection between humans, animals, and surrounding environment.

Keywords
Electronic Medical Record, Veterinary Informatics, Data Mining

1. Introduction

Animals, be they categorized as pets, livestock, or wildlife, stand as essential element in the evolution of human race for countless reasons. In particular, animal healthcare–related aspects play a prominent role because of their strict connections with human health. The monitoring of both wildlife and syntropic species' health state can provide in fact valuable information about (i) the quality of the environment they live in, and that they share with humans, in terms of pollution level, as well as food safety and traceability management; (ii) the occurring of zoonotic phenomena (for instance, leptospirosis and the recent COVID-19 pandemic). Furthermore, many non-infectious diseases (e.g. diabetes, cancer, and renal failure) are similar in both animals and humans [1]. Consequently, the need for an effective tracking of veterinary information to facilitate integration of animal medical data to support Public Health, has become essential. As a matter of fact, under the epidemiological perspective the advantages of using animals as sentinels or comparative models of human diseases are well known, as animals – or better, animal sentinels – may be sensitive indicators of environmental hazards and provide an early warning system for public health interventions [2]. With specific reference to Campania Region, this kind of studies are of particular concern due to the widely known so-called "Terra dei Fuochi/Land of Fires" phenomenon (see e.g. [3, 4]). An as important aspect relates then to the control of the zoonoses, i.e. those diseases that can be transmitted from the animals to the human beings via faeces, urine, saliva, or blood. It is the case of e.g. intestinal parasites and ticks (that use the animal as a vector), or rabies (transmitted via the saliva). Such risks have to be carefully taken into account when it comes to the cohabitation between humans and (conventional as well as non-

SEBD 2021: The 29th Italian Symposium on Advanced Database Systems, September 5-9, 2021, Pizzo Calabro (VV), Italy
EMAIL: oscar.tamburis@unina.it (O. Tamburis); elio.masciari@unina.it (E. Masciari); gerardo.fatone@unina.it (G. Fatone)
ORCID: 0000-0002-0130-7915 (O. Tamburis); 0000-0002-1778-5321 (E. Masciari); 0000-0003-2578-7420 (G. Fatone)

conventional) pets [5]. The implementation of integrated veterinary information management systems (VIMS) for the capture, storage, analysis and retrieval of data, provides the opportunity for the cumulative gathering of the knowledge, and the capability for its competent interpretation [6]. To this end, it becomes useful to resort to data mining computational methods for extracting knowledge also in the case of animal large databases. Among the most diffused data mining algorithms [7, 8], decision tree provides a tree-based classification for developing a predictive model according to independent variables [9]. In this paper the main results will be shown from the analysis of the data extracted from PONGO software ©, i.e. the first EMR solution implemented in the University Veterinary Teaching Hospital (it.: OVUD, acronym for Ospedale Veterinario Universitario Didattico) of the "Federico II" University of Naples, Italy. The main goal was to establish, by means of decision tree algorithm, a predictive model for an effective recognition of neoplastic diseases and zoonoses using clinical data, according to clinical, para-clinical, and demographic attributes. The investigation on the quality of clinical data of OVUD's patients is intended for helping, at least on a region-wide scenario, to find out the presence of specific connections between people's health, animal health, and their surrounding environment, thus conveying the specific Public Health dimension into the greater One (Digital) Health scenario [10].

2. Materials and Methods

2.1. Subjects

The data extracted from PONGO sw in form of MS Access DB relate to the general physical examination (GPE), that is the first visit performed from the veterinarian when the animal arrives to the hospital. The database contains about 10360 rows (one row per animal access) which span over a period going from 2010 to mid-2020. The visits were mainly performed on pets, i.e. dogs (n = 8925; 86%) and cats (n = 1181; 11%). Horses occurred to be treated in the hospital as well (n = 160; 2%). Only for a small part (n = 92; 1%) the animals examined belonged to other species (ducks, donkeys, bovines, buffaloes, goats, lagomorphs, rodents, tortoises, and birds). Besides animal species and date of the visit, the main fields of the DB also related to age and sex of the animal, main health issue (HI) acknowledged during the GPE, type of feeding (e.g. commercial vs. homemade), and vaccination status information. Also considered in the study were the kind of environments the animal used to live in (e.g. in an apartment, or outdoors), and the Italian province it came from. As for the latter point, the research was limited to the provinces of Campania Region, due to the marginal number of rows related to patients coming from other Italian regions. Table 1 reports the accesses to OVUD, based on the geographic provenance, for dogs, cats, and horses. Several OLAP operations [11,12] were performed on the mentioned dataset, in order to investigate the quality of clinical data of OVUD's patients for the considered time period. Given the situation, it was decided to focus the investigation only on dogs and cats.

2.2. Accesses per animal sex

Four types of sex specifications have to be considered for animals: male (M), castrated male (MC), female (F), spayed female (FS). Figure 1 reports the accesses to the OVUD of dogs and cats, respectively, for the time period considered. The number of rows/visits for which it was not possible to retrieve the sex of the animal, were also reported. Only in one case, the animal (dog) was reported as not visited after the access in the hospital. It has to be pointed out that the lower number of accesses registered in 2016 in both cases, was due to a partial stop of the OVUD activities, as a structural collapse interested at the end of 2015 part of the University Department that hosts the hospital itself. The number of male dogs' accesses is about twice as much the female accesses in almost all the years considered, with quite lower numbers for the neutered dogs. A different situation concerns cats, where the differences M/MC and F/FS tend to be proportionally shorter, sometimes in favour of the neutered exemplars.

Table 1
Distribution of dogs, cats, and horses that accessed the OVUD, according to the Italian provinces

Species	Province	#	%
	Avellino	145	2%
	Benevento	71	1%
	Caserta	753	8%
Dog	Napoli	6967	78%
	Salerno	444	5%
	Other Italian provinces	545	6%
	Avellino	22	2%
	Benevento	9	1%
	Caserta	68	6%
Cat	Napoli	975	83%
	Salerno	41	3%
	Other Italian provinces	66	6%
	Avellino	3	2%
	Benevento	7	4%
Horse	Caserta	14	9%
	Napoli	64	40%
	Salerno	49	31%

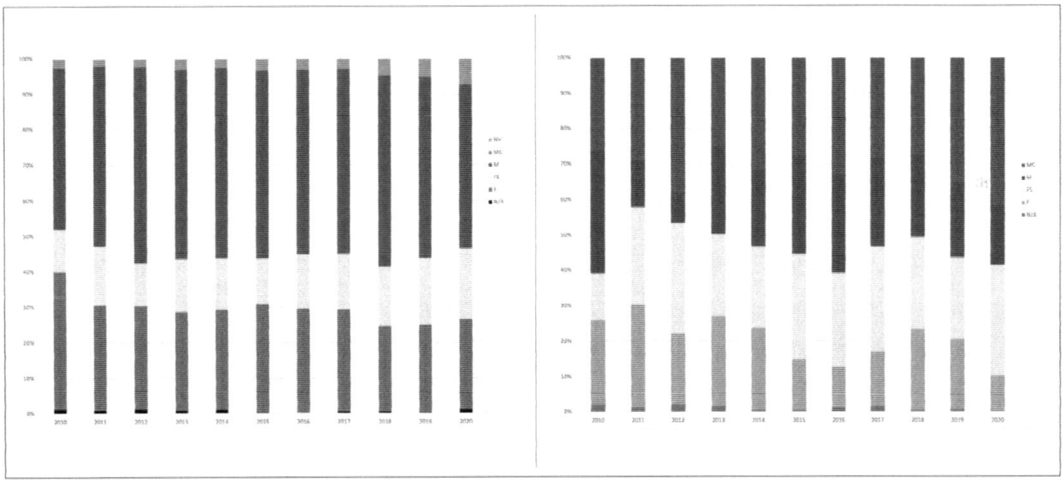

Figure 1: Accesses to OVUD of dogs (left) and cats (right)

2.3. Health issues per year

It was possible to identify about 140 different diagnoses from the GPE for the period considered. For mere space reasons, it was decided for both dogs and cats to investigate, for each year, only the three most relevant health issues (HIs), as reported in Tables 2 and 3. In case of HIs featuring the same occurrences, they were all considered. The only exception is for cats' HIs in 2012, where the occurrences for HI #3 were equal to 1 for a very large set of issues, so it was decided not to report it in the table. It can be noticed for dogs a diffuse presence of limping–related issues (N = 458), along with Neoplastic diseases (N = 263), and alopecia (N = 239). Injury of abdomen (N = 46), inspection of vomit (N = 46), and pain in eye (N = 40) appear instead among the most diffused issues reported for the cats that accessed the OVUD. The occurrences of such HIs during the years are reported in Table 4 and 5, and in Figure 2. The total number of occurrences are depicted in Figure 3. In both cases, it is worth noticing the presence of neoplastic diseases (dogs: N = 263; cats; N = 9) and firm lymph node–related (dogs: N = 95; cats; N= 3) diagnoses. Moreover, considering animals' age of birth (spanning from 1984 to 2020), it was possible to compare for each trimester the diagnoses of firm lymph nodes and neoplastic diseases. This revealed that the 44% cases of dogs of the same age, and the 5% cases of cats of the same age presented a number of occurrences of firm lymph node–related diagnoses greater or at least equal to neoplastic diseases diagnoses, thus inducing – at least for dogs – the reasonable hypothesis of an existing connection between the two pathologies. Furthermore, Figure 3 reports the occurrences of those diagnoses which can be somehow related to the transmission of zoonoses, from tetanus (N = 1 for dogs) to vomit (dogs: N = 254; cats: N = 53). The number of occurrences of such diagnoses is the 7% of the total occurrences registered in OVUD for dogs and cats for the period considered.

2.4. Dataset

A preliminary step of dataset cleansing was necessary, especially for what concerns the health diagnoses, as no form of clinical standardized terminology had been deployed. Moreover, for about 30% rows (N = 3729), such type of data was actually missing, and only in a limited number of cases it was possible to get to it anyway by means of the analysis of the remainder fields of the database. Eventually, the total number of participants considered in the model were 10108.

Health Issues (as already done for reported in Tables 1 and 2) were categorized according to the vet-SNOMED terminology [13, 14], as developed by the Veterinary Medical Informatics Laboratory at Virginia-Maryland College of Veterinary Medicine: for each of them, the corresponding Concept was identified, together with the related SNOMED hierarchy level, the Concept ID, and the Preferred Description (Synonym) ID [15, 16].

Table 2
The three most diagnosed health issues for dogs

Year	HI #1	HI #2	HI #3
2010	Limping	Injury of abdomen	Firm lymph node (on exam.)
2011	Limping	On exam. - inspection of vomit	Pain in eye; Skin lesion (on exam.); Cough
2012	Alopecia	Skin lesion (on exam.); Limping	On exam. - inspection of vomit
2013	Limping	Alopecia	On exam. - inspection of vomit
2014	Limping	Neoplastic disease	Alopecia
2015	Limping	Neoplastic disease	Alopecia
2016	Limping	Injury of abdomen; Alopecia	Firm lymph node (on exam.)
2017	Limping	Firm lymph node (on exam.); Alopecia	Neoplastic disease
2018	Limping	Injury of abdomen	Neoplastic disease
2019	Injury of abdomen	Cough; Neoplastic disease	Limping
2020	Injury of abdomen	Alopecia	On exam. - inspection of vomit

Table 3

The three most diagnosed health issues for cats

Year	HI #1	HI #2	HI #3
2010	On exam. - inspection of vomit; Pain in eye	Injury of abdomen	Urinary tract pain
2011	On exam. - inspection of vomit	Alopecia	Urinary tract pain
2012	On exam. - inspection of vomit Pain in eye	Firm lymph node (on exam.); Alopecia	.
2013	On exam. - inspection of vomit	Pain in eye; Injury of abdomen	Alopecia
2014	Pain in eye	Injury of abdomen	Urinary tract pain
2015	Alopecia; On exam. - inspection of vomit	Neoplastic disease	Skin lesion (on exam.); Pain in eye
2016	On exam. - inspection of vomit	Injury of abdomen	Alopecia
2017	Injury of abdomen	Skin lesion (on exam.)	On exam. - inspection of vomit Urinary tract pain; Neoplastic disease
2018	On exam. - inspection of vomit	Alopecia; Pain in eye; Injury of abdomen	Skin lesion (on exam.)
2019	Injury of abdomen	Cough	Pain in eye; Alopecia
2020	Injury of abdomen	Firm lymph node (on exam.)	Skin lesion (on exam.); Closed fracture of hip; Sore mouth

Table 4

Distribution of the three most diagnosed health issues per year, for dogs

Year	**Alopecia**	**Cough**	**Firm lymph node (on examination)**	**Injury of abdomen**	**Limping**	**Neoplastic disease**	**On examination - inspection**	**Pain in eye**	**Skin lesion (on examination)**
2010	0	0	12	13	17	0	0	0	0
2011	0	13	0	0	34	0	18	13	13
2012	13	0	0	0	8	0	7	0	8
2013	33	0	0	0	43	0	23	0	0
2014	42	0	0	0	57	50	0	0	0
2015	48	0	0	0	73	56	0	0	0
2016	38	0	34	38	40	0	0	0	0
2017	49	0	49	0	59	33	0	0	0
2018	0	0	0	59	68	58	0	0	0
2019	0	66	0	108	59	66	0	0	0
2020	16	0	0	17	0	0	15	0	0
TOT	**239**	**79**	**95**	**235**	**458**	**263**	**63**	**13**	**21**

Table 5
Distribution of the three most diagnosed health issues per year, for cats

Year	Alopecia	Closed fracture of hip	Cough	Firm lymph node (on examination)	Injury of abdomen	Neoplastic disease	On examination - inspection of vomit	Pain in eye	Skin lesion (on examination)	Sore mouth
2010	0	0	0	0	3	0	4	4	0	0
2011	4	0	0	0	0	0	5	0	0	0
2012	1	0	0	1	0	0	2	2	0	0
2013	4	0	0	0	8	0	10	8	0	0
2014	0	0	0	0	8	0	0	9	0	0
2015	8	0	0	0	0	5	8	4	4	0
2016	4	0	0	0	5	0	6	0	0	0
2017	0	0	0	0	7	4	4	0	5	0
2018	5	0	0	0	5	0	7	5	4	0
2019	8	0	9	0	12	0	0	8	0	0
2020	0	1	0	2	3	0	0	0	1	1
TOT	**34**	**1**	**9**	**3**	**51**	**9**	**46**	**40**	**14**	**1**

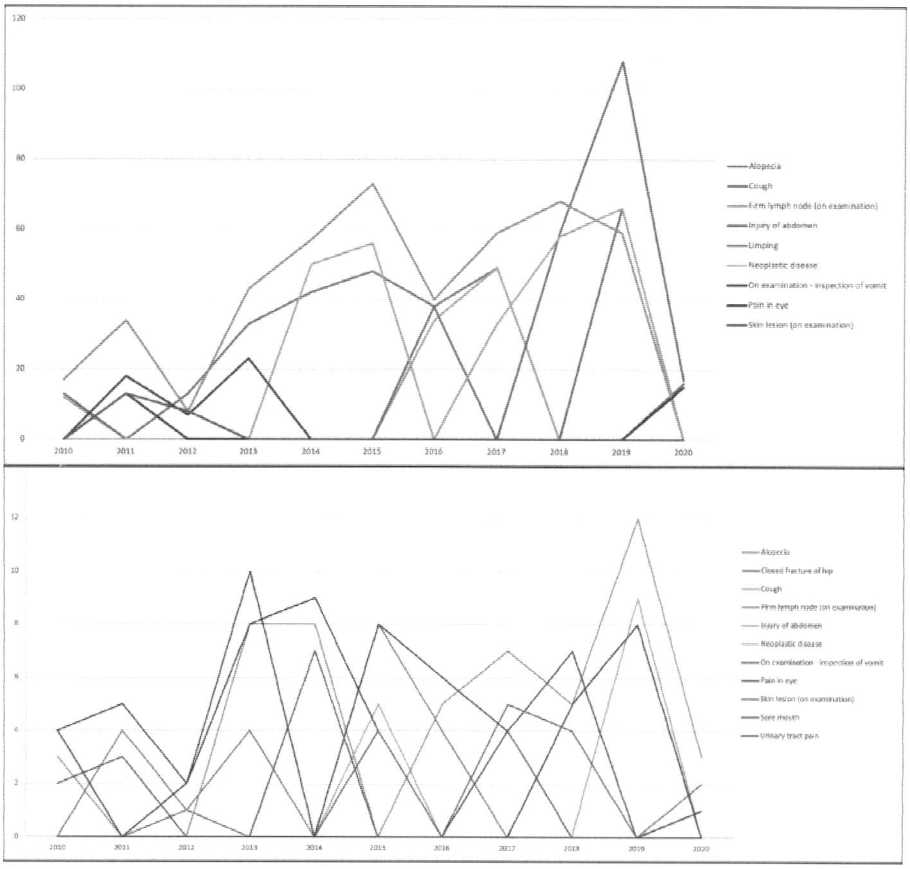

Figure 2: Distribution of the three most diagnosed HIs per year, for dogs (up) and cats (down)

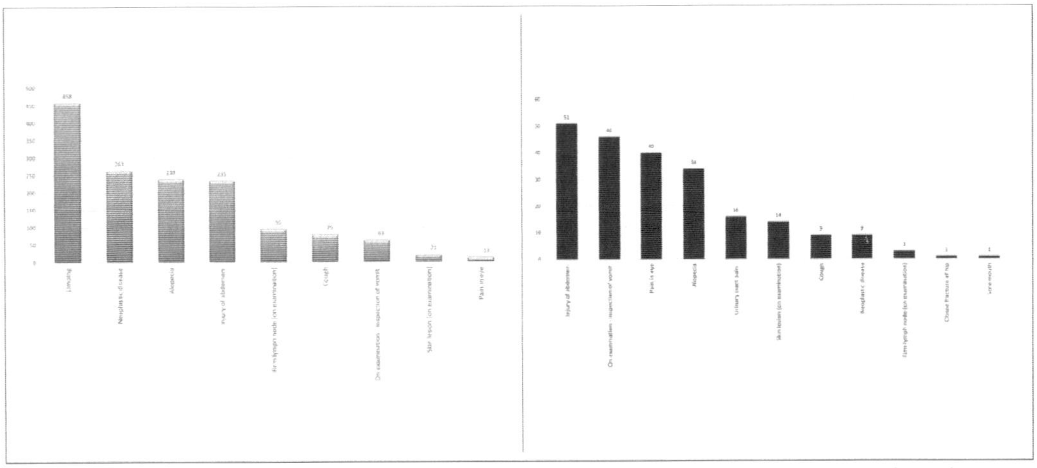

Figure 3: Total occurrences for the three most diagnosed HIs, for dogs (left) and cats (right)

Given the mentioned importance of identifying the presence of neoplastic diseases–related and/or zoonoses–related diagnoses, the need emerged to figure out a way to predict the presence of symptoms for both the issues considered – for both dogs and cats, who also happen to live very close to humans. In particular, according to what depicted in Figure 4, for what concerns zoonoses it was decided to consider for the analysis the diagnosis of "inspection of vomit".

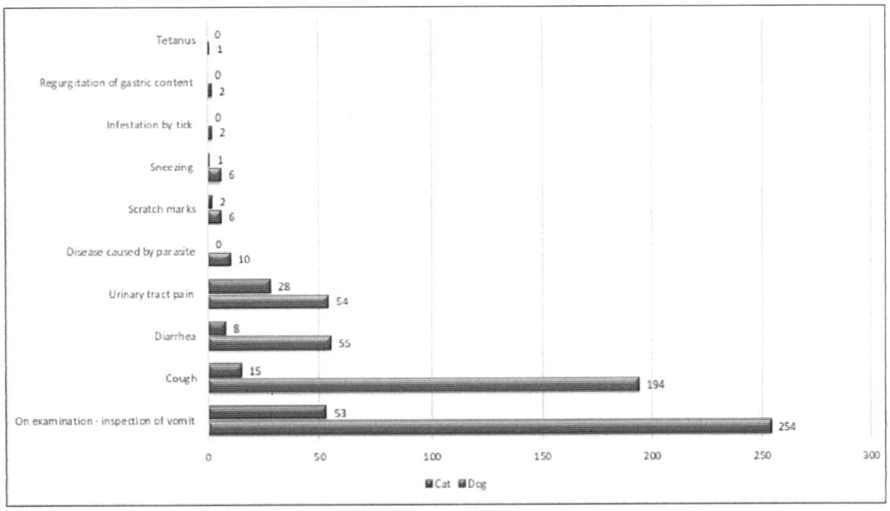

Figure 4: Total occurrences of zoonosis–related diagnoses, for both dogs and cats

Table 6 reports the vet-SNOMED classification for the two health issues considered in the study.

Table 6

Veterinary SNOMED classification of the investigated diseases

Type of Disease	Neoplastic Disease	On examination - inspection of vomit
Classification (Is a)	Disorder	Clinical finding
ConceptID (according to VTSL)	55342001	308637007
Preferred DescriptionID (according to VTSL and AAHA)	92007014	451951011
Acceptable synonym	Neoplasia	O/E - inspection of vomit
Synonym's DescriptionID	1231453017	2670302013

2.5. DT ID3 Feature selection algorithm

The implementation of a Decision Tree Algorithm (DT) appeared as the most suitable way to investigate the membership of the subjects to different categories (diagnosed with neoplastic disease, or not; diagnosed with vomit, or not), taking into account the values of specific attributes (predictor variables), which in our case were identified for both cases as: animal sex, diet, vaccination, feeding routines, and living environment (plus the eventual presence of diagnosis of firm lymph nodes, for neoplastic diseases).

In order to achieve these goals, a filter-based strategy using DT ID3 (Iterative Dichotomiser 3) was proposed [17]. As it is common in data mining methods to divide the dataset into two parts, also in our case the original sample was split into a training set (to train the model), and a test set (to evaluate the performance of DT ID3). In particular, the original Training dataset for the DT (oTrDS) featured all the accesses of dogs and cats to the OVUD between 2010 and 2018 (N = 8643; 86%), while the original Testing dataset (oTeDS) comprised the remaining accesses between 2019 and 2020 (N = 1465; 14%). The reason why it was not respected the common rule according to which oTrDS $\simeq$ 70% sampling data, and oTeDS $\simeq$ remaining 30%, mainly depends on two factors: (i) the reduced accesses to OVUD in 2016 due to the mentioned structure collapse, and; (ii) available data from year 2020 only cover the first six months.

Since the aim of the study was to make prediction for two kind of health issues, each per two animal species, four specific Training datasets (sTrDS) and four specific Testing datasets (sTeDS) were extracted from oTrDS and oTeDS, respectively. For each case, a confusion matrix was used to evaluate the performance of the DT for classification of participants. Accuracy, sensitivity, and specificity were then measured for comparison. For sake of simplification, decision tree and confusion matrix have been represented in the following for one case only (presence of symptoms for neoplastic disease in dogs). A comparison was instead conducted for the performances of all four algorithms.

3. Results

A decision tree was built starting from the sTrDS related to the recognition of neoplastic disease for dogs (N = 8927). The sTeDS (N = 1305) was used to evaluate the model. The input variables were animal sex, diet, vaccination, feeding routines, living environment, and eventual presence of diagnosis of firm lymph nodes.

As seen, since for dogs the possibility of a correlation was recognized between the diagnoses of neoplastic disease and firm lymph nodes, the number of subjects positive for both health issues (ND+ and L+) was reported in the algorithm. ID3 uses two metrics to measure the importance of the input variables, or features, such as entropy (the measure of the amount of uncertainty) and information gain (the difference between the entropy of the DS, and the one related to the single feature). So, be DS a given dataset, and X the set of variables in DS. For each $x \in X$, the less the entropy, the more the information gain. For each iteration, the algorithm selects the feature with the smallest entropy/largest information gain value. The final decision tree with size 15, 8 leaves and 5 layers is shown in Figure 5.

The evaluation of the tree was undertaken using confusion matrix on a testing dataset, as shown in Table 7. The algorithm had an Accuracy of 99%: of the 70 animals diagnosed as ND+ in the sTeDS, 60 were correctly classified using the DT. In a subordinate position, of the 50 animals diagnosed as L+, 37 were correctly identified. The specificity and sensitivity of the tree were equal to 99,2 and 1, respectively. The performance of DT was also reported in Table 8.

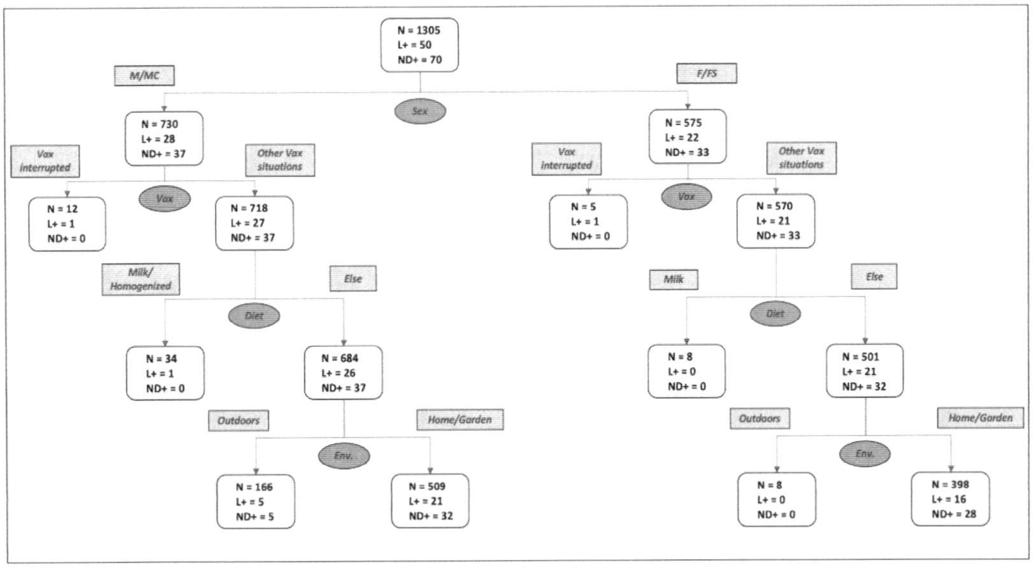

Figure 5: Decision Tree to evaluate the presence of symptoms for neoplastic disease in dogs

Table 7
Confusion Matrix of sTeDS related to the recognition of neoplastic disease for dogs

		Predicted Outcome	
		ND+	**ND–**
Expected Outcome	**ND+**	60 (TP)	10 (FP)
	ND–	0 (FN)	1235 (TN)

Table 8
Performance of the DT ID3 model for the case investigated

Variable	Decision Tree Model
Sensitivity (95% CI)	1 (93,9 – 1)
Specificity (95% CI)	99,2 (98,5 – 99,6)
Accuracy (95% CI)	99 (98,3 – 99,4)

An overall comparison was instead conducted between the performances of the algorithm for the four cases investigated, as reported in Table 9.

Table 9
Comparison of the performances of the DT ID3 algorithm for all the cases investigated

		Accuracy	Sensitivity	Specificity
Dogs	**Neoplastic Disease**	99%	100%	99,2%
	Zoonosis (Vomit)	100%	100%	100%
Cats	**Neoplastic Disease**	100%	100%	100%
	Zoonosis (Vomit)	100%	100%	100%

Although the numbers of cats-related diagnoses extracted from the PONGO DB were significantly lesser than the dogs-related ones, the overall results obtained confirmed anyway the validity of the data mining algorithm implemented, which turned as highly capable of modelling the process of healthcare provision [18], as well as of setting forth reliable measurements of system performance and outcomes [19].

4. Discussion and Conclusions

In this paper a decision tree algorithm was implemented, starting from the database of the University Veterinary Hospital of the Federico II University of Naples, to work out a predictive model for an effective recognition of neoplastic diseases and zoonoses using clinical data, according to clinical, para-clinical, and demographic attributes. The main scope was to investigate whether and at what extent relations can stand between human and animal health, and their surrounding environments. The whole set of disciplines broadly dealing with the such kind of "connecting chain" goes under the name of One Health (OH), introduced for the first time as part of the twelve "Manhattan Principles" calling for an international, interdisciplinary approach to prevent diseases [20] and specifically animal-human transmissible and communicable ones. In this spirit, the seminal idea of "One Health Informatics" (OHI) was proposed as connected to the deployment of big data analytics to support and improve public health and medical research and address issues related to e.g. biodiversity control, disease monitoring, or control of zoonoses [21, 22].

To this purpose, the evolution of timely solutions of Electronic Medical Records (EMRs) for pets (dogs and cats, mainly) allows achieving the same benefits as in human health, in terms of increased quality of care, better coordination among vet professionals, efficient care path design, etc. Seen under this comprehensive point of view, the bursting of dynamics connected to the emerging and re-emerging of infectious diseases, as well as the need to identify at global level risk factors and causes of health problems that arise at the human-animal-environment crossing, made even more remarkable the role of veterinarians towards the protection of human health.

This points out therefore the growing of veterinary informatics, as also encompassing the need for new paradigms, approaches and technologies to reinforce the capacity of traditional surveillance systems for prevention and control of zoonoses, in terms of i.e. inter-sectoral coordination, link between human and animal health data and consequent management of flows of reliable data and information, or proper use of infrastructures, systems and human resources to detect outbreaks [23].

5. References

[1] K.A. Smith-Akin, C.F. Bearden, S.T. Pittenger, E.V. Bernstam, E.V, Toward a veterinary informatics research agenda: an analysis of the PubMed-indexed literature, International journal of medical informatics, 76 (2007) 306-312.

[2] H. Vilhena, A.C, Figueira, F. Schmitt, A. Canadas, R. Chaves, A. Gama, P. Dias-Pereira, Canine and Feline Spontaneous Mammary Tumours as Models of Human Breast Cancer, in: M.R. Pastorinho, A.C.A. Sousa (Eds.), Pets as Sentinels, Forecasters and Promoters of Human Health, Springer, Cham, 2020, pp. 173-207.

[3] A. Zaccaroni, A. Corteggio, G. Altamura, M. Silvi, R. Di Vaia, C. Formigaro, G. Borzacchiello, Elements levels in dogs from "triangle of death" and different areas of Campania region (Italy), Chemosphere, 108 (2014) 62-69.

[4] S. Cavallo, F.P. Serpe, D. Rea, R. Pellicanò, M. D'Amore, C.D. Martinis, ..., L. Baldi, The Land of Fires in Campania: the effects of exposure to dioxins on the progression of human breast cancer in an innovative animal model, in: Proceedings of the XVIII Congresso Nazionale S.I. Di. LV, Società Italiana di Diagnostica di Laboratorio Veterinaria (SIDiLV), Perugia (PG), Italia, 2018, pp. 41-42.

[5] A. Mhlanga, Assessing the Impact of Optimal Health Education Programs on the Control of Zoonotic Diseases, Computational and Mathematical Methods in Medicine, 2020.

[6] B. Plavšić, D. Nedić, Z. Mićović, M. Tešić, S. Stanojević, R. Ašanin, ..., S. Milanović, Veterinary information management system (VIMS) in the process of notification and management of animal diseases Acta veterinaria, 59 (2009) 99-108.

[7] M. Ianni, E. Masciari, G.M. Mazzeo, M. Mezzanzanica, C. Zaniolo, Fast and effective Big Data exploration by clustering, Future Generation Computer Systems, 102 (2020) 84-94.

[8] E. Masciari, SMART: stream monitoring enterprise activities by RFID tags, Information Sciences, 195 (2012) 25-44.

[9] M.L. Bernardi, M. Cimitile, F. Martinelli, F. Mercaldo, A time series classification approach to game bot detection, in: Proceedings of the 7th International Conference on Web Intelligence, Mining and Semantics, 2017, pp. 1-11.

[10] A. Benis, O. Tamburis, C. Chronaki, A. Moen, One Digital Health: a unified framework for future health ecosystems, Journal of Medical Internet Research, 23 (2021) e22189.

[11] S. Pešić, T. Stanković, D. Janković, D.: Benefits of using OLAP versus RDBMS for data analyses in health care information systems, FACULTY OF ELECTRICAL ENGINEERING UNIVERSITY OF BANJA LUKA, 56 (2009).

[12] S. El Hajjami, M. Berrada, M. Harti, G. Diallo, Using Semantic Web Technologies and Multi-agent System for Multi-dimensional Analysis of Open Health Data, Journal of Information & Knowledge Management, 19 (2020) 205002.

[13] K.L. Zimmerman, J.R. Wilcke, J.L. Robertson, B.F. Feldman, T. Kaur, L.R. Rees, K.A. Spackman, SNOMED representation of explanatory knowledge in veterinary clinical pathology, Veterinary clinical pathology, 34 (2005) 7-16.

[14] H. Lerner, Conceptions of health and disease in plants and animals. Handbook of the Philosophy of Medicine. Dordrecht: Springer Science+ Business Media, 2017, pp. 287-301.

[15] SNOMED Homepage, URL: www.snomed.org.

[16] Veterinary Terminology Services Laboratory, URL: https://vtsl.vetmed.vt.edu.

[17] M. Tayefi, M. Tajfard, S. Saffar, P. Hanachi, A.R. Amirabadizadeh, H. Esmaeily, ..., M. Ghayour-Mobarhan, hs-CRP is strongly associated with coronary heart disease (CHD): A data mining approach using decision tree algorithm, Computer methods and programs in biomedicine, 141 (2017) 105-109.

[18] O. Tamburis, Bridging the gap between process mining and des modeling in the healthcare domain, in: Proceedings of the 2019 E-Health and Bioengineering Conference (EHB), Iasi, Romania, IEEE, 2019, pp. 1-4.

[19] D. Luzi, F. Pecoraro, O. Tamburis, Appraising Healthcare Delivery Provision: A Framework to Model Business Processes, Studies in health technology and informatics, 235 (2017) 511-515.

[20] J.S. Mackenzie, M. Jeggo, The One Health approach—Why is it so important?, Trop Med Infect Dis. 4 (2019) 88.

[21] H.C. Ossebaard, One health informatics, in: Proceedings of the 23rd International Conference on World Wide Web, 2014, pp. 669-670.

[22] G.V. Asokan, V. Asokan, Leveraging "big data" to enhance the effectiveness of "one health" in an era of health informatics, Journal of epidemiology and global health, 5 (2015) 311-314.

[23] J. Choi, Y. Cho, E. Shim, H. Woo, Web-based infectious disease surveillance systems and public health perspectives: a systematic review, BMC public health, 16 (2016) 1-10.

A Web Tool for the Semantic Integration of Heterogeneous and Complex Spreadsheet Tables

Sara Bonfitto[1], Luca Cappelletti[1], Elena Casiraghi[1], Paolo Perlasca[1], Fabrizio Trovato[2], Giorgio Valentini[1] and Marco Mesiti[1]

[1]*Dep. of Computer Science, Università di Milano, Via Celoria 18, 20133 Milano*
[2]*Area s.r.l., Via Torino 10/B, 12084 Mondovì*

Abstract
The acquisition and integration of data contained in spreadsheet tables is a complex task because they do not impose any regular structure on the organization of the data, or constraints on valid values. Moreover, mistakes can occur due to the passage from a format to another one or misspelled words in the original sources. The automatic extraction of their content, interpretation and integration is thus a complex task. In this paper, we outline the characteristics of a semi-automatic, interactive tool conceived for creating a knowledge base by extracting semantic information from heterogeneous spreadsheets.

Keywords
Heterogeneous Spreadsheet Tables, Semantic Table Interpretation, User Interfaces, Machine Learning

1. Introduction

The table understanding problem consists in the meaningful extraction of information from tabular data [1] contained in different kinds of files (HTML, pdf, csv, spreadsheets). As reported in a recent survey [2], many approaches have been proposed for the *localization* of the table(s) within a file, the *segmentation* of its cells, each with an eventually different size, the automatic identification of their *functional* role, in terms of either data cell or access key (i.e. the column headers or later stubs) and of their *structural* role (i.e. the identification of hierarchies on the access keys), and the *interpretation* of the table content. The interpretation of a table usually regards the transformation of its content in terms of well-known data models (like the relational model or RDF). Nowadays, different approaches for table understanding have been proposed that exploit machine learning (ML) techniques for inferring the table metadata by exploiting domain Ontologies and (automatically or manually) tagged knowledge bases (e.g. [3, 4, 5, 6]).

We have faced the table understanding problem in the context of a research project with an Italian debt collection agency. The agency daily receives spreadsheets in different formats (`csv`, `xls`, `xlsx`) from local authorities (e.g. municipalities, tax agency), each containing batches

SEBD 2021: The 29th Italian Symposium on Advanced Database Systems, September 5-9, 2021, Pizzo Calabro (VV), Italy
sara.bonfitto@unimi.it (S. Bonfitto); luca.cappelletti@unimi.it (L. Cappelletti); elena.casiraghi@unimi.it (E. Casiraghi); paolo.perlasca@unimi.it (P. Perlasca); fabrizio.trovato@team1994.it (F. Trovato); giorgio.valentini@unimi.it (G. Valentini); marco.mesiti@unimi.it (M. Mesiti)
0000-0002-9883-5561 (S. Bonfitto); 0000-0002-1269-2038 (L. Cappelletti); 0000-0003-2024-7572 (E. Casiraghi); 0000-0001-6674-2822 (P. Perlasca); 0000-0002-5694-3919 (G. Valentini); 0000-0001-5701-0080 (M. Mesiti)

with thousand of invoices to be rescued. These spreadsheets are large, heterogeneous, and do not follow any standard format or notation. Moreover, the labels used for the column headers, if not missing, do not belong to any pre-defined dataset and sometimes are not informative of the column content. Finally, spreadsheets often contain mistakes that need to be fixed. In this context, usual approaches for table understanding are not successful due to the following two reasons. First, they mainly rely on the homogeneity of the types of data contained in the columns of the identified table (i.e. columns containing only person names, or only date of births), and therefore exploit rules maximizing coherence in their cell segmentation methods, as well as in their structural and functional analysis algorithms; this is impossible in our scenario, where heterogeneity often characterizes both rows, columns, and even cells. In practice, it often happens that both rows and columns contain different types of information (e.g. the name of a person and the name of a company in the same column) and the information of a single invoice is contained in contiguous table rows. Moreover, each cell often contains complex string contents, which express multiple information (e.g. street number, street name, ZIP code and city can be extracted from the string "N. 3425 Stone Street, BN12HB - London"). Finally, current approaches rarely consider the presence of syntactic mistakes (e.g. the SSN number that does not fit the length constraint, or a misspelled city name) and semantic mistakes (e.g. a city in the wrong region, or the amount of a debt that does not match its detailed voices).

We believe that the development of an automatic technique for addressing all the mentioned issues, even if exploiting sophisticated ML techniques, would be unpractical. Therefore, we introduce a semi-automatic approach that combines data management approaches with ML techniques and intelligent user-interfaces to reduce the human effort in the extraction, cleaning and semantic characterization of the information contained in the invoices and their integration in a single and common knowledge base. Our human-in-the-loop approach heavily relies on the user-interaction to tune the prediction system depending on the feedback obtained while processing new spreadsheets. Easy-to-use graphical interfaces are thus fundamental for correcting mistakes and improving the overall performance of the system. To reach this goal, we propose the adoption of a three-phase approach. Phase I (Section 2) is responsible for the spreadsheet cleaning, the identification of the column types and the syntactic error correction. Phase II (Section 3) aims at creating a semantic characterization of the table content to be extracted from the spreadsheet and relies on the use of a domain Ontology (DO) and, when possible, a Knowledge Base (KB). Phase III (Section 4) relies on the construction of a KB containing the extracted information.

In the paper we use as running example the spreadsheet in Fig. 1 reporting traffic tickets which is organized in three parts: title lines, a table of data, and footer notes. Below the heading rows, a row contains the access keys to the columns (*column schema*). Column SSN/VAT contains the code identifying either individual or companies (it is an example of heterogeneous column containing values of two types). On the other side, the address column contains complex (string) contents expressing multiple information; a proper string parser must be defined to correctly extract all such information. Blanks and semi-blank rows can occur in the main table. Semi-blank rows usually contain totals or aggregated data. While some blank rows are sometimes used for aesthetic reasons, some others for delimiting correlated rows. This is the case of the two rows marked with a green border that represent an invoice with its the legal representative that must pay the invoice. Last but not least, different kinds of errors can occur in the spreadsheet.

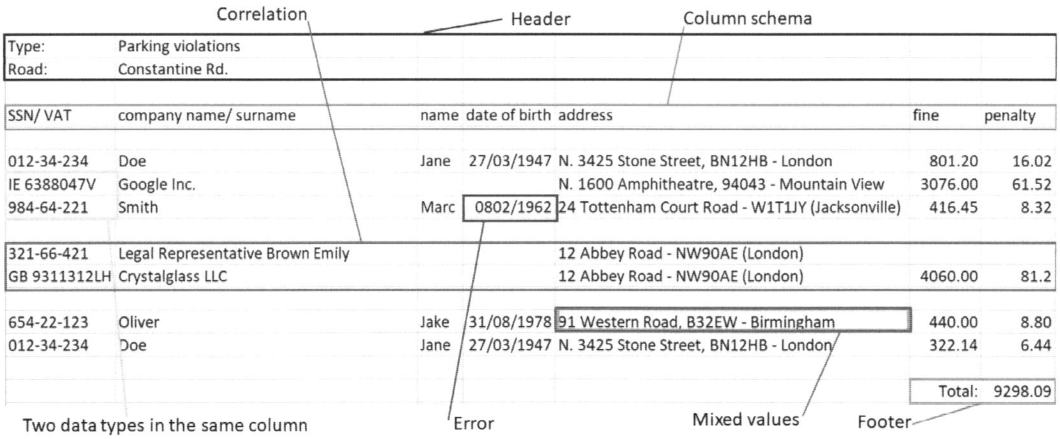

Figure 1: A spreadsheet example

2. Phase I: Extraction, Cleaning and Typing

The main purpose of this phase is to correct syntax errors occurring in the data, identifying the existing relations among table rows, and identifying basic types of each column and cell as detailed in the remainder of the section.

Table extraction. The table is extracted by using the approach described in [7]. Essentially, for the localization of the table, we consider the density of the information contained in the table w.r.t. external data. For the functional analysis of the cells, we use their position within the table and adopt dictionaries of already processed spreadsheets for identifying the column schema. For removing blank and semi-blank rows, predefined thresholds are used on the minimal number of non-empty cells in each row w.r.t. the number of columns.

Correlation between rows. For identifying correlation among table rows, we adopt a declarative pattern-based language, allowing the user to define rules, which express its knowledge about the existence of a relationship between consecutive rows. The rules can be specified through a GUI, and the user can decide the rules to be applied in processing a specific spreadsheet. More precisely, each rule is identified by a unique name $name$, and is applied to consecutive rows, the `current` row, r_i, and the `next` row, r_{i+1}. A rule is composed by a conjunction of basic *conditions* (that check for the existence of a relationship) and an *action* that expresses the way the information from the two rows should be joined when the condition is verified. The following two basic $condition$ can be specified: 1) $r[k]$ op v (named *basic* condition) requiring that the k-th cell in the row $r \in \{\texttt{current}, \texttt{next}\}$ is compared according to the operator op with a value v, where $op \in \{=, \neq, \texttt{startwith}, \texttt{endwith}\}$; 2) $\texttt{current}[k] = \texttt{next}[k']$ (named *equijoin* condition) imposing that the k-th cell of `current` row is equal to the k'-th cell of `next` row. $action$ is specified by a tuple $(conc, rel)$ determining the way in which r_i and r_{i+1} should be concatenated ($conc \in \{\texttt{natural}, \texttt{inverse}\}$) and the kind of relationship that exists among the two rows. The relationship can be: `extra`, representing further information about the invoice; `LR`, when the row contains the legal representative of the invoice; `heir` when the invoice is titled to a subject that is dead and one of his/her heirs should be contacted.

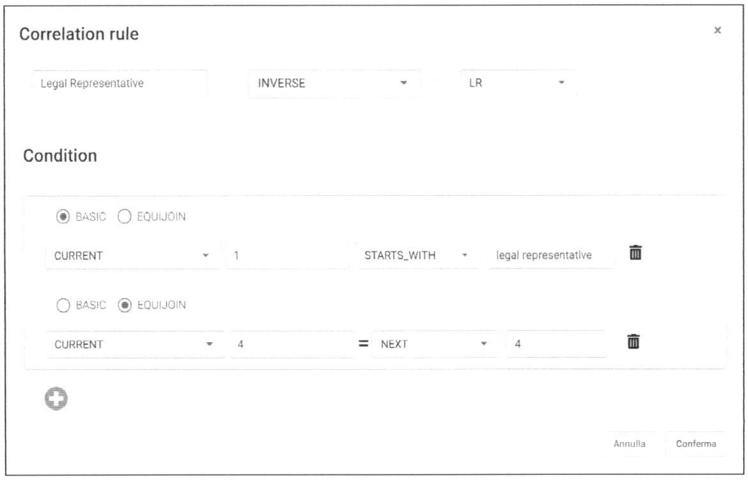

Figure 2: Correlation rule specification

Example 1. *In our scenario, a company is represented by a Legal Representative whose data are reported in the row above the one containing the invoice. To identify this situation, the rule in Fig. 2 presents two conditions: a basic one that identifies a cell whose value starts with* `Legal Representative`*, and an equijoin to verify that the two addresses are equal. Whenever a pair of rows satisfy the condition, the first row is concatenated after the second one (inverse order).*

Rules can be specified in advance, through a graphical interface (see Fig. 2), or on the fly, by clicking on the operations on tuples loaded in the interface in Fig. 3 (first column). In both cases, the table schema is duplicated and correlated rows are concatenated to form a single table line.

Type Inference. By applying the aforementioned techniques, a table $T = \langle S, V \rangle$ is extracted from the spreadsheet, where $S = [col_1, \ldots, col_j, \ldots, col_m]$ is the list of column names, and $V = \{r_1, \ldots, r_n\}$ is the set of table rows. Each row r_i, $1 \leq i \leq n$, is a list of values, and $r_i = [v_{i,1}, \ldots, v_{i,j}, \ldots, v_{i,m}]$, one for each column identified in the column schema.

At this stage, to discriminate the role of each cell within the table and to correctly assign a meaning to its content, a preliminary step is the identification of the column and cell types among those in our type system $\mathcal{T}$ composed of *simple*, *mixed* and *union* types (details in [7]). *Simple* types are basic domains and specific domains for our application (e.g. SSN, VAT, `emails`, `zip` codes). A *mixed* type (e.g. `address` column) is a record-type associated with different patterns used for extracting the record (in the case of `address` column, it is `rec(city, streetName, streetNumber, zip)`) from a string. *Union* types represent the occurrence of instances of different types in the same column and are denoted $union(t_1, \ldots, t_h)$ where $t_1, \ldots, t_h$ are simple or mixed types.

For type-inference we exploit decision trees, which are trained on synthetised table corpora, which have been automatically tagged with the types of our type system. The decision of using synthetised tables is firstly due to the fact that our tables use Italian language and are from a financial context; to the best of our knowledge, no such corpora exist yet. Secondly, our approach must be robust against mistakes, so that we have specifically developed the synthetizer in order to produce common mistakes we experienced in the first spreadsheets we received

#	SSN/ VAT	company name/ surname	name	date of birth	address	fine	penalty	correlation	SSN/ VAT_correlated	company name/ surname_correlated	address_correlated
	SSN, VAT	surname, comp...	name	date	mixed, text	decimal	decimal		SSN	company_name	text
1	012-34-234	Doe	Jane	27/03/1947	3425 Stone Street BN12HB London	801.2	16.02				
2	IE 6388047V	Google Inc.			1600 Amphitheatre 94043 Mountain View	3076	61.52				
3	984-64-221	Smith	Marc	0802/1962	24 Tottenham Court Road - W1T1JY (Jacksonville)	416.45	8.32				
4	GB 9311312LH	Crystalglass LLC			12 Abbey Road - NW90AE (London)	4060	81.2	LR	321-66-421	Legal Representative Brown Emily	12 Abbey Road - NW90AE (London)
5	654-22-123	Oliver	Jake	31/08/1978	91 Western Road B32EW Birmingham	440.00	8.80				
6	012-34-234	Doe	Jane	27/03/1947	3425 Stone Street BN12HB London	322.14	6.44				

Figure 3: Automatic Typing of the extracted table

(and tagged as `error`). The corpora consists of 10.000.000 synthetic tables that are randomly split 10 times in 8.000.000 documents for training and 2.000.000 for the validation set.

The decision tree works on a value $v_{i,j}$ represented by a vector u consisting of two parts: 1) $(u_{i,j,1}, \dots, u_{i,j,R})$ are Boolean values obtained by the application of basic-type recognizers on the value $v_{i,j}$ (several kinds of recognizers have been realized for each of the considered basic and mixed types); 2) $(avg_{j,1}, \dots, avg_{j,R})$ are average numbers of recognition for each type recognizer applied on the values occurring in the column j. The generated vectors are used for training a decision tree that predicts the type of each value contained in the table T.

In order to determine the type of each column, we cannot exploit a majority vote approach, because in our context we admit the presence of values belonging to a union type (as the case of the column SSN/VAT). For this reason, we have adopted an approach based on the frequency of the types in a column, where the types included in the union types are those that exceed a basic cutoff threshold. All the values whose type is not included in the union type are considered `error` for the current column.

Example 2. *Fig. 3 shows the result of the automatic type inference approach on our running example. White columns denote values of the same single type, whereas yellow cells denote empty values and red cells denote type mistakes w.r.t. the type identified for the column. Cells with mistakes need to be fixed by the user (also exploiting facilities made available in the platform for reducing the typing efforts). When more than one colour is used for the same column, it means that a union type was detected for such a column. Values of a mixed type are denoted by using different text colours (as in the address column where each sub-component has a different text colour).*

In the address column, there are also values that the ML algorithm was not able to extract because a non-supported pattern was used. In this case, the user exploits the interface in Fig. 4 for extracting the pattern. Note that, the identification of a correlated row led to the introduction of further columns w.r.t. those initially contained in the spreadsheet for representing all the information related to a single invoice in the same row. Further, a new column named `correlation` *has been introduced for representing the correlation typed identified by the rule.*

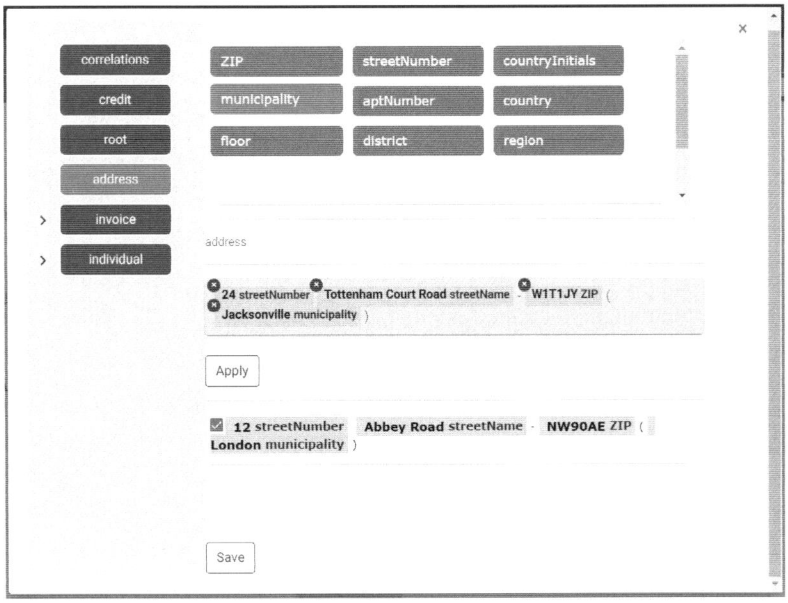

Figure 4: Assign or modify a type to single values

Interfaces for the manual typing and correction. The automatically identified types, however, may contain errors due to the occurrence of mistakes in the data or in the classification algorithm. Therefore, specific interfaces have been developed to make ease the correction. A key point of this manual modification is to consider the concept and properties of the Domain Ontology (details will be given in Section 3) in this way the human operator can give further information for the generation of the semantic description of the data contained in the table.

Fig. 4 shows the interface for altering the type associated with a single value (a similar interface is used for altering one of the types specified for a column). In the left panel, the Domain Ontology concepts are reported. Once a concept has been chosen, the list of its properties is shown in the top part of the interface, so that the user can use the selected property for labelling a portion of the value or the entire string. By assigning different properties to differing parts of the string, the pattern of a mixed type is identified. The identified pattern can thus be checked to other values of the same column (those sharing the same initial type). In this way, a single type specification can be applied to many values. Moreover, the identified pattern is stored in the system and made available for processing subsequent spreadsheets.

Preliminary experiments. To validate the type prediction algorithm we considered 40 spreadsheets offered by the debt collection agency. Each spreadsheet may contain errors and has around 100 rows and a variable number of columns (between 7 and 25). Starting from this original dataset, the ground truth dataset has been created by manual correction of the errors and subsequent type labelling. After processing the original documents as described in this section, the precision, recall, and F1 measures have been computed by taking into account the occurrences of mixed, union types, errors and empty values. We remark that the presence of union types requires to consider as true positives (TP) those cells whose predicted type corresponds to the manually assigned type, as false positives (FP) those cells whose predicted

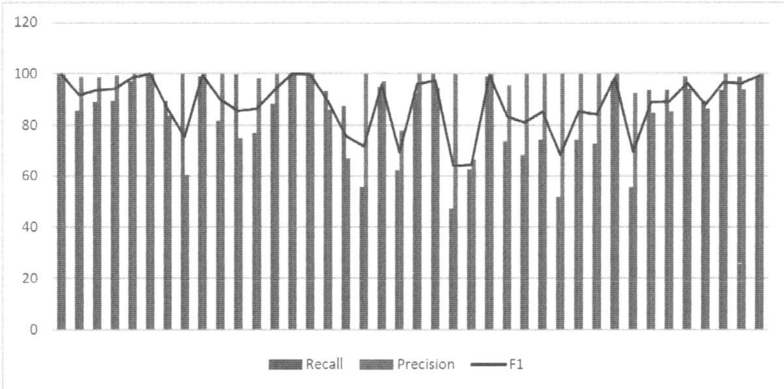

Figure 5: Recall, Precision and F1 of 40 documents

type does not match the manually assigned type (among those specified in the union type), as false negatives (FN) those cells for which an error has been predicted and the expected type is one of the union type, as true negatives (TN) those cells whose predictive type does not match those occurring in the union type.

The results are shown in Figure 5. For more than a half of all the documents we obtained a precision of 100%, while the lowest result is above the 60%; this result highlights that the system rarely identifies an error as a correct value. The recall of two-thirds of the documents is over the 85%, which means that most error cases are identified by the ML algorithm. The F1 measure is above 80% for 32 documents. In most cases, the mistakes of the ML algorithm (FN) are due to cells containing mixed types. As future work, we plan to exploit the user-defined patterns in the prediction system in order to incrementally reducing the user efforts in manual typing.

3. Phase II: Semantic Model Generation

The aim of this phase is to provide a *semantic description* of the spreadsheet tables by means of annotations w.r.t. a Domain Ontology. Even if many approaches have been proposed for this problem ([3, 4, 5, 6]), in our research we wish to face the presence of union types for table columns, which is generally neglected. Our semantic description is inspired to the one used in Karma [8] but differs because it is created starting from the types identified in Phase I and allows the extraction of several data from a column (while Karma only admits a 1:1 correspondence).

The Domain Ontology. Starting from the analysis of the information system currently used by the debt collection agency for the management of the invoices, we have developed a Domain Ontology containing the concepts and relationships useful for the considered scenario. Among them, we have identified the `invoice` concept, representing the document assigned by the local authority to the debt collection agency. The invoice contains many properties (e.g. the date in which it has been issued, the total amount) and is associated with a `subject`. Subjects can be classified in `individuals` and companys and can be associated with one of more `addresses`. Addresses can specify the residence/domicile of an individual or the legal/administrative office of a company. The invoice is associated with the detailed credit/debit voices (concept `details`) that the total amount to be rescued is composed of. Each invoice can be also associated with other subjects that are co-obligated in its payment (e.g. a legal representative or an heir). Formally, a Domain Ontology O consists of a set of Concepts $C = \{C_1, \ldots, C_n\}$. Concepts can be organized in a hierarchy of concepts: $C_1 \sqsubseteq C_2$ denotes that C_1 is subclass of C_2. Each Concept can have associated basic properties taken from a set $P = \{p_1, \ldots, p_m\}$; each property is associated with basic types of our type system $\mathcal{T}$; the properties of a concept C are denoted $P(C)$. Among the properties belonging to a class, we identified a subset of *mandatory properties.* These properties need to be specified for properly characterizing an individual of the concept and it is relevant for identifying the presence of instances of real world concepts in the KB (and thus avoiding the introduction of duplicates). Relationships can be identified among concepts and denoted by means of a set of roles R that identifies the kind of relationships that bind the individuals of two concepts. Some relationships can be considered mandatory to be identified in the semantic description (e.g. we cannot have an invoice without its subject and the corresponding address).

The Semantic Description of a table. The semantic description of a table $T = \langle S, V \rangle$ is a graph $(U_C, U_T, E_R, E_E, \phi_{E_R}, \phi_{E_E})$, where U_C is a multiset of concepts belonging to the Ontology, $U_C \subseteq C$, (we consider a multiset because a concept can appear more than once), U_T is a set of nodes corresponding to the columns in T ($U_T \subseteq S$), $E_R \subseteq U_C \times U_C$ are edges representing the relationships existing among concepts in V_C, and E_E are edges representing the extraction of values from the columns of T that are used for feeding properties of concepts in U_C. Moreover labeling functions ϕ_{E_R}, ϕ_{E_E} are introduced. The first one is used for assign to edges in E_R the name of the relationship that they represent (i.e. $\phi_{E_R} : E_R \rightarrow R$, where R is the set of relation names), whereas the second one is used for determining the type of values that can be extracted from a column of T, i.e. $E_E \times \mathcal{T} \rightarrow P$, where $P(C)$ is the set of properties. This function assigns to an edge (u_T, u_C) and a type $t \in \mathcal{T}$ a property among those specified for the concept associated with the vertex u_C. We remark that in our context more than one type of information can be extracted from the same column because of the presence of union and mixed types. In the case of union type, the extraction assumes the meaning of identifying different kinds of values in different rows. For mixed type, the extraction assumes the meaning of identifying a record from a string value of a table row.

Example 3. *The top part of Fig. 6 reports the semantic description obtained for our running example. In our web tool, this description is editable and the user can fix it or include other properties and relationships depending on the needs. The blue nodes represent the column of the table from which data are extracted. The green nodes represent classes. Edges among green nodes represent relationships available in the Domain Ontology, whereas, edges between green and blue nodes represent extraction rules. Whenever more than one edge arrives at the same blue nodes, it means that different alternative information (i.e. values of a union type) or a mixed value can be extracted.*

Semi-automatic Construction of Semantic Descriptions. Even if our graphical interfaces allow the manual creation of the semantic description starting from the types obtained at the end of phase I, this approach is tedious and does not take into account the semantic descriptions $s_1, \ldots, s_p$ already developed for other spreadsheets. Two approaches have been adopted for constructing a semantic description by relying on previous experience. First, each s_i ($1 \leq i \leq p$)

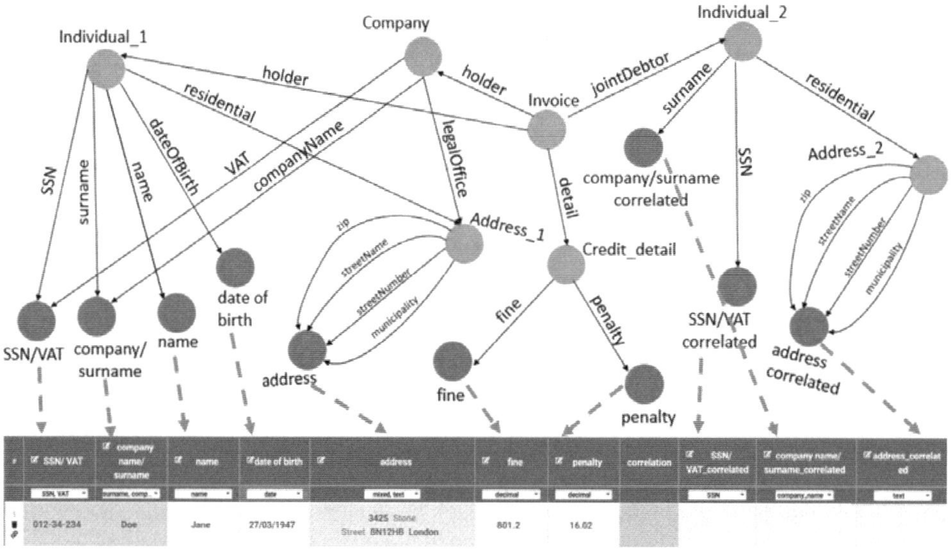

Figure 6: Mapping between the extracted table and the generated semantic description

is associated with an hash value obtained by applying an hash function on the ordered list of types obtained at the end of phase I. This value is used as an index for identifying a possible semantic description for the novel spreadsheet. This approach is adequate when the spreadsheets always adhere to a pre-defined structure. Another approach is to keep track of the types of the single columns and fragments of the semantic descriptions already associated with them. Whenever a column is labeled with a type, the fragments associated with it are collected and integrated into a single description. Since many combination of fragments could be possible, we adopt a scoring function that try to maximize the adoption of fragments extracted from types used in the same table. However, there is no guarantee that the final semantic description of all the the columns of the spreadsheet is correct. For this reason, the semantic description is drawn as a graph, and graphical facilities support the user for updating its representation.

4. Phase III: Construction of the Knowledge Base

At the end of the previous phase, we have constructed a semantic description of the information contained in the table extracted from the initial spreadsheet. The description characterizes the information contained in the table, but can also be used for transforming the table rows in instances of a KB that adhere to the constraints imposed by the Domain Ontology. In this way, the knowledge base becomes a data-store of the invoices treated by the debt agency and can be exploited for predicting the capacity of the invoice subjects in paying the due imports. Indeed, by combining the invoice information with the subjects' previous payments/not-payments, it is possible to predict when a given invoice will be positively rescued by a given subject.

In the transformation process, the following issues should be taken into account. First, the presence of union types and missed properties can lead to the generation of different semantic descriptions for each row of the table and special attention should be kept in generating

Algorithm 1 `GenerateInstances`

Input: A knowledge base KB, A semantic description S_D, A table $T = \langle S, V \rangle$
Output: KB enhanced with the content extracted from T

for each row of T **do**
  create a copy $\bar{S}_D = (U_C, U_T, E_R, E_E, \phi_{E_R}, \phi_{E_E})$ of S_D
  apply the extraction rule associated with ϕ_{E_E}
  assign the extracted value to the corresponding vertex in U_T
  for each class c in U_C **do**
    if all the properties in c have been removed and
     c is not involved in mandatory relationships **then**
      remove the class c and all the relationships in which it is involved
    end if
    if c still exists and mandatory properties in c are missing **then**
      include the mandatory properties with fake values
    end if
  end for
  Consider the updated structure $\bar{S}_D$, for creating the triples to include in KB
end for

consistent values according to our Domain Ontology. Second, when a mandatory property is missing in the considered row, this property should be included in any case in the semantic description and proper interfaces should be developed for supporting the user in fixing these properties. Finally, the data extracted from the spreadsheet should be included in the KB. Therefore, we need to identify overlapping with the instances of the KB that need to be integrated. The integration process should guarantee that coherent and correct information are maintained in the KB by exploiting well known properties of data quality [9].

The last problem is a well-known problem in the context of data quality (object identification problem [9]) and we plan to introduce facilities in this direction in the next release of our platform. For what concerns the first two issues, Algorithm 1 has been developed with the aim of generating the proper instances of the Domain Ontology that describe the single invoices contained in the data table. The algorithm works row by row on the table identified at the end of phase 1 (see Fig. 3) and allows the extraction of values according to the properties and classes identified in the semantic description. The algorithm takes into account the possibility that classes of the semantic description are not instantiated because alternative classes have been fed (due to the presence of union types). Moreover, the algorithm imposes the introduction of properties when they are mandatory in the Domain Ontology.

Example 4. *Fig. 7 reports the generated graph. Brown nodes represent invoices. An invoice is sometimes titled to individuals, other times to companies. In the case of the correlated tuples discussed in Example 1 for invoice 4 (the area highlighted on the top part of the figure), the invoice has been titled to a company and presents a legal representative (note that in this specific case, the two subjects share the same address). Finally, the subject Jane Doe (the area highlighted on the bottom part of the figure) is represented only once in the KB because the two instances of the subject share the same SSN, and so they are considered the representation of the same individual.*

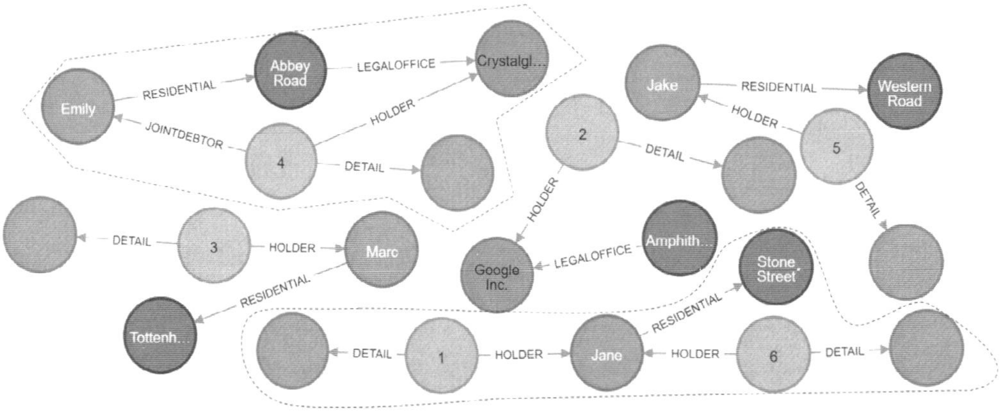

Figure 7: Knowledge base for the considered running example

5. Concluding Remarks

Both approaches for inferring simple data types and concepts of a knowledge base have been proposed in the literature. In the first category falls many studies, including wrangling tools [10, 11], software libraries (e.g. [12]) and probabilistic approaches (e.g. [13]) that exploit validation functions and regular expressions on data samples for inferring a single type. However, these approaches are able to infer a very limited number of types and usually do not work very well when missing and anomalous data occur in the sample. Many approaches are nowadays proposed for inferring concepts of a knowledge base by exploiting different pre-annotated corpora (e.g. [8, 14, 4]). However, the tolerance to mistakes is quite limited and in many cases they require that table values occur in the KB.

In this paper, we have proposed an approach that is not completely automatic but combines ML techniques, data management facilities and user-friendly interfaces for dealing with heterogeneous tables that can contain different kinds of mistakes. The approach has been tested on a collection of documents made available from the debt collection agency that needs to handle every day this kind of documents that are highly heterogeneous and with many mistakes. Our initial experiments prove the feasibility of the approach and the utility of our interfaces for easily fixing the mistakes and generating a consistent KB. The tool is not yet publicly available because it contains sensitive information, however interested readers can get in touch with us for a demo.

The work discussed in this paper can be extended in several directions. By means of the graphical interfaces described in Fig. 4 it is possible to define new patterns and include them in the ML process described in Section 2. This is an interesting research direction in the spirit of incremental learning and thus being able to adapt the model without the entire re-training. The extension of the learning facilities discussed in Section 3 for learning a semantic description from previous generated descriptions is another interesting research direction that can take advantage of the work discussed in [8]. Moreover, a systematic evaluation of the performances of the entire web application should be conducted. Furthermore, we wish to combine our approach for the construction of the semantic description of a table with the approaches proposed in

[3, 4, 5, 6] by taking into account the peculiarity of our domain. Finally, we also plan to apply the concepts discussed in this paper for dealing with other kinds of semi-structured data in order to semantically characterize data produced in heterogeneous sources (e.g. IoT data [15, 16], graphs [17], and tree-structured data) and represented in different models for their integration.

Acknowledgements. The authors wish to thank Giovanni Mancinelli for working on the implementation of the tool.

References

[1] M. Hurst, The Interpretation of Tables in Texts, Ph.D. thesis, Uni. of Edinburgh, 2000.

[2] S. Bonfitto, E. Casiraghi, M. Mesiti, Table understanding approaches for extracting knowledge from heterogeneous tables, WIREs Data Mining and Knowledge Discovery (2021). doi:https://doi.org/10.1002/widm.1407.

[3] Z. Zhang, Effective and efficient semantic table interpretation using tableminer$^+$, Semantic Web 8 (2017) 921–957. doi:10.3233/SW-160242.

[4] J. Chen, E. Jiménez-Ruiz, I. Horrocks, C. Sutton, Colnet: Embedding the semantics of web tables for column type prediction, in: AAAI Conf. on Artificial Intelligence, volume 33, 2019, pp. 29–36. doi:10.1609/aaai.v33i01.330129.

[5] S. Zhang, E. Meij, K. Balog, R. Reinanda, Novel entity discovery from web tables, in: Proc. of The Web Conf., ACM, 2020, p. 1298–1308. doi:10.1145/3366423.3380205.

[6] M. Cremaschi, F. D. Paoli, A. Rula, B. Spahiu, A fully automated approach to a complete semantic table interpretation, Future Gener. Comput. Syst. 112 (2020) 478–500. doi:10.1016/j.future.2020.05.019.

[7] S. Bonfitto, L. Cappelletti, F. Trovato, G. Valentini, M. Mesiti, Semi-automatic column type inference for csv table understanding, in: 47th Int. Conf. on Current Trends in Theory and Practice of Computer Science., Springer, 2021, pp. 535–549. doi:10.1007/978-3-030-67731-2.

[8] M. Taheriyan, et al. Learning the semantics of structured data sources, J. of Web Semantics (2016).

[9] C. Batini, M. Scannapieco, Data and Information Quality - Dimensions, Principles and Techniques, Data-Centric Systems and Applications, Springer, 2016. doi:10.1007/978-3-319-24106-7.

[10] Trifacta, Trifacta wrangler, 2020. URL: https://www.trifacta.com/.

[11] Google, Openrefine: A free, open source, powerful tool for working with messy data, 2020. URL: https://openrefine.org/.

[12] T. Petricek, G. Guerra, D. Syme, Types from data: Making structured data first-class citizens in f#, in: Proc. of 37th ACM SIGPLAN Conf. on Programming Language Design and Implementation, ACM, 2016, p. 477–490. doi:10.1145/2908080.2908115.

[13] I. Valera, Z. Ghahramani, Automatic discovery of the statistical types of variables in a dataset, in: Proc. of Machine Learning Research, volume 70, 2017, pp. 3521–3529.

[14] M. Hulsebos, et al. Sherlock: A deep learning approach to semantic data type detection, in: SIGKDD Int'l Conf. on Knowledge Discovery and Data Mining, ACM, 2019.

[15] S. Bonfitto, F. Hachem, E. G. Belay, S. Valtolina, M. Mesiti, On the bulk ingestion of iot devices from heterogeneous iot brokers, in: 2019 IEEE International Congress on Internet of Things (ICIOT), 2019, pp. 189–195. doi:10.1109/ICIOT.2019.00039.

[16] S. Valtolina, L. Ferrari, M. Mesiti, Ontology-based consistent specification of sensor data acquisition plans in cross-domain iot platforms, IEEE Access 7 (2019) 176141–176169. doi:10.1109/ACCESS.2019.2957855.

[17] M. Mesiti, Mergegraphs: a web-based system for merging heterogeneous big graphs, in: Proc. of the 17th Int'l Conf. on Information Integration and Web-based Applications & Services, ACM, 2015, pp. 1:1–1:10. doi:10.1145/2837185.2837211.

AMFLP: Adversarial Matrix Factorization-based Link Predictor in Social Graphs

Giuseppe De Candia[a], Tommaso Di Noia[a], Eugenio Di Sciascio[a] and Felice Antonio Merra[a]

[a]*Politecnico di Bari, Via Edoardo Orabona, 4, 70126 Bari BA, Italy*

Abstract

Nowadays, we are involved in virtual social interactions that create social networks. These networks can be used to study the behavior of individuals in terms of connections with other people by exploiting the historically recorded data, i.e., the friends on the Facebook platform. The link prediction (LP) task accomplishes the prediction of possible new user connections. In particular, inspired by the advances of the adversarial machine learning approaches in the computer vision domain, we propose an adversarial perturbation method on matrix factorization-based link prediction models, one of the most popular classes of LP methods. After verifying the performance deterioration caused by the adversarial model perturbation in preserving accurate LP performance, we propose an adversarial-based learning approach to robustify the MF-based method integrating the loss function with an adversarial regularization term. The proposed approach, named Adversarial Matrix Factorization-based Link Predictor (AMFLP), is tested on two real-world open-source datasets to prove the efficacy of the adversarial regularization technique in robustifying the model against the perturbations on the parameters without the deterioration on the overall link prediction performance.

Keywords

Adversarial Machine Learning, Link Prediction, Matrix Factorization

1. Introduction

Human beings need to be part of, and connected to, other humans from their family, to friends, from teammates to school colleagues. Everyone has to be connected to other people giving rise to subjectively and relatively small social networks that, analyzing their overall extension, generate a vast network that connects billions of people. In the digital era, many services are publicly available to give the chance to communicate instantly in every part of the world regardless of distances. These innovations have led, over the years, to the development of numerous virtual platforms that allow interaction between people, such as Twitter, Facebook, and Instagram. All these platforms are commonly named social networks. A social network can be modeled as a (social) graph, a structure composed of nodes, e.g., people, and links, e.g., connections between people. In the simple case, a link is a connection between nodes without side information— additional information related to the connection like the date two people got friendship relation in a platform.

SEBD 2021: The 29th Italian Symposium on Advanced Database Systems, September 5-9, 2021, Pizzo Calabro (VV), Italy
giuseppe.decandia@poliba.it (G. De Candia); tommaso.dinoia@poliba.it (T. Di Noia); eugenio.disciascio@poliba.it (E. Di Sciascio); felice.merra@poliba.it (F. A. Merra)

CEUR Workshop Proceedings (CEUR-WS.org)

Guessing how people's behavior and interests can make them decide to connect with new people are known as the link prediction (LP) task. In the last years, multiple works have addressed this task via machine learning (ML) approaches [1, 2, 3, 4]. While a deep focus has been dedicated to improving and proposing models to predict possible new connections in the best accurate way, the security of these models has raised interest only recently. Adversarial machine learning (AML), the field of study investigating the security of ML models, attracted great attention when ML-based computer vision systems used in an autonomous vehicle have been demonstrated to be easily fooled by perturbing a traffic sign in a human-imperceptible way [5, 6]. For instance, an ordinary image of a stop sign has been demonstrated to be perturbed by an adversary such that it will be classified by the vehicle as a different traffic sign making possible incidents [5]. However, while a recent part of research interest on AML in the social graph has been dedicated to investigating attack and defense approaches on altering the LP task by adding or modifying existing nodes and link [7, 8, 9], we found a lack of study on robustifying the model parameters of MF-based methods.

Inspired by the motivating scenario in recommender system domain [10], whose intuition is to find the minimal adversarial perturbation on model parameters to break the LP performance, lays down to the scenario where the easy addition of a new edge in the dataset graph, or the removal of an existing one, might cause a substantial variation of the model parameters with a consequent reduction in the reliability of the LP model. A real case example might be the suggestion of friends on social network platforms that are unlikely to be known from the users that are getting the friend suggestion, making her feel uncomfortable towards the platform's reliability. To investigate the possible existence of the weakness mentioned above, this work firstly proposes a gradient-based adversarial perturbation method against MF-based link predictors, i.e., the state-of-the-art model proposed by Equation (1), to test the performance degradation on the LP task. Then, it presents a novel approach, named Adversarial Matrix Factorization-based Link Predictor (AMFLP), by adopting an adversarial training approach to make the model more robust to the previously verified adversarial perturbation.

Our contributions can be summarized as follows:

1. we show that state-of-the-art MF model for the LP task might be adversarial modified dropping off their accuracy performance,
2. we propose an adversarial training procedure used into AMFLP to robustify a MF model against the previously defined adversary threat models;
3. we experiment on two real datasets to verify the efficacy of both the adversarial attack and defense methods on multiple accuracy measures.

2. Related Work

2.1. Link Prediction in Social Networks

A social network is a connections structure made up of social actors and links between them that can be visualized as a graph, where *nodes* represent people and *edges* correspond to interactions/relationships. The link prediction task in a social network scenario aims to predict the new connection between nodes. State of the art provides two ways to solve this problem [11]: *similarity-based approaches* and *learning-based approaches.* The *similarity-based approaches* use different similarity metrics to predict the existence of connections, while *learning-based approach* treats the link prediction problem as a binary classification task. We identify two main techniques to evaluate the similarities across nodes based on either node or topology metrics about the first category. Node-based metrics work considering that users tend to create relationships with people who are similar in education, religion, interests, and locations [12, 13, 14]. This insight is exploited for the assignment of a score to a pair of nodes —a high score indicates a high probability that two nodes will have a link. Topology-based metrics take advantage of the graph's topology using, for instance, neighbor-based metrics such as the Jaccard coefficient, the number of common neighbors, or the Salton-Cosine similarity [15]. On the other hand, the *learning-based approaches* solve the problem as a binary classification based. For instance, Scripps et al. [1] propose a discriminative learning mechanism to determine the most predictive attributes and topological features automatically. Menon et al. [3] propose one of the most used mechanisms extending the MF-based method while gathering the support of external side information. In this work, we investigate the robustness of learning-based approaches with interest in the widely used Menon et al. [3] proposal.

2.2. Adversarial Machine Learning

There is growing recognition that machine learning models are vulnerable to adversarial samples. Adversarial machine learning (AML) is the field of study for the security of ML models [16]. AML techniques aim to develop models or strategies that generate high-quality prediction results and are robust to malicious third parties, i.e., the adversaries. Adversaries could manipulate documents [17], images [18, 19], graph-data [20, 21, 22, 23], knowledge graphs [24], training data [25], and model parameters [10]. In particular, link predictions could be affected by attackers who adversarially modify observed topology or side information to hide target links. In [26], the authors study the vulnerability of centrality measures. Zhou et al. [8] experimentally analyze the robustness of several similarity metrics. Chen et al. [9] proposed an iterative gradient-based approach to simulate the construction of adversarial graph. Lin et al. [27] focus on evasion attack (test-time), crafting adversarial examples to deceive graph neural network LP models via optimized perturbation of the graph topology. While previous works have been focused on the insertion, or removal, of edges and nodes to alter the LP performance, we focus on analyzing the robustness of the learned model parameters.

3. Method

This study carries to the production of an adversarial defended MF-based approach, starting from the assessment of the adversarial risks of the Menon et al. [3] model. Below, we describe our attack and defense procedures.

3.1. Preliminaries.

The MF model under analysis factorizes the original adjacency matrix built up the historical node-node connections using also side information related to both the single node and the pair of nodes. The cost function minimized in Menon's model is defined as follow

$$\min_{U,\Lambda,V,w,b} \frac{1}{|\mathcal{O}|} \sum_{i=1}^{n} \sum_{j \in \mathcal{O}_i^+, k \in \mathcal{O}_i^-} \ell\left(L\left(u_i^T \Lambda \left(u_j - u_k\right) + b_i + b_j + x_i^T V x_j + w^T z_{ij}\right), 1\right) \tag{1}$$

where,

- $\mathcal{O}^+$ and $\mathcal{O}^-$ are the sets of known present and known absent dyads respectively,
- u_i and u_j are latent vectors relative to the node i and node j, extracted from the matrix $U \in \mathbb{R}^{n \times f}$ with n that represents the number of nodes and f the number of latent features;
- $\Lambda \in \mathbb{R}^{f \times f}$ is a square matrix such that $G \approx L(U \Lambda U^T)$, with G is the original adjacency matrix of the observed graph
- b_i and b_j are biases extracted from B, a $\mathbb{R}^n$ vector
- x_i and x_j are vectors extracted from the matrix X that includes moniadic information for each node in the graph
- V is a squared low rank matrix
- $z_{i,j}$ is a vector extracted from the matrix Z that contains dyadic information for each pair of nodes in the graph
- w is a learnable parameters multiplied by the term $z_{i,j}$.

In the previous equation, $L(\cdot)$ is the **link function** and $l(\cdot)$ is the **loss/objective function.** Following [3] we model

- $\boldsymbol{L}$ as a sigmoid function:

$$\sigma(Arg^{(i,j)}) = \frac{1}{1 + e^{-Arg^{(i,j)}}} \tag{2}$$

- $\boldsymbol{l}$ as cross entropy loss function:

$$\text{J(Arg)} = -\frac{1}{m} \cdot \frac{1}{n} \sum_{i=1}^{m} \sum_{j=1}^{n} ((y^{(i,j)} \log\left(\sigma(Arg^{(i,j)})\right) + (1 - y^{(i,j)}) \log(1 - \sigma(Arg^{(i,j)}))) \tag{3}$$

with $n = m$, and

$$Arg^{(i,j)} = u_i^T \Lambda u_j + b_i + b_j + x_i^T V x_j + w^T z_{ij} \tag{4}$$

Notice that to refer to the whole system we use Arg instead of $Arg^{(i,j)}$ that is only related to a generic couple of nodes. Such cost function, that indicates how big is the prediction error, is the guideline to make the learning of whole LP system. The learning of the model parameters is executed via stochastic gradient descent (SGD).

3.2. Attack: Gradient-based Adversarial Perturbation

After the definition of the model under attack, here we present the procedure to adversarially perturb its learned parameters. Following the study by Xiangnan He et al. [28] for recommendation task, we express the adversarial perturbation as follows:

$$\Delta_{Adv} = \arg\max J(Arg^{(i,j)} + \Delta) \tag{5}$$

with Δ as a generic noise on model parameters that must satisfy the constrain $\|\Delta\| \leq \epsilon$, where $\|\cdot\|$ is the L2 norm and ϵ is the budget magnitude for the maximum perturbation. The optimal solution for Δ_{Adv} is difficult to get but it is possible to employ the fast gradient method [5] to approximate the objective function around Δ as a linear function. We calculate the adversarial perturbation as follows

$$\Delta_{Adv} = \epsilon\frac{\Gamma}{\|\Gamma\|} \text{ where } \Gamma = \frac{\partial J(Arg^{(i,j)} + \Delta)}{\partial \Delta} \tag{6}$$

In the last expression, the adversarial noise is expressed in function of the parameter Γ and the parameter ϵ —the bounds of the perturbation. In the experimental section, we will present the effectiveness of this attack method on the tested MF-based LP model.

3.3. Defense: Adversarial Training

In the previous subsection, we explained how it is possible, at the inner loop level, to generate the perturbation Δ_{Adv} for each couple of nodes i and j, for each epoch. Differently from the classical learning updates, we must consider a novel objective function that introduced the adversarial regularization. We define

$$J_{Adv}(Arg^{(i,j)}) = J(Arg^{(i,j)}) + \eta J(Arg^{(i,j)} + \Delta_{Adv}) \tag{7}$$

as the objective function of the proposed Adversarial Matrix Factorization model for Link prediction (AMFLP). In Equation 7 the term $J(Arg^{(i,j)} + \Delta_{Adv})$ can be seen as a regularization term where η — the adversarial regularization coefficient— controls its strength.

To learn the adversarial regularized parameters of **AMFLP**, we introduce the characteristics of the adversarial training, also known as **minimax game** [29], that is expressed as

$$Arg^*, \Delta^* = \arg\min_{Arg}\max_{\Delta, \|\Delta\| \leq \epsilon} J(Arg) + \eta J(Arg + \Delta) \tag{8}$$

where the intuition is that, fixing the ϵ budget to perturb the model, the training has to proceed in two steps; first, it has to build the perturbation that maximizes the loss, then, after having added it into the model, it has to minimize the loss in this worst-case setting. The proposed learning algorithm is presented in Algorithm 1.

3.4. AMFLP Gradients

Here, we define the updates of the parameters to optimize the objective function in Equation 7. Using Equation 3 the whole objective function is

$$\begin{aligned} J_{Adv}(Arg^{(i,j)}) &= -(y^{(i,j)} \log\sigma(Arg^{(i,j)}) + (1 - y^{(i,j)})\log(1 - \sigma(Arg^{(i,j)}))) \\ &-\eta(y^{(i,j)} \log\sigma(Arg^{(i,j)} + \Delta_{Adv}) + (1 - y^{(i,j)})\log(1 - \sigma(Arg^{(i,j)} + \Delta_{Adv}))) \end{aligned} \tag{9}$$

Algorithm 1 AMFLP Training.

Set N : epochs; α: learning rate; ϵ: pert. budget; η: adv. reg. coeff.; K : num. updated parameters: m nd n are the number starting and ending nodes in the graph (i.e., $m = n$).

for *epoch* $= 1, 2, \dots, N$ **do**
    for $i = 1, 2, \dots, m$ **do**
        for $j = 1, 2, \dots, n$ **do**
            Calculate prediction: $Arg^{(i,j)}$
            Compute Γ and Δ_{Adv}
            Calculate perturbed prediction
            Calculate prediction's Sigmoid $\sigma(Arg^{(i,j)})$
            Calculate perturbed prediction's Sigmoid $\sigma(Arg^{(i,j)} + \Delta_{Adv})$
            Gradients Calculation
            for $k = 1, 2, \dots, K$ **do**
                $\Theta_k \leftarrow \Theta_k - \alpha((\sigma(Arg^{(i,j)}) - y)\frac{\partial Arg^{(i,j)}}{\partial \Theta_k} + \eta(\sigma(Arg^{(i,j)} + \Delta_{Adv}) - y^{(i,j)})\frac{\partial Arg^{(i,j)} + \Delta_{Adv}}{\partial \Theta_k})$
            end for
        end for
    end for
end for

Notice that the first addend of the function is the same as the original cost function that doesn't include the adversarial component. For this reason, and for the *linear property of the derivative*, we show the partial derivatives relatively to the second (adversarial) addend. The partial derivatives on the perturbed model is defined as

$$\frac{\partial J(Arg^{(i,j)} + \Delta_{Adv})}{\partial \Theta_k} = \eta(\sigma(Arg^{(i,j)} + \Delta_{Adv}) - y^{(i,j)})\frac{\partial Arg^{(i,j)} + \Delta_{Adv}}{\partial \Theta_k} \tag{10}$$

where Θ_k could be a model parameter (or a perturbation) that will be updated during the training.

Now is possible to go into more detail and derive the inner adversarial perturbed argument. In this case, the argument that coincides with the not normalized prediction includes the noise in the following explicit form:

$$Arg^{(i,j)} + \Delta = (u_i^T + \Delta^{u_i})\Lambda(u_j + \Delta^{u_j}) + b_i + b_j + (x_i^T + \Delta^{x_i})V(x_j + \Delta^{x_j}) + w^T z_{ij} \tag{11}$$

The derivatives to build the adversarial perturbations for the K-perturbed parameters are measured as shown in Table 1.

Table 1
Derivatives of Equation (10).

$\frac{\partial Arg^{(i,j)}+\Delta}{\partial u_i} = \Lambda(u_j + \Delta^{u_j})$	$\frac{\partial Arg^{(i,j)}+\Delta}{\partial u_j} = (u_i^T + \Delta^{u_i})\Lambda$	$\frac{\partial Arg^{(i,j)}+\Delta}{\partial b_i} = 1$
$\frac{\partial Arg^{(i,j)}+\Delta}{\partial \Lambda} = u_i u_j + \Delta^{u_i} u_j + \Delta^{u_j} u_i + \Delta^{u_i} \Delta^{u_j}$		$\frac{\partial Arg^{(i,j)}+\Delta}{\partial b_j} = 1$
$\frac{\partial Arg^{(i,j)}+\Delta}{\partial V} = x_i x_j + \Delta^{x_i} x_j + \Delta^{x_j} x_i + \Delta^{x_i} \Delta^{x_j}$		$\frac{\partial Arg^{(i,j)}+\Delta}{\partial w} = z_{ij}$
$\frac{\partial Arg^{(i,j)}+\Delta}{\partial \Delta^{u_i}} = \Lambda(u_j + \Delta^{u_j})$	$\frac{\partial Arg^{(i,j)}+\Delta}{\partial \Delta^{u_j}} = (u_i^T + \Delta^{u_i})\Lambda$	$\frac{\partial Arg^{(i,j)}+\Delta}{\partial \Delta^{x_i}} = V(x_j + \Delta^{x_j})$
$\frac{\partial Arg^{(i,j)}+\Delta}{\partial \Delta^{x_j}} = (x_i^T + \Delta^{x_i})V$		

4. Experiment

In this section, we aim to investigate the research questions:

RQ1: What is the effect of the adversarial perturbation strategy described in Section 3.2 on the accuracy performance of the state-of-the-art MF model for link prediction [3]?

RQ2: Is AMFLP, the MF-based model that integrates the defense strategy proposed in Section 3.3, more protected against the gradient-based perturbation of the model parameters?

To answer RQ1 and RQ2, first, we present the experimental settings, then, we report and discuss the experimental results of AMFLP.

4.1. Setup

4.1.1. Datasets.

We test AMFLP on two popular datasets for the link prediction task on social graphs: `Conflict` and (an extraction of) `Facebook`.

The first dataset, `Conflict`, is a dataset containing information about military disputes between countries [30] in the period 1990-2000. Following the experimental settings in [3], the directed graph is converted into an undirected graph with the result that the adjacency matrix (U) is symmetric. It contains features on both nodes and pairs of nodes (or dyads). Each node has three features, i.e., population, GDP, and polity, while each dyad has five features, e.g., countries' geographic distance. These features are anonymized and transformed in numerical values to be fed into AMFLP.

The second dataset, `Facebook`, is an anonymized collection of nodes, edges, and other side information relative to a sub-net of the social network platform. It has been released by Jure Leskovec and is publicly available [1]. The data, collected from a survey whose participants answered in the Facebook application, provide anonymized feature vectors. For instance, where the original dataset may have contained a feature "political=Democratic Party," the new data would contain "political=anonymized feature 1". Thus, it is possible to use the anonymized data to determine whether two users have the same political affiliations but not the specific party. We reduce the number of features to 19 using the ones that have preserved the 70% of

[1] http://snap.stanford.edu/data/ego-Facebook.html

Table 2
Statistics of the test datasets

Dataset	Nodes	$\mathcal{O}^+$	$\mathcal{O}^-$	$\frac{\mathcal{O}^+}{\mathcal{O}^-}$	Used Features
Conflict	130	320	16580	1:52	3
Facebook	792	28048	613240	1:22	19

variance using the principal component analysis. For instance, we remove features such as name, surname, the end date of a job, leaving the essential features such as spoken languages, hometown, education, attended school, and job position. The removal of 176 features makes the computation faster because of its square complexity. The statistics of the two datasets are summarized in Table 2. We split both datasets in training and test set, putting the 90% of links in the training set and the remaining 10% in the test set.

4.1.2. Evaluation Metrics

Since the link prediction task could be seen as a classification problem, predicting whether a connection between two nodes exists or not, it is possible to use accuracy measures. In particular, we compute the Accuracy (Acc), Area under the ROC Curve (AUC), and the Hit Ratio (HR) at three thresholds, i.e., 3, 7, and 10. Acc calculates how often predictions equal labels. AUC measures the probability that a randomly chosen missing link s given a higher similarity score than a randomly chosen pair of unconnected links. Note that AUC, differently from Acc, does not suffer from the unbalance data distribution problem [3]. HR@k computes the fraction of test nodes correctly guessed to be connected to one of the top-k predicted links. The Hr is a recall-based metric that helps to understand if increasing the analyzed cut-off of suggested nodes; the model can correctly predict a link connection after k attempts.

4.1.3. Reproducibility

We use a grid search with 8-fold cross-validation to train the experimented methods in order to find the best hyper-parameters on which to investigate the attack and defense performance. The explored hyper-parameters for both datasets are defined as follow $\alpha_U : \{0.05, 0.01\}$, $\alpha_\Lambda : \{0.05\}$, $\alpha_b : \{0.005, 0.0005\}$, $\alpha_V : \{0.05, 0.005\}$, $\alpha_w : \{0\}$, $\eta : \{1.0\}$, and $\epsilon : \{0.5\}$, where we set η and ϵ values following [10] and α_k is the learning rate used to update the k-th parameter. We train the standard MF model for N iterations. However, after $N/2$ training epochs, we fork the learning process in two ways. In the first training, we continue the standard training until the N-th epoch. In the second training, the one related to AMFLP, we perform the adversarial training procedure for the remaining $N/2$ epochs using the defense approach described in Section 3.3. We set $N = 1000$. After having explored the search space, we report in Section 4.2 the results measured on the best model with respect to the test set.

4.2. Results and Discussion

Table 3 reports the link prediction performance evaluated on `Conflict` and `Facebook`. For each dataset, we report three **Attack** settings: *No*, *Random*, and *Adversarial*. The first setting

Table 3
Results of random and adversarial attacks against MF and AMFLP.

Dataset	Conflict						Facebook					
Attack	*No*		*Random*		*Adversarial*		*No*		*Random*		*Adversarial*	
Model	MF	AMFLP	MF	AMFLP	MF	AMFLP	MF	AMFLP	MF	AMFLP	MF	AMFLP
Acc	.9790	.9790	.9790	.9800	.9670	.9740	.9555	.9555	.9555	.9555	.0008	.9410
AUC	.8666	.8666	.8666	.8666	.6600	.8420	.7960	.7850	.7920	.7851	0	.3190
HR@3	.0312	.0625	.0190	.0210	.0312	.0312	.0035	.0035	.0037	.0037	.0018	.0025
HR@7	.0937	.1250	.0581	.0512	.0625	.0312	.0110	.0114	.0122	.0130	.0074	.0110
HR@10	.1250	.2812	.0718	.0756	.0937	.0625	.0160	.0192	.0187	.0195	.0132	.0164

is related to the base model performance without any adversarial (or random) perturbation. *Random* attack bounded at ϵ is used as the **baseline** approach to verify if the adversarial attack procedure presented in Section 3.2 is not degrading the model performance due to the addition of random noise. The *Adversarial* column reports the results on the adversarial perturbations computed when $\epsilon = 0.5$. Finally, we report also two model: MF and AMFLP. In this section, we use the name MF to indicate the MF-based model proposed in [3].

4.2.1. Attack: analysis of the performance (RQ1).

Looking at Table 3 it is possible to focus on the three couple of columns, looking that in the case of *Random* attack, MF has a slight drop on Acc and AUC metrics. Conversely, analyzing the *Adversarial* attacks, we can observe that both metrics reduced much more than in the random attack setting. For instance, looking at the `Conflict` dataset, the AUC of MF goes down by more than 24% with the application of the adversarial perturbation, while it is not getting performance worsening when using random perturbations. This phenomenon is even more evident for the `Facebook` dataset, in which we observe that both Acc and AUC get values close to 0, making the model completely unreliable. Additionally, it is interesting to observe that the drop of accuracy performance can also be partially verifiable on the analysis of ranking-based metrics. Analyzing the result values for the `Facebook` dataset, we observe that HR@10 is 0.0160 in the no-attack setting on MF, and it is even increased to 0.192 in the random one, while, as expected, is reduced to 0.0164 with the use of the adversarial approach. At the same time, it can be observed in the other dataset that *Random* seems to be more potent in reducing the HR if compared to *Adversarial.* The reason is that the HR metric is a ranking-wise metric, while the adversarial mechanism is a score-based reduction approach that may have reduced the score of a possible link suggestion but not enough to put it below the top-*k* list. Indeed, the first two accuracy measures confirm that the *Adversarial* approach is the most effective one.

For the previous analysis of the attack performance, we can claim that *the gradient-based adversarial perturbation of model parameters can reduce the accuracy performance of a link prediction model.* Below, we verify the AMFLP performance to understand if we would have better performance under the same attack under the adversarial training setting.

4.2.2. Defense: analysis of the performance (RQ2).

Having assessed worrying deterioration performance due to adversarial perturbation, here we test if the use of the adversarial training procedure presented in Section 3.3 and used in AMFLP would guarantee a minor degradation of performance.

To verify the efficacy of AMFLP is necessary to compare the values of the *Adversarial* column for both datasets in Table 3. The accuracy and AUC results for `Conflict` show that the model AMFLP efficiently reduces the effects of the adversarial perturbation on the model parameters. For instance, the AUC value is 0.8520 for the attack against AMFLP, while 0.6600 for the attack on the no-defended model. Extending the analysis on the second tested dataset, i.e., `Facebook`, it can be observed that the goodness of the proposal defense is consistently confirmed. The complete worsening of the performance observed on the no-defended scenario is successfully improved in the defended one. For instance, the complete loss of Acc observed on MF is quite wholly solved with the Acc value equals to 0.9410 measured on AMFLP. Observing the hit ratio performance, it can be seen that, similarly to the observations made in Section 4.2.1, further improvements on the proposed approach might be helpful also to robustify rank-wise performance. Analyzing the general performance obtained in *No* attack columns, it can be claimed that the adversarial regularization of MF applied in AMFLP has not reduced the general performance of the model. Instead, we can observe that AMFLP might have even improved the model performance. For instance, HR@7 increases from 0.0937 to 0.1250 in the `Conflict` dataset, and from 0.0110 to 0.0114 in the `Facebook` one.

We can claim that the *adversarial training of a matrix factorization model to address the link prediction task can robustify the model against gradient-based adversarial perturbation while preserving, or even improving, the high accurate prediction performance.*

5. Conclusion

We have investigated the link prediction task, which, for instance, helps people to find new possible connections, e.g., friends on social networks. Inspired by the adversarial attacks in computer vision, e.g., an autonomous vehicle can turn left instead of stopping with a human-imperceptible perturbation of a traffic signal, we have investigated the security of matrix factorization-based link predictor. Firstly, we have proposed a perturbation technique that minimally alters the learned model parameters by reducing the accuracy performance in the link prediction task. Then, after having verified the weakness of MF-based models against the proposed adversary threat model, we have presented an adversarial training solution employing the minimax procedure. This procedure has been implemented in the proposed Adversarial Matrix Factorization-based Link Predictor (AMFLP). The goal is to build the perturbations that maximize the model loss and minimize the global objective, considering the possible deterioration caused by the perturbation. To verify the efficacy of the proposed attack and defense scenarios, we have tested two popular datasets, i.e., Conflict and Facebook, verifying that the proposed defensive strategy can robustify the model accuracy. Our results also open further investigation on how to improve even more the robustification performance. Additionally, we plan to extend this method to deep learning-based link-predictors to verify their possible weakness and the efficacy of the proposed robustification approach.

Acknowledgments

The authors acknowledge partial support of the projects: Servizi Locali 2.0, PON ARS01_00876 Bio-D, PON ARS01_00821 FLET4.0, PON ARS01_00917 OK-INSAID, H2020 PASSPARTOUT.

References

[1] J. Scripps, P. Tan, F. Chen, A. Esfahanian, A matrix alignment approach for link prediction, in: ICPR, IEEE Computer Society, 2008, pp. 1–4.

[2] J. Kunegis, A. Lommatzsch, Learning spectral graph transformations for link prediction, in: ICML, volume 382 of *ACM International Conference Proceeding Series*, ACM, 2009, pp. 561–568.

[3] A. K. Menon, C. Elkan, Link prediction via matrix factorization, in: Joint european conference on machine learning and knowledge discovery in databases, Springer, 2011, pp. 437–452.

[4] M. Pujari, R. Kanawati, Link prediction in complex networks by supervised rank aggregation, in: ICTAI, IEEE Computer Society, 2012, pp. 782–789.

[5] I. J. Goodfellow, J. Shlens, C. Szegedy, Explaining and harnessing adversarial examples, 2014. arXiv:1412.6572.

[6] P. D. McDaniel, N. Papernot, Z. B. Celik, Machine learning in adversarial settings, IEEE Secur. Priv. 14 (2016) 68–72.

[7] H. Dai, H. Li, T. Tian, X. Huang, L. Wang, J. Zhu, L. Song, Adversarial attack on graph structured data, in: ICML, volume 80 of *Proceedings of Machine Learning Research*, PMLR, 2018, pp. 1123–1132.

[8] K. Zhou, T. P. Michalak, Y. Vorobeychik, Adversarial robustness of similarity-based link prediction, in: ICDM, IEEE, 2019, pp. 926–935.

[9] J. Chen, X. Lin, Z. Shi, Y. Liu, Link prediction adversarial attack via iterative gradient attack, IEEE Trans. Comput. Soc. Syst. 7 (2020) 1081–1094.

[10] X. He, Z. He, X. Du, T. Chua, Adversarial personalized ranking for recommendation (2018) 355–364.

[11] P. Wang, B. Xu, Y. Wu, X. Zhou, Link prediction in social networks: the state-of-the-art, Sci. China Inf. Sci. 58 (2015) 1–38.

[12] C. G. Akcora, B. Carminati, E. Ferrari, User similarities on social networks, Soc. Netw. Anal. Min. 3 (2013) 475–495.

[13] A. Anderson, D. P. Huttenlocher, J. M. Kleinberg, J. Leskovec, Effects of user similarity in social media, in: WSDM, ACM, 2012, pp. 703–712.

[14] P. Bhattacharyya, A. Garg, S. F. Wu, Analysis of user keyword similarity in online social networks, Soc. Netw. Anal. Min. 1 (2011) 143–158.

[15] J. Repplinger, G.G. chowdhury. *Introduction to Modern Information Retrieval.* 3rd ed. london: Facet, 2010. 508p. alk. paper, $90 (ISBN 9781555707156). LC2010-013746, Coll. Res. Libr. 72 (2011) 194–195.

[16] L. Huang, A. D. Joseph, B. Nelson, B. I. Rubinstein, J. D. Tygar, Adversarial machine

learning, in: Proceedings of the 4th ACM workshop on Security and artificial intelligence, 2011, pp. 43–58.

[17] G. Goren, O. Kurland, M. Tennenholtz, F. Raiber, Ranking robustness under adversarial document manipulations, in: SIGIR, ACM, 2018, pp. 395–404.

[18] T. Di Noia, D. Malitesta, F. A. Merra, Taamr: Targeted adversarial attack against multimedia recommender systems, in: DSN Workshops, IEEE, 2020, pp. 1–8.

[19] V. W. Anelli, Y. Deldjoo, T. Di Noia, D. Malitesta, F. A. Merra, A study of defensive methods to protect visual recommendation against adversarial manipulation of images, in: SIGIR, ACM, 2021.

[20] Y. Sun, S. Wang, X. Tang, T. Hsieh, V. G. Honavar, Adversarial attacks on graph neural networks via node injections: A hierarchical reinforcement learning approach, in: WWW, ACM / IW3C2, 2020, pp. 673–683.

[21] N. Entezari, S. A. Al-Sayouri, A. Darvishzadeh, E. E. Papalexakis, All you need is low (rank): Defending against adversarial attacks on graphs, in: WSDM, ACM, 2020, pp. 169–177.

[22] D. Ding, M. Zhang, X. Pan, M. Yang, X. He, Improving the robustness of wasserstein embedding by adversarial pac-bayesian learning, in: AAAI, AAAI Press, 2020, pp. 3791–3800.

[23] D. Zügner, S. Günnemann, Adversarial attacks on graph neural networks via meta learning, in: ICLR (Poster), OpenReview.net, 2019.

[24] V. W. Anelli, Y. Deldjoo, T. Di Noia, E. Di Sciascio, F. A. Merra, Sasha: Semantic-aware shilling attacks on recommender systems exploiting knowledge graphs, in: ESWC, volume 12123 of *Lecture Notes in Computer Science*, Springer, 2020, pp. 307–323.

[25] Y. Deldjoo, T. Di Noia, E. Di Sciascio, F. A. Merra, How dataset characteristics affect the robustness of collaborative recommendation models, in: SIGIR, ACM, 2020, pp. 951–960.

[26] M. Waniek, T. P. Michalak, T. Rahwan, M. J. Wooldridge, Hiding individuals and communities in a social network, CoRR abs/1608.00375 (2016).

[27] W. Lin, S. Ji, B. Li, Adversarial attacks on link prediction algorithms based on graph neural networks, in: AsiaCCS, ACM, 2020, pp. 370–380.

[28] X. He, H. Zhang, M. Kan, T. Chua, Fast matrix factorization for online recommendation with implicit feedback (2016) 549–558.

[29] Y. Deldjoo, T. Di Noia, F. A. Merra, A survey on adversarial recommender systems: From attack/defense strategies to generative adversarial networks, ACM Comput. Surv. 54 (2021) 35:1–35:38.

[30] F. Ghosn, G. Palmer, S. A. Bremer, The mid3 data set, 1993—2001: Procedures, coding rules, and description, Conflict Management and Peace Science 21 (2004) 133–154. doi:10.1080/07388940490463861.

An Effective and Efficient Graph Representation Learning Approach for Big Graphs

Edoardo Serra[1], Mikel Joaristi[2], Alfredo Cuzzocrea[3], Selim Soufargi[4] and Carson K. Leung[5]

[1]*Computer Science Dept., Boise State University, Boise, ID, USA*
[2]*Computer Science Dept., Boise State University, Boise, ID, USA*
[3]*iDEA Lab, University of Calabria, Rende, Italy*
[4]*iDEA Lab, University of Calabria, Rende, Italy*
[5]*Computer Science Dept., University of Winnipeg, MB, Canada*

Abstract

In the Big Data era, large graph datasets are becoming increasingly popular due to their capability to integrate and interconnect large sources of data in many fields, e.g., social media, biology, communication networks, etc. Graph representation learning is a flexible tool that automatically extracts features from a graph node. These features can be directly used for machine learning tasks. Graph representation learning approaches producing features preserving the structural information of the graphs are still an open problem, especially in the context of large-scale graphs. In this paper, we propose a new fast and scalable structural representation learning approach called SparseStruct. Our approach uses a sparse internal representation for each node, and we formally proved its ability to preserve structural information. Thanks to a light-weight algorithm where each iteration costs only linear time in the number of the edges, SparseStruct is able to easily process large graphs. In addition, it provides improvements in comparison with state of the art in terms of prediction and classification accuracy by also providing strong robustness to noise data.

Keywords

Graph Representation Learning, Sparse Representation, Large-Scale Graph Structural Representation

1. Introduction

Many fields are naturally connected with graph structures, including social networks, biological interactions, and communication networks. With the advent of Big Data, there is a huge availability of large-scale graph datasets, on top of with making analytics (e.g., [1]), also considering privacy/security issues (e.g., [2]). Given this availability, there is a great need to apply machine learning techniques on large scale graphs.

Graph node representation learning is a powerful tool to automatically extract features from the nodes inside a graph. Such features are the input of standard machine learning tasks that can solve several node classification tasks (e.g., in [3] and [4] authors use graphs describing relationships between entities to identify malicious/bad actors inside such graphs).

SEBD 2021: The 29th Italian Symposium on Advanced Database Systems, September 5-9, 2021, Pizzo Calabro (VV), Italy
edoardoserra@boisestate.edu (E. Serra); mikeljoaristi@boisestate.edu (M. Joaristi); alfredo.cuzzocrea@unical.it (A. Cuzzocrea); selim.soufargi@unical.it (S. Soufargi); kleung@cs.umanitoba.ca (C. K. Leung)

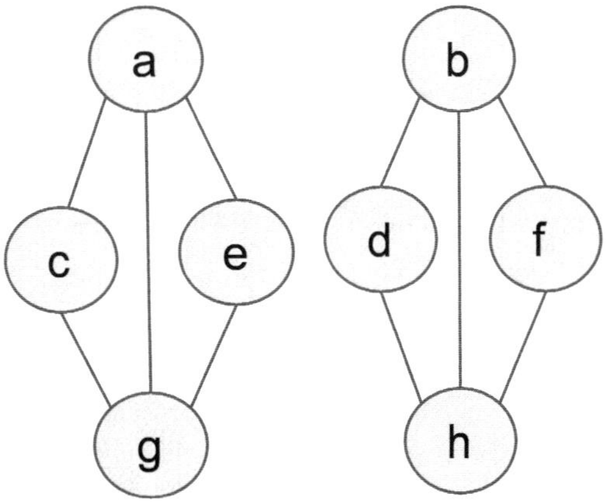

Figure 1: Structural vs. connectivity proximity.

More specifically, a graph node representation associates to each graph node a vector of hidden features. We consider only representation learning models trained with an unsupervised procedure that is independent to any specific machine learning task.

Unsupervised graph representation learning approaches are divided into connectivity and structure-based. Connectivity-based representation learning methods work on the assumption that nodes that are in proximity have similar representation, e.g., nodes a and c in Figure 1 are in proximity (it exists a short path connecting them) while nodes a and b are not. Instead, structural-based node representations assume that if two nodes have a similar structure, they should have the same representation, e.g., in Figure 1, nodes c and d are structurally identical even if they are not connected, the same for the nodes a and b.

Connectivity-based approaches are usually better for the task of edge prediction, while structural-based approaches are more suitable for node classification tasks [5]. This is because the structural representations helps the identification of structural patterns useful for the classification. Moreover, connectivity-based approaches in the case of two disconnected nodes (such as g and h) may have completely different representations even if, according to a specific classification task, these two nodes should have the same class.

The structural representation learning approaches already proposed in the literature, such as Struc2vec [5] and GraphWave [6], do not scale well on large graphs because their non linear execution time. In addition, as we show in our experimental section for some structural classification tasks, they sometimes present some poor performance. In this work, we propose a structural representation approach, called SparseStruct, that creates for each node a sparse representation that is condensed through a truncated singular value decomposition. The sparse representation is created with an iterative approach exploring the structure of a node, level by level. More specifically, this paper provides the following contributions: (*i*) we define SparseStruct, a structural representation learning approach with a convergent iterative procedure; (*ii*) we provide formal proof about the ability of SparseStruct to preserve the structural information of nodes; (*iii*) we prove that SparseStruct's execution time is linear on the size of the graph; (*iv*) from the experimental results, SparseStruct in all the experimental cases is comparable or better than the other approaches considered in terms of performance for regression and classification tasks.

2. Background

In this section, we first present a set of important notations and concepts that will be used throughout this work.

2.1. Graphs Basics and Vectorial Representation

Let $G = (V, E)$ be a unlabeled undirected graph, or network, where V denotes the set of nodes, and $E \subseteq (V \times V)$ denotes the set of edges connecting the nodes in G. $|V|$ and $|E|$ denote the number of nodes and edges contained in the graph respectively. The neighborhood of any node $u \in V$ is given by $nbr(u) = \{v|(u, v) \in E \quad or \quad (v, u) \in E\}$, and $|nbr(u)|$ denotes the size of this neighborhood or the node's degree. The diameter of a graph is commonly defined as the "longest shortest path" between any two nodes of the graph. More formally, the diameter is the length $max_(u, v)d(u, v)$ between any two graph nodes (u, v), where $d(u, v)$ is the distance between nodes u and v.

The representation of a node u is defined as $X_u \in \mathbb{R}^k$, where k is the desired size of the representation. Finally, the whole representation matrix is defined as $X \in \mathbb{R}^{|V|\times k}$. Graph representation learning methods require a notion of proximity between nodes in order to learn. These methods can, arguably, be classified into two groups based on the proximity notion they use, connectivity-based methods (K-order Proximity), and structure-based methods (Structural Role Proximity) [7].

3. Truncated SVD

Dimensionality reduction approaches are used to reduce the size of a set of features. Truncated SVD [8] is a Linear dimensionality reduction using Singular Value Decomposition to reduce the dimension. Contrary to Principal Component Analysis [9], Truncated SVD does not center the data before computing the singular value decomposition. Such difference makes this approach suitable to work with sparse matrices.

Truncated SVD has been widely applied on text analysis applications [10]. It is known as latent semantic analysis (LSA), and it is applied to term-document matrices. The result of such transformation is a "semantic" space of low dimensionality that contrasts the effects of synonymy and polysemy, i.e. when there are multiple meanings for the same word. Truncated SVD is also used in graphs by transforming the sparse graph adjacency matrix [11]. This produces a connectivity-based graph representations. In our work, we will show how to effetely use the truncated SVD procedure with a newly defined sparse matrix to produce a structural graph representation learning procedure.

The fastest solver for Truncated SVD is based on a randomized approach [12]. The time complexity for this approach is $O(k \times T_{mult} + (n + m) \times k^2)$, where k is the size of the reduced dimensional space, T_{mult} is the execution time of the sparse matrix multiplication with a vector, n is the number of rows in the sparse matrix, and m is the number of columns.

4. SparseStruct Algorithm

In this section, we provide the details of SparseStruct, described in Algorithm 1, that learns a structural node representation. SparseStruct is divided into two steps: **Step 1** (line 2) use an iterative procedure to create a sparse positive integer matrix where each row corresponds to a sparse vectorial representation of a specific node, and **Step 2** (line 3) uses the Truncated SVD to transform the sparse matrix in a smaller dense representation with k dimensions, (k represents the size of the learned output representation. The matrix M (line 3) represents the output of our algorithm.

Intuitively, at each iteration i of the process the algorithm determines the structural information of a generic node u, by considering all the possible structure combinations present in the graph at depth i. All these structures are indexed and used to describe a node's structure in terms of its neighboring nodes structures. The concatenation of all the sparse matrix through a horizontal stacking tells how the structures connected to a node changes step by step with the increase of the exploration depth. This process runs until no more change is detected by the algorithm. For this reason, we called the maximum number of iteration $explorationDepth$ (line 11).

More specifically, in this algorithm, we assume that each node of the graph has a unique identifier $id(v)$ from 0 to $|V| - 1$, and such identifier is the index of all the matrices (sparse and not) created in the algorithm. Then the final representation X_u learned for a generic node u is given by $M[id(u), :]$. The core part of Algorithm 1 is the iterative procedure $sparseMatrixGen$ that creates the structural representative sparse matrix SM, and it is inspired by the Weisfeiler-Lehman method for graph isomorphism testing [13]. At each iteration i, the $sparseMatrixGen$ method assigns to all the identical rows the same progressive identifier with the use of a hash tree index (line 12), and then create a sparse matrix SM^i where the value of the generic cell $SM^i[id(u), j]$ is the number of neighbor nodes of u that are indexed with the identifier j (lines 13-15). Each matrix SM^i has dimension $|V| \times |indexID(SM^i)|$ however its occupied memory space is less than $O(|E|)$. Each generated sparse matrix SM^i inside the while loop is added to the list L (line 17), and after the while loop, all the sparse matrices in L are horizontally stacked to create a unique sparse matrix called SM^{tot} that is the output of the method. The while loop (lines 11-25) iterates until the number of indexes generated (line 12) stops to grow at each iteration, or a maximum number of iterations is reached.

While this approach may, at first glance, seem space and time consuming depending on the number of iteration of the algorithm, in reality, we will show in the time and space complexities section that this is not the case. This is because of the fast convergence of our algorithm.

Our representation approach is able to preserve structural properties of the nodes in the graph (see Theorem 1).

Theorem 1. *Given a graph $G = (V, E)$, for each pair of nodes (u, v) having the same structure (i.e., the graphs extracted from a visit of u and v are isomorphic) the representations $M[id(u), :]$ and $M[id(v), :]$ are the same.*

In the following subsections, we show: (i) the optimality of the stopping criterion, and (i) the time and space complexity of our proposed approach, that under certain conditions are

Algorithm 1 SparseStruct representation learning algorithm.

```
1: function SparseStruct(G = (V, E), explorationDepth, k)
2:     SM = sparseMatrixGen(G, explorationDepth)
3:     M = TruncatedSVD(SM, k)
4:     return M
5: end function
6: function sparseMatrixGen(G = (V, E), explorationDepth)
7:     Initialize a sparse matrix SM^0 ∈ Z^{|V|×1} to zero
8:     Initialize an empty list L of sparse matrices.
9:     i = 1
10:    len = 0
11:    while i <= explorationDepth do
12:        index = IndexID(SM^i)
13:        Initialize a sparse matrix SM^i ∈ Z^{|V|×|index|} to zero
14:        for all (u, v) ∈ E do
15:            SM^i[id(u), index(SM^{i-1}[id(v), :])]+ = 1
16:        end for
17:        append SM^i on L
18:        if len = |index| then
19:            break
20:        else
21:            append SM^i on L
22:            len = |index|
23:            i = i + 1
24:        end if
25:    end while
26:    SM^tot = horizontalStack(L)
27:    return SM
28: end function
```

linear on the size of the graph.

4.1. Stopping Criterion

Theorem 1 and Theorem 2 prove that the stopping criteria (line 18) of the function *sparseMatrixGen* in Algorithm 1 is correct and avoids column duplications that do not add information to the generated sparse matrix.

Theorem 2. *In the function sparseMatrixGen, in Algorithm 1, for each i >= 0, for any pair of nodes a and b, if* $SM^i[id(a), :] \neq SM^i[id(b), :]$ *then also* $SM^{i+1}[id(a), :] \neq SM^{i+1}[id(b), :]$

Theorem 3. *Given the stopping iteration s, function sparseMatrixGen (in Algorithm 1) stops due to the condition in line 18, the column of the matrix* SM^{s-1} *can be reordered to be the same of* SM^s*. This implies that it does not need to continue the iterations since the newly generated sparse matrices will continue to have always the same information of* SM^{s-1}*.*

4.2. Time and Space Complexities

We describe the time and space complexities of Algorithm 1. The following theorem shows that, assuming the *explorationDepth* a constant, the method *sparseMatrixGen* has space and execution time linear in the number of edges of the graph times the number of iterations. Consequently, considering the $\min(explorationDepth, s)$ as a constant, our proposed method is linear (in space and time) on the graph size.

Theorem 4. *Let s be the iteration when the function sparseMatrixGen (in Algorithm 1) stops due to the condition in (line 18), the time and space complexity of the method sparseMatrixGen in Algorithm 1 is* $O(|E| \times \min(explorationDepth, s))$

The entire algorithm complexity depends on the cost to compute the sparse matrix plus the cost to apply the Truncated SVD on the aforementioned matrix. The following theorem gives an idea of the whole execution cost of the algorithm.

Theorem 5. *Let s be the iteration when the function sparseMatrixGen (in Algorithm 1) stops due to the condition in (line 18), the execution time of Algorithm 1) is* $O((|V|+|E|\times\min(explorationDepth, s))\times k^2)$

It is important to note that the execution time for the Truncated SVD is a pessimistic upper bound, as mentioned in [7], and, in average the execution time is small. In term of space complexity of the entire approach we have still $O(|v| + |E| \times \min(explorationDepth, s))$.

5. Experimental Results

In this section we present a set of experiments to empirically verify the capabilities of SparseStruct. We compare our approach with the following six well established techniques: node2vec [14], struc2vec [5], GraphWave [6], GraphSAGE [15], ARGA [16], and DRNE [17].

To test these approaches, we select a set of small to large-sized real-world graphs. They range from hundreds to thousands of nodes. The chosen graphs are:

- **Facebook348** [18]: This network is one of the ten available ego networks (id 348) of the Stanford ego-Facebook dataset. The network contains 224 nodes and 3,192 edges.
- **Air-traffic networks** [5]: In this set of networks, nodes represent airports and edges indicate the existence of commercial air traffic between them. We will use three different sized air-traffic networks: **Brazilian air-traffic network** (131 nodes and 1,038 edges), **European air-traffic network** (399 nodes and 5,995 edges), and **American air-traffic network**(1,190 nodes and 13,599 edges).
- **Wikipedia** [14]: This network contains the co-occurrence of words appearing in the first million bytes of the Wikipedia dump. The network contains 4, 777 nodes and 184, 812 edges.

All experiments used an Intel Xeon E5-2620 2.00GHz CPU with 128 GB of RAM memory and an Nvidia GeForce GTX 1080 Ti GPU with 11 GB of dedicated memory. SparseStruct is implemented in python and for all the other methods, we used the Python implementation provided by the authors and, unless otherwise stated, default parameters provided in the code and their documentation.

Table 1 PageRank (PR), HITS Authority/Hub (HITS), Degree Centrality (DC), Eigenvector Centrality (EC), Betweenness Centrality (BC), and Node Clique Number (NCN) centrality measure regression results.

Brazilian air-traffic network

	PR		HITS		DC		EC		BC		NCN	
	RMSE	R^2	RMSE	R^2	RMSE	R^2	RMSE	R^2	RMSE	R^2	RMSE	R^2
Degree	0.016	0.990	0.047	0.962	-	-	0.047	0.962	0.071	0.571	0.076	0.946
node2vec	0.183	0.111	0.229	0.203	0.192	0.137	0.229	0.203	0.141	-0.043	0.280	0.324
struc2vec	0.029	0.968	0.031	0.972	0.029	0.975	0.036	0.972	0.066	0.304	0.064	0.959
GraphWave	0.020	0.978	0.035	0.958	0.021	0.975	0.034	0.956	0.082	0.383	0.089	0.920
GraphSAGE	0.163	0.253	0.209	0.333	0.171	0.275	0.209	0.333	0.136	-0.070	0.258	0.425
ARGA	0.045	0.927	0.048	0.954	0.040	0.949	0.048	0.954	0.052	0.606	0.087	0.933
DRNE	0.016	0.991	0.037	0.974	**0.007**	0.998	0.037	0.973	0.071	0.569	**0.061**	**0.966**
SparseEmb	**0.009**	**0.997**	**0.008**	**0.999**	0.009	**0.998**	**0.008**	**0.999**	**0.049**	**0.766**	0.086	0.933

European air-traffic network

	PR		HITS		DC		EC		BC		NCN	
	RMSE	R^2	RMSE	R^2	RMSE	R^2	RMSE	R^2	RMSE	R^2	RMSE	R^2
Degree	0.020	0.983	0.034	0.973	-	-	0.034	0.973	0.067	0.522	0.113	0.850
node2vec	0.159	0.112	0.190	0.232	0.159	0.166	0.190	0.232	0.104	0.009	0.256	0.280
struc2vec	0.023	0.979	0.030	0.979	0.017	0.989	0.030	0.979	0.051	0.744	0.107	0.868
GraphWave	0.035	0.856	0.036	0.968	0.031	0.873	0.036	0.968	0.044	0.808	0.100	0.879
GraphSAGE	0.087	0.737	0.097	0.796	0.083	0.767	0.097	0.796	0.091	0.279	0.143	0.768
ARGA	0.016	0.991	0.025	0.986	0.015	0.992	0.025	0.986	0.035	0.874	0.096	0.897
DRNE	0.019	0.986	0.026	0.986	**0.007**	**0.998**	0.026	0.986	0.059	0.610	0.098	0.886
SparseEmb	**0.008**	**0.997**	**0.007**	**0.999**	**0.007**	**0.998**	**0.007**	**0.999**	**0.048**	**0.805**	**0.068**	**0.949**

American air-traffic network

	PR		HITS		DC		EC		BC		NCN	
	RMSE	R^2	RMSE	R^2	RMSE	R^2	RMSE	R^2	RMSE	R^2	RMSE	R^2
Degree	0.032	0.889	0.054	0.932	-	-	0.054	0.932	0.041	0.127	0.066	0.934
node2vec	0.065	0.554	0.113	0.716	0.278	0.273	0.113	0.716	0.043	0.230	0.129	0.770
struc2vec	0.026	0.921	0.033	0.971	0.011	0.995	0.033	0.971	0.038	-0.168	0.056	0.953
GraphWave	0.018	0.965	0.019	0.989	0.017	0.989	0.019	0.989	0.034	-0.212	0.032	0.983
GraphSAGE	0.040	0.844	0.044	0.966	0.047	0.920	0.044	0.956	0.044	0.216	0.061	0.947
ARGA	0.015	0.976	0.033	0.975	0.018	0.989	0.033	0.975	**0.022**	**0.628**	0.058	0.950
DRNE	0.024	0.941	0.031	0.973	0.010	0.973	0.010	0.996	0.034	-0.387	0.039	0.976
SparseEmb	**0.010**	**0.986**	**0.004**	**0.999**	**0.009**	**0.997**	**0.004**	**0.999**	0.035	0.553	**0.033**	**0.984**

Facebook348

	PR		HITS		DC		EC		BC		NCN	
	RMSE	R^2	RMSE	R^2	RMSE	R^2	RMSE	R^2	RMSE	R^2	RMSE	R^2
Degree	0.060	0.854	0.066	0.932	-	-	0.066	0.932	0.106	0.301	0.103	0.868
node2vec	0.137	0.524	0.148	0.713	0.131	0.647	0.148	0.713	0.117	0.118	0.153	0.705
struc2vec	0.044	0.947	0.047	0.964	0.023	0.988	0.047	0.964	0.098	0.387	0.086	0.908
GraphWave	**0.020**	**0.987**	0.027	0.988	0.013	0.995	0.027	0.988	0.090	0.476	0.085	0.910
GraphSAGE	0.161	0.312	0.168	0.624	0.152	0.507	0.168	0.624	0.126	-0.041	0.195	0.537
ARGA	0.032	0.964	0.027	0.990	0.018	0.993	0.027	0.990	**0.089**	**0.508**	**0.076**	**0.928**
NDRE	0.028	0.976	0.061	0.947	**0.004**	**0.999**	0.061	0.947	0.103	0.309	0.100	0.876
SparseEmb	0.037	0.937	**0.009**	**0.999**	0.007	**0.999**	**0.009**	**0.999**	0.107	0.313	0.092	0.894

Wikipedia

	PR		HITS		DC		EC		BC		NCN	
	RMSE	R^2	RMSE	R^2	RMSE	R^2	RMSE	R^2	RMSE	R^2	RMSE	R^2
Degree	0.006	0.951	0.010	0.960	-	-	0.010	0.959	0.009	0.001	0.062	0.900
node2vec	0.027	0.420	0.033	0.566	0.028	0.440	0.033	0.566	0.012	-1.94	0.129	0.573
struc2vec	0.007	0.945	0.007	0.976	0.007	0.951	0.007	0.976	0.008	-0.385	0.058	0.915
GraphWave	0.006	0.958	0.005	0.988	0.005	0.974	0.005	0.988	0.008	-1.265	0.051	0.932
GraphSAGE	0.033	0.131	0.044	0.223	0.033	0.138	0.044	0.223	0.022	-1.291	0.170	0.262
ARGA	0.005	0.975	0.005	0.987	**0.004**	**0.978**	0.005	0.987	0.006	0.114	0.047	0.944
DRNE	0.020	0.637	0.028	0.693	0.023	0.556	0.027	0.693	0.011	-3.47	0.078	0.845
SparseEmb	**0.004**	**0.977**	**0.004**	**0.992**	**0.004**	**0.978**	**0.004**	**0.994**	**0.005**	**0.092**	**0.042**	**0.955**

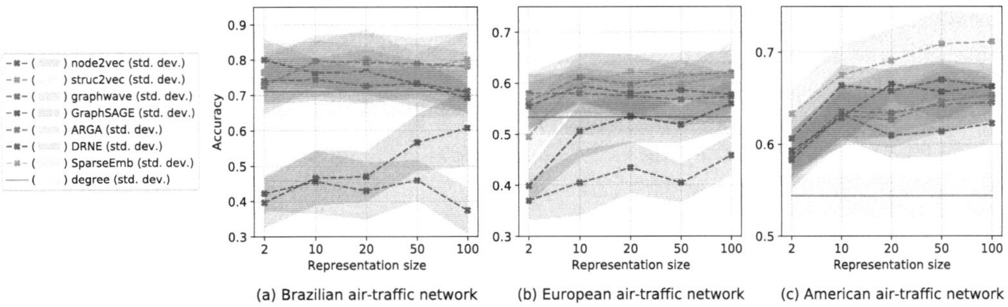

Figure 2: Accuracy (mean and standard deviation among the folds) prediction task vs. vectorial representation size.

5.1. Centrality Measure Regression Experiments

To evaluate the structural information encoded inside the generated representations, we propose a set of regression-based experiments where we use our representations to extract known centrality metrics. We consider the following centrality metrics: PageRank (PR), HITS Authority/Hub, Degree Centrality (DC), Eigenvector Centrality (EC), Betweenness Centrality (BC), and Node Clique Number (NCN).

To do so, we compute all the node representations and network metrics to generate the feature datasets and the ground truths to train and test the regression models. For the regression task, we use Support Vector Machine regression [19], and the optimal hyper-parameters (including kernel type) are selected with a grid-search approach and 10-fold cross-validation. The performance metrics we use are the Root Mean Square Error (RMSE) and the Coefficient of Determination (R^2), obtained as the average value computed over the results of the 10-folds.

In Table 1 are reported the results of each metric for each dataset and for each representation learning approach. As a baseline, we considered the degree of each node since one SM^1 generated by the sparseMatrixGen method in Algorithm 1 contains the degree of each node. Note that the results for the degree in the case of the degree centrality are not reported since two are the same.

From Table 1,SparseStruct is often outperforming all the other representation learning techniques or produce comparable results.

5.2. Classification

We test and compare SparseStruct and all the other considered approach with the node classification task. The node classification task consists in predicting a label for a set of unlabeled nodes. For these experiments, we selected the Brazilian, European, and American air-traffic networks from [5]. In order to test a structure-based classification setting, the datasets have been labeled according to each airport's activity level, where each airport activity is measured by the total number of airplane landings and takeoffs. Each airport on the datasets has been assigned with one of four possible activity levels. With these levels being the labels for our classification task. In order to assign each label, authors use the quartiles from the empirical airport activity distribution to split the dataset into four airport groups, each of these groups containing 25% of the total airports. The labels are ordered in increasing activity order, where group 1 contains airports with the least activity, and group 4 contains airports with the most activity. The resulting groups are used to label each node in the datasets. This process has been applied to each dataset separately. Given the representation provided by the different approaches, we used the Extra-Tree classifier [20]. As in the previous experiment, we decide the best model hyper-parameters by a combination of grid search and a 10-fold validation schema.

Figure 2 shows the accuracy (mean and standard deviation among the folds) result with different representation sizes: 2,10,20,50 and 100. Please note that the generated datasets are balanced, so mean accuracy among the fold and the standard deviation are accurate measurements. In Figure 2, we can observe that the SparseStruct is one of the best representation learning approaches in Brazilian and European air-traffic networks. While in the American air-traffic network, the SparseStruct clearly over-performs all the other approaches. In addition, in Figure 2, we can observe in SparseStruct has the desirable property that step by step, the representation size also increases the accuracy increases. This happens until, at a certain size, the performance is not going to change.

6. Conclusions and Future Work

In this paper, we proposed SparseStruct, a large-scale sparse structural representation learning approach for graph nodes. SparseStruct theoretically and empirically preserves the graph structure of each node, and it has a execution time linear in the size of the graph. In our experiments, SparseStruct is often superior or comparable to current state-of-art representation learning approaches on both classification and regression tasks.

Future works is mainly oriented to embed novel features of big data within our framework (e.g., [21, 22]).

Acknowledgements

This work is partially supported by NSERC (Canada) and University of Manitoba.

References

[1] A. Cuzzocrea, I. Song, Big graph analytics: The state of the art and future research agenda, in: Proceedings of the 17th International Workshop on Data Warehousing and OLAP, DOLAP 2014, Shanghai, China, November 3-7, 2014, ACM, 2014, pp. 99–101.

[2] A. Campan, A. Cuzzocrea, T. M. Truta, Fighting fake news spread in online social networks: Actual trends and future research directions, in: 2017 IEEE International Conference on Big Data, BigData 2017, Boston, MA, USA, December 11-14, 2017, IEEE Computer Society, 2017, pp. 4453–4457.

[3] M. Joaristi, E. Serra, F. Spezzano, Inferring bad entities through the panama papers network, in: 2018 IEEE/ACM International Conference on Advances in Social Networks Analysis and Mining (ASONAM), IEEE, 2018, pp. 767–773.

[4] M. Joaristi, E. Serra, F. Spezzano, Detecting suspicious entities in offshore leaks networks, Social Network Analysis and Mining 9 (2019) 62.

[5] L. F. Ribeiro, P. H. Saverese, D. R. Figueiredo, struc2vec: Learning node representations from structural identity, in: Proceedings of the 23rd ACM SIGKDD International Conference on Knowledge Discovery and Data Mining, ACM, 2017, pp. 385–394.
[6] C. Donnat, M. Zitnik, D. Hallac, J. Leskovec, Learning structural node embeddings via diffusion wavelets, in: Proceedings of the 24th ACM SIGKDD International Conference on Knowledge Discovery & Data Mining, ACM, 2018, pp. 1320–1329.
[7] D. Zhang, J. Yin, X. Zhu, C. Zhang, Network representation learning: A survey, IEEE transactions on Big Data (2018).
[8] P. C. Hansen, The truncatedsvd as a method for regularization, BIT Numerical Mathematics 27 (1987) 534–553.
[9] J. Shlens, A tutorial on principal component analysis, arXiv preprint arXiv:1404.1100 (2014).
[10] P. D. Turney, Mining the web for synonyms: Pmi-ir versus lsa on toefl, in: European conference on machine learning, Springer, 2001, pp. 491–502.
[11] A. C. Gilbert, J. Y. Park, M. B. Wakin, Sketched svd: Recovering spectral features from compressive measurements, arXiv preprint arXiv:1211.0361 (2012).
[12] N. Halko, P.-G. Martinsson, J. A. Tropp, Finding structure with randomness: Stochastic algorithms for constructing approximate matrix decompositions (2009).
[13] B. L. Douglas, The weisfeiler-lehman method and graph isomorphism testing, arXiv preprint arXiv:1101.5211 (2011).
[14] A. Grover, J. Leskovec, node2vec: Scalable feature learning for networks, in: Proceedings of the 22nd ACM SIGKDD international conference on Knowledge discovery and data mining, ACM, 2016, pp. 855–864.
[15] W. Hamilton, Z. Ying, J. Leskovec, Inductive representation learning on large graphs, in: Advances in neural information processing systems, 2017, pp. 1024–1034.
[16] S. Pan, R. Hu, G. Long, J. Jiang, L. Yao, C. Zhang, Adversarially regularized graph autoencoder for graph embedding, arXiv preprint arXiv:1802.04407 (2018).
[17] K. Tu, P. Cui, X. Wang, P. S. Yu, W. Zhu, Deep recursive network embedding with regular equivalence, in: Proceedings of the 24th ACM SIGKDD International Conference on Knowledge Discovery & Data Mining, 2018, pp. 2357–2366.
[18] J. Leskovec, A. Krevl, Snap datasets: Stanford large network dataset collection, 2014.
[19] C. Cortes, V. Vapnik, Support-vector networks, Machine learning 20 (1995) 273–297.
[20] P. Geurts, D. Ernst, L. Wehenkel, Extremely randomized trees, Machine learning 63 (2006) 3–42.
[21] A. Cuzzocrea, W. Wang, Approximate range-sum query answering on data cubes with probabilistic guarantees, J. Intell. Inf. Syst. 28 (2007) 161–197.
[22] A. Cuzzocrea, Accuracy control in compressed multidimensional data cubes for quality of answer-based OLAP tools, in: 18th International Conference on Scientific and Statistical Database Management, SSDBM 2006, 3-5 July 2006, Vienna, Austria, Proceedings, IEEE Computer Society, 2006, pp. 301–310.

A Knowledge-based Approach to Business Analysis for Process Innovation

Michele Missikoff

Istituto di Analisi dei Sistemi ed Informatica del CNR. Via dei Taurini 19, 00185 Rome, Italy

Abstract

This paper proposes a methodology for business process analysis, conceived in the context of business process (BP) innovation. The proposal, part of a more encompassing methodology referred to as *EasInnova*, addresses business process analysis as a knowledge management project. It is based on the progressive construction of a knowledge base about the business organization and, specifically, the process to be innovated. The method has been conceived to be easily adopted by business people without knowledge management experience, keeping them at the centre of the business analysis and, eventually, the application software development. After a brief description of the *EasInnova* methodology, the paper focuses on the acquisition and management of knowledge about the structural (avoiding the behavioural) aspects of the BP to be transformed, and the construction of the corresponding models. The method is characterised by a progressive approach. It consists in the production of a sequence of six different knowledge artefacts that go from more intuitive, and easy to be managed, plain text descriptions to a more structured semantic table, to a diagrammatic representation. The final knowledge artefact is represented by a BP ontology, i.e., a formal representation of the knowledge about the BP and is operating scenario.

Keywords

Business Analysis, Business Process Innovation, Knowledge Representation, Lexicon, Class Diagram, Ontology

1. Introduction

Enterprise innovation consists in the transformation of some business (e.g., organization, processes, products, services, etc.) in order to gain a given advantage (e.g., in terms of cost, time, quality). Within enterprise innovation, business process (BP) innovation [1] assumes a central position, in fact it cannot be considered in isolation with respect to other elements of the enterprise. Even if our initial focus is on the innovation of a specific BP, we need to consider other connected business elements, such as the documents, the organization, the enterprise structure, the roles and skills of the involved people. Conversely, if our focus is on, say, product innovation, then we are forced to change the involved processes as well. For these reasons, business process innovation is one of the most strategic field of a dynamic enterprise.

In this paper we propose a method for BP Analysis (BPA) that is positioned in the context of a methodology, called *EasInnova* [2], aimed at supporting business process innovation. *EasInnova* is based on the idea that process innovation is essentially a 'knowledge management affair'. In fact, to carry out a successful innovation, you need to start from a solid base of knowledge (about the enterprise, the process, various methods and tools, etc.) and, during the innovation activities, one of the major endeavours is the acquisition and organization of knowledge. Eventually, the outcome consists in the implementation of a new business solution, together with a rich, articulated body of

SEBD 2021: The 29th Italian Symposium on Advanced Database Systems, September 5-9, 2021, Pizzo Calabro (VV), Italy
EMAIL: Michele.missikoff@iasi.cnr.it
ORCID: 0000-0002-7972-5201

knowledge, (referred to as *InnoBok*, Innovation Body of Knowledge) [3] that remains as a strategic knowledge asset for the enterprise.

Seen the complexity of knowledge management in any (non-trivial) business innovation project, the *EasInnova* methodology proposes a set of guidelines, organised according to a vertical and a horizontal dimension.

Along the vertical dimension *EasInnova* adopts the Model-Driven Architecture (MDA) scheme [4] where enterprise knowledge, and the corresponding models, are organised according to three layers.

- Computation Independent Models (*CIM*),
- Platform Independent Models (*PIM*),
- Platform Specific Models (*PSM*).

Along the horizontal dimension, enterprise innovation take place following three stages: in the first stage, referred to as *AsIs*, the aim is to build models representing the existing business scenario. The second stage, business transformation (*BTran*), aims at identifying the issues, the possible solutions, and the activities necessary to move from *AsIs* to the new innovative scenario. The latter, referred to as *ToBe* scenario, aims at a full specification and modeling the innovative solution and the scenario resulting from its adoption. The three horizontal stages cut across the three MDA layers, giving place to the *EasInnova* matrix.

The rest of the paper is organised as follows. The next section proposes an overview of the EasInnova Methodology, followed, in Section 3, by the related work in the area of business process innovation. Then, in Section 4, we illustrate the BPA methodology by means of a running example. Finally, Section 5 presents the conclusions and some ideas for a future work.

2. The *EasInnova* methodology

As anticipated, the reference scheme of *EasInnova* is based on the matrix obtained by intersecting the two dimensions, i.e., the three vertical MDA layers and the three horizontal stages. In essence, we obtain the 3 x 3 *EasInnova* matrix defined as:

$$EI = (s_{i,j}) \tag{1}$$

where $(s_{i,j})$ represent the steps of the methodology,
with $i \in < CIM, PIM, PSM > and\ j \in < AsIs, BTran, ToBe >$.

The methodology provides a set of guidelines that an innovation team can follow by traversing the *EI* matrix left to right and top down. The traversal is primarily, but not strictly, in a sequence, since the knowledge produced in one step can be later amended when in a successive step additional knowledge is collected, refining the overall picture.

In this paper we focus on the first step, $s_{1,1}$, corresponding to the *AsIs* stage in the *CIM* Layer. The first step is particularly critical since it is where the current scenario is carefully analysed and (hopefully) understood. In such a step, we aim at building conceptual models of the business with a structural (static) perspective. We will also tackle actions and processes but only from a structural standpoint, i.e., considering all the elements of a BP and their relationships with other relevant entities (actors, documents, etc.), avoiding to model the business logic (i.e., the process flow) that will be later detailed in the PIM layer (while in the PSM layer all the implementation details will be provided.)

The *EasInnova* methodology is primarily addressed to business people, therefore we propose a set of knowledge artefacts sufficiently intuitive to be easily managed by people without a technical background. At the end, we will have a final step aimed at distilling the collected knowledge, essentially represented in an intuitive, informal way, into a business ontology. This last step, of a more technical nature, is an easily task for an ontology expert who will simply encode the knowledge into a formal representation, without altering the business models and the underlying vision.

The achievement of a BP ontology presents a number of advantages, such as the possibility of revising the informal models from a more formal standpoint. Then, once the knowledge is represented in a formal way (e.g., by using OWL), with a support of an ontology platform (we used Protégé) it is possible to carry out a number of automatic services, e.g., checking its formal consistency or the business (terminological) coherence of the various models (essentially, the coherent adoption and representation of the different business terms).

3. Related works

Business Process Innovation (BPI) includes, in its preliminarily phase, Business Analysis (BA) that is addressed in the first step of the *EasInnova* methodology: *EI(AsIs, CIM)*. BA is a discipline with a long tradition rooted in the business culture. With the advent of enterprise information systems, BA become an important part of Requirement Engineering and a must for a successful project of BPI. It has been indicated as Business Process Analysis (BPA) [5]: a territory of research and practice that traditionally belongs to business people, but that progressively attracted the attention of technical IT people. In early times, IT people were involved only at the end of this analysis process, when business requirement specifications were released.

Business people mainly addressed BPA following informal guidelines and producing informal process models [6]. Such approaches demonstrated a number of shortcomings in the development of enterprise information systems. One of the most severe is the Business/IT Alignment problem [7], i.e., the misalignment between business needs and services offered by an information system. Several efforts have been deployed to find a solution, but with a limited success [8]. One of the key causes is the separation between the BA performed by business experts and the successive analysis and specification carried out by IT experts. To solve this issue, the idea was to establish an early cooperation between business and IT experts, adopting rigorous and precise specifications in BP modeling. The expected advantage was to reduce the ambiguity of informal specifications, moving earlier the adoption of formal methods and the use of computer-supported services. Along this line, the adoption of a semantic approach started to emerge, with the proposal of knowledge-based solutions, business ontologies [9] and ontology-based enterprise models [10].

Ontology-based solutions for BPA, focused on business processes and their dynamic aspects, were proposed, like COBRA, a Core Ontology for Business pRocess Analysis [11], based on a Time Ontology. Another research line, with a wider scope, is represented by the adoption of ontologies and semantic web services for BP management, such as Semantic Business Process Management (SBPM) [12].

A different research line, rooted in the business culture, starts from a business standard, the Universal Business Language (UBL) [13] proposed by the international Organization for the Advancement of Structured Information Standards (OASIS). In essence, UBL is an open library of business components, such as Address, Price, Quantity, and business templates of the most common documents, such as Invoice, Order, Receipt, plus a number of standard process models (e.g., procurement). Roy et Al. [14] propose to associate a business ontology to UBL, modeling its components and templates, and the UBL process flow, with a logical formalism (essentially OWL).

Another interesting proposal is represented by BPMO [15], a BP Modeling Ontology that besides UBL considers also other business representation standards, including ebXML, conceived to allow the exchange of information among cooperating enterprises.

The literature is very rich and there are other important proposals that we omit for lack of space. But all the existing proposals had a limited practical impact, failing in the objective of convincing business people to adopt more rigorous and formal business modeling methods. We believe that there are several causes. The first is the clash of the business and the ontology cultures, with the pragmatism of the former and the formal approach of the latter. Then, the idea of building large, encompassing, enterprise ontologies turned out to be too complex, difficult to be built and to evolve over time. We believe that starting with a limited, local solution, e.g., a departmental or application ontology, would have more chances of success. Also, the idea of pushing extensive competencies of ontology principles and theories in the business world appears not practical. Then, there is a need for a methodology that supports business people in a progressive approach from informal to formal knowledge modeling. For these reasons, the paper presents a method that starts building simple intuitive models, in the form of textual specifications, progressively enriching such models producing structured, semantically tagged artefacts and, eventually, a first business ontology.

4. The CIM-AsIs step

The first *CIM-AsIs* step, aimed at BPA, mainly consists in carrying out a comprehensive business analysis of the current state of play. Such an analysis goes beyond the given BP and considers also other business elements, such as the actors who operate or superintend on the process, the documents that are exchanged among the actors, the data and information that are managed during the process. As anticipated, this preliminary analysis avoids considering the actual business flow, typically represented by a BP diagram. The focus is on the structural elements of the BP, e.g., activities, operation, and the links with the other cited elements (document, actors, etc.) In this way, we will collect a significant amount of enterprise knowledge. Such a knowledge will be used in the successive steps, starting from the *CIM-BTran* that is aimed at identifying the critical issues to be addressed in achieving BP innovation, and the transformations necessary to reach the new *CIM-ToBe* scenario. Both are the successive steps, not addressed in this paper, for which the knowledge collected in this step is a necessary base.

In this step the models that represent the enterprise knowledge can assume various forms, with different levels of details and formality. In particular, we have: (i) *plain text*, a narrative form of knowledge representation; (ii) *structured text*, e.g., itemised lists (bullet points, numbered lists, etc.) that collect and organise short statements; (iii) *tabular structures*, typically providing a matrix visualization of knowledge items; (iv) *diagrams*, where the knowledge is graphically represented, according to a given standard; (v) a formal representation of the business domain by means of a reference ontology.

4.1. The methodology presented with a running example

This step is aimed at collecting the knowledge and building static (structural) models of the current business scenario, creating the following knowledge artefacts that contribute to the construction of the first *CIM-AsIs* knowledge asset.

a) **BP Signature**. This is the first tabular artefact aimed at providing a synthetic description of the business process that we intend to innovate, gathering a few key information items about it.
b) **BP Statement**. A preliminary plain text description of the business scenario and the business process to be innovated, described in general terms (i.e., at an intensional level).
c) **BP Case**. A plain text description of an exemplar execution of the BP (i.e., at an extensional level). In essence, it represents one instance of the BP Statement.
d) **OPAALE Lexicon**. This is a structured terminology that provides a first semantic tagging of the key terms used in the two previous structures.
e) **UML Class Diagram**. The construction of the UML Class Diagram (CD) starts form the knowledge so far collected, modeling it in a graphical form. Such a graphical representation has a growing popularity, it is particularly useful to exchange the knowledge among people.
f) **CIM-AsIs ontology**. This is a formal representation of the analysed business process. It is the final knowledge artefact of this step.

Below we illustrate the details of the listed knowledge artefacts. To this end we adopt a running example concerning a pizza shop. The example will help to show the progression in complexity and formality in the acquisition of business knowledge to arrive, eventually, to the definition of the BP ontology.

BP Signature. The Table 1 organizes the key knowledge aimed at providing the essential information about the BP.

Table 1
BP Signature scheme

Knowledge items	Description
Name	<name of the business process>
Trigger	<event that causes the BP to start>
Key Actors	<most relevant actors that operate in the BP>
Key Objects	<most relevant objects involved in the BP>
Input	<objects required to start the BP>
Objectives	< objectives that the BP intends to achieve>
Output	<final deliverables released at the end of the BP>

Then we apply the above scheme to provide the first description of the pizza shop BP.

Table 2
PizzaShop BP Signature

Knowledge items	Description
Name	PizzaDelivery
Trigger	OrderArrived
Key Actors	Customer, Cook, DeliveryPerson
Key Objects	Order, Dough, Pizza, DeliveryVehicle
Input	Order
Objectives	Cook and deliver pizzas to customers
Output	Pizzas delivered

BP Statement. The text of the BP Statement is the synthesis of an interview to a (fictitious) pizza shop owner, whose business has name *PizzaPazza*.

> *My business, PizzaPazza, is a home delivery pizza shop. The customer fills in the order and then submits it to the shop, with the payment, by using our Web site. Making good pizzas requires good quality dough, produced in-house, and a careful baking of the pizza. To make clients happy, we need to quickly fulfil the order and the delivery person needs to know streets and how to speedily reach the customer's address.*

BP Case. This text reports a specific execution of the BP, i.e., it represents an instance of the PizzaShop BP.

> *John connects to the PizzaPazza Web site and places his order of two Napoli pizzas, providing also the payment. On the arrival of John's order at PizzaPazza, July, the cook, puts the order on the worklist. When the John's turn arrives, July prepares the ordered pizzas, cooks them, and alerts the delivery boy Ed to come and pick up the pizzas. Then, Ed takes the pizzas and starts his delivery trip, eventually achieving the delivery to John's home.*

4.2. Building a structured BP lexicon

Here, we start introducing the first semantic elements, extracting the terminology from the first three knowledge artefacts and organising them according to six semantic categories. To this end, we propose a semantically structured lexicon, referred to as OPAALE. The name comes from the six semantic categories that form its structure that is an evolution of a pre-existing proposal: OPAL [16].

(i) ***Object***: any passive entity with a lifecycle that follows to the CRUDA paradigm, i.e., the traditional *Create, Read, Update, Delete* (Martin, 1983 and Torim, 2012), to which we add *Archive* that is particularly relevant in business processes;
(ii) ***Process:*** a partially ordered set of tasks aimed to enact CRUDA operations on one or more business objects;
(iii) ***Actor:*** any active entity involved in one or more processes;
(iv) ***Attribute***: a property associated to one or more of the listed concepts;
(v) ***Link:*** a relationship between two of the listed concepts;
(vi) ***Event:*** a special object that causes the start of a BP instance, or that represents a milestone in its execution.

In Table 3 we report the OPAALE Lexicon built with the knowledge extracted from the BP descriptions (Signature, Statement and Case). Please note that here we do not mean to be complete, since the reported structures have mainly an illustrative purpose. Furthermore, we use the term 'lexicon' and not glossary since this structure collects the sole terminology without the description of terms.

Table 3
OPAALE Lexicon of the PizzaPazza BP

Categories	Business terms
Object	Pizza, Dough, Topping, Address, ...
Process	Cooking, MakingDough, PlacingOrder, AcceptingOrder, DeliveringPizza, Carrying, ...
Actor	PizzaShop, Customer, DeliveryPerson, ...
Attribute	Price, Quantity, PizzaKind, ...
Link	Customer-Order, Order-Pizza, DeliveryPerson-Pizza, Customer-Address, ...
Event	Order, DeliveredPizza, ...

To better clarify the elements of the Table 3, we provide a formal account of its content. Assuming that we have the full application lexicon F that gathers all the terms used to describe a Pizza business, then we introduce six predicates and a set theoretic account of the table content.

Firstly, we introduce the following predicates, each of which corresponds to a row in the above table:

object(x), evaluate true if *x* is an object;
process(x), evaluate true if *x* is an activity, an operation, a task, a process;
actor(x), evaluate true if *x* is an actor;
attribute(x), evaluate true if *x* is an attribute;
linked(x,y), evaluate true if the concepts represented by *x* and *y* exhibit a form of relatedness in the application domain.
event(x), evaluate true if *x* is an event.

Then we define the following subsets of $\mathcal{F}$:

$$O = \{\, o \in \mathcal{F} : object(o) \,\}$$

$$P = \{\, p \in \mathcal{F} : process(p) \,\}$$

$$A = \{\, a \in \mathcal{T} : actor(a) \,\}$$

$$AT = \{\, t \in \mathcal{T} : attribute(t) \,\}$$

$$E = \{\, e \in \mathcal{T} : event(e) \,\}$$

And the following relation:

$$L = \{\, (x,y) \in \mathcal{T} \times \mathcal{T} : linked(x,y) \wedge (\, ((actor(x) \wedge actor(y)) \vee (object(x) \wedge object(y)) \vee (actor(x) \wedge object(y)) \vee (actor(x) \wedge process(y)) \vee (\, (event(x) \wedge process(y))) \,\}$$

Please note that the above formalization does not intend to be complete (for sake of simplicity we left out the attributes that can be associated to all the other concepts), but we believe that it can help in the next steps, when building the Class Diagram and then the ontology. In this respect, in the *link* category we listed only the domain dependent terms, giving for granted the general conceptual modeling constructs, such as *partOf, ISA,* etc.

4.3. Building the Pizza Shop Class Diagram

Starting from the above knowledge artefacts, and in particular from the OPAALE Lexicon, we proceed in drawing the UML-Class Diagram (CD) of the Pizza Shop BP. The CD is built according to the following rules:

- Class Boxes are labelled with one of the terms in the classes of **Object** or **Actor**, or **Event**
- **Attribute** terms are listed within the box of the corresponding concept.
- Pairs of terms in the **Link** section are represented by arrows connecting two boxes. Such arrows can be representative of:
    a. *ISA*, if linking an object or an actor with its more general concept.
    b. *PartOf*, if linking an object or an actor that is a component of a more complex assembly to which it is part of.
    c. *Action*, if linking an actor with another actor or an object. Or an event to an actor. The action name is one of those listed in the **Process** section (we recall that the term Process in OPAALE is more general than 'business process', including various behavioural notions, such as task, operation, action, activity, function).
    d. An *Action* that goes from an *Event* (a special object) to the actor that is interested by such an event.

It is important to emphasise that all the names used in the UML-CD need to be already identified and reported in the OPAALE Lexicon. The concept (class) names are preceded by a tag indicating the corresponding OPAALE category. For sake of space, in this paper we report a fragment of the Class Diagram where the boxes include only the concept names (i.e., class names, in UML-CD jargon.)

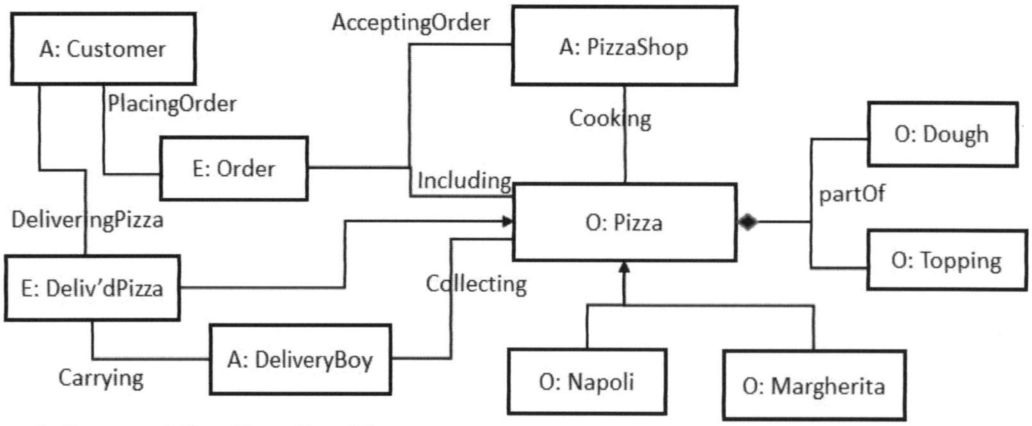

Figure 1: Excerpt of PizzaShop Class Diagram

Please note that in this *CIM-AsIs* step we need (possibly) to be precise, but we don't need to be neither formal nor complete. In fact, with *EasInnova*, we do not proceed linearly, but rather in a spiral way. For instance, when drawing a CD it may be the case that new terms, not yet identified, will emerge, then we go back to the OPAALE Lexicon adding the new terms to it, in order to keep the different models aligned.

The next knowledge artefact, the application ontology, represents the final outcome of the *CIM-AsIs* step of the *EasInnova* methodology.

4.4. Pizza shop BPA ontology

Adding an ontology to the knowledge artefacts already available presents various advantages. Firstly, the analyst need to revisit the knowledge collected so far to verify its consistency and (self) completeness. Then, the building of a formal representation, by means of a dedicated platform, such as Protégé, gives the possibility to apply a reasoner to prove the absence of (formal) inconsistencies.

In building the PizzaShop ontology we start from the terminology reported in the OPAALE lexicon and adopted in the Class Diagram. Please consider that the whole method has been conceived to allow business experts (without specific technical competencies) to directly manage all the previous knowledge artefacts. Only this last artefact requires competencies on ontology principles, even if the following rules provide effective guidelines in the ontology building endeavour.

- *Object, Actor* and *Event* terms are modelled as OWL *classes*
- *Attribute* terms are modelled as *datatype Properties*
- *Processes* are modelled as *Object Properties*, having *Actor* as *Domain* and *Object* or *Actor* as *Range*.
- *Links* are modelled as *Object Properties*, where *Domain* and *Range* are defined by the pair of terms reported in the table. The property label is assigned according to the label reported in the Class Diagram, in particular:
    - If the domain (i.e., the origin of the arrow) is an ***Actor*** term, we assume that an actor performs an action on another Object or Actor. Therefore, the label will be selected in the *Process class*.
    - If the domain is an ***Object***, we assume that the range is another object. Then the label will be, for instance, *partOf*. Or another relation among objects (e.g., *nextTo*).
    - If the domain is in ***Event***, then we adopt the predefined Object property '*triggering*' and the range is a Process.

In the figure below we report a fragment of the PizzaShop ontology that has been built by using the Protégé platform. For sake of space, it is a small fragment, but we believe that it can provide at least an intuition of the knowledge artefact that concludes the BPA activities in the *CIM-AsIs* step.

```
...
<http://webprotege.stanford.edu/#Customer>  rdf:type  owl:Class ;
    rdfs:subClassOf  <http://webprotege.stanford.edu/#Thing> ;
    rdfs:label "Customer"^^xsd:string.

<http://webprotege.stanford.edu/#Order>  rdf:type  owl:Class ;
    rdfs:subClassOf  <http://webprotege.stanford.edu/#Thing > ;
    rdfs:label  "Order"^^xsd:string .

<http://webprotege.stanford.edu/# Pizza>  rdf:type owl:Class ;
    rdfs:subClassOf  <http://webprotege.stanford.edu/#Thing > ;
    rdfs:label  "Pizza"^^xsd:string.

<http://webprotege.stanford.edu/# PlacingOrder >  rdf:type  owl:ObjectProperty ;
    rdfs:subPropertyOf  <http://webprotege.stanford.edu/#Process> ;
    rdfs:domain  <http://webprotege.stanford.edu/#Customer> ;
    rdfs:range  <http://webprotege.stanford.edu/#Order> ;
    rdfs:label  "PlacingOrder"^^xsd:string .
```

```
<http://webprotege.stanford.edu/# Choice>  rdf:type  owl:ObjectProperty ;
    rdfs:subPropertyOf  <http://webprotege.stanford.edu/#Link> ;
    rdfs:domain  <http://webprotege.stanford.edu/#Order> ;
    rdfs:range  <http://webprotege.stanford.edu/#Pizza> ;
    rdfs:label  "Including"^^xsd:string .
...
```

5. Conclusions and future work

In this paper we presented a method for BP analysis. This method is the first step, named CIM-AsIs, of the EasInnova methodology aimed at guiding business people in carrying out a business innovation project. The key objective of the methodology is to reduce to a minimum the role of technical experts providing to business people a central role in the whole innovation project, including the eventual development of a new software application.

The proposed method is based on the idea that business analysis essentially consists in the acquisition and modeling of knowledge about the application domain. Therefore, the method indicates a sequence of knowledge artefacts to be progressively built, from simple to complex ones, from informal to formal ones. Such a progression has been conceived so that five out of six knowledge artefacts can be easily built by business experts without the need of specific technical competences. Only the final artefact, the BP ontology, requires technical competencies. We believe that giving a central role to business experts has a number of advantages, first of all it contributes to solve the long-standing Business / IT alignment problem. Then, the proposed knowledge management approach appears easy to be adopted also by SMEs that, traditionally, lack of competencies and resources for such a kind of projects.

Our work will continue along two main lines. The first is to proceed with the next *EasInnova* steps. Firstly, *CIM-BTran* that, starting from the knowledge collected in the previous step, has the objective to identify the actual transformations needed to innovate the given business process. Then, the final step of the first *EasInnova* layer, *CIM-ToBe* aimed at providing a first sketch of the new scenario that will be built.

The second line of activities is the development of the *EasInnova* platform, a knowledge management environment that will support the business experts in all the steps needed to innovate a business process. To speed up the development we adopted a Low Code platform (BonitaSoft).

On the practical ground, the CIM steps are currently being experimented in a real world business context. It concerns an office of the central Italian Public Administration (Ragioneria Generale dello Stato). The first feedbacks that we are collecting encourage us to continue along the lines illustrated in this paper

6. References

[1] Markic, M., 2006. Process innovation: a precondition for business excellence. International Journal of Innovation and Learning, Vol.3, Issue 5 (2006). https://doi.org/10.1504/IJIL.2006.010483.

[2] Missikoff M., A Simple Methodology for Model-Driven Business Innovation and Low Code Implementation. ArXiv, Computer Science (2020). https://arxiv.org/abs/2010.11611.

[3] Missikoff, M., Canducci, M., Maiden, N. (Eds). "Enterprise Innovation: from Creativity to Engineering", Wiley-ISTE, 322 pages, August 2015. ISBN: 978-1-84821-851-2. DOI: 10.1002/9781119145622 (2015).

[4] Kleppe A., Warmer J., Bast W.. MDA Explained - The Model Driven Architecture: Practice and Promise. Addison - Wesley (2003).

[5] Carlos Pedrinaci, John Domingue, and Ana Karla Alves de Medeiros. A Core Ontology for Business Process Analysis. Proc. of ESWC: European Semantic Web Conference, LNCS 5021, Sproinger-Verlag, (2008).

[6] Ruth Sara Aguilar-Savén. Business process modelling: Revie wand frame work. Int. J. Production Economics 90, Elsevier, (2004).

[7] Wim Van Grembergen, Steven De Haes. a research Journey into Enterprise Governance of IT, Business/IT alignment and Value Creation. International Journal on IT/Business Alignment and Governance, 1(1), (2010).
[8] Lerina Aversano, Carmine Grasso, Maria Tortorella. A literature review of Business/IT Alignment Strategies. In CENTERIS 2012 - Conference on ENTERprise Information Systems, Elsevier (2012).
[9] Mark von Rosing and Wim Laurier. An Introduction to the Business Ontology. International Journal of Conceptual Structures and Smart Applications (IJCSSA), 3(1) (2015).
[10] Andersson B. et al. (2006) Towards a Reference Ontology for Business Models. In: Embley D.W., Olivé A., Ram S. (eds) Conceptual Modeling - ER 2006. Lecture Notes in Computer Science, vol 4215. Springer, Berlin, Heidelberg. https://doi.org/10.1007/11901181_36. (2006).
[11] Pedrinaci C., Domingue J., Alves de Medeiros A.K. (2008) A Core Ontology for Business Process Analysis. In: Bechhofer S., Hauswirth M., Hoffmann J., Koubarakis M. (eds) The Semantic Web: Research and Applications. ESWC 2008. LNCS 5021. Springer, Berlin, Heidelberg.
[12] Hepp, M., Leymann, F., Domingue, J., Wahler, A., Fensel, D.: Semantic business process management: A vision towards using semantic web services for business process management. In: Lau, F.C.M., Lei, H., Meng, X., Wang, M. (eds.) ICEBE, pp. 535–540. IEEE Computer Society, Los Alamitos (2005).
[13] W3C Recommendation. Universal Business Language v2.0. available at http://docs.oasis-open.org/ubl/cs-UBL-2.0/UBL-2.0.htm (2006).
[14] Roy, S., Sawant, K. & Ghose, A. K. Ontology modeling of UBL process diagrams using OWL. 2010 International Conference on Computer Information Systems and Industrial Management Applications (CISIM) (pp. 535-540). Piscataway, New Jersey, USA: IEEE (2010).
[15] Mark von Rosing, Wim Paul Remi Laurier, Simon Polovina. The BPM Ontology. In book: The Complete Business Process Handbook, Volume 1Publisher: Elsevier - Morgan Kaufmann (2015).
[16] D'Antonio F., Missikoff M., Taglino F. Formalizing the OPAL eBusiness ontology design patterns with OWL. Proceedings of the 3th International Conference on Interoperability for Enterprise Software and Applications, IESA 2007.

Hypergraph Data analysis with PAOHVis

Paolo Buono, Miguel Ceriani and Maria Costabile

University of Bari, via Orabona, 4, 70125 Bari, Italy

Abstract

Many data analysis activities exploit graphs to model complex relationships among data. Very often such relationships are better described using hypergraphs, whose edges can connect more than two nodes. Hypergraphs are suitable to model networks of business partners or co-authorship networks with multiple authors per article. This paper is about a technique that visualizes dynamic hypergraphs called PAOH (Parallel Aggregated ordered Hypergraph). It represents vertices as parallel horizontal bars and hyperedges as parallel vertical lines and shows the evolution of hypergraphs representing them in discrete Time Slots. PAOH is described in details in an article published in 2021 in IEEE Transaction on Visualization and Computer Graphics. It has been applied in several domains, such as ego-networks, co-authorship, as well as digital humanities, it is well-suited for medium-sized hypergraphs (50-500 vertices). PAOHVis is a tool, available online, that implements this technique. In this paper we briefly describe the tool and show the application of PAOH to the soccer domain, to support the analysis of players' contributions to the goals of a team.

Keywords

Data visualization, Network analysis, Sport

1. Introduction

A graph is a flexible data structure that is able to describe multifarious complex real world data and relationships. The visual representation of graphs is a challenging topic. By representing graphs as node-link diagrams there are several problems to face, in particular when the relationships involve more than two entities. An example is co-authorship networks, where relations are articles written by more than two authors. These kinds of networks can be more accurately modeled as hypergraphs where each relation may involve several nodes.

This paper illustrates a technique that visualizes dynamic hypergraphs, called PAOH (Parallel Aggregated ordered Hypergraph), which has been developed in the last few years. The article that describes all details of PAOH was first published online on August 2019, while its printed version appeared in January 2021 in IEEE Transaction on Visualization and Computer Graphics journal [1]. PAOH has been applied to various domains. An early version of the technique visualized co-authorships of EuroVis conferences from 2000 to 2015 [2]. An application to Digital Humanities visualized the business network of a 17th century French woman merchant [3]. An

SEBD 2021: The 29th Italian Symposium on Advanced Database Systems, September 5-9, 2021, Pizzo Calabro (VV), Italy

paolo.buono@uniba.it (P. Buono); paolo.buono@uniba.it (M. Ceriani); paolo.buono@uniba.it (M. Costabile)
http://ivu.di.uniba.it/people/buono.htm (P. Buono); http://ivu.di.uniba.it/people/ceriani.htm (M. Ceriani); http://ivu.di.uniba.it/people/costabile.htm (M. Costabile)
0000-0002-1421-3686 (P. Buono); 0000-0002-5074-2112 (M. Ceriani); 0000-0001-8554-0273 (M. Costabile)

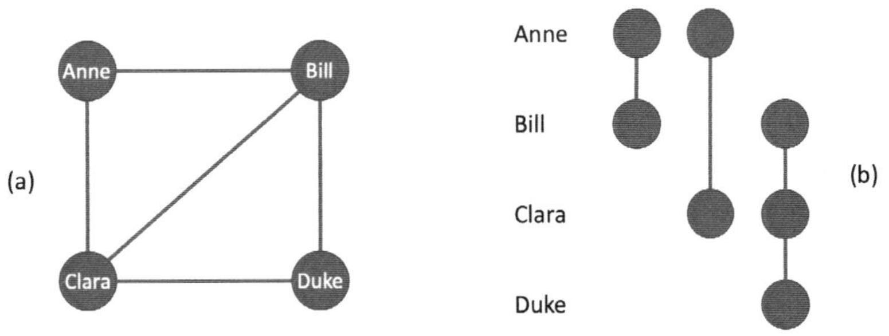

Figure 1: Co-authorships among four people shown with Node-Link and PAOH

extension of PAOH also considers ensemble clustering, analyzing a dataset related to authors' lineage in the VAST conference publication dataset [4].

A tool that implements this technique is called PAOHVis[1], and it is described in this paper; it is available online and its source code is open and maintained in a public repository[2]. After providing a simple example to illustrate the PAOH technique in Section 2, Section 3 describes some main features of PAOHVis using as case study the application of PAOH to the soccer domain, in order to support the analysis of players' contributions to the goals of a team. Section 4 provides conclusions and future works.

2. PAOH in short

PAOH was initially inspired by Biofabric [5], a technique that addresses the scalability of the hypergraph visualization but does not considers the network topology evolution over time, which in many cases is required. A technique that takes time into account is DyNetVis [6]; however, it considers time points instead of Time Slots as PAOH does, this do not allow to show different periods, which can be useful for the analysis. Another hypergraph visualization is Hyper-matrix [7]; in principle it is scalable but, when the number of nodes increases, the user loose details about the nodes. Even if there are other ways of visualizing hypergraphs, they are not scalable and thus they are not very significant (see for example [8]).

The PAOH technique is characterized by parallel hyperedges that are visualized along a time axis [1]. Vertices are ordered vertically according to a criterion. In order to give a simple example of the visualization, let us consider data about co-authorship. People are related if they are co-authors of a same publication. Since co-authors are often more than two, the usual node-link representation is not adequate. In Figure 1 (a), the authors are related because they share some publications, but it is not evident how many they share and which are the authors of each publication. Figure 1 (b) shows the PAOH visualization of the same co-authorship network. Each node is positioned vertically, in alphabetical order of the author name. All nodes involved in a co-authorship are connected by a vertical parallel line; this avoids edge crossing and well expresses the relationship that involve more than two people. It is evident that they

[1] https://www.aviz.fr/Research/Paohvis, last access: April 19th, 2021
[2] https://gitlab.inria.fr/aviz/paohvis

share three publications and who are the co-authors. The publications are visualized from left to right, chronologically.

Several definitions of dynamic graphs exist in the literature. The definition from the survey on dynamic graphs [9], is that a *dynamic graph* is a sequence of graphs $\{G_1, \cdots, G_n\} | G_i = (V, E_i), 1 \leq i \leq n$ sharing the same vertices but with a topology varying over time, in order to show how the relations evolve during time. A *hypergraph* G is a pair $G = (V, H)$, where V is the set of *vertices* and $H \subseteq \wp(V) \setminus \{\emptyset\}$ is the set of *hyperedges* (each hyperedge is a non-empty set of vertices). A *temporal hypergraph* is a sequence of hypergraphs $\{G_1, \cdots, G_n\} | G_i = (V, H_i), 1 \leq i \leq n$ that share the vertices and have the topology that varies over time. Each set of hyperedges H_i refers to a given Time Slot.

3. PAOHVis tool

In order to describe the PAOHVis tool that implements the PAOH technique, we refer to the soccer domain and more specifically, the challenge of visualizing discrete data about goal-leading shots and ball passes between players of the same soccer team. PAOH supports the study of the performance of players and teams in multiple contexts of varying granularity: multiple matches of the same team; all the teams and matches in a tournament; multiple tournaments at once. Soccer is today the most popular sport, with approximately 250 million players and 4 billion fans worldwide [10, 11]. As the concept of passes and scoring is common to many team sports, the described method is applicable to other team sports.

The dataset used for this application contains data from the first 26 weeks of the 2019-2020 season of the Italian Major league (Serie A)[3]. The data has been obtained by manual annotation from the *match highlights* video of each match, with the help of external sources for the players in the match. There are 20 teams in Serie A, 10 matches each week (each team plays once a week) during 26 weeks, for a total of 260 matches. In these matches 710 goals were scored and 353 players contributed at least a goal. The dataset also contains players' attributes: the team they are part of and their role in that team.

A *match phase* is composed of several passes among players of the same team, and is defined as a segment of a match in which a team keeps the possession of the ball. The phases of interest for this case study are those leading to successful scoring in the opponents' goal, called *goal-leading phases*. PAOH can be used also to show all phases of a match. To each phase, we associate information of the involved players and the match in which it happened. A phase is modeled as a hyperedge of a hypergraph and vertices are the players. In PAOHVis, all matches played in a week are grouped in a Time Slot, which is a hypergraph. The tournament is composed of the temporal sequence of all hypergraphs.

Figure 2 shows the user interface of PAOHVis. At the top of the app there is a green toolbar whose items refer to different sections of the tool; the orange item "View" is the one currently selected. At the center of the toolbar the name of the current dataset ("SerieA_1920_2.1.0-v2.4.json") is shown. The main area shows the dynamic hypergraphs. In Figure 2 players of two teams, i.e. Inter and Juventus, have been selected and shown ordered by the number of goal-leading phases they participated in. The players in the dataset can be filtered by team,

[3]Dataset available at: http://paovis.ddns.net/data/ItalianMajorLeague19-20.json, last visited: June 11th

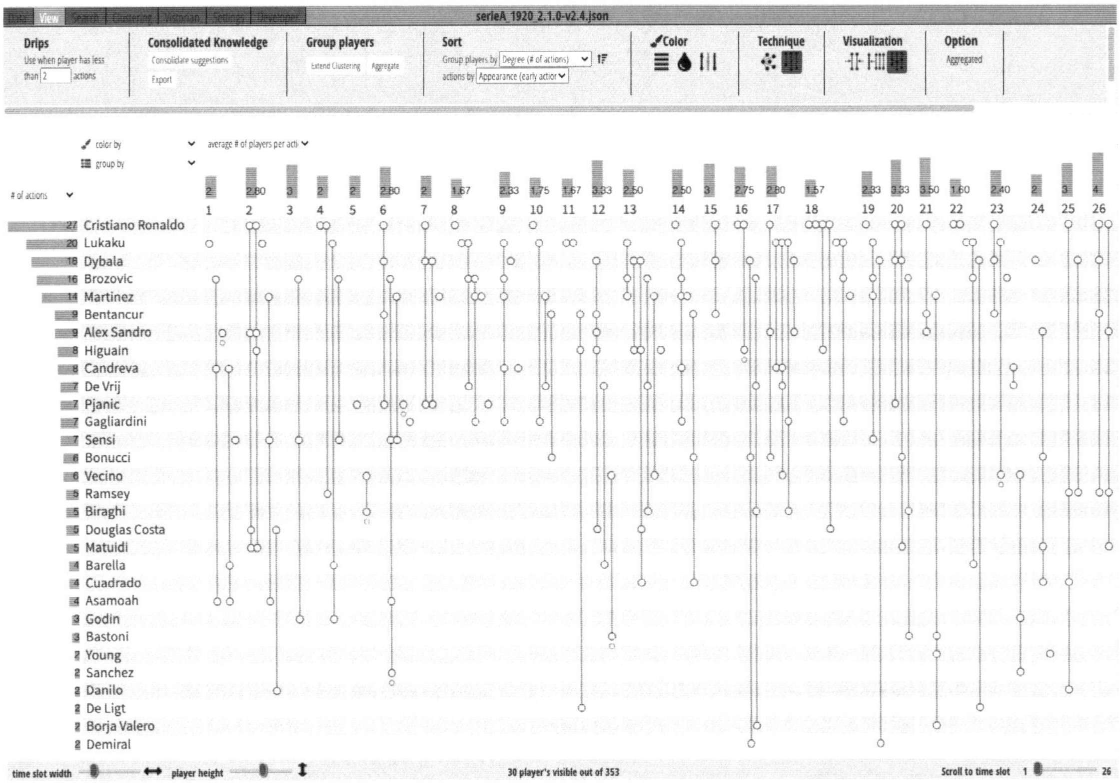

Figure 2: PAOHVis UI showing players of Inter and Juventus, two of the best teams in 2020 of "Serie A", the Major Italian league. The players are ordered by the number of goal-leading phases they participate.

player role, week. At the bottom of the user interface there are several controls through which the user can modify the visualized elements.

Among the several options *color by* and *group by* , visible on top left of the main area, revealed very useful. *color by* colors the vertices and their background while *group by* groups data according to a specific attribute selected by the user. For Example, the vertices in Figure 3 are colored by team and grouped by team. The updated screen now shows the attribute *team* chosen by the user. When the grouping is activated another column appears on the left of the players' names showing a label containing the group name.

Various sorting criteria are available, such as barycentric (the most connected players are vertically closer), degree (players are ordered vertically from the most to the less connected, as it is shown in Figure 2), group (players belonging to the same team appears together, as it is shown in Figure 3).

Figure 3 shows data about Inter and Juventus team. One player for each team has been highlighted by the user, respectively, Brozovic and Dybala. Both players did not participate much in goal-leading phases with the other principal attacker of the same team, respectively Lukaku and Cristiano Ronaldo. Indeed, Brozovic shares with Lukaku only 7 out of 20 goal-leading phases, similarly, Dybala shares only 7 out of 27 goal-leading phases. The two players are equivalent in terms of offensive capacity, both participated in a similar amount of goal-leading

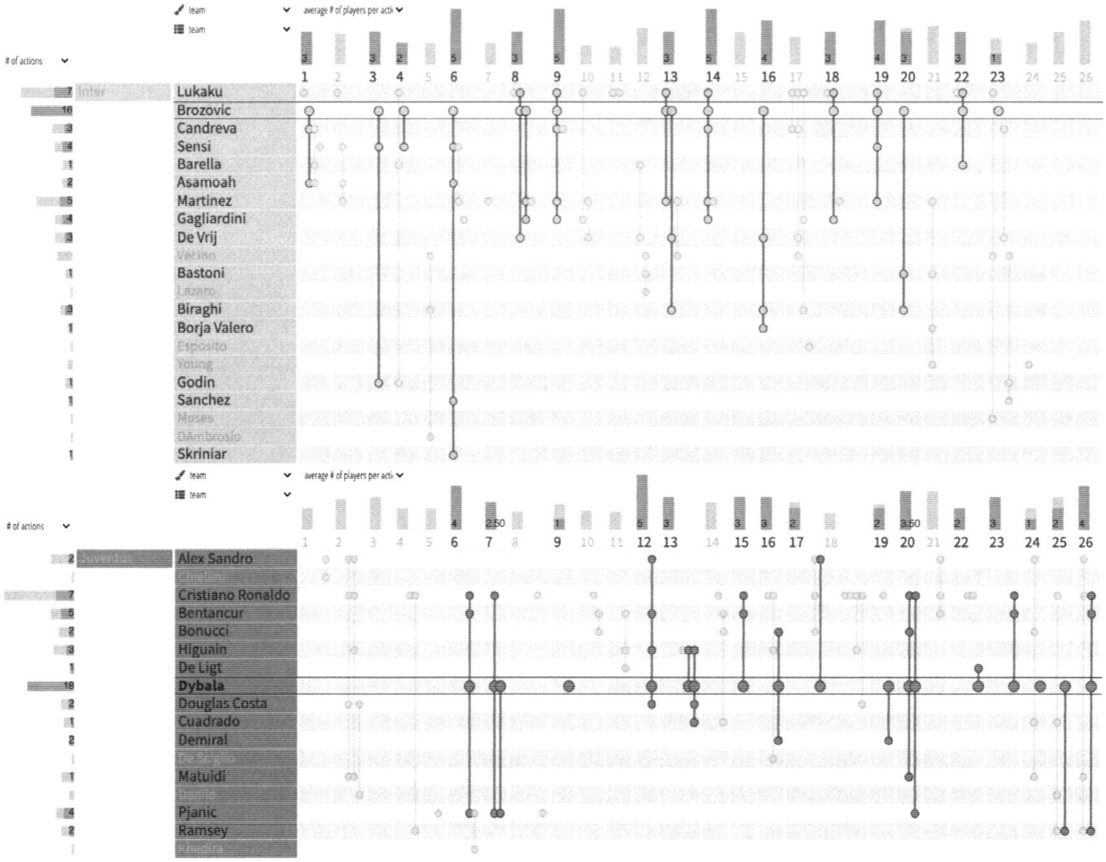

Figure 3: Comparison between two players of different teams: Brozovich (Inter) vs Dybala (Juventus).

phases (Brozovic 16 and Dybala 18) and both collaborated with most of their teammates. The single dots (one for Brozovic and two for Dybala) indicate free kicks. Grayed players never participate in goal-leading phases with the selected player. Brozovic does not pass the ball with 6 players (i.e. Vecino, Lazaro, Esposito, Young, Moses, D'Ambrosio), while Dybala with 4 players (i.e. Chiellini, De Sciglio, Danilo, Khedira). The total number of players participating in goal-leading phases is higher in the Inter team (21) than Juventus (17). This reveals that the Juventus attack uses globally fewer players that score more than Inter players. Finally, Brozovic is active until week 23, while Dybala plays since week 6 and intensifies his presence until the last week.

Figure 4 shows data of Hellas Verona team, which had three periods: week [1–9], the team scores low, week [10–23] the team is very active (Lazovic distinguished in most of the phases) and week [24–26] the team does not score at all. The horizontal histogram on the left (also visible in Figure 2 and Figure 3) reports the number of phases in which a player participated, while the histogram at the top reports, for each week, the number of players participating in goal-leading phases in the week.

PAOHVis offers also an aggregated view in which the representation is compacted by

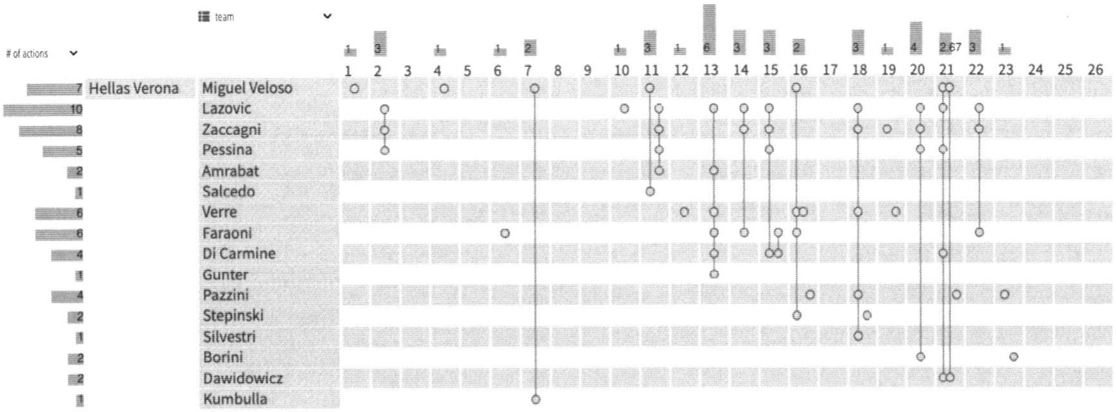

Figure 4: Goal-leading phases of Hellas Verona team. Three periods are visible: 1-9; 10-23; 24-26.

removing the horizontal constraint of weeks. This option leaves room for more data and it is useful when it is less important to know when a match occurs than to know who is involved in a goal-leading action. Figure 5 shows the aggregate view of Hellas Verona team. Three different moments of the interaction are reported, each has a different player highlighted: on the left, Miguel Veloso is highlighted; he participated in about a third of the goal-leading phases. In the middle and at the right Lazovic and Zaccagni are highlighted, respectively. These two players overlap a lot, which means they pass the ball a lot between them; on the contrary, Miguel Veloso is a more individualist player. More than a half of the players contributed to less than four goal-leading phases each. Such a group represent a third of the goal-leading phases, shown on the right of each of the three areas in Figure 5. Further information about the soccer domain and the use of PAOHVis in this domain is reported in [12].

PAOHVis offers many other features; we briefly described some of them. Time Slots are always displayed by their natural chronological order; however, within each Time Slot, the edges can be sorted differently. The edges can also be sorted according to their length. A packing algorithm optimizes the horizontal space by reorganizing hyperedges in each Time slot independently. It reuses the same horizontal position for hyperedges that do not overlap

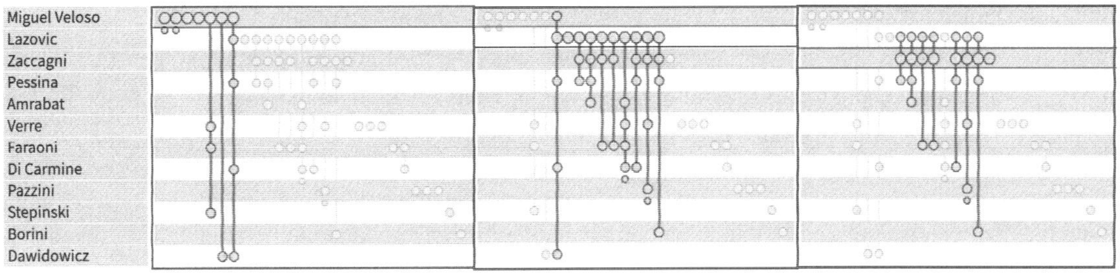

Figure 5: Aggregated view of Hellas Verona team. Each red box shows a player highlighted, from left to right: Veloso, Lazovic and Zaccagni

vertically. Optimizing packing is an NP-hard problem; PAOHVis uses the *first fit* bin packing approximation algorithm that inserts each edge in turn, from left to right, where it can fit without overlap [13] . The basic layout is monochrome so that the color can be used for specific needs. For example, the vertices background and the color of the dots can be used to indicate the vertices that belong to a category. Hovering over a hyperedge, similar hyperedges (those that share a similar set of vertices) are highlighted, in order to reveal recurrent relationships. Filtering helps reducing the size of the dataset. Double clicking on a vertex or searching a vertex name in the search box filters out all the vertices that are not connected to it. Faded dots reveal that visible vertices have relations with other vertices that have been filtered out. A specific filtering section has been added in the tool. It allows the user to apply various filters on attributes of the dataset.

4. Conclusions and future work

PAOH is a recent technique that is already appreciated in the InfoVis community. It is a unique tool that aims at helping people to analyze dynamic hypergraphs. It has successfully been adopted in several domains domains like the sport domain reported in this paper, in order to visualize goal-leading phases in soccer matches. As future work, the research will investigate how to improve the scalability of the PAOH technique. One direction is improving the clustering capabilities of PAOHVis to suggest aggregations and grouping similar teams or players. The challenge here is to find proper visualizations of the results and proper user interaction.

Acknowledgments

This work is partially supported by the Italian Ministry of University and Research, PON R&I 2014–2020 – Attraction and International Mobility (AIM) – project n. 1852414. The authors thank Alberto Rutigliano for his contribution in gathering the data analyzed in this article.

References

[1] P. Valdivia, P. Buono, C. Plaisant, N. Dufournaud, J.-D. Fekete, Analyzing dynamic hypergraphs with parallel aggregated ordered hypergraph visualization, IEEE TVCG 27 (2021) 1–13. doi:10.1109/TVCG.2019.2933196, date of publication: (Aug 2019).

[2] P. Valdivia, P. Buono, J.-D. Fekete, Hypenet: Visualizing dynamic hypergraphs, in: Proceedings of the Eurographics/IEEE VGTC Conference on Visualization: Posters, EuroVis '17, Eurographics Association, Goslar, DEU, 2017, p. 33–35. URL: https://doi.org/10.2312/eurp.20171162. doi:10.2312/eurp.20171162.

[3] P. Valdivia, P. Buono, C. Plaisant, N. Dufournaud, J.-D. Fekete, Using Dynamic Hypergraphs to Reveal the Evolution of the Business Network of a 17th Century French Woman Merchant, in: VIS 2018 - 3rd Workshop on Visualization for the Digital Humanities, Berlin, Germany, 2018. URL: https://hal.inria.fr/hal-01855675.

[4] A. Pister, P. Buono, J. D. Fekete, C. Plaisant, P. Valdivia, Integrating prior knowledge in mixed-initiative social network clustering, IEEE Transactions on Visualization and Computer Graphics 27 (2021) 1775–1785. doi:10.1109/TVCG.2020.3030347.
[5] W. J. Longabaugh, Combing the hairball with BioFabric: a new approach for visualization of large networks, BMC Bioinformatics 13 (2012) 275. URL: http://dx.doi.org/10.1186/1471-2105-13-275. doi:10.1186/1471-2105-13-275.
[6] C. D. G. Linhares, B. A. N. Travençolo, J. G. S. Paiva, L. E. C. Rocha, Dynetvis: A system for visualization of dynamic networks, in: Proceedings of the Symposium on Applied Computing, SAC '17, ACM, New York, NY, USA, 2017, pp. 187–194. URL: http://doi.acm.org/10.1145/3019612.3019686. doi:10.1145/3019612.3019686.
[7] M. T. Fischer, D. Arya, D. Streeb, D. Seebacher, D. A. Keim, M. Worring, Visual analytics for temporal hypergraph model exploration, IEEE Transactions on Visualization and Computer Graphics 27 (2021) 550–560. doi:10.1109/TVCG.2020.3030408.
[8] N. H. Riche, T. Dwyer, Untangling euler diagrams, IEEE Transactions on Visualization and Computer Graphics 16 (2010) 1090–1099. doi:10.1109/TVCG.2010.210.
[9] F. Beck, M. Burch, S. Diehl, D. Weiskopf, A Taxonomy and Survey of Dynamic Graph Visualization, Computer Graphics Forum 36 (2017) 133–159. URL: http://dx.doi.org/10.1111/cgf.12791. doi:10.1111/cgf.12791.
[10] F. I. de Football Association (FIFA), Fifa big count 2006: 270 million people active in football, ????. URL: https://resources.fifa.com/image/upload/big-count-estadisticas-520058.pdf?cloudid=mzid0qmguixkcmruvema.
[11] F. I. de Football Association (FIFA), 2018 fifa world cup russia - global broadcast and audience summary, ????. URL: https://resources.fifa.com/image/upload/2018-fifa-world-cup-russia-global-broadcast-and-audience-executive-summary.pdf?cloudid=njqsntrvdvqv8ho1dag5.
[12] B. Paolo, M. Ceriani, M. Costabile, P. Valdivia, Analyzing goal-leading actions in soccer with a visual tool, in: Proceedings of the 14th Biannual Conference of the Italian SIGCHI Chapter: Frontiers of HCI, CHItaly '21, accepted., 2021.
[13] E. G. Coffman, Jr., M. R. Garey, D. S. Johnson, Approximation Algorithms for Bin Packing: A Survey, in: D. S. Hochbaum (Ed.), Approximation Algorithms for NP-hard Problems, PWS Publishing Co., Boston, MA, USA, 1997, pp. 46–93. URL: http://dl.acm.org/citation.cfm?id=241938.241940.

A novel network-based methodology for analysis of COVID-19 data

Marianna Milano[1,2], Mario Cannataro[1,2]

[1]Department of Medical and Surgical Sciences, University of Catanzaro, Catanzaro, 88100, Italy
[2]Data Analytics Research Center, University of Catanzaro, Catanzaro, 88100, Italy

Abstract

The novel COVID-19 pandemic has posed unprecedented challenges to the society and the health sector all over the globe. Here, we present a new network-based methodology to analyze COVID-19 data measures and its application on a real dataset. The goal of the methodology is to analyze set of homogeneous datasets (i.e. COVID-19 data in several regions) using a statistical test to find similar/dissimilar dataset, mapping such similarity information on a graph and then using community detection algorithm to visualize and analyze the initial dataset. The methodology and its implementation as R function are publicly available at https://github.com/mmilano87/analyzeC19D. We evaluated diverse Italian COVID-19 data made publicly available by the Italian Protezione Civile Department at https://github.com/pcm-dpc/COVID-19/. We considered the data provided for each Italian region in two periods February 24-April 26, 2020 (1st wave), and September 28-November 29, 2020 (2nd wave) and then we compared two periods. Similarity matrices of Italian regions for ten COVID-19 data measures are built by using statistical analysis; then they are mapped to undirected networks. Each node represents an Italian region and an edge connects statistically similar regions. Finally, clusters of regions with similar behaviour were found using network-based community detection algorithms. Experiments depict the communities formed by Italian regions over time and the communities change with respect to the ten data measures and time.

Keywords

COVID-19, Network Analysis, Communities Detection

1. Introduction

The coronavirus (COVID-19) epidemic started in China, in November 2019 [1] and it has quickly spread in hundreds of countries in the world. COVID-19 disease is a viral infection produced by Sars-CoV-2, a new coronavirus [2]. The high transmissibility, the high level of infectivity [3] and an initial absence of a COVID-19 vaccine caused about a huge number of deceases. In March 2020, World Health Organization (WHO) declared COVID-19 as a serious epidemic. Thousands of cases of COVID-19 are recorded in Italy, and over 20,000 patients have died. In Italy, the first transmission of COVID-19 disease was reported on February, 2020. The outbreak of COVID-19 initiated in the Italian northern regions [4] and it spread rapidly in the rest of regions. Italy was seriously influenced by the epidemic with more than 3, 200, 000 infected and more than 115, 000 deaths that recorded at the end of April, 2021.

SEBD 2021: The 29th Italian Symposium on Advanced Database Systems, September 5-9, 2021, Pizzo Calabro (VV), Italy
m.milano@unicz.it (M. Milano); cannataro@unicz.it (M. Cannataro)
0000-0003-1561-725X (M. Milano); 0000-0003-1502-2387 (M. Cannataro)

In this work, we analyze the spread of the disease over time at a regional level by underlining difference among them. To this aim, in [5], we implemented a new methodology that is able to depict COVID-19 data as networks and to apply graph-based methods in order to evidence regions with similar behaviour along the time. In this work, we analyzed the evolution of the communities by considering a longer interval of time with the goal to highlight original clusters of regions with respect to COVID-19 data. We analyze the data released every day from the Italian Civil Protection. At first, we focus on the data provided on the period February 24-April 26, 2020. Then, we point out the period from September 28 to November 29, 2020. In detail, for each region, we considered ten daily provided data (e.g. total cases, deceased, see the rest of measures below) with the aim of assessing the behaviour of Italian regions respect to COVID-19 and highlighting which regions exhibit similar behaviour. To do this, we defined a new methodology to analyze those data, that comprises the four steps: i) Application of statistical test to identify the regions that present similar/dissimilar behaviour respect to COVID-19; ii) Building of similarity matrices; iii) Mapping of matrix of similarity into network whose each node is an Italian region and each edge depicts similarity connections; iv) Identification of communities by applying community detection algorithms.

The fundamental contribution of the paper consists of a new methodology that is able to depict COVID-19 data as networks and to apply graph-based methods in order to evidence regions with similar behaviour. The analysis enables to remarkably present the development of the communities over time, how the communities growth due to joining of regions or the communities reduce due to leaving of regions. This ensures to evaluate the changes of community coherence in relation to different data. The paper is designed as follows: Section 1 discusses the background on community detection on the network, Section 2 introduces the new methodology for network-based analysis, Section 3 discusses the use of our methodology on Italian COVID-19 data, Section 4 concludes the paper.

2. Methodology

We developed a new methodology for network-based analysis, where the input data are a collection of homogeneous measures (e.g. COVID-19 data in similar regions). The analysis pipeline consists of four steps:

1. **Definition of the similarity matrix.** In the first step the identification of similarity benchmark for the analyzed data is performed. Once similarity measure is applied to data, a similarity matrix is built. Let matrix M for dataset k, each (i, j) element represents a value obtained by performing a similarity measure.
   Given an input dataset $D_1 ... D_n$, where each D_i may contain one or more measured data $di_1^K ... di_n^K$, with 1...k time series. The similarity matrix for data $K = d_{ij}^K$ over a time period T is a matrix M where the value $M(i, j)$ is the similarity among the dataset D_i and the dataset D_i i.e. among $\{di_1^K ... di_n^K\}$ and $\{dj_1^K ... dj_n^K\}$; $(i, j) = 1 ... N$. In this work, the dataset i means the Region i.
2. **Converting similarity matrix to network**. In the second step the building of a similarity network is performed. According to the similarity matrix, a similarity threshold is fixed. Then, each similarity matrix $M(i, j)$ is mapped to a network N, whose nodes are

the Italian regions and the edges connect them when the similarity value among two regions (i,j), resulting in the matrix, exceeds the similarity threshold. Edges are weighted according to the similarity values. The lengths of the edges result inversely proportional to similarity values.

3. **Network analysis over time.** In the third step the building of the network at different time intervals is performed. Starting from consideration that the COVID-19 data present a temporal evolution, for each one, the corresponding networks at diverse time intervals and for an observation period are built. Furthermore, this step enables the visualization of the networks changes at different time.
4. **Community detection.** In the last step the extraction of the communities on the built networks is performed. The choice of an appropriate community detection algorithm is important to achieve the best results. Thus, an algorithm for community detection is applied to identify communities, i.e. groups of regions sharing similarity, on the networks related to different time intervals and for an observation period. Finally, this step enables the visualization of the community at different time changes.

Figure 1 shows the pipeline of methodology.

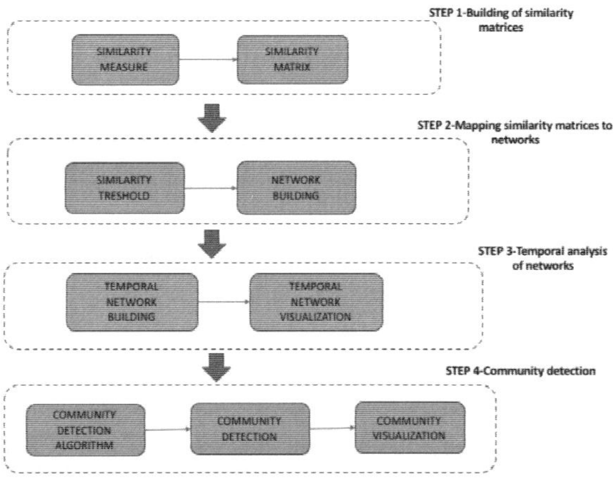

Figure 1: Methodology pipeline

3. Results

Our methodology presents a general design, for which it can be applied to analyze different types of data. In this work, we apply our methodology to analyze Italian COVID-19 dataset. We implement our algorithm using R software [6]. The algorithm is available at https://github.com/mmilano87/analyzeC19D. We chose igraph libraries [7] to perform the network analysis.

3.1. DataSet

We performed the analysis on COVID-19 dataset, released daily by the Italian Civil Protection at https://github.com/pcm-dpc/COVID-19 database. The overall database contains a dataset for each day, starting from February 24, 2020 and for each Italian region. The regions are: Abruzzo, Basilicata, Calabria, Campania, Emilia, Friuli, Lazio, Liguria, Lombardia, Marche, Molise, Piemonte, Puglia, Sardegna, Sicilia, Toscana, Umbria, Valle d'Aosta, Veneto, plus the autonomous provinces of Bolzano and Trento, for a total of 21 regions. The dataset of Regions in a time point (day) contains the following measurements:

- Hospitalised with Symptoms, relating to the count of COVID-19 patients in the hospital;
- Intensive Care, relating to the count of COVID-19 patients in Intensive Care Units;
- Total Hospitalised, relating to the sum of Hospitalised with Symptoms and Intensive Care measured;
- Home Isolation, relating to the count of subjects in quarantine at home;
- Total Currently Positive, relating to the count of COVID-19 positive subjects;
- New Currently Positive, relating to the daily count of COVID-19 positive subjects;
- Discharged/ Healed, relating to the count of healed or discharged from hospital subjects;
- Deceased, relating to the count of deaths;
- Total Cases, relating to the count of subjects affected by COVID-19;
- Swabs, relating to the count of test swab carried on COVID-19 positive subjects and on suspected COVID-19 positivity subjects.

The data have not been normalized with respect the number of people in a region.

The data occupies 169 Mbytes of memory.

3.2. Building of similarity matrices

We started to build the similarity matrices of each COVID-19 collected data. At first we focus on COVID-19 data related to the February 24-April 26, 2020 period.

Then, we analyze the COVID-19 data related to the September 29-November 24, 2020 period (that, for convenience, we called second observation period).

Initially, we used Pearson's chi-square test to evaluate the distribution of each type of data.

Since *p-value* resulted less than 0.05, we chose to applied non-parametric test for for subsequent analysis.

So, we recurred to the use of the Wilcoxon Sum Rank test to analyze the same type of data on the observation period, consisting of nine weeks and then, for single time intervals. The Wilcoxon test enables to assess the difference among to conditions when the samples are correlated. Thus, we used the Wilcoxon test to compare the Italian regions with the aim to evidence statistically similar distributions among them. After that, we constructed ten similarity matrices for all COVID-19 data and for each time interval, that report the statistical comparison among a couple of regions.

In detail, the (i,j) value of the matrix, related to data k (for example deceased data), describes the *p-value* of the Wilcoxon test achieved by applying the test on a given measure (e.g. the number of deceased) of the region i versus the region j in a given time interval. Lower *p-value* implies that two regions are different according to that measure. Otherwise, higher *p-value* implies that regions show a similarity according to that measure. We considered the conventional significance threshold of 0.05, and for this reason we built similarity matrices that contain only $p - values >= 0.05$. We mapped the $p - values < 0.05$ equal to zero. So, we considered the *p-value* as a measure of similarity.

3.3. Mapping similarity matrices to networks: Network building

We mapped each similarity matrix M(i,j) into a network N [8]. The nodes are the Italian regions, and the edges link two regions (i,j) when the *p-value* is greater than the threshold, otherwise (p-value < 0.05) none edge is added. Each edges is weighted according to *p-value* resulting from Wilcoxon test. In this way, the edge length results inversely proportional to similarity.

3.4. Network Visualization over time

We performed a temporal analysis by building ten networks related to the data measures (Hospitalised with Symptoms, Intensive Care data, Total Hospitalised, Home Isolation, Total Currently Positive, New Currently Positive, Discharged/ Healed, Deceased, Total Cases, Swab) by considering the period February 24 to April 26 (the observation period) and then, by building the networks of the same data at different time intervals. After that, we built the networks related to the second observation period and single weeks.

3.5. Temporal evolution of Communities

For each network related to different time intervals, our goal was the identification of regions that construct a community according to their similarity. For this aim, we used Walktrap community finding algorithm [9]. Walktrap is able to identify subgraphs with high density, i.e. communities, in a network through random walks. We selected Walktrap community detection algorithm because it outperforms other methods as discussed in [10]. For example, Figure 2 represents the evolution of Deceased Network Communities in the first observation period and Figure 3 the evolution the second observation period.

The results show that diverse data show dissimilar communities. In fact, each network related to different Italian COVID-19 data presents different detected communities. Furthermore, the results highlight that communities formed by regions evolves according to the diverse data. In particular, the different community structure grow due to joining of regions or the communities reduces due to leaving of regions. This enables to evaluate the changes of community according to to different data [5].

Figure 2 (a) presents the mined communities of Deceased Network at the end of the first week. The detected communities consist of: a considerable community formed by Emilia, Piemonte, Liguria, Campania, Abruzzo, Puglia, Valle d'Aosta, Umbria, Calabria, Sicilia, Campania, Trento, Lazio, Sardegna, Bolzano, Basilicata and Molise, Friuli; a single community formed by Lombardia: a single community represented by Veneto; and a single community consisting of Marche and Toscana.

By considering the networks built in the second observation period it is possible to note that the topology evolves from a sparse to a dense structure and this reflects on the discovered communities. For example, in Deceased Network, each region forms single community in single week and after three weeks, whereas, after five weeks, three communities are composed by two regions (Figure 3 (c)): (i) Marche and Lazio, (ii) Campania and Abruzzo, (iii) Sicilia and Friuli. After seven weeks (Figure 3 (d)), the Italian regions form single communities with the exception of three communities formed respectively by Umbria and Calabria, Campania and Abruzzo, Lazio and Marche and a community formed by three regions, Friuli, Sicilia, Trento.

4. Conclusion and Future Work

In conclusion, the aim of this work is to provide a network-based representation of the COVID-19 measures in order to evaluate the region behaviour on the basis of different data provided by Civil Protection. For this, we detected similar region related to COVID-19 data, and we mapped them in different networks. Then, we conducted a network-based analysis to identified communities of regions with similar behaviour. The present methodology is general and can be applied to the connection of data varying over time. Currently, the new methodology is available as R function. As future work, we plan to implement the methodology as an R package.

References

[1] Z. Wu, J. M. McGoogan, Characteristics of and important lessons from the coronavirus disease 2019 (covid-19) outbreak in china: summary of a report of 72 314 cases from the chinese center for disease control and prevention, Jama (2020).

[2] N. Zhu, D. Zhang, W. Wang, X. Li, B. Yang, J. Song, X. Zhao, B. Huang, W. Shi, R. Lu, et al., A novel coronavirus from patients with pneumonia in china, 2019, New England Journal of Medicine (2020).

[3] C. Huang, Y. Wang, X. Li, L. Ren, J. Zhao, Y. Hu, L. Zhang, G. Fan, J. Xu, X. Gu, et al., Clinical features of patients infected with 2019 novel coronavirus in wuhan, china, The Lancet 395 (2020) 497–506.

[4] A. Lai, A. Bergna, C. Acciarri, M. Galli, G. Zehender, Early phylogenetic estimate of the effective reproduction number of sars-cov-2, Journal of medical virology (2020).

[5] M. Milano, M. Cannataro, Statistical and network-based analysis of italian covid-19 data: Communities detection and temporal evolution, International journal of environmental research and public health 17 (2020) 4182.

[6] M. Milano, Computing languages for bioinformatics: R, Gribskov, M., Nakai, K. and Schonbach, C. (eds.), Encyclopedia of Bioinformatics and Computational Biology,Elsevier, Oxford: Elsevier. 1 (2019) 889–895.

[7] G. Csardi, T. Nepusz, et al., The igraph software package for complex network research, InterJournal, complex systems 1695 (2006) 1–9.

[8] G. Agapito, P. H. Guzzi, M. Cannataro, Challenges and opportunities for visualization and analysis of graph-modeled medical data, 2017. URL: https://doi.org/10.20944/preprints201710.0018.v1. doi:10.20944/preprints201710.0018.v1.

[9] P. Pons, M. Latapy, Computing communities in large networks using random walks, in: International symposium on computer and information sciences, Springer, 2005, pp. 284–293.

[10] F. B. de Sousa, L. Zhao, Evaluating and comparing the igraph community detection algorithms, in: 2014 Brazilian Conference on Intelligent Systems, IEEE, 2014, pp. 408–413.

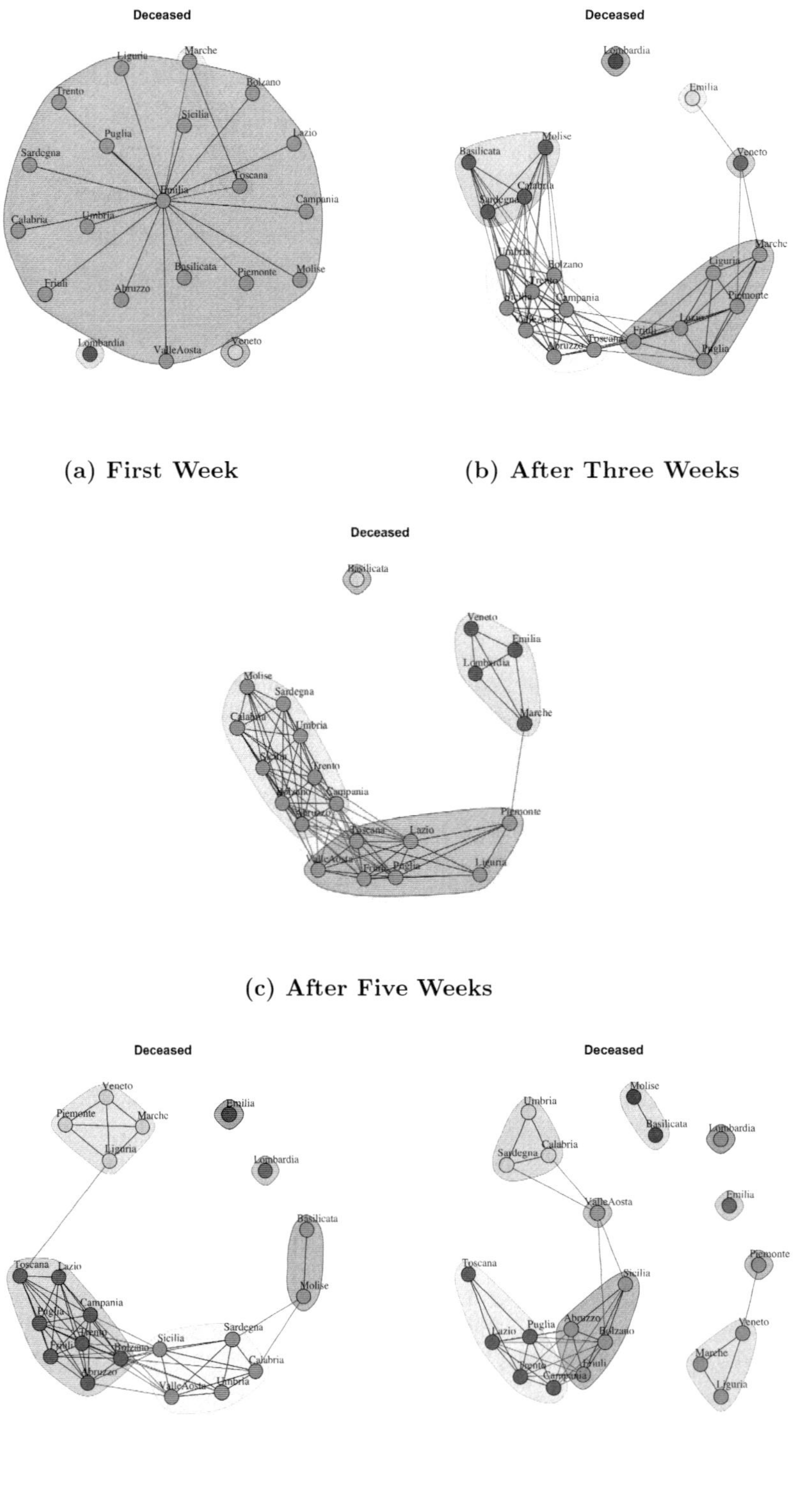

(a) First Week (b) After Three Weeks

(c) After Five Weeks

(d) After Seven Weeks (e) After Nine Weeks

Fig. 2. Evolution of Deceased Network Communities in the first observation period.

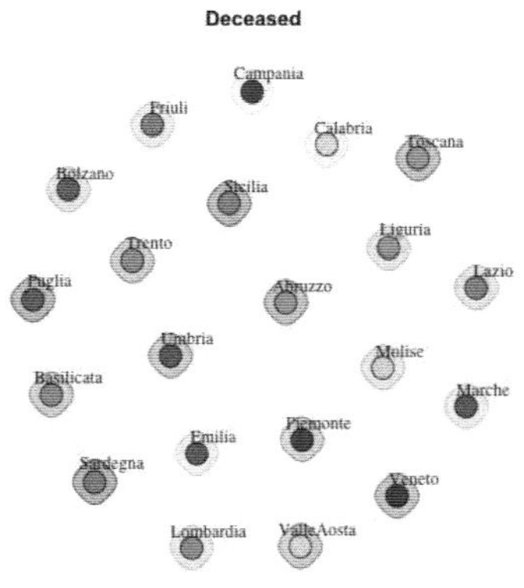

(a) First Week

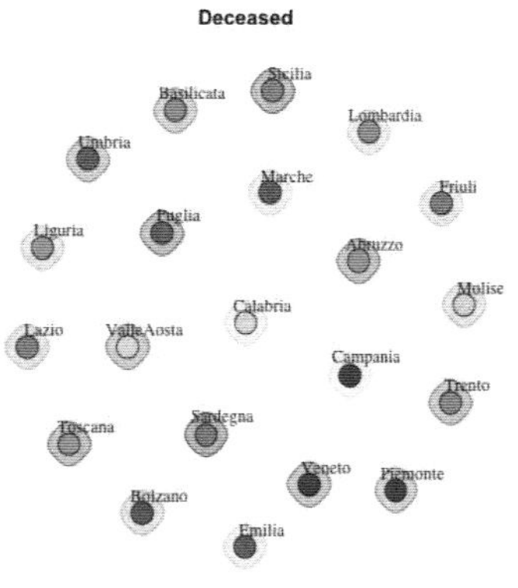

(b) After Three Weeks

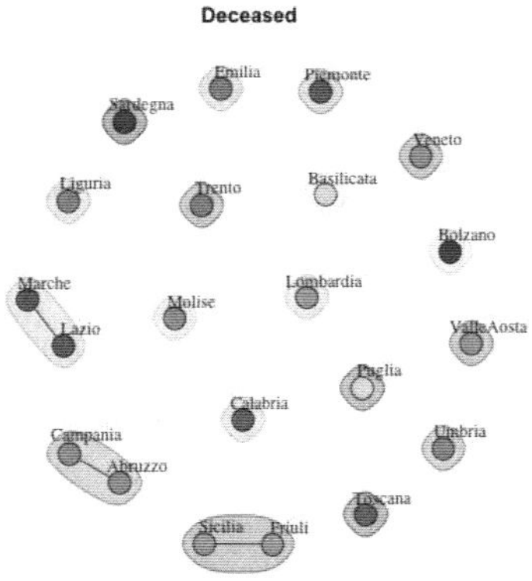

(c) After Five Weeks

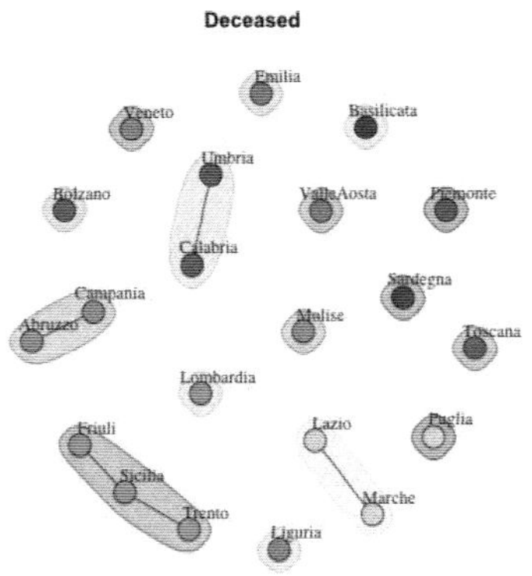

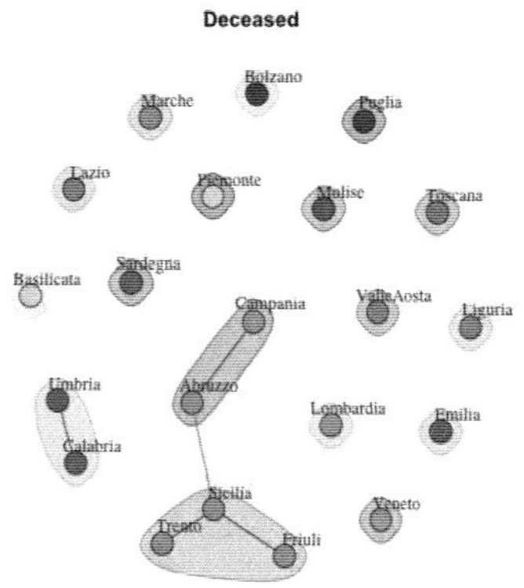

(d)After Seven Weeks (e)After Nine Weeks

Fig. 3. Evolution of Deceased Network Communities in the second observation period.

A collaborative Tool to Support Junior Developers in Secure Software Development

Maria Teresa Baldassarre[1], Vita Santa Barletta[1], Danilo Caivano[1], Giovanni Dimauro[1] and Antonio Piccinno[1]

[1] *University of Bari Aldo Moro, Via Orabona 4, 70125, Bari, Italy*

Abstract

In today's innovation and transformation scenarios, such as smart cities that transversally invest many technological fields and sectors of intervention, the security factor plays a primary role in software development projects. Currently, existing methodologies support developers only in the early stages of the software development life cycle (SDLC) and not in all of them. Therefore, it is necessary to provide operational guidelines in order to integrate privacy requirements and, consequently security, in software applications. Taking into account these needs, the research work presents a tool that supports team decisions to integrate privacy and security requirements in all software development phases regardless of the development methodology adopted.

Keywords

Privacy by Design, Human-Centered Privacy, Privacy Software Application

1. Introduction

Nowadays, organizations are undertaking increasingly complex projects in globalized, uncertain and dynamic environments [1]. Some of the factors that increase or generate project complexity are the emergence of new technologies [2], the growing sophistication of software project scopes characterized by challenging technical, time and cost requirements [3] and the increasing number of stakeholders involved [4]. Thus, to assure a successful software project [5], it is particularly important to stress concepts such as data and information security in all phases of the software development life cycle (SDLC) [6]. Software errors can be introduced by disconnections and miscommunications during planning, development, testing and maintenance of the components [7].

So, in order to satisfy security requirements, it becomes necessary to identify the key elements associated to the privacy and security-oriented software development, and to support decision making in all phases of the software life cycle.

Accordingly, this paper presents the key elements for privacy-oriented software development formalized in a knowledge base and a collaborative tool that integrates these elements. The tool supports decision making in all the software development lifecycle phases in order to integrate privacy and security requirements.

The paper is organized as follows. Section 2 discusses related works. Section 3 describes the tool and Section 4 reports the evaluation of collaborative tool and the obtained results. Finally, conclusions are given in Section 5.

SEBD 2021: The 29th Italian Symposium on Advanced Database Systems, September 5-9, 2021, Pizzo Calabro (VV), Italy
EMAIL: mariateresa.baldassarre@uniba.it (A. 1); vita.barletta@uniba.it (A. 2); danilo.caivano@uniba.it (A. 3); giovanni.dimauro@uniba.it (A. 4); antonio.piccinno@uniba.it (A. 5)
ORCID: 0000-0001-8589-2850 (A. 1); 0000-0002-0163-6786 (A. 2); 0000-0001-5719-7447 (A. 3); 0000-0002-4120-5876 (A. 4); 0000-0003-1561-7073 (A. 5)

2. Related Works

Software development requires integration of security and privacy to address threats related to cyber-attack [8]. So, for secure software development, it is particularly important to stress concepts such as data and information security in project activities which deal with or target aspects such as integrity, availability, and confidentiality [9,10]. This imposes, see for example the provisions on the subject dictated by the GDPR, "General Data Protection Regulation" [11], the adoption of processes and tools to mitigate the risks related to security and data privacy.

Privacy by Design [12] is a fundamental concept for software development as it requires data protection and the implementation of technical and organizational measures to protect the rights of users [13]. Confidentiality, integrity, availability, unlikability, transparency and intervenability are considered the six protection goals that provide a common scheme for addressing the legal, technical, economic and social dimension of privacy and data protection in complex IT systems [14].

The methodologies include two categories, *Security-based adaptations*, i.e., Privacy Engineering methodologies that are based and originated from security engineering methodologies, and *Privacy-Friendly systems* that aim to embed privacy into every step of the software development life cycle [15]. Therefore, a number of privacy requirements methodologies have been introduced in order to assist system designers and developers to analyze and elicit privacy requirements for different software systems and in different architectures [16].

LINDDUN [17] is a privacy threat modeling methodology that supports analysts in systematically eliciting and mitigating privacy threats in software architectures. The identified privacy threats are mapped with the existing privacy-enhancing technologies (PETs) [18]. PriS methods describes the effect of privacy requirements on business processes and facilitate the identification of the system architecture that best supports the privacy-related business processes [19]. SQUARE [20] security quality requirements engineering methodology supports the elicitation of privacy requirements at the early stages of software life cycle. It consists of nine steps which include what techniques will be used to elicit security requirements then categorize, prioritize, and inspect the requirements. STRAP [21] is a light-weight structured analysis of privacy vulnerabilities into the software development cycle. RBAC [22] method considers privacy requirements as constraints on permissions and user roles in order to define access control policies. PRIPARE introduces how privacy requirements should be incorporated into the software development life cycle [23].

Reviewing each of these methodologies, privacy requirements are addressed during the first phases of the SDLC, but never in all the phases. Therefore, it is necessary to integrate privacy in all phases of the development. Considering this need, the research work presents a tool to support the development team in all phases of the SDLC.

3. Collaborative Tool Proposal

Starting from the work illustrated in [24], the tool has been improved to overcome the limitations highlighted in the first experiment. It integrates the formalization of the privacy key elements in order to support decisions and choices in all phases of the software development (Figure 1). The five elements identified are Privacy by Design Principles, Privacy Design Strategies, Privacy Patterns, Vulnerabilities and Context.

Privacy by Design Principles [12] that describe the privacy model, each of which specify actions and responsibilities:

1. anticipate and prevent privacy-invasive events before they happen (*Proactive not Reactive*);
2. build privacy measures directly into any given ICT system or business practice by default (*Privacy as the Default*);
3. embed privacy into the design and architecture (*Privacy Embedded in to Design*);
4. accommodate all legitimate interests and objectives in a positive-sum manner, not through a zero-sum approach involving unnecessary trade-offs (*Full Functionality*);
5. ensure secure life-cycle management of information (*End-to-End Lifecycle Protection*);

6. keep component parts of systems and operations of business practices visible and transparent, to user and providers alike (*Visibility and Transparency*);
7. respect and protect interests of the individual, above all (*Respect for User Privacy*).

Privacy Design Strategies [25] that help IT architects to support Privacy by Design early in the software development life cycle. They are divided in two different categories:

- Data-Oriented Strategies focus on the privacy-friendly processing of the data (*Minimize, Hide, Separate, Abstract*).
- Process-Oriented Strategies focus on the process surrounding the responsible handling of personal data (*Inform, Control, Enforce, Demonstrate*).

Privacy Pattern [26] that underline the concept of pattern and can be used in all those situations where privacy is violated, and a user's personal data is no longer secure. Patterns are a literary format with which to capture the knowledge and experience of security experts, resulting in a structured document in the form of a template to which the security experts' knowledge is transferred [27,28].

Vulnerabilities within the code allow a malicious user to attack the application [7].

Context, that integrates *Architectural Requirements* to determine the flow of data within the system, components, roles and responsibilities; *Use Cases and Scenarios* to define all interactions within the system and protect the data from unauthorized reading and manipulation; and *Privacy Enhancing Technologies* (PETs) to protect the personal information handled by the applications.

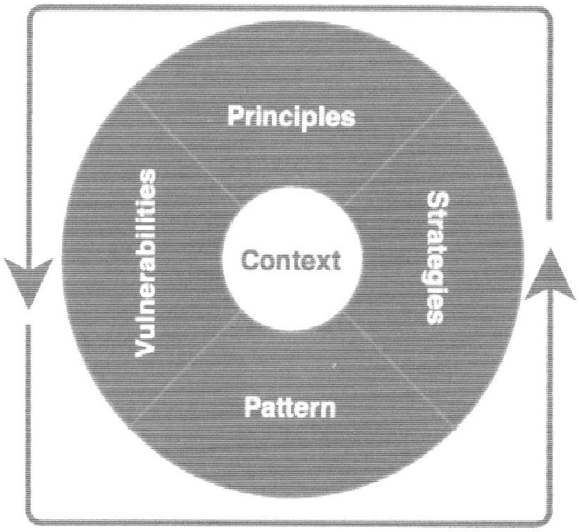

Figure 1: Privacy Knowledge Base: Key Elements

The collaborative tool supports the team's choices in all the software development phases in order to integrate security and privacy. At each stage of the SDLC, knowledge and skills are required to be able to develop a product that respects the principles of privacy and security by design. But many times, within the team certain knowledge are not present, such as knowing step by step the basic points of the GDPR [11] in order to provide a software product that is compliant. In order to overcome this limitation and provide operational guidelines to the development team, the tool allows you to select the necessary elements to be able to introduce privacy and security requirements throughout the software lifecycle. For example, starting from the vulnerabilities identified in the static code analysis the developer in addition to viewing a brief description of the vulnerability and an example, can also look at the privacy by design principles violated and view the privacy patterns that allow to mitigate the vulnerability and implement privacy strategies to correct the architectural flaws.

In Figure 2 are reported that OWASP Top 10 – 2017 [29], and the detail of Sensitive Data Exposure vulnerability. In addition, for each pattern identified for a particular vulnerability, it is shown how to implement it within a particular architecture chosen by the developer and on which he is working. If, for example, a privacy pattern or any other element of the knowledge base is not present, the team has the possibility to insert it in order to extend it. Figure 3 shows the addition of a pattern where it requires the title, which privacy strategy it implements, the context, the problem, the solution, the UML diagram, the vulnerability it mitigates, and the architecture.

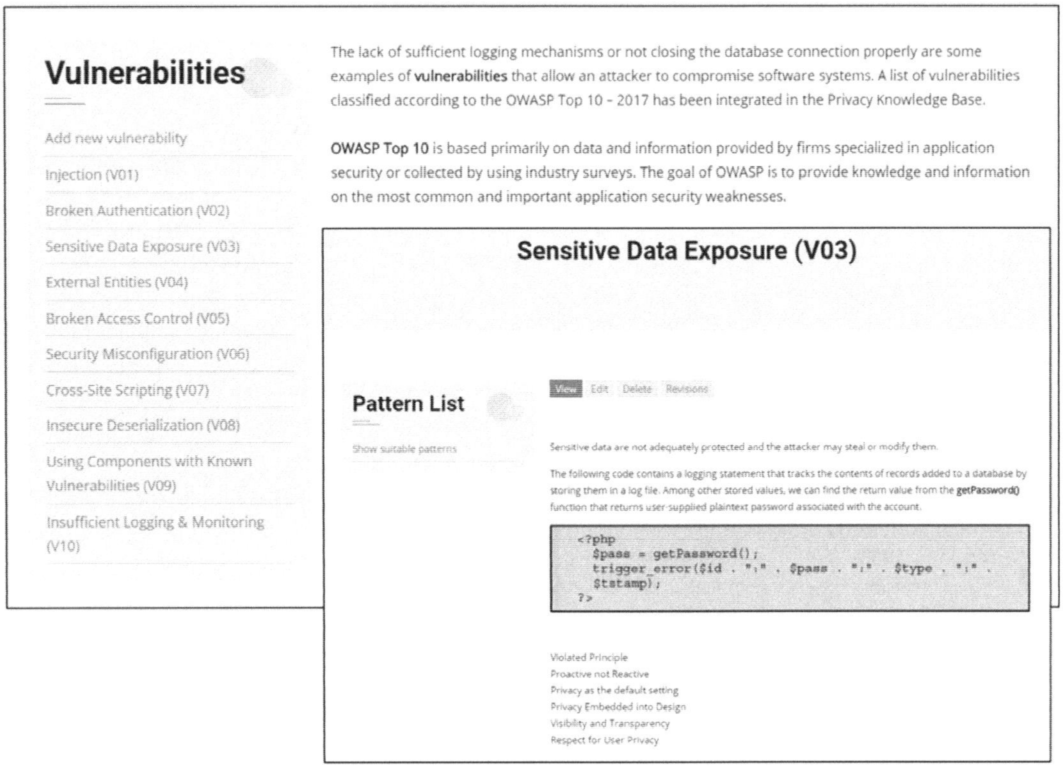

Figure 2: Vulnerabilities in Privacy Knowledge Base

Figure 3: Privacy Patterns in Privacy Knowledge Base

4. Evaluation

To evaluate the potential benefits of the tool in order to integrate privacy and security in software, we conducted a pilot experiment with 8 bachelor students in computer science, software engineering curriculum.

The students have taken the traditional software engineering course and have no expertise in both software development and in applying privacy oriented methodologies. The average is 22 years old. They were divided into 2 groups and asked to re-engineer a system developed by their colleagues in previous years during the software engineering course.

The system called "Civic Sense" allows a citizen to report failures, problems, malfunctions and, in general, events relevant to an entity that provides services or manages infrastructure of public interest (electricity, roads and streets, urban safety, etc.).

As in the previous study in which we involved junior developers [24], the tasks assigned to the two groups are the following:

- *Task 1*: Identify the principles of Privacy by Design violated by vulnerability.
- *Task 2*: Identify the Privacy Design Strategies to be implemented in the system to respect the principles of Privacy by Design.
- *Task 3*: Identify the privacy patterns that substantiate the Privacy Design Strategies.
- *Task 4*: Identify the Data Strategies Component to implement in Target Architecture in order to re-engineer the system from a privacy point of view.
- *Task 5*: Identify the Processes Component Strategies to implement in Target Architecture in order to re-engineer the system from a privacy point of view.

In order to perform the required tasks, each group was provided with a security report containing the list of vulnerabilities identified during the static code analysis of the system (Issue ID, Category, Severity, Short Description). The following is an example of the *Privacy Violation* category.

Abstract: The file loginn.php mishandles confidential information on line 12, which can compromise user privacy and is often illegal.

Explanation: Privacy violations occur when:

1. Private user information enters the program.
2. The data is written to an external location, such as the console, file system, or network.

Example: The following code contains a logging statement that tracks the contents of records added to a database by storing them in a log file. Among other values that are stored is the return value from the getPassword() function that returns user-supplied plaintext password associated with the account.

```
<?php
$pass = getPassword();
trigger_error($id . ":" . $pass . ":" . $type . ":" . $tstamp); ?>
```

The code in the example above logs a plaintext password to the application eventlog. Although many developers trust the eventlog as a safe storage location for data, it should not be trusted implicitly, particularly when privacy is a concern.

Private data can enter a program in a variety of ways:

- Directly from the user in the form of a password or personal information - Accessed from a database or other data store by the application
- Indirectly from a partner or other third party

Sometimes data that is not labeled as private can have a privacy implication in a different context. For example, student identification numbers are usually not considered private because there is no explicit and publicly-available mapping to an individual student's personal information. However, if a school generates identification numbers based on student social security numbers, then the identification numbers should be considered private.

Security and privacy concerns often seem to compete with each other. From a security perspective, you should record all important operations so that any anomalous activity can later be identified. However, when private data is involved, this practice can create risk.

Then, starting from the security report, the students carried out each task in order. Each task was done in different sessions, one for each task, and each session was done in parallel. This was done to prevent the two groups from communicating with each other and knowing in advance the task to be performed. In addition, each group was observed by a researcher.

Keeping in mind that the research goal is to support the development team in all phases of the security and privacy oriented software lifecycle, we did not set out to investigate the developers' productivity. The focus was to observe the interaction with the tool to operationally implement guidelines in privacy-oriented software development and collect information to improve the tool.

Table 1 and Table 2 present the results obtained using the tool in re-engineering Civic Sense.

All tasks were done correctly although Task 4 of Group A was not accomplish by the time limit. In each session, it was critical to observe task execution to understand user behavior in being able to retrieve the information needed in reengineering the system.

The students' feedback was positive in being able to use a single tool that would allow them to view all the information needed to integrate privacy and security requirements operatively. Figure 4 shows an example of the architecture with the identification of privacy patterns that implement the privacy design strategies.

And this was confirmed by the SUS [30] [31] questionnaire conducted after at the end of the five sessions and the execution of the various tasks. The SUS score obtained was 89,9.

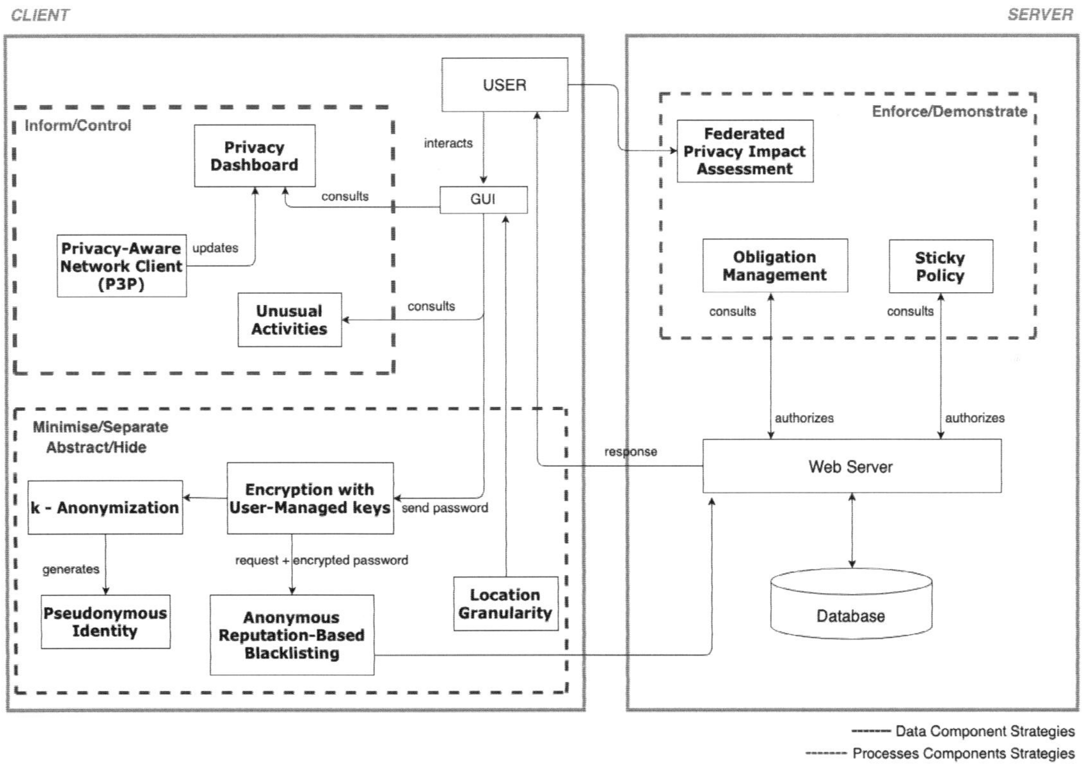

Figure 4: Target Architecture Result

Table 1
Task Results Group A

Task	Goal	Time limit	Time spent
Task 1	PbD violated	0h 30m	0h 21m
Task 2	Privacy Design Strategies to be implemented	0h 30m	0h 27m
Task 3	Privacy Patterns	1h 0m	0h 58m
Task 4	Data Component Strategies	1h 30m	**1h 33m**
Task 5	Process Component Strategies	1h 30m	1h 29m

Table 2
Task Results Group B

Task	Goal	Time limit	Time spent
Task 1	PbD violated	0h 30m	0h 29m
Task 2	Privacy Design Strategies to be implemented	0h 30m	0h 26m
Task 3	Privacy Patterns	1h 0m	0h 57m
Task 4	Data Component Strategies	1h 30m	1h 29m
Task 5	Process Component Strategies	1h 30m	1h 28m

5. Conclusions

In this research work, we analyzed the potential benefits of a collaborative tool that supports developers in order to integrate privacy and security in software development. The tool integrates the key elements identified in privacy-oriented software development (Principles of Privacy Design, Privacy Design Strategies, Privacy Patterns, Vulnerabilities, Context) and formalized in a knowledge base. The knowledge base shows that it is able to translate best practices for both secure application development and data privacy, into operational guidelines, software architectures and code structures to be used.

The tool allows to provide all the information needed to integrate privacy and security requirements during each stage of the re-engineering process. Students in the experimentation were positively supported despite not having specific skills in security by design and privacy by design. Indeed, the results demonstrate that the proposed tool supports developers in collaborative contexts integrating privacy and security in software development processes.

The positive results obtained by this study with bachelor students and the previous one with junior developers, encouraged us to plan for further case studies and evaluate developer's productivity with the collaborative tool.

6. References

[1] Barletta, V.S., Caivano, D., Dimauro, G., Nannavecchia, A., Scalera, M, (2020). Managing a Smart City Integrated Model through Smart Program Management. Appl. Sci. 2020, 10, 714. https://doi.org/10.3390/app10020714

[2] Pesare, E., Roselli, T., Rossano, V., Di Bitonto, P. (2015). Digitally enhanced assessment in virtual learning environments. Journal of Visual Languages & Computing, 31, 252-259. https://doi.org/10.1016/j.jvlc.2015.10.021

[3] Barletta, V.S.; Caivano, D.; Nannavecchia, A.; Scalera, M. A Kohonen SOM Architecture for Intrusion Detection on In-Vehicle Communication Networks. Appl. Sci. 2020, 10, 5062. https://doi.org/10.3390/app10155062

[4] Nonino F., Annarelli A., Gerosa S., Mosca P., Setti S., "Project Management: Driving Complexity", PMI® Italian Academic Workshop, (2018). ISBN 978-88- 9377-086-6

[5] Baldassarre M.T., Barletta V.S., Caivano D., Scalera M., (2019). Privacy Oriented Software Development. Communications in Computer and Information Science, 1010, pp. 18-32, https://doi.org/10.1007/978-3-030-29238-6_2

[6] Ellison, R. J., "Security and Project Management", 2006. Software Engineering Institute – Carnegie Mellon University

[7] Baldassarre, M.T., Barletta, V.S., Caivano, D., Scalera M., 2020. Integrating security and privacy in software development. *Software Qual J* (2020). https://doi.org/10.1007/s11219-020-09501-6

[8] Baldassarre, M. T., Barletta, V. S., Caivano, D., Raguseo, D., Scalera, M. (2019). Teaching Cyber Security: The Hack-Space Integrated Model. Proceedings of the *Third Italian Conference on Cyber Security*, Vol-2315, CEUR Workshop Proceedings.

[9] Jaccard, J. J., Nepal, S., "A survey of emerging threats in cybersecurity", Journal of computer and System Sciences, 2014. Volume 80, Issue 5, August 2014, pp. 973-993. https://doi.org/10.1016/j.jcss.2014.02.005

[10] Ardito, C.; Caivano, D.; Colizzi, L.; Dimauro, G.; Verardi, L. Design and Execution of Integrated Clinical Pathway: A Simplified Meta-Model and Associated Methodology. *Information* **2020**, *11*, 362. https://doi.org/10.3390/info11070362

[11] Regulation (EU) 2016/679 of the European Parliament and of the Council of 27 April 2016 on the protection of natural persons with regard to the processing of personal data and on the free movement of such data, and repealing Directive 95/46/EC.

[12] Cavoukian, A. (2010). Privacy by Design: The 7 Foundational Principles.

[13] Cavoukian, A. (2012). Operationalizing Privacy by Design: A Guide to Implementing Strong Privacy Practices. pp. 1–72.

[14] M. Hansen, M. Jensen and M. Rost (2015). Protection Goals for Privacy Engineering, IEEE Security and Privacy Workshops, San Jose, CA, 2015, pp. 159-166.

[15] Al-Slais, Y., 2020. Privacy Engineering Methodologies: A survey. International Conference on Innovation and Intelligence for Informatics, Computing and Technologies (3ICT), Sakheer, Bahrain, 2020, pp. 1-6, doi: 10.1109/3ICT51146.2020.9311949.

[16] Pattakou, A., Mavroeidi, A., Diamantopoulou, V., Kalloniatis, C., Gritzalis, S., 2018. Towards the Design of Usable Privacy by Design Methodologies. IEEE 5th International Workshop on Evolving Security & Privacy Requirements Engineering (ESPRE), Banff, AB, Canada, 2018, pp. 1-8, doi: 10.1109/ESPRE.2018.00007.

[17] Deng, M., Wuyts, K., Scandariato, R., Preneel, B., Joosen, W., 2011. A privacy threat analysis framework: supporting the elicitation and fulfillment of privacy requirements. *Requirements Engineering*, vol. 16, no. 1, pp. 3-32, 2011.

[18] Van Blarkom, G.W., Borking, J.J., and Olk, J.G.E. (2003). Handbook of Privacy and Privacy-Enhancing Technologies. The Case of Intelligent Software Agents. College Bescherming Bersoonsgegevens, ISBN 90-74087-33-7

[19] Kallpniatis, C., Kavakli, E., Gritzalis, S. (2008). Addressing privacy requirements in system design: the PriS method. *Requirements Engineering*, vol. 13, pp 241-255. Springer-Verlag. https://doi.org/10.1007/s00766-008-0067-3

[20] Mead, N.R., Stehney, T., 2005. Security quality requirements engineering (SQUARE) methodology, *ACM*, vol. 30, no. 4, pp. 1-7, 2005

[21] Jensen, C., Tullio, J., Potts, C., Mynatt, E.D., 2005. STRAP: a structured analysis framework for privacy, *Georgia Institute of Technology*, 2005.

[22] He, Q., Anton, A.I., 2003. A framework for modelling privacy requirements in role engineering, *In: Proceedings of REFSQ*, vol. 3, pp. 137-146, 2003.

[23] Notario, N., Crespo, A., Martin, Y. S., Del Alamo, J. M., Le Métayer, D., Antignac, T., Kung, A., et al. (2015). PRIPARE: Integrating Privacy Best Practices into a Privacy Engineering Methodology. *IEEE Security and Privacy Workshops*, San Jose, CA, pp. 151-158. https://doi.org/10.1109/SPW.2015.22

[24] Baldassarre, M.T., Barletta, V.S., Caivano, D., Piccinno, A., 2020. A Visual Tool for Supporting Decision-Making in Privacy Oriented Software Development. In Proceedings of the International Conference on Advanced Visual Interfaces (AVI '20). Association for Computing Machinery, New York, NY, USA, Article 45, 1–5. https://doi.org/10.1145/3399715.3399818
[25] Hoepman, J.-H. (2014). Privacy Design Strategies. In IFIP, ICT Systems Security and Privacy Protection (pp 446-459). Springer Berlin Heidelberg.
[26] Privacy Patterns, https://privacypatterns.org. Resource document. UC Berkeley, School of Information. Accessed 10 January 2020.
[27] M. Schumacher "B. Example Security Patterns and Annotations" in Security Engineering with Patterns, 2003, pp. 171-178.
[28] Moral-García, S., Ortiz, R., Moral-Rubio, S., Vela, B., Garzás, J., & Fernández-Medina, E. (2010). A new pattern template to support the design of security architectures.
[29] The Open Web Application Security Project, 2019. OWASP Top 10–2017. The Ten Most Critical Web Application Security Risks. https://www.owasp.org/index.php/Category:OWASP_Top_Ten_2017_Project.
[30] Brooke, J. "SUS - A quick and dirty usability scale.", in Usability evaluation in industry, CRC Press, 1996.
[31] Borsci, S., Federici, S., & Lauriola, M. (2009). On the dimensionality of the System Usability Scale: a test of alternative measurement models. Cognitive Processing, 10(3), 193-197. doi: 10.1007/s10339-009-0268-9

A Research Infrastructure for E-Health Big Data Analytics

Alessio Botta[1], Elio Masciari[1]

[1]*University of Napoli Federico II, Napoli, Italy*
alessio.botta@unina.it
[1]*University of Napoli Federico II, Napoli, Italy*
elio.masciari@unina.it

Abstract
In this paper, we present a research infrastructure, built within the Department of Excellence project in order to support a wide spectrum of big data analysis related to e-health. More in details we built a both a public cloud based infrastructure and a private cloud one in order to guarantee a high performance approach to researchers.

Keywords
Big Data Platform, Cloud Services for Big Data, Research Infrastructures.

1. Introduction

The Department of Electrical Engineering and Information Technologies - DIETI - of the University of Naples Federico II is the largest department in Southern Italy that works on issues relating to Information and Communication Technology (ICT). The scientific/disciplinary sectors (Settori Scientifico/Disciplinari in Italian or simply SSD) participating in the activities of DIETI have shown in the last round of Evaluation of the quality of research (VQR) 2011-2014 evaluation peaks of absolute excellence; very limited is in fact the number of SSD below the national average evaluation. With particular reference to the Area 09, ten SSD have received evaluations greater than or equal to the national average. The DIETI, unanimously, has therefore decided to develop in the next five years its research lines in the field of Information and Communication Technologies, especially with regard to the application of modern information technologies in the thematic areas of the so-called eHealth. From these premises it was natural to propose an innovative project called *ICT for Health* (ICTH in the following) within the Departments of Excellence call of the Italian Ministry of Research and University. The call financed 180 Excellence Departments in Italy, and DIETI was among the 14 ones with the maximum evaluation for the project, one of the only two cases in south Italy. ICTH has been financed with over 9 M Euros for a time span of five years.

Using the financial tools available for the project, DIETI is recruiting a full professor chosen by a panel of international experts from a short-list of candidates of excellence. This figure is responsible for coordinating and managing the entire project ensuring the success and

SEBD 2021: The 29th Italian Symposium on Advanced Database Systems, September 5-9, 2021, Pizzo Calabro (VV), Italy

achievement of all objectives. In addition, it is currently ongoing the recruitment of an associate professor and four Tenure-track Researchers (RTD-B) in order to strengthen the research areas that are described below. The ICT for Health project involves the strengthening of existing laboratories in the DIETI and the creation of a new experimental reality active on issues not present now within the DIETI, in order to create a network of laboratories to support the proposed research. Finally, a new doctorate school has been created, specific on the themes of the project in order to have, together with the development of the research activities, also the training of professionals ready to be employed in a socio-economic regional and national environment, particularly active in this field and whose annual European budget now exceeds 20 billion euros. In the following we will describe the requirements we would like to fulfill with our Big Data laboratory.

1.1. Research Agenda

The eHealth technologies and services in the coming decades will bring deep changes in the organization of the health care system, with the aim of improving the quality and efficiency of care and, at the same time, reducing costs. In the short term, the new technologies will have to integrate with the current structures that provide healthcare, but in the long term they will produce significant changes both in the internal organization and in the architecture of the buildings that will house the hospitals and healthcare facilities of the future. These facilities will need to be able to provide personalized therapies to patients, which may also be decentralized or delivered at home and monitored remotely. The ICT for Health departmental project, based on the pre-existing infrastructure of the DIETI laboratories and on the new laboratory to be built, is therefore developed along the following lines of scientific and technological research.

1.1.1. Sensing for Health

Smart transducers for the Internet of Everything environment will be developed, such as the electronic syringe, smart sensors to integrate robotic microsurgery devices, advanced biomedical instrumentation for automated and robotic surgery systems, and innovative systems for remote monitoring of patients' health status, both in hospitals or healthcare facilities (e.g., nursing homes for the elderly), and in private homes.

In particular, we will study solutions based on new sensors and wearable devices, wearable or implantable, which will allow to monitor the state of health even outside the traditional care centers. Particular attention will be paid to Exergaming technologies based on Serious Games, in which rehabilitation or treatment takes place through Augmented Reality applications, and Brain Computer Interfaces, with low training and response times, and low number of electrodes, for patients with high rates of disability. The topics of sensor development and their interaction in augmented vision systems will be experimentally developed within the new laboratory foreseen in the program.

1.1.2. Data for Health

The eHealth services and technologies generate huge amounts of data and information that, for their treatment, require the use of non-traditional methodologies and technologies: Cloud

Computing, Internet of Things and Big Data Analytics are the new paradigms underlying the new generation of systems for information management in eHealth. The data sources to be considered, in addition to having high volume, are also heterogeneous given their different types and origins [1]. The speed with which information is produced and stored, together with the aforementioned volume and variety, require systems and tools to collect, manage, and analyze the data and information produced by healthcare systems, directing research towards Big Data Analytics (BDA) methodologies and techniques [2].

The BDA in eHealth enables the transformation of a classical hypothesis-driven information analysis to an innovative data-driven one, able to identify non-trivial connections between heterogeneous data and information. This requires the need to investigate: (a) new cloud-based architectures that allow for the timely processing of information, from the Hadoop to the Spark Ecosystem; (b) new information management systems that integrate relational (SQL), non-relational (NoSQL) and new relational (newSQL) architectures; (c) use of descriptive, diagnostic, prescriptive and descriptive analysis techniques; (d) use of Data Mining tools and techniques on Massive Data Sets, including Deep Learning . In this context, equally important are digital infrastructures for data circulation and device interconnection, following the Internet of Things paradigm.

1.1.3. Logistics for Health

In-hospital logistics services impact 15-20% of operating costs. These services include moving patients, linen, meals, medications, equipment and samples between clinics, wards, operating rooms, laboratories and warehouses. Digitization, automation, and robotic technologies can optimize these processes through solutions that enable automated patient and material transport and automated hospital warehouse management. The main difference from factory logistics systems is the need to operate in man-made environments.

We aim at creating robotic systems capable of interacting with humans (patients, medical/nursing staff, visiting relatives) in an intuitive and safe manner. In the "hospital 4.0" model, the automation system for logistics represents a further integrated node within the ICT network for the management of services, whose architecture is typically distributed and whose management and analysis methodologies are typical of the Data Analysis presented in the previous point. Extending such integration also to a "smart grid" for the management of the utilities, it is possible to increase the energy efficiency of the logistics system. Such an integration also enables a notable containment of the peaks of demanded power to the net ("peak shaving"), with consequent containment of the expense for electric consumption. We want to evaluate the integration of methodologies typical of energy optimization with the management of logistics automation in order to ensure the safe performance of all critical operations by controlling and, if possible, optimizing energy consumption.

1.1.4. Robotics for Health

To ensure continuous and personalized care for patients in the wards or at their homes, solutions involving the use of nurse-robots will be investigated. These intelligent machines will help patients perform simple daily actions, facilitate remote monitoring and communication with medical staff or relatives, administer simple therapies, or can be used for entertainment (reading, storytelling, playing games) [3].

In addition to nursing robots, devices and control strategies for rehabilitation will be designed such as the development of virtual agents to be implemented in augmented reality that can interact with the patient through advanced techniques of automatic control and provide real-time data to medical staff through telemedicine strategies.

Robotics is already a widespread reality in several medical-surgical specialties. The use of tele-operated or computer-guided machines offers numerous advantages such as precision, repeatability, and tremor filtering [4]. Robots such as the da Vinci system for minimally invasive robotic surgery allow to improve and reduce the duration of the post-operative course of patients. The aim is to improve the capabilities of currently used robots through the use of new sensors, advanced image processing and sensory fusion techniques, computerized procedures for surgery planning based on pre-operative images or guidance through intra-operative image processing, virtual and augmented reality, and new human-robot interfaces [5, 6]. These interfaces, connected to analog or software simulators, will be used, thanks to the already structured collaboration of DIETI within the ICAROS center, for the training of surgeons. New sensorized surgical instruments will be designed and controlled inspired by the human manipulation capability. Anthropomorphic gripping instruments will be developed for both surgery and rehabilitation.

2. The Research Infrastructures

The laboratory is intended as an hub for collecting the computational and storage needs of researchers at Unina. More in details the goal is to provide a complete support in order to profitably leverage the skills of the laboratory team in order to create a room for exchanging ideas and providing multidisciplinary insight on how to build solid benchmarks for assessing research results in several fields. In the following, we will describe the two big data [7, 8, 9, 10, 11, 12, 13] infrastructures that will be available for researchers.

2.1. Public Cloud resources

The eHBDA laboratory in the Cloud is based on virtual infrastructures, i.e. Cloud services, consisting of the following main components: data collection, storage, processing and consumption. Below is a description of the elements composing our infrastructure.

Data collection module. It features 2 Instances of virtual machines each with 8 virtual cores with 3.0 Ghz Xeon Platinum processors providing the possibility to get access to a further increase in performance using Intel Turbo Boost technology equipped with 16 GB of RAM and 20 GB of SSD persistent storage.

Data storage module. It offers a managed Relational Database Service based on MySQL compatible technologies with a minimum space of 2 TB. The service includes the ability to automatically schedule and execute backups and make the necessary tools available for a possible restore; it is also possible to extend the single database instance in order to support Big Data analysis scenarios. The database service is implemented by virtual machines having the following characteristics: 8 virtual cores with Intel Xeon Ivy Bridge processors with the possibility of having memory bandwidth larger than 60000 MB/s and 122 GB of RAM.

It also provides a No SQL database service providing a storage space of 100 GB, with item size 20KB, data access times less than ten milliseconds, integrated backup and the ability to dynamically scale according to the workload without any service interruption. The Object Storage service guarantees high durability of objects provided in serverless mode and which can scale on demand. The service can also be used as a storage service for the implementation of a datalake. The service includes a storage space of at least 200GB, with the possibility of making at least 2000 Req/month and 2000 Put/month.

Furthermore, there is an in-memory cache service based, on Redis, with available space of at least 60GB. The service is implemented by virtual machines having the following features: 2 virtual cores and 15 GB of RAM.

Finally, a managed service for real-time data ingestion capable of receiving a data flow up to 1MB/s as input is available that allows integration with Spark to allow real-time processing of streaming data by Spark Streaming.

Data processing module. This module provides a managed data warehouse service, with the possibility of scaling (scale-out) the computing cluster in order to manage the increase in the volume of data to be processed. The solution includes back-up functionalities able to manage the DB saving even when the volumes managed grow suddenly. Overall, the computing cluster provide 8 TB of storage space and 8 vcore and 120 GB of RAM. The Business Intelligence service is implemented in IaaS mode by 4 virtual machine instances having the following characteristics each: 4 virtual cores with Xeon Broadwell processors, 30 GB of RAM, 100 GB of SSD persistent storage.

A Managed service for the implementation of a cluster based on Hadoop, Hive, Spark technologies (including the SparkSQL, Spark Mlib, Spark Streaming and GraphX extensions) is integrated with storage solutions for the implementation of the datalake both internal and external, allowing a decoupling of costs and resources dedicated to computing from those dedicated to data storage. The cluster solution is easily integrated with the tools used for the creation of NoSQL databases and Datawarehouse. There are 8 nodes of the Hadoop cluster having the following features: 8 virtual cores with Intel Xeon Ivy Bridge, 60 GB of RAM, 100 GB of storage space in SSD technology, directly attached to the instance plus 100GB of persistent storage.

Finally, a code service allows to write programs in the following languages: Node.js, (JavaScript), Python, Java (Java 8 compatible), and C # (.NET Core), and Go. It checks the limits (throttling) of the functions to prevent programming errors that can generate an unexpected increase in costs and and support the versioning of functions in order to change the definition "at a glance" without impact on the running processes.

Data consume module. The Business Intelligence service in fully managed mode allows the creation of dashboards and that allows integration with the data sources included in the configuration (Datalake, Datawarehouse, Relational Database). The service allows the drafting of fully customizable graphic dashboards, the definition of the analysis paths and the caching of the data in memory to allow a rapid exploration of the same. The service must have at least 10GB of stored data model. Business Intelligence service is based on technologies such as Kibana and Qlikview and supported by at least 2 instances of virtual machines each with the following configuration: 4 virtual cores with Xeon Platinum 3.0 Ghz processors with the possibility of accessing a further increase in performance using Intel Turbo Boost technology, 8 GB of RAM and 10 GB of SSD persistent storage.

2.2. Private Cloud resources

In order to provide users a broader choice of solutions to fulfill any research needs, we also built our own infrastructure for big data analysis. In the following, we will describe the main features of our infrastructure.

We have 10 compute nodes configured to have a cluster with this features: power supplies for at least 7500W, with at least two hot-swappable power supplies per node, 100 cores in total with 1.80GHz frequency and at least 11M cache per CPU, 1280 GB of total RAM, in banks of at least 32GB DDR4, 4.8 TB total hot plug SSD storage, with drives of at least 480GB, Hot-plug 10TB SAS/SATA storage, with disks of at least 1TB, RAID Controller and Onboard SATA Controller, PCIe x16 expansion slot in each node, Network connectivity of at least 20Gbps for each node and an aggregate (number of interfaces per node x speed per interface x number of nodes) of at least 200Gbps, remote management card on each node with at least 1Gbps dedicated interface, rack mount kit, which must be supplied as specified below.

The storage is guaranteed by 750TB SSD hard disks, having 500.000 IOPS, a latency of 10ms, a CPU with 12 Core, 2.40GHz, 30M Cache, connectivity rate of 4 x10 GbE + 4 x 1 GbE. We have the possibility to scale-up to 1PB with an availability of 99.9999% by a dedicated switch having 16 10GbE port, 2 25GbE/100GbE port.

In order to obtain a high performance level, we built a proper network infrastructure as follows. A Switch for the production network, including 3mt cables for connection to the nodes, with the following characteristics: 48 25GbE SFP28 ports + 6 100GbE ports, 3.6 Tbps (full-duplex) non-blocking, store and forward switching fabric, L2 and L3 Ethernet switching with support for QoS, features for IPv4 and IPv6, including support for OSPF and BGP routing, Support for OpenFlow v 1.3. A Switch for the management network with 48 1GbE Base-T ports + 4 10GbE ports and 3mt RJ45/RJ45 cables for connection to the nodes. Finally, we have 3 Rack 750x1200mm able to contain all the nodes described above (computing nodes, storage nodes and switches).

3. Conclusion

In this paper, we described the e-health laboratory we implemented at DIETI in order to support a variety of big data analyses for a broad set of application scenarios [14]. The goal of this paper is to provide a quick view of an actual infrastructure that could be used as a reference architecture for top-class applications.

Acknowledgments

Supported by the Ministry of University and Research for Department of Excellence Project.

References

[1] G. Aceto, A. Botta, A. Pescapé, C. Westphal, Efficient storage and processing of high-volume network monitoring data, IEEE Transactions on Network and Service Management 19 (2013) 1–14.

[2] K. Wang, Y. Shao, L. Shu, C. Zhu, Y. Zhang, Mobile big data fault-tolerant processing for ehealth networks, IEEE Network 30 (2016) 36–42.

[3] S. Chiaverini, B. Siciliano, L. Villani, A survey of robot interaction control schemes with experimental comparison, IEEE/ASME Transactions on Mechatronics 4 (1999) 273–285. doi:10.1109/3516.789685.

[4] A. Mashayekhi, S. Behbahani, F. Ficuciello, B. Siciliano, Influence of human operator on stability of haptic rendering: a closed-form equation, International Journal of Intelligent Robotics and Applications 4 (2020). doi:10.1007/s41315-020-00131-6.

[5] A. Botta, L. Gallo, G. Ventre, Cloud, fog, and dew robotics: Architectures for next generation applications, in: 2019 7th IEEE International Conference on Mobile Cloud Computing, Services, and Engineering (MobileCloud), IEEE, 2019, pp. 16–23.

[6] G. Stanco, A. Botta, G. Ventre, Dewros: a platform for informed dew robotics in ros, in: 2020 8th IEEE International Conference on Mobile Cloud Computing, Services, and Engineering (MobileCloud), IEEE, 2020, pp. 9–16.

[7] V. Persico, A. Pescapé, A. Picariello, G. Sperlí, Benchmarking big data architectures for social networks data processing using public cloud platforms, Future Generation Computer Systems 89 (2018) 98 – 109. URL: http://www.sciencedirect.com/science/article/pii/S0167739X17328303. doi:https://doi.org/10.1016/j.future.2018.05.068.

[8] D. Agrawal et al., Challenges and opportunities with big data. A community white paper developed by leading researchers across the United States (2012).

[9] V. R. Borkar, M. J. Carey, C. Li, Inside "Big Data Management": Ogres, Onions, or Parfaits?, in: International Conference on Extending Database Technology, 2012, pp. 3–14.

[10] T. Economist, Data, data everywhere, The Economist (2010).

[11] V. L. Heron, Michaeland Hanson, I. Ricketts, Open source and accessibility: advantages and limitations, Journal of Interaction Science 1 (2013) 1–10. URL: http://dx.doi.org/10.1186/2194-0827-1-2. doi:10.1186/2194-0827-1-2.

[12] Nature, Big data, Nature (2008).

[13] S. Mgudlwa, T. Iyamu, Integration of social media with healthcare big data for improved service delivery, SA Journal of Information Management 20 (2018). doi:10.4102/sajim.v20i1.894.

[14] G. Manco, E. Masciari, A. Tagarelli, A framework for adaptive mail classification, in: 14th IEEE International Conference on Tools with Artificial Intelligence (ICTAI 2002), 4-6 November 2002, Washington, DC, USA, IEEE Computer Society, 2002, p. 387. URL: https://doi.org/10.1109/TAI.2002.1180829. doi:10.1109/TAI.2002.1180829.

A short account of FAIR-DB: a system to discover Data Bias

(Discussion Paper)

Fabio Azzalini[1,2], Chiara Criscuolo[1] and Letizia Tanca[1]

[1]*Politecnico di Milano - Dipartimento di Elettronica, Informazione e Bioingegneria*
[2]*Human Technopole - Center for Analysis, Decisions and Society*

Abstract
Computers and algorithms are increasingly pervading our daily lives, therefore to trust these systems we have to make sure that the data they use are fair and without bias. As a result, Fairness has become a relevant topic of discussion within the field of Data Science, and technologies that accurately discover discrimination and bias present in datasets are of paramount importance.

In this work we present FAIR-DB (FunctionAl dependencIes to discoveR Data Bias), a novel framework to detect biases and discover discrimination in datasets. By exploiting various kinds of functional dependencies, our tool can identify those attributes in a database that encompass discrimination (e.g. gender, ethnicity or religion) and the ones that instead satisfy various fairness criteria.

We compared our framework with two state-of-the-art systems for detecting unfairness in datasets, obtaining overall similar results on a real-world dataset; specifically, the comparison highlighted that FAIR-DB not only provides very precise information about the groups treated unequally, but also that, in comparison with other existing tools, may obtain more insights regarding the bias present in datasets

Keywords
Fairness, Data Bias, Functional Dependencies

1. Introduction

In the recent years fairness has become an important topic of interest in the Data Science community. Indeed, computers and algorithms have made our lives efficient and easier, but among the prices we risk to pay is the possible presence of discrimination and unfairness in the decisions we make with their support [1]. Data Science technologies are based on data, and for them to be reliable we have to make sure that the data we feed them are fair and without bias: *data can be considered of good quality only if they conform to high ethical standard* [1]: to avoid (possibly unintentional) unethical behaviors and their consequences, data cleaning tools should also include *tools to discover bias in data* [2].

In this paper we present *FAIR-DB* [3], a framework that, by discovering and analyzing particular types of functional dependencies, can find unfair behaviors in a dataset and guide its correction. A *Functional Dependency* ($FD : X \rightarrow Y$) is a class of database integrity constraints that hold

SEBD 2021: The 29th Italian Symposium on Advanced Database Systems, September 5-9, 2021, Pizzo Calabro (VV), Italy
fabio.azzalini@polimi.it (F. Azzalini); chiara.criscuolo@polimi.it (C. Criscuolo); letizia.tanca@polimi.it (L. Tanca)
0000-0003-0631-2120 (F. Azzalini); 0000-0003-2607-3171 (L. Tanca)

[1]https://www.propublica.org/article/machine-bias-risk-assessments-in-criminal-sentencing

between two sets X and Y of attributes in a relation of a database. It specifies that the values of the attributes of X uniquely (or *functionally*) determine the values of the attributes of Y [4]. In a FD, X is called antecedent or left-hand-side (LHS) while Y is called consequent, or right-hand-side (RHS). In Conditional Functional Dependencies (or CFDs) [5], conditions are used to specify the subset of tuples on which a dependency holds: a CFD is a pair $(X \rightarrow Y, t_p)$, where $X \rightarrow Y$ is a standard functional dependency and t_p is a *pattern tuple* over the attributes in X and Y; for each A in $X \cup Y$, $t_p[A]$ is a constant *'a'* in *dom(A)*, or an unnamed variable '_'.
In this paper we consider Approximate Conditional Functional Dependencies (ACFDs), i.e., uncertain CFDs that hold only on a subset of the tuples, to detect biases and discover discrimination in the datasets subject to analysis, by recognizing cases where the value of a certain attribute (e.g. gender, ethnicity or religion) *frequently determines* the value of another one (such as range of the proposed salary or social state).

2. State of the Art

Most of the research done in the area of Data Science Ethics is carried out by the Machine Learning community; three possible approaches can be adopted when trying to enforce fairness in a data analysis application: *(i) preprocessing techniques*, i.e. procedures that, before the application of a prediction algorithm, make sure that the learning data are fair; *(ii) inprocessing techniques*, i.e. procedures that ensure that, during the learning phase, the algorithm does not pick up the bias present in the data, and *(iii) postprocessing techniques*, i.e. procedures that correct the algorithm's decisions with the scope of making them fair.
One of the first preprocessing techniques was presented by Pedreschi et al. [6]: exploiting the concept of association rules and custom metrics, the system can identify potentially discriminatory itemsets.
A project that provides the implementation of many interesting techniques is *AI Fairness 360: An Extensible Toolkit for Detecting, Understanding, and Mitigating Unwanted Algorithmic Bias* [7], this work presents a new open-source framework whose aim is to reach algorithmic fairness. The system tries to mitigate algorithmic bias by exploiting techniques that use statistical measures to compute fairness.
In the Machine Learning context, the majority of works that try to enforce fairness are related to a prediction task, and more specifically to classification algorithms in decision-making tools [8], [9], [7]. The main difference between these approaches and our framework, that solves unfairness adopting a *preprocessing technique*, is that our system does not need a classifier to work, because it is based on finding conditions (in form of approximate constraints) that are already present in the data, even though possibly with some level of approximation. Furthermore, building a classifier to solve the fairness problem requires the policy to be application-oriented, greatly limiting the applicability of these systems to scenarios where other tasks are needed.
A very interesting work on fairness in Machine Learning that employs a *preprocessing technique* is *Nutritional Labels for Data and Models* by Stoyanovich and Howe [10]. The authors developed an interpretability and transparency tool based on the concept of *Nutritional Labels*, drawing an analogy to the food industry, where simple and standardized labels convey information about the ingredients and the production processes. Nutritional labels are derived semi-automatically

as part of the complex process that gave rise to the data or model they describe. The final system is called *Ranking Facts*, and automatically derives nutritional labels for ranking. *Ranking Facts* is a collection of visual widgets, in particular, the *Fairness* widget quantifies whether the ranked output exhibit statistical parity (a particular definition of group fairness) with respect to one or more protected attributes.

3. Methodology

Before presenting the methodology we first introduce some fundamental notions that will accompany us along our discussion. Given a dataset D, the *support* of a CFD $\left(X \rightarrow Y, t_p\right)$ is defined as the proportion of tuples t in the dataset D which contain t_p, that is:

$$Support(X \rightarrow Y, t_p) = \frac{|t \in D; t_p \subseteq t|}{|D|}$$

The *confidence* is an indication of how often the CFD has been found to be true. Let $t_p = (x \cup y)$ where x is a tuple over X and y is a tuple over Y. The confidence value of a CFD $\left(X \rightarrow Y, t_p\right)$ is the proportion of the tuples t containing x which also contain y:

$$Confidence(X \rightarrow Y, t_p) = \frac{|t \in D; t_p \subseteq t|}{|t \in D; x \subseteq t|}$$

FAIR-DB is composed by the following main steps: *Data Preparation and Exploration*, *ACFD Discovery and Filtering*, *ACFDs Selection*, *ACFDs Ranking* and *ACFDs User Selection and Scoring*. In the next subsections we present each phase in detail, with the help of the following example:

Example 1. Running Example *For our experiments, we have used the U.S. Census Adult Dataset*[2] *[11], containing information about many social factors of US adults, like 'Income', 'Age', 'Workclass', 'Education', 'Education-Num' (i.e. the number of years already attended at school), 'Marital-Status', 'Race', 'Sex', (work) 'Hours-Per-Week', 'Native-Country', and some more.*

3.1. Data Preparation and Exploration

In this phase we import the data, perform (if needed) data integration and apply the typical data preprocessing steps (solve missing values, apply discretization etc.) needed to clean and prepare the data. As a last step of this first phase, *Data Visualization* can be of great help in analyzing the characteristics of the data; in fact, from the plots, a user can understand whether groups are present in the dataset and more specifically, if there is a majority class for a certain attribute, and if present can identify minorities.
This preliminary phase gives a general idea of the dataset, and during this step we can guesstimate the protected columns and identify, if present, the target variable of our study. Regarding the running example, we selected 'Sex', 'Race' and 'Native-Country' as protected attributes and 'Income' as target variable.

[2]https://archive.ics.uci.edu/ml/datasets/Adult

(Education-Degree='Middle-school') → Income='≤ 50K'
(Age-Range='15-30') → Income='≤ 50K'
(Education-Degree, Income='≤ 50K') → Native-Country
(Native-Country='NC-Hispanic') → Income='≤ 50K'
(Income='≤ 50K') → Native-Country='NC-US'

Table 1
CFD Discovery output

ACFD	Support	Difference
(Native-Country = 'NC-Hispanic') → (Income = '≤50K')	0.0439	0.1570
(Sex = 'Female') → (Income = '≤50K')	0.2874	0.1352
(Race = 'Black') → (Income = '≤50K')	0.0813	0.1190

Table 2
A few of the selected ACFDs using the *Difference metric*

3.2. ACFD Discovery and Filtering

In this phase we extract the ACFDs from the dataset, using the algorithm of [12]. The algorithm expects as input the following three parameters: *the (minimum) support threshold*, the *(minimum) confidence threshold*, and the size of the largest antecedent *maxSize*.
Given an instance D of a schema R, support threshold δ, confidence threshold ϵ, and maximum antecedent size α, the approximate CFDs discovery problem is to find all ACFDs ϕ: $\left(X \rightarrow Y, t_p\right)$ over R with: support(ϕ, D) $\geq \delta$, confidence(ϕ, D) $\geq \epsilon$ and $|X| \leq \alpha$. The ACFDs obtained are in this form: $(lhsAttr1 = v1, ..., lhsAttrN = vN) \rightarrow (rhsAttr = v)$.
The algorithm returns all the dependencies that satisfy the constraints.

Example 2. CFD Discovery *The algorithm, applied to the dataset resulting from the previous phase, finds 118 ACFDs. Table 1 reports a few of them.*
Now we filter the dependencies, discarding the ones that do not satisfy two constraints:

- all the attributes must be assigned a value (the ACFDs that contains only constants in both the LHS and RHS are called *Constant ACFDs*[13]);
- at least one protected attribute and the target variable have to be present inside the dependency, so that the ACFDs might show bias.

Example 3. ACFDs Filtering *From Table 1 we discarded the third dependency for not being a Constant ACFD and the first three dependencies for not containing any protected attribute. After this phase we are left with 84 of the original 118 dependencies.*

3.3. ACFD Selection

This phase is responsible for finding the dependencies that *actually reveal* unfairness in the dataset. To do so, we have devised an unfairness measure, called *Difference*, that indicates how much a dependency is *'unethical'*. The higher the difference, the more the ACFD reveals

an unfair behavior. In order to assess the unfair behavior of a dependency, we also take into consideration its support, that indicates the *pervasiveness* of the ACFD; unethical dependencies with high support will impact many tuples, and thus will be more important.
We define the *Difference* of a dependency ϕ as the difference between the confidence of ϕ and the confidence of the dependency computed without the protected attributes of the LHS of the ACFD. Let $\phi : (X \rightarrow Y, t_p)$ be an ACFD, and $Z = (X - \{ProtectedAttributes\})$, that is, the LHS of the dependency without its *protected attributes*, and let z be the restriction of t to Z. Then:

$$\text{Difference}(\phi) = \text{Confidence}(\phi) - \text{NoProtectedAttributeConfidence}(\phi)$$

where

$$\text{NoProtectedAttributeConfidence}(\phi) = \frac{|t \in D; t_p \subseteq t|}{|t \in D; z \subseteq t|}$$

That is:

$$\text{Difference}(\phi) = \frac{|t \in D; t_p \subseteq t|}{|t \in D; x \subseteq t|} - \frac{|t \in D; t_p \subseteq t|}{|t \in D; z \subseteq t|}$$

The *Difference* metric gives us an idea of how much the values of the protected attributes influence the value of Y.

Example 4. Difference score of a dependency *Analyzing the following dependency:* $\phi_1 : (Sex =' Female', Workclass =' Private') \rightarrow (Income =' \leq 50K')$ *we can compute the* Difference *as:* $Diff(\phi_1) : Conf(\phi_1) - Conf(\phi_1')$, *where* $\phi_1' : (Workclass =' Private') \rightarrow (Income =' \leq 50K')$. *Three different behaviors can emerge:*

- *If the Difference is close to zero, fairness is respected since it means that females are treated equally to all the elements of the population that have the same characteristics (without specifying the protected attribute).*
- *If the Difference is positive it means that the women that work privately and gain less than 50K dollars/year are overall treated worse than the generality of people that work privately and gain less than 50K dollars/year.*
- *If the Difference is negative the opposite situation is detected.*

Finally, we choose the ACFDs whose *Difference* is above the *minThreshold*, which means that there is a significant inequality between the group involved in the ACFD and the general behaviour of the population.

Example 5. Selected ACFDs *Table 2 reports three of the seventeen dependencies that satisfied the selection criteria along with their relevant metrics. From the example, "Hispanic", "Female" and "Black" groups suffer from discrimination with respect to the rest of the population, in fact, people that belong to one or more of these groups have an income that is below the 50000 dollars/year because of their nationality, sex or race.*

3.4. ACFD Ranking

In a real-world dataset, the number of ACFDs selected in the previous step could be very large, therefore for the user to look at all these dependencies would be a very demanding task to complete. Thus, it is necessary to order the dependencies according to some criterion, enabling the user to analyze the most important and interesting ones first, speeding up the process and reducing the cost. In our framework the user can order the dependencies according to one of the following criteria:

- *Support-based*: the support indicates the proportion of tuples impacted by the dependency; the higher the support, the more tuples are involved by the ACFD. Ordering dependencies by support highlights the *pervasiveness* of the dependency.
- *Difference-based*: this criterion highlights the dependencies where the values of the protected attributes influence most the value of their RHS, therefore this ordering privileges the *unethical aspect* of the dependencies.
- *Mean-based*: this method tries to combine both aspects of a dependency: the unethical perspective and its pervasiveness. Sorting the ACFDs using this criterion results in positioning first the dependencies that have the best trade-off between difference and support.

3.5. ACFD User Selection and Scoring

In this last phase the user selects from the ranked list N dependencies that are interesting for the research needs. Using only the N selected ACFDs, the framework computes two scores that summarize the properties of the entire dataset:

- *Cumulative Support*: is the percentage of tuples in the dataset involved by the selected ACFDs. The more this value is close to 1, the more tuples are impacted by unfair dependencies.
- *Difference Mean*: is the mean of all the *'Difference'* scores of the selected ACFDs. It indicates how much the dataset is unethical according to the dependencies selected. The greater the value, the higher the bias in the dataset.

Example 6. ACFDs User Selection and Scoring *The user chooses $N = 15$ ACFDs that are interesting according to her needs among the dependencies obtained after the ranking step. The total number of tuples involved by the ACFDs is 13296 while the total number of tuples in the dataset is 30169; this results in a Cumulative Support of 0.44. The Difference Mean is 0.16. These two scores indicate that a considerable number of tuples, 44%, show a behavior that is very different, on average 16%, from the fair one. Finally, a deeper analysis of the dependencies confirm that the dataset is unfair with respect to all the protected attributes; the groups more discriminated are: 'Female', 'Black', 'NC-Hispanic' and 'Amer-Indian-Eskimo'. Table 3 reports a few interesting ACFDs.*

(Sex = 'Female') → Income = '$\leq$ 50K'
(Race = 'Black') → Income = '$\leq$ 50K'
(Race = 'Amer-Indian-Eskimo') → Income = '$\leq$ 50K'
(Native-Country = 'NC-Hispanic') → Income = '$\leq$ 50K'

Table 3
A few user-selected dependencies from the U.S. Census Adult Income Dataset

4. Experimental Results

We now present the results obtained by *FAIR-DB* on a real-world dataset, and a comparison between our framework and the competitors presented in the Introduction chapter. The dataset we considered is the *U.S. Census Adult Income Dataset*, already briefly presented in Example 1. The version we considered contains 32561 tuples and 13 attributes, 5 of which are numerical and 8 are categorical.

4.1. *FAIR-DB* Results

We recall from Example 6 the results of *FAIR-DB* on the U.S. Census Adult Income Dataset, which scores a *Cumulative Support* of 0.44 and a *Difference Mean* of 0.16, indicating that many tuples show an unfair behavior. Specifically, the dataset highlights bias towards all the protected attributes: 'Sex', 'Race' and 'Native-Country'; a deeper analysis confirms that the most discriminated groups are: 'Female', 'Black', 'NC-Hispanic' and 'Amer-Indian-Eskimo'.

4.2. Comparison with competitors

The results obtained by *Ranking Facts*[10] and with *AI Fairness 360*[7] are in complete accordance with ours. *Ranking Facts* finds in the U.S. Census Adult Income Dataset unfair behaviors across all the three protected attributes with discrimination against: 'Female', 'Black', 'NC-Hispanic' and 'Amer-Indian-Eskimo'.
AI Fairness 360 analyzed fairness through statistical measures computed for two protected attributes: 'Race' and 'Sex' checking fairness only for one binary attribute at the time. For the most of statistical measures, the 'Race' attribute has a privileged group composed by 'White' people and a discriminated one composed by 'Not White' people, the 'Sex' attribute has a privileged group composed by 'Male' and a discriminated one composed by 'Female'.
The two competitors check fairness property only for one binary attribute at the time, while, since the ACFD technique can involve more than one attribute at a time, our tool can report information about subgroups fairness, actually detecting unfair behaviors at finer level of granularity; as a results *Ranking Facts* and *AI Fairness 360* do not contain information about the existing bias in minorities. This is very important, because the discrimination might be limited to some specific scenario (e.g. not all the women but only the black women working in the private sector), and this information is very useful to guide the phase of DB repair.
Finally, we present a theoretical comparison between *FAIR-DB* and the work by Pedreschi et al. [6]. Their system extracts association rules that signal potentially discriminatory itemsets. The process exploits a specific type of association rules that constrains the target class to be only on the RHS, as a result, the potentially discriminatory itemset can be only on the LHS; in

our approach the ACFDs found do not have this constraint. Finally, [6] does not involve user interaction, therefore the user cannot discard the rules that are not interesting for the specific investigation. Moreover, FAIR-DB provides as a final step a set of summarizing metrics that describes the overall degree of unfairness of the dataset.

5. Conclusion and Future Works

We presented *FAIR-DB*, a novel framework, that, through the extraction of a particular type of Functional Dependencies, can discover bias and discrimination present in a datasets.
Future works will include:, *(i)* the addition to the system of a dependency repair phase, that, starting from the selected ACFDs will correct the dataset removing all the unfair behaviors from it *(ii)* the study of dependencies with high confidence and low support to highlight interesting, not necessarily frequent, behaviors, *(iii)* the development of a graphical user interface to facilitate the interaction of the user with the system, *(iv)* the study of other classes of functional dependencies[5], *(v)* a deeper comparison with *Ranking Facts* and other similar methods.

References

[1] D. Firmani, L. Tanca, R. Torlone, Ethical dimensions for data quality, Journal of Data and Information Quality (JDIQ) (2019).

[2] J. Stoyanovich, B. Howe, H. Jagadish, Responsible data management, Proceedings of the VLDB Endowment (2020).

[3] F. Azzalini, C. Criscuolo, L. Tanca, FAIR-DB: Functional dependencies to discover data bias, Workshop Proceedings of the EDBT/ICDT 2021 (2021).

[4] S. Abiteboul, R. Hull, V. Vianu, Foundations of Databases, Addison-Wesley, 1995. URL: http://webdam.inria.fr/Alice/.

[5] L. Caruccio, V. Deufemia, G. Polese, Relaxed functional dependencies—a survey of approaches, IEEE Transactions on Knowledge and Data Engineering (2015).

[6] S. Ruggieri, D. Pedreschi, F. Turini, Data mining for discrimination discovery, ACM Transactions on Knowledge Discovery from Data (TKDD) 4 (2010) 1–40.

[7] R. K. Bellamy, K. Dey, M. Hind, S. C. Hoffman, S. Houde, K. Kannan, P. Lohia, J. Martino, S. Mehta, A. Mojsilović, et al., AI Fairness 360: An extensible toolkit for detecting and mitigating algorithmic bias, in: IBM Journal of Research and Development, IBM, 2019.

[8] J. A. Adebayo, et al., FairML: ToolBox for diagnosing bias in predictive modeling, Ph.D. thesis, Massachusetts Institute of Technology, 2016.

[9] F. Tramer, V. Atlidakis, R. Geambasu, D. Hsu, J.-P. Hubaux, M. Humbert, A. Juels, H. Lin, Fairtest: Discovering unwarranted associations in data-driven applications, 2017 IEEE European Symposium on Security and Privacy (2017).

[10] J. Stoyanovich, B. Howe, Nutritional labels for data and models., IEEE Data Eng. Bull. (2019).

[11] D. Dua, C. Graff, UCI machine learning repository, 2017. URL: http://archive.ics.uci.edu/ml.

[12] J. Rammelaere, F. Geerts, Revisiting conditional functional dependency discovery: Splitting the "C" from the "FD", Springer, 2018.

[13] W. Fan, F. Geerts, J. Li, M. Xiong, Discovering conditional functional dependencies, IEEE Transactions on Knowledge and Data Engineering (2010).

On Database Inconsistency Measures

(Discussion Paper)

Francesco Parisi[1], John Grant[2]

[1] *DIMES Department, University of Calabria, Italy*
[2] *University of Maryland at College Park, USA*

Abstract
Although there has been an extensive body of work on handling inconsistency in databases, little work has been done on measuring inconsistency. In this paper, we present inconsistency measures (IMs) for databases with denial constraints. Our database IMs are inspired by well-established methods to quantify inconsistency in propositional knowledge bases, but are tailored to the relational database context where data are generally the reason for inconsistency, not the integrity constraints. We investigate the complexity of some problems related to measuring inconsistency and briefly discuss other ideas concerning IMs.

Keywords
Relational database, Inconsistency measure, Denial constraints

1. Introduction

There is a growing number of applications where inconsistent information arises, often because data are obtained from multiple sources. This has led to an extensive body of work on handling inconsistent data, and in particular inconsistent databases. Approaches for dealing with inconsistent databases include consistent query answering frameworks [1, 2], inconsistency management policies [3, 4, 5], interactive data repairing and cleaning systems [6, 7, 8, 9], as well as interactive data exploration tools [10, 11]. However, little work has been done on measuring inconsistency in databases, a problem that in contrast has been extensively investigated for propositional knowledge bases [12, 13, 14, 15, 16].

Measuring the amount of inconsistency in a database can help in understanding the primary sources of conflicts as well as devising ways to deal with them. For instance, inconsistency measurement has recently been explored in [17] to quantify and understand inconsistency in bank holding company data w.r.t. four consistency rules (i.e., integrity constraints) specifically asserted for the considered domain. In general, quantifying and monitoring the amount of inconsistency helps to get information on the health status of data, whose quality is more and more important nowadays. Furthermore, measuring inconsistency makes it possible to compare the amount of inconsistency between various chunks of information. Indeed, inconsistency measures (IMs for

SEBD 2021: The 29th Italian Symposium on Advanced Database Systems, September 5-9, 2021, Pizzo Calabro (VV), Italy
fparisi@dimes.unical.it (F. Parisi); grant@cs.umd.edu (J. Grant)
0000-0001-9977-1355 (F. Parisi)

short) are important for inconsistency-tolerant integrity checking [18], where one wants to accept an update only if the measure of inconsistency of the old state does not increase in the new state.

Although the idea of measuring inconsistency was introduced more than 40 years ago, in [19], at that time it did not seem to be an important issue. The problem became more noticeable in the 1990s when it became possible to store large amounts of information. It was only in the early 2000s when several AI researchers started to investigate this issue systematically [16]. The bulk of this work since then has been for propositional knowledge bases, that is, where the information is presented as a set of formulas in propositional logic. In the last couple of years the work has been extended to other frameworks. [14] surveys what has been done so far and gives some extensions.

There are few works addressing the problem of measuring inconsistency in relational databases. [20] first developed single-dependency axioms for dirtiness functions quantifying inconsistency w.r.t. one functional dependency (FD)—a simple type of denial constraint—considered in isolation, and proposed an IM that satisfies these axioms. Then a single axiom for dirtiness functions that can handle multiple FDs was proposed, although such functions are supposed to be built on top of dirtiness functions for single FDs. The approach in [21, 22, 23] shows how database IMs can be applied to integrity checking [24, 18], relaxing repairs, and repair checking, which are applications that perfectly fit within our framework. However, the degrees of inconsistency defined in [23] form a partially ordered set; hence it is not always possible to compare the inconsistency of different databases. Finally, [25] proposes an IM based on an abstract repair semantics, where the degree of inconsistency depends on the distance between the database instance and the set of repairs, and an instantiation for cardinality-repairs that can be computed via answer-set programs [26].

Previous work has not investigated the problem of tailoring propositional IMs to relational data, as well as analysing postulates compliance and the complexity of the resulting IMs, which is the focus of our work [27]. We introduce new IMs for relational databases with *denial constraints*. These measures are inspired by IMs for propositional logic. However, we do not apply well-known methods for propositional logic directly, as done for instance in [28, 29]; rather, we use these methods as inspiration to define (by analogy) new IMs for databases. In particular, we introduce the database counterpart, namely $\mathscr{I}_x$ with $x \in \{B, M, \#, P, A, H, C, \eta\}$, of several propositional IMs I_x. Every *database IM* $\mathscr{I}_x$ measures the inconsistency by blaming database tuples only. This is different from measuring the inconsistency of a set of formulas, all of which have the same status, as is the case for propositional knowledge bases. This leads to some substantial differences between the two cases: for instance, some measures that are distinct for propositional knowledge bases become identical in our setting (namely $\mathscr{I}_C$ and $\mathscr{I}_H$). We investigate the complexity of the problems of deciding whether a given value is lower than (**LV**), greater than (**UV**), or equal to (**EV**) the inconsistency measured using a given IM $\mathscr{I}_x$. A summary of the complexity results obtained for these problems, as well as for the problem of computing the actual value of an inconsistency measure (**IM** problem), is reported in Table 1 (Section 2.4). We conclude the paper by discussing rationality postulates for IMs and outlining some directions for future work.

We assume the reader is familiar with the standard concepts of relational database and integrity constraint, and with the complexity classes used in the paper (see e.g. [30] for a comprehensive overview).

2. Database Inconsistency Measures

We use $\mathbf{D}$ to denote the set of all database instances over a fixed but arbitrary database scheme $\mathscr{DS}$. We say that a database instance D is consistent, meaning that D is consistent w.r.t. a fixed but arbitrary set $\mathscr{C}$ of denial constraints. A *denial constraint* is a first-order sentence of the form: $\forall \vec{x}_1, \ldots, \vec{x}_k\ [\neg R_1(\vec{x}_1) \vee \cdots \vee \neg R_k(\vec{x}_k) \vee \varphi(\vec{x}_1, \ldots, \vec{x}_k)]$ where: *(i)* $\forall i \in [1..k]$, $\vec{x}_i$ are tuples of variables and $R_i(\vec{x}_i)$ are atoms over $\mathscr{DS}$; and *(ii)* φ is a disjunction of built-in predicates of the form $\tau_i \circ \tau_j$ where τ_i and τ_j are variables in $\vec{x}_1, \ldots, \vec{x}_k$ or constants, and $\circ \in \{=, \neq, >, <, \geq, \leq\}$. We will write $[\neg R_1(\vec{x}_1) \vee \cdots \vee \neg R_k(\vec{x}_k) \vee \varphi(\vec{x}_1, \ldots, \vec{x}_k)]$ for a constraint (of arity k). For the sake of presentation, we will often omit the database scheme and the set of constraints in the terminology.

The idea of an inconsistency measure is to assign a nonnegative number to a knowledge base that measures its inconsistency[12, 13, 14, 15, 16]. We now define it for a database.

Definition 1 (Inconsistency Measure). *A function $\mathscr{I} : \mathbf{D} \rightarrow \mathbb{R}^{\geq 0}_{\infty}$ is an* **inconsistency measure** *if the following two conditions hold for all $D, D' \in \mathbf{D}$:*
1) ***Consistency****: $\mathscr{I}(D) = 0$ iff D is consistent;*
2) ***Monotony****: If $D \subseteq D'$, then $\mathscr{I}(D) \leq \mathscr{I}(D')$.*

Consistency and Monotony are called (rationality) postulates. Postulates are desirable properties for IMs and we will mention additional ones in Section 3. However, we require that a function on databases must at least satisfy these two postulates in order to be called an IM. Consistency means that all and only consistent databases get measure 0. Monotony means that the enlargement of a database cannot decrease its measure.

A **minimal inconsistent subset** of D is a set of tuples $X \subseteq D$ such that X is inconsistent (with respect to $\mathscr{C}$) and no proper subset of X is inconsistent. We denote by $\mathsf{MI}(D)$ the set of minimal inconsistent subsets of D. Similarly, a **maximal consistent subset** is a set of tuples Y that is consistent and no proper superset of Y is consistent. We write $\mathsf{MC}(D)$ for the set of maximal consistent subsets (of D). Any tuple that occurs in a minimal inconsistent subset is **problematic**; otherwise it is **free**. We use $\mathsf{Problematic}(D)$ and $\mathsf{Free}(D)$ to denote the sets of problematic and free tuples of D. A tuple t is **contradictory** if $\{t\}$ is inconsistent w.r.t. $\mathscr{C}$. We write $\mathsf{Contradictory}(D)$ for the set of contradictory tuples.

Example 1. *Consider the database scheme $\mathscr{DS}_{ex}$ consisting of the relation MealTicket(Number, Value, Holder, Date) whose instance contains the number, the value, the holder, and the issue date of meal tickets (one for each tuple) provided by a company to the employees. $\mathscr{C}_{ex}$ consists of the following denial constraints:*

- $c_1 = [\neg MealTicket(x_1, x_2, x_3, x_4) \vee x_2 > 0]$, *stating that the value (i.e., the amount of the ticket) of every tuple of MealTicket must be a positive number.*
- $c_2 = [\neg MealTicket(x_1, x_2, x_3, x_4) \vee \neg MealTicket(x_1, x_5, x_6, x_7) \vee x_2 = x_5]$, *i.e., the functional dependency Number→Value, stating that there cannot be two distinct tickets with the same number and different values.*
- $c_3 = [\neg MealTicket(x_1, x_2, x_3, x_4) \vee \neg MealTicket(x_1, x_5, x_6, x_7) \vee x_3 = x_6]$, *i.e., the functional dependency Number→Holder.*

- $c_4 = [\neg MealTicket(x_1,x_2,x_3,x_4) \vee \neg MealTicket(x_5,x_6,x_3,x_4) \vee \neg MealTicket(x_7,x_8,x_3,x_4) \vee x_1 = x_5 \vee x_1 = x_7 \vee x_5 = x_7]$, *stating the numerical dependency (see [31]) Holder, Date* $\rightarrow^2$*Number whose meaning is that for every holder and date there can be at most* 2 *meal ticket numbers.*

An instance D_{ex} *of* $\mathscr{DS}_{ex}$ *consisting of* 7 *tuples* $\vec{t}_1,\ldots,\vec{t}_7$ *is shown below.*

Number	*Value*	*Holder*	*Date*	*Tuple*
1001	*15*	*Matthew*	*2018-12-13*	$\vec{t}_1$
1001	*15*	*Matthew*	*2018-12-18*	$\vec{t}_2$
1001	*15*	*Sophia*	*2018-12-17*	$\vec{t}_3$
1004	*20*	*Sophia*	*2018-12-17*	$\vec{t}_4$
1005	*0*	*Alex*	*2018-12-18*	$\vec{t}_5$
1006	*10*	*Alex*	*2018-12-18*	$\vec{t}_6$
1007	*20*	*Alex*	*2018-12-18*	$\vec{t}_7$

Going through the integrity constraints we find that: 1) $\vec{t}_5$ *is inconsistent with* c_1*: it is a contradictory tuple; 2) no pair of tuples violates* c_2*; 3) the two pairs of tuples,* $\vec{t}_1$, $\vec{t}_3$, *and* $\vec{t}_2$, $\vec{t}_3$, *are inconsistent with* c_3*; 4) the three tuples* $\vec{t}_5$, $\vec{t}_6$, *and* $\vec{t}_7$ *together are inconsistent with* c_4*. Hence,* $\mathsf{MI}(D_{ex}) = \{\{\vec{t}_5\},\{\vec{t}_1,\vec{t}_3\},\{\vec{t}_2,\vec{t}_3\}\}$*. Note that* $\{\vec{t}_5,\vec{t}_6,\vec{t}_7\}$ *is not included because it contains* $\{\vec{t}_5\}$ *(and thus it is not minimal). Thus there are* 4 *problematic tuples in* D_{ex}*, and* 3 *free-tuples. Also,* $\mathsf{MC}(D) = \{\{\vec{t}_1,\vec{t}_2,\vec{t}_4,\vec{t}_6,\vec{t}_7\},\{\vec{t}_3,\vec{t}_4,\vec{t}_6,\vec{t}_7\}\}$.

2.1. Measures using Minimal Inconsistent Subsets

We start with the measures that rely on minimal inconsistent subsets and the related concepts defined above. We give the rationale for each measure below.

Definition 2 (Database Inconsistency Measures). *For a database D, the IMs* $\mathscr{I}_B$, $\mathscr{I}_M$, $\mathscr{I}_\#$, $\mathscr{I}_P$, $\mathscr{I}_A$, *and* $\mathscr{I}_H$ *are such that:*

- $\mathscr{I}_B(D) = 1$ *if D is inconsistent and* $\mathscr{I}_B(D) = 0$ *if D is consistent.*
- $\mathscr{I}_M(D) = |\mathsf{MI}(D)|$.
- $\mathscr{I}_\#(D) = \begin{cases} 0 & \text{if } D \text{ is consistent,} \\ \sum_{X \in \mathsf{MI}(D)} \frac{1}{|X|} & \text{otherwise.} \end{cases}$
- $\mathscr{I}_P(D) = |\mathsf{Problematic}(D)|$.
- $\mathscr{I}_A(D) = (|\mathsf{MC}(D)| + |\mathsf{Contradictory}(D)|) - 1$.
- $\mathscr{I}_H(D) = \min\{|X| \text{ s.t. } X \subseteq D \text{ and } \forall M \in \mathsf{MI}(D),\ X \cap M \neq \emptyset\}$.

$\mathscr{I}_B$ is also called the drastic measure [15]: 0 means consistent; 1 means inconsistent. So this measure simply distinguishes between consistent and inconsistent databases. $\mathscr{I}_M$ counts the number of minimal inconsistent subsets [15]. The rationale is that a minimal inconsistent subset represents a minimal inconsistency for a set of database tuples; hence this measure counts the number of such inconsistencies. $\mathscr{I}_\#$ also counts the number of minimal inconsistent subsets, but it gives larger sets a smaller weight. The reason for $I_\#$ in the propositional logic setting is that when a minimal inconsistent set contains more formulas than another minimal inconsistent set, the former is intuitively less inconsistent than the latter [15]. For instance, we can say that intuitively $\{a, \neg a\}$ is more inconsistent than $\{a, a \rightarrow b, b \rightarrow c, c \rightarrow d, \neg d\}$. In the database setting, this measure gives a higher value to the violations of constraints having smaller arity, that is, to violations due to a smaller sets of tuples. It is a way to differentiate between constraints. For instance, in Example 1 this measure gives a violation of c_1 the highest value, a violation of c_4 the lowest value, and a violation of c_2 or c_3 a middle value. $\mathscr{I}_P$ counts the number of tuples that are in one or more minimal inconsistencies [12]. $\mathscr{I}_A$ uses the cardinality of the set of maximal consistent subsets [12], i.e., of the set of database repairs [1]. Intuitively, the larger this set, the larger is the space of different ways to get consistency, the higher the degree of inconsistency. Contradictory tuples are added as they do not appear in any way in a maximal consistent set; then 1 must be subtracted to obtain $\mathscr{I}_A(D) = 0$ for a consistent D because every consistent database has a maximal consistent subset, namely D itself. $\mathscr{I}_H$ counts the minimal number of tuples whose deletion makes the database consistent [13]. Hence $\mathscr{I}_H$ can be written as $\mathscr{I}_H = \min\{|X| \; s.t. \; D \setminus X$ is consistent $\}$. In fact, both $\mathscr{I}_A$ and $\mathscr{I}_H$ link the inconsistency measurement to the ways of restoring consistency, an idea recently explored in [25, 26] where the degree of inconsistency depends on the distance between the database instance and the set of possible repairs under a given repair semantics.

Example 2. *The values of IMs for the database of our running example are as follows.*

- $\mathscr{I}_B(D_{ex}) = 1$ *as the database is inconsistent.*
- $\mathscr{I}_M(D_{ex}) = 3$ *as there are 3 minimal inconsistent subsets as given above.*
- $\mathscr{I}_\#(D_{ex}) = 1 + \frac{1}{2} + \frac{1}{2} = 2$ *as there is one minimal inconsistent subset of size* 1 *and two minimal inconsistent subsets of size* 2.
- $\mathscr{I}_P(D_{ex}) = 4$ *as there are* 4 *distinct tuples in* $\mathsf{MI}(D_{ex})$.
- $\mathscr{I}_A(D_{ex}) = 2$ *because there are* 2 *maximal consistent subsets.*
- $\mathscr{I}_H(D_{ex}) = 2$ *as the set* $\{\vec{t}_3, \vec{t}_5\}$ *intersects with each minimal inconsistent subset.*

2.2. A Measure using Three-valued Logic

The contension measure $\mathscr{I}_C$ [12] uses a three-valued (3VL) logic. A *3VL-interpretation* is a function i that assigns to each atom $R(\vec{t})$ in D one of the three truth values: T (*true*), F (*false*), or B (*both*). A 3VL-interpretation uses an ordering on the truth values where $F < B < T$ and $\wedge$ computes the minimum value while $\vee$ computes the maximum value; also $\neg(B) = B$. So, for example, $B \wedge F = F$ and $B \vee F = B$. Then, an interpretation i satisfies a formula iff the truth-value of the formula for i is T or B.

Given a database D with a set $\mathscr{C}$ of integrity constraints, a 3VL interpretation is a 3VL model iff all the constraints are satisfied and no atom $R(\vec{t}) \in D$ is assigned F. We use $\mathsf{Models}(D)$ to denote the set of 3VL models for a database D (with the integrity constraints in the background). Also, for a 3VL interpretation i we define $\mathsf{Conflictbase}(i) = \{R(\vec{t}) \mid i(R(\vec{t})) = B\}$, the tuples that have truth value B.

Definition 3 (Contension measure $\mathscr{I}_C$). *For database D, measure $\mathscr{I}_C$ is such that $\mathscr{I}_C(D) = \min\{|\mathsf{Conflictbase}(i)| \mid i \in \mathsf{Models}(D)\}$.*

Thus $\mathscr{I}_C$ counts the minimal number of tuples that if we could consider them both true and false would resolve all inconsistencies. For the database of our running example, we have that $\mathscr{I}_C(D_{ex}) = 2$ as the minimal number of B values for an interpretation occurs when $i(\vec{t}_1) = i(\vec{t}_2) = i(\vec{t}_4) = i(\vec{t}_6) = i(\vec{t}_7) = T$ and $i(\vec{t}_3) = i(\vec{t}_5) = B$.

In the propositional case, of the measures considered no 2 measures give the same result for all knowledge bases. But because of the special structure of databases, for database IMs there is an equality that does hold: $\mathscr{I}_C(D) = \mathscr{I}_H(D)$. In fact, $\mathscr{I}_C(D)$ counts the minimum number of tuples that need to be assigned B in order to get a 3VL model in $\mathsf{Models}(D)$. This is the same as the cardinality of the set $X \subseteq D$ having a non-empty intersection with every minimal inconsistent subset of D. It can be shown that no other pair of IMs considered in this paper is identical [27].

2.3. A Probabilistic Measure

Finally, we define the database counterpart of the probabilistic measure I_η that uses the **PSAT (probabilistic satisfiability)** concept [16]. A PSAT instance is a set, $\Gamma = \{\Pr(\phi_i) \geq p_i \mid 1 \leq i \leq m\}$, that assigns probability lower bounds to a set $\{\phi_1, \ldots, \phi_m\}$ of formulas; therefore $0 \leq p_i \leq 1$ for $1 \leq i \leq m$. A *probability function* over a set X is a function $\pi : X \to [0,1]$ such that $\sum_{x \in X} \pi(x) = 1$. Let Int be the set of all (classical) interpretations of the set of formulas and π a probability function over Int. The probability of a formula ϕ according to π is the sum of the probabilities assigned to the interpretations assigning T(rue) to ϕ, that is, $\Pr_\pi(\phi) = \sum_{i \in Int, i(\phi)=T} \pi(i)$ for every formula $\phi \in K$. A PSAT instance is *satisfiable* if there is a probability function π over Int such that $\Pr_\pi(\phi_i) \geq p_i$ for all $1 \leq i \leq m$.

Given a database D, a set of integrity constraints $\mathscr{C}$, and a probability threshold $\eta \in [0,1]$, we define the PSAT instance $\Gamma_{\mathscr{C},\eta}(D) = \{\Pr(R(\vec{t})) \geq \eta \mid R(\vec{t}) \in D\} \cup \{\Pr(g(c)) = 1 \mid g(c)$ is a ground constraint for $c \in \mathscr{C}\}$. Here, integrity constraints are assigned a probability equal to one, analogously to the case of probabilistic databases with integrity constraints (see e.g. [32]).

Definition 4 (Probabilistic measure $\mathscr{I}_\eta$). *Given a database D and a set of constraints $\mathscr{C}$, the inconsistency measure $\mathscr{I}_\eta$ is such that $\mathscr{I}_\eta(D) = 1 - \max\{\eta \in [0,1] \mid \Gamma_{\mathscr{C},\eta}(D)$ is satisfiable$\}$.*

Thus, $\mathscr{I}_\eta(D)$ is one minus the maximum probability lower bound η that one can consistently assign to all tuples in D. For our running example, we have that $\mathscr{I}_\eta(D_{ex}) = 1$ because the maximum probability that can be assigned to (contradictory) tuple $\vec{t}_5$ is 0.

2.4. Complexity of the Database Inconsistency Measures

We investigate the data-complexity of the three decision problems, which intuitively ask if a given rational value v is, respectively, lower than, greater than, or equal to the value returned by a given IM when applied to a given database. Observe that every IM returns a rational number, including $\mathscr{I}_\eta$ (as it can be shown by reasoning as in [16]).

Table 1
Complexity of **LV**, **UV**, **EV**, and **IM** problems.

Measure(s)	$\mathbf{LV}_{\mathscr{I}}(D,v)$	$\mathbf{UV}_{\mathscr{I}}(D,v)$	$\mathbf{EV}_{\mathscr{I}}(D,v)$	$\mathbf{IM}_{\mathscr{I}}(D)$
$\mathscr{I}_B, \mathscr{I}_M, \mathscr{I}_\#, \mathscr{I}_P$	P	P	P	FP
$\mathscr{I}_A$	PP	PP	PP	$\#P$-complete
$\mathscr{I}_H$, $\mathscr{I}_C$	$coNP$-complete	NP-complete	D^p-complete	$FP^{NP[\log n]}$-complete
$\mathscr{I}_\eta$	$coNP$-complete	NP-complete	D^p	FP^{NP}

Definition 5 (Lower (LV), Upper (UV), and Exact Value (EV) problems). *Let $\mathscr{I}$ be an IM. Given a database D over a fixed database scheme with a fixed set of denial constraints, and a value $v \in \mathbb{Q}^{>0}$, $\mathbf{LV}_{\mathscr{I}}(D,v)$ is the problem of deciding whether $\mathscr{I}(D) \geq v$. Given D and $v' \in \mathbb{Q}^{\geq 0}$, $\mathbf{UV}_{\mathscr{I}}(D,v')$ is the problem of deciding whether $\mathscr{I}(D) \leq v'$, and $\mathbf{EV}_{\mathscr{I}}(D,v')$ is the problem of deciding whether $\mathscr{I}(D) = v'$.*

We also consider the problem of determining the IM value.

Definition 6 (Inconsistency Measurement (IM) problem). *Let $\mathscr{I}$ be an IM. Given a database D over a fixed database scheme with a fixed set of denial constraints, $\mathbf{IM}_{\mathscr{I}}(D)$ is the problem of computing the value of $\mathscr{I}(D)$.*

The complexity of $\mathbf{LV}_{\mathscr{I}}(D,v)$, $\mathbf{UV}_{\mathscr{I}}(D,v)$, $\mathbf{EV}_{\mathscr{I}}(D,v)$, and $\mathbf{IM}_{\mathscr{I}}(D)$ is as given in Table 1 [27]. Interestingly, while the measures $\mathscr{I}_B$, $\mathscr{I}_M$, $\mathscr{I}_\#$, $\mathscr{I}_P$ become tractable in the database setting and the complexity of $\mathscr{I}_A$ decreases, the measures $\mathscr{I}_H$ and $\mathscr{I}_\eta$ remain as hard as in the propositional case [33] even under data complexity.

3. Discussion and Future Work

We have introduced a framework for measuring inconsistency in databases. We believe that the definition and investigation of IMs for databases benefit from our approach to the problem, which stems from what has been done in the past by the AI community.

In [27] we also introduced the database counterparts of six rationality *postulates* defined for propositional knowledge bases (in addition to Consistency and Monotony, cf. Definition 1). For instance, *Free-Tuple Independence* states that deleting/adding a free tuple does not change the IM value, while *Penalty* states that deleting a problematic tuple decreases the measure. Thus, IMs satisfying these postulates allow us to check if deleting a given tuple makes a database less inconsistent or not. *Super-Additivity* deals with the union of two disjoint databases, and states that the measure of the union is at least as great as the sum of the measures of the two databases. Thus, an IM satisfying Super-Additivity is able to separately count the inconsistency arising from different sources. Other postulates considered in [27] help in describing the behavior of IMs.

Some postulates violated in the propositional case become satisfied in the database case. Specifically, $\mathscr{I}_M$ satisfies all the postulates considered in [27]. One step down, we find $\mathscr{I}_\#$ which satisfies all the postulates but one. Next, $\mathscr{I}_P$ satisfies all the postulates but two. $\mathscr{I}_H$ which as said above coincides with $\mathscr{I}_C$ in our setting also satisfies all the postulates but two, though it turns out to be computationally hard. Notably $\mathscr{I}_M$, $\mathscr{I}_\#$, and $\mathscr{I}_P$ can be evaluated by standard SQL, meaning that measuring inconsistency using these measures scales as far as the database can answer queries in reasonable time.

Many interesting issues concerning IMs in databases remain unexplored. We have dealt with denial constraints, a common type of integrity constraint which can express for instance equality generating dependencies (e.g., functional dependencies). We plan to extend our work to other types of integrity constraints, and in particular to inclusion dependencies. Also, we plan to identify tractable cases for the hard measures, possibly exploiting connections with work done on inconsistent databases (e.g., results in [34] help in characterizing the complexity of $\mathscr{I}_A$), and devise efficient algorithms and index structures for evaluating IMs. The IMs we have considered work at the tuple-level, without distinguishing inconsistency arising from different attributes, which is another issue we want to address in the future. Moreover, we plan to investigate methods for measuring the degree of inconsistency of query answers by leveraging on our IMs (an recent proposal in this direction is [35]). Finally, another interesting direction for future work is considering incomplete information (e.g., databases with null values).

References

[1] M. Arenas, L. E. Bertossi, J. Chomicki, Consistent query answers in inconsistent databases, in: Proc. of Symposium on Principles of Database Systems (PODS), 1999, pp. 68–79.

[2] M. Calautti, L. Libkin, A. Pieris, An operational approach to consistent query answering, in: Proc. of Symposium on Principles of Database Systems (PODS), 2018, pp. 239–251.

[3] M. V. Martinez, F. Parisi, A. Pugliese, G. I. Simari, V. S. Subrahmanian, Inconsistency management policies, in: Proc. of KR, 2008, pp. 367–377.

[4] M. V. Martinez, F. Parisi, A. Pugliese, G. I. Simari, V. S. Subrahmanian, Efficient policy-based inconsistency management in relational knowledge bases, in: Proc. of Int. Conference on Scalable Uncertainty Management (SUM), 2010, pp. 264–277.

[5] M. V. Martinez, F. Parisi, A. Pugliese, G. I. Simari, V. S. Subrahmanian, Policy-based inconsistency management in relational databases, Int. J. Approx. Reas. 55 (2014) 501–528.

[6] B. Fazzinga, S. Flesca, F. Furfaro, F. Parisi, DART: A data acquisition and repairing tool, in: EDBT Workshop on Inconsistency and Incompleteness in Databases, 2006, pp. 297–317.

[7] S. Flesca, F. Furfaro, F. Parisi, Preferred database repairs under aggregate constraints, in: Proc. of Int. Conference on Scalable Uncertainty Management (SUM), 2007, pp. 215–229.

[8] S. Hao, N. Tang, G. Li, J. He, N. Ta, J. Feng, A novel cost-based model for data repairing, IEEE Trans. Knowl. Data Eng. 29 (2017) 727–742.

[9] J. He, E. Veltri, D. Santoro, G. Li, G. Mecca, P. Papotti, N. Tang, Interactive and deterministic data cleaning, in: Proc. of SIGMOD, 2016, pp. 893–907.

[10] T. Bleifuß, L. Bornemann, D. V. Kalashnikov, F. Naumann, D. Srivastava, DBChEx: Interactive exploration of data and schema change, in: Proc. of CIDR, 2019.

[11] A. Giuzio, G. Mecca, E. Quintarelli, M. Roveri, D. Santoro, L. Tanca, INDIANA: an interactive system for assisting database exploration, Inf. Syst. 83 (2019) 40–56.

[12] J. Grant, A. Hunter, Measuring consistency gain and information loss in stepwise inconsistency resolution, in: Proc. of ECSQARU, 2011, pp. 362–373.

[13] J. Grant, A. Hunter, Distance-based measures of inconsistency, in: Proc. of ECSQARU, 2013, pp. 230–241.
[14] J. Grant, M. V. Martinez, Measuring Inconsistency in Information, College Pub., 2018.
[15] A. Hunter, S. Konieczny, Measuring inconsistency through minimal inconsistent sets, in: Proc. of Principles of Knowledge Representation and Reasoning (KR), 2008, pp. 358–366.
[16] K. Knight, Measuring inconsistency, J. Philosophical Logic 31 (2002) 77–98.
[17] L. Fan, M. D. Flood, J. Grant, Measuring inconsistency in bank holding company data, in: Proc. of SIGMOD Workshop on Data Science for Macro-modeling with Financial and Economic Datasets (DSMM), 2019, pp. 5:1–5:5.
[18] H. Decker, D. Martinenghi, Inconsistency-tolerant integrity checking, IEEE Trans. Knowl. Data Eng. 23 (2011) 218–234.
[19] J. Grant, Classifications for inconsistent theories, Notre Dame J. Formal Log. 19 (1978) 435–444.
[20] M. V. Martinez, A. Pugliese, G. I. Simari, V. S. Subrahmanian, H. Prade, How dirty is your relational database? an axiomatic approach, in: Proc. of ECSQARU, 2007, pp. 103–114.
[21] H. Decker, Inconsistency-tolerant database repairs and simplified repair checking by measure-based integrity checking, Trans. L. S. Data Knowl. Cent. Syst. 34 (2017) 153–183.
[22] H. Decker, S. Misra, Database inconsistency measures and their applications, in: Proc. of Int. Conf. on Information and Software Technologies (ICIST), 2017, pp. 254–265.
[23] H. Decker, Measuring database inconsistency, in: J. Grant, M. V. Martinez (Eds.), Measuring Inconsistency in Information, College Publications, 2018, pp. 271–311.
[24] H. Decker, D. Martinenghi, Classifying integrity checking methods with regard to inconsistency tolerance, in: Proc. of Prin. and Pract. of Decl. Prog. (PPDP), 2008, pp. 195–204.
[25] L. E. Bertossi, Measuring and computing database inconsistency via repairs, in: Proc. of International Conference on Scalable Uncertainty Management (SUM), 2018, pp. 368–372.
[26] L. E. Bertossi, Repair-based degrees of database inconsistency, in: Proc. of Logic Programming and Nonmonotonic Reasoning (LPNMR), 2019, pp. 195–209.
[27] F. Parisi, J. Grant, On measuring inconsistency in relational databases with denial constraints, in: Proc. of European Conf. on Artificial Intelligence (ECAI), 2020, pp. 857–864.
[28] J. Grant, F. Parisi, Measuring inconsistency in a general information space, in: Proc. of Int. Symp. on Foundations of Information and Knowledge Systems (FoIKS), 2020, pp. 140–156.
[29] J. Grant, F. Parisi, General information spaces: measuring inconsistency, rationality postulates, and complexity, Ann. Math. Artif. Intell. (2021).
[30] C. H. Papadimitriou, Computational complexity, Addison-Wesley, 1994.
[31] J. Grant, J. Minker, Inferences for numerical dependencies, TCS 41 (1985) 271–287.
[32] S. Flesca, F. Furfaro, F. Parisi, Consistency checking and querying in probabilistic databases under integrity constraints, J. Comput. Syst. Sci. 80 (2014) 1448–1489.
[33] M. Thimm, J. P. Wallner, Some complexity results on inconsistency measurement, in: Proc. of Principles of Knowledge Representation and Reasoning (KR), 2016, pp. 114–124.
[34] E. Livshits, B. Kimelfeld, Counting and enumerating (preferred) database repairs, in: Proc. of Symposium on Principles of Database Systems (PODS), 2017, pp. 289–301.
[35] O. Issa, A. Bonifati, F. Toumani, Evaluating top-k queries with inconsistency degrees, Proc. VLDB Endow. 13 (2020) 2146–2158.

Benchmarking Approximate Consistent Query Answering

(Discussion Paper)

Marco Calautti[1], Marco Console[2] and Andreas Pieris[3]

[1] *DISI, University of Trento, Italy*
[2] *Sapienza, University of Rome, Italy*
[3] *University of Edinburgh, UK*

Abstract

Consistent query answering (CQA) aims to deliver meaningful answers when queries are evaluated over inconsistent databases. Such answers must be certainly true in all repairs, which are consistent databases whose difference from the inconsistent one is somehow minimal. A more informative notion is the percentage of repairs in which a candidate answer is true, called relative frequency. Computing this percentage is intractable in general, but for the relevant setting of conjunctive queries and primary keys, data-efficient randomized approximation schemes exist. Our goal is to perform a thorough experimental evaluation and comparison of those approximation schemes and provide new insights on which technique is indicated depending on key characteristics of the input.

1. Introduction

A database is inconsistent if it does not conform to its specifications given in the form of constraints. There is a consensus that inconsistency is a real-life phenomenon that arises due to many reasons such as integration of conflicting sources. With the aim of obtaining conceptually meaningful answers to queries posed over inconsistent databases, Arenas, Bertossi, and Chomicki introduced in the late 1990s the notion of Consistent Query Answering (CQA) [1]. The key elements underlying CQA are (1) the notion of *repair* of an inconsistent database D, that is, a consistent database that differs somehow minimally from the original database D, and (2) the notion of query answering based on *certain answers*, i.e., answers that are entailed by every repair. Here is a simple example taken from [2]:

Example 1. *Consider the single relation* Employee(id, name, dept) *where the attribute* id *is the key of the relation* Employee. *Consider also the database D consisting of the tuples:*

$$(1, \text{Bob}, \text{HR}) \quad (1, \text{Bob}, \text{IT}) \quad (2, \text{Alice}, \text{IT}) \quad (2, \text{Tim}, \text{IT}).$$

Observe that the above database is inconsistent w.r.t. the key constraint since we are uncertain about Bob's department, and the name of the employee with id 2. *In this case, to devise a repair, we only need to keep one of the two atoms that are in a conflict. In this way, we obtain a $\subseteq$-maximal subset of D that is consistent. Consider now the Boolean query that asks whether employees* 1 *and*

SEBD 2021: The 29th Italian Symposium on Advanced Database Systems, September 5-9, 2021, Pizzo Calabro (VV), Italy
marco.calautti@unitn (M. Calautti); console@diag.uniroma1.it (M. Console); apieris@inf.ed.ac.uk (A. Pieris)

CEUR Workshop Proceedings (CEUR-WS.org)

2 *work in the same department. This query is true only in two repairs, thus, according to certain answers, is not entailed.* ■

CQA has been extensively studied both in theory (see, e.g., [3, 4, 5]), and in practice (see, e.g., [6, 7]). Nevertheless, the CQA approach comes with a conceptual limitation. The notion of certain answers only says that a candidate answer is entailed by *all* repairs, or is not entailed by *at least one* repair. But, as it has been frequently observed (e.g., see [2, 8, 9]), the former is too strict, while the latter is not very useful in a practical context.

A Refined Approach. A simple step in obtaining more information for a candidate answer is to consider its relative frequency, i.e., the percentage of repairs that entail the answer [2]. In Example 1, the relative frequency of the empty tuple (i.e., the only candidate answer for Boolean queries) is 50% since, out of four repairs in total, only two satisfy the query. However, computing this simple measure is #P-hard, even in data complexity, i.e., when the query and the constraints are fixed, and even if we focus on conjunctive queries and primary keys [10]. Hence, the way to proceed is to give up exact solutions, and target approximations.

Data-efficient Approximations. Approximation algorithms have been crucial for tackling intractable problems in different areas of Data Management. Examples are in the context of approximating certain answers over incomplete databases, where different approximation algorithms have been devised and experimentally evaluated [11, 12, 13]. In the case of inconsistent databases, data-efficient randomized algorithms exist, in the relevant setting of conjunctive queries and primary keys, that approximate the relative frequency of a candidate answer within a desired error, with high probability [2]. These rely on techniques that have been originally proposed to approximate the number of satisfying assignments of DNF Boolean formulas [14]. However, no corresponding infrastructure for experimentally evaluating such techniques exists.

Main Objective. The main objective of this work is to provide a benchmark for these randomized approximation schemes, when considering primary keys and conjunctive queries, covering a wide range of scenarios, and exploit this benchmark to asses how the performance of the approximation schemes is affected by key parameters of the input.[1]

2. Preliminaries

Relational Databases. A *schema* $\mathbf{S}$ is a finite set of relation symbols (or predicates) with associated arity. A *database* D over a schema $\mathbf{S}$ is a set of facts of the form $R(\bar{t})$, where $R \in \mathbf{S}$, and $\bar{t} = t_1, \ldots, t_n$ is a tuple of terms that are drawn from a countably infinite set $\mathbf{C}$ of constants. We write $\mathsf{dom}(D)$ for the *active domain* of D, that is, the set of constants occurring in D.

Primary Key Constraints. A *key constraint* (or *key*) κ over a schema $\mathbf{S}$ is an expression $\mathsf{key}(R) = \{1, \ldots, m\}$, where $R \in \mathbf{S}$ has arity n, and $m \leq n$; we also call it an R-key. A database D satisfies κ if, for every $R(\bar{t}), R(\bar{s}) \in D$, $\bar{t}[i] = \bar{s}[i]$ for each $i \in \{1, \ldots, m\}$ implies $\bar{t} = \bar{s}$. We say that D is *consistent* w.r.t. a set Σ of keys, written $D \models \Sigma$, if D satisfies each key in Σ; otherwise, it is *inconsistent*. A set of *primary keys* Σ is a set of keys such that, for each predicate R, Σ has at most one R-key. For $\alpha = R(c_1, \ldots, c_n)$, the *key value* of

[1] An extended version of this paper has been accepted to PODS 2021, and can be found at https://tinyurl.com/f8sev5pj. Source code and test scenarios can be found at https://gitlab.com/mcalautti/cqabench.

α w.r.t. Σ, denoted $\mathsf{key}_\Sigma(\alpha)$, is defined as $\langle R, \langle c_1, \ldots, c_m \rangle\rangle$, if $\mathsf{key}(R) = \{1, \ldots, m\} \in \Sigma$, and $\langle R, \langle c_1, \ldots, c_n \rangle\rangle$ otherwise. Let $\mathsf{block}_\Sigma(\alpha, D) = \{\beta \in D \mid \mathsf{key}_\Sigma(\beta) = \mathsf{key}_\Sigma(\alpha)\}$, and $\mathsf{block}_\Sigma(D) = \{\mathsf{block}_\Sigma(\alpha, D) \mid \alpha \in D\}$. A *repair* of D w.r.t. Σ is a database obtained by choosing one fact from each $B \in \mathsf{block}_\Sigma(D)$. We denote the set of repairs of D w.r.t Σ as $\mathsf{rep}(D, \Sigma)$.

Conjunctive Queries. A *conjunctive query* $Q(\bar{x})$ over a schema $\mathbf{S}$ is a first-order expression of the form $\exists \bar{y}\, (R_1(\bar{z}_1) \wedge \cdots \wedge R_n(\bar{z}_n))$ that mentions only atoms over $\mathbf{S}$, and has free variables $\bar{x}$. For a tuple $\bar{t} \in \mathbf{C}^{|\bar{x}|}$, $Q(\bar{t})$ denotes Q after replacing the i-th variable in $\bar{x}$ with the i-th constant in $\bar{t}$. A *homomorphism* from Q to a database D is a function h from the set of variables and constants in Q to $\mathsf{dom}(D)$ that is the identity over $\mathbf{C}$ such that $R_i(h(\bar{z}_i)) \in D$ for every $i \in [n]$. We use $Q \xrightarrow{h} D$ to say that h is a homomorphism from Q to D. The answer to $Q(\bar{x})$ over a database D, denoted $Q(D)$, is the set of tuples $\{h(\bar{x}) \in \mathsf{dom}(D)^{|\bar{x}|} \mid Q(\bar{x}) \xrightarrow{h} D\}$.

Consistent Query Answering. Consider a database D, a set Σ of primary keys, and a CQ $Q(\bar{x})$. The *relative frequency* of a tuple $\bar{t} \in \mathsf{dom}(D)^{|\bar{x}|}$ w.r.t. D, Σ and Q is the ratio $\mathsf{R}_{D,\Sigma,Q}(\bar{t}) = |\{D' \in \mathsf{rep}(D, \Sigma) \mid \bar{t} \in Q(D')\}| / |\mathsf{rep}(D, \Sigma)|$. Our main problem is:

PROBLEM :	CQA
INPUT :	A database D, a set Σ of primary keys, and a CQ $Q(\bar{x})$.
OUTPUT :	The set $\{(\bar{t}, \mathsf{R}_{D,\Sigma,Q}(\bar{t})) \mid \bar{t} \in \mathsf{dom}(D)^{|\bar{x}|} \text{ and } \mathsf{R}_{D,\Sigma,Q}(\bar{t}) > 0\}$.

That is, output, for each candidate answer tuple $\bar{t}$, its relative frequency, when this is not zero. We dub the problem of computing $\mathsf{R}_{D,\Sigma,Q}(\bar{t})$, given $D, \Sigma, Q, \bar{t}$, RelativeFreq. We know that RelativeFreq is #P-hard, in data complexity. Clearly, having an efficient way of approximating the relative frequency of a tuple will immediately provide an algorithm for approximately solving CQA. Hence, in the rest, we focus on RelativeFreq.

Approximate CQA. A *(data-efficient) randomized approximation scheme* for the problem RelativeFreq is a randomized algorithm A that takes a database D, a set Σ of primary keys, a CQ $Q(\bar{x})$, a tuple $\bar{t} \in \mathsf{dom}(D)^{|\bar{x}|}$, and numbers $\epsilon > 0$ and $0 < \delta < 1$, runs in polynomial time in $||D|| + ||\bar{t}||$,[2] $1/\epsilon$ and $\log(1/\delta)$, and produces a random variable $\mathcal{A}$ such that $\Pr(|\mathcal{A} - \mathsf{R}_{D,\Sigma,Q}(\bar{t})| \leq \epsilon \cdot \mathsf{R}_{D,\Sigma,Q}(\bar{t})) \geq 1 - \delta$.

3. Approximation Schemes

In principle, an approximation scheme for RelativeFreq would require to access the input database D. However, doing this naively is prohibitive in practice since, in general, D is very large. However, an approximation scheme for RelativeFreq only needs a small part of the database, which we call synopsis. In what follows, let $D, \Sigma, Q(\bar{x}), \bar{t}$ be a database, a set of primary keys, a CQ and a tuple in $\mathsf{dom}(D)^{|\bar{x}|}$, respectively.

The (Σ, Q)-*synopsis of* D *for* $\bar{t}$ is the pair $(\mathcal{H}, \mathcal{B})$, where $\mathcal{H} = \{h(Q) \mid Q(\bar{t}) \xrightarrow{h} D, \text{ and } h(Q) \models \Sigma\}$ and $\mathcal{B} = \{\mathsf{block}_\Sigma(\alpha, D) \mid \alpha \in \cup_{H \in \mathcal{H}} H\}$. That is, the (Σ, Q)-synopsis of D for $\bar{t}$ collects all the consistent homomorphic images of $Q(\bar{t})$ in D (the set $\mathcal{H}$), and the blocks of the atoms occurring in a consistent homomorphic image of $Q(\bar{t})$ in D (the

[2] As usual, for a syntactic object o, we write $||o||$ for its size.

set $\mathcal{B}$). We also let $\mathsf{db}(\mathcal{B}) = \{\{\alpha_1, \ldots, \alpha_n\} \mid \langle \alpha_1, \ldots, \alpha_n \rangle \in \times_{B \in \mathcal{B}} B\}$, i.e., the set of databases that can be formed by keeping exactly one atom from each member B of $\mathcal{B}$. Finally, $\mathsf{R}_{(\mathcal{H},\mathcal{B})} = |\{I \in \mathsf{db}(\mathcal{B}) \mid H \subseteq I \text{ for some } H \in \mathcal{H}\}| |\mathsf{db}(\mathcal{B})|$.[3]

We show that the (Σ, Q)-synopsis of a database D for a tuple $\bar{t}$ can be efficiently constructed, and it contains enough information that allows us to compute the relative frequency of $\bar{t}$.

Lemma 2. *If $(\mathcal{H}, \mathcal{B})$ is the (Σ, Q)-synopsis of D for $\bar{t}$, then :1) $(\mathcal{H}, \mathcal{B})$ can be computed in polynomial time in $||D|| + ||\bar{t}||$; 2) $\mathsf{R}_{D,\Sigma,Q}(\bar{t}) = \mathsf{R}_{(\mathcal{H},\mathcal{B})}$; 3) $\mathsf{R}_{D,\Sigma,Q}(\bar{t}) = 0$ iff $\mathcal{H} = \emptyset$.*

3.1. Monte Carlo Approach

Let $(\mathcal{H}, \mathcal{B})$ be the (D, Σ)-synopsis of some tuple $\bar{t}$ and let Sample be a randomized procedure that with input $(\mathcal{H}, \mathcal{B})$, computes a random number in $[0, 1]$. Being randomized, its output is determined by the underlying sampling space obtained from $(\mathcal{H}, \mathcal{B})$. $\mathsf{Sample}(\mathcal{H}, \mathcal{B})$ produces a random variable, and a crucial problem for us is computing its expected value $\mathbb{E}[\mathsf{Sample}(\mathcal{H}, \mathcal{B})]$.

$\mathbb{E}[\mathsf{Sample}(\mathcal{H}, \mathcal{B})]$ can be approximated by performing the following: (1) $S := 0$, (2) for N times do the following: $S := S + \mathsf{Sample}(\mathcal{H}, \mathcal{B})$, and finally (3) return S/N.

It is clear that as long as we increase the number N of iterations in the above procedure, the ratio S/N is a better approximation of $\mathbb{E}[\mathsf{Sample}(\mathcal{H}, \mathcal{B})]$. From [15], we know that we can compute the *minimum* number (up to constant factors) of iterations N such that the above algorithm approximates $\mathbb{E}[\mathsf{Sample}(\mathcal{H}, \mathcal{B})]$ within a given error ϵ, and with probability at least $1 - \delta$, for some given $0 < \delta < 1$. By exploiting this approach in the algorithm discussed above, we obtain the algorithm MonteCarlo[Sample], which is parametrized with a randomized procedure Sample. Let $||\mathcal{H}, \mathcal{B}|| = |\mathcal{H}| + \max_{H \in \mathcal{H}}\{||H||\} + ||\mathcal{B}||$. From [15], we know that:

(*) *If* Sample *runs in polynomial time in $||\mathcal{H}, \mathcal{B}||$ and $\mathbb{E}[\mathsf{Sample}(\mathcal{H}, \mathcal{B})] > 1/\mathsf{pol}(||\mathcal{H}, \mathcal{B}||)$, when $\mathbb{E}[\mathsf{Sample}(\mathcal{H}, \mathcal{B})] > 0$, for some polynomial* pol, *then* MonteCarlo[Sample] *is a data-efficient randomized approximation scheme for computing* $\mathbb{E}[\mathsf{Sample}(\mathcal{H}, \mathcal{B})]$.[4]

By combining the above property and Lemma 2, an approximation scheme for RelativeFreq can be obtained by devising the right sampling procedure Sample.

Natural Sampling Space. The first sampler, which we call SampleNatural, takes as input $(\mathcal{H}, \mathcal{B})$, and has $\mathbb{E}[\mathsf{SampleNatural}(\mathcal{H}, \mathcal{B})] = \mathsf{R}_{(\mathcal{H},\mathcal{B})}$, i.e., its expected value precisely coincides with the relative frequency. This sampler simply performs the following: *1)* sample a database $I \in \mathsf{db}(\mathcal{B})$ uniformly at random (u.a.r.); *2)* if $H \subseteq I$, for some $H \in \mathcal{H}$, output 1, otherwise output 0. We can prove that SampleNatural enjoys (*) and $\mathbb{E}[\mathsf{SampleNatural}(\mathcal{H}, \mathcal{B})] = \mathsf{R}_{(\mathcal{H},\mathcal{B})}$. By Lemma 2, the algorithm that constructs the (D, Σ)-synopsis $(\mathcal{H}, \mathcal{B})$ of $\bar{t}$, and runs MonteCarlo[SampleNatural] with input $(\mathcal{H}, \mathcal{B})$, is an approximation scheme for RelativeFreq. This algorithm is called Natural.

Symbolic Sampling Space. An alternative sampler is one whose expected value, on input $(\mathcal{H}, \mathcal{B})$, is a number from which $\mathsf{R}_{(\mathcal{H},\mathcal{B})}$ can be derived. We devise a slightly more complex sampling space, called symbolic, by exploiting ideas from [14]. Let $H_1, \ldots, H_n$ be an arbitrary order-

[3] In case $\mathcal{H} = \emptyset$, we let $\mathsf{R}_{(\mathcal{H},\mathcal{B})} = 0$.

[4] In a data-efficient randomized approximation scheme for EV[Sample] the output to be approximated is $\mathbb{E}[\mathsf{Sample}((\mathcal{H}, \mathcal{B}))]$, and the running time must be polynomial in $||\mathcal{H}, \mathcal{B}||$ (and $1/\epsilon$ and $\log(1/\delta)$), as these are the parameters of a synopsis that depend on the database.

ing (e.g., lexicographical) among the databases of $\mathcal{H}$. For each $i \in [n]$, $\mathcal{I}^i_{\mathcal{H},\mathcal{B}}$ is set of all $I \in \mathsf{db}(\mathcal{B})$ such that $H_i \subseteq I$. Our sampling space is defined as $\mathcal{S}^{\bullet}_{\mathcal{H},\mathcal{B}} = \left\{(i, I) \mid i \in [n] \text{ and } I \in \mathcal{I}^i_{\mathcal{H},\mathcal{B}}\right\}$.

Our second sampler, called SampleKL, performs the following: *1)* sample $(i, I) \in \mathcal{S}^{\bullet}_{\mathcal{H},\mathcal{B}}$ u.a.r., *2)* if there is no $j < i$ s.t. $(j, I) \in \mathcal{S}^{\bullet}_{\mathcal{H},\mathcal{B}}$, then output 1, otherwise output 0. We can prove that SampleKL enjoys (*) and that its expected value is $r/|\mathcal{S}^{\bullet}_{\mathcal{H},\mathcal{B}}|$, where r is the numerator of $\mathsf{R}_{(\mathcal{H},\mathcal{B})}$. Hence, we consider the algorithm KL, that constructs the (D, Σ)-synopsis $(\mathcal{H}, \mathcal{B})$ of $\bar{t}$, runs the algorithm MonteCarlo[SampleKL] with input $(\mathcal{H}, \mathcal{B})$, and multiplies its output by $|\mathcal{S}^{\bullet}_{\mathcal{H},\mathcal{B}}|/|\mathsf{db}(\mathcal{B})|$. By Lemma 2, KL is an approximation scheme for RelativeFreq.

One can devise a slightly different sampler, called SampleKLM, that has a lower variance in general w.r.t. SampleKL. Using SampleKLM in place of SampleKL, as discussed above, we obtain the approximation scheme for RelativeFreq called KLM.

3.2. Union of Sets Approach

An approximation scheme, called *self-adjusting coverage algorithm* was presented in [14] for the *union of sets problem*, which takes a description of $n \geq 1$ sets $S_1, \ldots, S_n$, and the output is $|\bigcup_{i\in[n]} S_i|$. For space reasons, we do not present this algorithm, but only show how RelativeFreq reduces to this problem. We first construct the (Σ, Q)-synopsis of D for $\bar{t}$, $(\mathcal{H}, \mathcal{B})$. Then, since $\bigcup_i \mathcal{I}^i_{\mathcal{H},\mathcal{B}}$ is the numerator of the ratio $\mathsf{R}_{(\mathcal{H},\mathcal{B})}$, we approximate the value $|\bigcup_i \mathcal{I}^i_{\mathcal{H},\mathcal{B}}|$ via the self-adjusting coverage algorithm of [14], by seeing $(\mathcal{H}, \mathcal{B})$ as the description of the sets $\mathcal{I}^i_{\mathcal{H},\mathcal{B}}$, for each i. Then, dividing the result by $|\mathsf{db}(\mathcal{B})|$ will give an approximation of $\mathsf{R}_{(\mathcal{H},\mathcal{B})}$. This, together with Lemma 2, provides an approximation scheme for RelativeFreq, which we dub Cover.

4. The Benchmark

Implementation. Note that to compute the approximate relative frequency of each candidate tuple $\bar{t}$, the corresponding synopsis must be computed first, regardless of the chosen algorithm. We show we can construct the set $\mathsf{syn}_{\Sigma,Q}(D)$ of all pairs $(\bar{t}, S)$, with S the (D, Σ)-synopsis of $\bar{t} \in \mathsf{dom}(D)^{|\bar{x}|}$, with $\mathsf{R}_{D,\Sigma,Q}(\bar{t}) > 0$, via a single SQL query, obtained by a careful rewriting of the original query Q. We call this initial precomputation of $\mathsf{syn}_{\Sigma,Q}(D)$ the *preprocessing step*. For implementing the approximation schemes, we extended the framework of [16] of approximation algorithms for the number of satisfying assignments of DNF formulas.

Experimental Setting. To effectively evaluate our algorithms, our test scenarios must expose how the running time of the approximation schemes is affected by key input parameters like the inconsistency of the database, and the number of joins in the query.

Data Generator. We generate databases using the dbgen tool of the TPC-H benchmark. Databases of varied size can be generated by providing a *scale factor* as input. Since the generated databases are consistent w.r.t. the underlying constraints we will later inject inconsistency via a noise generator that we developed.

Query-aware Noise Generator. General-purpose noise generators exist in the literature; see, e.g., [17]. However, all such tools are query-oblivious, i.e., do not take into account any query: if we generate noise by randomly adding facts to the database, considering only the primary keys, it is likely that we will not affect the evaluation of the query (and hence the synopses), as in general, databases are much larger than the actual synopses.

Given $D, \Sigma, Q(\bar{x})$, a percentage $0 < p < 1$ and an integer interval $[l, u]$, our noise generator constructs the set $\mathsf{syn}_{\Sigma,Q}(D)$, and for each $(\bar{t}, (\mathcal{H}, \mathcal{B}))$, randomly chooses $\ell = \lceil p \cdot |\mathcal{B}| \rceil$ blocks $B_1, \ldots, B_\ell$, and for each B_i, adds to D a random number $t \in [l, u]$ of tuples having the same key value as the one of B_i. These tuples are constructed by reusing existing tuples from D, and by changing their key value. This ensures that the new tuples preserve the join patterns of D.

Query Generator. To generate our stress test queries we exploit a recent query generator [18], which we call *static query generator* (SQG) since it can control static query parameters, such as the number of joins, and the number of free variables (i.e., output variables). As we also want to precisely control the *size* of the synopsis, we also consider some dynamic query parameters.

Letting $\mathsf{syn}_{\Sigma,Q}(D) = \{(\bar{t}_i, (\mathcal{H}_i, \mathcal{B}_i))\}_{i \in [n]}$ for some $n \geq 1$, we consider the *homomorphic size* of Q w.r.t. D defined as $|\bigcup_{i=1}^{n} \mathcal{H}_i|$, which measures how large is the portion of D that can affect any (D, Σ)-synopsis in $\mathsf{syn}_{\Sigma,Q}(D)$. Since synopses in $\mathsf{syn}_{\Sigma,Q}(D)$ can have different sizes, it is natural to consider the *average* size of a (Σ, Q)-synopsis in $\mathsf{syn}_{\Sigma,Q}(D)$ as a key parameter, which is given by $\frac{|\bigcup_{i=1}^{n} \mathcal{H}_i|}{|\mathsf{syn}_{\Sigma,Q}(D)|}$. We normalize the above to a number in the interval $(0, 1)$ by considering its inverse. We call this number the *balance of* Q *w.r.t.* D. The closer the balance to 1 (resp., 0) is, the smaller (resp., larger) the average size of a (Σ, Q)-synopsis is.

We developed a query generator, called dynamic, that modifies a query generated by the SQG so that it has a desired balance w.r.t. the given database D.

Test Scenarios. For our test scenarios we consider the TPC-H schema, denoted $\mathbf{S}_{\mathrm{H}}$, and the set Σ_{H} of primary keys over $\mathbf{S}_{\mathrm{H}}$ coming with the TPC-H benchmark. We generated a large set of database-query pairs P_{H} as follows: (1) First, we generated a (consistent) database D_{H} over $\mathbf{S}_{\mathrm{H}}$, using scale factor 1GB. The database contains roughly 9M tuples. (2) For each number of joins $j \in [5]$, we generated 5 base CQs Q_j^i, with $i \in [5]$, having j joins, using SQG, producing a set $\mathcal{Q}$ of 25 CQs. Using our query-aware noise generator, for each $Q \in \mathcal{Q}$, we generated 10 inconsistent databases $D_Q[p]$, using noise levels $p \in \{0.1, 0.2, \ldots, 1\}$, and the same block interval $[2, 5]$. (4) Finally, for each $Q \in \mathcal{Q}$, and for each $D_Q[p]$, we generated 11 variations of Q, denoted $Q_p[q]$, having balance $q \in \{0, 0.1, 0, 2, \ldots, 1\}$ w.r.t. $D_Q[p]$, where balance $q = 0$ means the query $Q_p[q]$ is Boolean. P_{H} is then the set of pairs $\{(D_Q[p], Q_p[q]) \mid Q \in \{Q_j^i\}_{i,j \in [5]}, p \in \{0.1, \ldots, 1\}$ and $q \in \{0, 0.1, \ldots, 1\}\}$, containing 2750 database-query pairs.

We considered different scenarios (subsets of P_{H}) by fixing all parameters but one. *Noise scenarios*: The sets $\mathsf{Noise}[q, j]$ of all pairs of P_{H}, where the balance level (q) and the number of joins (j) are fixed. *Join scenarios*: The sets $\mathsf{Join}[p, q]$ of all pairs of P_{H}, where the noise level (p) and the balance level (q) are fixed. *Balance scenarios*: The sets $\mathsf{Balance}[p, j]$ of all pairs of P_{H}, where the noise level (p) and the number of joins (j) are fixed.

Hardware and execution. For the experiments we used two Desktop PCs each with an Intel(R) Core(TM) i5-8500 CPU@3.00GHz processor, 16GB RAM, 500GB mechanical drive, running Xubuntu 19.04 64-bit. All databases are stored in a PostgreSQL 11.5 instance. The approximation schemes and the preprocessing step are implemented in C++ and SQL, respectively.

We fixed $\delta = 0.25$ and $\epsilon = 0.1$, i.e., 75% confidence and 10% error. We report the time required to execute each algorithm over the synopses of *all* output tuples, excluding the time of the preprocessing step since it is the same for all the approximation schemes. Each data point

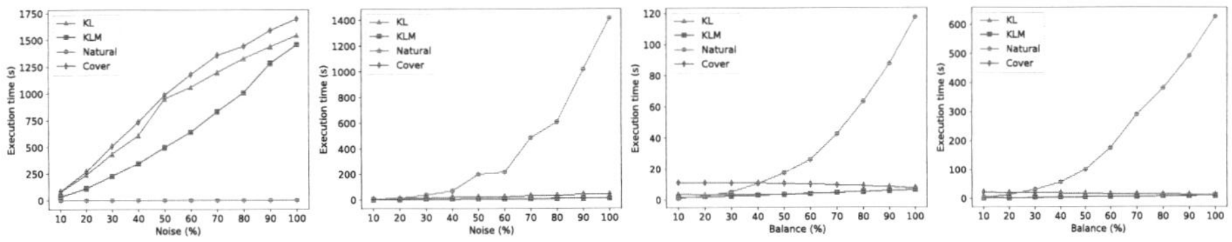

(a) Noise$[0, 3]$ (b) Noise$[0.5, 3]$ (c) Balance$[0.2, 3]$ (d) Balance$[0.4, 3]$

Figure 1: Noise and balance scenarios - Noise$[balance, joins]$, and Balance$[noise, joins]$

in a plot of Fig. 1 is the average runtime over all the CQs for that X-axis value; due to space constraints, here we report only some representative noise and balance scenarios (see Fig. 1).

5. Take-home Messages

Our analysis reveals a striking difference between Boolean and non-Boolean CQs.

The Boolean Case. Here, Natural is the best performer, no matter the noise and the number of joins in the query, whereas Cover is the worst. Only in the case of CQs with many joins Cover is comparable to KL(M), but in any case, Natural is the way to go. This is mainly due to the fact that for Boolean queries, the (only) synopsis is very large in general, and thus the relative frequency is very high. Hence, since Natural directly estimates the value of the relative frequency via the natural sampling space, requires less samples to obtain a good estimate.

The Non-Boolean Case. In this case, KLM is the way to go in almost all the scenarios, i.e., for any level of noise and for any level of (non-zero) balance of the query. Only for CQs with many joins, and high noise, KL is comparable to KLM. Nevertheless, KL is never going to outperform KLM in practice. The worst algorithms for non-Boolean CQs are Natural and Cover. They perform similarly for low levels of noise, balance and joins, but, in general, Natural is the slowest. The reson for this outcome is that for higher values of balance, the average size of a synopsis is low, which then implies that the relative frequency of the corresponding tuple is usually close to 0, hence, sampling from the symbolic space helps avoiding to perform a large number of samples like Natural does. Moreover, the low-variance sampler of KLM lets the algorithm find the optimal number of samples earlier than KL, on average.

Practical Applicability. In most of our experiments, the preprocessing step took less than 30 seconds. Furthermore, for modest scenarios, which is what we expect to face in practice, the running time of the best performing approximation scheme is in the order of seconds. We also considered larger databases, up to 120M tuples (15GBs), for which the overall running time of the preprocessing step is encouraging (considering the weak machines used): it is in the order of minutes, while the best approximation algorithm for each case always performs in the order of seconds. Thus, we believe applying approximate CQA in practice is not an unrealistic goal.

Acknowledgments

Part of Calautti's and Console's work was done while they were research associates at the University of Edinburgh. Console has been partially supported by MIUR under the PRIN 2017 project "HOPE" (prot. 2017MMJJRE), and by the EU under the H2020-EU.2.1.1 project TAILOR, grant id. 952215. Pieris was supported by the EPSRC grant EP/S003800/1 "EQUID".

References

[1] M. Arenas, L. E. Bertossi, J. Chomicki, Consistent query answers in inconsistent databases, in: PODS, 1999, pp. 68–79.

[2] M. Calautti, M. Console, A. Pieris, Counting database repairs under primary keys revisited, in: PODS, 2019, pp. 104–118.

[3] P. Koutris, J. Wijsen, Consistent query answering for primary keys in logspace, in: ICDT, 2019, pp. 23:1–23:19.

[4] B. ten Cate, G. Fontaine, P. G. Kolaitis, On the data complexity of consistent query answering, Theory Comput. Syst. 57 (2015) 843–891.

[5] S. Greco, C. Molinaro, I. Trubitsyna, Computing approximate query answers over inconsistent knowledge bases, in: IJCAI, 2018, pp. 1838–1846.

[6] A. A. Dixit, P. G. Kolaitis, A sat-based system for consistent query answering, in: SAT, 2019, pp. 117–135.

[7] A. Fuxman, E. Fazli, R. J. Miller, Conquer: Efficient management of inconsistent databases, in: SIGMOD, 2005, pp. 155–166.

[8] S. Greco, C. Molinaro, Probabilistic query answering over inconsistent databases, Ann. Math. Artif. Intell. 64 (2012) 185–207.

[9] M. Calautti, L. Libkin, A. Pieris, An operational approach to consistent query answering, in: PODS, 2018, pp. 239–251.

[10] D. Maslowski, J. Wijsen, A dichotomy in the complexity of counting database repairs, J. Comput. Syst. Sci. 79 (2013) 958–983.

[11] N. Fiorentino, S. Greco, C. Molinaro, I. Trubitsyna, ACID: A system for computing approximate certain query answers over incomplete databases, in: SIGMOD, 2018, pp. 1685–1688.

[12] S. Greco, C. Molinaro, I. Trubitsyna, Approximation algorithms for querying incomplete databases, Inf. Syst. 86 (2019) 28–45.

[13] M. Console, P. Guagliardo, L. Libkin, E. Toussaint, Coping with incomplete data: Recent advances, in: PODS, 2020, pp. 33–47.

[14] R. M. Karp, M. Luby, N. Madras, Monte-carlo approximation algorithms for enumeration problems, J. Algorithms 10 (1989) 429–448.

[15] P. Dagum, R. M. Karp, M. Luby, S. M. Ross, An optimal algorithm for monte carlo estimation, SIAM J. Comput. 29 (2000) 1484–1496.

[16] K. S. Meel, A. A. Shrotri, M. Y. Vardi, Not all FPRASs are equal: Demystifying FPRASs for DNF-counting, Constraints 24 (2019) 211–233.

[17] P. C. Arocena, B. Glavic, G. Mecca, R. J. Miller, P. Papotti, D. Santoro, Messing up with BART: Error generation for evaluating data-cleaning algorithms, PVLDB 9 (2015) 36–47.

[18] M. Benedikt, G. Konstantinidis, G. Mecca, B. Motik, P. Papotti, D. Santoro, E. Tsamoura, Benchmarking the chase, in: PODS, 2017, pp. 37–52.

Preference-based Inconsistency-Tolerant Query Answering under Existential Rules

(Discussion Paper)

Marco Calautti[1], Sergio Greco[2], Cristian Molinaro[2] and Irina Trubitsyna[2]

[1]*DISI, University of Trento, Italy*
[2]*DIMES, University of Calabria, Italy*

Abstract

Query answering over inconsistent knowledge bases is a problem that has attracted a great deal of interest over the years. Different inconsistency-tolerant semantics have been proposed, most of which are based on the notion of *repair*, that is, a "maximal" consistent subset of the database. In general, there can be several repairs, so it is often natural and desirable to express preferences among them. In this paper, we propose a framework for querying inconsistent knowledge bases under user preferences for existential rule languages. We provide generalizations of popular inconsistency-tolerant semantics taking preferences into account and study the data and combined complexity of different relevant problems.

1. Introduction

The problem of querying inconsistent knowledge bases has been investigated for many years. Different inconsistency-tolerant semantics have been proposed in the literature, that is, approaches to provide meaningful query answers despite the knowledge base being inconsistent.

Several popular semantics rely on the notion of *repair*, which is a "maximal" consistent subset of the database. Since inconsistency can be resolved in different ways, in general there are multiple repairs, which are then used in various ways to determine "valid" query answers. For instance, the *ABox repair (AR)* semantics [1, 2] considers a query answer valid if it can be inferred from each of the repairs of the knowledge base. The *intersection of repairs (IAR)* semantics [2] considers an answer valid if it can be inferred from the intersection of the repairs. The *intersection of closed repairs (ICR)* semantics [3] considers an answer valid if it can be inferred from the intersection of the closures of the repairs. We illustrate these semantics in our running example below.

Example 1. *Consider a knowledge base* (D, Σ) *describing orders in a restaurant, where* D *is the following database:*

$$\{\mathsf{meat}(\mathsf{beef}), \mathsf{order}(\mathsf{o}), \mathsf{main}(\mathsf{o}, \mathsf{beef}), \mathsf{side}(\mathsf{o}, \mathsf{cheese}), \mathsf{drink}(\mathsf{o}, \mathsf{red}), \mathsf{drink}(\mathsf{o}, \mathsf{beer}), \mathsf{dessert}(\mathsf{o}, \mathsf{cake}), \mathsf{dessert}(\mathsf{o}, \mathsf{pie})\},$$

SEBD 2021: The 29th Italian Symposium on Advanced Database Systems, September 5-9, 2021, Pizzo Calabro (VV), Italy
marco.calautti@unitn (M. Calautti); greco@dimes.unical.it (S. Greco); cmolinaro@dimes.unical.it (C. Molinaro); trubitsyna@dimes.unical.it (I. Trubitsyna)

stating that beef is a meat dish and o *is an order; furthermore, order* o *has beef for the main course, cheese as side dish, red wine and beer as drinks, and cake and pie as desserts. The ontology* Σ *contains the following dependencies:*

$$\begin{aligned}
&\sigma_1\colon \mathsf{main}(X,Y), \mathsf{meat}(Y) \rightarrow \mathsf{hasMeat}(X),\\
&\sigma_2\colon \mathsf{drink}(X,\mathsf{red}) \rightarrow \mathsf{hasWine}(X),\\
&\sigma_3\colon \mathsf{drink}(X,\mathsf{beer}) \rightarrow \mathsf{hasBeer}(X),\\
&\sigma_4\colon \mathsf{drink}(X,Y) \rightarrow \mathsf{hasDrink}(X),\\
&\sigma_5\colon \mathsf{main}(X,Y) \rightarrow \exists Z\, \mathsf{side}(X,Z),\\
&\nu_1\colon \mathsf{hasBeer}(X), \mathsf{hasWine}(X) \rightarrow \bot,\\
&\nu_2\colon \mathsf{hasBeer}(X), \mathsf{dessert}(X,Y) \rightarrow \bot,\\
&\nu_3\colon \mathsf{hasBeer}(X), \mathsf{side}(X,\mathsf{cheese}) \rightarrow \bot,\\
&\nu_4\colon \mathsf{hasWine}(X), \mathsf{dessert}(X,\mathsf{cake}), \mathsf{dessert}(X,\mathsf{pie}) \rightarrow \bot.
\end{aligned}$$

The existential rules σ_1–σ_4 *specify when an order includes a meat dish, wine, beer, and a drink, respectively. Then,* σ_5 *says that a main course always comes with a side dish. The negative constraints* ν_1–ν_3 *say that beer cannot be included in an order together with wine, or a dessert, or cheese. Finally,* ν_4 *says that an order cannot include wine, cake, and pie all together.*

The knowledge base is clearly inconsistent and admits the following four repairs: $R_1 = D \setminus \{\mathsf{drink}(\mathsf{o},\mathsf{beer}), \mathsf{dessert}(\mathsf{o},\mathsf{cake})\}$, $R_2 = D \setminus \{\mathsf{drink}(\mathsf{o},\mathsf{beer}), \mathsf{dessert}(\mathsf{o},\mathsf{pie})\}$, $R_3 = D \setminus \{\mathsf{side}(\mathsf{o},\mathsf{cheese}), \mathsf{drink}(\mathsf{o},\mathsf{red}), \mathsf{dessert}(\mathsf{o},\mathsf{pie}), \mathsf{dessert}(\mathsf{o},\mathsf{cake})\}$, *and* $R_4 = D \setminus \{\mathsf{drink}(\mathsf{o},\mathsf{red}), \mathsf{drink}(\mathsf{o},\mathsf{beer})\}$. *The query* $Q = \exists X,Y\, \mathsf{dessert}(X,Y)$, *asking if some dessert has been ordered, is not entailed under the AR semantics, as repair* R_3 *does not include any dessert. Thus,* Q *is not entailed also under the IAR and ICR semantics.* □

The AR, IAR, and ICR semantics have been extensively studied for both description logics (DLs) and existential rule languages. In each semantics, all repairs are equally important, and there is no way to prefer one over another. However, in many applications it is natural and desirable to express preferences, e.g., when one data source is more reliable than another, or when information is time-stamped and more recent facts are preferred over earlier ones.

To deal with the scenarios discussed above, we propose a framework for querying inconsistent knowledge bases under user preferences. We enrich knowledge bases with preference rules, so as to narrow down the set of repairs to a set of *preferred* ones. We then define preferred counterparts of the AR, IAR, and ICR semantics by looking only at preferred repairs.[1]

Example 2. *Consider again the scenario of Example 1. Suppose we would like to express preferences among repairs in such a way that the presence of some items in an order determines what other items are preferred. In our framework, one could specify this kind of preferences by means of the following set* Π *of* preference rules*:*

$$\begin{aligned}
&\rho_1:\quad \mathsf{hasWine}(X) \succ \mathsf{hasBeer}(X) \leftarrow \mathsf{hasMeat}(X),\\
&\rho_2:\quad \mathsf{dessert}(X,\mathsf{cake}) \succ \mathsf{dessert}(X,\mathsf{cherries}) \leftarrow \mathsf{main}(X,Y),\\
&\rho_3:\quad \mathsf{dessert}(X,\mathsf{pie}) \succ \mathsf{dessert}(X,\mathsf{cake}) \leftarrow \exists Y \mathsf{hasDrink}(X), \mathsf{side}(X,Y).
\end{aligned}$$

[1] An extended version of this paper has been accepted to KR 2020 [4].

The first preference rule says that when an order includes meat, wine is preferred over beer. The second preference rule states that when an order includes a main course, cake is preferred over cherries. The third preference rule says that when an order includes a drink and some side dish, pie is preferred over cake.

We will see later that R_1 and R_4 (cf. Example 1) are the repairs that best satisfy the above preference rules, and thus they are preferred. *Only preferred repairs are considered in the definition of* preferred *inconsistency-tolerant semantics. Thus, for instance, query Q of Example 1 is entailed under our* preferred *AR, IAR, and ICR semantics.* □

2. Preliminaries

We briefly recall some basics on existential rules from the Datalog$^{\pm}$ family [5] and inconsistency-tolerant semantics for querying inconsistent knowledge bases.

General. We assume a set $\mathbf{C}$ of *constants*, a set $\mathbf{N}$ of *labeled nulls*, and a set $\mathbf{V}$ of *variables*. A *term* t is a constant, null, or variable. We also assume a set of *predicates*, each associated with an *arity*, i.e., a non-negative integer. An *atom* has the form $p(\mathbf{t})$, where p is an n-ary predicate, and $\mathbf{t}$ is a tuple of n terms. An atom containing only constants is also called a *fact*. Conjunctions of atoms are often identified with the sets of their atoms. An *instance* I is a (possibly infinite) set of atoms $p(\mathbf{t})$, with $\mathbf{t}$ a tuple of constants and nulls. A *database* D is a finite instance with only constants. A *homomorphism* is a substitution h from terms to terms that is the identity on $\mathbf{C}$ and maps $\mathbf{N}$ to $\mathbf{C} \cup \mathbf{N}$. With abuse of notation, homomorphisms are applied also to (sets/conjunctions of) atoms. A *(Boolean) conjunctive query* (BCQ) Q has the form $\exists \mathbf{X} \varphi(\mathbf{X})$, where $\mathbf{X}$ is a tuple of variables, and $\varphi(\mathbf{X})$ is a conjunction of atoms over the variables in $\mathbf{X}$ without nulls. An instance I *satisfies* Q, denoted $I \models Q$, if there is a homomorphism h with $h(\varphi(\mathbf{X})) \subseteq I$.[2]

Dependencies. A *tuple-generating dependency (TGD)* σ is a first-order formula of the form $\forall \mathbf{X} \forall \mathbf{Y}\, \varphi(\mathbf{X}, \mathbf{Y}) \rightarrow \exists \mathbf{Z}\, p(\mathbf{X}, \mathbf{Z})$, where $\mathbf{X}$, $\mathbf{Y}$, and $\mathbf{Z}$ are pairwise disjoint tuples of variables, $\varphi(\mathbf{X}, \mathbf{Y})$ is a conjunction of atoms over $\mathbf{X}, \mathbf{Y}$, and $p(\mathbf{X}, \mathbf{Z})$ is an atom, all without nulls; $\varphi(\mathbf{X}, \mathbf{Y})$ is the *body* of σ, denoted $body(\sigma)$, while $p(\mathbf{X}, \mathbf{Z})$ is the *head* of σ, denoted $head(\sigma)$. For clarity, we consider single-atom-head TGDs; however, our results extend to TGDs with a conjunction of atoms in the head. An instance I satisfies σ, written $I \models \sigma$, if the following holds: whenever there exists a homomorphism h such that $h(\varphi(\mathbf{X}, \mathbf{Y})) \subseteq I$, then there exists $h' \supseteq h|_{\mathbf{X}}$, where $h|_{\mathbf{X}}$ is the restriction of h on $\mathbf{X}$, such that $h'(p(\mathbf{X}, \mathbf{Z})) \in I$. A *negative constraint (NC)* ν is a first-order formula $\forall \mathbf{X}\, \varphi(\mathbf{X}) \rightarrow \bot$, with $\mathbf{X}$ a tuple of variables, $\varphi(\mathbf{X})$ is a conjunction of atoms over $\mathbf{X}$, without nulls, called the *body* of ν and denoted $body(\nu)$, and $\bot$ denotes the truth constant $false$. An instance I satisfies ν, written $I \models \nu$, if I does not satisfy the BCQ $\exists \mathbf{X} \varphi(\mathbf{X})$. Negative constraints that are not satisfied can be represented via hypergraphs [6].

Given a set Σ of TGDs and NCs, I satisfies Σ, written $I \models \Sigma$, if I satisfies each TGD and NC of Σ. For brevity, we omit the universal quantifiers in front of TGDs and NCs, and use the comma for conjoining atoms. Given a class of TGDs $\mathcal{L}$, we denote by $\mathcal{L}_{\bot}$ the formalism obtained

[2]We focus on Boolean queries for clarity, but all our results immediately extend to non-Boolean conjunctive queries.

by combining $\mathcal{L}$ with arbitrary NCs. Finite sets of TGDs and NCs are also called *programs*, and TGDs are also called *existential rules.*

Knowledge Bases. A *knowledge base* is a pair (D, Σ), where D is a database and Σ is a program. The set of *models* of $KB = (D, \Sigma)$, denoted $mods(KB)$, is the set of instances $\{I \mid I \supseteq D \wedge I \models \Sigma\}$. We say that KB is *consistent* if $mods(KB) \neq \emptyset$, otherwise KB is *inconsistent.* We say that KB *entails* a BCQ Q, denoted $KB \models Q$, if $M \models Q$, for each $M \in mods(KB)$. The *data complexity* considers only the database as part of the input, while the *combined complexity* considers everything as part of the input.

The Datalog$^{\pm}$ languages that we consider to guarantee decidability are among the most frequently analysed in the literature, namely, linear (L) [5], guarded (G) [7], sticky (S) [8], and acyclic TGDs (A), along with the "weak" (proper) generalizations weakly sticky (WS) [8] and weakly acyclic TGDs (WA) [9], as well as their "full" (i.e., existential-free) proper restrictions linear full (LF), guarded full (GF), sticky full (SF), and acyclic full TGDs (AF), respectively, and full TGDs (F) in general. We refer to [10] for an overview of the complexity of BCQ entailment for the above languages.

Inconsistency-Tolerant Semantics. We now recall the AR, IAR, and ICR semantics.

Let $KB = (D, \Sigma)$ be a knowledge base. A *repair* of KB is an inclusion-maximal subset R of D such that (R, Σ) is consistent. We use $Rep(KB)$ to denote the set of all repairs of KB. The *closure* $Cn(KB)$ of KB is the set of all facts (thus containing constants only) entailed by D and the TGDs of Σ. KB entails a BCQ Q under the

- AR *semantics* if $(R, \Sigma) \models Q$, for each $R \in Rep(KB)$.
- IAR *semantics* if $(D_I, \Sigma) \models Q$, where $D_I = \bigcap\{R \mid R \in Rep(KB)\}$.
- ICR *semantics* if $(D_C, \Sigma) \models Q$, where $D_C = \bigcap\{Cn((R, \Sigma)) \mid R \in Rep(KB)\}$.

We refer to [10] and [11] for an overview of the complexity of AR- and IAR-/ICR-query answering, respectively, for different TGD languages and complexity measures.

3. Preference Rules

In this section, we introduce the syntax and semantics of *preference rules*, which allow users to express preferences among repairs. The aim is to use such rules to identify a set of *preferred repairs* among all possible ones, and use only the preferred repairs for AR, IAR, and ICR entailment.

Syntax. The syntax of preference rules is as follows.

Definition 3. *A* preference rule ρ *is an expression of the form*

$$p(\mathbf{X}) \succ q(\mathbf{Y}) \leftarrow \exists \mathbf{Z}\, \varphi(\mathbf{Z}, \mathbf{W}),$$

where $\mathbf{X}$, $\mathbf{Y}$, $\mathbf{Z}$, *and* $\mathbf{W}$ *are tuples of variables such that* $\mathbf{X} \cap \mathbf{Z} = \mathbf{Y} \cap \mathbf{Z} = \emptyset$, $p(\mathbf{X})$ *and* $q(\mathbf{Y})$ *are atoms over the variables* $\mathbf{X}$ *and* $\mathbf{Y}$, *respectively, and* $\varphi(\mathbf{Z}, \mathbf{W})$ *is a (possibly empty) conjunction of atoms over the variables* $\mathbf{Z} \cup \mathbf{W}$, *all without nulls.* □

In the previous definition, the right-hand (resp., left-hand) side of $\leftarrow$ is called the *body* (resp., *head*) of ρ and is denoted as $body(\rho)$ (resp., $head(\rho)$). Intuitively, the head expresses a preference among two atoms, while the body expresses a precondition for such a preference to be applied. A preference rule ρ is *ground* if all its variables are existentially quantified, that is, it has the form $p(\mathbf{a}) \succ q(\mathbf{b}) \leftarrow \exists \mathbf{Z}\, \varphi(\mathbf{Z}, \mathbf{c})$, with $\mathbf{a}$, $\mathbf{b}$, $\mathbf{c}$ tuples of constants and $\mathbf{Z}$ a tuple of variables. A *preference program* is a finite set of preference rules. A prioritized knowledge base combines a knowledge base with a preference program.

Definition 4. *A* prioritized knowledge base $\mathcal{K}$ *is a triple* (D, Σ, Π), *where* D *is a database,* Σ *is a program, and* Π *is a preference program.* □

We say that $\mathcal{K}$ is *consistent* (resp., *inconsistent*) iff the knowledge base (D, Σ) is consistent (resp., inconsistent). The set of all repairs of $\mathcal{K}$, denoted $Rep(\mathcal{K})$, is the set of all repairs of (D, Σ). An example of prioritized knowledge base $\mathcal{K} = (D, \Sigma, \Pi)$ is the one presented in Examples 1–2.

Semantics. Consider a prioritized knowledge base $\mathcal{K} = (D, \Sigma, \Pi)$. We use $\mathbf{C}_{\mathcal{K}}$ to denote the set of all constants appearing in $\mathcal{K}$ (that is, appearing in D, Σ, or Π). A *ground instance* of a preference rule $\rho \in \Pi$ is a ground preference rule derived from ρ by replacing every non-existential variable with a constant in $\mathbf{C}_{\mathcal{K}}$, with multiple occurrences of the same variable being replaced with the same constant. We use $grnd(\rho)$ to denote the set of all ground instances of ρ, and define $grnd(\Pi) = \bigcup_{\rho \in \Pi} grnd(\rho)$. To define preferred repairs, we first need to define when a repair satisfies a ground preference rule.

Intuitively, a repair R satisfies a ground preference rule ρ iff whenever R (together with the ontology) entails the body of ρ, the head of ρ is fulfilled by R. We formally define these notions below. For a prioritized knowledge base $\mathcal{K} = (D, \Sigma, \Pi)$, by consistent subset R of D we mean a set $R \subseteq D$ such that (R, Σ) is consistent.

Definition 5. *Let* $\mathcal{K} = (D, \Sigma, \Pi)$ *be a prioritized knowledge base,* R *a consistent subset of* D*, and* ρ *a ground preference rule in* $grnd(\Pi)$ *of the form* $p(\mathbf{a}) \succ q(\mathbf{b}) \leftarrow \exists \mathbf{Z}\, \varphi(\mathbf{Z}, \mathbf{c})$. *We say that* R fulfills $p(\mathbf{a}) \succ q(\mathbf{b})$ *(w.r.t.* $\mathcal{K}$*) iff* $(R, \Sigma) \models q(\mathbf{b})$ *implies* $(R, \Sigma) \models p(\mathbf{a})$. *We say that* R satisfies ρ *(w.r.t.* $\mathcal{K}$*) iff* $(R, \Sigma) \models \exists \mathbf{Z}\, \varphi(\mathbf{Z}, \mathbf{c})$ *implies* R *fullfils* $p(\mathbf{a}) \succ q(\mathbf{b})$ *w.r.t.* $\mathcal{K}$. □

Notice that we do not transitively close preferences. In contrast, we look for an explicit preference rule saying that $p(\mathbf{a})$ is preferred over $q(\mathbf{b})$. A transitive closure would require (iteratively) adding a ground preference rule $A \succ C \leftarrow body_1, body_2$ for each pair of ground preference rules $A \succ B \leftarrow body_1$ and $B \succ C \leftarrow body_2$, which can yield an exponential blow-up in the number of preference rules. Nonetheless, if needed, transitivity can still be stated by explicitly including a transitive closure in Π.

For a repair R of a prioritized knowledge base $\mathcal{K} = (D, \Sigma, \Pi)$, we use $\mathcal{S}(R, \mathcal{K})$ to denote the set of all preference rules in $grnd(\Pi)$ that are satisfied by R (w.r.t. $\mathcal{K}$). We define preferred repairs as follows.

Definition 6. *A repair* R *of a prioritized knowledge base* $\mathcal{K}$ *is* preferred *iff there is no repair* R' *of* $\mathcal{K}$ *s.t.* $\mathcal{S}(R, \mathcal{K}) \subsetneq \mathcal{S}(R', \mathcal{K})$. *The set of all preferred repairs of* $\mathcal{K}$ *is denoted as* $PRep(\mathcal{K})$. □

Thus, preferred repairs satisfy an inclusion-maximal set of ground preference rules. Other criteria are possible, such as defining preferred repairs as those that satisfy a cardinality-maximal set of preference rules. All such approaches are interesting, in much the same way as cardinality and set-inclusion maximality are both interesting when defining (standard) repairs. We plan to investigate other criteria in future work.

Example 7. *Consider the prioritized knowledge base $\mathcal{K} = (D, \Sigma, \Pi)$ and repairs R_1–R_4 of Examples 1–2. First of all, note that only ground preference rules in $grnd(\Pi)$ whose body contains order* o *can be differently satisfied by R_1–R_4, as the body of any other ground preference rule in $grnd(\Pi)$ is never entailed by (R_i, Σ), for each $i \in \{1, 2, 3, 4\}$. Thus, such preference rules are satisfied by all repairs. Hence, we can focus on these three ground preference rules:*

$$\rho'_1 : \mathsf{hasWine}(\mathsf{o}) \succ \mathsf{hasBeer}(\mathsf{o}) \leftarrow \mathsf{hasMeat}(\mathsf{o}),$$
$$\rho'_2 : \mathsf{dessert}(\mathsf{o}, \mathsf{cake}) \succ \mathsf{dessert}(\mathsf{o}, \mathsf{cherries}) \leftarrow \mathsf{main}(\mathsf{o}, \mathsf{beef}),$$
$$\rho'_3 : \mathsf{dessert}(\mathsf{o}, \mathsf{pie}) \succ \mathsf{dessert}(\mathsf{o}, \mathsf{cake}) \leftarrow \exists Y \mathsf{hasDrink}(\mathsf{o}), \mathsf{side}(\mathsf{o}, Y).$$

Notice that ρ'_1 is applicable in all repairs. Repairs R_1 and R_2 satisfy ρ'_1 because they both contain red wine; R_4 satisfies ρ'_1 because it does not include any wine or beer; R_3 does not satisfy ρ'_1 because it includes beer and no wine.

The preference rule ρ'_2 is applicable in all repairs as well, and it is satisfied by all of them, essentially because none of them contain dessert(o, cherries).

Finally, R_1, R_3, and R_4 satisfy ρ'_3, while R_2 does not. Thus, R_1 and R_4 satisfy all preference rules, while R_2 and R_3 do not, and thus R_1 and R_4 are preferred. □

We now provide our inconsistency-tolerant semantics over preferred repairs.

Definition 8. *A prioritized knowledge base $\mathcal{K} = (D, \Sigma, \Pi)$ entails a BCQ Q under the*

- *PAR* semantics *if $(R, \Sigma) \models Q$, for every $R \in PRep(\mathcal{K})$.*
- *IPAR* semantics *if $(D_I, \Sigma) \models Q$, where $D_I = \bigcap\{R \mid R \in PRep(\mathcal{K})\}$.*
- *ICPR* semantics *if $(D_C, \Sigma) \models Q$, where $D_C = \bigcap\{Cn((R, \Sigma)) \mid R \in PRep(\mathcal{K})\}$.* □

Example 9. *Consider again the prioritized knowledge base $\mathcal{K}$ and the query Q from Examples 1–2. The preferred repairs of $\mathcal{K}$ are $PRep(\mathcal{K}) = \{R_1, R_4\}$ (cf. Example 7). Then, $\mathcal{K}$ entails Q under the PAR, IPAR, and ICPR semantics, while Q is not entailed under any of the standard inconsistency-tolerant semantics.* □

4. Complexity Results

We performed a thorough study of the data and combined complexity of the "preferred" variant of classical problems in the context of querying inconsistent knowledge bases. The first problem, which we dub Preferred Repair Checking (PRC), given a prioritized knowledge base $\mathcal{K}$ and a database D', asks whether $D' \in PRep(\mathcal{K})$. The remaining problems, called S-Entail, with $S \in \{\text{PAR, IPAR, ICPR}\}$, given a prioritized knowledge base $\mathcal{K}$ and a BCQ Q, ask whether $\mathcal{K}$ entails Q under the S semantics.

Language	PRC		PAR		IPAR		ICPR	
	Data	Comb.	Data	Comb.	Data	Comb.	Data	Comb.
L, LF, AF		PSPACE		PSPACE		PSPACE		PSPACE
SF		EXP		EXP		EXP		EXP
F, GF		EXP		EXP		EXP		EXP
WA	coNP	2EXP	Π_2^p	2EXP	Π_2^p	2EXP	Π_2^p	2EXP
S		EXP		EXP		EXP		EXP- 2EXP
A		P^{NEXP}		P^{NEXP}		P^{NEXP}		P^{NEXP}- EXP^{NEXP}
G, WS		2EXP		2EXP		2EXP		2EXP- 3EXP

Table 1
Data and combined complexity of preferred repair checking and preferred entailment.

Table 1 reports the data and combined complexity of the above problems, when considering different TGD languages. A single complexity class in a cell refers to a completeness result, while two classes C_1-C_2 refer to C_1-hardness and C_2-membership.

In the data complexity, the use of preference rules incurs an increase of complexity w.r.t. the standard setting with no preferences: the data complexity goes from membership in P to coNP-completeness. For the AR and ICR semantics, the data complexity goes from coNP-completeness of the standard setting to Π_2^p-completeness of our preferred framework. For the IAR semantics, the data complexity increases from membership in AC^0 or coNP-completeness (depending on the language) to Π_2^p-completeness. In the combined complexity, moving from the classical semantics to the preferred ones does not yield an increase of complexity, except for the languages S, A, G, and WS under the ICPR semantics. Indeed, despite our efforts, in such cases, we did not manage to obtain completeness results. We point out that some of our results immediately extend to other TGD languages. For example, the Π_2^p memberships in data complexity also hold for TGDs classes for which the so-called skolem chase always terminates, e.g. see [12, 13] – for such classes, classical BCQ entailment is always tractable in data complexity.

5. Conclusion

Expressing preferences is a common need in various domains, such as querying inconsistent knowledge bases [14, 15], game theory [16], and answer set programming [17]. We have proposed a framework for querying inconsistent knowledge bases under existential rules in the presence of user preferences. We have analyzed the data and combined complexity of different relevant problems for a wide range of existential rule languages.

Related work. In the context of logic programming, logic programs have been combined with preferences so as to determine a set of *preferred answer sets*—e.g., see [17, 18]— while we use preferences to determine a set of preferred repairs.

Another related framework are *(existential) active integrity constraints* (EAICs) [19], i.e. integrity constraints that also specify the updates that are allowed to restore consistency when the constraint is violated. *Founded* repairs are those repairs obtained by applying only allowed updates. This expresses a sort of hard preference by partitioning conflicting facts into allowed and non-allowed ones, while our framework allows us to express preferences among arbitrary facts, and thus do not forbid any fact a priori.

Future work. An interesting direction for future work is to extend our analysis to the *fixed-program combined complexity*, that is, when the ontology is assumed to be fixed, and to the *bounded-arity combined complexity*, that is, when it is assumed that the maximum arity of the predicates is bounded by an integer constant. Another direction for future work is to apply preferences rules to different kinds of repairs, e.g., cardinality-maximal ones. Also, it would be interesting to extend the notion of an *explanation*, already investigated under existential rules [20, 21], to our framework with preferences. Finally, considering the intractability of our reasoning tasks, another interesting direction is to consider approximations, i.e., compute a subset of query answers over our semantics in polynomial time, as done in the context of querying incomplete databases [22, 23]. Moreover, one could also consider the counting variants of the PAR semantics, i.e., to count the number of preferred repairs that entail the query (together with the TGDs). This is a more refined measure providing useful insights when the query is not entailed by *every* preferred repair and has been thoroughly studied in the database setting for different integrity constraints, e.g., see [24, 25, 26, 27].

References

[1] M. Arenas, L. E. Bertossi, J. Chomicki, Consistent query answers in inconsistent databases, in: Proc. PODS, 1999, pp. 68–79.

[2] D. Lembo, M. Lenzerini, R. Rosati, M. Ruzzi, D. F. Savo, Inconsistency-tolerant semantics for description logics, in: RR, 2010, pp. 103–117.

[3] M. Bienvenu, On the complexity of consistent query answering in the presence of simple ontologies, in: Proc. AAAI, 2012, pp. 705–711.

[4] M. Calautti, S. Greco, C. Molinaro, I. Trubitsyna, Preference-based inconsistency-tolerant query answering under existential rules, in: KR, 2020, pp. 203–212.

[5] A. Calì, G. Gottlob, T. Lukasiewicz, A general Datalog-based framework for tractable query answering over ontologies, J. Web Sem. 14 (2012) 57–83.

[6] G. Gottlob, E. Malizia, Achieving new upper bounds for the hypergraph duality problem through logic, in: Proc. LICS, 2014, pp. 43:1–43:10.

[7] A. Calì, G. Gottlob, M. Kifer, Taming the infinite chase: Query answering under expressive relational constraints, J. Artif. Intell. Res. 48 (2013) 115–174.

[8] A. Calì, G. Gottlob, A. Pieris, Towards more expressive ontology languages: The query answering problem, Artif. Intell. 193 (2012) 87–128.

[9] R. Fagin, P. G. Kolaitis, R. J. Miller, L. Popa, Data exchange: semantics and query answering, Theor. Comput. Sci. 336 (2005) 89–124.

[10] T. Lukasiewicz, M. V. Martinez, A. Pieris, G. I. Simari, From classical to consistent query answering under existential rules, in: Proc. AAAI, 2015, pp. 1546–1552.

[11] T. Lukasiewicz, E. Malizia, C. Molinaro, Complexity of approximate query answering under inconsistency in Datalog+/–, in: Proc. IJCAI, 2018, pp. 1921–1927.
[12] M. Calautti, S. Greco, C. Molinaro, I. Trubitsyna, Logic program termination analysis using atom sizes, in: Proc. IJCAI, volume 2015-January, 2015, pp. 2833–2839.
[13] M. Calautti, S. Greco, I. Trubitsyna, Detecting decidable classes of finitely ground logic programs with function symbols, ACM Trans. Comput. Log. 18 (2017) 28:1–28:42.
[14] M. Bienvenu, C. Bourgaux, F. Goasdoué, Querying inconsistent description logic knowledge bases under preferred repair semantics, in: Proc. AAAI, 2014, pp. 996–1002.
[15] S. Staworko, J. Chomicki, J. Marcinkowski, Prioritized repairing and consistent query answering in relational databases, Ann. Math. Artif. Intell. 64 (2012) 209–246.
[16] G. Greco, E. Malizia, L. Palopoli, F. Scarcello, Non-transferable utility coalitional games via mixed-integer linear constraints, J. Artif. Intell. Res. 38 (2010) 633–685.
[17] G. Brewka, I. Niemelä, M. Truszczynski, Answer set optimization, in: Proc. IJCAI, 2003, pp. 867–872.
[18] S. Greco, I. Trubitsyna, E. Zumpano, On the semantics of logic programs with preferences, J. Artif. Intell. Res. 30 (2007) 501–523.
[19] M. Calautti, L. Caroprese, S. Greco, C. Molinaro, I. Trubitsyna, E. Zumpano, Existential active integrity constraints, Expert Syst. Appl. 168 (2021) 114297.
[20] İ. İ. Ceylan, T. Lukasiewicz, E. Malizia, A. Vaicenavicius, Explanations for query answers under existential rules, in: Proc. IJCAI, 2019, pp. 1639–1646.
[21] T. Lukasiewicz, E. Malizia, C. Molinaro, Explanations for inconsistency-tolerant query answering under existential rules, in: Proc. AAAI, 2020, pp. 2909–2916.
[22] N. Fiorentino, S. Greco, C. Molinaro, I. Trubitsyna, ACID: A system for computing approximate certain query answers over incomplete databases, in: Proc. SIGMOD, 2018, pp. 1685–1688.
[23] S. Greco, C. Molinaro, I. Trubitsyna, Approximation algorithms for querying incomplete databases, Inf. Syst. 86 (2019) 28–45.
[24] S. Greco, C. Molinaro, Probabilistic query answering over inconsistent databases, Ann. Math. Artif. Intell. 64 (2012) 185–207.
[25] S. Greco, C. Molinaro, I. Trubitsyna, Computing approximate query answers over inconsistent knowledge bases, in: IJCAI, 2018, pp. 1838–1846.
[26] M. Calautti, M. Console, A. Pieris, Counting database repairs under primary keys revisited, in: D. Suciu, S. Skritek, C. Koch (Eds.), Proc. PODS, ACM, 2019, pp. 104–118.
[27] E. Livshits, B. Kimelfeld, J. Wijsen, Counting subset repairs with functional dependencies, J. Comput. Syst. Sci. 117 (2021) 154–164.

A system for translating natural language questions into SPARQL queries with neural networks: Preliminary results

(Discussion Paper)

Manuel Alejandro Borroto[1], Francesco Ricca[1] and Bernardo Cuteri[1]

[1]*University of Calabria, Via Pietro Bucci, Rende, Cosenza, 87036, Italy*

Abstract

The development of knowledge bases has gathered nowadays large volumes of information concerning multiple domains. Unfortunately, access to this information is complicated for those users unfamiliar with the SPARQL query language and the knowledge base definition. In this paper, we present preliminary results on a system for automatic translation of natural language questions into SPARQL queries. Our method uses Neural Machine Translation and Named Entity Recognition tasks that complement each other to obtain a final query ready to be executed. We demonstrate the potential of our approach by presenting its results on the Monument dataset, which is a recently released dataset for Question Answering on the well-known DBpedia knowledge base.

Keywords

Knowledge base, Question Answering, Neural network

1. Introduction

Today we live in what is known as the Digital Age. How knowledge is generated and shared has changed dramatically, digital formats and the internet have made information much more accessible than the old non-virtual format. As evidence of this, we now have vast and complex knowledge bases which allow gathering large volumes of information through the intercommunication of thousands of datasets referring to various domains in what is known as Linked Data. This means that the people have access to a large amount of information never thought, and the DBpedia [1] project is a real example of that, which is one of the most popular knowledge bases nowadays.

The problem is that the search and retrieval of the information stored in this way can be a hard task for lay users because it is necessary to know the structure of the knowledge base and the appropriate query languages, such as SPARQL [2]. As a result, natural language Question Answering (QA) has taken a central role in the area of the Semantic Web to address such issues. A group of QA approaches, especially the most recent, have begun to take advantage of the

SEBD 2021 - The 29th Italian Symposium on Advanced Database Systems, September 5-9, 2021, Pizzo Calabro (VV), Italy

manuel.borroto@unical.it (M. A. Borroto); francesco.ricca@unical.it (F. Ricca); bernardo.cuteri@unical.it (B. Cuteri)

0000-0001-8218-3178 (F. Ricca); 0000-0001-5164-9123 (B. Cuteri)

great development achieved by Deep Learning and started to use deep neural networks to tackle the problem, proposing systems for the automatic translation from natural language questions to SPARQL queries, removing all technical complexity to the final users.

In this context, we propose a system for the automatic translation of natural language questions into SPARQL queries. More specifically we employ LSTM [3] neural networks due to the proven effectiveness for Natural Language Processing that they have demonstrated. The system is consists of two parts. The first one translates the questions in natural language into a SPARQL template using an LSTM encoder-decoder model, which is the state-of-the-art for these types of tasks [4]. Whereas the second part is a model for Named Entity Recognition [5], also based on LSTM networks, and responsible for extracting the entities from the question to finally combine the results and create a SPARQL query ready to be executed. Besides, we introduce a formal definition of a dataset format that greatly reduces the output space and is essential for the proper functioning of the system and also allows us to tackle the problem with the out-of-vocabulary (OOV) words of the training set, a major weakness of the majority of the related approaches today.

We demonstrate the potential of our approach by presenting its results on the Monument dataset, which is a recently released dataset for Question Answering on the well-known DBpedia knowledge base.

The remainder of the paper is structured as follows. Section 2, we talk about related works. In section 3, we go into the particular details of our approach. Section 4 focuses on the discussion of experiments and results. Finally, we provide some conclusions and aspects for future work.

2. Related Work

Pattern-based. The idea of employing query patterns for mapping questions to SPARQL-queries was already exploited in the literature [6, 7]. The approach presented by Pradel and Ollivier [6] also adopts named entity recognition but applies a set of predefined rules to obtain all the query elements and their relationships. The approach by Steinmetz et. al [7] has 4 phases, firstly, the question is parsed and the main focus is extracted, then general queries are generated from the phrases in natural language according to predefined patterns, and finally, makes a subject-predicate-object mapping of the general question to triples in RDF. Despite both of the above-mentioned approaches performed well in selected benchmarks, they rely on patterns and rules defined manually for all existing types of questions. A limit that is not present in our proposal.

Deep Learning-based. In the Seq2SQL approach [8] an LSTM Seq2Seq model is used to translate from natural language to SQL queries. The interesting thing about this approach is that they use *Reinforcement Learning* to guide the learning. The usage Encoder-Decoder model based in LSTM with an attention mechanism to associate a vocabulary mapping between natural language and SPARQL also was proposed in the literature [9] obtaining good results.

The *Neural SPARQL Machines (NSpM)* [10] approach is based on the idea of modifying the SPARQL queries to treat them as a foreign language. To achieve this, they encoded the brackets, URIs, operators, and other symbols, making the tokenization process easier. The resulting dataset was introduced in a Seq2Seq model responsible for performing the question-query mapping. The same authors created the *DBNQA dataset*[11], and their model was tested on a subdomain referring to monuments and evaluated using the purely syntactic BLEU score [10]. As a consequence, it performs well in reproducing the syntax of the gold query but is less able to generalize to unseen natural language questions and OOV words when compared with our approach.

The query building approach by Chen et al. [12] features two stages. The first stage consists of predicting the query structure of the question and leverages the structure to constrain the generation of the candidate queries. The second stage performs a candidate query rank. As in our approach, Chen et al. [12] uses BiLSTM networks, but query representation is based on abstract query graphs.

Also, we report that eight different models based on RNNs and CNNs were compared by Yin and colleagues [13]. In this large experiment, the ConvS2S [14] model proved to be the best.

For completeness, we studied another related line of work that aims to translate the natural language questions into SQL queries. The work proposed by Yu et. al [15] introduces a large-scale, complex, and cross-domain semantic parsing and text-to-SQL dataset. To validate the work contribution, they used the proposed dataset to train different models to convert text to SQL queries. Most of the models were based on a Seq2Seq architecture with attention, demonstrating an adequate performance. Another interesting case of study is the editing-based approach for text-to-SQL generation introduced by Zhang et. al [16]. They implement a Seq2Seq model with Luong's attention, using BiLSTMs and BERT embeddings. The approach demonstrates to perform well on SParC and Spider datasets, outperforming the related work in some cases.

Our architecture addresses the issues connected with the translation resorting to specific tools, an aspect that is not present in mentioned works. Moreover, existing approaches based on NMT do nothing special to deal with OOV words.

3. Translating Natural Language Questions to SPARQL

Knowledge bases (KB) are a rich source of information related to a great variety of domains, which can be accessed by experts of formal query languages. The potential of exploiting knowledge bases can be greatly increased by allowing any user to query the ontology by posing questions in natural language.

In this paper, this problem is seen as the following Natural Language Processing task: Given an RDF knowledge base O and a question Q_{nat} in natural language (to be answered using O), translate Q into a SPARQL query $S_{Q_{nat}}$ such that the answer to Q_{nat} can be obtained by running $S_{Q_{nat}}$ on the underlying ontology O.

The starting point is a training set containing a number of pairs $\langle Q_{nat}, G_{Q_{nat}} \rangle$, where Q_{nat} is a natural language question, and $G_{Q_{nat}}$ is a SPARQL query, called the *gold query*. The gold query is a SPARQL query that models (i.e., allows to retrieve from O) the answers to Q_{nat}. The training set has to be used to learn how to answer questions posed in natural language using O, so that, given a question in natural language Q_{nat}, the QA system can generate a query $S'_{Q_{nat}}$ that is equivalent to the gold query $G_{Q_{nat}}$ for Q_{nat}, i.e., such that

Table 1
$\langle Question, Query\rangle$ pair for *Who painted the Mona Lisa?*

Question	Query
Who painted the Mona Lisa?	select ?a where {dbr:Mona_Lisa dbo:author ?a.}

$answers(S'_{Q_{nat}}) = answers(G_{Q_{nat}})$.[1] In particular, we approach this problem as a machine translation task, that is, we compute $S'_{Q_{nat}}$ as $S'_{Q_{nat}} = Translate(Q_{nat})$, where $Translate$ is the translation function implemented by our QA System, called *sparql-qa.*

In the remainder, we first present an intermediate format conceived to boost the training time of the entire process and reduce the impact of words that reference individuals that are not mentioned in the training set, in turn, we describe our translation modules that take as input the dataset in the new format.

3.1. A new data set format

In general, NL to SPARQL datasets are composed of a set of pairs $\langle Q_{nat}, G_{Q_{nat}}\rangle$. In such a common type of representation, the named entities found in the question are typically represented directly by their URIs in the SPARQL query, but this transformation is hard to learn from mere examples, and the trained system would fail if the transformation can not be described as simple rules. This is an issue, especially in large ontologies, where there is a huge number of resources.

A dataset in QQT is composed of a set of triples in the form $\langle Question, QueryTemplate, Tagging\rangle$, where $Question$ is a natural language question, and $Tagging$ marks which parts of $Question$ are entities, and $QueryTemplate$ is a SPARQL query template with the following modifications: (i) The KB resources are replaced by one or more variables; (ii) A new triple is added for each variable in the form *"?var rdfs:label placeholder"*. $Placeholders$ are meant to be replaced by substrings of $Question$ depending on $Tagging$.

In Table 1 we show an example of a $\langle Q_{nat}, Q_{sparql}\rangle$ pair for the question *Who painted the Mona Lisa?*, while Table 2 shows the corresponding $\langle Question, QueryTemplate, Tagging\rangle$ triple in the QQT format.

In table 2 the term *$1* denotes a placeholder, where 1 means that it has to be replaced by the first entity occurring in the question, that is *Mona Lisa* as represented by B and I in *Tagging*. Note that, in the QQT format, the query template does not contain any DBpedia resource, thus the learning model (which is the neural network in our case) does not need to understand that

[1]Note that we are interested in computing the answers and not in syntactically reproducing the gold query.

Table 2
$\langle Question, QueryTemplate, Tagging\rangle$ triple for *Who painted the Mona Lisa?*

Question	QueryTemplate	Tagging
Who painted the Mona Lisa?	select ?a where { ?w dbo:author ?a. ?w rdfs:label $1 }	O O O B I O

Mona Lisa stands for the *dbr:Mona_Lisa* resource and the $QueryTemplate$ is exactly the same for all questions asking the author of a given artwork.

3.2. The translation modules

Our approach consists of two deep neural networks, the first one specialized in Neural Machine Translation (NMT) based on the well-known Seq2Seq [4] model and the second one used for extracting the entities from the question using the Named Entity Recognition (NER) technique.

3.2.1. Neural Machine Translation

The network focused on NMT is used to translate the question into a SPARQL $QueryTemplate$. The network is based on an Encoder-Decoder model with *Luong's attention* [17], in which the Encoder extracts semantic content from the question in natural language and encodes it into a fixed-dimensional vector representation V. Instead, the Decoder tries to decode V into a sequence in the output language ($QueryTemplate$).

The Encoder is composed of an input layer that receives a question in natural language converted into a sequence of word-embeddings obtained by mean of FastText [18], in the form $\{x_1, x_2, ..., x_t\}$, where x_t is the vector representation of the word t in the sentence. Next, we use a Bidirectional LSTM (BiLSTM) to summarize $\{x_1, x_2, ..., x_t\}$ into V, in forward and reverse orders. V is formed by concatenating the last hidden states in the two directions.

On the other hand, during the training process, the Decoder is responsible for calculating the word-embeddings of the output language tokens (SPARQL), which is used together with the vector V, provided by the Encoder, as input to a Luong-Decoder layer. This layer is responsible for decoding the sentence supported by the attention mechanism. Finally, the values are feed to a Fully Connected Network with a Softmax activation function that predicts the output sequence by calculating the conditional probability over the output vocabulary. Figure 1 shows the described network architecture.

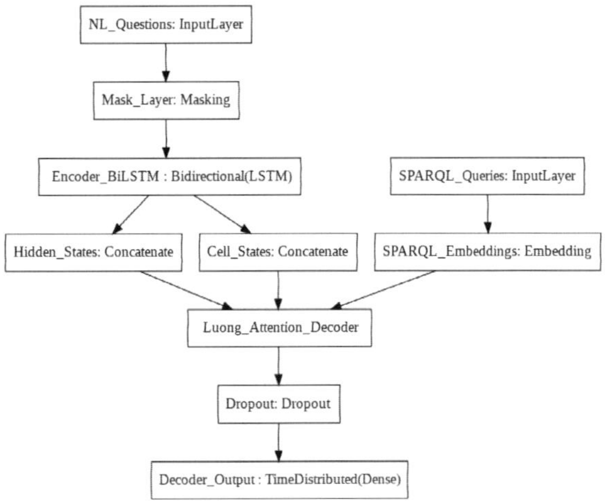

Figure 1: NMT neural network architecture

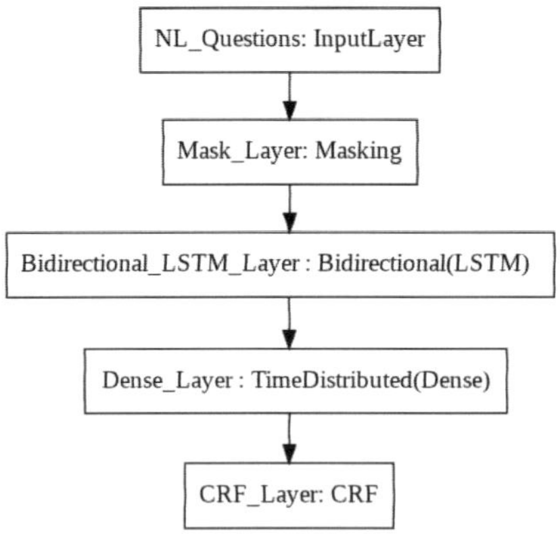

Figure 2: NER neural network architectu-re

3.2.2. Named Entity Recognition

To perform the entity recognition, we created a BiLSTM-CRF [5] network that constitutes state-of-the-art for this type of task. In this case, we again used FastText to obtain the word-embeddings and deal with OOV words. The model is composed of an input layer that receives the sequences of embeddings, followed by a BiLSTM connected to a Fully Connected layer. Finally, the information flows through a CRF layer that predicts the final sequence of tags. Figure 2 shows the described network architecture.

Finally, we mixed the results of both networks to obtain the final query $S'_{Q_{nat}}$. Here, the placeholders in the $QueryTemplate$ are replaced by the corresponding entities obtained with the NER network.

To better understand how *sparql-qa* works, we can translate, for example, the question: *Where is Washington Monument located?* First, the question is cleaned and split into tokens and then converted into a sequence of fastText word-embeddings. Then, the sequence is processed by the two networks used by our system. The NMT network translates the question into the corresponding *QueryTemplate*:

```
SELECT DISTINCT ?a WHERE { ?w dbo:location ?a . ?w rdfs:label $1 }
```

successively the NER network calculates the tagging sequence: $O\,O\,\boldsymbol{B}\,\boldsymbol{I}\,O$, where it is indicated that the entity to be considered is *Washington Monument* (Positions 2 and 3 of the tagging sequence, respectively). Finally, in the composition phase, the results are mixed, obtaining the final query:

```
SELECT DISTINCT ?a WHERE { ?w dbo:location ?a .
                           ?w rdfs:label "Washington Monument"@en }
```

It is important to note that the previous example describes the translation operation in general terms and does not go into the more complicated details of the process.

4. Experiments on Monument dataset

Setup. The Monument dataset was proposed as part of the Neural SPARQL Machines (NSpM) [10] research. It contains 14,778 question-query pairs about the instances of type monument present in DBpedia.

We compared our system with the state-of-the-art, thus, we have trained the Learner Module of NSpM as it was done in [10], where the authors proposed two instances of the Monument dataset that we will denote by Monumet300 and Monument600 containing 8,544 and 14,788 pairs, respectively. In both cases, the dataset split fixes 100 pairs for both validation and test set and keeps the rest for the training set. All the data is publicly available in the NSpM GitHub project.[2]

We have implemented our system, called *sparql-qa*, by using Keras, a well-known framework for machine learning, on top of TensorFlow. We trained the networks by using Google Collaboratory, which is a virtual machine environment hosted in the cloud and based on Jupyter

[2]https://github.com/LiberAI/NSpM/tree/master/data

Table 3
Comparison on Monument datasets.

	Mon300			Mon600		
	P	R	F1	P	R	F1
NSpM	0.860	0.861	0.852	0.929	0.945	0.932
sparql-qa	0.78	0.78	0.78	0.791	0.791	0.791

Notebooks. The environment provides 12GB of RAM and connects to Google Drive. To train our system, we first performed hyperparameter tuning focused on three metrics: embedding-size of the target language, batch size, and LSTM hidden units. The task was performed by using a grid search method. We set the number of epochs to 5, shuffling the dataset at the end of each one. After tuning, we set the hyperparameters of the two networks as follows: embedding-size is set to 300, LSTM hidden units are set to 96, and batch size is set to 64.

For comparing performance, we adopted the macro precision, recall, and F1-score measures, which are the most used ones to assess this kind of system.

Results. Results of the execution reported in Table 3 show that *sparql-qa* performs reasonably well, reaching F1-score values greater than 0.7. On the other hand, NSpM achieves better results.

We have investigated why our system could not provide an optimal answer for some questions. This analysis evidenced that the performance of our approach is mainly affected by problems in the dataset. Indeed, there is a set of questions that lacks context to determine specific expected URIs. For example, for the question *"What is Washington Monument related to?"* our system uses "Washington Monument", but the gold query uses the specific URI: *Washington_Monument_(Baltimore).* Note that there is no reference to Baltimore in the question text, and there are Washington Monuments also in Milwaukee and Philadelphia, according to DBPedia. Surprisingly, the compared system can often use the specific URI of the gold query even without context. Thus, we run another experiment to better outline the issue. We create a new test set of 200 pairs by using the templates provided by NSpM and a randomly selected set of unseen monument entities extracted from DBpedia. Table 4 shows that our approach has the same good performance (F1 score greater than 0.78) and performs much better than NSpM that is not able to generalize to deal with OOV (F1 of 0.11).

Another cause that affects our approach is the correctness with which the named entities are written. Sometimes the entities mentioned in the question do not match the *rdfs:label* property value, and sometimes they are referenced using acronyms. In these cases, our system will not give the expected answers because it cannot reference the right DBpedia resources. To address

Table 4
Comparison with OOV entities on Monument datasets.

	Mon300			Mon600		
	P	R	F1	P	R	F1
NSpM	0.097	0.123	0.101	0.11	0.11	0.11
sparql-qa	0.795	0.795	0.795	0.785	0.785	0.785

these issues, we plan to use *Named Entity Linking (NEL)* [19], which allows us to determine accurately which DBpedia resources are present in the question.

Finally, for completeness, we report that the intermediate format allows us to save 40% of training time.

5. Conclusions and Future Work

The paper presents preliminary results on an approach for querying SPARQL knowledge bases by using natural language. We combine in our system both neural machine translation and named entity recognition modules and focus on attenuating the impact of the OOV words, an important issue that is not well considered in existing approaches. Our system showed good preliminary results on the Monument dataset and demonstrated a more general and robust behavior than state-of-the-art approaches.

In future work, we plan to extend our system to improve translation performance by integrating other NLP tools, such as Named Entity Linking and BERT contextual word embeddings. We also plan to extend our experiments by considering other well-known QA benchmarks.

Acknowledgments

This work was partially supported by the Italian Ministry of Economic Development (MISE) under projects "MAP4ID - Multipurpose Analytics Platform 4 Industrial Data", N. F/190138/01-03/X44.

References

[1] J. Lehmann, R. Isele, M. Jakob, A. Jentzsch, D. Kontokostas, P. N. Mendes, S. Hellmann, M. Morsey, P. Van Kleef, et al., Dbpedia–a large-scale, multilingual knowledge base extracted from wikipedia, Semantic Web 6 (2015) 167–195.

[2] W3C, Semantic web standards, 2014. URL: https://www.w3.org.

[3] S. Hochreiter, J. Schmidhuber, Long short-term memory, Neural Computation 9 (1997) 1735–1780.

[4] I. Sutskever, O. Vinyals, Q. V. Le, Sequence to sequence learning with neural networks, in: NIPS, 2014, pp. 3104–3112.

[5] Z. Huang, W. Xu, K. Yu, Bidirectional LSTM-CRF models for sequence tagging, CoRR abs/1508.01991 (2015).

[6] C. Pradel, O. Haemmerlé, N. Hernandez, Natural language query interpretation into sparql using patterns, 2013.

[7] N. Steinmetz, A. Arning, K. Sattler, From natural language questions to SPARQL queries: A pattern-based approach, in: BTW, volume P-289 of *LNI*, Gesellschaft für Informatik, Bonn, 2019, pp. 289–308.

[8] V. Zhong, C. Xiong, R. Socher, Seq2sql: Generating structured queries from natural language using reinforcement learning, CoRR abs/1709.00103 (2017).

[9] F. F. Luz, M. Finger, Semantic parsing natural language into SPARQL: improving target language representation with neural attention, CoRR abs/1803.04329 (2018).
[10] T. Soru, E. Marx, D. Moussallem, G. Publio, A. Valdestilhas, D. Esteves, C. B. Neto, SPARQL as a foreign language, SEMANTiCS 2017 - Posters and Demos (2017). URL: https://arxiv.org/abs/1708.07624.
[11] A. Hartmann, E. Marx, T. Soru, Generating a large dataset for neural question answering over the DBpedia knowledge base (2018).
[12] Y. Chen, H. Li, Y. Hua, G. Qi, Formal query building with query structure prediction for complex question answering over knowledge base, in: IJCAI, 2020.
[13] X. Yin, D. Gromann, S. Rudolph, Neural machine translating from natural language to SPARQL, CoRR abs/1906.09302 (2019).
[14] J. Gehring, M. Auli, D. Grangier, D. Yarats, Y. N. Dauphin, Convolutional sequence to sequence learning, in: ICML, volume 70 of *Proc. of ML Research*, PMLR, 2017, pp. 1243–1252.
[15] T. Yu, R. Zhang, K. Yang, M. Yasunaga, D. Wang, Z. Li, J. Ma, I. Li, Q. Yao, S. Roman, et al., Spider: A large-scale human-labeled dataset for complex and cross-domain semantic parsing and text-to-sql task, arXiv preprint arXiv:1809.08887 (2018).
[16] R. Zhang, T. Yu, H. Y. Er, S. Shim, E. Xue, X. V. Lin, T. Shi, C. Xiong, R. Socher, D. Radev, Editing-based sql query generation for cross-domain context-dependent questions, arXiv preprint arXiv:1909.00786 (2019).
[17] M. Luong, H. Pham, C. D. Manning, Effective approaches to attention-based neural machine translation, arXiv preprint arXiv:1508.04025 (2015).
[18] P. Bojanowski, E. Grave, A. Joulin, T. Mikolov, Enriching word vectors with subword information, TACL 5 (2017) 135–146.
[19] W. Shen, J. Wang, J. Han, Entity linking with a knowledge base: Issues, techniques, and solutions, IEEE Transactions on Knowledge and Data Engineering 27 (2014) 443–460.

sMARE: An Enhanced Query Performance Prediction Evaluation Approach

(Discussion Paper)

Guglielmo Faggioli[1], Oleg Zendel[2], J. Shane Culpepper[2], Nicola Ferro[1] and Falk Scholer[2]

[1]*University of Padova, Padova, Italy*
[2]*RMIT University, Melbourne, Australia*

Abstract

QPP has been studied extensively in the IR community over the last two decades. Nevertheless, the Query Performance Prediction (QPP) field still lacks sound theoretical evaluation methodologies. In this work*, we re-examined the existing evaluation methodology commonly used for QPP, and propose a new approach. Our key idea is to model QPP performance as a distribution instead of relying on point estimates. Our work demonstrates important statistical implications and overcomes key limitations imposed by the currently used correlation-based point-estimate evaluation approaches. This, in turns, enables the use of ANalysis Of VAriance (ANOVA) models for comparative analyses, permitting deeper analyses on the QPP models performance, and allowing to measure interactions between multiple factors.

1. Introduction

The Information Retrieval (IR) community has long recognized the importance of applying statistical tests to evaluation results. Although best practices continue to evolve, conference and journal guidelines and discussion papers [2] have led the community to appreciate the importance of a more theoretically grounded evaluation. While this has led to higher quality analytical comparisons in many IR-related fields, not all areas have adopted the practice. An example of a common IR problem that might benefit from alternative evaluation techniques is Query Performance Prediction (QPP). The goal of QPP is to estimate the effectiveness of a retrieval system in response to a query when no relevance judgments are available [3]. The most widely-used method for evaluating QPP approaches is based on the strength of a relationship between per-topic prediction scores, and the actual per-topic system effectiveness as measured using a standard IR effectiveness metric, usually Average Precision (AP). Such association is measured using a correlation coefficient: a QPP approach that achieves a higher correlation value than another is taken to be the superior approach. This evaluation method compares QPP effectiveness at a very high level, with the performance of a QPP approach over a whole set of topics being summarized just by a correlation coefficient as a *point value.* In order to statistically validate the results, by relying on repeated randomized topic sampling, we can test whether or

*This is an extended abstract of [1], best full paper award.

SEBD 2021: The 29th Italian Symposium on Advanced Database Systems, September 5-9, 2021, Pizzo Calabro (VV), Italy

not the correlation coefficients for two different QPP methods are significantly different from each other. However, it is important to note that this approach is fundamentally different from the pair-wise significance test used for system retrieval effectiveness, which is now common practice in IR evaluation exercises. Motivated by these observations, we re-examine how QPP efficacy can be analyzed using a more fine-grained approach – by modeling the performance of QPP techniques as *distributions*. This approach has also previously been applied successfully in system evaluation exercises. A distribution-based model can be constructed as follows. First, an estimate of the performance for each system-topic combination is computed using a traditional performance measure, such as AP. Then, all of the topics for a collection are used to model the performance distribution. Note that this is fundamentally different from a classical QPP evaluation approach.

In this work, we propose an evaluation approach (dubbed scaled Mean Absolute Rank Error (sMARE)) which has several appealing properties: it allows formal inferential statistics to be applied, which generalizes the results to the entire population of topics; it allows the behavior of a QPP approach to be more clearly isolated, for example through confidence intervals; and, it enables factor decomposition, which in turn allows us to measure the relative contributions to observed effectiveness systematically. We also incorporate recent work in retrieval effectiveness on query variation and reformulation of each topic [4] into our framework, which allows a more fine-grained sampling of retrieval performance, and to estimate interaction between systems, topics and query formulations, which is not possible using only a single point estimate.

Our work focuses on two related research questions: (**RQ1**) How can statistical analysis and testing be applied to QPP evaluation exercises? (**RQ2**) What factors contribute to improving or reducing the performance of a QPP model?

2. Related Work

Retrieval performance can vary widely across different systems, even for a single query [3]. *Pre-retrieval predictors* analyze query and corpus statistics prior to retrieval [5] while *post-retrieval predictors* also analyze the retrieval results [6]. Predictors are typically evaluated by measuring the correlation coefficient between the AP values attained with relevance judgments and the values assigned by the predictor. Such evaluation methodology is based on a *point estimate* and have been shown to be unreliable when comparing multiple systems, corpora and predictors [7]. Hauff et al. [7] demonstrate that higher correlation does not necessarily attest to better prediction, and used Root Mean Square Error (RMSE) in their evaluation. When computing the Confidence Interval (CI) for Pearson's linear correlation in the evaluation using multiple previously reported pre-retrieval predictors, Hauff et al. [7] found that many of the predictors had overlapping CIs, and concluded that they were not significantly different from the best performing predictor. Also of interest, recent work using query variations for QPP [4] has demonstrated that the relative prediction quality of predictors can vary with respect to the effectiveness of the queries used to represent the topics, and we explore such observation further using advanced statistical instrumentation.
One principled approach that can be used in IR evaluation is ANOVA[8, 9, 10]. ANOVA is commonly used to assess the presence of statistically significant differences in mean performance

observed when using different experimental conditions. This technique can be operationalized as a General Linear Mixed Model (GLMM), where a response variable, called $Data$, is linearly modeled into two parts: the experimental conditions (the $Model$) and the $Error$: $Data = Model + Error$. The $Model$ includes a subject component (which in IR evaluation often corresponds to the topic), one or more factors, which are the different experimental conditions (e.g, the entire system, or its components), and possibly their interactions. Specific factors might be *nested* inside others: in the following analyses, query formulations are a nested factor of the topic, since each formulation represents a single topic and cannot be used to represent others. The ANOVA approach is particularly useful in our work as it allows us to break down the variance observed in the data, assigning it to the factors that caused it [9].

3. Experimental Analysis

In our analyses, we use the TREC Robust 2004 (Robust04) Ad Hoc [11] collection. We enrich the set of queries for the corpus using publicly available human-curated query variants for each topic [12].[1] Our experiments use a Grid of Points (GoP) of runs, using 4 different stoplists (`atire`, `zettair`, `indri`, `lingpipe`), plus the `no stop` approach and 2 different stemmers, (`lovins`, `porter`) plus a `no stem` approach. All the runs were produced using the query-likelihood model. We experimented with the following pre-retrieval qpp models: SCQ, AvgSCQ, MaxSCQ, SumVAR, AvgVAR, MaxVAR [13], AvgIDF [14], MaxIDF [15]. Concerning post-retrieval qpp models, we considered the followings: Clarity [5], NQC [16], WIG [17], SMV [18]. We duplicate the number of post-retrieval methods, considering, for each of them, their UEF [19] counterpart. Such QPP models have been selected since they are the most well-known and representative. In total, 240 different predictor-system combinations were generated for the Robust04 collection. For predictors which required hyper-parameters, we considered those previously observed to be effective [16]. We apply Average Precision (AP) to measure the effectiveness of the different retrieval pipelines.

3.1. Traditional QPP evaluation using correlations

Prior work on QPP has relied primarily on a single evaluation paradigm: the QPP generates a candidate list where the queries are ranked by their prediction values. The correlation between such list and a list induced using a reference measure, such as AP, is then considered as measure of quality of the QPP model.

Figure 1a shows the performance of 16 different QPP models when using this common evaluation approach – Kendall's τ correlation in this case – with 95% confidence intervals shown as well. In this example, the results are generated for a specific retrieval pipeline, using the `indri` stoplist and `porter` stemmer. To compute the confidence intervals (at significance level $\alpha = 0.05$), we used a bias-corrected and accelerated bootstrap procedure with 10,000 samples. Observe that when using title queries only (orange bars), there is a large degree of overlap between the different QPP approaches. The pairwise comparison using the data from Figure 1a (title queries only), shows that 57 pairs of predictors are found to be significantly

[1] http://culpepper.io/publications/robust-uqv.txt.gz

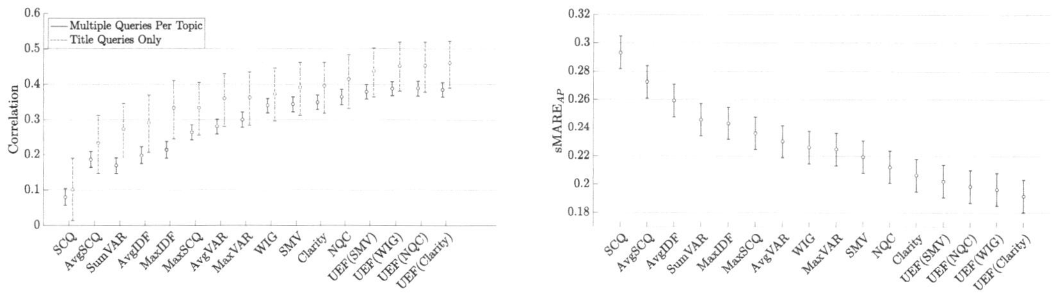

(a) Prediction quality of the selected QPP models on ROBUST04 (Confidence Intervals computed with Kendall's τ), using either title queries or all available formulations.

(b) Confidence Intervals of AP induced scaled Mean Absolute Rank Error (sMARE$_{AP}$) from $\mathrm{MD0}_{micro}$ on the ROBUST04 title queries.

Figure 1: Quality and Confidence Intervals of the selected QPP models using the traditional approach (left) and the sMARE$_{AP}$ measure (right).

different, out of 120 total pairs of QPP models (47.5%). This suggests that using confidence intervals does indeed make it difficult to decide which QPP system is the best performing, as suggested by [7].

In addition to using the traditional title queries, we also explore the scenario of using multiple formulations, which allows us to produce replicas for the same experimental conditions (i.e., the retrieval system or the QPP model used) on the same subject (i.e., the topic). While the performance is generally lower when using multiple topic formulations (the blue bars shown in Figure 1a), there is a high degree of similarity between the ordering of the QPP models for multiple query formulations to the ordering for title-only (Kendall's tau correlation between using title-only versus multiple queries per topic is 0.98, $p < 0.0001$). Overall, the bootstrap intervals are substantially larger if a traditional title-only evaluation approach is used, which makes it less suitable for determining if any single system is a clear winner, while using multiple queries does induce smaller intervals and better discriminative power between the QPP approaches.

3.2. ANOVA modeling and analysis of QPP

To support a more detailed analysis of QPP methods and associated factors, we now explore the use of ANOVA. Instead of computing the correlations between the complete lists, we measure the difference, for each query, in the rank position assigned by a QPP method and the ground truth rank position assigned by AP. Ties in ranks are broken using the average of tie rank spans, as is the default in many statistical applications. Observe that this transitions us from *point estimates* of a single correlation value for the two lists over a whole set of topics to a *distribution* of the rank differences between the two lists for each query in the set. In order to scale the scores to the range $[0, 1]$ we divide them by the number of samples. The error, labeled as AP induced scaled Absolute Rank Error (sARE$_{AP}$), for each query is:

$$\text{sARE}_{AP}(q_i) := \frac{|r_i^p - r_i^e|}{|Q|}, \quad (1)$$

where r_i^p and r_i^e are the ranks assigned by the predictor and the evaluation metric respectively for query i; Q is the set of queries. For each predictor $\mathcal{P}$, we can calculate the sMARE$_{AP}$ as follows:

$$\text{sMARE}_{AP}(\mathcal{P}) := \frac{1}{|Q|} \sum_{q_i \in Q} \text{sARE}_{AP}(q_i). \quad (2)$$

Note that sMARE$_{AP}$ can be seen as a derivation of *Spearman's Footrule distance*, making it a metric for the full rankings instead of a correlation. Among the properties of Spearman's Footrule distance, Diaconis and Graham [20] list that it is bounded between $[0, \lfloor 0.5n^2 \rfloor]$, where n is the length of the ranking. Since both sARE$_{AP}$ and sMARE$_{AP}$ are normalized by the number of queries, sMARE$_{AP}$ is bounded between $[0, 0.5]$. The proposed metric presents a Kendall's τ correlation coefficient with the original metric higher than 0.99 ($p < 0.0001$) for all configurations.

We are in a position to introduce our first ANOVA model which will enable a more comprehensive experimental analysis of the results.

$$y_{iqrs} = \mu + \tau_i + \gamma_q + \delta_r + \zeta_s + \varepsilon_{iqrs} \quad (\text{MD0}_{micro})$$

where: $y_{i...}$ is the performance (sARE$_{AP}$) on the i-th topic (using the specified QPP pipeline); μ is the *grand mean*; τ_i is the effect of the i-th topic (represented with the title query formulation); γ_q, δ_r, and ζ_s are the effect of the q-th stoplist, the r-th stemmer, and the s-th QPP model; ε_{iqrs} is the error component. Such ANOVA shows that all factors are significants. Furthermore, we observe a large size ω^2 effect for the topic ($\omega^2_{<topic>} = 0.410$). Both the stoplist and the stemmer factors are significant, but with a negligible effect ($\omega^2_{<stoplist>} = 0.001$ and $\omega^2_{<stemmer>} = 0.004$), while the QPP model displays a small effect ($\omega^2_{<qpp\ model>} = 0.036$). Based on the results of this analysis, we also ran a Tukey's Honestly Significant Difference (HSD) post-hoc analysis to test for pairwise differences. Figure 1b shows the Tukey's HSD confidence intervals for sMARE$_{AP}$ over the different QPP models.

When comparing Figure 1a (orange bars) and Figure 1b, we can observe that there is less overlap between the CIs, in particular, we observe that, by computing the p-values for the pairwise comparisons, out of 120 pairs of predictors, 96 of them are significantly different (80.0%). Thus, compared to the results observed for the bootstrap-based approach, we are able to differentiate between 68.4% more pairs of predictors. The "Topic" factor is responsible for the largest part of the variance; this is in line with results from IR effectiveness evaluation (see for example Tague-Sutcliffe and Blustein [21]). Thus, the estimation of the performance for a specific QPP model can vary significantly as it is dependent on properties of the underlying collection (performance differences in topics/queries). By removing the contribution of the topics from the global variance, ANOVA removes any volatility in the underlying experimental data allowing the relative performance of predictors to be compared more precisely. When using only correlations aggregated across all topics, such information is lost, while an ANOVA analysis facilitates more discriminative performance comparisons between systems by systematically accounting for each factor separately.

Table 1
$\mathrm{MD1}_{micro}$ ANOVA applied on ROBUST04 collection. ω^2 for non-significant factors is ill-defined and thus not reported.

Source	SS	DF	MS	F	p-value	$\hat{\omega}^2_{\langle fact \rangle}$
Topic	1840.082	248	7.420	1293.936	<0.001	0.518
Formulation(Topic)	1746.213	996	1.753	305.749	<0.001	0.504
Stoplist	1.179	4	0.295	51.402	<0.001	0.001
Stemmer	10.622	2	5.311	926.188	<0.001	0.006
QPP model	305.796	15	20.386	3555.233	<0.001	0.151
Topic*Stoplist	40.224	992	0.041	7.071	<0.001	0.020
Topic*Stemmer	154.200	496	0.311	54.216	<0.001	0.081
Topic*QPP model	2051.688	3720	0.552	96.182	<0.001	0.542
Frm.*Stoplist	87.110	3984	0.022	3.813	<0.001	0.036
Frm.*Stemmer	312.955	1992	0.157	27.398	<0.001	0.150
Frm.*QPP model	3348.894	14940	0.224	39.091	<0.001	0.656
Stoplist*Stemmer	0.059	8	0.007	1.288	0.2444	—
Stoplist*QPP model	0.901	60	0.015	2.618	<0.001	<0.001
Stemmer*QPP model	4.850	30	0.162	28.195	<0.001	0.003
Error	1555.757	271312	0.006			
Total	11460.530	298799				

3.3. ANOVA modeling of multiple queries and interactions

One of the most interesting aspects of our framework is the capability to compute the effect sizes of interactions between factors. This is achieved using $\mathrm{MD1}_{micro}$

$$\begin{aligned} y_{ijqrs} &= \mu + \tau_i + \nu_{j(i)} + \gamma_q + \delta_r + \zeta_s + (\tau\gamma)_{iq} + (\tau\delta)_{ir} + (\tau\zeta)_{is} \\ &+ (\nu\gamma)_{j(i)q} + (\nu\delta)_{j(i)r} + (\nu\zeta)_{j(i)s} + (\gamma\delta)_{qr} + (\gamma\zeta)_{qs} + (\delta\zeta)_{rs} + \varepsilon_{ijqrs} \end{aligned} \qquad (\mathrm{MD1}_{micro})$$

which extends $\mathrm{MD0}_{micro}$ to include $\nu_{j(i)}$ to represent the effect of the j-th query formulation for the i-th topic. Moreover, this model considers all of the possible two-way interactions which are now computable using the replicates provided by the multi-query topic formulations.

Table 1 presents the ANOVA summary statistics for $\mathrm{MD1}_{micro}$. In this analysis we add the query formulations as a nested factor for each topic, in this case we randomly chose 5 for each topic.[2] The table empirically shows that the largest differences in QPP performance are due to the topics, and their formulations. The effect for the QPP factor is medium-sized. The significance of the stoplist and stemmer factors suggests that they affect the overall prediction quality, and practitioners should consider all possible factors when comparing and contrasting QPP performance for a corpus. We are now in a position to observe the interaction between topics (and their query formulations) and the predictors, which is large, indicating that important differences between QPP model performance exists within reformulations of a single topic. Finding the QPP model where interactions are smallest is valuable in practice as this corresponds

[2]The topic with the minimal number of query formulations had 5 formulations.

to be choosing a model that is most robust to query reformulation. Additionally, this enables a series of additional analyses, such as a failure analysis for topics with the largest interaction with a QPP model.

4. Conclusion

We have presented a novel evaluation framework for QPP. The framework estimates the performance of QPP on every topic as the distance between its predicted rank - computed using the QPP – and the expected one – measured through AP (or any other traditional IR measure). This allows us to obtain a distribution of performance for the QPP over the different topics. Furthermore, our framework makes use of multiple query formulations for each topic to enhance the power of our analyses. Together, the use of multiple query formulations and the distributional representation of the performance enables carrying out more accurate studies. In particular, we showed that it is possible to rely on the statistical properties of ANOVA and corresponding post hoc procedures to better identify pairs of QPP approaches that are statistically significantly different. The newly proposed framework also enables the analysis of interaction effects for QPP models and topics, allowing failure analyses and a deeper understanding into how a QPP model works. Our framework can be extended and adapted to different investigation needs. The two-way ANOVA described in $\mathrm{MD0}_{micro}$ is sufficient to determine if QPP models are significantly different, and has the added benefit of relying on a statistically-sound framework. In future work, we plan to study additional components of the evaluation framework, such as the impact of the ranking methods which are used to establish "ground truth" performance; new factors that influence QPP systems such as the ranking approach used in the post-retrieval QPP; and the effects of using multiple corpora, in order to more comprehensively model and understand corpus and QPP interactions.

References

[1] G. Faggioli, O. Zendel, J. S. Culpepper, N. Ferro, F. Scholer, An Enhanced Evaluation Framework for Query Performance Prediction, in: Proc. ECIR, 2021, pp. 115–129.

[2] N. Fuhr, Some Common Mistakes In IR Evaluation, And How They Can Be Avoided, SIGIR Forum 51 (2017) 32–41.

[3] D. Carmel, E. Yom-Tov, Estimating the Query Difficulty for Information Retrieval, Morgan & Claypool Publishers, USA, 2010.

[4] O. Zendel, A. Shtok, F. Raiber, O. Kurland, J. S. Culpepper, Information Needs, Queries, and Query Performance Prediction, in: Proc. SIGIR, 2019, p. 395–404.

[5] S. Cronen-Townsend, Y. Zhou, W. B. Croft, Predicting Query Performance, in: Proc. SIGIR, 2002, pp. 299–306.

[6] J. A. Aslam, V. Pavlu, Query Hardness Estimation Using Jensen-Shannon Divergence Among Multiple Scoring Functions, in: Proc. ECIR, 2007, pp. 198–209.

[7] C. Hauff, L. Azzopardi, D. Hiemstra, The Combination and Evaluation of Query Performance Prediction Methods, in: Proc. ECIR, 2009, pp. 301–312.

[8] D. Banks, P. Over, N.-F. Zhang, Blind Men and Elephants: Six Approaches to TREC data, Information Retrieval 1 (1999) 7–34.
[9] N. Ferro, G. Silvello, A General Linear Mixed Models Approach to Study System Component Effects, in: Proc. SIGIR, 2016, pp. 25–34.
[10] G. Faggioli, N. Ferro, System effect estimation by sharding: A comparison between anova approaches to detect significant differences (2021).
[11] E. M. Voorhees, Overview of the TREC 2004 Robust Track, in: Proc. TREC, 2004.
[12] R. Benham, J. S. Culpepper, Risk-Reward Trade-offs in Rank Fusion, in: Proc. ADCS, 2017, pp. 1:1–1:8.
[13] Y. Zhao, F. Scholer, Y. Tsegay, Effective Pre-retrieval Query Performance Prediction Using Similarity and Variability Evidence, in: Proc. ECIR, 2008, pp. 52–64.
[14] S. Cronen-Townsend, Y. Zhou, W. B. Croft, A Language Modeling Framework for Selective Query Expansion, Technical Report, 2004.
[15] F. Scholer, H. E. Williams, A. Turpin, Query Association Surrogates for Web Search, J. Assoc. Inf. Sci. Technol. 55 (2004) 637–650.
[16] A. Shtok, O. Kurland, D. Carmel, F. Raiber, G. Markovits, Predicting Query Performance by Query-Drift Estimation, ACM Trans. Inf. Syst 30 (2012) 1–35.
[17] Y. Zhou, W. B. Croft, Query Performance Prediction in Web Search Environments, in: Proc. SIGIR, 2007, p. 543–550.
[18] Y. Tao, S. Wu, Query Performance Prediction By Considering Score Magnitude and Variance Together, in: Proc. CIKM, 2014, p. 1891–1894.
[19] A. Shtok, O. Kurland, D. Carmel, Using Statistical Decision Theory and Relevance Models for Query-Performance Prediction, in: Proc. SIGIR, 2010, pp. 259–266.
[20] P. Diaconis, R. L. Graham, Spearman's Footrule as a Measure of Disarray, J. Royal Stat. Soc. 39 (1977) 262–268.
[21] J. M. Tague-Sutcliffe, J. Blustein, A Statistical Analysis of the TREC-3 Data, in: Proc. TREC, 1994, pp. 385–398.

A data-driven context-based approach for modelling Resilient Cyber Physical Production Systems

(Discussion Paper)

Ada Bagozi[1], Devis Bianchini[1] and Valeria De Antonellis[1]

[1]*University of Brescia, Dept. of Information Engineering, Via Branze 38, 25123 - Brescia (Italy)*

Abstract

In modern Cyber Physical Production Systems (CPPS) workers interact with hybrid networked cyber and engineered physical elements that record data (e.g., using sensors), analyse them using connected services and support decision making, according to the Human-In-the-Loop paradigm. In this paper we present an approach for modelling Resilient Cyber Physical Production Systems (R-CPPS). The approach is conceived as: (i) data-driven, because recovery actions, modelled in a service-oriented architecture, are activated by sensor data measures collected on the CPPS subsystems and the surrounding production environment; (ii) context-based, since recovery services are associated with the steps of the production process as well as with the hierarchical organisation of the CPPS components involved in the recovery actions. The approach provides runtime selection of services, where the sensor data measures are used as service inputs and service outputs are displayed to the operators who supervise the CPPS subsystem on which recovery actions must be performed, enabling fast and effective resilience also in a Human-In-the-Loop scenario. The feasibility of the approach is demonstrated in a food industry case study.

Keywords

Resilient cyber physical production system, context-aware resilience, service-oriented architecture, Human-In-the-Loop

1. Introduction

Cyber Physical Systems (CPS) are hybrid networked cyber and engineered physical elements that record data (e.g., using sensors), analyse them using connected services, influence physical processes and interact with human actors using multi-channel interfaces. Examples of CPS interacting with humans in industrial production are Cyber Physical Production Systems (CPPS), where workers supervise the operations of industrial work centers, according to the Human-In-the-Loop paradigm [1]. In this paper, the design of Resilient CPPS (R-CPPS) is addressed. Resilience in CPPS is even more challenging since it must be performed both on single work centers and at the shop floor level across connected components. For example, let's consider the production line shown in Figure 1, to produce biscuits starting from the recipe and ingredients.

SEBD 2021: The 29th Italian Symposium on Advanced Database Systems, September 5-9, 2021, Pizzo Calabro (VV), Italy

a.bagozi@unibs.it (A. Bagozi); devis.bianchini@unibs.it (D. Bianchini); valeria.deantonellis@unibs.it (V. De Antonellis)

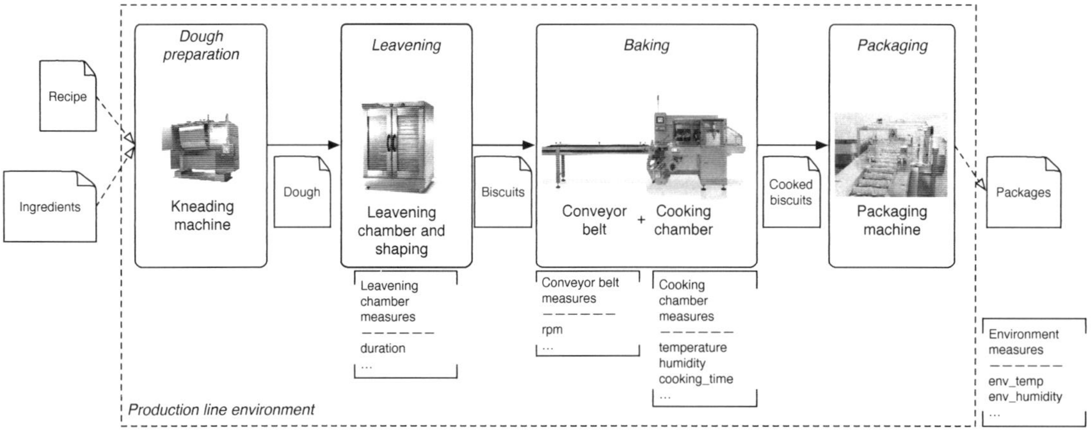

Figure 1: Production process for the food industry case study.

In the process, the dough is prepared by a kneading machine and let rise in a leavening chamber. Once the biscuits are ready to be baked, they are placed in the oven. The oven is composed of a conveyor belt and the cooking chamber. By regulating the velocity of the belt through the rpm of the rotating engine, it is possible to setup the cooking time of the biscuits. The temperature and the humidity of the cooking chamber can be regulated as well. Finally, other measures can be gathered at the shop floor level, such as the temperature and the humidity of the production line environment.

In modern digital factories work centers are fully connected, therefore changes in one of them may require recovery actions on the others. For example, an anomaly on the rotating engine of the conveyor belt might cause the cookies to burn and a possible recovery action can be triggered to modify the temperature of the cooking chamber to face a longer cooking time. Similarly, the effects of environment humidity on the dough entering the oven must be considered. Finally, recovery actions sometimes require an interaction with operators (e.g., the substitution of some parts in the production line should be authorised). Therefore, the effects of recovery services should be visualised nearby the involved work centers only, in order to give useful insights to on-field operators who supervise the involved components.

To address the above mentioned complexity of the domain, we propose a service-oriented approach for modelling R-CPPS, in line with recent approaches for the design of resilient CPS [2]. The approach is conceived as: (i) *data-driven*, because recovery actions, modelled in a service-oriented architecture, are activated by sensor data measures collected on the CPPS and the surrounding production environment; (ii) *context-based*, since recovery services are associated with the steps of the production process as well as with the hierarchical organisation of the CPPS components. The approach provides runtime selection of services, where the sensor data measures are used as service inputs and service outputs are displayed to the operators supervising the CPPS subsystem on which recovery actions must be performed, enabling fast and effective resilience also in a Human-In-the-Loop scenario. The approach described in this paper has been presented in details in [3].

The paper is organised as follows: in Section 2 related work are discussed; Section 3 describes the context model; in Section 4 the recovery services selection procedure is presented; in Section 5 we describe implementation and experimental validation; finally, Section 6 closes the paper.

2. Related Work

A recent ever growing interest has been devoted to resilience challenges in industrial plants, often related with the notion of self-adaptation, as witnessed by an increasing number of surveys [4, 5].

Resilience/self-adaptation specifically designed for CPPS has been addressed in [6, 7, 8, 9, 10]. Authors in [6] propose a failure predictive tool based on the dynamic principal component analysis (DPCA) and the gradient boosting decision trees (GBDT), a supervised machine learning algorithm. Authors in [7] address resilience in a micro factory adopting a digital twin (DT) to perform simulation on the monitored system and reinforcement learning (RL)-based production control method. In [8, 9] ad-hoc resilience solutions are provided, focusing on single systems to monitor, without considering the effects of resilience across connected components. Compared to these approaches, our solution introduces a context model, apt to relate recovery services with work centers organised in the fully connected hierarchy of smart machines (from connected devices up to the whole production line at shop floor level). The adoption of context-awareness to implement resilience on single CPS has been investigated in the Context-Aware Resilience for Cyber Physical Systems (CAR) project (`http://www.msca-car.eu`), where resilience patterns have been implemented by combining recovery actions. Authors in [10] propose an approach for resilient CPPS that uses a simulation-based decision support system to automatically select the best recovery action based on KPIs (e.g., Overall Equipment Efficiency) measured on the whole production process. With respect to [10], our approach uses the context model to explicitly relate different kinds of recovery services to the product that is being created, the involved work centers and production process phases. Moreover, a continuous evolution of the service ecosystem is realised through the design of new services in case of unsuccessful or missing recovery actions. Authors in [2] share with us the service-oriented viewpoint. With respect to them, we add here the context model and we propose a set of context-driven phases to identify critical conditions and improve the selection of recovery services.

3. Context Model

In Figure 2 we report a simplified schema of the context model to support resilience in CPPS. In the proposed model, the *Context* is described by the *Product* that is being produced (e.g., a certain type of biscuits), the production *Process* (e.g., biscuits baking process) and the *Environment Parameters* that may influence the production (e.g., the environment temperature and humidity). A *Process* is associated with *Services* and is performed by one or more *components*, that cooperate to successfully complete the production. For example, the biscuits baking process involves the kneading machine to prepare the dough, the leavening chamber to prepare biscuits, the oven to bake the biscuits. Components can be organised hierarchically (according to the hierarchy levels

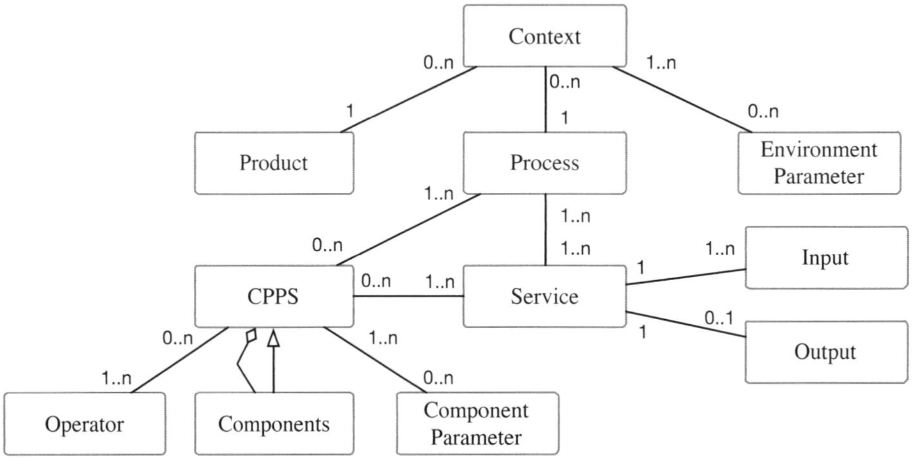

Figure 2: Resilient CPPS context model.

dimension of the RAMI 4.0 reference architectural model, IEC 62264/IEC 61512 standards): for example, the oven is composed of the conveyor belt and the cooking chamber. *Services* represent recovery actions to be executed on a component or the whole CPPS to ensure resilience. A component is supervised by at least one *Operator* and can be monitored and controlled through a set of *Component Parameters* (e.g., the oven temperature). Both *Environment Parameters* and *Component Parameters* are used to monitor the behaviour of a *CPPS* in a given *Context*.

A recovery service S_j is associated with a CPPS (or one of its components) and is described as a tuple

$$S_j = \langle n_{S_j}, IN_{S_j}, out_{S_j}, type_{S_j}, CPPS_{S_j} \rangle \tag{1}$$

where: (i) n_{S_j} is the service name; (ii) IN_{S_j} is the set of input parameters; (iii) out_{S_j} is an optional service output; (iv) $type_{S_j}$ is the service type; (v) $CPPS_{S_j}$ is the component or the whole CPPS associated with the service. Service I/O can be either Component or Environment Parameters.

Flexibility of service-oriented architectures enables to include and dynamically add different types of services. For instance, a recovery service may implement the function that relates one or more input parameters with the output one. We refer to this type of service as "re-configuration". The following service

```
setOvenTemperature(ConveyorBelt.rpm) → CookingChamber.temperature
```

represents a re-configuration service to set the cooking chamber temperature when the conveyor belt rpm changes, to avoid cookies overheating. When a re-configuration is not an applicable solution (e.g., if the service returns a cooking chamber temperature out of an acceptable range of values), other recovery actions must be applied, such as to replace or repair the conveyor

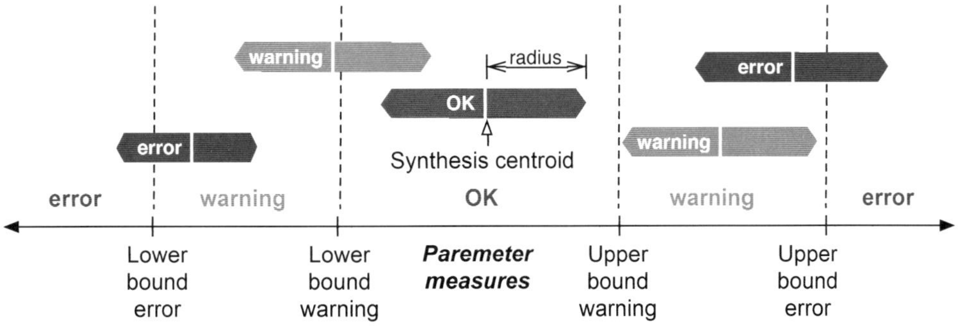

Figure 3: Warning and error parameters bounds to detect the system status.

belt. An example of "component substitution" service would be the following:

```
replaceConveyorBeltRotatingEngine(ConveyorBelt.rpm) → void
```

that has no output parameter to modify. This service is associated with the conveyor belt. Other service information (e.g., execution cost, time) can be used to guide the automatic selection of the proper recovery actions. The examples of recovery service types considered here is not exhaustive and may be extended [11]. Recovery services can be exposed in different ways, for example as web services, invoked from a local library, integrated in the administrative shell of work centers according to the RAMI4.0 specification.

4. Selection of relevant recovery services

Once an anomalous event (corresponding to a critical condition) is detected on one of the CPPS components, the event is used to identify recovery services to be applied on the involved component or connected ones. Recovery services are automatically identified by inspecting their inputs. In particular, a recovery service is relevant if one of its input parameters has been classified in the `error` (reactive resilience) or `warning` status (proactive resilience), as summarised in Figure 3. In order to face the volume of data streams collected from monitored CPPS and to avoid misleading anomaly detection due to noise and false outliers, that may affect single measures, anomaly detection is performed by applying the IDEAaS approach described in [12]. Roughly speaking, a summarised representation of collected measures, called *syntheses*, is incrementally built. Each synthesis contains measures collected when the observed system is operating in the same working conditions. Moreover, the following conditions must hold on the relevant recovery service: *(a)* if the service type is "re-configuration", the value of its output parameters must not exceed any parameter bound; *(b)* if the service type is "component substitution", an alternative machinery or component ready to be used in substitution must be available and associated with the service.

As an example, the `setOvenTemperature` service is relevant if an anomaly has been detected on the values of rotating engine rpm in the conveyor belt. Since the service type in this case is "re-configuration", the value of the service output resulting from its automatic execution

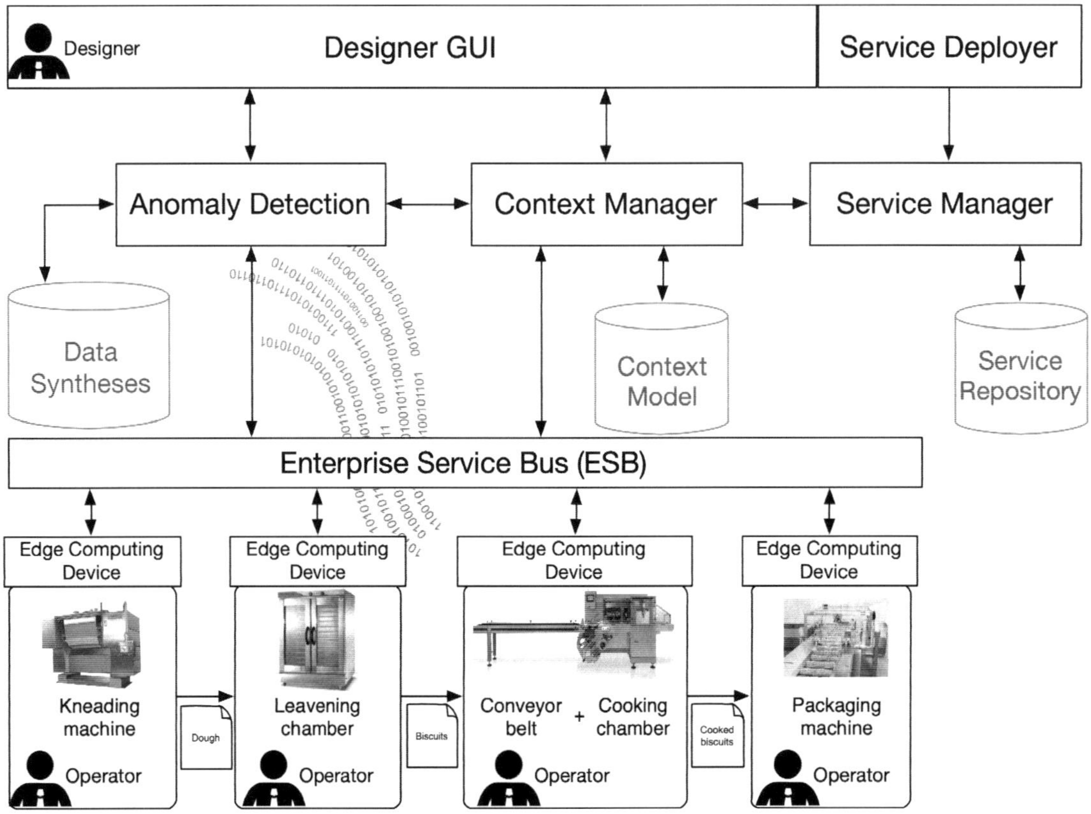

Figure 4: Approach architecture.

must be compliant with parameter bounds of the cooking chamber temperature. The relevant service is then automatically executed to operate on the component or the whole CPPS (for re-configuration services) or to proceed with a physical substitution of the affected part (for component substitution services). The system will present all the necessary information to guide the maintenance operator during the substitution. In fact, we remark that another feature of the approach is that the information about the recovery actions to undertake, as results of recovery services execution, is visualised nearby the involved work center, providing insights to operators who supervise those components, avoiding information flooding towards operators that may hamper their working efficiency. A prototype operator interface is detailed in [3].

5. Implementation and preliminary evaluation

The approach described in this paper has been integrated with the IDEAaS anomaly detection module and the resulting architecture is sketched in Figure 4. During anomaly detection, the `Context Manager` is invoked in order to contextualise the incoming data. To this purpose, the `Context Manager` will provide the following information: *(i)* an identifier for the context; *(ii)* a set of parameters, either *Environment or Component parameters*, to be analysed; *(iii)* the observed CPPS; *(iv)* the product that is being produced; *(v)* the running process. Such information is extracted from the *Context Model* database.

Collected measures in the context are properly summarised as syntheses by applying IDEAaS data summarisation techniques. Furthermore, syntheses are processed in order to detect anomalies and are stored in the *Data Syntheses* database. Summarised data are visualised: *(a)* on the `Designer GUI` to let the designer monitor the overall evolution of the CPPS; *(b)* on the `Edge Computing Device` of the involved component (operator interface), to let the on-field operator to better understand the behaviour of the component. Moreover, when anomalous conditions are detected, the `Context Manager` is notified with the identifier of the context and the list of critical parameters on which the anomaly occurred, together with their measures. The `Context Manager` will search for relevant recovery services, associated with the component in the context. Once relevant recovery services have been identified, the `Context Manager` launches the execution of the services by interacting with the `Service Manager`, which is responsible for services registration in the *Service Repository* and for their execution. The result of the services execution is sent to the operator supervising the component.

A proof-of-concept validation of the approach to demonstrate its applicability is being performed. In particular, processing time required to promptly detect anomalies and activate recovery actions services (a potential bottleneck for the whole approach) is investigated. We run experiments on a MacBook Pro Retina, with an Intel Core i7-6700HQ processor, at 2.60 GHz, 4 cores, RAM 16GB. For measures of parameters collected every 200ms, average response time per measure necessary to apply data summarisation and anomaly detection is within 0.12 ms. We also quantified the capability to detect anomalies on the collected measures using the Pearson Correlation Coefficient (PCC) $\in [-1, +1]$, that estimates the correlation between the real variations and the detected ones. In the experiment, the best PCC value is higher than 0.85, that represents an acceptable correlation.

6. Conclusions

In this paper, we addressed resilience in Cyber Physical Production Systems, where recovery services are activated by sensor data measures (*data-driven*) and are selected according to a *context model*, that relates services with the steps of the production process as well as with the hierarchical organisation of the involved CPPS components. A validation of the approach is being performed on a real dataset that we should pre-process appropriately (e.g., sensitive information must be removed or anonymised) before making it available to the community as a benchmark for future work comparison. Future efforts will be devoted to the improvement of service selection criteria, for example defining a cost model and using simulation-based modules to predict the effects of recovery actions on the production process, like the one described in [10]. Finally, modelling of other kinds of recovery services is being considered.

References

[1] D. Nunes, J. Silva, F. Boavida, A Practical Introduction to Human-in-the-Loop Cyber-Physical Systems, Wiley IEEE Press, 2018.

[2] N. Bicocchi, G. Cabri, F. Mandreoli, M. Mecella, Dynamic digital factories for agile supply chains: An architectural approach, Industrial Information Integration 15 (2019) 111–121.

[3] A. Bagozi, D. Bianchini, V. De Antonellis, Designing Context-Based Services for Resilient Cyber Physical Production Systems, in: 21st Int. Conf. on Web Information Systems Engineering (WISE), 2020, pp. 474–488.

[4] D. Ratasich, F. Khalid, F. Geissler, R. Grosu, M. Shafique, E. Bartocci, A Roadmap Toward the Resilient Internet of Things for Cyber-Physical Systems, IEEE Access 7 (2019) 13260–13283.

[5] J. Moura, D. Hutchison, Game Theory for Multi-Access Edge Computing: Survey, Use Cases, and Future Trends, IEEE Communication Surveys and Tutorials 21 (2019) 260–288.

[6] Y. Zhang, X. Beudaert, J. Argandoña, S. Ratchev, J. Munoa, A cpps based on gbdt for predicting failure events in milling, The International Journal of Advanced Manufacturing Technology 111 (2020) 341–357.

[7] K. T. Park, Y. H. Son, S. W. Ko, S. D. Noh, Digital twin and reinforcement learning-based resilient production control for micro smart factory, Applied Sciences 11 (2021).

[8] R. Barenji, A. Barenji, M. Hashemipour, A multi-agent RFID-enabled distributed control system for a flexible manufacturing shop, Advanced Manufacturing Technology 71 (2014) 1773–1791.

[9] B. Vogel-Hauser, C. Diedrich, D. Pantförder, P. Göohner, Coupling heterogeneous production systems by a multi-agent based cyber-physical production system, in: Proc. of 12th IEEE Int. Conf. on Industrial Informatics (INDN), 2014, pp. 713–719.

[10] N. Galaske, A. R, Disruption Management for Resilient Processes in Cyber-Physical Production Systems, Procedia CIRP 50 (2016) 442 – 447.

[11] G. Pumpuni-Lenss, T. Blackburn, A. Garstenauer, Resilience in Complex Systems: An Agent-Based Approach, Systems Engineering 20 (2017) 158–172.

[12] A. Bagozi, D. Bianchini, V. D. Antonellis, M. Garda, A. Marini, A Relevance-based approach for Big Data Exploration, Future Generation Computer Systems 101 (2019) 51 – 69.

Some experiments on activity outlier detection

(Discussion Paper)

Michele Ianni[1], Elio Masciari[2]

[1]*Università della Calabria, Italy*
[2]*Università Federico II, Napoli, Italy*

Abstract
The rise of cyber crime observed in recent years calls for more efficient and effective data exploration and analysis tools. In this respect, the need to support advanced analytics on activity logs and real time data is driving data scientist' interest in designing and implementing scalable cyber security solutions. However, when data science algorithms are leveraged for huge amounts of data, their fully scalable deployment faces a number of technical challenges that grow with the complexity of the algorithms involved and the task to be tackled. Thus algorithms, that were originally designed for classical scenarios, need to be redesigned in order to be effectively used for cyber security purposes. In this paper, we explore these problems and then propose a solution which has proven to be very effective in identifying malicious activities.

Keywords
Cybersecurity, Data Compression, Activity Analysis, Cluster Analysis

1. Introduction

Monitoring activities is a crucial and often underused method in the task of documenting, assessing and preventing risk. Either if we talk about a large computer network or a single machine or even a small IoT device, we face the problem of handling a high volume of data that is generated continuously. This data could be related to network activity, software logs, user interaction, hardware monitoring to cite a few. By carefully analyzing this endless stream of information, it could be possible to thwart many kinds of cyberattacks, even before they happen [1].

Cybercrime is on the rise, annual damage from cyberattacks is set to hit 6 trillion dollar in 2021 [2], this is twice the amount of annual damage from cybercrime recorded in 2016. Many attacks follow well known patterns and many malicious software are just a variant of existing menaces, however, even the simplest form of cyberattacks are still dangerous nowadays. It is important to notice that many attacks could be detected in the very early stages, or even prevented at all, if all the information available could be analyzed in a fast and reliable way [3]. In this respect, activity monitoring is a crucial component of comprehensive cybersecurity. The technologies in the field of Big Data analysis and the advances of computing capabilities led to

SEBD 2021: The 29th Italian Symposium on Advanced Database Systems, September 5-9, 2021, Pizzo Calabro (VV), Italy
michele.ianni@univr.it (M. Ianni); elio.masciari@unina.it (E. Masciari)
0000-0003-0562-7462 (M. Ianni)

new possibilities in the difficult task of extracting sensitive information from huge amounts of data [4]. Moreover, activity data has an inestimable value in cybersecurity as the information extracted can easily be leveraged in order to better frame the legitimate actions performed thus easily recognizing and blocking unwanted interactions.

Nowadays, especially in business scenarios, the attackers could be insiders, even employees sometimes, who (consciously or not) could endanger the sensitivity of data, or damage the software/hardware architecture by opening holes that can be exploited by attackers [5]. Misconfigured services, unpatched binaries, unknown vulnerabilities are all issues who constantly jeopardize the security of our computers, leaving big holes open which can be used by attackers to easily infiltrate. By analyzing logs and monitoring activities in real time, many of these holes could be detected before an unauthorized user could spread your valuable information [6].

How Is Activity Monitoring Useful In The Event Of An Attack? If a cyberattack occurs, activity logs provide a roadmap to the origin of the attack and what agents were directly involved. Each log can provide further details about where the cyberattackers may be going next, how to prevent further attacks and what can be done to secure your system after the threat has been eliminated. It is important to notice that, in the majority of the cases, the domain experts are able to classify malicious actions and safe ones. This is usually a straightforward task that is performed in several different types of security systems, from intrusion detection systems to blacklist based access control. Unfortunately, the task of identifying and marking malicious actions is not always easy. As a matter of fact, even if we could enumerate all malicious actions, we may found that many malicious activities are the result of the execution of several actions that, when analyzed individually, are usually considered safe. This allows to understand why simple blacklists are usually not enough to keep a system safe. System administrators are overwhelmed by a continuous stream of logs that is very difficult to tackle. It is worth noticing that, in managing this huge amount of data, it is likely to miss small amounts of relevant actions, that could be related to an attack. Indeed, the actions related to an attack represent an almost invisible fraction, in terms of size, hidden in endless logs as a needle in a haystack. Thus, it is straightforward to note that the analysis of the activity logs became an infeasible task to be performed manually, on the contrary it is mandatory to use anomaly detection techniques in order to early detect any possible threat.

In this paper, we leverage the prime numbers based encoding scheme described in [7] in order to efficiently and effectively identify suspicious activities by means of a proper outlier detection strategy. More in detail, our contribution can be summarized as follows:

- SCOUT: a hierarchical approach for quick identification of outlying activities;
- A deep experimental evaluation of the proposed approach that confirmed the validity of our proposal.

2. Computing Outliers on Activity Logs

In order to identify outlying activities after they are encoded as explained in [7], we leverage a fast hierarchical approach, that combines the benefits of the divisive and agglomerative approaches. Fig. 1 illustrates the operations performed by our algorithm SCOUT. The input

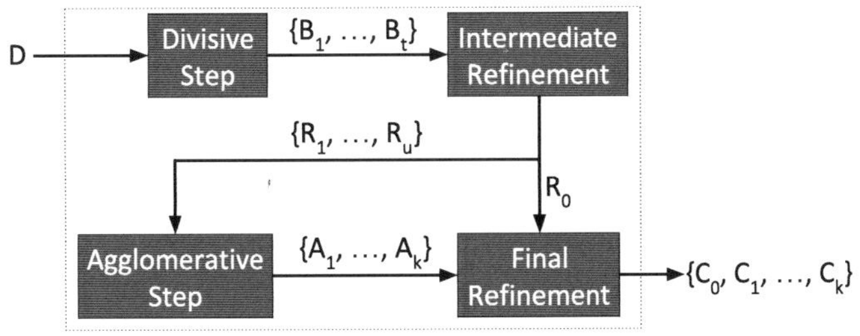

Figure 1: The four Steps of the SCOUT Algorithm

dataset D is first partitioned into a set of rectangular blocks $\{B_1, \ldots, B_t\}$ by means of a top-down divisive procedure. Those blocks are then refined in the next step, whose result is a new partitioning of the points of D, $\{R_0, R_1, \ldots, R_u\}$, where R_0 contains points that are classified as outliers, and each of the remaining u sets represents a cluster. These u clusters are processed in the third step, through a bottom-up agglomerative procedure, whose result is a new partitioning of the points in $R_1 \cup \ldots \cup R_u$ into the sets $A_1, \ldots, A_k$, where $k \leq u$, obtained by possibly merging groups of clusters in $\{R_1 \cup \ldots \cup R_u\}$ into one only cluster of $\{A_1, \ldots, A_k\}$. Finally, the new clusters in output from the agglomerative step and the outliers R_0 in output from the previous, are refined, thus obtaining the final set of well-rounded clusters, $\{C_1, \ldots, C_k\}$, and the set of outliers C_0. In our running example of Fig. 2, we show how the successive steps of SCOUT applied to the two-dimensional data distribution of Fig. 2(a), produce the results shown in Fig. 2(b–e). Thus, Fig. 2(b), (c), (d), and (e) show the results produced, respectively, by the steps of Fig. 1, which are described in detail in the following.

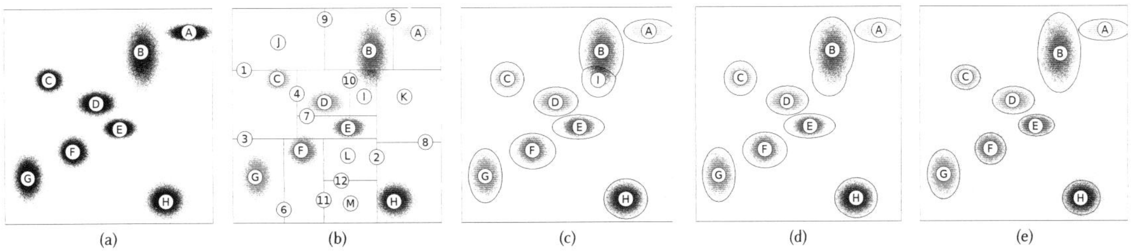

Figure 2: A two-dimensional data set with 8 clusters (a), its partitioning after the divisive step (b), the intermediate refinement (c), the agglomerative step (d), and the final refinement (e).

The divisive step of SCOUT performs a top-down partitioning of the data set to isolate blocks whose points are as much as possible close to each other: this is equivalent to minimizing the $WCSS$ of the blocks, an objective also pursued by the vast majority of algorithms tailored for outlier detection. As the clustering algorithm at the basis of the outlier detection strategy have been described in details in [8, 9] we do not report here the complete description except a brief overview of the approach focusing on the goal of this paper, i.e., the. outlier detection phase. Indeed, the divisive phase described above partition the overall space into (A) several blocks containing clusters, and (B) zero or more blocks that only contain **outliers** and noise points. We also see that blocks of type A will only contain a single cluster since blocks containing several clusters were split according to the "when in doubt split" philosophy used in the divisive phase. To better understand this approach, we report the details of the refinement step in order to better explain the details of the outlier detection strategy. More in detail, SCOUT seeks to realize the objectives of (I) identifying the blocks that contain only outliers, and (II) generating well-rounded clusters for the remaining blocks. Task (I) is performed by using the observation that (a) the density of blocks containing only outliers is low, and (b) the density of such blocks is rather uniform because of the random nature of noise and outliers.

Algorithm 1: The algorithm for identifying outlier blocks

```
Procedure identifyOutlierBlocks(B)
    Input: B = {B_1, ..., B_t}: a set of t blocks
    Output: o: an array of t boolean values, where o_i = true ⇔ B_i is classified as outlier block
    begin
        o ← an array [o_1, ..., o_t] of t boolean;
        den ← an array [d_1, ..., d_t] containing the densities of blocks in B;
        v ← an array [v_1, ..., v_{t-1}] containing t-1 numbers;
        sort(den);
        for i ← 1 to t − 1 do
            v[i] ← den[i + 1]/den[i];
        end
        vt ← average(v) + standardDeviation(v); vi ← 1;
        while vi < t ∧ v[vi] ≤ vt do
            vi ← vi + 1;
        end
        dt ← den[vi]; // the maximum density an outlier block may have
        for i ← 1 to t do
            o[i] ←density(B_i)≤ dt ∧ aroundCentroidDensity(B_i)< 2×density(B_i);
        end
        return o;
    end
```

The pseudo-code is reported in Algorithm 1. SCOUT checks condition (a) first by sorting the densities of blocks and detecting discontinuity in density between blocks that are contiguous in that ordering. That is, if den is an array containing the density values of the t blocks yielded by the divisive step, sorted in ascending order, we compute an array v with $t - 1$ values, such that $v[i] = den[i + 1]/den[i]$. Then, if vi outlier-blocks are present, the first $vi - 1$ values of v will be approximately equal to 1, while $v[vi]$ will be 'quite large'. Through a number of experiments, extensive empirical evaluation shows that a good threshold for value of v to be considered 'quite large' is provided by average value of v plus its standard deviation. Thus, with vi the smallest value index for which the v-value exceeds this threshold, we classify all blocks with density above $dt = den[vi]$ as cluster blocks. Then, we test the other blocks using condition (b), i.e., we test the blocks that are suspected to be outlier blocks because of their low density. This additional verification step is needed because large density differences between cluster blocks cannot be always excluded (e.g., because of large differences in the volume of those blocks). Therefore, a small hypercube is taken around the centroid of each block being checked for condition (b), as depicted in Figure 3, and if the density in the hypercube is less than twice the density of the whole block, this is classified as an outlier block (Fig. 3(a)); otherwise it is classified as a cluster block (Fig. 3(b)). The size of the hypercube used for this check is such that, for each dimension, the edge of the hypercube is $1/10$ of that of the whole block on the same dimension. The rationale of this the criterion can be understood by considering that for an

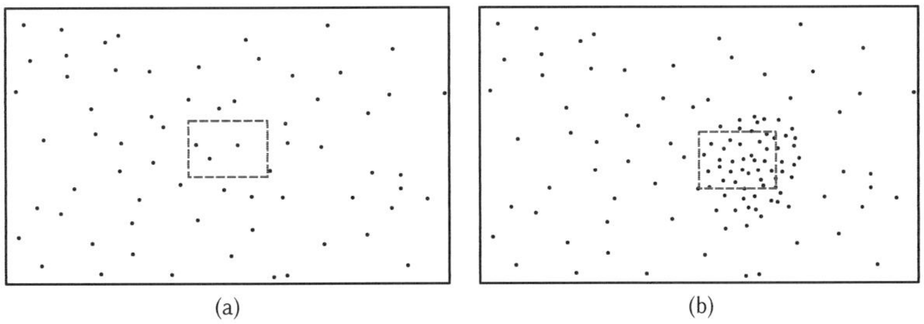

Figure 3: A block containing only outliers (a) and a block containing a cluster (b).

outlier-block, where data are randomly distributed, it is very unlikely that the density around centroid is twice the global density while in a cluster-block, the density around centroid is very likely to be twice the global density. For instance, these tests applied to our running example in Fig. 2(b) have classified blocks "J", "K", "L" and "M" as outlier-blocks.

Having thus identified all the cluster blocks, we can now proceed with task (II) and materialize the centroids of their clusters and assign each point to the cluster with the nearest centroid. To this end, we use a weighted function of the distance between points on each dimension. Specifically, we measure the distance of a point $\mathbf{p} = (p_1, \ldots, p_d)$ from a cluster-blocks C with centroid $(c_1, \ldots, c_d)$ as

$$dist^{\star}(\mathbf{p}, C) = \sum_{i=1}^{d} \left(\frac{\|p_i - c_i\|}{r_i} \right)^2$$

where r_i is the radius of the cluster along the i-th dimension, which is estimated by the usual $3{\times}\sigma$ criterion [10] used to separate core points from outliers:

$$r_i = 3 \cdot \sqrt{\frac{WCSS_i(C)}{n}}$$

where n is the number of points inside C and $WCSS_i(C)$ is the variance of the i-th coordinates of the points in C. Observe that $dist^{\star}(\mathbf{p}, C) = 1$ defines an ellipsoid whose center is the centroid of C and whose radius on the i-th dimension is r_i. Therefore, we can now classify each point in the sample set as either belonging to a particular cluster or as an outlier by assigning each point $\mathbf{p}$ to the cluster C which minimizes $dist(\mathbf{p}, C)$, provided that this minimum distance is less than or equal to 1; otherwise $\mathbf{p}$ is classified as outlier. The final output is thus a quite simple and explainable set of points that are marked as outliers.

3. Experimental Evaluation

In this section, we will describe the experimental assessment for our framework. First, we introduce the pre-elaboration steps that are needed on the dataset before running our tests as the activity logs usually contains a huge amount of information that could be not partitioned in sessions or single user activities. More in detail, when dealing with transactional data, a tuple is a collection of features, an activity record instead is an ordered set (i.e., a sequence) of time-stamped actions. Moreover, log data are usually recorded in a variety of different formats, and they can be built from several domains. As we deal with activity logs composed of different types of actions we define a mapping function from the domains of actions to logs.

Definition 3.1. Let ACT be a set of actions contained in an activity logs, a function $L : O \rightarrow ACT$ mapping each action to its activity log (or set of activity logs) is called a *labeling* function.

We point out here, that due to privacy reasons, real datasets are usually anonymized, nevertheless, in the experimental section we performed a proper labeling of activities in order to obtain a meaningful experimental assessment for our approaches. More in detail, we ran our experiments on several dataset whose naming convention are different for each action, thus, we omit here to describe the labeling function we used as they are quite straightforward (by using name permutation or punctuation) but we mention here their existence to clarify that a proper mapping is always computed as pre-elaboration step especially when same action could have different name in different sessions in order to have a fair comparison.

3.1. Results

For the experimental evaluation we used two different datasets.

The first dataset source is the widely used KDD Cup 1999 Data [11] which contains more than seven million connection records. A connection is a sequence of TCP packets starting and ending within a time interval during which, data flows to and from a source IP address to a target IP address under some well defined protocol. Each connection is labeled as either normal, or as an attack, with exactly one specific attack type. Each connection record consists of about 100 bytes. Attacks fall into four main categories: i) *DOS*: denial-of-service, e.g. syn flood; ii) *R2L*: unauthorized access from a remote machine, e.g. guessing password; iii) *U2R*: unauthorized access to local superuser (root) privileges, e.g., various "buffer overflow" attacks; iv) *probing*: surveillance and other probing, e.g., port scanning. As regards the second dataset, referred from now on as "synthetic", in order to perform fine tuning tests, we developed a logging system based on the `strace` Linux command that captures the system calls invoked by a malicious software we created ad-hoc. The generated log contains the timestamp, the user performing the call, the name of the call, and its parameters. We further enriched the information contained in the logs by running our logging system on many different applications, using different users, so that the results contains information related both to normal usage of the operating system and to malicious activity. It is important to notice that each dataset described above contains labels that are used to mark malicious actions. However, since we are dealing with activities which we defined as a sequence of several atomic actions, we consider an activity as a malevolent one if it is a sequence of actions containing at least one malicious action. The first task in our experimental evaluation is, then, identifying activities in our datasets. This task can be done using different metrics and considerations, and, in most of the cases, is strictly related to the specific log we are working on. The actions included in a given activity are, in fact, determined by means of multiple factors like the user performing the action, the timestamp, the relationship with a software session, a network connection, the type of the action performed and so on. More in detail, we built activities by specifying a fixed length and then (eventually) padding them as explained in previous section. We compared the performances on well-established

Measure	*Derivations*	*KDD Cup*	*Synthetic*
Sensitivity	$\frac{TP}{TP+FN}$	0.9700	0.9920
Specificity	$\frac{TN}{FP+TN}$	0.8829	0.9920
Precision	$\frac{TP}{TP+FP}$	0.9868	0.9920
Negative Predictive Value	$\frac{TN}{TN+FN}$	0.7656	0.9920
False Positive Rate	$\frac{FP}{FP+TN}$	0.1171	0.0080
False Discovery Rate	$\frac{FP}{FP+TP}$	0.0132	0.0080
False Negative Rate	$\frac{FN}{FN+TP}$	0.0300	0.0080
Accuracy	$\frac{TP+TN}{P+N}$	0.9613	0.9920
F1 Score	$\frac{2TP}{2TP+FP+FN}$	0.9783	0.9920
Matthews Correlation Coefficient	$\frac{TP*TN-FP*FN}{\sqrt{(TP+FP)*(TP+FN)*(TN+FP)*(TN+FN)}}$	0.8011	0.9840

Table 1: KDD Cup and Synthetic datasets

evaluation described in table 1 where *TP, FP, TN, FN* respectively mean True Positive, False Positive, True Negative and False Negative.

In Figure 1, we report the results obtained for the KDD and Synthetic datasets.The performances are quite interesting due to the peculiar features of our approach, especially when observing that the percentage of threats that are not identified correctly (and the percentage of normal activities marked as malicious as well) is negligible.

4. Conclusion and Future Work

In this paper we discussed SCOUT, an algorithm for clustering based outlier detection for activity logs. Our goal is to overcome the limitation of classical approaches for outlier detection that do not apply well to activity logs as each activity is a sequence of actions and the definition of a proper metric for evaluating anomalous actions could be quite difficult. In this respect, we leverage a simple yet effective encoding that allow us to easily represent complex activities as real numbers. After the encoding phase, we perform an effective outlier detection based on cluster analysis. We evaluated our algorithm on several datasets by performing an accurate pre-elaboration step in order to make them more effective. The results obtained show a very good effectiveness of our strategy on all the datasets being tested thus confirming the soundness of our approach. As a future work, we plan to test other encoding strategies as well as more refined outlier functions in order to further improve our (already satisfactory) performances.

References

[1] J. Babbin, Security log management: identifying patterns in the chaos, Elsevier, 2006.
[2] S. Morgan, Cybercrime to cost the world $10.5 trillion annually by 2025, 2020. URL: https://cybersecurityventures.com/hackerpocalypse-cybercrime-report-2016/.

[3] J. Jang-Jaccard, S. Nepal, A survey of emerging threats in cybersecurity, Journal of Computer and System Sciences 80 (2014) 973–993.

[4] P. Zikopoulos, C. Eaton, et al., Understanding big data: Analytics for enterprise class hadoop and streaming data, McGraw-Hill Osborne Media, 2011.

[5] E. E. Schultz, A framework for understanding and predicting insider attacks, Computers & Security 21 (2002) 526–531.

[6] K. Kent, M. Souppaya, Guide to computer security log management, NIST special publication 92 (2006) 1–72.

[7] M. Ianni, E. Masciari, A compact encoding of security logs for high performance activity detection, in: 29th Euromicro International Conference on Parallel, Distributed and Network-Based Processing, PDP 2021, Valladolid, Spain, March 10-12, 2021, IEEE, 2021, pp. 240–244. URL: https://doi.org/10.1109/PDP52278.2021.00045.

[8] M. Ianni, E. Masciari, G. M. Mazzeo, M. Mezzanzanica, C. Zaniolo, Fast and effective big data exploration by clustering, Future Generation Computer Systems 102 (2020) 84–94.

[9] M. Ianni, E. Masciari, G. M. Mazzeo, C. Zaniolo, Clustering goes big: Clubs-p, an algorithm for unsupervised clustering around centroids tailored for big data applications, in: 2018 26th Euromicro International Conference on Parallel, Distributed and Network-based Processing (PDP), IEEE, 2018, pp. 558–561.

[10] T. Zhang, R. Ramakrishnan, M. Livny, Birch: An efficient data clustering method for very large databases, in: SIGMOD, 1996, pp. 103–114.

[11] S. Hettich, Kdd cup 1999 data, The UCI KDD Archive (1999).

A Two-Step Network Intrusion Detection System for Multi-Class Classification

(Discussion Paper)

Giuseppina Andresini[1], Annalisa Appice[1,2] and Donato Malerba[1,2]

[1]*Dipartimento di Informatica, Università degli Studi di Bari Aldo Moro via Orabona, 4 - 70126 Bari - Italy*
[2]*Consorzio Interuniversitario Nazionale per l'Informatica - CINI*

Abstract

A network intrusion detection system aims to discover any unauthorised access to computer networks by analysing the network traffic for signs of malicious activity. In this paper, we present a two-step system for network intrusion detection. The first step comprises a Triplet network that processes the flow-based characteristics of the historical network traffic data to learn an embedding space, where distances between samples labelled with opposite classes are greater than distances between samples labelled with the same class. We take adavantage of this embedding space to separate the normal samples from the malicious ones. The second step uses a multi-class eXtreme Gradient Boosting classifier to recognize the attack family of the detected malicious flows. The experiments prove the effectiveness of the proposed system as it leads to higher accuracy when compared to several, recent competitors.

Keywords

Network Intrusion Detection, Deep metric learning, Triplet network, Autoencoder

1. Introduction

Network intrusion detection is a crucial cyber-security problem, where deep learning is recognised as a relevant approach to learn signs of malicious activity [1, 2, 3, 4, 5]. In this study, we illustrate a two-step network intrusion detection system that first recognises signs of malicious activities in the network traffic and then classifies the malicious type of these activities.

In the first step, we resort to deep learning to analyse the flow-based characteristics of the network traffic data. In particular, we resort to an intrusion detection model that is trained through a Triplet network [6]. This is an emerging deep learning network that combines deep learning and metric learning. A Triplet network is commonly trained taking triplet samples as input. Every triplet is commonly composed of a training sample selected as an anchor, a training sample labelled in the same class as the anchor and a training sample labelled in the opposite class. Then, the Triplet network learns an embedding space, where distances between samples labelled with opposite classes are greater than distances between samples labelled with

SEBD 2021: The 29th Italian Symposium on Advanced Database Systems, September 5-9, 2021, Pizzo Calabro (VV), Italy
giuseppina.andresini@uniba.it (G. Andresini); annalisa.appice@uniba.it (A. Appice); donato.malerba@uniba.it (D. Malerba)
0000-0002-5272-644X (G. Andresini); 0000-0001-9840-844X (A. Appice); 0000-0001-8432-4608 (D. Malerba)

the same class. Although, the Triplet network is emerging as a relevant approach to separate samples belonging to opposite classes, existing approaches based on Triplet networks commonly suffer from poor convergence. In particular, the Triplet network convergence problem is mainly caused by a random selection of samples for the triplet construction in the training set [7]. In fact, the traditional Triplet network implementations randomly select a single training sample labelled in the same class as the anchor and a single training sample labelled in the opposite class.

To overcome the convergence affecting traditional Triplet networks, we resort to an innovative triplet construction strategy. The original contribution of this work is reported in [8]. This strategy uses autoencoders [9] instead of traditional sampling to derive both the positive and negative information for the triplet construction. Specifically, we train two separate autoencoders on historical normal network flows and attacks, respectively. We construct every triplet by considering the positive and negative pseudo-samples that are the unique reconstructions of the considered anchor restored through the two autoencoders. We note that, basing the triplet construction, and consequently the triplet-learned embedding, on the pseudo-samples reconstructed through these two autoencoders, we are able to exploit possible patterns existing among the normal and attack classes, given the class of the anchor sample of the triplet.

As the learned embedding moves each flow close to its reconstruction, restored with the autoencoder associated with the same class as the flow, and away from its reconstruction, restored with the autoencoder of the opposite class, we are able to perform a predictive stage assigning each new flow to the binary class (normal or attack) associated with the autoencoder that restores the closest reconstruction of the flow in the embedding space.

In the second step, we use a multi-class classifier to perform the task of attack type classification, in addition to attack detection. To this aim, we use a multi-class eXtreme Gradient Boosting classifier trained on attack samples only, in order to recognize the attack family of the detected malicious flows.

This paper is organised as follows. The formulated two-step network intrusion detection system is described in Section 2, while the implementation details are illustrated in Section 3. The NSL-KDD dataset considered for the empirical validation and the findings in the evaluation of the proposed network intrusion detection system are discussed in Section 4. Finally, Section 5 refocuses on the purpose of the research and draws conclusions.

2. The two-step system

The detailed description of the training and predictive stage are reported in Sections 2.1 and 2.2, respectively. The block diagram of the proposed system is reported in Figure 1

2.1. Training stage

Let us consider $\mathcal{D} = \{(\mathbf{x}_i, y_i)\}_{i=1}^{N}$ as a set of N training samples, where each $\mathbf{x}_i \in \mathbb{R}^D$ is a row vector corresponding to an input network flow defined over D features, and y_i is the corresponding binary label denoting a *normal* or an *attack* sample.

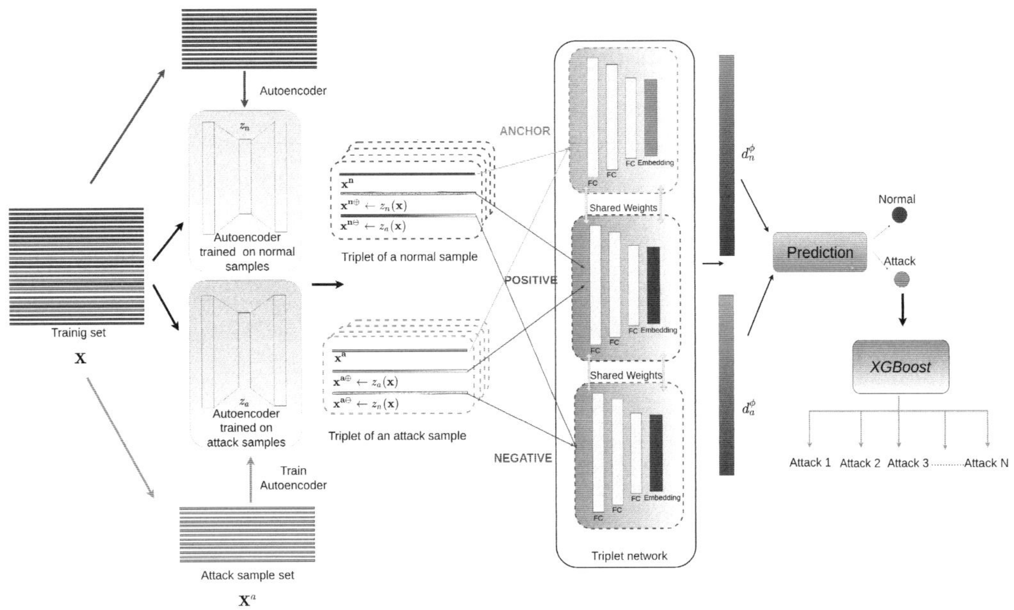

Figure 1: Architecture of the two-step system (Triplet network + XGBoost).

In the first step, we train a Triplet network using autoencoders to built triplets. Let $\mathbf{X} = [\mathbf{x}_1, \ldots, \mathbf{x}_N]^\top \in \mathbb{R}^{N \times D}$ denote the data matrix of N D-dimensional random variables $\mathbf{x} \in \mathbb{R}^D$, so that $\mathbf{X}^n = \mathbf{X}_{|y_i = normal}$, resp. $\mathbf{X}^a = \mathbf{X}_{|y_i = attack}$, represent the subset of samples in $\mathbf{X}$, whose label is normal, resp. attack. We process $\mathbf{X}^n$ and $\mathbf{X}^a$ separately to learn two independent autoencoders, denoted as normal autoencoder z_n and attack autoencoder z_a, respectively. We use both autoencoders to construct the two triplet counterparts of each anchor.

In principle, the normal autoencoder z_n should aid in recovering a denoised representation of $\mathbf{X}$, which highlights attacks as anomalies. Based upon this consideration, normal flows can be considered as positive samples, while attacks can be seen as negative samples from the normal autoencoder z_n. Vice-versa, the attack autoencoder z_a aids in recovering a denoised representation of $\mathbf{X}$, which highlights normal flows as anomalies. Therefore, the autoencoder z_a can see normal flows as negative samples and attacks as positive samples from its point of view. This conjecture inspires the idea of using the representations of $\mathbf{X}$ reconstructed through both z_n and z_a to derive the unique positive and negative component of each triplet. Following this idea, let us consider a training sample $\mathbf{x}$ assigned to the label $\mathbf{y} = normal$ as the anchor. We build $\mathbf{x}^\oplus = z_n(\mathbf{x})$ as the positive triplet counterpart of $\mathbf{x}$, and $\mathbf{x}^\ominus = z_a(\mathbf{x})$ as the negative triplet counterpart of $\mathbf{x}$, respectively. Vice-versa, let us consider a training sample $\mathbf{x}$ assigned to the label $\mathbf{y} = attack$ as the anchor. We build $\mathbf{x}^\oplus = z_a(\mathbf{x})$ as the positive triplet counterpart of $\mathbf{x}$, and $\mathbf{x}^\ominus = z_n(\mathbf{x})$ as the negative triplet counterpart of $\mathbf{x}$, respectively.

By leveraging the collection of sample triplets constructed from $\mathbf{X}$, we train a Triplet network that embeds every triplet component into a d-dimensional Euclidean space $\phi\colon \mathbb{R}^D \mapsto \mathbb{R}^d$ learned to better quantify the similarity between sample components within each triplet. This

Triplet network processes $\mathbf{x}$, $\mathbf{x}^{\oplus}$ and $\mathbf{x}^{\ominus}$ across three base feed-forward networks with shared parameters. The network learns the embedding $\phi\colon \mathbb{R}^D \mapsto \mathbb{R}^d$ by optimising a triplet loss function. This loss function minimises the distance between the embedding vectors of both the anchor $\mathbf{x}$ and its positive triplet counterpart $\mathbf{x}^{\oplus}$, while it maximises the distance between the anchor $\mathbf{x}$ and its negative triplet counterpart $\mathbf{x}^{\ominus}$. We compute the soft-margin triplet loss proposed in [10].

In the second step, we train a multi-class eXtreme Gradient Boosting (XGBoost) classifier to classify the attacks into specific categories. This type of disentanglement into different attack types is important for the network administrator who can take appropriate responsive steps depending on the type of the intrusion detected. Based upon the analysis conducted in [11], we select XGBoost as an appropriate multi-class classifier for this scope. It is trained on the feature space $\mathbf{X}$ on the attack samples labelled with the specific attack category.

2.2. Testing stage

Let us consider a query sample $\mathbf{x} \in \mathbb{R}^D$. First the sample reconstructions $z_n(\mathbf{x})$ and $z_a(\mathbf{x})$ are restored through both the normal autoencoder z_n and the attack autoencoder z_a, respectively. Then the Euclidean distance is computed to compare $\mathbf{x}$ to both $z_n(\mathbf{x})$ and $z_a(\mathbf{x})$, respectively. The Euclidean distance is computed within the embedding space ϕ, so that:

$$d_n^{\phi}(\mathbf{x}) = \|\phi(\mathbf{x}) - \phi(z_n(\mathbf{x}))\|^2, \quad (1)$$

$$d_a^{\phi}(\mathbf{x}) = \|\phi(\mathbf{x}) - \phi(z_a(\mathbf{x}))\|^2. \quad (2)$$

If $d_a^{\phi}(\mathbf{x}) < d_n^{\phi}(\mathbf{x})$, then $\mathbf{x}$ is classified as an attack, while the attack type is predicted with the classification model trained with XGBoost. Otherwise $\mathbf{x}$ is classified as a normal network flow. Finally, if $\mathbf{x}$ is classified as an attack.

3. Implementation details

The triplet network is implemented in Python 2.7. The source code is available online.[1] The deep neural network architectures are developed in Keras 2.3[2] – a high-level neural network API with TensorFlow[3] as the back-end. The pre-processing step includes the operation to scale the input numeric features, using the Min-Max scale (as implemented in the Scikit-learn 0.22.2 library[4]). In addition, the pre-processing includes the implementation of the one-hot-encoder mapping of the categoric attributes. We conduct an automatic hyper-parameter optimization using the tree-structured Parzen estimator algorithm, as implemented in the Hyperopt library [12]. This hyper-parameter optimization is performed by using 20% of the entire training as a validation set. In particular, we randomly select the validation set with the stratified sampling procedure. We automatically choose the configuration of the parameters, which achieves the

[1] https://github.com/gsndr/RENOIR

[2] https://keras.io/

[3] https://www.tensorflow.org/

[4] https://scikit-learn.org/stable/modules/generated/sklearn.preprocessing.MinMaxScaler.html

Table 1
Hyper-parameter search space.

	Autoencoders	Triplet network
batch size	$\{2^5, 2^6, 2^7, 2^8, 2^9\}$	$\{2^5, 2^6, 2^7, 2^8, 2^9\}$
learning rate	[0.0001, 0.01]	[0.0001, 0.01]
dropout	[0,1]	[0,1]
#neurons for hidden layer	-	$\{2^7, 2^8, 2^9\}$

best validation loss. The values of the hyper-parameters, automatically explored with the tree-structured Parzen estimator, are reported in Table 1.

Each autoencoder architecture comprises 3 fully-connected (FC) layers of $32 \times 16 \times 32$ neurons and one dropout layer, in order to prevent the overfitting phenomenon. The mean squared error (*mse*) is used as the loss function. The classical rectified linear unit (*ReLu*) is selected as the activation function for each hidden layer, while for the last layer the *Linear* activation function is used. The Triplet network is implemented with three base feed-forward networks with shared weights. Each base network is a deep neural network with three intermediate layers (with the number of neurons chosen with the hyper-parameter optimization), an embedding layer with 512 neurons and two dropout layers. The (*ReLu*) function is selected as the activation function for each hidden layer, while for the embedding layer the *Sigmoid* activation function is used. The *Sigmoid* activation function is commonly used for the embedding layer [13] instead of a *Linear*, in order to guarantee that each dimension will be between 0 and 1. This architecture assigns samples to the binary normal or attack classes by returning the Euclidean distance returned by the embedding layers.

The multi-class classifier XGBoost is integrated from xgboost.XGBoostClassifier,[5] by adopting the default parameter set-up reported in the documentation.[6]

4. Empirical evaluation

We analyse the effectiveness of the proposed methodology also in a multi-class scenario of network intrusion detection. To this purpose, we consider the multi-class version of the dataset NSL-KDD.[7] This dataset is introduced in [14] as a revised version of KDDCUP99, which is obtained by removing the duplicate samples from KDDCUP99. The multi-class NSL-KDD comprises normal flows and four categories of attack: Denial of Service Attack (DoS), User to Root Attack (U2R), Remote to Local Attack (R2L) and Probing Attack. For this experiment we adopt the original data setting described in [14], that includes KDDTrain$^+$ as the training set and KDDTest$^+$ as the testing set. The number of samples collected in both the training and testing sets for each category is reported in Table 2. We note that both U2R and R2L are rare attacks. We select this dataset as it include zero-days attacks in the testing set, and despite it is an old dataset, it has been recently used in the evaluation of various multi-class intrusion detection methods. Table 3 reports Precision, Recall and F-score achieved by the proposed method on each class.

[5]https://xgboost.readthedocs.io/en/latest/index.html
[6]https://xgboost.readthedocs.io/en/latest/parameter.html
[7]https://www.unb.ca/cic/datasets/nsl.html

Table 2
Number of samples per category in both KDDTrain+ and KDDTest+.

Dataset	Total	DoS	Probe	R2L	U2R	Normal
KDDTrain+	125973	45927 (37%)	11656 (9.11%)	995 (0.85%)	52 (0.04%)	6734 (53%)
KDDTest+	22544	7458 (33%)	2421 (11%)	2754 (12.1%)	200 (0.9%)	9711 (43%)

Table 3
Triplet network + XGBoost: Precision, Recall and F-score per class in NLS-KDD

Class	Precision	Recall	F-score
DoS	96.1	82.5	88.8
Probe	76.4	85.8	80.8
R2L	95.2	48.0	63.8
U2R	62.5	7.5	13.4
Normal	77.8	96.3	86.1

For the comparative study, we consider the performance of several recent competitors that handle the same multi-class problem addressed here, by integrating various techniques to deal with multi-class attacks. In particular, we consider: (1) Deep learning multi-class competitors with Siamese networks [15] [8] and XGBoost: SIAM-IDS[16][11] and I-SiamIDS [11]. (2) Deep learning multi-class competitors with rare data augmentation: DSSTE+AlexNet[17], IGAN-IDS[18] and ID-CAVE[19]. (3) Deep Reinforcement Learning competitors: AESMOTE[20] and AE-RL[21]. The results of Macro-Average F1, Micro-Average F1 and Weighted F1 of both the multi-class configurations of Triplet network + XGBoost and its competitors are reported in Table 4. No values of the Macro-Average F1 are reported in the reference papers for DSSTE+AlexNet, IGAN-IDS, AESMOTE and AE-RL.

We note that SIAM-IDS and I-SiamIDS are the nearest-related competitors to our method. This is an expected outcome, as both algorithms use a deep learning methodology based on a deep metric architecture for the binary classification and resort to a multi-class XGBoost-based re-classification of the attacks. So, this experiment contributes to assess the effectiveness of our Triplet network-based method in separating normal samples from attacks. In addition, it highlights that resorting to XGBoost for the attack classification can achieve good performance. On the other hand, our method also outperforms the remaining competitors, that have been defined in the recent literature to deal with the multi-class problem in the imbalanced scenario of NSL-KDD. The only exception is IGAN-IDS, that uses a deep Generative Adversarial Network process to generate new samples for the minority classes. Therefore, this improvement is achieved at the cost of a complex process of augmentation of the training set. In any case, this result suggests that new milestones may be reached in the future by injecting Generative Adversarial Learning mechanisms into multi-class network intrusion detection.

[8] Siamese networks learn a contrastive loss to quantify similarity between sample pairs.

Table 4
Results of the Macro-average F1, the Micro-Average (OA) and the weighted F1 obtained by our method compared with several competitors that perform multi-class classification in NSL-KDD. The best results are in bold. The results of the competitors are collected from the reference papers. "-" denotes that no value is reported in the reference paper.

Algorithm	Macro-Average F1	Micro-Average (OA)	Weighted F1
Triplet+XGBoost	**66.58**	83.91	83.05
SIAM-IDS[16][11]	56.14	76.96	75.28
I-SiamIDS[11]	66.54	79.90	78.49
DSSTE+AlexNet[17]	-	82.84	81.66
IGAN-IDS[18]	-	**84.45**	**84.17**
AESMOTE[20]	-	82.09	82.43
AE-RL[21]	-	80.16	79.40
ID-CAVE[19]	59.27	80.10	79.08

5. Conclusion

In this paper we present an innovative Triplet network approach that takes advantage of autoencoder information for effective network intrusion detection. In addition, the attack samples identified with the first step through the Triplet network are input to the second step composed of the multiclass eXtreme Gradient Boosting for the classification of the detected malicious activity into attack categories. In general, this study provides the evidence that the Triplet network, originally formulated for a binary task, may also be combined with multi-class attack classifiers to have potential in the multi-class scenario. In any case, this conclusion paves the way for a systematic investigation of the topic in the future.

6. Acknowledgments

We acknowledge the support of the MIUR-Ministero dell'Istruzione dell'Università e della Ricerca through the project "TALIsMan -Tecnologie di Assistenza personALizzata per il Miglioramento della quAlità della vitA" (Grant ID: ARS01_01116), PON RI 2014-2020 funding scheme, as well as the project "Modelli e tecniche di data science per la analisi di dati strutturati", funded by the University of Bari "Aldo Moro".

References

[1] D. S. Berman, A. L. Buczak, J. S. Chavis, C. L. Corbett, A survey of deep learning methods for cyber security, Information 10 (2019) 1–35.
[2] G. Andresini, A. Appice, N. D. Mauro, C. Loglisci, D. Malerba, Multi-channel deep feature learning for intrusion detection, IEEE Access 8 (2020) 53346–53359.
[3] G. Andresini, A. Appice, F. Caforio, D. Malerba, Improving cyber-threat detection by moving the boundary around the normal samples, in: Y. Maleh, Y. Baddi, M. Shojaafar, M. Alaza

(Eds.), Machine Intelligence and Big Data Analytics For Cybersecurity Applications, Studies in Computational Intelligence, 2021, pp. 105–127.

[4] G. Andresini, A. Appice, D. Malerba, Nearest cluster-based intrusion detection through convolutional neural networks, Knowledge-Based Systems 216 (2021) 106798.

[5] Gan augmentation to deal with imbalance in imaging-based intrusion detection, Future Generation Computer Systems 123 (2021) 108–127.

[6] E. Hoffer, N. Ailon, Deep metric learning using triplet network, in: A. Feragen, M. Pelillo, M. Loog (Eds.), Similarity-Based Pattern Recognition, Springer International Publishing, Cham, 2015, pp. 84–92.

[7] B. Yu, T. Liu, M. Gong, C. Ding, D. Tao, Correcting the triplet selection bias for triplet loss, in: V. Ferrari, M. Hebert, C. Sminchisescu, Y. Weiss (Eds.), Computer Vision – ECCV 2018, Springer International Publishing, Cham, 2018, pp. 71–86.

[8] G. Andresini, A. Appice, D. Malerba, Autoencoder-based deep metric learning for network intrusion detection, Information Sciences (2021).

[9] C. C. Aggarwal, Neural Networks and Deep Learning - A Textbook, 2018.

[10] A. Hermans, L. Beyer, B. Leibe, In Defense of the Triplet Loss for Person Re-Identification, arXiv preprint arXiv:1703.07737 (2017) 1–17.

[11] P. Bedi, N. Gupta, V. Jindal, I-siamids: an improved siam-ids for handling class imbalance in network-based intrusion detection systems, Applied Intelligence 51 (2021) 1133–1151.

[12] J. Bergstra, D. Yamins, D. D. Cox, Making a science of model search: Hyperparameter optimization in hundreds of dimensions for vision architectures, in: ICML, 2013, pp. 115–123.

[13] C. Deng, Z. Chen, X. Liu, X. Gao, D. Tao, Triplet-based deep hashing network for cross-modal retrieval, IEEE Transactions on Image Processing PP (2018) 1–1.

[14] M. Tavallaee, E. Bagheri, W. Lu, A. A. Ghorbani, A detailed analysis of the KDD CUP 99 data set, in: CISDA, 2009, pp. 1–6.

[15] H. O. Song, Y. Xiang, S. Jegelka, S. Savarese, Deep metric learning via lifted structured feature embedding, in: Computer Vision and Pattern Recognition (CVPR), 2016, pp. 4004–4012.

[16] P. Bedi, N. Gupta, V. Jindal, Siam-ids: Handling class imbalance problem in intrusion detection systems using siamese neural network, Procedia Computer Science 171 (2020) 780 – 789. Third International Conference on Computing and Network Communications (CoCoNet'19).

[17] L. Liu, P. Wang, J. Lin, L. Liu, Intrusion detection of imbalanced network traffic based on machine learning and deep learning, IEEE Access 9 (2021) 7550–7563.

[18] S. Huang, K. Lei, Igan-ids: An imbalanced generative adversarial network towards intrusion detection system in ad-hoc networks, Ad Hoc Networks 105 (2020) 1–11.

[19] M. Lopez-Martin, B. Carro, A. Sanchez-Esguevillas, J. Lloret, Conditional variational autoencoder for prediction and feature recovery applied to intrusion detection in iot, Sensors 17 (2017) 1–17.

[20] X. Ma, W. Shi, Aesmote: Adversarial reinforcement learning with smote for anomaly detection, IEEE Transactions on Network Science and Engineering (2020) 1–1.

[21] G. Caminero, M. Lopez-Martin, B. Carro, Adversarial environment reinforcement learning algorithm for intrusion detection, Computer Networks 159 (2019) 96 – 109.

Increasing protection and autonomy in the IoT through a two-tier blockchain framework

(Discussion Paper)

Enrico Corradini[1], Serena Nicolazzo[2], Antonino Nocera[3], Domenico Ursino[1] and Luca Virgili[1]

[1]*Department of Information Engineering, Polytechnic University of Marche*

[2]*Daisy Lab, Politechnic University of Marche*

[3]*Department of Electrical, Computer and Biomedical Engineering, University of Pavia*

Abstract

In this paper, we propose an approach that uses a two-tier blockchain framework and a trust-based protection mechanism to increase the security and autonomy of smart objects in the IoT. The proposed approach groups the involved smart objects into suitable communities. The two blockchains perform different, but complementary, tasks. Indeed, the first-tier blockchain is local and records probing transactions performed to evaluate the trust of one smart object in another. Periodically, after a time window, the probing transactions are aggregated to determine the reputation of each smart object within its community and the trust of one community in each of the others. These values are stored in the second-tier blockchain. This paper describes the proposed approach, the underlying framework, the behavior, the security model and a test carried out to evaluate its performance.

Keywords

Internet of Things, Blockchain, Protection, Autonomy, Reliability, Trust, Reputation,

1. Introduction

In recent years, the Internet of Things (IoT) paradigm has become increasingly successful and pervasive. However, at the same time, it has posed new challenges. Indeed, the IoT involves the presence of a large number of smart objects cooperating with each other. These objects are often characterized by constraints on storage, computational capability, criticality and sensitivity of used services and applications. At the same time, they show a great dynamism. In this scenario, the protection of smart objects and the possibility of granting them autonomy represent two challenges that must be faced simultaneously.

As for *protection*, [1] presents an approach to address this issue when it comes to privacy. It partially hides object features, but allows for their full usage to support inter-object communication. However, this approach does not provide a scalable, reliable and secure framework

SEBD 2021: The 29th Italian Symposium on Advanced Database Systems, September 5-9, 2021, Pizzo Calabro (VV), Italy

e.corradini@pm.univpm.it (E. Corradini); serena.nicolazzo.sn@gmail.com (S. Nicolazzo); antonino.nocera@unipv.it (A. Nocera); d.ursino@staff.univpm.it (D. Ursino); l.virgili@pm.univpm.it (L. Virgili)

https://kmitd.github.io/ilaria/ (S. Nicolazzo)

0000-0002-1140-4209 (E. Corradini); 0000-0003-2719-9526 (S. Nicolazzo); 0000-0003-2120-2341 (A. Nocera); 0000-0003-1360-8499 (D. Ursino); 0000-0003-1509-783X (L. Virgili)

for the IoT devices. As for *autonomy*, in order to make objects independent from each other during their interactions, it is necessary to include a solution allowing objects to add/remove contacts, and to identify which features/services are provided by other objects [2]. Moreover, it is crucial to design a mechanism assessing the ability of an object to correctly provide the necessary features/services. The previous reasoning shows that protection and autonomy are two strongly correlated aspects whose effective management requires the definition of trust and reputation mechanisms. However, due to the peculiarities of the IoT scenario discussed above, existing solutions for sensors or P2P networks are not directly applicable [3].

To achieve a fully distributed solution in this context, each smart object should be able to build a representation of the behavior of other objects in the IoT. To this end, it should be capable of unambiguously knowing the sequence of actions of its peers. To achieve this goal, the blockchain technology is unanimously recognized as one of the most effective strategy [4]. However, even the only monitoring of the public ledger is a heavy and expensive task for smart objects with a low computational capability in presence of a high volume of transactions. To overcome this problem, some authors have proposed to adopt approaches based on the use of a validity window and the aggregation of historical data within it. However, if the volume of transactions is big, this approach may be too expensive and unfeasible for the IoT [5].

This paper aims at providing a contribution in this setting. In fact, it proposes a two-tier blockchain framework to increase the protection and autonomy of smart objects in the IoT. Following the intuition proposed in [1], our approach organizes smart objects into communities. Moreover, it uses the local first tier of the framework to manage the reputation of each smart object within the community it belongs to. It also uses a validity window, coupled with a lightweight blockchain, to face the high transaction volume. The organization of objects in communities allows our approach to control the size of the blockchain, thus avoiding excessive loads for smart objects. Finally, it uses the second global tier to record aggregate data related to communities, as well as the trust values that each community assigns to the others. To implement the tasks of our approach, we leverage the blockchain's smart contract technology. It has already been successfully used in the context of the IoT, e.g., to implement single and multi-party authentication for an IoT device (see [6] for an example).

The outline of this paper is as follows: Section 2 describes the proposed framework. Section 3 illustrates our security model. Section 4 presents an experimental comparison with two other approaches. Finally, Section 5 draws conclusions and takes a look at some possible future developments.

2. Technical description of our approach

In our model, the main actor is the smart object. It has a profile characterized by: *(i)* an identifier; *(ii)* a set of features regarding it; *(iii)* a set of services it offers; *(iv)* the information that other smart objects need for communicating with it (e.g., its MAC and IP addresses, etc.). The smart objects of our framework can be partitioned into communities, based on some rules. Each smart object belongs to exactly one community. A source smart object can communicate with a target one through suitable transactions. These last can be classified in: *(i) ordinary*, if the source requests a service/feauture to the target; *(ii) probing*, if the source (called trustor) wants to test what the target (called trustee) declared to assess its reliability. Transactions can also be *intra-community* (resp., *inter-community*) if they involve smart objects from the same community (resp., from different communities).

Each community has an associated local blockchain that records information about transactions having one of its smart objects as trustor. The overall IoT has associated a global blockchain, which records aggregate information produced periodically from probing transactions recorded in the local blockchains. Specifically, the global blockchain stores: *(i)* the list of smart objects belonging to each community and, for each of them, the corresponding reputation scores; *(ii)* the trust of each community in the others of the IoT.

The interaction mechanisms between smart objects allows each of them to understand which features/services can be provided by another one with which it is in contact [7]. To allow a smart object to asses whether another one is reliable in providing the features/services it advertises, we adopt the approach of [8] based on probing transactions. To certify them, we use a blockchain-based solution. Adopting blockchains in the IoT context poses important challenges concerning the large number of nodes involved, the large amount of data generated, and the low computational power of many smart objects. As specified in the Introduction, to address these challenges, our approach leverages a two-tier blockchain framework. It groups smart objects into appropriate communities, based on certain criteria. Within these communities, smart objects adopt control mechanisms to identify anomalous behaviors and make interactions as secure as possible. Our approach is independent of the way communities are built. It only requires that smart objects in a community should have some level of redundancy in the features/services offered.

Thus, the first layer of the framework is a blockchain underlying a community; it represents a local public ledger storing all the probing transactions performed within the community. There are several approaches to implement lightweight blockchains for the IoT context [9, 10] that could be adopted to create this layer. In our case, we could use any of them, for instance IOTA (www.iota.org), which supports smart contracts via the QUBIC protocol [11]. The second layer of the framework is a global blockchain that involves the whole IoT and only stores the *aggregate* information of the different communities. It could be implemented with any blockchain, such as Ethereum (www.ethereum.org) or HyperLedger (www.hyperledger.org). In Figure 1, we report the general architecture of our approach.

In order to limit the volume of transactions to be analyzed, communications between devices take place within time windows, where the devices perform ordinary and probing transactions. These last are randomly generated; each smart object can decide to test another one belonging to its community with a certain probability, while considering the features and services offered by it. The reliability of the tested smart object can be verified thanks to the support of other smart objects belonging to the same community of the tester and providing the same feature/service. These tests compute the trust scores associated with smart objects in their communities, and all of them are stored in their corresponding local blockchain. Figure 2 shows a summary representation of our intra-community probing scheme and the computation of the trust of a trustor tr_i in a trustee te_j.

After a defined time window, the reputation of each smart object in its community is derived, thanks to the aggregation of the results of its probing transactions. A smart contract of the blockchain is responsible for the reputation computation. The results of this task, which consists

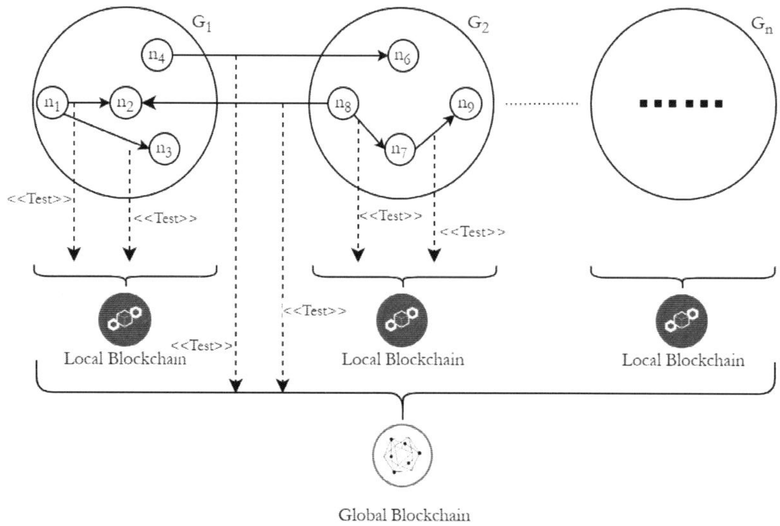

Figure 1: General architecture of our approach

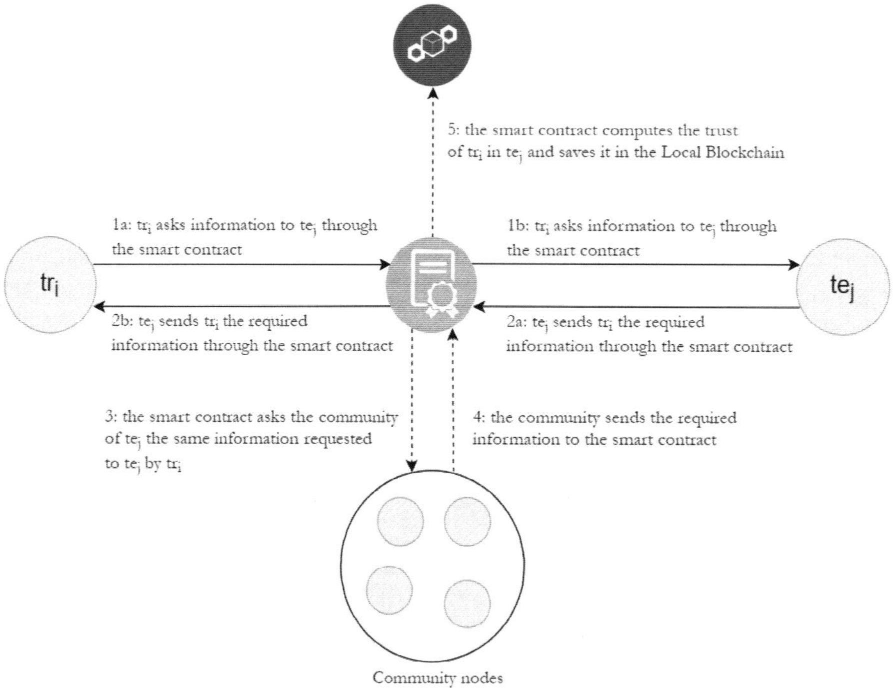

Figure 2: Computation of the trust of a trustor tr_i in a trustee te_j

of the list of community members and the corresponding reputation scores, is published in the global blockchain (see Figure 3). Smart objects having a reputation below a certain threshold are automatically removed from their community.

Our approach also provides protection during the interactions between objects from different communities. Specifically, when two objects from different communities contact each other,

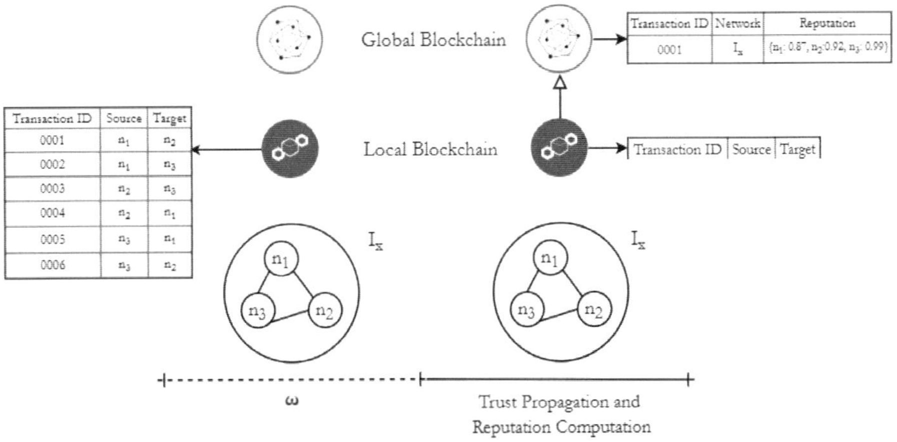

Figure 3: Transaction aggregation and computation of the reputation of the smart objects of a community

one of them may undergo a test with a certain probability. To perform this test, the tester object requests a feature/service among those provided by the tested object. This request is also sent to other objects in the same community of the tested object. The test result is stored in the local blockchain of the community of the tester object. After a certain time window, the results of the tests performed by the smart objects belonging to different communities are aggregated. Following this reasoning, it is possible to obtain a trust value of a community towards other communities with which at least one transaction between the corresponding objects has taken place. These trust values are also saved in the global blockchain.

Thanks to the information stored in the global blockchain, when a smart object o_{i_k} of a community C_k wants to interact with a smart object o_{j_q} of a community C_q, $C_q \neq C_k$, o_{i_k} can compute the reliability of o_{j_q} taking into account the reputation of o_{j_q} within C_q and the trust of C_k in C_q.

3. Security Model

In this section, we present the security model associated with our framework. Preliminarily, we highlight that it is based on the assumption that a sufficient number of nodes are available in such a way as to successfully implement our approach. Therefore, our model does not consider anomalous situations or the startup time, in which the number of nodes available in the framework is less than the minimum required.

In the analysis of security properties, we will consider that our threat model includes the following assumptions: *(i)* At most t smart objects can collude to break the security properties of the protocol; *(ii)* the size of all the pruned support partitions is greater than t; *(iii)* an attacker cannot control a whole group of smart objects; moreover, she cannot own all the smart objects providing a certain service; *(iv)* an attacker has no additional knowledge derived from any direct physical access to smart objects; *(v)* the blockchain technologies adopted to implement both the local and the global tiers are compliant with the standard security requirements already adopted for common blockchain applications. As for the first assumption, we recall that probing transactions are produced collaboratively by several smart objects in our protocol. Some of them might be corrupted, but, according to [12], we assume the honesty of the majority of them.

In the following, we report the list of the security properties that our framework must assure (due to space limitations, we cannot report here the corresponding security analysis):

- *Resistance to the attacks to local and global blockchains* conceived to find vulnerabilities in them.
- *Resistance to self-promoting attacks*, occurring when a smart object manipulates its own reputation to increase it falsely and promote itself.
- *Resistance to whitewashing or self-serving attacks*, occurring when a malicious smart object, with a compromised reputation, tries to quickly degrade the latter with the goal of being removed from the framework and asking to rejoin it again with a fresh start.
- *Resistance to slandering or bad-mouthing attacks*, occurring when one or more attackers try to manipulate the reputation of other smart objects by reporting false data.
- *Resistance to opportunistic service attacks*, occurring when a malicious smart object can provide good or bad services opportunistically.
- *Resistance to ballot stuffing attacks*, occurring when an attacker tries to boost the reputation of bad objects providing good recommendations for them.
- *Resistance to Denial of Service (DoS) attacks*, occurring when an attacker tries to prevent a reputation system from operating properly by flooding it with an excessive number of transactions.
- *Resistance to orchestrated attacks*, occurring when malicious smart objects orchestrate their actions and leverage several of the previous strategies to perform a coordinated and multi-faced attack, which can change over time.

4. Experimental comparison with other approaches

In this section, we compare our approach with other related strategies proposed in the past literature. The related approaches we selected have many similarities with our own in both the reference scenario and the adopted methodologies; instead, their goal is different.

The first approach we selected concerns an intrusion detection system protecting smart devices in vehicular networks [13]. The authors proposed to group the nodes into "clusters", so that security is achieved through the collaboration of nodes inside the identified protected zones. This approach and ours are very similar in two aspects, even if their goals are different. The former is the definition of a security model operating on smart devices and the IoT, whereas the latter is the usage of groups and clusters of things (corresponding to communities of smart objects in our model). The second approach we considered focuses on the modeling of a scheme for grouping objects in such a way as to preserve their privacy [1]. The modeled scheme guarantees the protection of user's privacy in all the IoT scenarios where the knowledge of the object characteristics may lead to attacks based on the collection of user habits and behaviors.

A way to compare the approaches of [13] and [1] with ours consists of measuring the communication delay introduced by them against the community size. In our approach, we

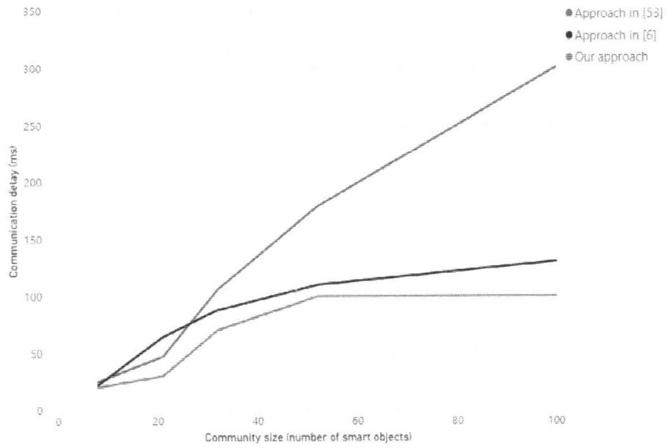

Figure 4: Comparison of the average delay against the community size between our approach and the ones of [13] ad [1]

defined this parameter as the average difference, in terms of delivery time, between a scenario adopting our approach and another not adopting it. Figure 4 shows the results obtained. As we can see, the average delay introduced by our approach ranges from 20 ms to 100 ms. The delay of [13] ranges between 24 ms and 170 ms, whereas the one of [1] ranges from 22 ms to 300 ms. This result tells that our approach is clearly comparable with, and even better performing than, the ones described in [13] and [1]. In conclusion, we can say that our approach returns satisfactory results still keeping low the IoT overhead.

5. Conclusion

In this paper, we proposed an approach adopting a two-tier blockchain framework and a trust-based protection mechanism for increasing the security and autonomy of smart objects in the IoT. The proposed approach and the results obtained are not to be intended as an ending point. By contrast, they represent a starting point for further future activities. For example, we plan to combine our approach with other community-based strategies aiming at ensuring the privacy of smart objects and their owners. The ultimate goal of such a task would be the definition of a single solution handling both privacy and security in the IoT.

References

[1] S. Nicolazzo, A. Nocera, D. Ursino, L. Virgili, A privacy-preserving approach to prevent feature disclosure in an iot scenario, in: Future Generation Computer Systems, volume 105, 2019, pp. 1–8. IEEE.

[2] J. Quevedo, M. Antunes, D. Corujo, D. Gomes, R. Aguiar, On the application of contextual iot service discovery in information centric networks, Computer Communications 89 (2016) 117–127. Elsevier.

[3] F. Buccafurri, G. Lax, S. Nicolazzo, A. Nocera, Accountability-Preserving Anonymous Delivery of Cloud Services, in: Proc. of the International Conference on Trust, Privacy and Security in Digital Business (TRUSTBUS 2015), Springer, 2015, pp. 124–135.

[4] M. Shen, X. Tang, L. Zhu, X. Du, M. Guizani, Privacy-Preserving Support Vector Machine Training over Blockchain-Based Encrypted IoT Data in Smart Cities, IEEE Internet of Things Journal (2019). IEEE.

[5] S. Huh, S. Cho, S. Kim, Managing IoT devices using blockchain platform, in: Proc. of the International Conference on Advanced Communication Technology (ICACT'17), PyeongChang, Korea, 2017, pp. 464–467. IEEE.

[6] M. Khan, K. Salah, IoT security: Review, blockchain solutions, and open challenges, Future Generation Computer Systems 82 (2018) 395–411. Elsevier.

[7] S. Bandyopadhyay, M. Sengupta, S. Maiti, S. Dutta, A survey of middleware for Internet of Things, in: Recent trends in wireless and mobile networks, 2011, pp. 288–296. Springer.

[8] F. Buccafurri, L. Coppolino, S. D'Antonio, A. Garofalo, G. Lax, A. Nocera, L. Romano, Trust-Based Intrusion Tolerant Routing in Wireless Sensor Networks, in: Proc. of the International Conference on Computer Safety, Reliability and Security (SAFECOMP 2014), Springer, Firenze, Italy, 2014, pp. 214–229.

[9] M. Rehman, N. Javaid, M. Awais, M. Imran, N. Naseer, Cloud based secure service providing for IoTs using blockchain, in: Proc. of the IEEE Global Communications Conference (GLOBCOM 2019), Puako, Hawaii, USA, 2019, pp. 1–7.

[10] A. Dwivedi, G. Srivastava, S. Dhar, R. Singh, A decentralized privacy-preserving healthcare blockchain for IoT, Sensors 19 (2019) 326. Multidisciplinary Digital Publishing Institute.

[11] T. Moellers, IOTA-based Business Model Configurations, https://www.alexandria.unisg.ch/257117/ (2018).

[12] P. Fouque, G. Poupard, J. Stern, Sharing decryption in the context of voting or lotteries, in: Proc. of the International Conference on Financial Cryptography (FC'00), Anguilla, Anguilla, 2000, pp. 90–104. Springer.

[13] M. Aloqaily, S. Otoum, I. A. Ridhawi, Y. Jararweh, An intrusion detection system for connected vehicles in smart cities, Ad Hoc Networks 90 (2019) 101842. Elsevier.

Extraction of Medical Concepts from Italian Natural Language Descriptions

(Discussion Paper)

Patrizia Agnello[1], Silvia Maria Ansaldi[1], Fabio Azzalini[2,3], Giovanni Gangemi[2], Davide Piantella[2], Emanuele Rabosio[3] and Letizia Tanca[2]

[1]*INAIL - Dipartimento Innovazioni Tecnologiche*
[2]*Politecnico di Milano - Dipartimento di Elettronica, Informazione e Bioingegneria*
[3]*Human Technopole - Center for Analysis, Decisions and Society*

Abstract

In this paper we present a Natural Language Processing (NLP) pipeline to automatically extract medical concepts from a free text written in a language other than English. To do so, we use common NLP techniques and the metathesaurus of Unified Medical Language System (UMLS). Specifically, our goal is to automatically extract ontological concepts representing which part of the human body is injured and what is the nature of the injury, given an Italian textual description of a work accident. We start by partitioning the text into tokens and assigning to each token its part-of-speech, and then use an appropriate tool to extract relevant concepts to be searched within UMLS. We tested our system on a public large repository containing textual descriptions of work accidents produced by INAIL. Experimental results confirm that our system is able to correctly extract relevant medical concepts from texts written in Italian.

Keywords

Ontology, EHR, NLP, Work accident

1. Introduction

The term Electronic Health Records (EHRs) describes the concept of a comprehensive, cross-institutional, and longitudinal collection of healthcare data, trying to group the entire clinical life of a patient [1]. EHRs store information both in structured (e.g. diagnosis codes, laboratory results, etc) and unstructured (e.g. clinical notes, discharge summaries, etc.) formats. Unstructured data usually contain a more complete, and broader, view of the patient's conditions, as well as additional valuable information that would be difficult to represent in a structured manner (e.g. social history, special conditions, etc.). To leverage all the advantages of a systematic adoption of EHRs, many technical and non-technical requirements must be fulfilled [2], such as

SEBD 2021: The 29th Italian Symposium on Advanced Database Systems, September 5-9, 2021, Pizzo Calabro (VV), Italy

p.agnello@inail.it (P. Agnello); s.ansaldi@inail.it (S. M. Ansaldi); fabio.azzalini@polimi.it (F. Azzalini); giovanni.gangemi@mail.polimi.it (G. Gangemi); davide.piantella@polimi.it (D. Piantella); emanuele.rabosio@fht.org (E. Rabosio); letizia.tanca@polimi.it (L. Tanca)
0000-0003-0631-2120 (F. Azzalini); 0000-0003-1542-0326 (D. Piantella); 0000-0003-3722-7789 (E. Rabosio); 0000-0003-2607-3171 (L. Tanca)

privacy, data security, portability, performance, maintainability, reliability, interoperability, and usability.

In this work we focus on the natural-language texts included in EHRs, since unstructured data analytics is one of the most challenging task of EHRs automated analysis. Our main contributions are the development of a system capable of automatically extracting medical ontological concepts from an Italian natural language text, and the experimental evaluation of our system using a real-world dataset regarding work injuries.

The paper is organized as follows. Section 1 gives an overview of the problem, Section 2 reviews the state of the art regarding medical concept extraction, Section 3 describes our methodology, Section 4 presents the experiments and, finally, Section 5 concludes the paper.

2. State of the Art

Concept extraction from natural language texts related to clinical information consists of three phases [3]: (1.) Identification of concept mentions such as medications, drugs, anatomical parts, and diseases; (2.) Coreference resolution regarding relationships between different mentions referring to the same entity; and (3.) Extraction of relationships between concepts.

We now briefly describe one of the most complete medical ontology system (UMLS) and two state-of-the-art frameworks for clinical concept extraction: *cTAKES* and *MetaMap*.

2.1. Unified Medical Language System

The *Unified Medical Language System (UMLS)* [4] is a compendium of many controlled vocabularies in the biomedical sciences, produced and distributed by the National Library of Medicine (NLM). It also provides a mapping structure among these vocabularies and thus allows to translate among the various terminology systems. It can be therefore considered a comprehensive thesaurus and ontology of biomedical concepts.

UMLS is composed by three modules: Metathesaurus, Semantic Network, and Specialist Lexicon. We now provide a brief explanation of each of these modules.

2.1.1. Metathesaurus

The Metathesaurus of UMLS includes over one million biomedical concepts and five million concept names, enclosing many vocabularies such as ICD-10, SNOMED CT, MeSH, and more. The Metathesaurus is structured to facilitate the identification of synonyms between concepts, also in different languages ensured by leveraging hierarchical concept identifiers, in turn linked to:

- Concepts (CUI): identifying the meaning to be expressed, it never changes over time, no matter the updates in the vocabularies.
- Strings (SUI): each string representing a concept is assigned with a permanent string identifier. Any character variation (e.g. case sensitivity, punctuation, etc.) will result in a different SUI, for each language. A SUI can in principle be linked to more than one CUI.
- Atoms (AUI): being building blocks of the Metathesaurus, atoms represent specific entries in the vocabularies included in UMLS. An AUI is linked to one and only one CUI.

<table>
<tr><th>CONCEPT (CUI)</th><th>TERMS (LUIs)</th><th>STRINGS (SUIs)</th><th>ATOMS (AUIs)</th></tr>
<tr><td rowspan="5">C0004238</td><td rowspan="3">L0004238
(preferred)</td><td rowspan="2">S0016668
Atrial Fibrillation</td><td>A0027665
MSH:AtrialFibrillation</td></tr>
<tr><td>A0027667
PSY:AtrialFibrillation</td></tr>
<tr><td>S0016669
Atrial Fibrillations</td><td>A0027668
MSH:AtrialFibrillations</td></tr>
<tr><td rowspan="2">L0004237
(synonym)</td><td>S0016899
Auricular Fibrillation</td><td>A0027930
PSY:AuricularFibrillation</td></tr>
<tr><td>S0016900
Auricular Fibrillations</td><td>A0027932
MSH:AuricularFibrillations</td></tr>
</table>

Figure 1: Hierarchical concept identifiers of UMLS, as reported in [5]

- Lexical terms (LUI): a lexical term comprises different strings (i.e. SUI) that are lexical variants or minor variants. This layer is often used to reduce the computational complexity of exploration and for a more effective concept lookup. It is currently available for all the English strings, and only partially for other languages.

2.1.2. Semantic Network

The Semantic Network provides a consistent categorization of all concepts represented in the Metathesaurus along with a set of useful relationships between these concepts. The network contains 133 semantic types and 54 relationships. Each concept in the Metathesaurus is assigned one or more semantic types, which are linked to one another through semantic relationships. The major semantic types are *organisms, anatomical structures, biologic function, chemical, events, physical objects*, etc.

The possible relationships between semantic types range from simple ⟨*is-a*⟩ hierarchies to complex associations, such as ⟨*physically related to*⟩, ⟨*spatially related to*⟩, ⟨*co-occurs with*⟩. Relationships can be derived from associations already present in the vocabularies (*intra-source* relationships) or they can connect concepts from different vocabularies (*inter-source* relationships), including not only synonyms. Inter-source relationships enhance the integration of all the vocabularies present in UMLS and enable an easy exploration of the resulting ontology. A subset of the Semantic Network with ⟨*is-a*⟩ relationships is shown in Figure 2.

2.1.3. Specialist Lexicon

Specialist Lexicon is a module of UMLS that addresses the high degree of variability in natural language words, allowing the abstraction of lexical variants. It covers general English lexicon and many biomedical terms, including syntactic, morphological, and orthographic information. Since only English words are covered by this module, we adopted a different approach for Italian Natural Language Processing, which we will describe in Section 3.

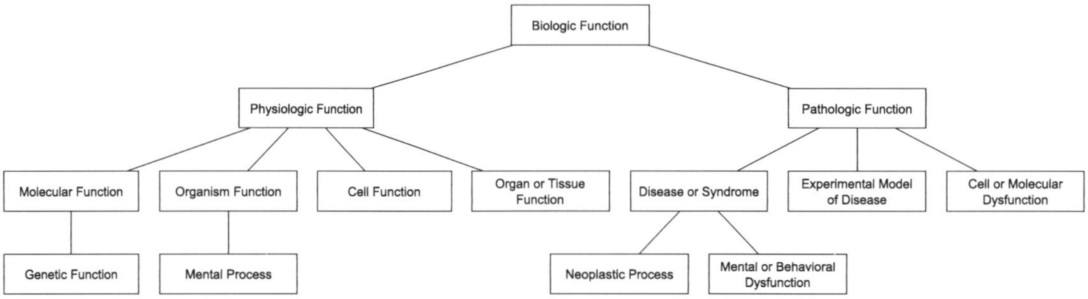

Figure 2: A portion of UMLS Semantic Network

2.2. cTAKES

Apache *clinical Text Analysis and Knowledge Extraction System* [6] (cTAKES, for short) is an open-source framework for knowledge extraction from clinical texts, exploiting NLP techniques including rule-based and machine learning approaches. It leverages a pipeline of six components. First of all the text is divided into sentences by the *sentence boundary detector*, a component which extends OpenNLP sentence detector [7]. Each sentence is then *tokenized* taking into consideration also context-specific occurrences (e.g. dates, time intervals, etc.). Each token is then *normalized* leveraging tools part of UMLS Specialist Lexicon (described in Section 2.1.3), in order to map each token in a normalized form with respect to many lexical properties (e.g. inflection, diacritics, symbols, stop words, etc.). Both the normalized and the original occurrences are maintained for further analysis. After a *part-of-speech tagging*, the *named entity recognition annotator* component performs a terminology-agnostic dictionary lookup on a subset of UMLS Metathesaurus (described in Section 2.1.1), searching all the noun-phrases identified and their respective unnormalized occurrences.

2.3. MetaMap

MetaMap was developed by the National Library of Medicine (NLM) with the goal of mapping biomedical text to the UMLS Metathesaurus [8]. It relies on a pipeline similar to cTAKES, apart from the leveraging of relationships and hierarchical identifiers, present in UMLS Metathesaurus, to better identify synonyms and lexical variants of the tokenized texts.

2.4. Comparison between cTAKES and MetaMap

A comparison between cTAKES and MetaMap has already been investigated in [9]: the results of the experiments proved that cTAKES slightly outperforms MetaMap, with the exception of texts in which abbreviations are present. It has been shown that abbreviations are quite common in natural language texts written by doctors and both tools have difficulties in correctly identify their correct meanings. With MetaMap, however, it is possible to partially solve this problem, specifying a list of strings that will be treated as special tokens. This possibility is

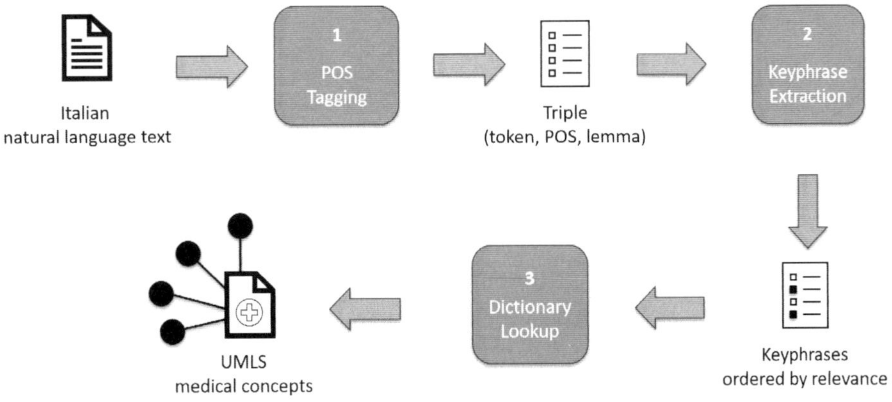

Figure 3: The framework of our system

not particularly investigated in the cited experimental comparison, and could be the subject of future studies.

The main disadvantage of both cTAKES and MetaMap, with respect to our study, is that they are strongly English-centric, since they both rely on UMLS Specialist Lexicon which, as we already described in Section 2.1.3, fully covers only the English language.

3. Methodology

We now present the methodology of our system. The final goal is to automatically extract ontological concepts representing which part of the human body is injured and what is the nature of the injury, given an Italian textual description of a work accident. Figure 3 displays the three phases of our workflow: Part-of-Speech (POS) Tagging, Keyphrase Extraction and Dictionary Lookup.

The first phase receives as input a textual description representing the dynamic of an accident and gives as output a preprocessed and enriched representation of the input text. Specifically, Tint takes as input a raw text in Italian and performs a series of natural language processing operations. Tint (The Italian NLP Tool) [10] is an open-source Java-based pipeline for Natural Language Processing (NLP) in Italian. It is very fast and accurate, and implements most of the common linguistic tools, such as part-of-speech tagging and dependency parsing. This first phase is necessary since the next stage needs the text divided into tokens, lemmas and parts of speech in order to continue the execution.

Example 1: Given the following accident description: "Erano in corso attività di produzione di acciaio. Mentre un agganciamento del nastro trasportatore vibrovaglio alla motopala, a causa di una manovra pericolosa rimaneva con le braccia in contrasto tra le due macchine decedendo per contusione al fegato", the pipeline produces the tagged text visible in Table 1.

The second phase receives as input the tagged text with lemmas and POS, and returns as output a new series of keyphrases ordered by importance and frequency. This step uses a tool called Keyphrase Digger (KD) [11] which analyzes the text file with tokens, lemmas and pos and returns as a result a new text file with a series of keyphrases ordered by importance and

Table 1
A possible output of phase 1

Token	POS	Lemma
Erano	Verb	essere
in	Preposition	in
corso	Noun	corso
attività	Noun	attività
di	Preposition	di
produzione	Noun	produzione
di	Preposition	di
acciaio	Noun	acciaio

frequency. Keyphrases are n-grams of different length, both single and multi-token expressions, which capture the main concepts of a given document [12]. Keyprhase extraction is essential to understand the topic covered in long text and has many applications, especially when integrated into pipelines, like this one, that perform more complex tasks.

Example 2: After the second phase the pipeline extracted the following concepts: "produzione di acciaio", "nastro trasportatore vibro", "contusione al fegato", "vaglio alla motopala" and "manovra pericolosa".

As can be seen from Example 2, not all the concepts extracted from the accident description contain information regarding the part of the body and the nature of the incident. The third and last phase, exploiting the Rest API provided by the UMLS, allows the system to query various databases and to discard all the concepts that do not relate to the medical field. This phase can be divided into two distinct sub-phases:

- Concept lookup: we create a query that queries UMLS to get the medical concept. We use as input every possible combination of the keyphrases obtained in the previous step.
- Semantic type lookup: after obtaining the medical concept, we check if it belongs to one of these four semantic types, which represent nature and location of an injury.

Example 3: After the third phase the only keyphrase not discarded is "contusione al fegato".

4. Experiments

We tested our system on the accident descriptions contained in the InforMo dataset [13] made available by INAIL, a repository containing the results of a survey on mostly fatal accidents occurring during work time. This dataset contains 636 entries, each with detailed information on the incident. Concepts are extracted from the description written in natural language in the questionnaire (called dynamic) by those who compiled it. In the original questionnaire there is not always consistency between what is written in the dynamic section and the nature and location of the lesion's attributes. As an example, we may find the concept "skull injury" in the dynamic of the accident, and "contusion" manually written as the nature of the injury. These two concepts might be considered as synonyms for someone who is filling out the questionnaire, but in an ontology they are two different concepts. To solve this problem, we decided to manually create a Golden Truth, analyzing all the dynamics to understand what could be extracted from them.

For each text, our system must extract two concepts that will form a pair constituting the nature and location of an injury. What is extracted is compared with the golden truth to assess the accuracy of the framework. What we want to achieve is an exact extraction of the nature-location pair directly from the textual description of the accident.

After analyzing each textual description, we have evidence to say that most of the times when a nature-location pair is present in the text, it is in the same period, so we analyze each period. If a couple is present in a period of the text we keep it, otherwise we delete the couple. This allowed to greatly reduce the extracted concepts while keeping the performance unchanged.

To evaluate the performance of our pipeline we used recall, precision and F1-score, whose definitions are reported reported here:

$$\text{Recall} := \frac{TP}{TP+FN} \quad \text{Precision} := \frac{TP}{TP+FP} \quad \text{F1-Score} := 2 \cdot \frac{\text{Precision} \cdot \text{Recall}}{\text{Precision} + \text{Recall}}$$

TP represents a correctly guessed nature-location pair, the FP instead are all those incorrect but still extracted, FN are those that are mistakenly not recognized as a match.

In the UMLS query we can specify a parameter called "searchType" which can take two different values: "words" (by default) or "exact". With the first, a similarity search is carried out, resulting in the list of concepts most similar to the one given in input, ordered by decreasing similarity. With the second, on the other hand, a result is obtained only if the input word really exists in the database. We tested the system checking both of these parameters so as to understand which is the best one. In the Table 2 we list the results in the two cases. The results

Table 2
Experimental results

	exact	words
Recall	**0.90**	0.85
Precision	**0.51**	0.20
F1-Score	**0.65**	0.32

show that the "exact" case is better than the second. A deeper analysis highlights that this it is due to the fact that in the second case many more concepts are extracted, most of which are quite different from the original one.

5. Conclusion and Future Work

In this paper we presented a methodology for extracting medical concepts from accident descriptions written in natural language, specifically tailored for the Italian language. The system, still being in a preliminary phase, suffers from some limitations: *(i)* there is a strong dependence on UMLS and its provided APIs, this often makes the system pretty slow in its computation *(ii)* the experimental campaign carried out is pretty limited, this may cause problems in the applicability of the framework to other input sources.

Acknowledgements

This work has been funded by INAIL within the BRiC 2018, ID09 framework, project RECKON.

References

[1] B. Shickel, P. J. Tighe, A. Bihorac, P. Rashidi, Deep ehr: a survey of recent advances in deep learning techniques for electronic health record (ehr) analysis, IEEE journal of biomedical and health informatics 22 (2017) 1589–1604.

[2] A. Hoerbst, E. Ammenwerth, Electronic health records, Methods Inf Med 49 (2010) 320–336.

[3] Y. Wang, L. Wang, M. Rastegar-Mojarad, S. Moon, F. Shen, N. Afzal, S. Liu, Y. Zeng, S. Mehrabi, S. Sohn, et al., Clinical information extraction applications: a literature review, Journal of biomedical informatics 77 (2018) 34–49.

[4] O. Bodenreider, The Unified Medical Language System (UMLS): integrating biomedical terminology, Nucleic Acids Research 32 (2004) D267–D270. doi:10.1093/nar/gkh061.

[5] National Library of Medicine, UMLS reference manual, https://www.ncbi.nlm.nih.gov/books/NBK9676/, 2021. Online; accessed 24-April-2021.

[6] G. K. Savova, J. J. Masanz, P. V. Ogren, J. Zheng, S. Sohn, K. C. Kipper-Schuler, C. G. Chute, Mayo clinical text analysis and knowledge extraction system (ctakes): architecture, component evaluation and applications, Journal of the American Medical Informatics Association 17 (2010) 507–513.

[7] Apache Software Foundation, openNLP website, https://opennlp.apache.org/, 2021. Online; accessed 28-April-2021.

[8] A. R. Aronson, F.-M. Lang, An overview of metamap: historical perspective and recent advances, Journal of the American Medical Informatics Association 17 (2010) 229–236.

[9] R. Reátegui, S. Ratté, Comparison of metamap and ctakes for entity extraction in clinical notes, BMC medical informatics and decision making 18 (2018) 13–19.

[10] A. Palmero Aprosio, G. Moretti, Tint 2.0: an all-inclusive suite for nlp in italian, Proceedings of the Fifth Italian Conference on Computational Linguistics CLiC-it 10 (2018) 12.

[11] G. Moretti, R. Sprugnoli, S. Tonelli, Digging in the dirt: Extracting keyphrases from texts with kd, CLiC it 198 (2015).

[12] P. D. Turney, Learning algorithms for keyphrase extraction, Information retrieval 2 (2000) 303–336.

[13] INAIL, Informo dataset, https://www.inail.it/sol-informo/, 2021. Online; accessed 28-April-2021.

The POOR-MAD approach: Preferred Objects Over Rich, Multi-Attribute Data

(Discussion Paper)

Paolo Ciaccia[1], Davide Martinenghi[2] and Riccardo Torlone[3]

[1]Dipartimento di Informatica - Scienza e Ingegneria, Università di Bologna, Viale Risorgimento, 2, 40136 Bologna, Italy
[2]Dipartimento di Elettronica, Informazione e Bioingegneria, Politecnico di Milano, Via Ponzio, 34/5, 20133 Milano, Italy
[3]Dipartimento di Ingegneria, Università Roma Tre, Via della Vasca Navale, 79, 00146 Roma, Italy

Abstract

Preferences about objects of interest are often expressed at different levels of granularity, not always matching the level of detail of stored data. For instance, we prefer rock to pop music, yet scheduled concerts only cite the name of the performer, with no reference to the musical genre. In this paper, we address this common mismatch by leveraging the vast amounts of data organized in taxonomies (such as those found in electronic catalogs and classification systems). We present a model to represent preferences and state the desirable properties of preference propagation, such as the fact that more specific preferences always prevail over more generic ones. We then illustrate an approach for propagating preferences along taxonomies complying with the stated properties and show how the best objects can thereby be identified.

1. Introduction

The information available in digital form is growing so fast that the search for data of interest (for attending events, buying products, planning a trip, etc.) is becoming increasingly difficult over time. For this reason, there has recently been a huge effort to develop effective methods and tools able to automatically suggest to any individual the items that better match what he/she is looking for [1]. In this framework, the availability of preferences, explicitly expressed by the users or somehow automatically derived from their actions, has been always considered an important ingredient [2, 3]. Unfortunately, preferences and data do not always match perfectly, even when they refer to the same domain of interest. This is mainly due to the fact that, usually, preferences are expressed in generic terms whereas data is very specific, as shown in the next example.

SEBD 2021: The 29th Italian Symposium on Advanced Database Systems, September 5-9, 2021, Pizzo Calabro (VV), Italy

paolo.ciaccia@unibo.it (P. Ciaccia); davide.martinenghi@polimi.it (D. Martinenghi); riccardo.torlone@uniroma3.it (R. Torlone)
http://www-db.deis.unibo.it/~pciaccia/ (P. Ciaccia); https://martinenghi.faculty.polimi.it (D. Martinenghi); http://www.dia.uniroma3.it/~torlone/ (R. Torlone)

Example 1. We are planning to reserve tickets for a series of concerts for which a general schedule is available, like the one in Figure 1. We prefer rock to pop concerts, yet we prefer a performance by Madonna to a rock concert. Due to work commitments, we also prefer concerts in August rather than in September. Furthermore, as for the concert venue, during autumn we prefer indoor places to stadiums. And, given two concerts by the same artist, we prefer to save money (say, if a concert costs less than 40$, then we prefer it to a concert by the same artist that costs more than 100$, whereas for intermediate prices other considerations are relevant). For the same reason, we would like to buy tickets only for (a subset of) the "best" available alternatives. ■

Concerts

Artist	Day	Venue	Price ($)	
Bruce Springsteen	10/05/2019	Verona Arena	70	t_a
Madonna	24/06/2019	Verona Arena	35	t_b
Madonna	21/07/2019	Blue Note, Milan	120	t_c
Eminem	12/08/2019	Unipol Arena, Bologna	60	t_d
Rihanna	10/10/2019	Blue Note, Milan	50	t_e
Bruce Springsteen	30/10/2019	Stadio Olimpico, Rome	100	t_f

Figure 1: A set of concerts.

The example highlights that: (i) preferences can be expressed at different levels of detail, even for the same "dimension" of the problem (e.g., seasons vs months for the time dimension), and (ii) in general, preferences do not match the level of detail of data. Moreover, preferences can be conflicting when changing the level of detail (rock is better than pop, yet Madonna, a pop singer, is preferred to rock artists). Finally, additional knowledge is needed to choose the best alternatives using preferences. For instance, we need to know that `Unipol Arena` is an indoor place, whereas `Verona Arena` is a Roman amphitheater (thus an outdoor place).

This problem can be tackled by leveraging the great availability of shared and public taxonomies, that is, collection of terms in a domain arranged hierarchically according to an inclusion relationship (e.g., product catalogs, book classifications, biological categorizations, etc.). For instance, the availability of a classification of music artists according to different musical genres would allow us to understand that a preference on rock artists *propagates* to Springsteen.

In this paper, which is an extended abstract of [4], we present a principled approach to the problem of finding the best objects stored in a data repository on the basis of a set of preferences that are defined at a level of detail that does not match that of the data. As a preliminary step, we adopt a data model for representing taxonomies of values in specific domains (e.g., time or location) and propose a preference model for tuples over a given set of taxonomies. We then identify the general properties of preference propagation in the taxonomies, in particular, the fact that more specific preferences prevail over more generic ones. Thus, in the example above, a Madonna concert takes precedence over a Springsteen concert even if, in general, we prefer rock to pop. We then illustrate an algorithm for propagating preferences along taxonomies, complying with the stated properties. Finally, we present a technique for selecting the best tuples according to the propagated preferences. This technique would select tuples t_b and t_d as the best alternatives among the tuples in Figure 1 given the preferences discussed in Example 1.

2. Preliminaries

2.1. Data Model

First of all, it is useful to remind that a *partial order* $\leq$ on a domain V is a subset of $V \times V$, whose elements are denoted by $v_1 \leq v_2$, that is: reflexive ($v \leq v$ for all $v \in V$), antisymmetric (if $v_1 \leq v_2$ and $v_2 \leq v_1$ then $v_1 = v_2$), and transitive (if $v_1 \leq v_2$ and $v_2 \leq v_3$ then $v_1 \leq v_3$).

Our data model is a natural extension of the relational model in which the values in each domain can be arranged hierarchically according to a *taxonomy* [5, 6]. Each taxonomy is represented by a partial order $\leq_L$ on over a set L of *levels*, each of which includes a set of values at a certain degree of granularity. For instance, a *time* taxonomy can be organized in levels such as day, month, season, and year, with day $\leq_L$ month $\leq_L$ year and day $\leq_L$ season. For each pair of levels $l_1 \leq_L l_2$ in a taxonomy, we then assume the existence of a function $\mu_{l_1}^{l_2}$, called *level mapping*, that maps each value in l_1 to a value in l_2. For instance, we have: $\mu_{\text{day}}^{\text{month}}(23/07/2019) = 07/2019$. The level mappings induce a partial order $\leq_V$ on the values of a taxonomy where $v_1 \leq_V v_2$ if $l_1 \leq_L l_2$ and $\mu_{l_1}^{l_2}(v_1) = v_2$.

Example 2. Portions of the taxonomies relevant to our working example on concerts are shown in Figure 2. For the *location* of a concert we consider levels Venue, VenueType, and InOut. The values of this taxonomy are organized in the poset shown in Figure 3, where the level mappings are represented by arrows. ■

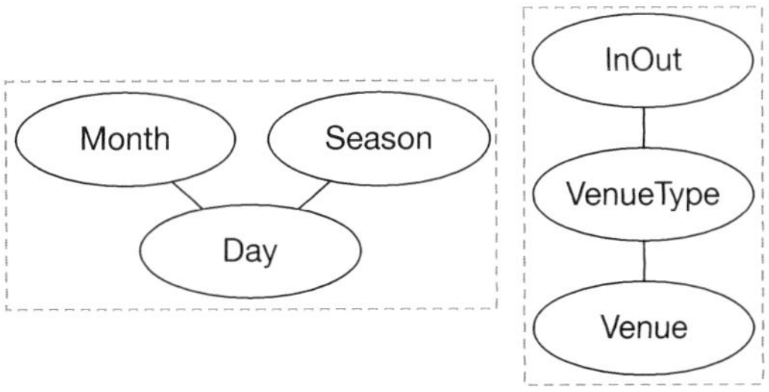

Figure 2: The taxonomies for our working example

The main constructs of the data model are the t-schema, the t-tuple, and the t-relation, which are natural extensions of the analogous notions in the relational model in which data domains can be taxonomies. For instance, a catalog of concerts in Italy can be represented by the t-relation shown in Figure 1 over the taxonomies in Figure 2 where we have used the levels as names of the attributes, assuming for simplicity that level names are unique. A partial order can than also be defined over t-schemas and t-tuples as follows: $S_1 \leq_S S_2$ if for each $l_i \in S_2$ there is an element $l_j \in S_1$ such that $l_j \leq_L l_i$ and $t_1 \leq_t t_2$ if: (i) $S_1 \leq_S S_2$, and (ii) for each $l_i \in S_2$ there is an element $l_j \in S_1$ such that $t_1[l_j] \leq_V t_2[l_i]$. Note that S_2 may have fewer

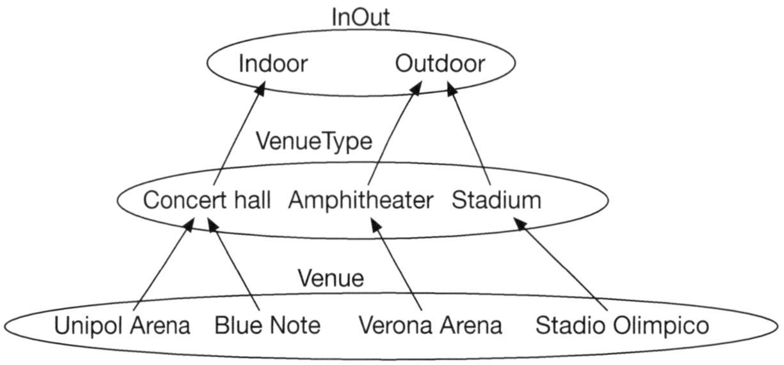

Figure 3: A taxonomy for concerts' locations

attributes than S_1. However, we assume without loss of generality that they have the same set of attributes, since we can add to S_2 the missing attributes at the top level of the taxonomy.

2.2. Preference Model

In our approach preferences are represented by a binary relation $\succeq$ over t-tuples as follows: given a collection of taxonomies $\{T_1, \ldots, T_k\}$ and a pair of t-tuples t_1 and t_2 over $\mathcal{T} = T_1 \times \ldots \times T_k$, if $t_1 \succeq t_2$ then we say that t_1 is *(weakly) preferable* to t_2. If $t_1 \succeq t_2$ and $t_2 \not\succeq t_1$ we say that t_1 is *strictly preferable* to t_2, denoted $t_1 \succ t_2$. Then, the "best" t-tuples in a t-relation r according to the preference relation $\succeq$ can be selected by means of the *Best* operator $\beta_{\succeq}(r) = \{t \in r \mid \nexists t' \in r, t' \succ t\}$ [7].

We express preferences in a logic-based language, so that $t_1 \succeq t_2$ iff they satisfy the *preference formula* $F(t_1, t_2)$: $t_1 \succeq t_2 \Leftrightarrow F(t_1, t_2)$. In particular, we consider formulas in which only built-in predicates are present and quantifiers are omitted, also called *intrinsic preference formulas* (ipf) [2]. Furthermore, without loss of generality, we assume that F is in Disjunctive Normal Form (DNF) and call each disjunct of F a *preference clause*, i.e.: $F(t_1, t_2) = \bigvee_{i=1}^{n} P_i(t_1, t_2)$.

Example 3. The preferences informally stated in Example 1 can be expressed by the formula $F(t_1, t_2) = P_1(t_1, t_2) \vee \ldots \vee P_5(t_1, t_2)$, where:

$$
\begin{aligned}
P_1(t_1, t_2) = \;& (t_1[\text{Genre}] = \texttt{rock}) \wedge (t_2[\text{Genre}] = \texttt{pop}) \\
P_2(t_1, t_2) = \;& (t_1[\text{Artist}] = \texttt{Madonna}) \wedge (t_2[\text{Genre}] = \texttt{rock}) \\
P_3(t_1, t_2) = \;& (t_1[\text{Artist}] = t_2[\text{Artist}]) \wedge \\
& (t_1[\text{PriceRange}] = \texttt{cheap}) \wedge (t_2[\text{PriceRange}] = \texttt{expensive}) \\
P_4(t_1, t_2) = \;& (t_1[\text{Season}] = \texttt{autumn}) \wedge (t_2[\text{Season}] = \texttt{autumn}) \wedge \\
& (t_1[\text{InOut}] = \texttt{indoor}) \wedge (t_2[\text{VenueType}] = \texttt{stadium}) \\
P_5(t_1, t_2) = \;& (t_1[\text{Month}] = \texttt{august}) \wedge (t_2[\text{Month}] = \texttt{september})
\end{aligned}
$$

■

3. Propagation of Preferences

The initial preference relation $\succeq$ completely ignores the structure of the poset on t-tuples $\leq_t$, thus it treats $\mathcal{T}$ as if it were a "flat" domain. This is because $\succeq$ includes all and only those preferences $t_1 \succeq t_2$ such that the attribute values of t_1 and t_2 satisfy the preference formula, yet it does not take into account the taxonomies. The key observation justifying the *downward propagation* of preferences, is that, given a target t-schema S, by exploiting the hierarchical organization of $\mathcal{T}$ it is possible to extend $\succeq$ with more preferences that involve t-tuples with t-schemas S_i, with $S \leq_S S_i$.

Let $\succeq_{\mathsf{D}}$ denote the binary relation obtained by propagating, in some way to be described, the preferences in $\succeq$. The basic idea underlying propagation is that, if we have t-tuples t'_1 and t'_2 such that $t'_1 \succeq t'_2$, then this preference can be downward propagated to all t-tuples t_1 and t_2 such that $t_1 \leq_t t'_1$ and $t_2 \leq_t t'_2$. For instance, consider the t-schema in Figure 1 and the preference clause $P_1(t_1, t_2) = t_1[\mathsf{Genre}] = \mathsf{Rock}) \wedge (t_2[\mathsf{Genre}] = \mathsf{Pop})$. From P_1 we can obtain through propagation the preferences $t_a \succeq_{\mathsf{D}} t_b$ and $t_a \succeq_{\mathsf{D}} t_c$, since Bruce Springsteen is a rock artist whereas Madonna is a pop singer.

In terms of logical formulas, downward propagation with respect to the target t-schema S can be easily obtained by exploiting the level mappings. For instance, consider clause $P_5(t_1, t_2)$ in Example 3. This can be rewritten as:

$$(\mu_{\mathsf{Day}}^{\mathsf{Month}}(t_1[\mathsf{Day}]) = \mathtt{august}) \wedge (\mu_{\mathsf{Day}}^{\mathsf{Month}}(t_2[\mathsf{Day}]) = \mathtt{september})$$

so that it is applicable to values at the Day level. In order to simplify the notation, in the following level mappings are understood and we use $=_{\mathsf{D}}$ in place of $=$ to allow comparisons between values at different levels (similarly for other comparison operators, eg., $\leq$ would become $\leq_D$). Thus, the above clause can be more conveniently written as:

$$t_1[\mathsf{Day}] =_{\mathsf{D}} \mathtt{august} \wedge t_2[\mathsf{Day}] =_{\mathsf{D}} \mathtt{september}.$$

Given an input formula F, we denote by F_{D} the formula rewritten by means of level mappings.

3.1. Transitively Closing the Formula

Downward propagation does not guarantee that $\succeq_{\mathsf{D}}$ is a transitive relation, even because the very input relation $\succeq$ is not necessarily transitive. Although one may be tempted to circumvent this problem by adopting an algorithm for non-transitive preferences [8], algorithms of this type can discard a sub-optimal t-tuple t only if the t-relation r contains a t-tuple t' that is *directly* (rather than transitively) better than t.

Our approach is to transitively closing formula F_{D} with respect to the t-tuple domain $\mathcal{T}$, as described in [2] for the base case of flat domains.[1] The presence of taxonomies requires to extend the basic scheme adopted in [2], as the following example illustrates.

[1] Notice that the transitive closure of an ipf is finite and still an ipf [2].

Example 4. Given the formula $F(t_1, t_2) = P_5(t_1, t_2) \vee P_4(t_1, t_2)$, where P_4 and P_5 are as in Example 3, by means of downward propagation we obtain the formula:

$$\begin{aligned} F_{\mathsf{D}}(t_1, t_2) = \; & (t_1[\mathsf{Day}] =_{\mathsf{D}} \texttt{august} \wedge t_2[\mathsf{Day}] =_{\mathsf{D}} \texttt{september}) \vee \\ & (t_1[\mathsf{Day}] =_{\mathsf{D}} \texttt{autumn} \wedge t_2[\mathsf{Day}] =_{\mathsf{D}} \texttt{autumn} \wedge \\ & t_1[\mathsf{Venue}] =_{\mathsf{D}} \texttt{indoor} \wedge t_2[\mathsf{Venue}] =_{\mathsf{D}} \texttt{stadium}). \end{aligned}$$

Now, since some september days are in autumn, it is sound to add to the transitive closure of F_{D}, a formula that will be denoted as F_{DT}, the clause:

$$t_1[\mathsf{Day}] =_{\mathsf{D}} \texttt{august} \wedge t_2[\mathsf{Day}] =_{\mathsf{D}} \texttt{autumn} \wedge t_2[\mathsf{Venue}] =_{\mathsf{D}} \texttt{stadium}.$$

■

We observe that F_{D} uses level mappings in order to understand when preferences expressed at different levels can be transitively combined. Indeed, this is the only additional complexity with respect to the procedure given in [2]. In particular, similarly to what done in Example 4, we have to compare values at different levels in a taxonomy (e.g., september and autumn) and determine if they have a non-empty intersection (so that the transitive step can be applied).

3.2. Computing the Result with Specific Preferences

The propagation scheme described in the previous section is unable to deal with conflicting preferences, one of which is *more specific* than the other. In our working example, we have a generic preference for rock concerts over pop concerts (clause P_1), yet we also have a more specific preference stating that a performance by Madonna takes precedence over any rock concerts (clause P_2). Thus, according to P_1 we would have, among others, $t_a \succeq_{\mathsf{DT}} t_b$, whereas P_2 would yield $t_b \succeq_{\mathsf{DT}} t_a$, thus making t_a and t_b indifferent. We argue that giving the same importance to both preferences contradicts the intuition, as the more specific preference should take precedence over the more generic one.

We now detail how, given a formula F_{DT}, we can effectively solve conflicts by maintaining only more specific preferences.

If $F_{\mathsf{DT}}(t_1, t_2)$ holds, we look at the clause P_i that evaluates to **true**[2] and, for each involved attribute, we consider the original level it has for both t_1 and t_2 (remind that F_{DT} has been obtained by applying level mappings). If an attribute does not appear in P_i we set its level to the top level of its taxonomy (henceforth simply indicated by $\top$).

Example 5. Consider t-tuples t_a and t_b in Figure 1 and clause $P_2(t_1, t_2) = (t_1[\mathsf{Artist}] = \texttt{Madonna}) \wedge (t_2[\mathsf{Genre}] = \texttt{rock})$. Note that $P_2(t_b, t_a)$ holds and the original levels when evaluating P_2 for t_a are $(\mathsf{Genre}, \top, \top, \top)$, while those for t_b are $(\mathsf{Artist}, \top, \top, \top)$. ■

Overall, this leads to *a pair of t-schemas*, $\mathsf{spp}(t_1, t_2) = \langle \mathsf{sig}_{1,2}(t_1), \mathsf{sig}_{1,2}(t_2) \rangle$. Notice that $\mathsf{sig}_{1,2}(t_1)$ is the t-schema for t_1 when we test if t_1 is preferred to t_2, which, in general, is different from $\mathsf{sig}_{2,1}$, i.e., the t-schema for t_1 when we test if t_2 is preferred to t_1. This motivates the use of subscripts.

[2]Generalization to the case in which more than one clause is **true** is immediate.

Algorithm 1: Computing the best t-tuples in r.

Input: *t-relation* r *with t-schema* $S = \{A_1 : l_1, \ldots, A_k : l_k\}$, *formula* F_{DT}.
Output: $\beta_{\succ_{\mathsf{DT}}}$.

let $Best := \emptyset$
for each $t \in r$
  let $Opt :=$ **true**
  for each $t' \in Best$
    cases
      $F_{\mathsf{DT}}(t,t') \wedge (F_{\mathsf{DT}}(t',t) \wedge t = \textsc{MoreSpecificPref}(t,t') \vee \neg F_{\mathsf{DT}}(t',t))$: $Best := Best \setminus \{t'\}$
      $F_{\mathsf{DT}}(t',t) \wedge (F_{\mathsf{DT}}(t,t') \wedge t' = \textsc{MoreSpecificPref}(t,t') \vee \neg F_{\mathsf{DT}}(t,t'))$: **let** $Opt :=$ **false**; **break**
  if Opt **then** $Best := Best \cup \{t\}$
return $Best$

When also $F_{\mathsf{DT}}(t_2, t_1)$ holds, i.e., we have a conflict, we compare $\mathsf{spp}(t_1, t_2)$ and $\mathsf{spp}(t_2, t_1) = \langle \mathsf{sig}_{2,1}(t_2), \mathsf{sig}_{2,1}(t_1) \rangle$ and conclude that the first preference is more specific than the second iff $\mathsf{sig}_{1,2}(t_1) \leq_S \mathsf{sig}_{2,1}(t_1)$ and $\mathsf{sig}_{1,2}(t_2) \leq_S \mathsf{sig}_{2,1}(t_2)$, with at least one t-schema being strictly more specific.

Example 6. Assume we are comparing t-tuples t_a and t_b in Figure 1. From clause P_1 in Example 3 ($P_1(t_1, t_2) = (t_1[\mathsf{Genre}] = \mathtt{rock}) \wedge (t_2[\mathsf{Genre}] = \mathtt{pop})$) we derive that $t_a \succeq_{\mathsf{DT}} t_b$, whereas $t_b \succeq_{\mathsf{DT}} t_a$ follows from clause P_2. For the first preference we have $\mathsf{spp}(t_a, t_b) = \langle (\mathsf{Genre}, \top, \top, \top), (\mathsf{Genre}, \top, \top, \top) \rangle$, whereas for the second we have $\mathsf{spp}(t_b, t_a) = \langle (\mathsf{Artist}, \top, \top, \top), (\mathsf{Genre}, \top, \top, \top) \rangle$. Although for t_a the two t-schemas are the same, for t_b Artist is strictly more specific than Genre, thus t_b is strictly preferred to t_a. ■

In order to compute the best results according to the (transitively closed) rewritten formula F_{DT} we can use any algorithm developed for returning the best objects in a strict partial order, such as those in [9, 7], by suitably adapting it to work in our scenario. Algorithm 1 is such an adaptation of the well-known BNL algorithm [9]. In the algorithm the "specificity test" is performed by the procedure $\textsc{MoreSpecificPref}(t, t')$, which returns t if the preference $t \succeq_{\mathsf{DT}} t'$ is more specific than $t' \succeq_{\mathsf{DT}} t$, t' in the opposite case, and **nil** otherwise.

4. Conclusions

In this paper we have studied preference propagation along several taxonomies, when the levels at which preferences are stated and that of the stored data differ. The preference model we have proposed is able to deal with conflicting preferences in an effective way, thus propagating only the most specific preferences.

The specificity principle we use in this paper was also considered in [10, 11], although on a preference model using strict rather than weak preferences and in a different scenario regarding preferences combined across different *contexts* (not preference formulas): if $a \succ b$ holds in context c, and $b \succ a$ in context c', then $a \succ b$ prevails if c is more specific than c'. The problem of dealing with preferences defined on different schemas, which is the main focus of the present paper, was not addressed at all in [10, 11].

The interplay between specificity and transitivity is studied in depth in [12].

Propagation of preferences in OLAP systems is considered in [13], where an algebraic language is adopted. Propagation occurs along hierarchies of levels, however no issue concerning combination of conflicting preferences is considered. Unlike most works studying the problem of managing *qualitative* preference queries on databases [3], in which the preference relation is a strict partial order $\succ$, in this paper we have considered "weak" preferences $\succeq$. This choice originates from the observation that, while propagating preferences between different t-schemas, transitivity cannot be guaranteed and a transitive closure is needed. However, enforcing transitivity might lead to cycles, which are harmless in our model but cannot occur in strict partial orders.

Future work includes the study of efficient methods for computing the transitive closure of the preference formula, the development of ad hoc algorithms for determining the best objects that scale over very large datasets, and an experimental evaluation on real-world scenarios.

References

[1] F. Ricci, L. Rokach, B. Shapira, Introduction to recommender systems handbook, in: Recommender Systems Handbook, Springer, 2011, pp. 1–35.

[2] J. Chomicki, Preference formulas in relational queries, TODS 28 (2003) 427–466.

[3] K. Stefanidis, G. Koutrika, E. Pitoura, A survey on representation, composition and application of preferences in database systems, TODS 36 (2011) 19:1–19:45.

[4] P. Ciaccia, D. Martinenghi, R. Torlone, Finding preferred objects with taxonomies, in: ER, 2019, pp. 397–411.

[5] D. Martinenghi, R. Torlone, Querying databases with taxonomies, in: ER, 2010, pp. 377–390.

[6] D. Martinenghi, R. Torlone, Taxonomy-based relaxation of query answering in relational databases, VLDB J. 23 (2014) 747–769.

[7] R. Torlone, P. Ciaccia, Which are my preferred items?, in: RPEC, 2002, pp. 217–225.

[8] C. Y. Chan, H. V. Jagadish, K. Tan, A. K. H. Tung, Z. Zhang, Finding k-dominant skylines in high dimensional space, in: SIGMOD, 2006, pp. 503–514.

[9] S. Börzsönyi, D. Kossmann, K. Stocker, The skyline operator, in: ICDE, 2001, pp. 421–430.

[10] P. Ciaccia, D. Martinenghi, R. Torlone, Foundations of context-aware preference propagation, J. ACM 67 (2020) 4:1–4:43.

[11] P. Ciaccia, R. Torlone, Modeling the propagation of user preferences, in: ER, 2011, pp. 304–317. *Best paper award.*

[12] P. Ciaccia, D. Martinenghi, R. Torlone, Preference queries over taxonomic domains, Proceedings of the VLDB Endowment (2021) to appear.

[13] M. Golfarelli, S. Rizzi, P. Biondi, myOLAP: An approach to express and evaluate OLAP preferences, TKDE 23 (2011) 1050–1064.

Using Descriptions for Explaining Entity Matches

(Discussion Paper)

Matteo Paganelli[1], Paolo Sottovia[2], Antonio Maccioni[3], Matteo Interlandi[4] and Francesco Guerra[1]

[1]*DIEF - University of Modena and Reggio Emilia, Modena, Italy*
[2]*Huawei Research. Munich, Germany*
[3]*Independent Researcher, USA*
[4]*Microsoft Research, Seattle, USA*

Abstract

Finding entity matches in large datasets is currently one of the most attractive research challenges. The recent interest of the research community towards Machine and Deep Learning techniques has led to the development of many and reliable approaches. Nevertheless, these are conceived as black-box tools that identify the matches between the entities provided as input. The lack of explainability of the process hampers its application to real-world scenarios where domain experts need to know and understand the reasons why entities can be considered as match, i.e., they represent the same real-world entity. In this paper, we show how *data descriptions*—a set of compact, readable and insightful formulas of boolean predicates—can be used to guide domain experts in understanding and evaluating the results of entity matching processes.

Keywords

data explanation, data exploration, data profiling, outliers

1. Introduction

Entity Matching (EM) is a long-lasting problem in the database research community. Recently, approaches based on Machine Learning (ML) and Deep Learning (DL) have been proposed. They conceive EM as a binary classification problem [1] applied on datasets whose records describe pairs of entities. Since the first proposals (see related work in Section 4), they have proved to be very effective. Nevertheless, the application of ML and DL approaches in real scenarios is hampered not only by the need for a significant amount of labeled data for their configuration and training, but also for the lack of explainability of the results they provide.

We have already introduced and showcased *(data) descriptions*, i.e. compact, readable and insightful structures formed by *predicates* expressed on the attribute values and able to effectively explain the content of large and complex datasets, in [2, 3]. We have experimentally

SEBD 2021: The 29th Italian Symposium on Advanced Database Systems, September 5-9, 2021, Pizzo Calabro (VV), Italy

matteo.paganelli@unimore.it (M. Paganelli); paolo.sottovia@huawei.com (P. Sottovia); antonio.maccioni@gmail.com (A. Maccioni); matteo.interlandi@microsoft.com (M. Interlandi); francesco.guerra@unimore.it (F. Guerra)
http://morespace.unimore.it/francescoguerra/ (F. Guerra)
0000-0001-8119-895X (M. Paganelli); 0000-0001-7116-9338 (P. Sottovia); 0000-0002-5756-8321 (M. Interlandi); 0000-0001-6864-568X (F. Guerra)

Entity ID	Song Name	Artist Name	Album Name	Genre	
1	I Ai n't Livin ' Long Like This	Chris Janson	Take It to the Bank - EP	Country	e_1
2	I Ai n't Livin ' Long Like This	Chris Janson	Take It to the Bank (EP)	Country	e_1
3	I Ai n't Livin ' Long Like This	Chris Janson	Take It to the Bank - EP	Country	e_1
4	Billy	Keith Urban	Keith Urban In The Ranch	Country	e_2
5	I Ca n't Go There (Acoustic Version)	Kenny Chesney	No Shoes, No Shirt, No Problems	Country	e_3
6	I Ca n't Go There (Acoustic Version)	Kenny Chesney	No Shoes, No Shirt, No Problems	Country	e_3
7	I Ca n't Go There (Acoustic Version)	Kenny Chesney	No Shoes, No Shirt, No Problems	Urban Cowboy	e_3
8	Afire Love	Ed Sheeran	x	Pop	e_4
9	Afire Love	Ed Sheeran	x	Pop	e_4
10	Afire Love	Ed Sheeran	x	Pop	e_4

Table 1
The *Entity Matches from the iTunes-Amazon Dataset*

demonstrated the effectiveness of *descriptions* in performing many tasks of data exploration. The aim of this paper is to show how they can be useful in another field, making a (large) dataset describing the result of an EM task understandable at a glance by domain expert users.

Running Example. Let us introduce Table 1 containing a sample of entity matches obtained by applying a generic EM approach to a sample of the *iTunes-Amazon* dataset published in the Magellan library[1] and by transitively extending the results through a connected components algorithm (i.e., according to the literature [4], we consider entities as referring to the same real-world entity when the matching elements form a clique). Each record represents a song with a list of characteristics (`Entity Id`, `Song Name`, `Artist name`, `Album Name`, and `Genre`). The extra-column on the right shows the result of the application of the EM process, which is able to recognize four distinct songs from the nine in the Table. A domain expert who needs to validate the result of the EM task has to manually inspect the dataset to figure out the reasons for the computed matches. Data descriptions can support the process since they are able to concisely represent any arbitrary set of data tuples.

Example 1. *D_1 is a description of the dataset represented in Table 1 obtained conjoining a list of predicates, each characterizing the same attribute of the dataset with the related values. We called `M_E` the extra-column recording the identifier of the resulting entity from the matching task. In this example, the description covers the entire dataset (all the tuples are represented by D_1) and is built upon only an attribute of the original dataset (i.e., `Song_Name`). Moreover, D_1 partitions the dataset into four clusters, each one representing a unique entity resulting from the EM process. The description based on the `Song_Name` attribute is then useful to understand if the EM Model is able to perform a correct identification of entities: for each entity a different song name is displayed thus confirming the correct subdivision into distinct entities of the dataset entries. Other descriptions for the same dataset are possible, built upon other attributes, dividing the datasets into other partitions and using more attributes for each partition (e.g., the dataset can be grouped by `Genre` and described with the `Album Name`).*

D_1 :($M\_E \in \{e_1\}$) $\bigwedge$ *Song Name* $\in$ {I Ai n't Livin ' Long Like This}) $\bigvee$
($M\_E \in \{e_2\}$ $\bigwedge$ *Song Name* $\in$ {Billy}) $\bigvee$

[1] https://github.com/anhaidgroup/deepmatcher/blob/master/Datasets.md

$(M_E \in \{e_3\} \bigwedge Song\ \ Name \in \{$I Ca n't Go There (Acoustic Version)$\}) \bigvee$
$(M_E \in \{e_4\} \bigwedge Song\ \ Name \in \{$Afire Love$\})$

Building the Descriptions: A principled approach. The data descriptions are generated according to three main principles. The first states that *it is more explicative to think of a dataset as the composition of different groups of related tuples.* Attributes of a dataset carry different degrees of relevance for users who want to understand the content of datasets and glean insight from their data. Some attributes have intrinsic value because, for example, they can identify entities in a domain (e.g., the attribute `EntityID` in the dataset of Table 1) or because they allow identifying specific features of the entities (e.g., the attributes `Album Name`, `Artist Name` in the dataset). On the other hand, the importance of certain attributes may depend on the users: on their specific interests motivating the dataset exploration and on their knowledge of the domain. Nevertheless, in this case study the idea is to generate data descriptions representing entity matches, and it is therefore natural to partition the dataset around clusters of matching entities. We call *d-formula* the conjunction of predicates describing a partition. A *description* is formally a non-empty disjunctive-normal formula of d-formulas (one for each partition).

The exploration of a dataset as well as the analysis of entity matches can be conducted for different purposes. In some cases, users want an accurate and complete, yet readable, representation of the whole dataset, able to precisely explain the reasons that led to the generation of those clusters of matching entities. In other cases, a general profile of the dataset is enough for the user, who needs only to broadly know why entity possible match in that domain. The description represents, in these latter cases, an overview that ignores infrequent values. Often, instead, there are users who are interested in finding possible mistakes, i.e., entities in the same clusters with values which are not consistent with the ones of other entities in the same cluster. These values can be infrequent values, or outliers, but can also represent possible mistakes. The second driving principle is that *we can accommodate the multi-faceted goals of data explanation by relaxing the concept of coverage in the descriptions.* Our approach allows users to interactively change the coverage of the expected descriptions (intended as the percentage of the total number of tuples that are true for the description), thus making them able to satisfy all possible needs.

Finally, the quality of a description is influenced by the subjectivity of the users and the tasks where the description has to be applied. A prolix description can be suitable for a user who wants to interpret a matching model, but, at the same time, be poor for another one who only needs to know the main features of a type of entity. *The third driving principle is to consider user preferences for qualifying descriptions.* We follow this principle by: (1) defining a series of dimensions that characterize the descriptions; (2) we let the users indicate their preferential value for these dimensions. Specifically, we identified three dimensions for characterizing a description from a user perspective: *coverage* , *degree*, and *diversity.* The *coverage* is the percentage of items covered by a description in each partition where the dataset is divided. Through the coverage, the users select from one extreme (i.e., low coverage) if they want to find the peculiarities for each cluster of matching items (i.e.. possible mistakes); from the other (i.e. high coverage), if they want to describe the common features for all the entities in a matching group. The *degree* refers to the number of predicates used to describe each cluster of entities. Intuitively, a description with lower *degree* tends to be much easier to read. The *diversity* measures how often attributes are shared in describing different clusters of matching

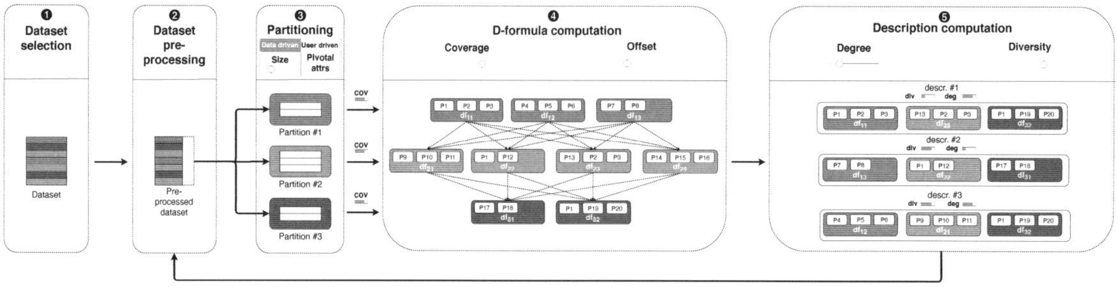

Figure 1: The process for generating descriptions.

entities. While repetitions of a set of attributes in different partitions increase readability, they could reduce the fine-grained representation of partitions.

The rest of the paper is organized as follows. Section 2 summarizes the approach for building the descriptions, Section 3 shows the application to the entity matching task, Section 4 provides some related work, and finally Section 5 sketches out some conclusion.

2. The Approach

The description generation process is interactive: users can specify their preference parameters—namely *coverage*, *degree* and *diversity*—and the system generates the best description according to these preferences. The user can repeatedly vary the preferences and generate further descriptions until the explanation need is fulfilled.

Figure 1 illustrates the 5 steps driving the user in the generation process of descriptions. First of all, the user starts the process by uploading a new dataset (❶). Once the dataset is selected, the user can specify the attributes of interest that must be considered by the system when generating the descriptions (❷, by default all attributes are used). Next, the user is guided through the UI into the 3 major phases in which the actual descriptions are generated.

In the first phase (❸), the input dataset is partitioned such that the tuples that are expected to be described together reside in the same group. The user is in charge to select how to partition the dataset. If the dataset describes the results of an EM task, the partition should be defined on an extra value identifying the clusters of matching entities.

The generation of the d-formulas (conjunction of predicates) happens during the second phase (❹). For each partition, the number of possible d-formulas is exponential over the number of attributes' values. Generating all possible d-formulas is, therefore, prohibitively expensive. As explained in Section 2.1, we adopt a heuristic procedure that allows us to prune d-formulas that are less relevant for the task at hand. In the last phase (❺), the actual descriptions are computed by combining d-formulas over different partitions. Intuitively, we assemble the top-k descriptions that maximize a scoring function computed on the generated d-formulas that takes into account the user preferences of degree, and diversity. This problem can be solved with a dynamic programming approach: in Section 2.2 we will employ a variant of the Viterbi Algorithm called *LVA* [5] (a.k.a. *List Viterbi*), although any other algorithm can be used.

2.1. Building d-formulas

The approach starts building all feasible and relevant d-formulas for each partition. The number of candidate predicates for each partition depends on the size of the active domain of the attributes in the partition. Therefore, the complexity of this phase is $\mathcal{O}\left(\rho \times \prod_{a \in A} (2^{|adom_p(a)|})\right)$, where A is the set of the attributes, ρ is the number of partitions and $|adom_p(a)|$ is the aforementioned size. Given the complexity for generating all possible d-formulas, we follow a heuristic process that generates the most relevant candidate d-formulas only. We adopt two heuristics, one for pruning prolix d-formulas, and one for pruning d-formulas and predicates with undesirable selectivity.

2.1.1. Heuristic 1 - pruning prolix d-formulas

A low degree is specified when the user prefers a small number of predicates and, conversely, a high degree is for users who prefer descriptions with wide d-formulas. We push the degree intent of the users into the process of building d-formulas in order to early-prune d-formulas that do not meet such a requirement. This limits the number of predicates to evaluate, and it improves the efficiency of the process.

2.1.2. Heuristic 2 - pruning d-formulas with undesirable selectivity.

The coverage parameter (cov) indicates the desired percentage of tuples that make a d-formula true. Heuristic 2 transforms the coverage value indicated by the user input parameter value into an interval $[\text{cov}_l, \text{cov}_u]$ of admissible coverage values. The width of the interval is proportional to the coverage itself given that $\text{cov}_l = \text{cov} - \textit{offset}(\text{cov})$, $\text{cov}_u = \text{cov} + \textit{offset}(\text{cov})$ and $\textit{offset}(\text{cov}) = 0.14 * \text{cov}^2$. As for Heuristic 1, we push the coverage interval into the process of generating d-formulas for early pruning.

2.1.3. Generating d-formulas.

The approach adopted for generating all possible and relevant d-formulas takes in input the list of partitions, the list of dataset attributes, the desired coverage, and degree. The d-formulas of each partition are computed separately. First, we generate the *atomic predicates* (i.e., predicates with only one value). Atomic predicates are generated only if they are within the expected coverage as defined by Heuristic 2. Then the atomic predicates are combined together to generate conjunctions of predicates. The resulting d-formulas, for each partition, are then returned as output.

When combining the predicates together, an internal routine makes sure that only those valid combinations (i.e., d-formulas) for Heuristic 2 are actually returned. The combination of the input predicates is organized in a lattice which is dynamically generated using a loop. In each iteration, we generate one level of the lattice (the *n*-th) by combining pairs of the previously generated predicates into one d-formula. Only combinations of predicates whose coverage is within the interval defined by Heuristic 2 are kept for the next level of the lattice. The generation of the lattice ends when the threshold, as per Heuristic 1, is reached or when it is no longer possible to generate predicates.

2.2. Building top-k descriptions

Selecting the best d-formulas in isolation does not necessarily lead to the best descriptions. We need to search for the optimal set of d-formulas across partitions that all together best fit the users' needs. To achieve this, we use dynamic programming: our current implementation is based on the *List Viterbi Algorithm* [5]. Viterbi Algorithm and its variants require to model the search space as a trellis. We build a vertical slice for each partition. The nodes in the slice are the d-formulas we have found in the previous phase. Nodes of a slice are connected to all the nodes of the next slice via weighted edges. A path represents a list of d-formulas, with at most one d-formula for partition. The algorithm is used to find the best full path.

Viterbi needs an objective function w to score a path, which intuitively represents the score of the (intermediate) descriptions we are computing.

We introduce a scoring function which measures (1) the adherence between the features of the description and the expectation of the user (expressed with a preference on level of coverage, degree and diversity); and (2) the goodness of the chosen attribute in describing the partitions. Other techniques can be evaluated. For example, we experimented also with the Smooth Local Search [6] with no improvement in the performance.

3. Applying Descriptions to the EM scenario

When we need to explain entity matches, it is natural to create descriptions with a d-formula for each cluster of matching entities. The use of descriptions enables the computation of different types of explanation, obtained by varying the preferences of coverage, degree and diversity specified by the user.

What do these entities represent? When users are interested in understanding the main features of the entities in the dataset, they have to select settings with high coverage values. These configurations generate descriptions where d-formulas aim to represent the clusters of matching entities as whole units. Descriptions with high degree tend to create d-formulas with more predicates. Descriptions with high diversity tend to use different attributes in the predicate lists of different d-formulas.

Example 2. *D_1 in Example 1 is a description with high coverage, low degree and low diversity. All clusters of matching entities shown in Table 1 are represented and the user can understand that the values of* `Song Name` *qualify the entities. D_2 is an example of a description with high coverage, low degree and high diversity. In this case, the approach tries to select different attributes for describing each partition.*

D_2 : ($M\_E \in \{e_1\}$ $\bigwedge$ `Song Name` $\in$ {I Ai n't Livin ' Long Like This}) $\bigvee$
($M\_E \in \{e_2\}$ $\bigwedge$ `Artist Name` $\in$ {Keith Urban}) $\bigvee$
($M\_E \in \{e_3\}$ $\bigwedge$ `Song Name` $\in$ {I Ca n't Go There (Acoustic Version)}) $\bigvee$
($M\_E \in \{e_4\}$ $\bigwedge$ `Genre` $\in$ {Pop})

Descriptions with high degree tend to use the largest number of possible attributes for each partition. Clearly, degree and diversity are related dimensions and when the dataset has a low dimensionality as in Table 1, the generated descriptions cannot accomplish both the requirement.

Is this a mistake? When users are interested in discovering possible mistakes in clusters of matching entities, they need to generate low coverage descriptions, that apply only to a small portion for each partition. As before for high coverage descriptions, degree and diversity are used to qualify the d-formulas generated.

Example 3. *D_3 is a description with low coverage, low degree and low diversity. It describes a unique partition, i.e., the cluster of matching entities e_3. In this cluster, the entity with `Entity id` 7 has a genre which is different from the ones of the other entities in the same cluster. This can be a possible mistake that the domain expert needs to check. Note that D_3 shows the information about cluster e_3, since it is not possible to generate low coverage d-formulas for the other partitions.*

D_3 :M_E $\in \{e_3\} \bigwedge$ Song Name $\in$ {I Ca n't Go There (Acoustic Version)} $\bigwedge$ Genre $\in$ {Urban Cowboy}

In this case, the expert will probably validate the cluster, since all songs in e_3 actually refer to the same real-world item. Nevertheless, let us suppose that the EM model erroneously generates a cluster of matching entities which is the concatenation of the entities in e_1 and e_2. D_4 is a low coverage description for this new cluster. In this case, the item reported by this description will probably be evaluated by an expert as a mistake, since the song with `Entity id` 4 is completely different from the other ones.

D_4 :M_E $\in \{e_1 + e_2\} \bigwedge$ Song Name $\in$ {Billy} $\bigwedge$ Genre $\in$ {Country}

4. Related Work

Describing datasets. Explanation systems help users in gaining knowledge on the behavior of systems, experiments or query answers [7], and "black box" complex models [8]. Explanations typically assume the form of association rules, decision lists and decision sets [9]. Our approach performs data explanation since it creates partitions from a dataset and builds rules that provide users with an explanation of their content. The paper develops a subgroup discovery technique for performing data explanation and exploration on structured datasets [10].

Explainable Entity Matching. Entity matching [11] represents one of the main steps of data integration and has been under study for several years. Many techniques have been proposed: from the more traditional rule-based approaches to the most recent machine learning and deep learning methods. Rule-based approaches [12] are intrinsically interpretable, however, the identification of the most effective set of matching rules is a complex and non-trivial task [13]. EM approaches based on Deep Learning (e.g., DeepER [14], DeepMatcher [15], DITTO [16] and many others [17]) have been demonstrated particularly effective. Nevertheless, they require a significant amount of annotated data, they need a complex configuration, and there is no direct interpretation of their behavior, affecting their usability in business environments. There are typically two alternative approaches for providing explanation of AI techniques [18]: 1) applying explanation systems to interpret their behavior a-posteriori or 2) building models that are interpretable by design, i.e. models that base their decisions on humanly interpretable "structures / components". The main approaches in EM (e.g., *LIME* [19] and *SHAP* [20], *Mojito* [21] and *Landmark Explanation* [22]) belong to the first area.

5. Conclusion

This discussion paper shows how *data descriptions* can be used for evaluating an EM task. In particular, descriptions can be used to generate an overview of the main features of the entities in the dataset or for discovering outliers, which can be the symptom of a mistake in the approach. Interested readers can found further details of the approach and a deep evaluation in [2, 3].

References

[1] P. Christen, Data Matching - Concepts and Techniques for Record Linkage, Entity Resolution, and Duplicate Detection, Data-Centric Systems and Applications, Springer, 2012.

[2] M. Paganelli, P. Sottovia, A. Maccioni, M. Interlandi, F. Guerra, Explaining data with descriptions, Inf. Syst. 92 (2020).

[3] M. Paganelli, P. Sottovia, A. Maccioni, M. Interlandi, F. Guerra, Understanding data in the blink of an eye, in: CIKM, ACM, 2019, pp. 2885–2888.

[4] D. Firmani, B. Saha, D. Srivastava, Online entity resolution using an oracle, Proc. VLDB Endow. 9 (2016).

[5] N. Seshadri, C.-E. W. Sundberg, List viterbi decoding algorithms with applications, IEEE Transactions on Communications 42 (1994).

[6] U. Feige, V. S. Mirrokni, J. Vondrák, Maximizing non-monotone submodular functions, SIAM J. Comput. 40 (2011) 1133–1153.

[7] A. Meliou, S. Roy, D. Suciu, Causality and explanations in databases, PVLDB 7 (2014) 1715–1716.

[8] R. Guidotti, A. Monreale, S. Ruggieri, F. Turini, F. Giannotti, D. Pedreschi, A survey of methods for explaining black box models, CSUR 51 (2018) 93.

[9] H. Lakkaraju, S. H. Bach, J. Leskovec, Interpretable decision sets: A joint framework for description and prediction, in: SIGKDD, 2016, pp. 1675–1684. URL: http://doi.acm.org/10.1145/2939672.2939874.

[10] M. Atzmueller, Subgroup discovery, Wiley Interdiscip. Rev. Data Min. Knowl. Discov. 5 (2015) 35–49.

[11] G. Papadakis, G. Mandilaras, L. Gagliardelli, G. Simonini, E. Thanos, G. Giannakopoulos, S. Bergamaschi, T. Palpanas, M. Koubarakis, Three-dimensional entity resolution with jedai, Information Systems 93 (2020).

[12] R. Singh, V. V. Meduri, A. K. Elmagarmid, S. Madden, P. Papotti, J. Quiané-Ruiz, A. Solar-Lezama, N. Tang, Synthesizing entity matching rules by examples, Proc. VLDB Endow. 11 (2017) 189–202.

[13] M. Paganelli, P. Sottovia, F. Guerra, Y. Velegrakis, Tuner: Fine tuning of rule-based entity matchers, in: CIKM, ACM, 2019, pp. 2945–2948.

[14] M. Ebraheem, S. Thirumuruganathan, S. R. Joty, M. Ouzzani, N. Tang, Distributed representations of tuples for entity resolution, Proc. VLDB Endow. 11 (2018) 1454–1467.

[15] S. Mudgal, H. Li, T. Rekatsinas, A. Doan, Y. Park, G. Krishnan, R. Deep, E. Arcaute, V. Raghavendra, Deep learning for entity matching: A design space exploration, in: SIGMOD Conference, ACM, 2018, pp. 19–34.

[16] Y. Li, J. Li, Y. Suhara, A. Doan, W.-C. Tan, Deep entity matching with pre-trained language models, Proc. VLDB Endow. 14 (2020) 50–60. URL: https://doi.org/10.14778/3421424.3421431. doi:10.14778/3421424.3421431.

[17] U. Brunner, K. Stockinger, Entity matching with transformer architectures - A step forward in data integration, in: EDBT, OpenProceedings.org, 2020, pp. 463–473.

[18] M. Du, N. Liu, X. Hu, Techniques for interpretable machine learning, Commun. ACM 63 (2020) 68–77.

[19] M. T. Ribeiro, S. Singh, C. Guestrin, " why should i trust you?" explaining the predictions of any classifier, in: Proceedings of the 22nd ACM SIGKDD, 2016, pp. 1135–1144.

[20] A. Ghorbani, J. Y. Zou, Data shapley: Equitable valuation of data for machine learning, in: ICML, volume 97 of *Proceedings of Machine Learning Research*, PMLR, 2019, pp. 2242–2251.

[21] V. D. Cicco, D. Firmani, N. Koudas, P. Merialdo, D. Srivastava, Interpreting deep learning models for entity resolution: an experience report using LIME, in: aiDM@SIGMOD, ACM, 2019, pp. 8:1–8:4.

[22] A. Baraldi, F. D. Buono, M. Paganelli, F. Guerra, Using landmarks for explaining entity matching models, in: EDBT, OpenProceedings.org, 2021, pp. 451–456.

Automatic Entity Labeling through Explanation Techniques

(Discussion Paper)

Silvana Castano[1], Alfio Ferrara[1], Donatella Firmani[2], Jerin George Mathew[3] and Stefano Montanelli[1]

[1]*Università degli Studi di Milano*
[2]*Università degli Studi Roma Tre*
[3]*Università di Roma Sapienza*

Abstract

Entity resolution (ER) aims at matching records that refer to the same real-world entity, e.g., the same product sold by different websites. Recent solutions to this problem have reached unprecedented accuracy. Nonetheless, due to intrinsic limitations of automatic testing methods, it is known among researchers and practitioners that a significant manual effort is still required in production environments for verification and cleaning of ER results. In order to facilitate such activity, we are developing the E2L methodology (**E**ntity **to** **L**abels) for automatic computation of human-readable labels of identified entities. Given a selection of entities for which the user wants to compute labels, E2L first extracts relevant features by training a classifier on the ER results, then it leverages the notion of *black-box model explanation* to select the most important terms for the classifier, and finally it uses those terms to compute labels. In this paper we report our first experiences with E2L. Preliminary results on a real-world application scenario show that E2L labels can provide an accurate description of entities and a natural way for humans to assess the trustworthiness of ER results at a glance.

1. Introduction

Entity Resolution (ER) is the task of finding records in a collection that refer to the same real-world entity. Recent works have investigated the application of machine learning (ML) and deep learning (DL) techniques, demonstrating impressive prediction accuracy [1]. Nonetheless, in production environments, humans are still required to manually inspect the entities identified by the ER process, in order to assess their trustworthiness. This can be a gruesome activity, especially when large datasets are considered, with entities consisting of hundreds of records. For this reason, tools for supporting the manual inspection of ER results and speeding up the search for possibly mismatched records are strongly demanded. Within this space, we focus on the problem of computing human-readable textual *labels* of identified entities, such as those in Table 1, which represent a natural way to support human comprehension of what is inside each clustered entity.

SEBD 2021: The 29th Italian Symposium on Advanced Database Systems, September 5-9, 2021, Pizzo Calabro (VV), Italy
silvana.castano@unimi.it (S. Castano); alfio.ferrara@unimi.it (A. Ferrara); donatella.firmani@uniroma3.it (D. Firmani); mathew@diag.uniroma1.it (J. G. Mathew); stefano.montanelli@unimi.it (S. Montanelli)

ID	Description	Resolution	Battery
1	Cannon EOS 1100D - Buy	32 mp	NULL
1	Camera Canon EOS 1100D	32000000 p	NP-400
1	...	...	...
2	Sony Ebay 4.7 stars	A7	NULL
2	...	...	...

(a)

ID	Entity Label
1	Canon EOS 1100D
2	Sony A7

(b)

Table 1
(a) Sample records from the dataset in our experiments. (b) Labels returned by E2L. The column entity "ID" shows the result of the ER process.

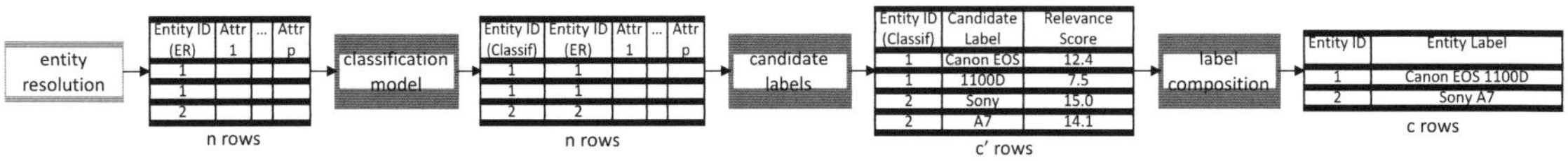

Figure 1: The E2L approach. The E2L components are shown in blue.

Already available solutions for analogous tasks (see Section 4) typically require some form of human intervention, such as, providing external knowledge (e.g., vocabularies) or a selection of sample labels for training. Fully-automated solutions instead are based on token frequencies (e.g., TF-IDF) which may perform poorly in datasets with skewed entity size distribution. Our main intuition is to exploit (i) recent methods to process natural language such as [2, 3] to discover meaningful patterns in the association between records and entities with no human effort, and (ii) recent *explainable techniques* such as [4] to reveal such patterns and make them human-readable, by selecting the salient information.

In this paper, we formalize these intuitions by presenting the E2L (**E**ntity **to** **L**abels) approach and report our experiences with a real world application scenario [5] where ER results need to be manually curated. Our current implementation, featuring two representative text classification methods [3, 2] and one popular explanation method [4] can achieve promising results and highlight errors in the ER results. A repository with all our data and scripts is publicly available for download at https://github.com/jermathew/E2L.

2. The E2L methodology

Let $R = \{r_1, \ldots, r_n\}$ be a collection of *record descriptions* referring to a set of entities $\hat{E} = \{e_1, \ldots, e_c\}$ with $n > c$. Each record $r \in R$ is related to an entity $e \in \hat{E}$, also referred as a *cluster* of records. Given two records $r_1 \in R, r_2 \in R$, we refer to them as *matching* records if they are associated to the same entity.

Our methodology, that we call E2L (**E**ntity **to** **L**abels), comprises the sequence of modules in Figure 1 as described below.

1. Classification model. Given a set of entities $E \subseteq \hat{E}$ that ought to be manually checked by the final user, E2L trains a classifier to learn a function $M : R \to E$, such that $M(r) = e$ denotes that the record $r \in R$ is associated with the entity e. In order to build the training set, we use standard text processing (e.g., stop-words removal) and *tokenization* techniques to represent a record $r \in R$ as sequence of tokens $T(r) = [t_1, \ldots, t_s]$. Resulting tokens can be either single terms (e.g. `Canon`) or *noun chunks*. A noun chunk provides a singleton representation of a composite noun (e.g., `digital camera`, `USA warranty`). Note that this step requires no human effort as association between records and entities required for training are selected directly from the input ER results.

2. Candidate labels. Each element $l \in \bigcup_{r \in R \text{ s.t. } M(r)=e} T(r)$ represents a *candidate label* for the entity e. Given an entity e, this module computes a real-valued *relevance score* ρ_l for each candidate label l by leveraging a *black-box explanation technique* over model M. Intuitively, consider a token $t \in T(r)$ and let $\hat{r}$ correspond to the record r without t. The candidate labels module assigns higher relevance score to tokens that yields more consistently $M(\hat{r}) \neq M(r)$, for all r s.t. $M(r) = e$. Specifically, we use LIME [4] as our black-box explanation technique. In order to compute relevance scores for a given record r and a model M, LIME creates a new set of records R_p by randomly removing tokens from r. In R_p, records are represented as binary vectors where each dimension corresponds to a different token. Then, given a class $e \in E$, each $r' \in R_p$ is labeled accordingly to whether $M(r') = e$ or not. Finally, LIME fits a linear model on R_p. Weights of the linear model represent how much each token contributed to $M(r)$. Given an entity e, the output of this module is a sorted list of candidate labels and associated relevance scores $L^e = [(l_1, \rho_{l_1}), (l_2, \rho_{l_2}), \ldots], \rho_{l_i} \geq \rho_{l_{i+1}}$.

We now describe the candidate labels module in more details. Let $R_e \subseteq R$ be the set of records that M associates to a given entity e, that is $R_e = \{r \in R \mid M(r) = e\}$. For each record $r \in R_e$ we submit its tokens $T(r)$ to the black-box explanation function in order to get their relevance scores $L_r^e = \{\langle t, \rho \rangle : t \in T(r), \rho \in \mathbb{R}\}$. Tokens with positive relevance are then sorted by non-increasing relevance value and selected until their cumulative relevance is greater or equal to a user-specified fraction $\beta \in [0, 1]$ of the total. As a result a selection $L_r^{e'} \subseteq L_r^e$ of tokens is obtained for the record r. The set of candidate labels L^e consists of the union of the selected tokens $L_r^{e'}$ for each $r \in R_e$, and, for each label t, the label relevance $L^e[t]$ is the sum of the relevance scores of $L_r^{e'}[t]$ over all the records in $r \in R_e$. We repeat these steps for each entity $e \in E$

Running the aforementioned steps can be infeasible if (i) R_e contains a massive number of records or (ii) records in R_e consist of thousands of tokens. In both cases, the black-box explanation function could take a significant amount of time to process R_e. In order to address both points, we include in E2L a record sampling step and a token sampling step – described below – to be optionally executed before the black-box model explanation computation.

(i) During the record sampling step, we aim at picking a subset $R'_e \subseteq R_e$ such that the tokens in R'_e cover most of the relevant tokens in R_e. In order to do so, we run the *k-means* clustering algorithm with parameter k_r on a vector representation [1] of the input records R_e and then, for each cluster, we select the closest record to its centroid based on ℓ^2-norm. As a result, we obtain k_r vectors from which we retrieve the corresponding records, which collectively make up R'_e. The value k_r, corresponding to the sample size, is set such that as the number of records $|R_e|$ grows, the fraction of sampled records decreases via linear interpolation.

[1]The selected vector representation can be arbitrarily chosen, e.g a tf-idf vector representing a record r or the mean word embedding of its constituent tokens

(ii) During the token sampling step, given a record $r \in R_e$ we aim at picking a selection $T'(r) \subseteq T(r)$ of its most representative tokens. To that end, given a record $r \in R_e$ we sort its tokens $T(r)$ based on their Term Frequency (TF) in decreasing order, prioritizing noun chunks over singleton text tokens. Afterwards, we select the top k_t tokens as those to be included in the sample for the record r. Analogously to the record sampling step, the value k_t is set via linear interpolation so that as the number of tokens in $T(r)$ grows, the fraction of selected tokens decreases.

3. Label composition. Candidate labels and associated relevance scores are finally processed to return to the user a label for each entity. Given a user parameter k, we return as label the composition (e.g concatenation) of the top k labels in L^e.

3. Experiences with E2L

The E2L approach is evaluated on the `camera` dataset in the Alaska Benchmark, an end-to-end benchmark tailored for a variety of tasks related to Data Integration, including ER [5], and has been recently used for the 2020 SIGMOD Programming Contest[2] and for the two editions of the DI2KG challenge[3]. The dataset comprises i) a set of camera descriptions collected over different web sources, and ii) a manually-curated ground truth consisting of camera names (i.e., brand name and model name) for each description, such that multiple descriptions can refer to the same camera. In the evaluation, we take into account the 20 entities with the highest number of records, ranging from 184 to 53 records per entity. The resulting dataset consists of 2171 records. We use the `page_title` attribute from each description to compose a dataset (hereinafter called Alaska dataset) as a list of <page_title>,<model_name> pairs, where <model_name> represents the correct label expected for each group of descriptions referring to the same camera. The longest `page_title` field in the dataset contains 42 words, while the shortest one contains 3 words.

Our experiments were performed on a server environment using an Intel Xeon E5-2966 v4 CPU, 512 GB of RAM, and 4 NVIDIA Tesla P100-SXM2 GPUs. The operating system is Ubuntu 17.10.

Classification model. We exploited two models, a LSTM-based neural network [6] and a pretrained DistilBERT model [2], and we generated two versions of E2L, namely E2L-Bert and E2L-Glove. The LSTM-based network consists of a pre-trained embedding layer based on GloVe [3] followed by a bidirectional LSTM (Bi-LSTM) layer whose memory dimension is 100. The output of the last time step in the Bi-LSTM is then fed to a fully connected layer of size 64 using ReLu as the activation function. Finally, the resulting output is passed to a fully connected layer of size 20 where softmax is used as the activation function. As for the second model, we leveraged the Transformers library [4] to set up a pretrained DistilBERT model for a multiclass classification task. This model comprises two parts: the body, consisting in a pretrained DistilBERT model, and a classification head on top of the body whose last layer consists in a fully connected layer

[2]http://www.inf.uniroma3.it/db/sigmod2020contest

[3]http://di2kg.inf.uniroma3.it

[4]https://github.com/huggingface/transformers

of size 20 with softmax as the activation function.

Baselines. As baselines for comparison against E2L, we exploit two different approaches for entity labeling, named TFIDF and BART. The choice of TFIDF is motivated by the fact that this is almost a standard solution for terminology retrieval and it provides good results on the entity labeling task. The choice of BART is motivated by the idea of comparing E2L against a solution for document summarization, based on the idea that summarizing entity descriptions is an effective way to enforce entity labeling. Both approaches start by joining the `page_title` fields referring to the same camera name in the Alaska dataset. This way, we obtain a set P of 20 pseudo-descriptions, one for each camera. These pseudo-descriptions are then tokenized by exploiting the same procedure used in E2L.

- For the TFIDF baseline, we compute Tf-Idf on P. Then, for each pseudo-description $p \in P$, tokens are sorted by their Tf-Idf weights in descending order.
- As for the BART baseline, we feed each $p \in P$ to a pretrained BART model, namely `BART.large.cnn` [7]. As a result, we obtain a summary of p, that is a concise and shorter version of b. Then, we tokenize and process the summary as in the E2L approach. Tokens are sorted according to their position.

3.1. Experimental comparison

Let be $L^e_m = [(l_1, \rho_{l_1}), (l_2, \rho_{l_2}), \dots]$ a list of candidate labels for the entity e produced by the approach m, either one of the E2L versions or one of the baselines, sorted by their relevance score ρ_l from the most relevant to the less relevant. For each label e, we know the gold label t_e (i.e., the correct camera name) and we aim to evaluate the capability of E2L to build t_e by combining the candidate labels in L^e_m. Moreover, we aim to assess how many of the L^e_m labels we need to employ to obtain exactly the gold label t_e. The effectiveness of an entity labeling solution can be measured by observing how many candidate labels are required to obtain the gold label. The lower is the number of needed candidates (taken with relevance score in descending order), the higher is the effectiveness. According to this, the quality of each approach is measured as follows. First, we create the set T_{t_e} of the tokens in the gold label t_e, by extracting single terms (i.e., separated by spaces). Then, we do the same for the most relevant candidate label l_1, by defining T_{l_1} as the set of tokens of l_1. Given T_{t_e}, we define $T^m_1 = T_{l_1}$ and we evaluate precision (P^m_1) and recall (R^m_1) of m at candidate 1 as:

$$P^m_1 = \frac{\mid T_{t_e} \cap T^m_1 \mid}{\mid T^m_1 \mid}; \; R^m_1 = \frac{\mid T_{t_e} \cap T^m_1 \mid}{\mid T_{t_e} \mid}$$

This process is repeated for each of the k top candidate labels produced by m. At each step $k > 1$, we define T^m_k as:

$$T^m_k = T^m_{k-1} \cup T_{l_k}.$$

The F1-measure (F^m_k) at k is the harmonic mean of P^m_k and R^m_k. By exploiting these measures of precision and recall at k, we can easily check when the gold label t_e has been completely obtained (i.e., the k value where we have $R^m_k = 1$) and how many wrong tokens we have

	Avg. P^*_m	$P^*_m = 1$	$P^*_m = 1$ (fraction)
TFIDF	0.84	12	0.6
BART	0.71	7	0.35
E2L-Glove	0.86	14	0.7
E2L-Bert	**0.92**	**17**	**0.85**

Table 2
Precision at full coverage.

Merged Clusters	TFIDF	E2L-Bert
canon eos 7d (178), nikon 1 j3 (54)	canon eos 7d 013803117493 ebay 18	canon eos 7d 1 nikon j3
nikon d610 (79), nikon d3300 (79), nikon 1 j1 (78)	10 j1 nikon d610 ebay	j1 d610 nikon d3300
nikon d5200 (144), nikon d5100 (137), nikon d7000 (130)	nikon d7000 16 d5100	d7000 d5100 d5200 nikon

Table 3
Clusters are denoted by their gold label and cluster sizes are reported between parentheses.

collected during the process (i.e., P^m_k). Thus, we measure the overall quality of E2L and the baselines through the notion of *Precision at full coverage* (P^*_m) that is defined as follows:

$$P^*_m = P^m_k : R^m_k = 1$$

In Table 2, we report the values of precision at full coverage (P^*_m) for all the approaches, together with the number and fraction of entities that are correctly retrieved when recall is equal to 1 (i.e., $P^*_m = 1$), which means that the gold label has been not only completely retrieved by also retrieved by not introducing any noisy token, that is with no errors. The experimental results show that the use of black-box explanation techniques in E2L allows to extract relevant terminology for composing the correct label of entities as a final stage in a ER process. Indeed, if the statistical techniques seem to be effective for retrieving relevant terminology, they appear also to be more prone to introduce noisy terms in the candidate labels. On the other hand, data summaries, especially for text, tend to produce longer descriptions that are not enough synthetic to be taken as a good entity label. By contrast, the terms found by E2L appear as a good compromise in that they are more specifically related to the entities at hand, but also short enough to be useful for the task of labeling entities.

ER errors. Limitations of statistical techniques such as TFIDF are even clearer when there are errors in the input ER results. Consider for instance *entity merge errors*, where different real-world entities are mis-clustered as one entity. Table 3 reports preliminary results on a selection of clusters with different sizes from our Alaska dataset. Specifically, we considered clusters of different sizes, merged them, and computed labels with TFIDF and E2L-Bert. In the table, we show the labels with k equal to the size of the gold label for each of the considered merged clusters. In presence of merge errors, statistical techniques like TFIDF fail at identifying relevant terminology for all the sub-clusters in the merged cluster, while E2L-Bert can return the labels corresponding to the merged entities, thus supporting manual inspection of results and error detection.

4. Related work

Works related to the proposed E2L approach are about *entity labeling* as well as *machine learning interpretation.*

Entity labeling. A number of solutions has been proposed in the literature for entity labeling intended as the problem of finding a representative label to a set of records that refers to the same real-world object. A common solution is based on the idea to rely on an external knowledge base that works as a reference vocabulary for selecting the most appropriate label to assign to a given entity [8]. Entity labeling can be considered as a task of semantic data mining where labels emerge from record descriptions and they are selected according to the results of text processing techniques usually based on conventional information retrieval metrics (e.g., [9]). Machine learning techniques are also employed for entity labeling [10]. Automatic solutions to entity labeling can be integrated within *human-in-the-loop* workflows where domain experts are involved to validate the results of automated solutions (e.g., [11]).

Machine learning interpretation. In the recent years there was a surge of interest in the novel field of *interpretability* (see [12]). Explanation techniques can be distinguished between *black-box* and *white-box*. The former come with a model-agnostic interface while the latter rely on the internal mechanisms of the model. In E2L, we adopt LIME [4] that is a widely-employed black-box method. Other methods in the same category include SHAP [13] and Anchor [14].

5. Future Work

In this paper, we presented the E2L approach to entity labeling based on the use of techniques for classification and model explanation. Our current implementation features two representative text classification methods [3, 2] and one popular explanation method [4]. We plan as future works the inclusion of a wider choice of text classification and the inclusion of more explanation methods, such as SHAP [13] and Anchor [14].

Furthermore, a limitation of the current approach is that it depends on the ability of a supervised classifier to capture the entity properties. In principle, if the classifier is underperforming, the extracted labels can be less satisfactory. A simple solution could consists in training an ensemble of different models (as opposed to a single classifier) and select labels by using a voting system. A more sophisticated solution could be to model the ER process as a binary model indicating whether two records are matching and then apply directly the explanation engine, analogously to [15]. This can be non-trivial and it is left as future work. Indeed (i) computing pair-wise explanations exhaustively can be unfeasible for large datasets and (ii) different record pairs in the same entity can be matched for different reasons (e.g., some camera pairs could share only the model name while others could share not only the model name but also other technical specifications) and thus important tokens may vary significantly among pairs.

References

[1] Y. Li, J. Li, Y. Suhara, A. Doan, W.-C. Tan, Deep entity matching with pre-trained language models, arXiv:2004.00584 (2020).

[2] V. Sanh, L. Debut, J. Chaumond, T. Wolf, Distilbert, a distilled version of bert: smaller, faster, cheaper and lighter, arXiv:1910.01108 (2019).

[3] J. Pennington, R. Socher, C. D. Manning, Glove: Global vectors for word representation, in: EMNLP, 2014, pp. 1532–1543.

[4] M. T. Ribeiro, S. Singh, C. Guestrin, "Why Should I Trust you?" Explaining the Predictions of Any Classifier, in: KDD, 2016, pp. 1135–1144.

[5] V. Crescenzi, A. De Angelis, D. Firmani, M. Mazzei, P. Merialdo, F. Piai, D. Srivastava, Alaska: A flexible benchmark for data integration tasks, arXiv:2101.11259 (2021).

[6] S. Hochreiter, J. Schmidhuber, Long short-term memory, Neural computation 9 (1997) 1735–1780.

[7] M. Lewis, Y. Liu, N. Goyal, M. Ghazvininejad, A. Mohamed, O. Levy, V. Stoyanov, L. Zettlemoyer, Bart: Denoising sequence-to-sequence pre-training for natural language generation, translation, and comprehension, arXiv preprint arXiv:1910.13461 (2019).

[8] D. Dou, H. Wang, H. Liu, Semantic Data Mining: A Survey of Ontology-based Approaches, in: ICSC, 2015, pp. 244–251.

[9] X. Sun, Y. Xiao, H. Wang, W. Wang, On Conceptual Labeling of a Bag of Words, in: Int. Joint Conference on Artificial Intelligence, 2015.

[10] F. N. C. de Araújo, V. P. Machado, A. H. M. Soares, R. de M.S. Veras, Automatic Cluster Labeling Based on Phylogram Analysis, in: IJCNN, 2018, pp. 1–8.

[11] D. R. Karger, S. Oh, D. Shah, Efficient Crowdsourcing for Multi-class Labeling, in: SIGMETRICS, 2013, pp. 81–92.

[12] Z. C. Lipton, The Mythos of Model Interpretability, ACM Queue 16 (2018) 31–57.

[13] S. M. Lundberg, S.-I. Lee, A Unified Approach to Interpreting Model Predictions, in: Advances in Neural Information Processing Systems, 2017, pp. 4765–4774.

[14] M. T. Ribeiro, S. Singh, C. Guestrin, Anchors: High-precision Model-agnostic Explanations, in: Proc. of the 32th AAAI Conf. on Artificial Intelligence, 2018.

[15] V. D. Cicco, D. Firmani, N. Koudas, P. Merialdo, D. Srivastava, Interpreting deep learning models for entity resolution: an experience report using LIME, in: aiDM@SIGMOD, 2019, pp. 8:1–8:4.

A software pipeline for pre-processing and mining EEG signals: application in neurology

(Discussion Paper)

Chiara Zucco[1], Barbara Calabrese[1], Miriam Sturniolo[2], Antonio Gambardella[2] and Mario Cannataro[1]

[1]*Department of Medical and Surgical Sciences, University "Magna Græcia", Catanzaro*
[2]*Mater Domini Polyclinic, University "Magna Græcia", Catanzaro*

Abstract
Psychogenic non-epileptic seizures (PNES) resemble epileptic seizures, but they do not show the characteristic electrical discharges associated with epileptic seizures. Long term video monitoring combined with EEG recording is the gold standard in clinical practice, but this methodology is quite expensive and time-consuming. This paper presents a software pipeline to discriminate short-term interictal EEG from PNES and epileptic patients. The pipeline supports EEG signals pre-processing, features selection and classification. A first case study concerning the classification of 75 EEG (healthy, PNES and epileptic subjects) is under evaluation.

Keywords
EEG, Psychogenic Non-Epileptic Seizures, Machine Learning, pre-processing

1. Introduction

Psychogenic non-epileptic seizures (PNES) are sudden behavioural changes mimicking epileptic seizures but without EEG ictal patterns, caused by psychic alterations [1], [2]. PNES have been associated to a dysfunction in the processing of psychological or social distress, abuse during childhood or severe traumatic events [3], [4]. In [5], the authors reported an aggravation of the seizure frequency in PNES patients, a vulnerable group of people during this pandemic COVID-19.

Misdiagnosis with epilepsy may lead to treatments through antiepileptic drugs (AEDs) with the risk of iatrogenic morbidity and elevated cost for the patient and Health Care Systems [6]. It has been discovered that the correct diagnosis of PNES is usually delayed for an average of seven years [7], with a profound impact on patients and caregivers quality of life. The gold standard for PNES diagnosis is represented by the visual examination of seizures captured during video-electroencephalography (video-EEG), either spontaneously or provoked by intermittent photic stimulation (IPS) suggestion techniques. These methods are time-consuming and ethically

SEBD 2021: The 29th Italian Symposium on Advanced Database Systems, September 5-9, 2021, Pizzo Calabro (VV), Italy
zucco@unicz.it (C. Zucco); calabreseb@unicz.it (B. Calabrese); sturniolom@yahoo.it (M. Sturniolo); a.gambardella@unicz.it (A. Gambardella); cannataro@unicz.it (M. Cannataro)
0000-0003-0048-0457 (C. Zucco); 0000-0003-2123-8221 (B. Calabrese); 0000-0001-7384-3074 (A. Gambardella); 0000-0003-1502-2387 (M. Cannataro)

disputable; thus, since the experts evaluate no definite criterion, visual analysis of EEG signals is insufficient. The International League Against Epilepsy (ILAE), using a consensus review of literature, evaluated fundamental diagnostic approaches, including detailed history and seizures description, EEG, video-EEG, neurophysiology, neuroimaging, hypnosis, and neuro-humoral monitoring [6].

To the best of our knowledge, only a few studies have investigated semi-automatic or automatic machine learning-based approaches for discrimination between epileptic and PNES subjects by only considering EEG recordings. The current study is one of the few in which an EEG dataset, without any correlated video-EEG PNES marker, has been analyzed to discriminate PNES via EEG.

Specifically, this paper proposes a novel and semi-automatic pipeline to discriminate PNES subjects from epileptic subjects based on the extraction of spectral features and classification through a Machine Learning-based approach. To design a software pipeline that allows discrimination, we have implemented different classifiers, i.e. Support Vector Machine (SVM), Linear Discriminant Analysis (LDA), Bayesian Network (BN). In this work, we have analyzed EEG recordings of twenty-five PNES subjects, twenty-five healthy volunteer subjects and twenty-five epileptic patients.

The paper is organized as follows: Section 2 presents the background relative to EEG analysis and classification, focusing on PNES discrimination; Section 3 describes experimental EEG acquisitions. Section 4 presents and discusses the proposed software pipeline, highlighting the features of software modules. Finally, Section 5 concludes the paper.

2. Background on EEG analysis and classification

The EEG signals are random and non-stationary and may contain valuable information about the brain state with millisecond temporal resolution. However, it isn't effortless to disentangle information from these signals directly in the time domain by observing them. EEG spectrum contains some characteristic waveforms that fall primarily within five frequency bands: delta (1--4 Hz), theta (4--8 Hz), alpha (8--13 Hz), beta (13--30 Hz) and gamma (30–60 Hz). Many efforts have been made for automatic and semi-automatic EEG processing by exploiting several algorithms that operate in time, frequency, or the time-frequency domain. Among the time domain (TD) features, Mean Absolute Value (MAV), Zero Crossings (ZC), Slope Sign Changes (SSC) and Waveform Length (WL) are some examples. Fourier Transform (FT) and Power Spectral Analysis (PSD) are the most common features extracted in the frequency domain. The most used methods are Wavelet Transform (WT) and Hilbert - Huang Transform in the time-frequency domain.

There are many studies on EEG data analysis. The work [8] describes a new method to identify seizures in EEG signals using feature extraction in time-frequency distributions (CFDs). In [9], the authors analyze the differences in power spectral density between healthy subjects and schizophrenic patients in various frequency bands. Moreover, frequency and time-frequency approaches have been applied for analysis of patients with brain damage [10], automatic detection of epileptic seizures [11] and, also, early detection of mild cognitive impairment and Alzheimer's disease [12].

Various data mining techniques such as Association Rule, classification, regression, and clustering have been used in the literature. Support vector machine (SVM) is a machine learning model used for classification, and regression analysis [13].

Differential diagnosis cannot rely only on clinical features of PNES because most of the signs fit with epileptic seizures. Longer duration, gradual onset, asynchronous movement, closed eyes, lateralized head movement contribute to a complex clinical pattern of PNES. These events are involuntary and out of the patient's conscious control. PNES patients mimic the different type of epileptic seizures but no epileptic seizures electrophysiological patterns. Thus discrimination would be useful to aid neurologist diagnosis and consequently assign the right pharmacological treatment. The prevalence of PNES is high in selected populations: 5--20% in outpatient epilepsy populations [14], [15]. 10--40 % of patients referred to tertiary epilepsy centers for medically refractory seizures [16]. Making PNES diagnosis is soupy with medico-legal hazards, and it is hard to prove [17].

EEG recordings alone are not sufficient to diagnose PNES: an ictal scalp EEG may show no epileptic features during simple partial seizures or mesial frontal lobe seizures. The latter may be easily mistaken for PNES. The differentiation between non-epileptic seizures and healthy subject can be difficult. Therefore, a good knowledge of the semiology of PNES is essential for the early screening of patients for video-EEG monitoring (VEM) and correct interpretation of the examination. PNES should also be differentiated from physiological, non-epileptic events such as syncope, cataplexy, migraine, paroxysmal movement disorders, breath-holding spells, stable ictal heart rate [18].

Additionally, VEM monitoring is highly time-consuming and labour intensive and therefore is relatively expensive and limited in availability; thus, alternative diagnostic procedures are necessary.

Despite many efforts made, no bio-marker of PNES has yet been identified. In [19], the authors sustain patients with PNES have a stable frequency of rhythmic movements, about (5Hz), which produces a stable rhythmic artefact on the EEG with little variation or evolution. Bolen et al. [20] have noted significantly more multifocal abnormalities in frontal, temporal, parietal, occipital, cerebellar and brainstem brain regions PNES patients.

Continuous wavelet transform is used in [21] to process CNT and PNES EEG signal.

In [22], a machine learning (ML) pipeline for classifying EEG epochs of PNES and healthy controls is introduced. This software pipeline consisted of a semi-automatic signal processing technique and a supervised ML classifier to aid the discriminative clinical diagnosis of PNES. Statistical features like the mean, standard deviation, kurtosis, and skewness were extracted from a power spectral density (PSD) map split up into the five conventional EEG rhythms. Finally, we evaluated three different supervised ML algorithms, namely, the Support Vector Machine (SVM), Linear Discriminant Analysis (LDA), and Bayesian network (BN), to perform EEG classification tasks for control vs PNES subjects. The algorithm's performance was evaluated on a dataset of 20 EEG signals (10 PNES and 10 control), achieving an average accuracy above 90 %.

3. EEG signals acquisition

The data under evaluation were collected from the Operative Unit of Neurology, Mater Domini Polyclinic, University of Catanzaro, Italy. In this study, we analyzed EEG recordings from 25 patients with PNES, 25 healthy patients referred to as CNT and 25 epileptic patients. PNES diagnosis was made based on a typical episode recorded during video-EEG, with EEG showing neither concomitant ictal activity nor post-ictal. Healthy controls did not suffer from any neurological disorder and had a normal neurological examination. None of the subjects was on chronic medication or had received any drug up to 24 hours before EEG acquisition. The study was conducted following the Declaration of Helsinki and formally approved by the local Medical Research Ethics Committee. Participants were comfortably seated in a semi-darkened room and with open eyes. The technician kept the subject alert in order to prevent drowsiness.

EEG recordings were conducted in poorly light-room using 19 Ag/AgCl surface electrodes placed according to the International 10/20 System. Recordings were performed with a Xltek® Brain Monitor EEG Amplifier with a sampling rate of 256 Hz; high-pass filter at 0.5 Hz and a low-pass filter at 70 Hz, plus a 50 Hz notch filter. All of the EEG signals were recorded using a montage with the following channels layout: Fp1, Fp2, F3, F4, C3, C4, P3, P4, O1, O2, F7, F8, T3, T4, T5, T6, Fz, Cz and Pz, and reference in Pz.

All the electrode-skin impedance has been kept below 5 KΩ. The EEG data were recorded in a resting condition. Each participant was seated in a comfortable chair in an electrically and acoustically shielded room. EEG artefacts were rejected through a semi-automatic procedure: (i) first artefacts components were individuated through clinical (visual) inspection; (ii) all signal segments affected by evident artifactual components are cut off from raw EEG data.

4. EEG software pipeline

The architecture of the proposed EEG software pipeline (written in Python language) presents the following modules:

- Pre-processing: this module performs digital filtering and semi-automatic artefact rejection;
- Features extraction: Power Spectral Density (PSD) function is evaluated for each channel by using Welch's method. From PSD functions, cumulative power coefficients in clinical bands are calculated to build features vector to fed in input to the classifiers;
- Features selection: searches for the most significant features for classification;
- EEG classification: the framework implements different machine learning approaches, such as Support Vector Machine, Bayesian Networks and Linear Discriminant Analysis to discriminate PNES EEG from CNT EEG.

The rest of the section details the features of each module.

4.1. EEG Pre-processing

In general, EEG signals are contaminated by environmental noise or even distorted by artefacts. Removing noise is an important step in EEG signals processing. A correct data cleaning may improve the signal to noise ratio and helps to disentangle the most informative features from the signal. Even if different semi-automatic approaches have been proposed for EEG pre-processing, in clinical practice, the rejection of artefacts is performed manually by trained neurologists by discarding contaminated EEG epochs. Therefore, the pre-processing stage is operator-dependent, tedious and time-consuming.

In this study, each EEG recording was checked by a trained neurologist to marker noise and artefact corrupted epoch. Subsequently, all EEG data were pre-processed using digital filtering techniques. Specifically, we have used a Butterworth band-pass filter (0.1-70 Hz) and a notch filter (cut-off frequency 50 Hz) to reduce high-frequency artefacts and power-line interference.

4.2. EEG Features Extraction

After the pre-processing step, the next step in the EEG software pipeline is the features extraction stage. As mentioned before, features extraction aims to extract relevant information contained in the signals. One of the most used features extractor in EEG signals processing is the Power Spectral Density (PSD) analysis. Different methods for PSD estimation have been reported in the literature. We have chosen Welch's method.

Welch Spectrum Welch's method is a well-known non-parametric method for PSD estimation. Let be $x[n]$, $n = 0, \cdots, N-1$ are the samples from an EEG segment. To estimate the Welch's spectrum of this segment, three basic steps are applied:

- First, divide the original EEG time series into N sections (possibly overlapped O) of equal lengths M;

$$x\lfloor n \rfloor = x\lfloor n + iO \rfloor \qquad i = 0, \dots K-1, \text{ and } n = 0, \dots N-1 \tag{1}$$

- Apply a window to each section and then calculate the periodogram on the windowed sections (modified periodograms). The periodogram is defined as:

$$\tilde{S}_{xx}(k) = \frac{1}{N} \left| \sum_{n=0}^{N-1} x(n) e^{-\frac{2\pi jkn}{N}} \right|^2. \tag{2}$$

- Average the modified periodograms from the K sections in order to obtain an estimator of the spectral density.

$$P_{yx}(f) = \frac{1}{K} \sum_{i=0}^{K-1} P_i(f) \tag{3}$$

Where P_{yx} estimates the cross power spectral density of two discrete-time signals, x and y, the Welch method eliminates the tradeoff between spectral resolution and variance by allowing the segments to overlap. If a high-frequency resolution is desired, one can only split the record into a small number N of segments of length L. In system identification, the number of segments K is typically 2,3, 6. Unfortunately, a small number of segments K implies a higher variance of the estimated power spectrum. Therefore, it is worth looking into methods using overlapping sub-records for reducing the variance as the main processing algorithm remains unchanged. Our analysis uses a segment with 50% overlap for the first step and the Hamming window in the second step.

In this paper, power spectral density (PSD) of classical frequency bands from around 1 Hz to 70 Hz were used as features. Specifically, delta (1-4 Hz), theta (4-8 Hz), alpha (8-13 Hz), beta (13-30 Hz), gamma (30-70 Hz) bands have been considered.

The main processing steps of our feature extraction approach are:

- Power Spectral Density (PSD) was estimated trough Welch method;
- from PSD matrix output, we selected five frequency sub-bands;
- for each band we computed cumulative power.

All features extracted are arranged into a vector, known as a features vector.

4.3. Features Selection and EEG Classification

Features selection is useful in the presence of high-dimensional data as it reduces the space of the features. This module is still under implementation. To discriminate CNT EEG from PNES EEG, we have implemented three supervised Machine Learning algorithms. The classi⊠ers used in this paper are the SVM, LDA, and BNs.

The SVM algorithm is based on the statistical learning theory. An SVM [23] constructs a separating hyperplane or a set of hyperplanes in a high dimensional space. Intuitively, a good separation is achieved by the hyperplane with the largest distance to the nearest training data points of any class (so-called functional margin).

Bayesian networks (BNs) [20], also known as belief networks, belong to probabilistic graphical models (GMs). These structures are used to extract knowledge about an uncertain domain. Each node in the graph represents a random variable, while the edges between the nodes represent probabilistic dependencies among the corresponding random variables. The graph dependencies are estimated by using known statistical and computational methods. Hence, Bayesian Networks provide a simple definition of independence between any two distinct nodes.

LDA classifier is one of the classification methods that finds an optimal linear transformation that maximizes the class separability. LDA generates a linear combination of data sets that allows the largest mean differences between the desired classes. It works well when the feature vector is multivariate normally distributed in each class group, and different groups have a common covariance.

5. Conclusions

The main contribution of this paper is a comprehensive software pipeline written in Python for the acquisition, pre-processing and classification of EEG signals. A first experimentation of the pipeline in the classification of PNES vs epileptic subject is under evaluation by the clinical team of the Neurology Unit of the University Magna Græcia of Catanzaro. The preliminary results show that a features selection phase is necessary to improve the performance of the classification.

References

[1] N. M. G. Bodde, J. L. Brooks, G. A. Baker, P. A. J. M. Boon, J. G. M. Hendriksen, O. G. Mulder, A. P. Aldenkamp, Psychogenic non-epileptic seizures–definition, etiology, treatment and prognostic issues: a critical review, Seizure 18 (2009) 543–553.

[2] S. Gasparini, M. Campolo, C. Ieracitano, N. Mammone, E. Ferlazzo, C. Sueri, G. G. Tripodi, U. Aguglia, F. C. Morabito, Information Theoretic-Based interpretation of a deep neural network approach in diagnosing psychogenic Non-Epileptic seizures, Entropy 20 (2018) 43.

[3] G. Baslet, A. Roiko, E. Prensky, Heterogeneity in psychogenic nonepileptic seizures: understanding the role of psychiatric and neurological factors, Epilepsy Behav. 17 (2010) 236–241.

[4] A. A. Uliaszek, E. Prensky, G. Baslet, Emotion regulation profiles in psychogenic non-epileptic seizures, Epilepsy Behav. 23 (2012) 364–369.

[5] A. R. B. G. M. R. d. S. B. P. A. Valente, K.D., The covid-19 outbreak and pnes: The impact of a ubiquitously felt stressor, Epilepsy Behavior 117 (2021).

[6] W. C. LaFrance, Jr, S. R. Benbadis, Avoiding the costs of unrecognized psychological nonepileptic seizures, Neurology 66 (2006) 1620–1621.

[7] M. Reuber, T. Kral, M. Kurthen, C. E. Elger, New-onset psychogenic seizures after intracranial neurosurgery, Acta Neurochir. 144 (2002) 901–7; discussion 907.

[8] C. Guerrero-Mosquera, A. M. Trigueros, J. I. Franco, A. Navia-Vázquez, New feature extraction approach for epileptic EEG signal detection using time-frequency distributions, Med. Biol. Eng. Comput. 48 (2010) 321–330.

[9] Y. Akbar, S. N. Khotimah, F. Haryanto, Spectral and brain mapping analysis of EEG based on pwelch in schizophrenic patients, in: Journal of Physics: Conference Series, volume 694, 2016, p. 012070.

[10] M. P. Davey, J. D. Victor, N. D. Schiff, Power spectra and coherence in the EEG of a vegetative patient with severe asymmetric brain damage, Clin. Neurophysiol. 111 (2000) 1949–1954.

[11] A. T. Tzallas, M. G. Tsipouras, D. I. Fotiadis, Epileptic seizure detection in EEGs using Time–Frequency analysis, IEEE Trans. Inf. Technol. Biomed. 13 (2009) 703–710.

[12] J. C. McBride, X. Zhao, N. B. Munro, C. D. Smith, G. A. Jicha, L. Hively, L. S. Broster, F. A. Schmitt, R. J. Kryscio, Y. Jiang, Spectral and complexity analysis of scalp EEG characteristics for mild cognitive impairment and early alzheimer's disease, Comput. Methods Programs Biomed. 114 (2014) 153–163.

[13] I. Guler, E. D. Ubeyli, Multiclass support vector machines for EEG-Signals classification, 2007.

[14] A. A. Leis, M. A. Ross, A. K. Summers, Psychogenic seizures: ictal characteristics and diagnostic pitfalls, Neurology 42 (1992) 95–99.

[15] GATES, J. R, The classification and treatment of nonepileptic events, Epilepsy and behavior (1991).

[16] R. Martin, J. G. Burneo, A. Prasad, T. Powell, E. Faught, R. Knowlton, M. Mendez, R. Kuzniecky, Frequency of epilepsy in patients with psychogenic seizures monitored by video-EEG, Neurology 61 (2003) 1791–1792.

[17] S. R. Benbadis, Nonepileptic behavioral disorders, 2013.
[18] C. Opherk, L. J. Hirsch, Ictal heart rate differentiates epileptic from non-epileptic seizures, Neurology 58 (2002) 636–638.
[19] A. Vinton, J. Carino, S. Vogrin, L. MacGregor, C. Kilpatrick, Z. Matkovic, T. O'Brien, Convulsive nonepileptic seizures have a characteristic pattern of rhythmic artifact distinguishing them from convulsive epileptic seizures, Epilepsia 45 (2004) 1344–1350.
[20] R. D. Bolen, E. H. Koontz, P. B. Pritchard, 3rd, Prevalence and distribution of MRI abnormalities in patients with psychogenic nonepileptic events, Epilepsy Behav. 59 (2016) 73–76.
[21] S. Gasparini, E. Beghi, E. Ferlazzo, M. Beghi, V. Belcastro, K. P. Biermann, G. Bottini, G. Capovilla, R. A. Cervellione, V. Cianci, G. Coppola, C. M. Cornaggia, P. De Fazio, S. De Masi, G. De Sarro, M. Elia, G. Erba, L. Fusco, A. Gambardella, V. Gentile, A. T. Giallonardo, R. Guerrini, F. Ingravallo, A. Iudice, A. Labate, E. Lucenteforte, A. Magaudda, L. Mumoli, C. Papagno, G. B. Pesce, E. Pucci, P. Ricci, A. Romeo, R. Quintas, C. Sueri, G. Vitaliti, R. Zoia, U. Aguglia, Management of psychogenic non-epileptic seizures: a multidisciplinary approach, Eur. J. Neurol. 26 (2019) 205–e15.
[22] G. Varone, S. Gasparini, E. Ferlazzo, M. Ascoli, G. G. Tripodi, C. Zucco, B. Calabrese, M. Cannataro, U. Aguglia, A comprehensive machine-learning-based software pipeline to classify eeg signals: A case study on pnes vs. control subjects, Sensors 20 (2020).
[23] K.-R. Muller, K. R. Muller, S. Mika, G. Ratsch, K. Tsuda, B. Scholkopf, An introduction to kernel-based learning algorithms, 2001.

Cataplexy Detection: Neurologists, You Are Not Alone!

(Discussion Paper)

Ilaria Bartolini[1], Andrea Di Luzio[1]

[1]Department of Computer Science and Engineering (DISI), Alma Mater Studiorum, University of Bologna, Italy

Abstract

Narcolepsy with cataplexy is a severe lifelong disorder characterized, among the others, by the sudden loss of bilateral face muscle tone triggered by emotions (cataplexy). In this extended abstract, we present two methodologies for the automatic analysis of patients' videos able to assist neurologists in diagnosing the disease and/or detecting attacks. Indeed, recent findings demonstrated that the detection of abnormal motor behaviors in video recordings of patients undergoing emotional stimulation is effective in characterizing the disease symptoms. Such motor behaviors (ptosis, mouth opening, head drop) are however to be discovered by neurologists through manual inspection of patients' videos. Automatic content-based video analysis is clearly of immediate help here. Experimental results conducted on real data support the effectiveness of the presented automated techniques.

Keywords

Video-based classification of cataplexy, automatic video content analysis, motor behavior patterns, data analysis for health

1. Introduction

Narcolepsy with cataplexy is a rare disorder mainly arising in young adults/children characterized by daytime sleepiness, sudden loss of muscle tone while awake triggered by emotional stimuli (cataplexy), hallucinations, sleep paralysis, and disturbed nocturnal sleep [13]. A recent approach for the detection of the disease is based on an analysis of video recordings of patients undergoing emotional stimulation made *on-site* by medical specialists [16]. According to this methodology, cataplexy is present if any of three abnormal motor behaviors is detected in the patient video: *ptosis* (a drooping or falling of the upper eyelid), *head drop*, and *smile/mouth opening* [13]. Such patterns are, however, still to be manually detected by neurologists through visual inspection of videos. This is due to the complete absence of automatic technological solutions able to properly support neurologists in such a delicate task.

It is evident that a tool able to detect the "correct" facial expression changes (i.e., the disease symptoms) from video recordings of patients would be able to automatically identify the presence of the disease. This could be extremely helpful, not only to support neurologists in diagnosing the disease, but also in monitoring everyday activities in a non-invasive way to

SEBD 2021: The 29th Italian Symposium on Advanced Database Systems, September 5-9, 2021, Pizzo Calabro (VV), Italy

ilaria.bartolini@unibo.it (I. Bartolini); andrea.diluzio2@unibo.it (A. Di Luzio)

provide early warnings in the event of the insurgence of a crisis. Indeed, it is well known that the synergistic use of Machine Learning (ML) techniques can help in alleviating the burden of the medical specialist in analyzing patient data, thus improving diagnostic consistency and accuracy [10].

In [2], we introduced the CAT-CAD (Computer Aided Diagnosis for CATaplexy) tool, which exploits ML techniques for the automatic analysis of video recordings made on patients undergoing emotional stimulation through the vision of funny movies designed to evoke the laughter. By means of a user friendly GUI, CAT-CAD effectively supports neurologists with (1) the automatic detection of disease symptoms, and thus in the disease recognition/monitoring, and (2) advanced functionalities for video playback and browsing/retrieval. CAT-CAD is the first tool to allow the automatic recognition of cataplexy symptoms based on the analysis of patients' video recordings.

In this extended abstract, we report details on the video analyzer for the automatic detection of cataplexy symptoms. This component of the CAT-CAD system is built on top of SHIATSU, a general and extensible framework for video retrieval which is based on the (semi-)automatic hierarchical semantic annotation of videos exploiting the analysis of their visual content [3], and exploits features managed through the Windsurf software library [4].

After reviewing some background information, we detail the methodologies used to automatically analyze videos: a pattern-based technique able to recognize facial patterns and a novel approach based on convolutional neural networks (Section 2). Finally, we provide results obtained from an extensive experimental evaluation to compare the performance of the two video analysis approaches, using a benchmark containing recordings from real patients (Section 3) and conclude (Section 4).

1.1. Background and Related Work

Narcolepsy with cataplexy usually arises in adolescence or young adulthood, but the diagnosis is typically established after a long period with a mean delay (across Europe) from symptom onset to diagnosis of 14 years [12]. The diagnosis delay is due not only to the failure to recognize the symptoms of the disease, but also to the misinterpretation of cataplexy phenomena as the expression of other disorders, such as episodes of loss of consciousness of epileptic nature, force reductions due to neuromuscular disorder or behavioral disorders of childhood psychiatric or neuropsychiatric relevance.

Few scientific studies have considered the video-polygraphic features of cataplexy in adult age and only recently the motor phenotype of childhood cataplexy has been described exclusively using video recordings of the attacks evoked by watching funny cartoons [13]. These studies showed that in the context of the physiological response to the laughter there are the distinctive elements of cataplexy, called *motor behaviors patterns*, particularly evident at the level of the *facial expression changes*. In particular, the three most recurrent motor phenomena (often displayed by patients affected by the disease) are ptosis, head drop, and smile/mouth opening [13].

To the best of our knowledge, CAT-CAD is the first study about the automatic recognition of cataplexy by exploiting patient video recordings. However, automatic detection of facial motor phenomena similar to the ones used to diagnose cataplexy is commonly used in other contexts. For example, the detection of eyelid closure, head pose, or mouth opening is useful for the automatic recognition of fatigue/drowsiness in vehicle drivers [11, 9, 6]. The "verbatim" use of such techniques in the context of cataplexy diagnosis is however inappropriate, since the peculiar motor patterns are somewhat different, even if they can be detected using similar facial features.

2. The CAT-CAD Video Analyzer

The core of the CAT-CAD tool is the real-time analysis of patients' videos to detect the presence of disease symptoms (i.e., ptosis, head drop, and smile/mouth opening). Two different approaches were developed to perform video analysis, with the idea of comparing their relative performance and possibly combining them to achieve the best possible result in recognizing the different motor phenomena:

- The *Pattern-Based* approach (Section 2.1) is built on the automatic detection of facial features in video frames.
- The *Deep Learning* approach (Section 2.2) exploits three convolutional neural networks, each trained to detect a specific motor phenomenon.

2.1. Video Analyzer: Pattern-Based Approach

The first video analyzer to be implemented in CAT-CAD for the detection of cataplexy motor phenomena exploits facial landmarks, as detected by OpenFace [1]. The first step of the pattern characterization process consists in detecting and extracting patients' facial landmarks of interest from each video frame; this is necessary because it is safe to assume that different patients have different facial features. Using OpenFace on each single video frame we are thus able to extract, for each video, a time series of multi-dimensional feature vectors, each vector characterizing the facial landmarks extracted from a single frame.

2.1.1. Ptosis

Ptosis is a drooping or falling of the upper eyelid. This, however, should not be mistaken as a (regular) eye blink. For this, ptosis is detected whenever eyes are closed for a period of time longer than a typical blink. For each frame, a 12-dimensional feature vector is extracted, containing the (x, y) coordinates of six landmarks characterizing the shape of the eye. The *Eye Aspect Ratio* (EAR) can then be defined as the ratio of the eye *height* to the eye *width* (averaged for left and right eye). EAR is partially invariant to head pose and fully invariant to uniform image scaling and in-place face rotation. The semantics of EAR are as follows: when an eye is closing, EAR approaches zero, whereas when the eye is completely open, EAR attains its maximum value (which varies from person to person). Therefore, we define the presence or absence of ptosis by measuring the length of the time series corresponding to a "long enough" sequence of frames with closed eyes (EAR lower than a threshold).

2.1.2. Head Drop

For head drop, a 8-D feature vector is extracted from each frame, including the (x, y) coordinates of the two landmarks characterizing the external corner of each eye and the one that is immediately below the tip of the nose and the rotation of the head around X and Z axes. The Center of Gravity (CoG) of the three landmarks is then used to measure rotation around the Y axis. Head drop is then detected if rotation around one of the three axes exceeds a threshold.

2.1.3. Smile/Mouth Opening

For the third motor phenomenon, a 8-D feature vector is extracted for each frame, containing (x, y) coordinates of four landmarks characterizing the shape of the mouth. The *Mouth Aspect Ratio* (MAR) can then be defined as the ratio of the mouth *width* to the mouth *height*. Like EAR, MAR is partially invariant to head pose and fully invariant to uniform image scaling and in-place face rotation. When the mouth is closed, MAR attains its maximum value (which varies from person to person), while if the mouth is completely open, MAR reaches its lowest value; intermediate values characterize various types of smile. We thus consider the cataplectic mouth opening as present if the current MAR is lower than a threshold, indicating that the patient is smiling widely or opening her mouth.

2.2. Video Analyzer: Deep Learning Approach

The alternative video analysis tool is based on convolutional neural networks (CNNs). The CNN architecture used in this work is based on the DeXpression Network [7], which achieves excellent performance in expression recognition, and has been implemented using TensorFlow (https://www.tensorflow.org/).

Our CNN architecture consists of three different types of blocks:

1. an *Input Block*, which performs image pre-processing,
2. a *Feature Extraction Block*, inspired by the architectural principles introduced by GoogleNet [15], which is repeated four times, and
3. an *Output Block*, which is used to produce the result class from the features extracted by previous layers.

We have trained three different networks, one for each motor phenomenon to be recognized. The three networks share the same architecture, but the learned weights are clearly different, due to the use of different training classes. It is clear that, for this approach, each frame is analyzed per se, and no considerations on frame sequences, like duration of eyelids closing or of head drop, can be extrapolated, contrary to the pattern-based approach. The three neural networks have been trained for 8 epochs each, for a total time of about 12 hours.

For each video frame, the face of the patient is first detected by means of OpenFace and then cropped. The resulting image is converted to grayscale and downsized to produce images of 320×320 pixels. Cropping of the images was necessary in order to provide the CNN with only face details (thus avoiding that the surrounding environment would distract the learning).

3. Experimental Evaluation

The benchmark used for our experimental evaluation consists of a population of patients of the Outpatient Clinic for Narcolepsy of the University of Bologna, who were assessed for the presence of cataplexy by way of a neurophysiological and biological diagnosis [16].

The first (experimental) group of patients includes 14 subjects displaying symptoms of the disease. Training of video analyzers has been performed using an inter-patient separation scheme, where patients have been randomly assigned to non-overlapping training and test sets, by respecting sex and age distribution. In particular, 11 patients have been included in the training set (thus, their entire videos have been used to train each analyzer), while the remaining 3 patients have been exploited to test the accuracy of the tool.

The second group includes 44 different subjects that show no sign of the disease. Among those, 14 patients have been selected as a control group so as to follow the same sex and age distribution of the experimental group.

For the deep-learning approach, data augmentation was performed by adding, to each training set frame, seven additional images by performing: (i) 3 *rotations* with a random angle between -45° and $+45^\circ$, (ii) 3 *translations* with a random shift between -50 and 50 pixels, and (iii) 1 *horizontal flipping*. The final training sets consists of 191140 labeled images for ptosis, 61216 labeled images for head-drop, and 108196 labeled images for mouth opening.

3.1. Performance Measures

To objectively evaluate the performance of our analyzers, each frame can be labeled according to a confusion matrix as correctly and incorrectly recognized for each of the two classes available (in our case, motor phenomenon actually present or absent). The four possible outcomes are tp (true positive, a frame where the symptom is correctly detected as present), fn (false negative, symptom wrongly not detected), tn (true negative, symptom correctly not detected) and fp (false positive, symptom wrongly detected as present). From the confusion matrix, the performance measures used in our experiments are defined as follows.

Recall/Sensitivity (R) is defined as the fraction of the frames showing signs of the disease (positives) that are correctly identified: $R = \frac{tp}{tp+fn}$. R is therefore used to measure the accuracy of a technique in recognizing the presence of the disease.

Specificity (S) is the fraction of frames not showing the disease (negatives) that are correctly classified: $S = \frac{tn}{tn+fp}$. S thus expresses the ability of a technique to avoid false alarms (which can lead to expensive/invasive exams).

Precision (P) is another popular metric, besides R and S, which are the fundamental prevalence-independent statistics. P is defined as the fraction of correct positively classified frames and assesses the predictive power of the classifier: $P = \frac{tp}{tp+fp}$.

Accuracy (A) measures the fraction of correct decisions, to assess the overall effectiveness of the algorithm: $A = \frac{tp+tn}{tp+fp+fn+tn}$.

Balanced Score (F_1) is a commonly used measure, combining P and R in a single metric computed as their harmonic mean: $F_1 = 2\frac{1}{\frac{1}{P}+\frac{1}{R}} = \frac{2 \cdot tp}{2 \cdot tp + fp + fn}$.

For the pattern-based approach, thresholds used for the detection of ptosis, head drop, and mouth opening were chosen as the ones providing the best classifying performance on the test set [8]. To this end, a Receiver Operating Characteristics (ROC) graph is used for each threshold, and the threshold value maximizing the harmonic mean of R and S measures is chosen as the optimal one: this represents a metric for imbalanced classification, seeking an equilibrium between the two measures [14].

3.2. Overall Performance

Tables 1 and 2 show the performance of the proposed classification techniques over cataplectic/non-cataplectic patients, respectively: figures values were obtained by averaging individual values weighted by the recordings' length. Tables report classification results for the detection of the three symptoms as well for the overall cataplexy which, we remind, is recognized as present if any of the three motor pattern is detected for a particular frame. To compare the performance of the two alternative video analyzers, results in tables show in boldface the best value obtained in any of the five considered performance measures (specificity only for the control group).

	pattern-based					deep learning				
motor phenomenon	R	S	P	A	F_1	R	S	P	A	F_1
ptosis	**0.72**	**0.84**	**0.82**	**0.78**	**0.77**	0.71	0.67	0.68	0.69	0.70
mouth opening	**0.78**	0.76	0.75	**0.76**	**0.77**	0.72	**0.81**	**0.79**	0.76	0.75
head drop	0.60	**0.94**	**0.89**	**0.77**	**0.72**	**0.67**	0.81	0.78	0.74	0.72
overall	**0.75**	**0.79**	**0.79**	**0.77**	**0.77**	0.70	0.74	0.73	0.72	0.71

Table 1
Performance of the proposed approaches for cataplectic patients.

	pattern-based	deep learning
motor phenomenon	S	S
ptosis	**0.99**	0.83
mouth opening	**0.98**	0.83
head drop	**0.99**	0.81
overall	**0.98**	0.66

Table 2
Specificity of the proposed approaches for non-cataplectic subjects.

Above results led us to draw the following considerations:

- The pattern-based approach lead to significantly superior results with respect to its deep learning counterpart. In particular, for cataplectic subjects the former attains the best performance in 85% of the metrics (17 out of $4 \times 5 = 20$ performance measures).

- When considering specific motor phenomena, the pattern-based approach consistently outperforms the deep learning approach in detecting ptosis, while the latter sports superior measures only for specificity and precision in detecting mouth opening and for recall in head drop detection.
- The superior specificity of the pattern-based technique is confirmed in non-cataplectic subjects, with an overall specificity at 98%.

A possible explanation for the inferior performance of the deep learning approach is the fact that such approach cannot discriminate between quick and long eye blinks/head drops, due to the fact that each frame is analyzed individually by the CNN. It is therefore likely that the higher number of false positives is because the CNN wrongly detects "regular" eye blinks or head movements as ptosis or head drop.

For the case of non-cataplectic subjects, it is interesting to note that the performance of the deep learning approach for the overall detection of cataplexy is sensibly worse than those attained for the single motor phenomena. For such patients, false positives for ptosis, head drop, and mouth opening are present in different frames. Indeed, due to the absence of positive cases, the set of false positive frames for the overall cataplexy coincides with the union of frames wrongly classified by any specific motor phenomenon detector.

Finally, we include a brief discussion about efficiency of the proposed techniques. On our experimental setup, which involved a commodity (low-end) machine, we were able to extract EAR, CoG and MAR descriptors in real-time for each video frame. Clearly, this is the more time consuming operation for the pattern-based approach, thus it is proven that the whole process of automatic detection can be performed on-line during a single emotional stimulated video recording session. On the other hand, our current implementation of the deep learning approach is only capable to obtain a throughput of 18.5 frame/s, thus being unable to attain real-time performance (recall that the frame rate of videos is 30 frame/s). The reason for this measure is the following: when analyzing a single frame, about 50% of the time is spent in detecting the position of the patient face, about 25% in cropping the image (retaining only the face), and 25% for the classification of the frame by the three neural networks. The bottleneck of the whole computation is clearly the face detection phase, which we implemented using the OpenFace library, instead of using other faster methods (such as the well-known Haar-Cascade filter). This choice was carried out starting from the consideration that quicker filters often fail to identify the face within the image, especially in videos with excessive head movement, which is the common case for cataplectic subjects.

4. Conclusions

In this extended abstract, we reported details on the video analyzer of CAT-CAD for the automatic detection of cataplexy symptoms (ptosis, head drop, and smile/mouth opening). Two different approaches are introduced for the detection of disease symptoms: the Pattern-Based approach is based on analysis of facial features, using the OpenFace framework, while the Deep Learning approach uses CNNs, as implemented by TensorFlow. An extensive comparative experimental evaluation conducted on a benchmark of real patients recordings demonstrated the accuracy of the proposed techniques. When comparing the effectiveness of the two video analyzers we introduced to detect cataplexy symptoms, the pattern-based approach achieves superior performance. One of the possible explanations for the inferior detection accuracy of the deep learning approach is the fact that 2D CNNs are unable to properly take into account the temporal dimension that correlates subsequent frames in a video. The use of 3D CNNs could be an interesting way to pursue, and we plan to consider their inclusion in CAT-CAD.

References

[1] T. Baltrušaitis, A. Zadeh, L. Yao Chong, L.-P.; Morency, OpenFace 2.0: Facial Behavior Analysis Toolkit, in: Proceedings of FG 2018, Xi'an, China, May 2018.

[2] I. Bartolini, A. Di Luzio, CAT-CAD: A Computer-Aided Diagnosis Tool for Cataplexy, Computers, 2021, 10(4).

[3] I. Bartolini, M. Patella, C. Romani, SHIATSU: Tagging and Retrieving Videos Without Worries, Multimedia Tools and Applications, 2013, 63(2).

[4] I. Bartolini, M. Patella, G. Stromei, The Windsurf Library for the Efficient Retrieval of Multimedia Hierarchical Data, in: Proceedings of SIGMAP 2011, Seville, Spain, July 2011.

[5] I. Bartolini et al, Automatic Detection of Cataplexy, Sleep Medicine, 2018, 52.

[6] L.M. Bergasa et al, Analysing Driver's Attention Level Using Computer Vision, in: Proceedings of ITSC 2008, Beijing, China, June 2008.

[7] P. Burkert et al, DeXpression: Deep Convolutional Neural Network for Expression Recognition, arXiv, September 2015.

[8] T. Fawcett, An Introduction to ROC Analysis, Pattern Recognition Letters, 2006, 27(8).

[9] J. Jo, H.G. Jung, K. Ryoung, J. Kim, Vision-Based Method for Detecting Driver Drowsiness and Distraction in Driver Monitoring System, Optical Engineering, 2011, 50(12).

[10] L. Lazli, M. Boukadoum, O.A. Mohamed, A Survey on Computer-Aided Diagnosis of Brain Disorders through MRI Based on Machine Learning and Data Mining Methodologies with an Emphasis on Alzheimer Disease Diagnosis and the Contribution of the Multimodal Fusion, Applied Sciences, 2020, 10.

[11] B. Mandal, L. Li, G.S. Wang, J. Lin, Towards Detection of Bus Driver Fatigue Based on Robust Visual Analysis of Eye State, IEEE Transactions on Intelligent Transportation Systems, 2017, 18(3).

[12] F. Pizza et al, Clinical and Polysomnographic Course of Childhood Narcolepsy with Cataplexy, Brain, 2013, 136(12).

[13] G. Plazzi et al, Complex Movement Disorders at Disease Onset in Childhood Narcolepsy with Cataplexy, Brain: A Journal of Neurology, 2011, 134(12).

[14] F. Provost, Machine Learning from Imbalanced Data Sets 101, in: Proceedings of the AAAI'2000 Workshop on Imbalanced Data Sets, 68(2000), Austin, TX, July 2000.

[15] C. Szegedy et al, Going Deeper with Convolutions, in: Proceedings of CVPR 2015, Boston, MA, June 2015.

[16] S. Vandi et al, A Standardized Test to Document Cataplexy, Sleep Medicine, 2019, 53.

Sentiment Analysis of medical questionnaires to improve adherence to telemonitoring programs

(Discussion Paper)

Chiara Zucco[1], Clarissa Paglia[2], Sonia Graziano[3], Sergio Bella[2] and Mario Cannataro[1]

[1]*Data Analytics Research Center, Department of Medical and Surgical Sciences, University Magna Græcia, Catanzaro, Italy*
[2]*Unit of Cystic Fibrosis, Bambino Gesù Children's Hospital, Rome, Italy*
[3]*Unit of Clinical Psychology, Bambino Gesù Children's Hospital, Rome, Italy*

Abstract

Although it is widely known that high adherence to telemedicine and in particular home telemonitoring programs lead to an improvement in the patient's quality of life, a reduction in hospitalizations, and the containment of healthcare costs, poor adherence is a widespread problem, especially in chronic diseases. Guided by the intuition that the sentiment, i.e., the degrees of positiveness/negativeness, expressed by patients through their responses to ad-hoc designed questionnaires, may be related to their adherence and can be used to predict poor adherence levels, this work describes an integrated software architecture for the online provision, collection, and analysis of questionnaires or surveys and summarizes some preliminary results already presented in our previous work.

Keywords

Text Mining, Sentiment Analysis, Web-based questionnaire, Telemedicine.

1. Introduction

All the set of health services providing medical care in patients' daily living environment are subsumed under the umbrella of telemedicine, which strongly relies on the support of information and telecommunication technologies [2].

Common goals of telemedicine programs range from the increment of patient empowerment to the reduction of healthcare costs [3].

Telemedicine and, specifically, home telemonitoring systems have shown themselves to be cost-effective [4] and to provide an improvement in patients' quality-of-life, in terms, for instance, of significant reduction of both mortality and length of stay of patients in progressive care unit [5], significant improvement of glycemic control for patients with diabetes [6]. However, a telemonitoring program's effectiveness is affected by the extent to which the patient follows medical protocols in terms of frequency and/or dosage [7], namely the adherence levels and, consequently, the degrees of drop-out. In fact, poor adherence is a widespread problem,

SEBD 2021: The 29th Italian Symposium on Advanced Database Systems, September 5-9, 2021, Pizzo Calabro (VV), Italy
chiara.zucco@unicz.it (C. Zucco); clarissa.paglia@opbg.net (C. Paglia); sonia.graziano@gmail.com (S. Graziano); sergio.bella@opbg.net (S. Bella); cannataro@unicz.it (M. Cannataro)

CEUR Workshop Proceedings (CEUR-WS.org)

especially in chronic diseases. Therefore, several studies have been carried out to investigate variables related to poor adherence [9],[8],[10].

Adherence levels may be measured in different suitable ways. Here, adherence is intended as the rate of performed monitoring events w.r.t. the ideal number of events, suggested by the telemonitoring protocol, while the degrees of drop-out refer to the percentage of patients the abandon the telemedicine or the telehomecare program they were enrolled in, generally due to poor adherence.

The proposed architecture is intended as a contribution that can help the context of home telemonitoring programs. The basic idea is to integrate within a telehomecare system an online survey instrument that, by collecting textual answers written by patients enrolled in a telemonitoring program, can extract useful features capable of early predict drop-out due to poor adherence.

The system encompasses a novel analysis approach that leverages lexicon-based sentiment analysis techniques [11] and exploits the inferred polarity as a numerical feature to enhance further statistical or machine learning analysis.

To the best of our knowledge, no specific research has been published, nor a system architecture has been proposed that would explicitly monitor changes in patient's opinion across time through the repeated administration of a questionnaire, using the polarity associated with answers to open-ended question as a numerical feature, in a telehomecare system.

Additionally, the paper will present a case study application of the system architecture to discuss whether a predictive relationship, in terms of Granger-causality test modeling, may be assessed between patient adherence in a cystic fibrosis telehomecare program and their opinion about the program they are enrolled in.

The rest of the paper is organized as follows: Section 2 describes the methodology behind the proposed approach and the case-study application. Section 3 provides insights related to collected data and presents the Granger-causality hypothesis tests results and discusses it.

Finally, Section 4 concludes the paper and outlines future works.

2. Materials and methods

In this Section, some preliminary information related to the case study, a description of the experimental protocol used and the analysis pipeline's proposal are presented.

2.1. Experimental protocol and Dataset description

The data analyzed in the present case study application were collected from the Cystic Fibrosis Unit, Bambino Gesù Children's Hospital, Rome, Italy. In this study, 169 online surveys sent by 38 cystic fibrosis patients (F/M=20/18, age= 28.7 ± 9.91, age range= $14 - 49$) recruited among patients already enrolled in a telemedicine program (years of enrollment = 5.9 ± 3.9) were collected and analyzed at five different survey epochs.

The enrollment criteria include patients more than 12 years old with cystic fibrosis who will access the Cystic Fibrosis Unit in ordinary, daytime, or outpatient hospitalization. All patients who have undergone a transplant (liver/lung) were excluded from the study.

The study was formally approved by the local Medical Research Ethics Committee.

2.2. Administration of questionnaire

From June 2019, 38 enrolled patients were asked to complete, every three months, an online questionnaire designed ad-hoc by the clinical team. In the following, each set of surveys submission will be indicated as an epoch.

The Telemedicine Drop-Out (TDO) questionnaire consists of 15 blocks of closed, mixed, and open-ended items with yes/no constraints, and it has been administered through a self-hosted web-based survey instrument built on top of LimeSurvey[1]. The TDO survey was designed as an online, structured version of the interview led by the medical team within the telemedicine program, extended with a series of open-ended questions, whose objective was to infer polarity or, in perspective, to extract emotions from the relative answers [12].

In order to administer surveys to patients, LimeSurvey is set up as a highly customizable, free, and responsive online survey tool. It also provides various API functions through the LimeSurvey RemoteControl 2 (LSRC2). The survey structure and the participants are created through the user interface provided by LimeSurvey. The collection of survey answers is automatized using the Python library Limepy that provides a Python wrapper for the LSRC2 API and the Python library Schedule to automatically update the responses. The DBMS server is MySQL.

As already stated, adherent patients need to transmit the results of the spirometry test at least twice a week. For each survey administration, i.e. survey epoch, the patient's adherence score (Adh-score) to the telemonitoring program was assessed as the total number of spirometry transmissions sent during a three months window starting from the month before until the month subsequent to the survey administration, averaged by twice the total number of weeks following. More in details, let suppose that a survey was carried at month t, then Adh-score$_t$ = $\frac{nS_{t-1}+nS_t+nS_{t+1}}{2(w_{t-1}+w_t+w_{t+1})}$ where nS_{t-1}, nS_t, nS_{t+1} refer to the number of spirometry trasmissions sent at month $t-1, t, t+1$ respectively, while w_{t-1}, w_t, w_{t+1} refer to the number of weeks in the month $t-1, t, t+1$ respectively.

Patients that strictly follow medical advice have a related Adh-score≥ 1. In the following, the percentage of Adh-score, i.e. Adh-score (%) will be considered. Therefore, $0 \leq$ Adh-score (%) = Adh-score $*$ 100 and Adh-score (%)>100 for patients with high rates of adherence. The clinical team provided the number of transmissions per month.

2.3. System architecture

The system architecture encompasses three independent modules, connected in a cascade-fashion. In future works, the modules are supposed to be integrated using a unique user interface. Figure 1 shows the overall architecture for the system, that is organized as three logical levels: i.e. i) data collection, ii) data integration, and iii)data analysis.

The general pipeline for the analysis of textual data, i.e. answers to open-ended questions, involves: **Text preprocessing :** includes standard NLP (Natual Language Processing) techniques, i.e. tokenization, stop word removal, and lemmatization. The preprocessing step has been executed by using *SpaCy*[2] a popular library for Natural Language Processing in Python,

[1]https://www.LimeSurvey.org/

[2]https://spacy.io/

which provides a set of preprocessing algorithms also for the Italian language. **Feature extraction:** to each open-ended free-text answer, a polarity score in the range $[-1, 1]$ has been assigned through the VADER [13] lexicon-based method adapted to the Italian language and considered as a numerical feature. **Statistical hypothesis testing:** data have been sorted by respondents and survey submission date and, for each open-ended question, the sequence of assigned polarity was modeled as a time series, as the sequence of Adh-scores. Augmented Dickey-Fuller Test [14] was used to check for stationarity while Granger-causality hypothesis test model [15] was examined to discuss the existence of directed causal interactions between the polarity score associated with free-text answers and adherence. **Data visualization:** to provide useful insights and summarize patient answers, different visualization techniques have been used. In particular, preprocessed free-text answers have been visualized through word clouds, while a graph shows the time-series of polarity scores at different submission epochs.

img/architecture-eps-converted-to.pdf

Figure 1: The modules of the system architecture, implemented as three independent levels connected to each other in cascade. The architecture is designed to be cyclical, as the system is used for each scheduled administration of the survey.

VADER (Valence Aware Dictionary for sEntiment Reasoning) [13] is a lexicon-based sentiment analysis engine that combines lexicon-based methods with a rule-based modeling consisting of 5 human validated rules.

Starting from a classical lexicon-based approach, the VADER engine's core step is the identification of some general grammatical and syntactic heuristics to identify semantic shifters, i.e. words that increase, decrease or change the polarity orientation of another word. In particular, five heuristics for sentiment polarity shifters have been identified: i.e.punctuation; capitalization; a list of degree modifiers which encompasses noun, adjective, adverbs know to impact sentiment intensity by increasing or decreasing it; contrastive particles and negations.

To extend VADER to the Italian language, Sentix [16], a lexicon that automatically extends the SentiWordNet annotation to the Italian synsets provided in MultiWordNet [17], has been considered.

Among the five heuristics designed in VADER, only three needed to be adapted to the Italian language since the shifter role of capitalization of words and exclamation marks is used as intensifiers for both languages. Words belonging to the VADER set of negation words were translated in the Italian language, and the set was then extended by retrieving MultiWordNet synset terms for each word, while contrastive particle "but" has been simply translated to Italian.

Among the intensifier sets, VADER also considered a few idioms, but, due to discrepancies across different languages, idioms were not considered.

Granger-causality is a statistical hypothesis testing model to determine if there is a directed relationship between two time-series [15]. A time series X is said to Granger-cause Y if it can be shown that there is a statistically significant improvement in predicting future values of Y by using past values of X (i.e. lagged values of X) and Y, compared to predictions based only on past values of Y.

The possibility to relate past values of X to Y's actual values is in virtue of a lag factor. Here, the Granger-causality test was computed for X's lagged values. All the lags ranging from one to four were tested, where four is the number of considered submission epochs minus one.

Here, the considered alternative hypothesis is that the polarity-score time-series associated with each considered open-ended question Granger-cause the time-series of adherence. The level of significance was set at 5%, i.e. *p-value* < 0.05. The Granger-causality test assumes the hypothesis that the investigated time-series are stationary. Therefore the augmented Dickey-Fuller method was exploited to check stationarity conditions [14].

3. Results and discussion

A comprehensive analysis of the responses to the TDO survey is beyond the scope of this study. Instead, only answers to two open-ended questions collected from the TDO survey will be discussed, namely: i) **Q1** - "What do you think about telemedicine?", and **Q2** - "Since you joined the telemonitoring program, what has improved the quality of your life?". A polarity score ranging in $[-1, 1]$ has been inferred by adapting the VADER framework to the Italian language and considered as a numerical feature for each set of answers.

3.1. Testing Granger-causality

Three time-series have been considered, i.e. polarity score related to Q1 and Q2 respectively and the time-series of Adh-scores. The augmented Dickey-Fuller test showed that for all the three considered time-series the stationarity condition holds (p-value= 4.6124e-18, p-value= 3.2185e-07, p-value= 0.0035 respectively).

Two Granger-causality tests were performed to check whether Q1 Granger-causes Adh-score and whether Q2 Granger-causes Adh-score. Moreover, since all the three series are considered contemporaneously, we also need to check whether Adh-score Granger-causes Q1 and whether Adh-score Granger-causes Q2. Three different test-statistics, i.e. F-test, chi2, and likelihood-ratio were considered, with the number of lags varying from one to four. Table 1 and Table 2 show the results in terms of p-values. It can be seen that both Q1 and Q2 Granger-causes Adh-score for lag=1. On the other hand, Adh-score appears to not Granger-causes Q1 or Q2.

Therefore, the results suggest the existence of a predictive relationship between the polarity scores series associated with Q1 and the polarity score series associated with Q2 w.r.t. the Adh-score.

Table 1

Q1 and Adh-score: p-value of Granger-causality test performed with three different statistics and four different lags.

	Q1⟶ Adh-score			**Adh-score⟶ Q1**		
	F-test	Chi2 test	Likelihood-ratio	F-test	Chi2 test	Likelihood-ratio
1	**0.0368**	**0.0339**	**0.0350**	0.4076	0.4027	0.4031
2	0.0998	0.0908	0.0936	0.6667	0.6585	0.6592
3	0.1063	0.0917	0.0963	0.6628	0.6479	0.6496
4	0.2032	0.1760	0.1833	0.8200	0.8061	0.8064

Table 2
Q2 and Adh-score: p-value of Granger-causality test performed with three different statistics and four different lags.

	Q2⟶ Adh-score			Adh-score⟶ Q2		
	F-test	Chi2 test	Likelihood-ratio	F-test	Chi2 test	Likelihood-ratio
1	**0.0020**	**0.0016**	**0.0028**	0.9970	0.9969	0.9969
2	**0.0174**	**0.0141**	**0.0155**	0.7455	0.7390	0.7394
3	0.0547	0.0446	0.0482	0.8235	0.8148	0.9154
4	0.0865	0.0685	0.0744	0.7566	0.7387	0.7406

The results are consistent with the hypothesis that the polarities extracted from patients' opinion on telemedicine may help predict their average adherence one epoch after the survey administration.

4. Conclusions

In the present paper, a system architecture for the extraction of emotional states from textual contents, designed to support the monitoring of patients with chronic disease has been presented. The main goal of the proposed system is basically to implement a methodology to capture the underlying opinions that chronic patients have about the program they are enrolled in and to investigate whether these features may help in the early prediction of patients drop-out from the telemedicine program.

The proposed system is designed in an end-to-end fashion to provide support through the whole process, including the implementation of the questionnaire, the survey administration at scheduled intervals, as well as the analysis. Specific contributions are: i)the design of a self-hosted web-based survey instrument built on top of Limesurvey for the management of online inquiries over time; ii)an analysis pipeline that exploits sentiment analysis techniques to infer a sentiment polarity score for each open-ended answer and uses it as a numerical feature (to the best of our knowledge, this is the first time that this kind of approach has been proposed); iii)the validation of both the survey instrument and the analysis pipeline, that have been applied to collect and analyze 169 TDO survey responses sent by 38 patients enrolled in a home telemonitoring program provided by the Cystic Fibrosis Unit at the "Bambino Gesu" Children Hospital in Rome, Italy.

Limitations to the present analysis may be found in the small amount of data collected up-to-date, which does not consent the investigation of changes for a single patient through time.

Nevertheless, the promising results encourage us to further investigate the potentiality of the proposed architecture and the analysis pipeline with the aim to develop, as future work, a predictive system for the early detection of poorly-adherent patients that may also alert doctors to contact patients and eventually update/personalize their telemedicine program (e.g. in terms of timing, technological equipment, psychological counseling, etc.)

References

[1] Zucco, C., Paglia, C., Graziano, S., Bella, S., & Cannataro, M.: Sentiment Analysis and Text Mining of Questionnaires to Support Telemonitoring Programs. Information, 11(12), 550 (2020)

[2] Ryu, S. Telemedicine: Opportunities and Developments in Member States: Report on the Second Global Survey on eHealth 2009 (Global Observatory for eHealth Series, Volume 2); *Healthc. inf. res.*; *18*, 153 (2012).

[3] Nielsen, M.K.; Johannessen, H. Patient empowerment and involvement in telemedicine. *J. Nurs. Educ. Pract.*, *9*, 54–58 (2019).

[4] Delgoshaei, B.; Mobinizadeh, M.; Mojdekar, R.; Afzal, E.; Arabloo, J.; Mohamadi, E. Telemedicine: A systematic review of economic evaluations. *Med J. Islam. Repub. Iran (MJIRI)*, *31*, 754–761 (2017).

[5] Armaignac, D.L.; Saxena, A.; Rubens, M.; Valle, C.A.; Williams, L.M.S.; Veledar, E.; Gidel, L.T. Impact of Telemedicine on Mortality, Length of Stay, and Cost Among Patients in Progressive Care Units: Experience From a Large Healthcare System. *Critical care medicine*, *46*, 728 (2018).

[6] Polisena, J.; Tran, K.; Cimon, K.; Hutton, B.; McGill, S.; Palmer, K. Home telehealth for diabetes management: a systematic review and meta-analysis. *Diabetes, Obesity and Metabolism*, *11*, 913–930 (2009).

[7] Osterberg, L., & Blaschke, T.: Medication Adherence. New England Journal of Medicine, 353, 487-497 (2005)

[8] Gorst, S.L.; Armitage, C.J.; Brownsell, S.; Hawley, M.S. Home telehealth uptake and continued use among heart failure and chronic obstructive pulmonary disease patients: a systematic review. *Annals of Behavioral Medicine*, *48*, 323–336 (2014).

[9] Mathes, T., Jaschinski, T., & Pieper, D.: Adherence influencing factors–a systematic review of systematic reviews. Archives of Public Health, 72(1), 1–9 (2014)

[10] Tagliente, I.; Solvoll, T.; Murgia, F.; Bella, S. Telemonitoring in cystic fibrosis: A 4-year assessment and simulation for the next 6 years. *Interact. J. Med. Res.*, *5*, (2016).

[11] Zucco, C.; Calabrese, B.; Agapito, G.; Guzzi, P.H.; Cannataro, M. Sentiment analysis for mining texts and social networks data: Methods and tools. *Wiley Interdisciplinary Reviews: Data Mining and Knowledge Discovery*, p. e1333 (2019).

[12] Zucco, C.; Bella, S.; Paglia, C.; Tabarini, P.; Cannataro, M. Predicting abandonment in telehomecare programs using Sentiment Analysis: a system proposal. 2018 IEEE International Conference on Bioinformatics and Biomedicine (BIBM). IEEE, 1734–1739 (2018).

[13] Hutto, C.; Vader, G.E. A parsimonious rule-based model for sentiment analysis of social media text. In Proceedings of the Eighth International AAAI Conference on Weblogs and Social, Ann Arbor, MI, USA, 1–4 (2014).

[14] Dickey, D.A.; Fuller, W.A. Distribution of the estimators for autoregressive time series with a unit root. *J. Am. Stat. Assoc.*, *74*, 427–431 (1979).

[15] Granger, C.W. Testing for causality: A personal viewpoint. *J. Econ. Dyn. Control*, *2*, 329–352 (1980).

[16] Basile, V.; Nissim, M. Sentiment analysis on Italian tweets. In *Proceedings of the 4th*

Workshop on Computational Approaches to Subjectivity, Sentiment and Social Media Analysis, Atlanta, Georgia, 14 June 2013; Association for Computational Linguistics: Atlanta, Georgia; 100–107 (2013).

[17] Pianta, E.; Bentivogli, L.; Girardi, C. *MultiWordNet: Developing an Aligned Multilingual Database*; In Proceedings of the First International Conference on Global WordNet, Mysore, India, 293–302 (2002).

EmbDI: Generating Embeddings for Relational Data Integration

(Discussion Paper)

Riccardo Cappuzzo[1], Paolo Papotti[1] and Saravanan Thirumuruganathan[2]

[1]EURECOM, France
[1]EURECOM, France
[2]QCRI, Qatar

Abstract

Deep learning techniques have been used with promising results for data integration problems. Some methods use *pre-trained* embeddings that were trained on a large corpus such as Wikipedia. However, they may not always be an appropriate choice for enterprise datasets with custom vocabulary. Other methods adapt techniques from natural language processing to obtain embeddings for the enterprise's relational data. However, this approach blindly treats a tuple as a sentence, thus losing a large amount of contextual information present in the tuple. We propose algorithms for obtaining *local embeddings* that are effective for data integration tasks on relational databases. We describe a graph-based representation that allows the specification of a rich set of relationships inherent in the relational world. Then, we propose how to derive sentences from such a graph that effectively "describe" the similarity across elements (tokens, attributes, rows) in the datasets. The embeddings are learned based on such sentences. Our experiments show that our framework, EmbDI, produces promising results for data integration tasks such as entity resolution, both in supervised and unsupervised settings.

Keywords

Data Integration, Word Embeddings

1. Introduction

The problem of data integration concerns the combination of information from heterogeneous relational data sources, which is recognized as an expensive task for humans [1]. While traditional approaches require substantial effort from domain scientists to generate features and labeled data or domain specific rules, there has been increasing interest in achieving accurate data integration with deep learning methods to reduce the human effort. Embeddings have been successfully used for this goal in data integration tasks such as entity resolution [2, 3, 4, 5, 6, 7], schema matching [8, 9], identification of related concepts [10], and data curation in general [1]. Typically, these works fall into two dominant paradigms based on how they obtain word embeddings. The first is to reuse *pre-trained* word embeddings computed on a generic corpus

SEBD 2021: The 29th Italian Symposium on Advanced Database Systems, September 5-9, 2021, Pizzo Calabro (VV), Italy
riccardo.cappuzzo@eurecom.fr (R. Cappuzzo); paolo.papotti@eurecom.fr (P. Papotti); sthirumuruganathan@hbku.edu.qa (S. Thirumuruganathan)
0000-0003-0651-4128 (P. Papotti)

for a given task. The second is to build *local* word embeddings that are specific to the dataset. These methods treat each tuple as a sentence by reusing the same techniques for learning word embeddings employed in natural language processing.

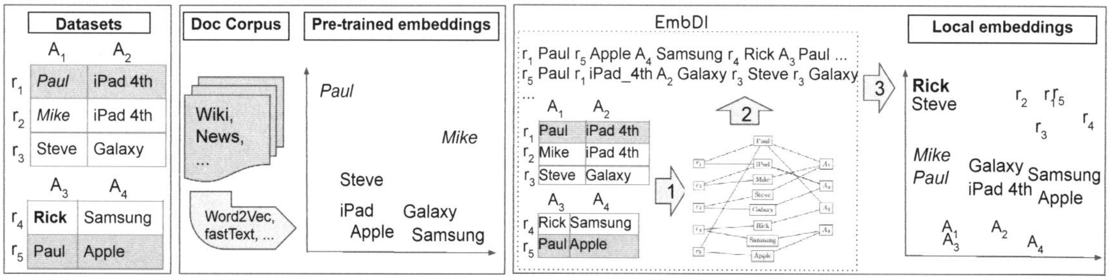

Figure 1: A vector space learned from text (prior methods) and from data (EmbDI).

However, both approaches fall short in some circumstances. Enterprise datasets contain custom vocabulary, as in the small datasets in the left-hand side of Figure 1. The pre-trained embeddings do not capture the semantics expressed by these datasets and do not contain embeddings for the word "Rick". Approaches that treat a tuple as a sentence miss a number of signals such as attribute boundaries, integrity constraints, and so on. Moreover, existing approaches do not consider the generation of embeddings from heterogeneous datasets, with different attributes and alternative value formats. These observations motivate the generation of *local* embeddings for the *relational* datasets at hand. We advocate for the design of such local embeddings that leverage both the relational nature of the data and the downstream task of data integration.

Tuples are not sentences. Simply adapting embedding techniques originally developed for textual data ignores the richer set of semantics inherent in *relational* data. Consider a cell value $t[A_i]$ of an attribute A_i in tuple t, e.g., "Mike" (in italic) in the first relation from the top. Conceptually, it has a semantic connections with both other attributes of tuple t (such as "iPad 4th") and other values from the domain of attribute A_i (such as "Paul", also in italic in the figure).

Embedding generation must span different datasets. Embeddings must be trained using heterogeneous datasets, so that they can meaningfully leverage and surface similarity across data sources. A notion of similarity between different types of entities, such as tuples and attributes, must be developed. Tuple-tuple and attribute-attribute similarity are important features for data integration.

There are multiple challenges to overcome. First, it is not clear how to encode the semantics of the relational datasets in the embedding learning process. Second, datasets may share limited amount of information, have different schemas, and contain a different number of tuples. Finally, datasets are often incomplete and noisy. The learning process is affected by low information quality, generating embeddings that do not correctly represent the semantics of the data.

We introduce EmbDI, a framework for building relational, local embeddings for data integration that introduces a number of innovations to overcome the challenges above. We identify crucial components and propose effective algorithms for instantiating each of them. EmbDI is designed to be modular so that anyone can customize it by plugging in other algorithms and benefit from the continuing improvements from the deep learning and database communities. The two main contributions in our solution are the following.

1. Graph Construction. We use a compact tripartite graph-based representation of relational datasets that effectively represents syntactic and semantic data relationships. Specifically, we use three types of nodes. *Token* nodes correspond to the unique values found in the dataset. *Record Id* nodes (RIDs) represent a unique token for each tuple. *Column Id* nodes (CIDs) represent a unique token for each column/attribute. These nodes are connected by edges based on the structural relationships in the schema. This graph is a compact representation of the original datasets that highlights overlap and explicitly represent the primitives for data integration tasks, i.e., records and attributes.

2. Embedding Construction. We formulate the problem of obtaining local embeddings for relational data as a graph embeddings generation problem. We use random walks to quantify the similarity between neighboring nodes and to exploit metadata such as tuple and attribute IDs. This method ensures that nodes that share similar neighborhoods will be in close proximity in the final embeddings space. The corpus that is used to train our local embeddings is generated by materializing these random walks.

In this discussion paper, we report results for the entity resolution task and refer the reader to the extended version for more experiments [11].

Outline. Section 2 introduces background about embeddings. Section 3 highlights the main challenges and details the major components of the framework. Section 4 concludes the paper by reporting experiments validating our approach.

2. Background

Embeddings. Embeddings map an entity to a high dimensional real valued vector. The mapping is performed in such a way that the geometric relation between the vectors of two entities represents their co-occurrence/semantic relationship. Algorithms used to learn embeddings rely on the notion of "neighborhood": if two entities are similar, they frequently belong to the same contextually-defined neighborhood. When this occurs, the algorithm forces the vectors that represent the two entities to be close to each other in the vector space.

Word Embeddings [12] are trained on a large corpus of text and produce as output a vector space where each word in the corpus is represented by a vector. The vectors for words that occur in similar context – such as SIGMOD and VLDB – are in proximity to each other. Popular architectures for learning embeddings include continuous bag-of-words (CBOW) or skip-gram (SG).

Node embeddings [13] map graph nodes to a high dimensional vector space so that the likelihood of preserving node neighborhoods is maximized. One way to achieve this is by performing random walks starting from each node. Node embeddings are often based on the SG model, as it maximizes the probability of observing a node's neighborhood given its embedding. By varying the type of random walks used, one obtains diverse types of embeddings.

Embeddings for Relational Datasets. Termite [10] projects tokens from structured and unstructured data into a common representational space that could then be used for identifying related concepts. RetroLive [14] produces embeddings that combine relational and semantic information through a retrofitting strategy. There has been prior work that adopt embeddings for specific tasks like entity matching [2, 3] and schema matching [9]. Our goal is to learn relational embeddings tailored for data integration that can be used for multiple tasks.

3. Challenges and Proposed Solution

Consider the scenario where one utilizes pre-trained embeddings, such as word2vec, for the tokens in two small datasets, as reported in Figure 1. Pre-trained embeddings suffer from a number of issues when we use them to model the relations.

1. A number of words, such as "Rick", in the dataset are not in the pre-trained embedding. This is especially problematic for enterprise datasets where tokens are often unique and not found in pre-trained embeddings.

2. Embeddings might contain geometric relationships that exist in the corpus they were trained on, but that are missing in the relational data. For example, the embedding for token "Steve" is closer to tokens "iPad" and "Apple" even though it is not implied in the data.

3. Relationships that do occur in the data, such as between tokens "Paul" and "Mike", are not observed in the pre-trained vector space.

Learning local embeddings from the relational data often produces better results. However, computing embeddings for non integrated data sources is a non trivial task. This becomes especially challenging in settings where data is scattered over different datasets with heterogeneous structures, different formats, and only partially overlapping content. Prior approaches express such datasets as sentences to be consumed by word embedding methods. However, we find that these solutions are still sub-optimal for downstream data integration tasks.

3.1. Constructing Local Relational Embeddings

Our framework, EmbDI, consists of three major components, as depicted in the right-hand side of Figure 1.

1. In the *Graph Construction* stage, we transform the relational dataset in a compact tripartite graph that encodes various relationships inherent in it. Tuple and attribute ids are treated as first class citizens.

2. Given this graph, the next step is *Sentence Construction* through the use of biased random walks. These walks are carefully constructed to avoid common issues such as rare words and imbalance in vocabulary sizes. This produces as output a series of sentences.

3. In *Embedding Construction*, the corpus of sentences is passed to an algorithm for learning word embeddings. Depending on available external information, we optimize the graph and the workflow to improve the embeddings' quality.

Why construct a Graph? Prior approaches for local embeddings seek to directly apply an existing word embedding algorithm on the relational dataset. Intuitively, all tuples in a relation are modeled as sentences by breaking the attribute boundaries. The corpus of sentences for each tuple in the relation is then used to train the embedding. This approach produces embeddings that are customized to that dataset, but it also ignores signals that are inherent in relational data. We represent the relational data as a graph, thus enabling a more expressive representation with a number of advantages. First, it elegantly handles many of the various relationships between entities that are common in relational datasets. Second, it provides a straightforward way to incorporate external information such as "two tokens are synonyms of each other". Finally, a graph representation enables a unified view over different datasets that is invaluable for learning embeddings for data integration.

Simple Approaches. Consider a relation R with attributes $\{A_1, A_2, \ldots, A_m\}$. Let t be an arbitrary tuple and $t[A_i]$ the value of attribute A_i for tuple t. A naive approach is to create a chain graph where tokens corresponding to adjacent attributes such as $t[A_i]$ and $t[A_{i+1}]$ are connected. This will result in m edges for each tuple. Of course, if two different tuples share the same token, then they will reuse the same node. However, relational algebra is based on set semantics, where the attributes do not have an inherent order. So, simplistically connecting adjacent attributes is doomed to fail. Another extreme is to create a complete subgraph, where an edge exists between all possible pairs of $t[A_i]$ and $t[A_{i+1}]$. Clearly, this will result in $\binom{m}{2}$ edges per tuple. This approach results in the number of edges is quadratic in the number of attributes and ignores other token relationships such as "token t_1 and token t_2 belong to the same attribute".

Relational Data as Heterogeneous Graph. We propose a graph with three types of nodes. *Token* nodes correspond to the content of each cell in the relation. Multi-word tokens may be represented as a single entity, get split over multiple nodes or use a mix of the two strategies. *Record Id* nodes (RIDs) represent tuples, *Column Id* nodes (CIDs) represent columns/attributes. These nodes are connected by edges according to the structural relationships in the schema.

Consider a tuple t with RID r_t. Then, nodes for tokens corresponding to $t[A_1], \ldots, t[A_m]$ are connected to the node r_t. Similarly, all the tokens belonging to a specific attribute A_i are connected to the corresponding CID, say c_i. This construction is generic enough to be augmented with other types of relationships. Also, if we know that two tokens are synonyms (e.g. via wordnet), this information could be incorporated by reusing the same node for both tokens. Note that a token could belong to different record ids and column ids when two different tuples/attributes share the same token. Numerical values are rounded to a number of significant figures decided by the user, then they are assigned a node like regular categorical values; null values are not represented in the graph.

Graph Traversal by Random Walks. To generate the distributed representation of every node, we produce a large number of random walks and gather them in a training corpus where each random walk corresponds to a sentence. Random walks allows a richer and more diverse set of neighborhoods than the encoding of a tuple as a *single* sentence. For example, a walk starting from node 'Paul' could go to node A_3, and then to node 'Rick'. This walk implicitly defines the neighborhood based on attribute co-occurrence. Similarly, the walk from 'Paul' could go to 'r_5' and then to 'Apple', incorporating the row level relationships. Our approach is agnostic to the specific type of random walk used. To better represent all nodes, we assign a "budget" of random walks to each of them and guarantee that all nodes will be the starting point of at least as many random walks as their budget. After choosing the starting point T_i, the random walk is generated by choosing a neighboring RID of T_i, R_j. The next step in the random walk will then be chosen at random among all neighbors of node R_j, for example by moving on C_a. Then, a new neighbor of C_a will be chosen and the process will continue until the random walk has reached the target length. We use uniform random walks in most of our experiments to guarantee good execution times on large datasets, while providing high quality results.

Embedding Construction. The generated sentences are then pooled together and used to train the embeddings algorithm. Our approach is agnostic to the actual word embedding algorithm used. We piggyback on the plethora of effective embeddings algorithms such as word2vec, GloVe, fastText, and so on. We discuss the hyperparameters for embedding algorithms such as learning method (either CBOW or Skip-Gram), dimensionality of the embeddings, and size of context window in the full version of the paper.

Using Embeddings for Integration. Once the embeddings are trained, they can be used for common data integration tasks. We describe *unsupervised* algorithms that employ the embeddings produced by EmbDI to perform tasks widely studied in data integration. The algorithms exploit the distance between embeddings of Column and Record IDs for schema matching and entity resolution, respectively; details are reported in the full version of the paper [11].

4. Experiments

We show the positive impact of our embeddings for entity resolution, more results on multiple data integration tasks are reported in the full version of the paper. Experiments have been conducted on a laptop with a CPU Intel i7-8550U, 8x1.8GHz cores and 32GB RAM.

Datasets and Pre-trained Embeddings. We used 8 datasets from the literature [15, 2, 3, 16] and a dataset with a larger schema (IM) that we created starting from open data (https://www.imdb.com/interfaces/, https://grouplens.org/datasets/movielens/). For the majority of the scenarios, less than 10% of the distinct data values are overlapping across the two datasets.

Pre-trained word embeddings have been obtained from fastText [17]. We relied on state of the art methods to combine words in tuples and to obtain embeddings for words that are not in the pre-trained vocabulary [2].

Algorithms. We test four algorithms for the generation of local embeddings. All local methods make use of our tripartite graph and exploit record and column IDs in the integration tasks. The first method is Basic, which creates embeddings from permutations of row tokens and sentences with samples of attribute tokens. The second method is Node2Vec [13], a widely used algorithm for learning node representation on graphs. Given our graph as input, it learns vectors for all nodes. The third method is Harp [18], a state of the art algorithm that learns embeddings for graph nodes by preserving higher-order structural features. This method represents general meta-strategies that build on top of existing neural algorithms to improve performance. The fourth method is EmbDI, as presented in Section 3.1 (https://gitlab.eurecom.fr/cappuzzo/embdi), with walks (sentences) of size 60, 300 dimensions for the embeddings space, the Skip-Gram model in word2vec with a window size of 3, and different tokenization strategies to convert cell values in nodes (details reported in the full paper).

We also test our local embeddings in the *supervised* setting with a state of the art ER system (DeER_L), comparing its results to the ones obtained with pre-trained embeddings (DeER_P). As baseline for the *unsupervised* case, we use our matching algorithm with pre-trained embeddings (FASTTXT).

Metrics. We measure the quality of the results w.r.t. hand crafted ground truth tuple pairs with precision, recall, and their combination (F-measure).

	Unsupervised						Supervised (5% labelled)		Task specific (5% labelled)	
	Pretrain	Local								
	FASTTXT	EMBDI-S	EMBDI-F	EMBDI-O	NODE2VEC	HARP	DeER_P	DeER_L	DeER_P	DeER_L
BB	0.59	0.50	0.82	**0.86**	**0.86**	**0.86**	0.51	0.53	0.54	0.58
WA	0.58	0.59	0.75	**0.81**	mem	0.78	0.58	0.62	0.62	0.63
AG	0.18	0.14	0.57	0.59	0.70	**0.71**	0.53	0.56	0.58	0.62
FZ	0.99	0.98	0.99	0.99	**1.00**	**1.00**	**1.00**	**1.00**	**1.00**	**1.00**
IA	0.10	0.09	0.09	0.11	mem	0.14	0.76	0.81	0.77	**0.82**
DA	0.72	0.95	0.94	0.95	0.87	**0.97**	0.84	0.89	0.86	0.90
DS	0.80	0.85	0.75	**0.92**	mem	0.81	0.80	0.87	0.82	0.91
IM	0.31	0.90	0.64	0.94	mem	**0.95**	0.82	0.88	0.84	0.91

Table 1
F-Measure results for Entity Resolution (ER).

ER Results. We study both unsupervised and supervised settings. To enable baselines to execute these datasets, we aligned the attributes with the ground truth. EMBDI can handle the original scenario where the schemas have not been aligned with a limited decrease in ER quality.

Results in Table 1 for unsupervised settings show that EMBDI-O embeddings obtain the best quality results in three scenarios and second to the best in four cases. In every case, local embeddings obtained from our graph outperform pre-trained ones. For supervised settings, using local embeddings instead of pre-trained ones increases the quality of an existing system. In this case, supervised DEER SHOWS an average 5% absolute improvement in F-measure with 5% of the ground truth passed as training data. The improvements decrease to 4% with more training data (10%). Local embeddings obtained with the BASIC method lead to 0 rows matched.

Compared to NODE2VEC and HARP, the execution of EMBDI is much faster and is able to compute local embeddings for all small and medium size datasets in minutes on a commodity laptop. For example, it takes 2 minutes for 7.4k tuples and 19 minutes for 25k tuples versus 40 and 12 minutes with HARP, respectively. EMBDI embedding creation takes on average about 80% of the total execution time, while graph generation takes less than 1%, and sentence creation the remaining 19%.

Acknowledgement This work has been partially supported by the ANR grant *ANR-18-CE23-0019* and by the IMT *Futur & Ruptures* program “AutoClean”.

References

[1] S. Thirumuruganathan, N. Tang, M. Ouzzani, A. Doan, Data curation with deep learning, EDBT (2020).

[2] M. Ebraheem, S. Thirumuruganathan, S. Joty, M. Ouzzani, N. Tang, Distributed representations of tuples for entity resolution, PVLDB 11 (2018) 1454–1467.

[3] S. Mudgal, H. Li, T. Rekatsinas, A. Doan, Y. Park, G. Krishnan, R. Deep, E. Arcaute, V. Raghavendra, Deep learning for entity matching: A design space exploration, in: SIGMOD, 2018.

[4] C. Zhao, Y. He, Auto-em: End-to-end fuzzy entity-matching using pre-trained deep models and transfer learning, in: WWW, 2019, pp. 2413–2424.

[5] Ö. Ö. Çakal, M. Mahdavi, Z. Abedjan, CLRL: feature engineering for cross-language record linkage, in: EDBT, 2019, pp. 678–681.

[6] J. Kasai, K. Qian, S. Gurajada, Y. Li, L. Popa, Low-resource deep entity resolution with transfer and active learning, arXiv preprint arXiv:1906.08042 (2019).

[7] R. Singh, V. V. Meduri, A. K. Elmagarmid, S. Madden, P. Papotti, J. Quiané-Ruiz, A. Solar-Lezama, N. Tang, Synthesizing entity matching rules by examples, Proc. VLDB Endow. 11 (2017) 189–202.

[8] R. C. Fernandez, E. Mansour, A. A. Qahtan, A. Elmagarmid, I. Ilyas, S. Madden, M. Ouzzani, M. Stonebraker, N. Tang, Seeping semantics: Linking datasets using word embeddings for data discovery, in: ICDE, 2018.

[9] C. Koutras, M. Fragkoulis, A. Katsifodimos, C. Lofi, Rema: Graph embeddings-based relational schema matching, SEA Data workshop (2020).

[10] R. C. Fernandez, S. Madden, Termite: a system for tunneling through heterogeneous data, arXiv preprint arXiv:1903.05008 (2019).

[11] R. Cappuzzo, P. Papotti, S. Thirumuruganathan, Creating embeddings of heterogeneous relational datasets for data integration tasks, in: SIGMOD, ACM, 2020.

[12] J. Turian, L. Ratinov, Y. Bengio, Word representations: a simple and general method for semi-supervised learning, in: ACL, ACL, 2010, pp. 384–394.

[13] A. Grover, J. Leskovec, node2vec: Scalable feature learning for networks, in: SIGKDD, ACM, 2016, pp. 855–864.

[14] M. Günther, M. Thiele, E. Nikulski, W. Lehner, Retrolive: Analysis of relational retrofitted word embeddings, EDBT (2020).

[15] C. Gokhale, S. Das, A. Doan, J. F. Naughton, N. Rampalli, J. W. Shavlik, X. Zhu, Corleone: hands-off crowdsourcing for entity matching, in: SIGMOD, 2014.

[16] S. Das, P. S. G. C., A. Doan, J. F. Naughton, G. Krishnan, R. Deep, E. Arcaute, V. Raghavendra, Y. Park, Falcon: Scaling up hands-off crowdsourced entity matching to build cloud services, in: SIGMOD, 2017.

[17] P. Bojanowski, E. Grave, A. Joulin, T. Mikolov, Enriching word vectors with subword information, TACL 5 (2017) 135–146.

[18] H. Chen, B. Perozzi, Y. Hu, S. Skiena, HARP: hierarchical representation learning for networks, CoRR abs/1706.07845 (2017). URL: http://arxiv.org/abs/1706.07845. arXiv:1706.07845.

Towards an Access Control Model for Knowledge Graphs

(Discussion Paper)

Marco Valzelli[1], Andrea Maurino[1], Matteo Palmonari[1] and Blerina Spahiu[1]

[1]*Department of computer systems and communication, University of Milano - Bicocca, Milano, Italy*

Abstract

Nowadays Knowledge Graphs are a common way to integrate and manage large amount of information. This involves also sensitive domains like security, so the management of access control on these graphs became crucial. Due to their dimension, Knowledge graphs are often stored using NoSQL solutions, that have very poor support to access control. In this paper a distributed and secure Knowledge graph management system is presented. The system supports both open and closed access control and its architecture guarantees the secure access of very large knowledge graph by means of query transformation.

Keywords

access control, knowledge graph, NoSQL, security

1. INTRODUCTION

In 2012 Google introduced the Knowledge Graph (KG in the follow) as a new technology to improve its famous search engine. Basically, it is a graph that contains all the main named-entity of the world and the relations between them, so that the search engine is able to identify the subject of the query and suggest all object or features related to it. Since their introduction, KGs have been largely used by a lot of big and small companies (e.g. Amazon, Facebook and so on), but they are also used in several research domains as a way to describe in a common and shared way the knowledge of a given field. Several companies are now aggregating the knowledge stored in both structured and unstructured sources into a unique, comprehensive KG, for a better data management. It is worth noting that a KG can be considered as an evolution of the traditional data integration approach, and as a consequence the size of KG is bigger than previous solutions.

As the uses case of KG increase, they start to include also very sensitive data like for cybersecurity purposes [1], in the military sector [2] the law enforcement sector [3], but also civilian cases like the medical one [4, 5]. For example in this last case, the KG includes all information related to doctors, patients, diseases and so on. Some people may access the KG in order to analyze correlation among clients but they cannot access to personal details of patients, while

SEBD 2021: The 29th Italian Symposium on Advanced Database Systems, September 5-9, 2021, Pizzo Calabro (VV), Italy
m.valzelli@campus.unimib.it (M. Valzelli); andrea.maurino@unimib.it (A. Maurino); matteo.palmonari@unimib.it (M. Palmonari); blerina.spahiu@unimib.it (B. Spahiu)

another person e.g. a doctor can access his patients' information but s/he cannot see information about others doctors. So, the explosion of KG raises new issues wrt. the preservation of relevant information from unauthorized access and their growing request for scalability at a higher level.

Currently, there is no common opinion about how to represent a KG. Among others, RDF is one of the most adopted description languages, SPARQL is the query language for RDF model and many systems for managing RDF data (also called triple store) are available. However there are proposals to implement an access control mechanism in RDF [6, 7, 8], but they are not scalable nor flexible and, most important not implemented in commercial triple store. Recently, others graph models like the Labelled Property Graph model (LPG from now on) has been used to represent knowledge graphs.

In this extended abstract, we propose a solution for enabling access control of large KG in a scalable way. The scalability issue is solved by means of Janusgraph[1] a distributed and scalable property graph. We provide a systematic translation of RDF concepts in terms of property graph model. Then we define an access control method based on logical description of KG and users in terms of property graph model; our solution support a subset of SPARQL query languages by optimizing Gremlinator [9] a software layer able to translate a SPARQL query into a property graph query.

The paper is organized as follows: in section 2 we report the most important contribution of literature and industrial solution for the access control problem applied to graphs, while in section 3 we provide a more formal description of the problem. Section 4 presents the proposed access control method and in section 5 the implementation of the model is shown. Finally in section 6 we draw conclusion and discuss future works.

2. Related Work

The great success of graphs as data model is very recent, but in the past we can find that trees, a particular type of graph, have been used as a data structure on which apply access control. With the need to store data comes along the need to provide an access control framework. An example is XML, a format widely used to exchange information across the web, on which has been proposed an access control model[10]. Starting from 2001 with the birth of the semantic web [11], the RDF semantic graph framework provided an efficient way to store big amounts of data in a graph format. RDF datasets usually are meant to be shared across the web, so no access control models have been provided. Since the users of RDF endpoints are often anonymous, the literature offers many proposals of context-based access control frameworks. One of these [12] also suggests an interesting mechanism for the creation of view on the graph based on the composition of allow/deny rules. The researches in this area also proposes to define policies through ontologies and to apply these policies using ontological reasoning. Research in this area also tried to address particular aspects of this technology like distribution [6, 13], federation [14] inference of new information [15] and possible solutions to the scalability problem [7]. Also more traditional access control models like DAC (Discretionary Accesss Control) have been implemented [8]. Although there are significant literature for access control in RDF Graphs [16], these approaches cannot be directly applied in other graph contexts as they focus on different

[1]janusgraph.org

aspects or heavily rely on ontological reasoning, that is usually provided only by native RDF stores.

Available NoSQL tools were not designed with security and privacy criterion and still lack in this aspect [17, 18]. Just a small part of these solutions support access control features, and only for specific types of policies, like RBAC (Role-Based Access Control). Also notable is the case of Accumulo[2] where access control at cells level is provided.

Graph model is supported by several NoSQL products, but in a very different way from RDF systems. While the letters are based on triples, the former adopt the property graph model. Graph database can be divided into native, where data is physically stored in terms of nodes and edges, and the hybrid, that provides a property graph model but rely on a different storage model like the wide-column.

Neo4J is the most common native graph database and it implements the LPG model. It still has only basic security and access control features: it allows to define user role and their privileges[3], but not at a fine-grained level.

The only significant work in the property graph context [19] has designed an access control model defining how users or groups of users can access and manipulate data. However, it has some drawbacks like lack of flexibility and redundancy. In fact, you can only describe positive permissions and you have to define them for every node, so it's not clear how the model can be applied with inheritance and conflicts. Furthermore, this work and the neo4j proposal has both the characteristic that they requires quite complex algorithm to be evaluated, so their scalability is in doubt. A different approach has been proposed in the Tinkerpop community[4] where the evaluation mechanism of authorizations has been integrated in the Graph-DMBS but it checks for access control metadata in every edge and node, so it needs a certain redundancy both in the stored data and in the interrogation, impacting on the performance of the system.

3. Considered Use Cases

In the past years the literature on access control, thanks to a great adoption in commercial DBMS, has defined a variety of policies one can implement[20]. We focus on three main kind of policies for access control, that are: **DAC, MAC**, and **RBAC**. The former provides for a direct rights specification between users and resources. The letter allows to assign rights to users based on their roles, while MAC provides access to the resources based on the clearance level of the user, following the need-to-know principle (closed policy): a subject should only be given access rights that are required to carry out the subject's duties.

These access control policies were designed to be mutually exclusive, but instead we want to combine and use them at the same time. We extend it by adding more abstraction also over resources, borrowing the notion of classes from RDF ontologies. In fact, groups of users and roles are ways to assign the same rights to more users at the same time, saving memory and maintainability time. We pursue the same objective over resources by giving the possibility to define access rights over entity classes and then propagate them using inheritance mechanisms.

---

[2]https://accumulo.apache.org/

[3]neo4j.com/blog/role-based-access.-control-neo4j-enterprise/

[4]archive.fosdem.org/2019/schedule/event/graph_access_control_tinkerpop

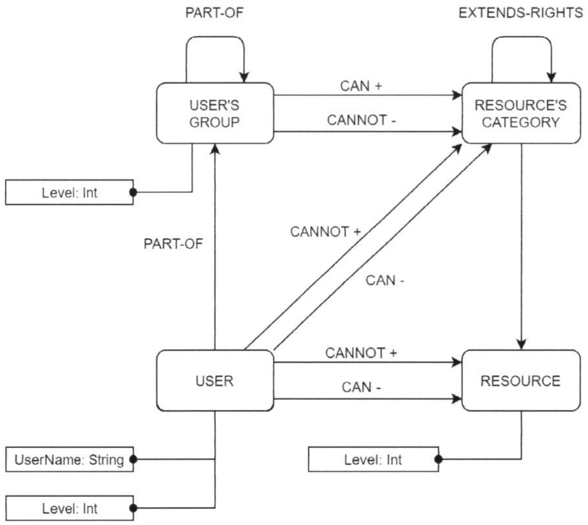

Figure 1: Graph pattern for the access control framework. "Can" and "Cannot" edges cannot be present simultaneously

For example, let's consider the case of a national security agency fighting terrorism. It KG includes classes like Person, Organization and Work. We call this extended graph of the domain Graph. It should be noted that we can use relations between classes as a way to extend access rights between instances that belongs to those classes. In fact, if is defined a relation between "Criminal" and "Document" classes and a user has access to a specific criminal profile, probably she will have access also to his related documents (except for clearance). It is possible to represent as a graph also users, that can be grouped by departments of the agency or their roles. We call this part of the graph the User's graph. According to our scenario, we want to specify only what a user can view, adopting a closed policy. That can be done on the base of both her role and groups,as foreseen by RBAC policy. Probably, different departments of the organization investigate different areas of the world, so they have to be able to view only a small portion of the graph. In addition, we may want to cover also particular cases (like temporary operation) that allows access to specific documents, by means of DAC rules. Moreover, all those rules have to match a user's clearance level (MAC).

4. Access Control Model

The proposed access control model has the goal to design a security mechanism that is reusable for many different policies, especially both the cases of open and closed policies. Our approach is focused on giving or not access to resource. More specific rights like own, delete, modify can be built on the top of our model.

The idea behind our model is to exploit all the flexibility of the LPG model so we do not give a rigid data structure, but only some graph patterns to follow, as can be seen in figure 1. Three are the main part of our model: the user's subgraph, the resource's subgraph and the authorization's edges between them.

In the user's subgraph users are represented by nodes with properties such as the clearance level. They can be grouped in groups by linking them to users' group nodes. This mean they will inherit the access rights of the group. Then, groups can be grouped themself iteratively. In the same way users can be grouped by roles' node. Potentially these types of nodes can coexist, but this will lead to a more complex rights administration.

As we mentioned before, we use relation between classes as a way to extends rights between instances. In fact, it is a common situation that some objects are semantically dependents to another object, that we call resource category. Our intuition is to use this kind of relation between classes to automatically insert specific "extends_rights" edges between their instances.

Finally, we can specify access rights between users or user's groups and resource's classes with authorization edges. In our model we want to allow both open and closed policies, so these edges can have opposite meanings. With closed policies access' rights are usually assigned with the "need to know" principle, which is that a user has to be given access to the resources strictly necessary to carry out his duties, and everything else is forbidden. On the contrary, using open policies are specified resources where a user has not access and all that is not specified is allowed.

In addition, our model provides for particular policy specification using exception edges, that are authorization edges between user and resource in contrast to those between users' groups and resources' categories. Imposing this constrain we ensure to allow expressiveness without leading to too much complexity.

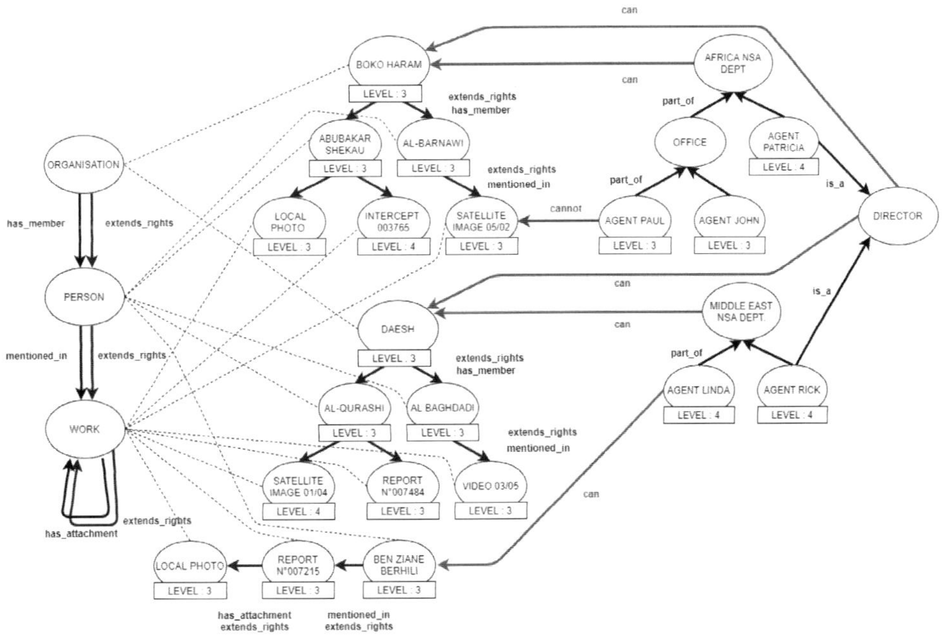

Figure 2: example of KG integrated with the users' Graph and the authorization edges

Determining which node a user can access with a traversal has many advantage:

- The graph model has great readability and also inheritance mechanism are easy to understand

- You can specify a great variety of policies with a few edges and attributes
- Full-scan are not needed as you can just use edges to reach resources you are or not allowed to access
- Maintainability is also simplified. For example, if a user wants to know which users have access to an object, she can exploit the reverse path used during the resource's access mentioned before

As an example of the above mentioned concepts let consider figure 2 whose Domain Graph is taken from DBpedia. The user's graph is linked to the Domain Graph with specific edges, and it is also integrated by AC edges itself. Let's clarify their meanings:

- Green edges represent the positive "can_view" permission.
- Red edges represent the negative "cannot_view" permission.
- Blue edges represent the extend rights relation.

This last relation can be defined between specific classes of the Domain Graph Ontology. For example, we specify that the relation "mentioned_in" extends the access rights from entity of type "Person" to entity of type "Work". Then we can use automatic procedure to add the access control attribute "extends_rights" to all the edges "mentioned_in" between entities of the classes defined before. The graph shown in figure 2 allow to describe the follow access rules:

- The department "Africa NSA" is allowed to view all information about Boko Haram organisation, but:
  - The object "Intercept 003765" cannot be seen from agent Paul and agent Patricia due to too low clearence level
  - The object "Satellite image 05/02" cannot be seen from agent Paul due to a "cannot" edge.
- The department "Middle East NSA" is allowed to view all Daesh organisation and Boko Hara is and affiliated organization.
- Agent Rick and agent Patricia are Director of their department, and this allows them to have full access to both organisation

Moeover, let assume that the agency found a connection between Daesh and the drug dealer Ben Ziane Berhily, who supplies daesh amphetamine. Agent Linda is now allowed to view Ben Ziane data with an exception specified with the "can" edge.

5. Implementation

For the implementation of our access control model, we rely on Tinkerpop [5], which is an Apache project that provides several services and is compatible with fairly all the most common graph products. The most useful feature of this framework for our purposes is the SubGraphStrategy, which is a traversal strategy that allows to create a virtual subgraph based on given constraints. What this method really does is to provide an automatic mechanism that, given a user query,

[5]tinkerpop.apache.org/

verify at every step if the initial constraints are satisfied. Since we use a pattern-based approach integrated with exceptions, we cannot use constraints based on attributes.

Our solution is to split the process into a two step. First, we retrieve all the IDs of the resource a user can access, then we use this list as a constraint for the traversal strategy. This prevents us to check for many different conditions at every step using a more immediate check like equality between IDs.

6. Conclusions and Future Work

We find out that in the state of the art there are not efficient, flexible and general-purpose access control models for Knowledge graphs. We propose an approach based on graph traversal over specific patterns and on the creation of a subgraph using a Tinkerpop feature to address this issue. This is a preliminary model on the top of which it has to be build a more complete access control policy that includes write, delete and own rights. We left as a future work also an extensive test of the scalability of the model.

References

[1] A. Piplai, et al., Creating cybersecurity knowledge graphs from malware after action reports (2019).

[2] F. Liao, L. Ma, D. Yang, Research on construction method of knowledge graph of us military equipment based on bilstm model, in: International Conference on High Performance Big Data and Intelligent Systems, IEEE, 2019, pp. 146–150.

[3] P. Szekely, et al., Building and using a knowledge graph to combat human trafficking, in: International Semantic Web Conference, Springer, 2015, pp. 205–221.

[4] M. Rotmensch, Y. Halpern, A. Tlimat, S. Horng, D. Sontag, Learning a health knowledge graph from electronic medical records, Scientific reports 7 (2017) 1–11.

[5] L. Shi, et al., Semantic health knowledge graph: Semantic integration of heterogeneous medical knowledge and services, BioMed research international 2017 (2017).

[6] L. Kagal, T. Finin, A. Joshi, A policy based approach to security for the semantic web, in: International semantic web conference, Springer, 2003, pp. 402–418.

[7] F. Abel, other, Enabling advanced and context-dependent access control in rdf stores, in: The Semantic Web, Springer, 2007, pp. 1–14.

[8] S. Kirrane, Linked data with access control, in: Workshop on. pp, volume 14, 2015, p. 23.

[9] H. Thakkar, D. Punjani, J. Lehmann, S. Auer, Two for one: Querying property graph databases using sparql via gremlinator, in: International Workshop on Graph Data Management Experiences & Systems (GRADES) and Network Data Analytics (NDA), 2018, pp. 1–5.

[10] E. Damiani, S. De Capitani di Vimercati, S. Paraboschi, P. Samarati, A fine-grained access control system for xml documents, ACM Transactions on Information and System Security (TISSEC) 5 (2002) 169–202.

[11] T. Berners-Lee, J. Hendler, O. Lassila, et al., The semantic web, Scientific american 284 (2001) 28–37.

[12] R. Stojanov, S. Gramatikov, I. Mishkovski, D. Trajanov, Linked data authorization platform, IEEE Access 6 (2017) 1189–1213.

[13] J. Hollenbach, J. Presbrey, T. Berners-Lee, Using rdf metadata to enable access control on the social semantic web, in: Workshop on Collaborative Construction, Management and Linking of Structured Knowledge, volume 514, 2009, p. 167.

[14] M. Goncalves, M.-E. Vidal, K. M. Endris, Pure: A privacy aware rule-based framework over knowledge graphs, in: International Conference on Database and Expert Systems Applications, Springer, 2019, pp. 205–214.

[15] A. Jain, C. Farkas, Secure resource description framework: an access control model, in: Symposium on Access control models and technologies, ACM, 2006, pp. 121–129.

[16] S. Kirrane, A. Mileo, S. Decker, Access control and the resource description framework: A survey, Semantic Web 8 (2017) 311–352.

[17] E. Sahafizadeh, M. A. Nematbakhsh, A survey on security issues in big data and nosql, Advances in Computer Science: an International Journal 4 (2015) 68–72.

[18] A. A. Alotaibi, R. M. Alotaibi, N. Hamza, Access control models in nosql databases: An overview (2019).

[19] C. Morgado, G. B. Baioco, T. Basso, R. Moraes, A security model for access control in graph-oriented databases, in: International Conference on Software Quality, Reliability and Security, IEEE, 2018, pp. 135–142.

[20] R. S. Sandhu, P. Samarati, Access control: principle and practice, IEEE communications magazine 32 (1994) 40–48.

Multi-Sorted Inverse Frequent Itemsets Mining for Generating Realistic No-SQL Datasets

(Discussion Paper)

Domenico Saccà[1], Edoardo Serra[2] and Antonino Rullo[1]

[1]*DIMES Department, University of Calabria, 87036 Rende, Italy*
[2]*Department of Computer Science, Boise State University, Boise, ID 83725, USA*

Abstract

The development of novel platforms and techniques for emerging "Big Data" applications requires the availability of real-life datasets for data-driven experiments, which are however not accessible in most cases for various reasons, e.g., confidentiality, privacy or simply insufficient availability. An interesting solution to ensure high quality experimental findings is to synthesize datasets that reflect patterns of real ones. A promising approach is based on inverse mining techniques such as inverse frequent itemset mining (IFM), which consists of generating a transactional dataset satisfying given support constraints on the itemsets of an input set, that are typically the frequent and infrequent ones. This paper describes an extension of IFM that considers more structured schemes for the datasets to be generated, as required in emerging big data applications, e.g., social network analytics.

Keywords

IFM, No-SQL, Itemset Mining

1. Introduction

Emerging "Big Data" platforms and applications call for the invention of novel data analysis techniques that are capable to effectively and efficiently handle large amount of data [1]. There is therefore an increasing need to use real-life datasets for data-driven experiments that are often not available for two main reasons: (i) *ownership* (i.e., they are often proprietary and out of reach for academic research), and (ii) *privacy* (they may include sensible data as it happens for many research areas, e.g., epidemiology, public health, social science, study of the behavior of large populations of individuals under natural scenarios, as well as under human interventions).

The two above limitations can be overcome by the design of "realistic" synthetic datasets that capture key attributes and activities of real ones without violating confidentiality [2].

In this paper we use an inverse data mining approach to generate an artificial NoSQL transactional dataset that reflects the patterns of a real one: the patterns can be thought of as a compressed representation of the original dataset and are first discovered by data mining techniques, and they are next used to generate a "realistic" pattern-preserving dataset.

SEBD 2021: The 29th Italian Symposium on Advanced Database Systems, September 5-9, 2021, Pizzo Calabro (VV), Italy

domenico.sacca@unical.it (D. Saccà); edoardoserra@boisestate.edu (E. Serra); n.rullo@dimes.unical.it (A. Rullo)
0000-0003-3584-5372 (D. Saccà); 0000-0003-0689-5063 (E. Serra); 0000-0002-6030-0027 (A. Rullo)

A well-known inverse approach refers to the classical data mining problem of extracting the set of the *frequent/infrequent itemsets* from a transaction database. The related literature is rather rich and covers almost three decades: after the seminal papers in the nineties [3, 4], additional aspects have been studied in the last two decades. The perspective of the frequent itemset mining problem can be naturally inverted as follows: we are be given in advance a set of itemsets together with their frequency as constraints and our goal is to compute a transactional database satisfying the above constraints. This problem, called the *inverse frequent itemset mining* problem (`IFM`), has been introduced in the context of defining generators for benchmarks of mining algorithms [5], and has been subsequently reconsidered in privacy preserving contexts [6, 7]. A reformulation of `IFM` in terms of frequencies instead of supports has been introduced in [8, 9] with the name `FREQSAT` and many variants of it have been proposed as well.

The original `IFM` formulation does not introduce any constraint on infrequency. A simple solution to exclude unexpected frequent itemset from a feasible solution is the formulation proposed in [10], which is called $\mathtt{IFM}_S$: only itemsets listed in the set S of constraints can be included as transactions in $\mathcal{D}$. A more general version of `IFM` with infrequency support constraint ($\mathtt{IFM}_\mathtt{I}$ for short), has been proposed in [11], where every infrequent itemset may occur a small number of times.

In order to enlarge the domain of `IFM` to NoSQL applications, an extension of `IFM` has been proposed in [12] that considers more structured schemes for the datasets to be generated, as required by emerging big data applications, e.g., social network analytics. A many-sorted extension of `IFM` called ms-`IFM` is defined by replacing the basic simple schema $R(K, A)$ with a more general NoSQL schema $R(K, A_1, \dots, A_p, A_1, \dots, A_q)$, where K is the table key, $A_1, \dots, A_p$ are single-valued attributes, and $A_1, \dots, A_q$ are multi-valued attributes. This problem reduces to classical `IFM` when $p = 0$ and $q = 1$, i.e., there is exactly one multi-valued attribute.

In this paper we describe the formal definition of ms-`IFM` of [12] and illustrate a method for solving ms-`IFM` that has been shown to be effective by means of a number of experiments. The solver is based on large-scale linear programming and generalizes the approach used in [11] to solve $\mathtt{IFM}_\mathtt{I}$.

2. Many-Sorted IFM

Let a NoSQL *relation* $R(K, A_1, \dots, A_p, A_{p+1}, \dots, A_{p+q})$ be given, where K is the table key, $A_1, \dots, A_p$ are classical single-valued (SV) attributes and $A_{p+1}, \dots, A_{p+q}$ are multi-valued (MV) attributes. We assume that the attributes are ordered, i.e., K is the first attribute, A_1 the second attribute, A_{p+1} the $(1 + p + 1)$-th attribute and so on. For each i, $1 \le i \le p + q$, let $\mathcal{A}_i$ be the finite domain for the attributes A_i and $|\mathcal{A}_i| = n_i$. We assume that the values of every domain $\mathcal{A}_i$ (called *items*) are given in input – they are SV items or MV items depending on whether the attribute A_i is SV or MV. On the other hand, the domain $\mathcal{K}$ of the key K is countably infinite and, then, its values are not listed.

Let $\dot{n} = \sum_{i=1}^{p} n_i$, $\ddot{n} = \sum_{i=p+1}^{p+q} n_i$ and $n = \dot{n} + \ddot{n}$. A NoSQL *tuple* on R is of the form $t = [k, a_1, \dots, a_p, g_1, \dots, g_q]$, where $k \in \mathcal{K}$, for each i, $1 \le i \le p$, $a_i \in \mathcal{A}_i$ (a_i is an *item* of t) and for each i, $1 \le i \le q$, $g_i \subseteq \mathcal{A}_{p+i}$ (g_i is an *itemset* of t). Items and itemsets are called *values* of t. A NoSQL *table* on R is a finite set of NoSQL tuples.

A *many-sorted transaction* T is a $(p+q)$-tuple $[a_1, \ldots, a_p, g_1, \ldots, g_q]$ where the key attribute value is dropped out from a NoSQL tuple. It follows that a many-sorted transaction can be transformed into a tuple simply by inventing a key for it. Given any attribute A_i in R and a many-sorted transaction T, T_{A_i} denotes the value of T for the attribute A_i (e.g., $a_i \in \mathcal{A}_i$ if $i \leq p$ or $g_{i-p} \subseteq \mathcal{A}_i$ if $i > p$).

Let $\mathcal{T}$ be the set of all many-sorted transactions. The cardinality of $\mathcal{T}$ is $n_{\mathcal{T}} = 2^{\ddot{n}} \cdot \prod_{i=1}^{p} \dot{n}_i$. A *many-sorted dataset* $\mathcal{D}$ is set of pairs $(T, \delta^{\mathcal{D}}(T))$, where T is a many-sorted transaction and $\delta^{\mathcal{D}}(T)$ is the number of occurrences of T. $\mathcal{D}$ can be transformed into a NoSQL table $T_{\mathcal{D}}$ by making $\delta^{\mathcal{D}}(T)$ tuple duplicates of each many-sorted transaction T. The *cardinality* of $\mathcal{D}$, denoted as $|\mathcal{D}|$, is the number of pairs in $\mathcal{D}$ and the *size* of $\mathcal{D}$ is $\delta^{\mathcal{D}} = |T_{\mathcal{D}}| = \sum_{T \in \mathcal{D}} \delta^{\mathcal{D}}(T)$. We stress that in general $\delta^{\mathcal{D}} \gg |\mathcal{D}|$. From now on, we shall omit the term *many-sorted* whenever it is clear from the context.

A *sub-transaction* S is a $(p+q)$-tuple $[a_1, \ldots, a_p, g_1, \ldots, g_q]$ on R for which the domain of each SV attribute is extended with $\perp$, which stands for a null value. Let $\perp(S)$ denote the number of null values in S – a transaction T can be also seen as a sub-transaction type for which $\perp(T) = 0$. The *length* of S, denoted as $l(S)$, is the number of values different from $\perp$ and $\emptyset$. A sub-transaction S *subsumes* a transaction T (written $S \sqsubseteq T$) if for each SV attribute A_i, either $S.A_i = \perp$ or $S.A_i = T.A_i$, and for each MV attribute A_i, $S.A_i \subseteq T.A_i$. Observe that if S happens to be a transaction then every transaction T for which $S \sqsubseteq T$ has the same SV items as S, whereas its MV itemsets are supersets of the corresponding itemsets in S. In the classical `IFM` setting, every transaction type S coincides with an itemset and the transactions T subsumed by S are all itemsets for which $S \subseteq T$. This analogy explains why we write $S \sqsubseteq T$ for transaction subsumption.

Given a sub-transaction S for which $l(S) > 0$ and two integers σ_1 and σ_2 for which $0 \leq \sigma_1 \leq \sigma_2$, $\gamma = \langle S, \sigma_1, \sigma_2 \rangle$ represents a *frequency support constraint* defined as: a database $\mathcal{D}$ satisfies γ (written as $\mathcal{D} \models \gamma$) if: $\sigma_1 \leq \sum_{T \in \mathcal{D} \wedge S \sqsubseteq T} \delta^{\mathcal{D}}(T) \leq \sigma_2$. An *infrequency support constraint* γ is a pair $\langle S, \sigma \rangle$ and is actually a shorthand for the frequency support constraint $\langle S, 0, \sigma \rangle$. The upper bound σ will be simply referred to as $\gamma_{\#}$. A (frequency or infrequency) support constraint γ for which $l(\gamma_S) = 1$ is called a *domain support constraint*. Given a set Π of support constraints, a database $\mathcal{D}$ satisfies Π (written as $\mathcal{D} \models \Pi$), if for each $\gamma \in \Pi$, $\mathcal{D} \models \gamma$.

Example. Individuals are characterized by the SV attributes *Gender*, *Location* and *Age* and by the MV attributes *Groups* and *Events*: an individual may belong to various groups and may attend a number of events. A transaction $I = [Male, Rome, 25, \{g_1, g_4\}, \{e_1, e_3\}]$ represents a 25-year old male individual located in Rome who belongs to the groups g_1 and g_4 and attends the events e_1 and e_3. The transaction $J = [Female, Rome, 20, \{g_1, g_2\}]$ represents an individual who does not attend any event. Note that, as the attributes do not define a key, there may exist several occurrences of the same individual. Examples of constraints are:

– $\langle [Male, Rome, \perp, \{g_1, g_2\}, \emptyset], 10000, 20000 \rangle$ fixes the range for the overall duplicate number of male individuals who are located in Rome and are participating to at least the groups g_1 and g_2;

– $\langle [Female, \perp, 25, \{g_1, g_2\}, \{e_1, e_3\}], 500, 1000 \rangle$ fixes the range for the overall duplicate number of 25-year old female individuals who are participating to at least the groups g_1 and g_2 and

attending at least the events e_1 and e_3;
Infrequency constraints:
– $\langle[\bot, Cosenza, \bot, \{g_1, g_2\}, \emptyset], 100\rangle$ states that the number of individuals located at Cosenza in a feasible dataset who are participating to at least the groups g_1 and g_2 is at most 100;
– $\langle[\bot, \bot, \bot, \emptyset, \{e_1, e_2\}], 10000\rangle$ states that the number of individuals attending at least the events e_1 and e_2 is at most 10000;
– $\langle[\bot, \bot, \bot, \{g_1\}, \emptyset], 100000\rangle$ is a domain support constraint stating that the number of individuals participating to at least the group g_1 is at most 100000. □

From now on, we assume that the following sets of constraints are given: (1) a set Σ of *frequency support constraints* with cardinality $m = |\Sigma| > 0$ and (2) a set $\widehat{\Sigma}$ of *infrequency support constraints* with cardinality $\widehat{m} = |\widehat{\Sigma}| \geq 0$. Let $\breve{\Sigma} = \Sigma \cup \widehat{\Sigma}$ and $\breve{m} = |\breve{\Sigma}| = m + \widehat{m}$.

Observe that, as the number of infrequency constraints could be very large, they are not induced as for the $\mathtt{IFM_I}$ case [11]. but explicitly defined. The drawback of this formulation is that it is not anymore excluded to eventually obtain undesired frequent itemsets. But an accurate choice of explicit infrequent itemsets may reduce this risk.

Definition. Given R, $\breve{\Sigma} = \Sigma \cup \widehat{\Sigma}$, and an integer $\mathtt{size} > 0$, the *multi-sorted inverse frequent itemset mining problem*, shortly denoted as ms–IFM, consists of finding a many-sorted dataset $\mathcal{D}$ on R such that both $\delta^{\mathcal{D}} = \mathtt{size}$ and $\mathcal{D} \models \breve{\Sigma}$ (or of eventually stating that there is no such a dataset). If the integer constraint for the number of duplicates for a transaction of a database $\mathcal{D}$ is relaxed (i.e., it is a rational number), the problem is called *relaxed* ms–IFM. □

By assuming that items, constraint bounds and size are stored using a constant amount of space, the input size of the problem is $\mathcal{O}(\, n + \breve{m}\,(p + q\,\ddot{n} + 1) + m\,)$. It is easy to see that ms–IFM reduces to the $\mathtt{IFM_I}$ problem if $p = 0$ and $q = 1$, i.e., there exists exactly one non-key attribute in R and this attribute is of MV type, say G. A transaction is then any itemset on the domain $\mathcal{G}$ of G. The next result shows that the complexity of ms–IFM and of relaxed ms–IFM.

Proposition. The decision version of ms–IFM is in PSPACE and NP-hard and the decision version of relaxed ms–IFM is NP-complete. □

Note that the higher complexity of the $\mathtt{IFM_I}$ problem, which has been proved to be NEXP-complete in [11], derives from the task of discovering "minimal" itemsets that must be enforced to be infrequent: in $\mathtt{IFM_I}$ minimal infrequent itemsets are computed by the resolution algorithm, whereas they are assumed to be part of the input for ms–IFM.

To solve the relaxed ms-IFM, in the next sections we define formulate ms-IFM as a linear program and present an extension of the classical simplex algorithm for its resolution.

2.1. Linear Program Formulation

We select an ordering of all *many-sorted transactions* in $\mathcal{T}$, say $\{T_1, \ldots, T_{n_\mathcal{T}}\}$. We use the vector $v = [1, \ldots, n_\mathcal{T}]$ to list all possible non-empty *many-sorted transaction* indices. Let the vector $s = [i_1, \ldots, i_m, j_1, \ldots, j_{\widehat{m}}]$ represent the indices of the frequency support constraints in Σ and the infrequency support constraint $\widehat{\Sigma}$. Let l and u be two vectors of m integers such that for each $j, 1 \leq j \leq m$, $l_j = \sigma^J_{min}$ and $u_j = \sigma^J_{max}$, where $J = \gamma_{\tilde{s}_j}$ is the j-th frequency support constraints in Σ according to the ordering fixed by s. Let u' be the vector of $\widehat{m}$ integers such that for each $j, m \leq j \leq m + \widehat{m}$, $u'_j = \sigma^J_{max}$, where $J = \gamma_{\tilde{s}_j}$ is the j-th infrequency support constraints in Σ according to the ordering fixed by s. Let x be a vector of $n_{\mathcal{T}}$ non-negative rational variables whose meaning is that its j-the coordinate, x_j, denotes the number of duplicates for the many-sorted transaction T_j. We consider a $(m + \widehat{m}) \times n_{\mathcal{T}}$ matrix A where for each $i, 1 \leq i \leq m + \widehat{m}$, and for each $j \in v$, $a_{ij} = 1$ if $S \sqsubseteq T_j$ where $\gamma_{s_i} = \langle S, \sigma_1, \sigma_2 \rangle$ or $a_{ij} = 0$ otherwise. As usual, we introduce a vector w of $2m + 1$ non-negative rational number artificial variables, whose values represent the costs of violating some support constraints.

The relaxed linear formulation of the ms-IFM is the following:

$$\texttt{LP}: \text{ minimize} \sum_{i=1}^{2m+1} w_i \quad \text{- subject to}$$

$$w_i + \sum_{j \in v} a_{ij} x_j \geq l_i \qquad 1 \leq i \leq m$$

$$w_{m+i} - \sum_{j \in v} a_{ij} x_j \geq -u_i \qquad 1 \leq i \leq m$$

$$-\sum_{j \in v} a_{ij} x_j \geq -u'_j \qquad m+1 \leq i \leq m+m'$$

$$w_{2m+1} + \sum_{j \in v} x_j \geq \texttt{size} \qquad -\sum_{j \in v} x_j \geq \texttt{size}$$

For solving the linear program we use the *column generation* approach (see e.g. [13]), which is an extension of the simplex method for dealing with linear programs with a large number of variables. The column generation simplex solves a linear program without explicitly including all columns (i.e., variables), in the coefficient matrix but only a subset of them with cardinality equal to the number of rows (i.e., constraints). Columns are dynamically generated by solving an auxiliary optimization problem called the *pricing problem.*

The linear program to be solved is denoted as the *master problem* (MP). In our case the MP problem consists of $r = 2m + m' + 2$ rows and $c = 2^n + 2m$ columns.

The linear program with only a subset of the MP columns with cardinality c' equal to the number r of rows is called the *restricted master problem* (RMP). Then, the restricted master problem is the master problem with a subset of columns w.r.t. the original master problem. From the theory of the simplex algorithm we know that a basic solution for a linear program is an assignment of the variables that satisfy the constraints and where only r (number of rows are activated) variables are assigned with a value greater or equal than zero (i.e., the variables in the basic solution), the reaming ones are zero. Starting from an initial basic solution, the simplex algorithm will iteratively find the optimal basic solution. Since each variable is assigned to a column, it turns out that if the RMP contains the columns associated to the variables in the optimal base solutions of the MP, then the RMP will return the same solution. Then the column generation approach is an iterative algorithm that working on the restricted master problem will keep the number of columns bounded and iterates till the RMP does not contain the columns associated with optimal base solution of the MP.

The column generation method looks for an optimal basis as within the simplex algorithm. It starts from an initial basis and moves from a current basis to a new one by adding a new basic column with a negative reduced cost (*iteration step*). Primal feasibility is maintained and the objective function is non-increasing during this search. The reduced cost of a column can be computed by using the current dual variables. The task of providing a column with a negative reduced cost, or certifying that there is not such a column, is delegated to the pricing problem. If there is no column with a negative reduced cost, then the algorithm terminates and the current basis is optimal.

The crucial task is the formulation and resolution of the pricing problem that is done by using integer linear program. Due to page restrictions, we defer this issue to the full paper [12].

2.2. Empirical evaluation of Many-Sorted IFM

To evaluate the accuracy of the solutions computed by our ms-IFM approximated approach, we show that synthetic data can successfully replace original data in an analytics task, in particular *classification*, which is the problem of identifying to which of a set of categories (subpopulations), a new observation belongs to, on the basis of a training set of data containing observations and whose categories membership is known [14]. To this end, we set up a classification problem by representing a transactional dataset with a standard dataset for classification, where each item corresponds to a binary attribute (i.e., 1 if present and 0 otherwise). To create several different classification tasks for each dataset used in the experiments, we selected the top-k most frequent items. For each of such items, we consider this item as the dependent feature (i.e., the binary attribute that we want to classify) and the remaining top-k items as the independent features (i.e., the input of the classification model). For each synthetic dataset generated by ms–IFM techniques, we train a classification model for each of the top-k most frequent items and we test the trained model on the original dataset.

In the experiments, we use 3 different classification models [14]: *Logistic Regression, Decision Tree,* and *Random Forest.* All of these models are trained with datasets and specific procedures to balance the training sets are executed. For each model and for each dataset, we compute the accuracy of the classification model, which was first trained and tested on the original dataset. The accuracy computed while testing classification on the original dataset (denoted as *original accuracy*) can be assumed to be the best classification accuracy value that any synthetic dataset generation approach can achieve.

To create instances for our ms-IFM, we used the Yelp dataset [15] to extract a No-SQL table. In particular, each transaction of the No-SQL table represents a business in Yelp (e.g., restaurant, hospital, etc.). In total there are 101,824 transactions. The table has 4 attributes: STARS (the average number of stars for each businesshis – a SV attribute with 9 values), STATE (the state where the business is located – a SV attribute with 50 values), CATEGORIES (the categories to which a particular business belongs – a MV value attribute with 397 distinct values, e.g., garage, restaurant, space for kids, etc.). To create the frequency and infrequency support many-sorted constraints, we converted this NOSQL table in a transactional dataset.

Table 1
Accuracy for the 30-top frequent items with $s(\%) \in \{1.2, 1.6\}$

classifier	Original	$S(\%) = 1.2$	$S(\%) = 1.6$
Logistic Regression	0.99	0.93	0.93
Decision Tree	0.99	0.85	0.84
Random Forest	0.99	0.92	0.92

In Table 1, we report the average classification results obtained for 30-top frequent items in the two different datasets obtained by means of two selected supports.

From Table 1 it is possible to see that the synthetic datasets generated are pretty close to the original dataset in term of accuracy. In addition, we did not observe a strong variation when the support changes. Further accuracy evaluations are reported in [12].

3. Conclusion

The *Inverse Frequent itemset Mining* (IFM) problem consists of generating a transactional database satisfying given support constraints on some itemsets, which are typically the frequent ones. In order to enlarge the application domain, an extension of IFM, called multi-sorted IFM (ms-IFM), has been introduced in [12] that considers more structured schemes for the datasets to be generated, as required in emerging big data applications, e.g., social network analytics.

This paper has given an overview of $ms-$IFM problem definition, linear program formulation, resolution using a column generation algorithm (an extension of the simplex method for dealing with linear programs with a large number of variables), and an experimental evaluation of the capability of the synthetic datasets to perform the data mining task of classification with an accuracy close to the one achieved with the original datasets.

References

[1] K. Michael, K. W. Miller, Big Data: New Opportunities and New Challenges [Guest editors' Introduction], Computer 46 (2013) 22–24. doi:http://doi.ieeecomputersociety.org/10.1109/MC.2013.196.

[2] H. Wu, Y. Ning, P. Chakraborty, J. Vreeken, N. Tatti, N. Ramakrishnan, Generating Realistic Synthetic Population Datasets, ACM Trans. Knowl. Discov. Data 12 (2018) 45:1–45:22. URL: http://doi.acm.org/10.1145/3182383. doi:10.1145/3182383.

[3] R. Agrawal, T. Imieliński, A. Swami, Mining Association Rules Between Sets of Items in Large Databases, in: Proceedings of the 1993 ACM SIGMOD International Conference on Management of Data, SIGMOD '93, ACM, New York, NY, USA, 1993, pp. 207–216.

[4] D. Gunopulos, R. Khardon, H. Mannila, H. Toivonen, Data mining, Hypergraph Transversals, and Machine Learning, in: A. O. Mendelzon, Z. M. Özsoyoglu (Eds.), Proceedings of the 16-th ACM SIGMOD-SIGACT-SIGART Symposium on Principles of Database Systems, PODS '97, ACM Press, 1997, pp. 209–216.

[5] T. Mielikainen, On Inverse Frequent Set Mining, in: Proceedings of 2nd Workshop on Privacy Preserving Data Mining, PPDM '03, IEEE Computer Society, Washington, DC, USA, 2003, pp. 18–23.
[6] R. Agrawal, R. Srikant, Privacy-preserving Data Mining, in: Proceedings of the 2000 ACM SIGMOD International Conference on Management of Data, SIGMOD '00, ACM, New York, NY, USA, 2000, pp. 439–450. doi:10.1145/342009.335438.
[7] X. Wu, Y. Wu, Y. Wang, Y. Li, Privacy Aware Market Basket Data Set Generation: A Feasible Approach for Inverse Frequent Set Mining, in: Proceedings of SIAM International Conference on Data Mining, SDM' 05, SIAM, Philadelphia, PA, USA, 2005, pp. 103–114.
[8] T. Calders, Computational Complexity of Itemset Frequency Satisfiability, in: Proceedings of the twenty-third ACM SIGMOD-SIGACT-SIGART Symposium on Principles of Database Systems, PODS '04, ACM, New York, NY, USA, 2004, pp. 143–154. doi:10.1145/1055558.1055580.
[9] T. Calders, The Complexity of Satisfying Constraints on Databases of Transactions, Acta Informatica 44 (2007) 591–624.
[10] A. Guzzo, D. Saccà, E. Serra, An Effective Approach to Inverse Frequent Set Mining, in: Proceedings of the 2009 Ninth IEEE International Conference on Data Mining, ICDM '09, IEEE Computer Society, Washington, DC, USA, 2009, pp. 806–811. URL: http://dx.doi.org/10.1109/ICDM.2009.123. doi:10.1109/ICDM.2009.123.
[11] A. Guzzo, L. Moccia, D. Saccà, E. Serra, Solving Inverse Frequent Itemset Mining with Infrequency Constraints via Large-scale Linear Programs, ACM Trans. Knowl. Discov. Data 7 (2013) 18:1–18:39. URL: http://doi.acm.org/10.1145/2541268.2541271. doi:10.1145/2541268.2541271.
[12] D. Saccà, E. Serra, A. Rullo, Extending Inverse Frequent Itemsets Mining to Generate Realistic Datasets: Complexity, Accuracy and Emerging Applications, Data Min. Knowl. Discov. 33 (2019) 1736–1774. URL: https://doi.org/10.1007/s10618-019-00643-1. doi:10.1007/s10618-019-00643-1.
[13] P. C. Gilmore, R. E. Gomory, A Linear Programming Approach to the Cutting-Stock Problem, Operations Research 9 (1961) 849–859. URL: http://or.journal.informs.org/cgi/doi/10.1287/opre.11.6.863.
[14] J. Han, M. Kamber, Data Mining: Concepts and Techniques, Kaufmann, San Francisco, CA, USA, 2005. URL: http://www.amazon.com/Data-Mining-Concepts-Techniques-Management/dp/1558604898.
[15] Yelp Challenge, 2017. URL: https://www.yelp.com/dataset.

Spice-Up your Coding Lessons with the ACME Approach

(Discussion Paper)

Giansalvatore Mecca[1], Donatello Santoro[1], Nazzareno Sileno[1] and Enzo Veltri[1]

[1]*Università degli Studi della Basilicata (UNIBAS), Potenza, Italy*

Abstract

It is nowadays considered a fundamental skill for students and citizens the capacity of undertaking a problem-solving process in various disciplines (including STEM, i.e. science, technology, engineering and mathematics) using distinctive techniques that are typical of computer science. These abilities are usually called Computational Thinking and at the roots of them stands the knowledge of coding. With the goal of encouraging Computational Thinking in young students, we discuss tools and techniques to support the teaching and the learning of coding in school curricula. It is well known that this problem is complex due to the fact that it requires abstraction capabilities and complex cognitive skills such as procedural and conditional reasoning, planning, and analogical reasoning. In this paper, we present ACME ("Code Animation by Evolved Metaphors") that stands at the foundation of the Diogene-CT code visualization environment and methodology. We discuss visual metaphors for both procedural and object-oriented programming. Based on them, we introduce a playground architecture to support teaching and learning of the principles of coding. To the best of our knowledge, this is the first scalable code visualization tool using consistent metaphors in the field of Computing Education Research (CER).

Keywords

Coding Tools and Techniques, Learning Environments, Educational Support, Computers and Education

1. Introduction and Motivation

The ability to face problem-solving challenges of STEM disciplines is nowadays universally considered as a crucial skill [1, 2, 3]. *Computational Thinking* has been defined as the capacity of undertaking a problem-solving process in various disciplines using techniques that are distinctive of computer science [4]. At the core of these techniques stand the skill of computer programming, commonly called *coding*. Coding abilities are a fundamental building block of any computational-thinking based approach to teaching. In view of this, this paper illustrates a new method and tools to simplify the teaching and learning of coding. This is a complex problem, that poses several important challenges. The prominent one is that acquiring coding skills requires abstraction capabilities: the conceptualization of the data, the choice of a proper representation, the algorithms development, the semantics of the program (the execution of a program consists of a sequence of actions executed by the machine, and for novice programmers,

SEBD 2021: The 29th Italian Symposium on Advanced Database Systems, September 5-9, 2021, Pizzo Calabro (VV), Italy
giansalvatore.mecca@unibas.it (G. Mecca); donatello.santoro@unibas.it (D. Santoro); nazzareno.sileno@gmail.com (N. Sileno); enzo.veltri@unibas.it (E. Veltri)
0000-0002-1189-1481 (G. Mecca); 0000-0002-5651-8584 (D. Santoro); 0000-0001-9947-8909 (E. Veltri)

this is done within a "black box"). Moved by these motivations our ACME approach [5] makes several important contributions towards the goal of fostering the ACME adoption of innovative tools and methods to teach computer programming:

- It introduces a set of consistent metaphors to introduce the concepts of programming. By adopting the metaphors, instructors can work with students through the concepts of programming with a very concrete, visually perceivable counterpart to all of the inner workings of a programming language, in order to ease the approach of students to coding, reduce their cognitive load and the "black box" effect associated with source code. The metaphors consider both introductory coding, i.e., procedural-programming concepts like variables, assignments, control structures and so on, i.e., programming-in-the-small, and object-oriented programming concepts like components, classes, objects, responsibilities and messages, i.e., programming-in-the-medium. This is an important feature of our method, that can be adopted as a holistic approach to building a complex coding curriculum.
- In addition to this methodology, we present a set of tools. The basic building blocks for our toolset are represented by animation actions and animation programs. The metaphors are translated into a library of animation actions over an animation scene. The scene contains the main actors of the animation – like the mechanical arm or the calculator, and their possible interaction. Each animation action animates one basic operation carried out by the processor or virtual machine during the execution of a piece of code, as a set of visible actions of the actors on the scene. In this way, each execution of a target program becomes an animation program on the scene.
- We develop an engine for animation-program execution. This allows to construct and run animation programs offline, or in detached mode. In this mode, the animation program is not directly attached to the target-program source code, and therefore it does not depend directly on the target programming language. This has the advantage of leaving instructors with ample flexibility in choosing programming languages, possibly allowing them to mix and compare programs in different languages.
- In addition to offline mode, we also develop a complex development environment to run animations in online or attached mode. The development environment supports the full cycle of Java source code development and execution, with the important addition of automatically generating animation actions and animation programs for the target code. To do this, we develop a complex infrastructure that represents one of the main technical contributions of our ACME approach.

The ACME methodology and Diogene-CT tools are the product of a long experience with innovative methods for teaching programming conducted over the last 15 years within introductory programming courses at the University of Basilicata. In the last couple of years, the adoption of animation programs has been successfully tested both the "Procedural Programming" course and in the "Object-Oriented Programming" course. This allowed us to gain precious insights into their strength and limitations, and to refine and significantly improve the method.

2. ACME-Approach

We intend to exploit the advantages of earlier approaches within our proposal, while at the same time removing the limitation connected to the scope of the programming platform [6, 7, 8]. We use the two main intuitions from previous work: (a) immediate visualization of the effect of instruction and (b) program as a way to bring the computer to a visually clear target state. But, we also deeply transform them, by constructing our metaphor based on the actual workings of a programming language rather than some fictional microworld or external physical robot.

We develop a methodology and a toolset capable of providing visual feedback for arbitrary programs written using programming languages of state-of-the-art platforms (primarily Java), and both for introductory procedural-programming, and more complex object-oriented programming.

The methodology is based on two different but interrelated metaphors. The first is centered around the main constructs of procedural programming, like storing value by a variable or evaluating a mathematical expression. The second one is constructed around the principles of object-oriented programming, like constructing objects of exchanging messages for method invocation.

The set of tools developed within the project supports different usage scenarios. In fact, Diogene-CT is both a teaching methodology and a set of executable tools. Teachers may decide to only adopt the teaching methodology (the ACME metaphors) as a basis for their lectures, or also the tools that come with it.

The animator tool may be run both in *offline* and *online* mode. In offline mode the teacher typically develops some code, then picks up a usage scenario for it – e.g., calculating the size of the circle given its radius, with a radius of 3 cm – and uses the Diogene-CT animator to give life to the execution of that particular usage scenario, in an offline fashion for the actual execution of the code. Much more challenging is the online mode, in which the Diogene-CT animator is provided with a piece of source code written in Java and allows the student to run the code and interact with it while animating all events triggered by the code.

These ideas are described in the following subsections.

2.1. The Mechanical Arm Metaphor for Procedural Programming

The aim is to teach the basic concepts of any programming language, like variables, assignments, control structures and so on. Based on this idea, we introduce a metaphor for the execution of code instructions based on the use of mechanical arms. A typical scene generated by the animator for this metaphor is shown in Figure 1.

The main elements (characters of the scene) of the metaphor are as follows: (a) The RAM is represented as a large spreadsheet of cells that can be named and can store values, to represent variables; (b) The ALU is exemplified as a calculator capable of performing the computations required in numerical and Boolean algebra; (c) The standard input and standard output are represented by pipes connected to the keyboard and console screen. Animations show streams of characters flowing through these pipes when they are activated; (d) The actions performed by the processor are depicted as movements of a group of mechanical arms. The mechanical arm represents an execution context, typically a function, and is responsible for animating

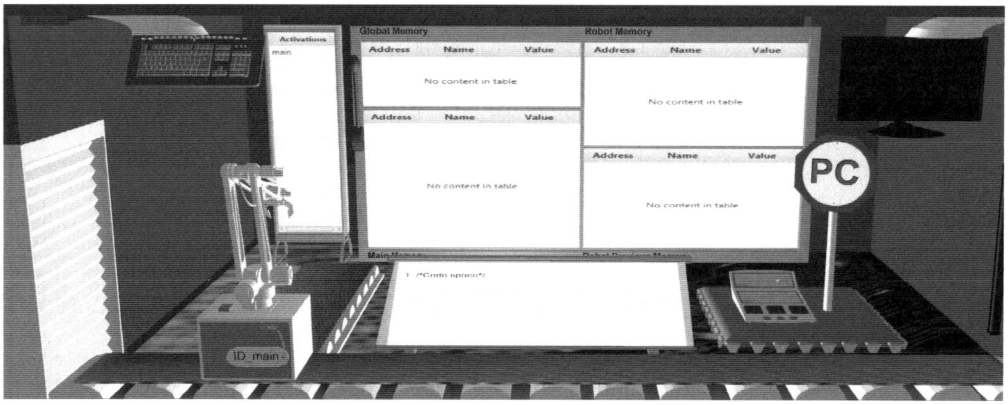

Figure 1: Procedural Programming staging area

operations carried out by the processor or virtual machine, like changing the contents of the memory spreadsheet; operating the calculator to perform computations; activating the pipes to the console or from the keyboard; (e) to highlight the importance of the control flow and the role of control structures, a lollipop sign indicates at any moment of the animation the number of the next instruction that the mechanical arm is supposed to execute. Each instruction causes a set of actions by the mechanical arm on the scenes, guided by the lollipop. Students can see all of the intermediate states of the program animation, and this removes the "black box" effect associated with the traditional execution of code by the machine, and makes it more transparent to students, adding the immediate feedback effect that is typical of robots and microworlds. At the same time, it is highly flexible and can scale from simple, toy examples to complex computations.

The execution of a program consists of a sequence of actions carried out by the machine. The semantics of the program is expressed through the following commands (typically used by the instructors to generate animations in detached mode): show line number and show code line, cell value writer, passing arguments, use calculator, throw an exception, fetch from stdin and push to stdout. To each command correspond an animation of the scene that involves one or more characters.

2.2. The Robot-Community Metaphor for Object-Oriented Programming

The main goal of the project is to bring students to the level of mastering advanced technologies, and primarily object-oriented programming. Experience tells that learning object-oriented method is challenging, even for students that have already acquired basic programming skills. Basic programming – or programming-in-the-small – deals with learning the main instructions offered by the programming language, the techniques to represent data using the program variables, and the process of code development and execution. This is what our mechanical-arm metaphor is focused on. Moreover, object-oriented programming requires that students acquire proper knowledge of programming-in-the-medium techniques, that is, how to organize the code of an application as a set of components – classes and objects, how to assign responsibilities to components, and how to exchange messages among them. In the end, each component will be described in terms of basic instructions, but the choice and design of components is a crucial design step per se.

We develop a second robot-like metaphor to handle this transition. A typical scene of this second kind is reported in Figure 2.

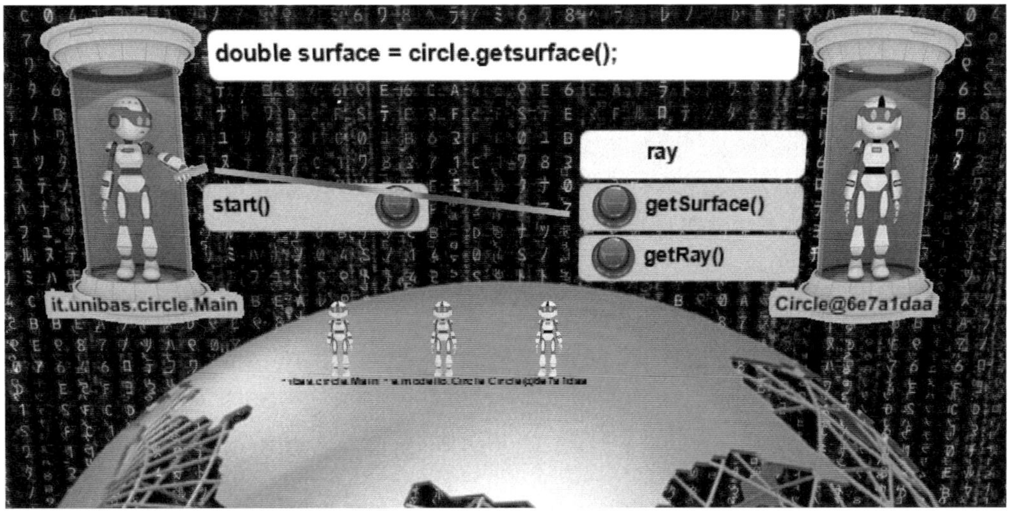

Figure 2: Object Oriented Programming staging area

More specifically, we design a metaphor of object-oriented applications as communities of cooperating robot, each robot being a component (class of objects); the typical concepts of object-oriented programming (reference, message, method, package, binding etc.) will be explained in terms of this metaphor. Every time a class constructor or a static method is executed the robot girl that symbolizes the class is materialized into the holographic tube. It semantically represents a generic OOP class and its animations tend to illustrate the class behaviors: static or objects method invocations, properties usage, and constructors' execution. Thus, the robot boy is generated by the robot girl. Every time a class instance is instantiated or an object reference is used, the robot boy representing the object is materialized into the holographic tube. It semantically represents a generic OOP object and its animations tend to illustrate the object behaviors (i.e.: static or object method invocations and properties usage). The use of the remote control semantically represents the object reference and the exchange of messages. The laser light reaches the opposite part of the scene lighting up methods or properties of the referenced element. The remote control helps learners understand the basic elements of object-oriented programming. The fundamental mechanism of the program execution is the exchange of messages among components. The heap that is represented as a surface on a globe is the element of the metaphor that represents the town where robots live and interact. When a class is first used or every time a new object is instantiated, their little avatar is positioned on the globe. The existence of the little elements allows learners to explore the state of the components and to keep track of the changes. The use of the broom semantically illustrates the garbage collector execution.

The main stage where the metaphor actors play together is composed of background elements that represent the virtual world of robots. The communities of cooperating robots are the places where classes and objects are picked up and materialized in the holographic tubes. The white rectangle on top is used to show the single running source code line.

As for the robot arm metaphor, there is a list of commands to animate all the Robot-Community metaphor aspects. The semantics of the program is expressed through the following commands: create a new object, zoom to the component, component message, garbage collector and the end component execution.

The Diogene-CT animator is designed to tightly integrate the two metaphors, in such a way that students may animate a piece of object-oriented code to have a high-level view of the cooperative behavior or objects, and at any moment zoom into the behavior of every single instruction by switching to the procedural, mechanical-arm animation to have a low-level view of the execution of the actual instructions.

2.3. Offline - Online Mode

At the core of the project stands the Diogene-CT animator. This is the module responsible for generating the actual visual animation of the code. The animator relies on a library of actions: (a) The action library for procedural programming includes all primitives needed to animate the moves of the mechanical arm, e.g., to change the status of the memory, to use the calculator, to access the keyboard and so on. (b) The action library for object-oriented programming includes the primitives to create new objects, send a message to a class, send a message to an object and so on.

Actions can be composed to form animation programs. The main intuition behind the use of Diogene-CT is to generate an animation program for each execution of the target program. This can be done in two different modes, depending on whether the animator has access to the source code or not.

The simplest usage of the Diogene-CT animator is in offline mode. In this mode, the animator runs separately from the target program, i.e., it does not require to have access to the actual source code. This animator program needs to be built by hand, stored in a file with the appropriate format, and fed to the animator. The animation program is independent from the programming language.

As an alternative, Diogene-CT provides the online or attached animation mode. In this mode, the animator works as a fully-fledged application-development environment, in the sense that it has access to the actual source code. The code can be edited within the environment and run. During execution, the animator captures all events triggered by the target program and animates them on the fly, i.e., it dynamically builds the corresponding animation program. Actions and animations are automatically generated based on the interactive execution of the target program.

3. Conclusions: Lessons Learned

Our experiences with the ACME approach in introductory coding courses, both for procedural and object-oriented programming, have shown that the ACME metaphors and Diogene-CT approach can be highly effective. At the same time, they have provided precious insights about possible developments of the tool.

We typically use quite heavily the tool and the metaphor in the first part of the Procedural-Programming course. This part usually covers approximately 40 hours of teaching, with 2:1 lessons to lab ratio, and goes from introductory concepts, like variables and data types, to functions, modular programming, arrays and lists. In the course of these initial lessons, the animations give students a very concrete perspective on the actual operational semantics of instructions, and allow instructors to discuss in great detail both simple concepts – like variables or parameter passing – and more complex ones, like recursion or pointers. The tool, when used in attached mode, also greatly helps student in debugging their first attempts at solving simple exercises, by providing a clear and graphical depiction of their logical errors.

However, we have noticed that, as soon as students become more experienced with coding and start dealing with medium-complexity tasks – like developing menu-based user interfaces, or writing algorithms on collections – they tend to rely less on the tool. In fact, the robot-arm metaphor may become boring when applied to very large codebases, since its perspective is very fine-grained, and therefore medium and upper-level students may get the impression that it slows them.

To solve this problem, in the second half of the course we tend to use the tool essentially in detached mode. We record videos of long animations of medium-complexity code, and then cut the full videos to extract the most significant parts that can be useful to students. In this respect, we believe that it would be very useful to introduce breakpoints, in the style of debuggers, to enable users to fast-track to specific points within the code, and a trace-like function to start and stop the generation of animations at these points.

The tool is perceived as a very useful addition again as soon as students are exposed to object-oriented programming. The introduction to objects and classes usually covers approximately 20 hours of our Object Oriented programming course, also in this case with a 2:1 lessons to lab ratio. Throughout these lessons, the possibility of exploring code executions by looking at the sequence of messages and the heap state in typically appreciated by students. Similarly, the tool be very useful when introducing concepts like object hierarchies and binding. In these cases, Diogene-CT can be used to emphasize the implicit association between object in a hierarchy through the "super" property.

Again, when projects become more complex and the heap increases in size the tool tends to become somehow less effective. Also in this case, debugger-like functionalities would very useful in order to restrict the collection of objects to focus animations on.

It is important to emphasize that not all important concepts can be properly addressed using Diogene-CT alone. For example, methodological guidelines like information hiding, the notion of interface vs implementation can only indirectly be emphasized during animations. Similarly, the comparison of strictly algorithmic aspects, like, for example, hashing vs sorting, is not among the main goals of Diogene-CT.

In this respect, we believe that Diogene-CT can be effectively used in conjunction with other tools, like, for example, algorithm visualization tools or UML-based code-visualization tools to complement and reinforce their abstractions.

In conclusion, ACME methodology and the associated tool Diogene-CT can support teaching and learning computer-programming skills in school curricula of the secondary grade and higher. Diogene-CT represents the first of a new breed of approaches, that we called code-animation environments.

We also conducted some experiments and users study [5] at the University of Basilicata. Based on that experience we obtained largely positive feedback, thus confirming the effectiveness of the approach.

References

[1] S. Marginson, R. Tytler, B. Freeman, K. Roberts, Stem: country comparisons: international comparisons of science, technology, engineering and mathematics (stem) education. final report. (2013).

[2] G. Siekmann, P. Korbel, Defining stem skills: review and synthesis of the literature, in: NCVER, Commonwealth of Australia, 2016.

[3] H. Watt, Session d: Promoting girls' and boys' engagement and participation in senior secondary stem fields and occupational aspirations (2016).

[4] J. M. Wing, Computational thinking, Communications of the ACM 49 (2006) 33–35.

[5] G. Mecca, D. Santoro, N. Sileno, E. Veltri, Diogene-ct: tools and methodologies for teaching and learning coding, International Journal of Educational Technology in Higher Education 18 (2021) 12. URL: https://doi.org/10.1186/s41239-021-00246-1. doi:10.1186/s41239-021-00246-1.

[6] M. U. Bers, L. Flannery, E. R. Kazakoff, A. Sullivan, Computational thinking and tinkering: Exploration of an early childhood robotics curriculum, Computers & Education 72 (2014) 145–157.

[7] B. Harvey, Computer Science Logo Style: Symbolic Computing, volume 1, MIT press, 1997.

[8] H. Tsalapatas, O. Heidmann, R. Alimisi, E. N. Houstis, Game-based programming towards developing algorithmic thinking skills in primary education, 2012.

The Case for Multi-task Active Learning Entity Resolution

(Discussion Paper)

Giovanni Simonini, Henrique Saccani[†], Luca Gagliardelli, Luca Zecchini, Domenico Beneventano and Sonia Bergamaschi

Università degli Studi di Modena e Reggio Emilia, Italy
<name.surname>@unimore.it
[†] *247673@studenti.unimore.it*

Abstract

Entity Resolution (ER) is a multi-task process that aims to detect different records in dirty datasets that refer to the same real-world entity. It is a building block for any data integration and cleaning framework. The state-of-the-art ER approaches heavily rely on supervised Machine Learning, hence on the availability of training data—which is notoriously hard to get in many contexts. To overcome this burden, many Active Learning (AL) strategies have been applied to every single task of ER to minimize the amount of training data by judiciously choosing which data to label.

Yet, no study has been conducted to apply AL to ER in a holistic way. This paper aims to fill this gap by experimentally studying on real-world datasets how to tackle ER as a *multi-task* AL problem and provides guidelines on how to balance AL on the different ER tasks to get better results.

Keywords

Entity Resolution, Active Learning, Data Integration

1. Introduction

1.1. Entity Resolution with Active Learning

Identifying records in datasets that refer to the same real-world entity is a fundamental task in data cleaning and data integration—known as *Entity Resolution* (ER).

State-of-the-art ER methods heavily rely on Machine Learning [1], hence on the availability of training data. One way to alleviate this problem is to employ Active Learning (AL), to judiciously choose the data to label so to minimize the human intervention, which is typically the bottleneck [2, 3, 4, 5]. As a matter of fact, AL is commonly employed for training binary classifiers to determine if a pair of records is a match or not. We call these classifiers *matchers*. The basic idea is that for pairs of records we can compute similarity/distance measures (e.g., string similarities of the attributes, such as Jaccard index) that allow to represent them as vectors of features. Then, some of these pairs are labeled by humans to provide a *training*

SEBD 2021: The 29th Italian Symposium on Advanced Database Systems, September 5-9, 2021, Pizzo Calabro (VV), Italy
0000-0002-3466-509X (G. Simonini); 0000-0001-5977-1078 (L. Gagliardelli); 0000-0002-4856-0838 (L. Zecchini); 0000-0001-6616-1753 (D. Beneventano); 0000-0001-8087-6587 (S. Bergamaschi)

set for a classifier (e.g., Random Forest, SVM, etc.). AL aims to select the pairs that, once employed to train the learner, will increase its accuracy the most. The major shortcoming is that computing a feature vector for all possible pairs of records in a dataset is typically computationally unbearable, due to its inherently quadratic complexity. Thus, *blocking* is employed for discarding pairs of records that most likely will not match. The basic idea is to employ "cheap" similarity (*blocking*) functions that work as surrogates for the "expensive" one employed by the matchers. Also for blocking we can learn *blocking* functions employing standard Machine Learning classifiers [6]—which can be combined with AL.

1.2. Contribution

To date, employing AL-based matchers and blocking for the same ER task has always been studied as separate problems [7]. In this paper, we aim to investigate how a practitioner should allocate her "budget" for labeling data (i.e., a number of instances she is willing to label due to time constraints) between blocking and matching to achieve the best final result for her ER task at hand. Our preliminary results suggest that modeling ER as a *multi-task Active Learning* problem can actually lead to better-quality performance than simply splitting the budget between the two tasks. In Section 4 we demonstrate it on 4 real-world well-known datasets, showing that in some cases a multi-task AL approach can achieve results as good as a state-of-the-art Deep Learning ER algorithm trained with a significantly higher amount of labeled pairs.

2. Related Work

Entity Matching (EM) can be interpreted as a binary classification problem applied to record pairs, labeled as matches or non-matches. AL application to classification tasks has been covered in literature [8] with the goal of maximizing the classification accuracy while minimizing the required human labeling effort. However, state-of-the-art solutions for EM, like Magellan [9] or DeepMatcher [10], do not exploit AL, relying in some cases on other methods to achieve this result (e.g., transfer learning [11]).

If the oracle is a human annotator, AL can be considered as a case of a human-in-the-loop, situation discussed in EM literature [12]. Significant approaches to this problem move from the idea of using crowdsourcing for EM tasks [13, 12]: it is the case of Falcon [3], which proposes the idea of hands-off crowdsourcing (HOC), using the crowd in the major tasks of the EM process.

AL for EM is often faced as a problem of choosing the best combination of example selector and classifier [7]. In many cases, related work focuses either on matching (considering blocking as a separated pre-processing step) [14], or on blocking [15]; when both steps are considered (e.g., Falcon), the different tasks of the EM pipeline are still treated separately, lacking a holistic approach. In fact, even if multi-task AL has already been used for other tasks [16], at the best of our knowledge, it was never applied to data cleaning before our study.

3. Study Methodology

3.1. Active Learning ER pipeline

Figure 1 summarizes the setting of our study: we define two budgets, one for the blocking and one for the matching, which the user should use to label data in an ER pipeline. These two budgets represent the number of records that have to be labeled in each step to train a classifier that is used to discriminate whether a pair is a match or not. In the first *blocking phase*, we employ features that are cheap to be extracted (orders of magnitude less expensive than string similarities).

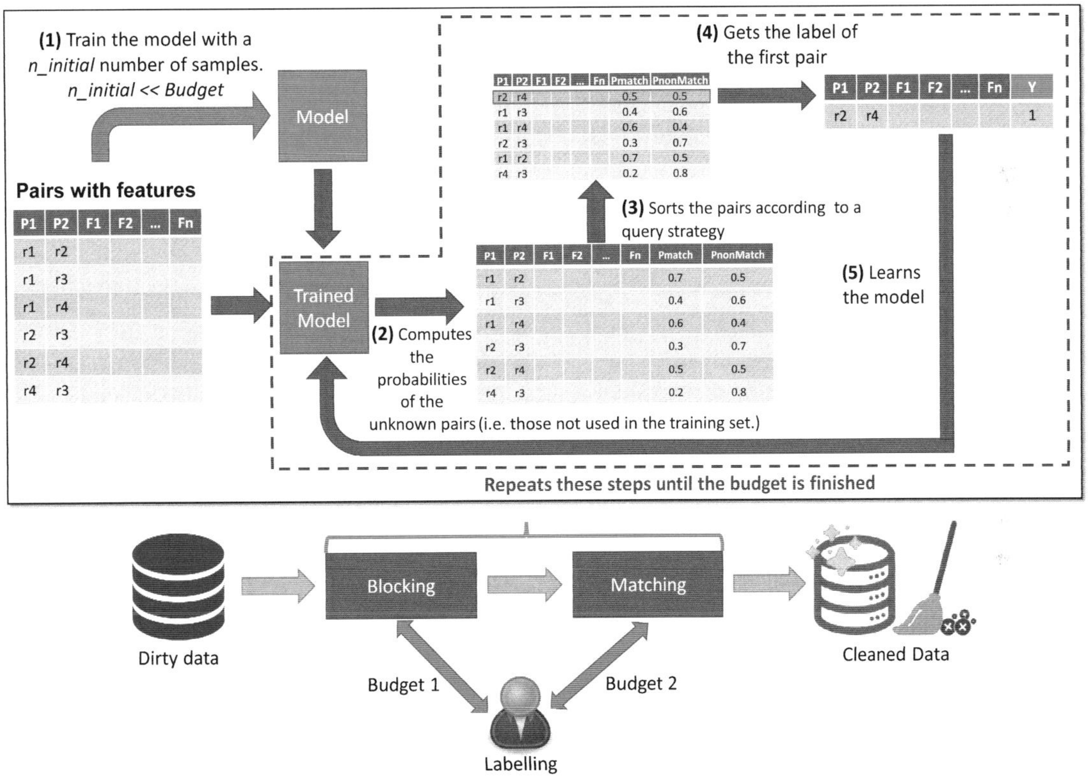

Figure 1: ER pipeline. The upper part of the figure represents the AL process that is executed once for *blocking* and once for *matching*.

Remember that the goal of blocking is indeed to avoid expensive comparisons. Thus, for each pair, we compute a set of features exploiting blocking functions—details below. These features are used to train a classifier with AL using *budget 1*: first, the classifier is trained with a minimal number of samples randomly chosen, then until the budget is consumed the classifier is trained by asking a user to label the most important pairs. At each iteration, the AL algorithm chooses the pairs to be labeled that are more informative, i.e., that will improve the most the accuracy of the classification model once labeled.

At the end of this process, only the pairs that are classified as candidates are kept. In the *matching phase* the same approach is applied, but using a different set of features that are based on expensive—more accurate—string similarity measures. Thus, a classifier is trained with AL using *budget 2* and applied to all the non-labeled pairs to detect all the matching pairs. Of course, the *matcher* is trained also with the pairs labeled in the blocking phase since already available.

3.2. Blocking and Matching Framework

We define an *entity profile* p_i as a tuple composed of a unique identifier and a set of *name-value* pairs. We call *profile collection* P a set of profiles. Two profiles $p_i, p_j \in P$ are called *matches* if they refer to the same real-world object. Thus, Entity Resolution (ER) is the task of identifying all the matches, given P.

We employed a schema-agnostic redundant blocking technique (i.e. Token Blocking [17]) combined with meta-blocking [6]. We choose this setting because it has been proven to be an efficient and effective blocking technique, which does not require parameter tuning and works also when the schema alignment is not complete (or present at all). Given a profile collection P, Token Blocking generates an inverted index for each token appearing in the profiles; then, it considers each entry of that index as a block. This means that two profiles appear together in a block if they share at least one token, and they will share as many blocks as many are the tokens that they share. The set of resulting blocks is called block collection B.

We indicate with $|B|$ the number of blocks $b_k \in B$ and with $||b_k||$ the number of comparisons $\langle p_i, p_j \rangle$ involved by the block b_k. From B we extract the set of features $\mathcal{F}$ as described by Papadakis et al. in [6]. Computing these features from B is orders of magnitude faster than computing string-based similarities, hence being the ideal candidate method for generating the features in the blocking phase. Thus, for each comparison in B we extract a feature vector, which can be used for Active Learning. In particular, we employed the best feature set as reported in [6] and summarized in Table 1—notation in Table 2.

Name	Formula/Description
Node Degree (ND)	Number of non-redundant comparisons involving a profile p_i.
Jaccard Similarity (JS)	$JS(p_i, p_j) = \frac{\lvert B_{i,j}\rvert}{\lvert B_i\rvert + \lvert B_j\rvert - \lvert B_{i,j}\rvert}$
Co-occurrence Frequency-Inverse Block Frequency (CFIBF)	$CFIBF(p_i, p_j) = \lvert B_{i,j}\rvert \cdot log\frac{\lvert B\rvert}{\lvert B_i\rvert} \cdot log\frac{\lvert B\rvert}{\lvert B_j\rvert}$
Reciprocal Aggregate Cardinality of Common Blocks (RACCB)	$RACCB(p_i, p_j) = \sum_{b_k \in B_{i,j}} \frac{1}{\lVert b_k\rVert}$

Table 1
Features employed in the blocking phase.

Symbol	Description
P	Profile collection, a set of profiles.
p_i	An entity profile $p_i \in P$
B	Block collection obtained by appling Token Blocking on P
$\lvert B\rvert$	Number of blocks $b_k \in B$
$\langle p_i, p_j \rangle$	A comparison, i.e. two entity profiles that co-occurs in a block
$\lVert b_k\rVert$	Number of comparisons involved by the block b_k
B_i	Blocks in which is contained an entity profile p_i

Table 2
Important symbols used throughout the paper.

3.3. Matching

For the matching phase, we employed common similarity/distance functions for computing feature records of pairs of candidate matches. We employed simple heuristic that has been shown to work well on all the datasets: *(i)* for attributes with long string values (i.e., >20 characters), we computed token-based measures (namely: Jaccard similarity, Dice similarity, Overlap coefficient, and Cosine similarity); *(ii)* for attributes with short string values (i.e., <20 characters), we computed character-based measures (namely: Levenshtein distance and Needleman–Wunsch distance); *(iii)* for numeric attributes, we computed the ratio $\delta num = min(a,b)/max(a,b)$, for all non-null values and values different from 0.

4. Experiments

4.1. Datasets

In Table 3 we report the characteristics of the employed datasets—commonly used as ER benchmark datasets [6, 10, 13, 18].

We divided them into two main groups:

(a) *structured datasets*, where the attributes are completely aligned and the attribute values are mostly short, carrying specific information about a certain domain (e.g., Title of a journal, or Venue of a conference);

(b) *dirty datasets*, where some information is scattered among attributes (e.g., one may find the Brand of a product in the attribute Title) and also composed of log text describing in plain English some characteristics of the entity (e.g., Description of a product).

Name	#dataset1	#dataset2	#matches	#attributes	type
DblpAcm	2.6k	2.3k	2.2k	4	structured
ScholarDblp	2.5k	61.3k	2.3k	4	structured
AbtBuy	1.1k	1.1k	1.1k	3	dirty
AmazonGoogleProd.	1.4k	3.3k	1.3k	4	dirty

Table 3
Datasets characteristics.

4.2. Setup

As binary classifier, we employ Random Forest[1], and uncertainty-based sampling as AL strategy[2], for both blocking and matching employing the features described in Section 3. We choose this Machine Learning (ML) algorithm for its interpretability and because it has been proven to work well for ER [9]. We consider two sets of budgets for labeling: 100 and 500. This means that for each experiment the AL for blocking and matching can ask to label 100 and 500 instances respectively, in total. These are representative of two typical scenarios: one where the practitioner has limited time to label instances and the other where she has more time (or more collaborators).

[1]https://scikit-learn.org/stable/modules/ensemble.html#forest
[2]https://modal-python.readthedocs.io/en/latest/

4.3. Results

In our experiment, we allocate a different share of AL budget for the blocking and the matching classifier by varying 10% at a time. The results are summarized in Figure 2, grouped by type of dataset (i.e., structured vs. dirty).

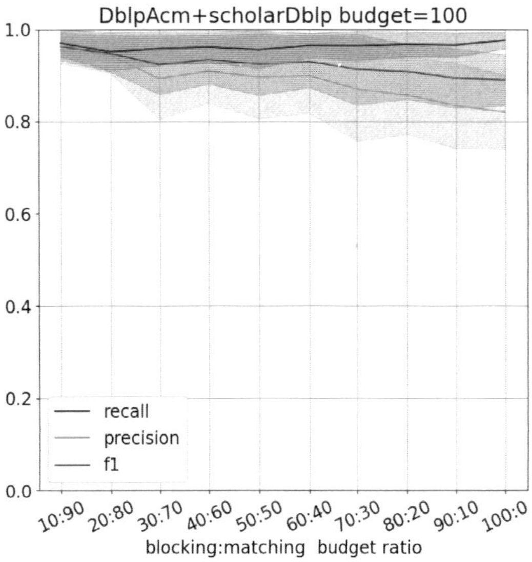

(a) Structured datasets with budget=100

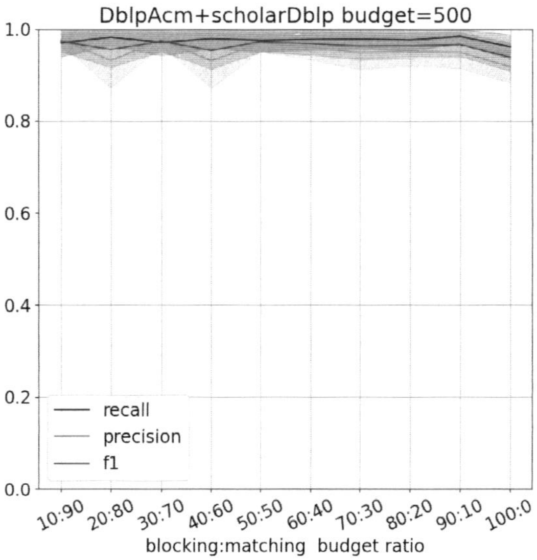

(b) Structured datasets with budget=500

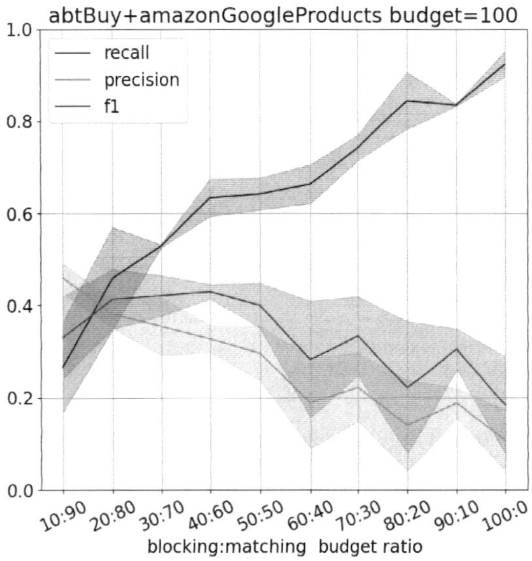

(c) Dirty datasets with budget=100

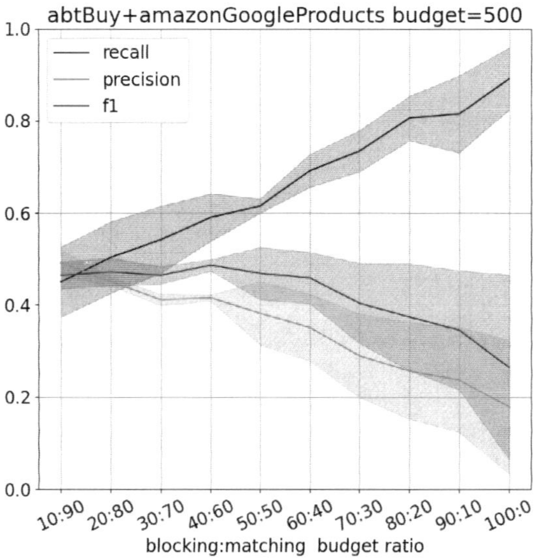

(d) Dirty datasets with budget=500

Figure 2: Results summary. Recall, Precision, and F1-score varying the percentage of the budget allocated to the AL algorithm for blocking and matching.

The results show how with just a little amount as 100 labels, AL can learn an effective ER pipeline for all the datasets: these results in some cases are almost as good as those that can be obtained with a complex Deep Learning (DL) model and thousands of labeled data, and better than those that can be obtained with traditional ML methods[3].

4.3.1. Structured datasets.

For the structured datasets, with just 100 labels as budget for AL we can achieve almost the highest results published so far. Both DeepMatcher [10] and Magellan [9] (respectively DL and traditional ML state-of-the-art ER tools) are able to reach a 0.984 F-score on the structured DblpAcm dataset, but they require a significant amount of labeled data (more than 9k labeled pairs), while we can achieve a 0.981 F-score exploiting 100 labeled examples (0.990 if using 500). Similarly, for ScholarDblp, our AL reaches a 0.939 (0.972) F-score with a budget of 100 (500) labels, while DeepMatcher achieves a 0.947 F-score with more than 20k labeled pairs.

4.3.2. Dirty datasets.

For dirty datasets, our AL method manages to compete with state-of-the-art solutions relying on a budget of just 500 labeled examples: on AmazonGoogleProducts and AbtBuy, DeepMatcher yields a F-score of 0.693 and 0.628, respectively (trained with more than 6k labeled pairs), while AL achieves 0.463 and 0.521—which is 0.03 lower than Magellan for the former and 0.09 higher for the latter.

4.3.3. Takeaway.

Overall, the results in Figure 2 suggest also that the budget for blocking and matching should be split with a 40:60 ratio, which seems to work well for all the datasets.

5. Conclusions

We investigate the problem of ER as a multi-task Active Learning problem. Surprisingly, we find that AL can be employed to easily achieve state-of-the-art performance with basically no feature engineering and with a very common ML algorithm. Further, our preliminary results suggest that employing only 40% of the budget for labeling pairs for AL-based blocking and the rest of the budget for the AL-based matching seems to be the best configuration for all the datasets. We are currently studying how to combine different AL strategies, ML methods and blocking techniques (*involving loose schema information* [19]), to provide a more depth analysis of the problem.

References

[1] A. Doan, P. Konda, P. Suganthan G. C., Y. Govind, D. Paulsen, K. Chandrasekhar, P. Martinkus, M. Christie, Magellan: toward building ecosystems of entity matching solutions, Commun. ACM 63 (2020) 83–91.

[3] We refer to the results reported in [10].

[2] J. Wang, T. Kraska, M. J. Franklin, J. Feng, CrowdER: Crowdsourcing Entity Resolution, PVLDB 5 (2012) 1483–1494.
[3] S. Das, P. Suganthan G. C., A. Doan, J. F. Naughton, G. Krishnan, R. Deep, E. Arcaute, V. Raghavendra, Y. Park, Falcon: Scaling Up Hands-Off Crowdsourced Entity Matching to Build Cloud Services, in: SIGMOD, ACM, 2017, pp. 1431–1446.
[4] E. K. Rezig, L. Cao, G. Simonini, M. Schoemans, S. Madden, N. Tang, M. Ouzzani, M. Stonebraker, Dagger: A data (not code) debugger, in: CIDR, 2020.
[5] E. K. Rezig, L. Cao, M. Stonebraker, G. Simonini, W. Tao, S. Madden, M. Ouzzani, N. Tang, A. K. Elmagarmid, Data civilizer 2.0: A holistic framework for data preparation and analytics, PVLDB 12 (2019) 1954–1957.
[6] G. Papadakis, G. Papastefanatos, G. Koutrika, Supervised Meta-blocking, PVLDB 7 (2014) 1929–1940.
[7] V. V. Meduri, L. Popa, P. Sen, M. Sarwat, A Comprehensive Benchmark Framework for Active Learning Methods in Entity Matching, in: SIGMOD, ACM, 2020, pp. 1133–1147.
[8] B. Settles, Active Learning Literature Survey, University of Wisconsin-Madison Computer Sciences Technical Report 1648 (2009).
[9] P. Konda, S. Das, P. Suganthan G. C., A. Doan, A. Ardalan, J. R. Ballard, H. Li, F. Panahi, H. Zhang, J. F. Naughton, S. Prasad, G. Krishnan, R. Deep, V. Raghavendra, Magellan: Toward Building Entity Matching Management Systems, PVLDB 9 (2016) 1197–1208.
[10] S. Mudgal, H. Li, T. Rekatsinas, A. Doan, Y. Park, G. Krishnan, R. Deep, E. Arcaute, V. Raghavendra, Deep Learning for Entity Matching: A Design Space Exploration, in: SIGMOD, ACM, 2018, pp. 19–34.
[11] Y. Li, J. Li, Y. Suhara, A. Doan, W. Tan, Deep Entity Matching with Pre-Trained Language Models, PVLDB 14 (2020) 50–60.
[12] D. Firmani, B. Saha, D. Srivastava, Online Entity Resolution Using an Oracle, PVLDB 9 (2016) 384–395.
[13] B. Mozafari, P. Sarkar, M. J. Franklin, M. I. Jordan, S. Madden, Scaling Up Crowd-Sourcing to Very Large Datasets: A Case for Active Learning, PVLDB 8 (2014) 125–136.
[14] K. Qian, L. Popa, P. Sen, Active Learning for Large-Scale Entity Resolution, in: CIKM, ACM, 2017, pp. 1379–1388.
[15] G. Dal Bianco, M. A. Gonçalves, D. Duarte, BLOSS: Effective meta-blocking with almost no effort, Inf. Syst. 75 (2018) 75–89.
[16] Y. Zhang, Q. Yang, A Survey on Multi-Task Learning, CoRR abs/1707.08114 (2017). arXiv:1707.08114.
[17] G. Papadakis, G. M. Mandilaras, L. Gagliardelli, G. Simonini, E. Thanos, G. Giannakopoulos, S. Bergamaschi, T. Palpanas, M. Koubarakis, Three-dimensional Entity Resolution with JedAI, volume 93, 2020, p. 101565.
[18] L. Gagliardelli, S. Zhu, G. Simonini, S. Bergamaschi, Bigdedup: a big data integration toolkit for duplicate detection in industrial scenarios, in: 25th International Conference on Transdisciplinary Engineering (TE2018), volume 7, NLD, 2018, pp. 1015–1023.
[19] D. Beneventano, S. Bergamaschi, L. Gagliardelli, G. Simonini, *BLAST2*: An Efficient Technique for Loose Schema Information Extraction from Heterogeneous Big Data Sources, ACM JIDQ 12 (2020) 18:1–18:22.

An Inductive Framework for Semi-supervised Learning

(Discussion Paper)

Shuyi Yang[1,2], Dino Ienco[3], Roberto Esposito[1] and Ruggero G. Pensa[1]

[1]*University of Turin, Italy*
[2]*Intesa Sanpaolo, Turin, Italy*
[3]*INRAE, UMR TETIS, Montpellier, France*

Abstract

Semi-supervised learning is crucial in many applications where accessing class labels is unaffordable or costly. The most promising approaches are graph-based but they are transductive and they do not provide a generalized model working on inductive scenarios. To address this problem, we propose a generic framework for inductive semi-supervised learning based on three components: an ensemble of semi-supervised autoencoders providing a new data representation that leverages the knowledge supplied by the reduced amount of available labels; a graph-based step that helps augmenting the training set with pseudo-labeled instances and, finally, a classifier trained with labeled and pseudo-labeled instances. The experimental results show that our framework outperforms state-of-the-art inductive semi-supervised methods.

Keywords

semi-supervised learning, graph-based algorithms sep inductive methods

1. Introduction

Prediction is one of the most important outcomes of any machine learning algorithm, but its accuracy strongly depends on the amounts and quality of labeled instances and, unfortunately, labeling is a cost-intensive manual activity requiring time, money, and expertise. Hence, labeling often turns out to be unaffordable for many organizations and, consequently, only small amounts of labeled instances are available for training. Semi-supervised learning aims at mitigating the above-mentioned problem by leveraging the so-called *smoothness* and *cluster* assumptions: if two data instances are close to each other or belong to the same cluster in the input distribution, then they are likely to belong to the same class [1]. Graph-based models constitute one of the main families of semi-supervised techniques [2]. They leverage the manifold assumption: the graphs, typically nearest neighbor graphs built upon the local similarity between data points, provide a lower-dimensional representation of the high-dimensional input data.

SEBD 2021: The 29th Italian Symposium on Advanced Database Systems, September 5-9, 2021, Pizzo Calabro (VV), Italy
shuyi.yang@unito.it (S. Yang); dino.ienco@inrae.fr (D. Ienco); roberto.esposito@unito.it (R. Esposito); ruggero.pensa@unito.it (R. G. Pensa)
0000-0002-8736-3132 (D. Ienco); 0000-0001-5366-292X (R. Esposito); 0000-0001-5145-3438 (R. G. Pensa)

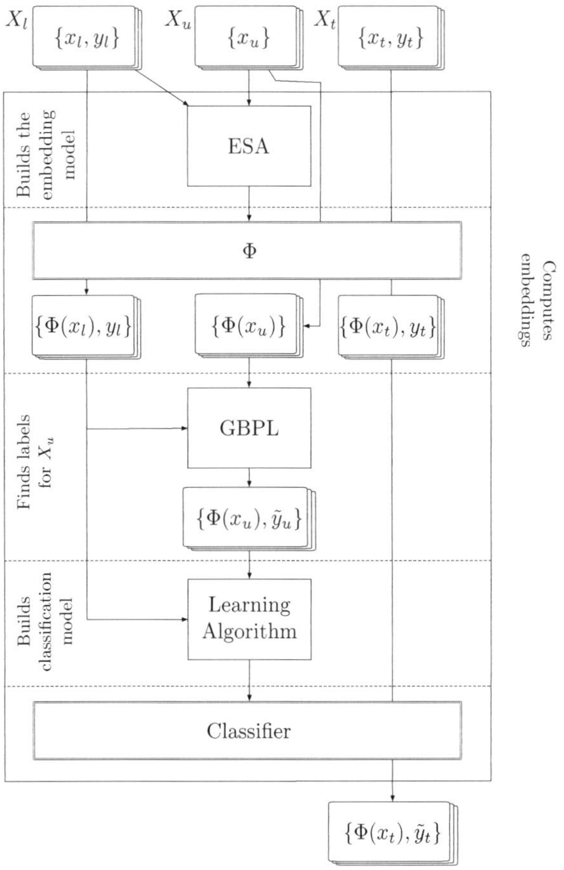

Figure 1: The proposed framework.

Unfortunately, graph-based methods are transductive [2], i.e., they do not construct any classification model and the prediction is limited to exactly those data instances that are already available during the training phase. Therefore, graph-based methods are unable to classify new data examples, unless they are trained again on the augmented dataset. A second limitation concerns the construction of the graph: in general, this phase is completely unsupervised even though, for some instances, labels are available. When the cluster assumption is not completely satisfied, this could lead to poor prediction results. In this paper, we present a novel graph-based semi-supervised framework, ESA*, that improves in the areas mentioned above: it takes into account the information carried out by labeled instances during the graph construction and is designed to work properly in inductive settings.

Our approach (sketched graphically in Fig. 1) first constructs a new representation using a semi-supervised autoencoder that takes all labeled and unlabeled training data as input. The representation learnt by the semi-supervised autoencoder, for both labeled and unlabeled training data, are then processed by a graph-based semi-supervised algorithm that propagates the label information from labeled to unlabeled data instances. This procedure provides pseudo-labels for the set of unlabeled instances. We propose two variants of our framework: the first, ESA^{LP}, is based on a graph-based label propagation algorithm [3]; the second one, ESA^{GAT}, exploits a graph convolutional neural network with masked self-attention layers [4]. All training instances (labeled and unlabeled with pseudo-labels) are then used to train a classification model, which can perform prediction for new unseen examples as well. We show that our approach outperforms state-of-the-art approaches and is competitive towards state-of-the-art transductive methods, even with extremely small amounts of labeled instances. A more in-depth presentation of our proposal is reported in the full version of this paper [5].

2. Inductive graph-based semi-supervised learning

In a semi-supervised learning setting, in addition to labeled instances, unlabeled ones are introduced as part of available data during the training phase: let $X_l \in \mathbb{R}^{n_l \times f}$ be the matrix of n_l labeled samples each with f predictors and y_l be the corresponding labels, then a supplementary matrix $X_u \in \mathbb{R}^{n_u \times f}$ representing n_u unlabeled instances is also provided without the corresponding y_u labels. Generally, the number n_l of labeled instances is limited and much smaller than the number n_u of unlabeled instances. Our framework aims to provide an inductive semi-supervised learning algorithm by leveraging graph-based semi-supervised learning in order to augment the amount of labeled instances to train a supervised classifier.

As shown in Figure 1, our framework consists of different parts: embedding computation, pseudo-labeling of unlabeled instances, and classification. In the embedding computation part, we train an ensemble of neural networks to extract a latent representation for each instance. These representations are used to build a graph over labeled and unlabeled instances so that a graph-based model can be employed to provide a pseudo-label for each unlabeled instance. Finally, labeled instances and pseudo-labeled ones are both used to train a supervised classification model.

In order to extract the data embeddings, an Ensemble of Semi-supervised Autoencoders (ESA) [6] is trained on both labeled and unlabeled data. The loss function we use to learn the internal parameters of the SSAE is a combination of reconstruction and classification loss. More formally

$$L_{\text{SSAE}} = L_{\text{AE}} + \lambda L_{\text{CL}} \tag{1}$$

where

$$L_{\text{AE}} = \frac{1}{n_l + n_u} \sum_{x_i \in X_l \cup X_u} ||x_i - D(E(x_i|\theta_E)|\theta_D)||^2, \tag{2}$$

$$L_{\text{CL}} = -\frac{1}{n_l} \sum_{x_i \in X_l} \sum_{c=1}^{|C|} y_{lic} \cdot \log(CL(E(x_i|\theta_E)|\theta_{CL})_c), \tag{3}$$

and θ_E, θ_D and θ_{CL} are respectively the set of parameters of the encoder, decoder and classification layer, y_{lic} is the c-th element of the i-th row of y_l, $CL(\cdot)_c$ is the c-th element of the output vector of *CL* and λ is a parameter that controls the importance of the classification loss. In our architecture the encoder has an input layer followed by other two hidden layers; the decoder has one hidden layer of the same size of the first hidden layer of the encoder and an output layer. The size of the input layer, the output layer and the classification layer are respectively fixed to f, f and $|C|$, while $size_{hidden}$ and $size_{bottleneck}$ (respectively, the size of the hidden layer and that of the bottleneck one) can be varied. In order to get diverse and multi-resolution representations, similarly as in [6], we train K independent SSAEs, each with the sizes of the layers extracted randomly from the intervals $\frac{f}{2} \leq size_{hidden} < f$ and $\frac{f}{4} \leq size_{hidden} < \frac{f}{2}$. Once the ensemble is trained we obtain the new representations $\Phi(X_l)$, $\Phi(X_u)$ of X_l and X_u by concatenating the embeddings of these K SSAEs:

$$\Phi(\cdot) = ||_{k=1}^{k=K} E_k(\cdot|\theta_{E_k}) \tag{4}$$

where $||$ is the stack (concatenation) operator and E_k and θ_{E_k} are respectively the encoder of the k-th SSAE and its weights.

Given the latent representations, a kNN graph structure can be derived from the data points of $X_l \cup X_u$: embedding representations are nodes and two of them can be considered connected if both of them belong to the top k nearest neighbors of each other, respectively.

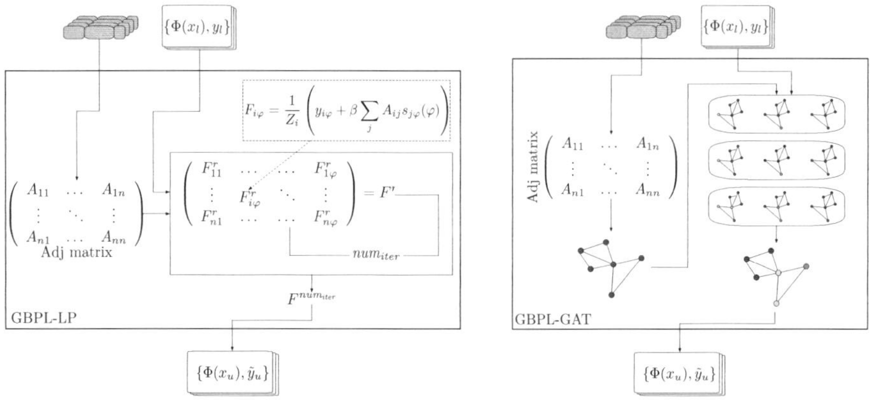

(a) ESA^{LP} (b) ESA^{GAT}

Figure 2: A graphical representation of the label propagation strategy of ESA^{LP} (a) and ESA^{GAT} (b)

At this point we perform graph-based pseudo-labeling (GBPL) to assign pseudo class labels to unlabeled instances. To this purpose, any graph-based semi-supervised learning algorithm (GBSSL) can be applied to infer the labels of the unlabeled portion of data $\tilde{y}_u$ by propagating the class information from the labeled data y_l over the graph constructed on the embeddings. Successively, a supervised classifier (SC) can be trained leveraging the union of the labeled data $(\Phi(X_l), y_l)$ with the pseudo-labeled one $(\Phi(X_u), \tilde{y}_u)$ as training set. In prediction, we first compute the latent representation of unseen data $\Phi(X_t)$ with the trained ESA, then we make predictions with the supervised classifier SC. It is worth pointing out that during the entire process, the transductive GBSSL process is used only during the training phase to provide pseudo-labels of the unlabeled data (as in wrapper methods) in order to help the supervised classifier to generalize better. Therefore, our approach, hereinafter referred as $\text{ESA}^{\star}$, is inductive. In the next two sections, we present two variants adopting different strategies to perform pseudo-labeling based on different graph-based semi-supervised learning approaches.

2.1. Pseudo-labeling based on confidence-aware label propagation

In this section we introduce the first variant of our framework for semi-supervised learning (see Figure 2(a)). The adopted strategy consists in instantiating the graph-based pseudo-labeling (GBPL) part with a confidence-aware label propagation algorithm working on both homophily and heterophily networks [3]. In the following we provide the details of this strategy, which we name ESA^{LP}. Given the adjacency matrix A, ESA^{LP} computes the probability distribution over the classes as the solution of $F_{i\varphi} = \frac{1}{Z_i}\left(y_{i\varphi} + \beta \sum_j A_{ij} s_{ji}(\varphi)\right)$, where $F_{i\varphi}$ is the probability that i-th instance has label φ, Z_i is a normalization term, $y_{i\varphi}$ is the prior belief of i-th instance having label φ, $0 < \beta$ represents the importance of the neighborhood's influence, A_{ij} is the i, j entry of the adjacency matrix and $s_{ji}(\varphi)$ represents how intense the node j believes that the node i has class φ. More formally, $s_{ji}(\varphi) = \sum_l F_{jl} H_{l\varphi}$, where H is the modulation matrix. If $H_{l\varphi}$ is low then class l has a low correlation with the class φ, on the contrary, if it is high these two classes have a strong correlation. On homophily networks, H is the identity matrix, while on heterophily networks it can be designed empirically. In our experiments we assume that the graph obtained by the embeddings of ESA is a homophily network. We can rewrite the the last equation in matrix form and in an iterative way, i.e., $F^{r+1} = Z^{-1}(Y + \beta A F^r H)$, where $Z = I + \beta D$ and D is the node degrees diagonal matrix. Once obtained the adjacency matrix A of labeled and unlabeled instances, as described in the previous section, we initialize F^0 as a $(n_l + n_u) \times |C|$ matrix of zeros. Then we apply the iterative formula num_{iter} times to obtain $F^{num_{iter}}$, which represents the probability distributions of the instances over the classes. From $F^{num_{iter}}$ we extract only the predictions of X_u and keep the original labels for X_l. They are then used to feed a classifier SC.

2.2. Pseudo-labeling based on graph attention networks

For the second variant, we consider a completely different approach leveraging the convolution operation with graph attention networks (GAT) [4], which are able to capture different levels of importance of features of neighborhood nodes in the kNN graph built upon the embeddings computed by ESA. We call this strategy ESA^{GAT} and provide the details below (a graphical representation is given in Figure 2(b)).

Given the set of nodes, each represented by a b-dimensional real numbers array obtained from the ESA embedding process or as a result of a previous convolutional layer, we can compute the self-attention on nodes as $e_{ij} = a(Wh_i, Wh_j|\aleph)$, where $h_i, h_j \in \mathbb{R}^b$ are the embeddings of instance i and j, W is a $b' \times b$ shared linear transformation matrix, and $a : \mathbb{R}^{b'} \times \mathbb{R}^{b'} \rightarrow \mathbb{R}$ is the attentional mechanism consisting in a feedforward layer with weights $\aleph$ and LeakyReLU activation [7]. Each e_{ij} is computed only for connected nodes (masked attention) so that the graph structure is embedded into the coefficients. The attention coefficients are then normalized using the softmax function, i.e., $\alpha_{ij} = \frac{\exp e_{ij}}{\sum_{\iota \in N(i)} \exp e_{i\iota}}$, with $N(i)$ representing the nodes connected to the node i. The new representation of the node i through the attention layer is then computed as $h_i' = \sigma\left(\sum_{j \in N(i)} \alpha_{ij} W h_j\right)$, with σ a non linear transformation. As in ESA, we can concatenate the outputs of different independent attention layers in order to employ a multi-head attention mechanism. To do that, once the ESA embeddings are obtained, we can apply the last formula multiple times: from the point of view of the neural network structure, the mechanism is realized by adding additional convolutional layers, each with its own weights to be trained and the number of nodes of the last layer should be equal to the number of classes.

3. Experiments

We assess the behavior of our framework under different settings, using Random Forests (RF) as final classifier. Thirteen publicly available real-world classification datasets, encompassing a wide variety of application scenarios, have been considered in our experiments. They exhibits different sizes (from 178 to 70 000 instances) and dimensionality (from 12 to 1087 features). Nine datasets (ANTIVIRUS, LANDSAT, MADELON, MALWARE, PARKINSON, SONAR, SPAMBASE, WAVEFORM, WINE) are from the UCI Machine Learning Repository[1], four are well-known

[1]http://archive.ics.uci.edu/ml

image datasets (USPS [8], MNIST[2], FMNIST[3], COIL20[4]). Each dataset is randomly split into three parts: labeled instances (p% of the dataset), unlabeled instances ($(70 - p)$% of the dataset), and test instances (30% of the dataset). The random split is stratified so that each dataset maintains the same proportion of labels as in the original datasets. Every supervised model is trained on labeled instances only and evaluated on test instances, while all semi-supervised models are trained both on labeled instances and unlabeled ones and evaluated on the test instances. During the experiments we vary the percentage p of labeled instances to study how the performances change when the portion of labeled instances increases in both supervised and semi-supervised models.

To obtain more robust performance indicators, for each combination of dataset, percentage p and model, we evaluate 25 different random splits as described above and then take the average performances. The model is re-trained for each of the 25 different splits and new predictions are made on every different test set. As performance index, we consider the micro-averaged F1-score computed on the test set. In all evaluations of the experiments, we compute detailed performance results for each dataset, but here we report a summary of the results (Figure 3). The latter is obtained as follows: for a given percentage p of labeled instances, we compute the average ranks across all the dataset for each algorithm, according to the micro-averaged F1 score, and then we plot them for increasing values of $p\%$. This allows us to obtain an overall picture of the relative performances of all competitors considered in our study. In the following, we present and discuss the results for each experiment.

3.1. Comparative analysis w.r.t. inductive methods

In the first experiment, we compare two configurations of our framework to four well-known supervised methods (Random Forests, Multilayer Perceptron, SVM and DRM [9]) and two recent state-of-the-art semi-supervised approaches: interpolation consistency training (ICT) [10] and ladder networks (LN) [11]. From the obtained results (Figure 3(a)), it emerges that, for every percentage of labeled examples, on average, the two variants of our framework outperform all other methods, including the four fully supervised classifiers considered in this study. It is worth noting that, in contrast, the two competing semi-supervised methods (*ICT* and *LN*) are not able to outperform the supervised competitors with the same consistency. The micro-averaged F1 score of *ICT* is below the one of RF, for any given value of p. Ladder networks (*LN*) are ranked third with less than 2% of labeled samples, but RF is still competitive w.r.t. *LN* despite the fact that it does not take advantage of unlabeled instances. Finally, it is worth pointing out that, not surprisingly, when the number of labeled instances increases, the differences between semi-supervised methods and fully supervised ones decrease.

3.2. Comparative analysis w.r.t. transductive methods

We compare two configurations of our framework to two state-of-the-art transductive semi-supervised approaches: structured graph learning with multiple kernel (SGMK) [12] and robust

[2]http://yann.lecun.com/exdb/mnist/
[3]https://github.com/zalandoresearch/fashion-mnist
[4]https://www.cs.columbia.edu/CAVE/software/softlib/coil-20.php

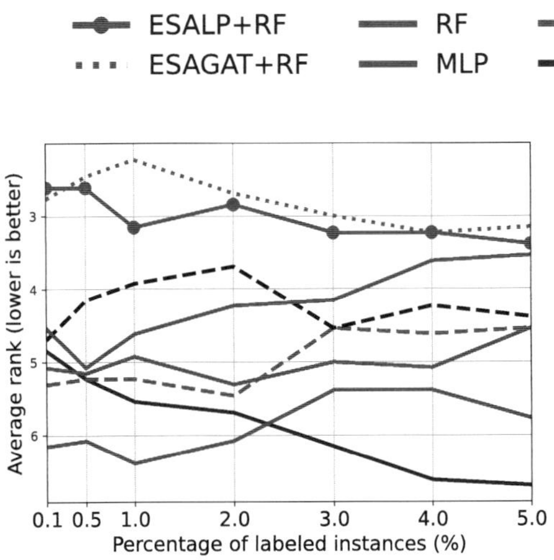

(a) ESA* vs inductive methods

(b) ESA* vs transductive methods

Figure 3: Average rank according to micro-averaged F1-measure in the experiments.

graph construction (RGC) [13]. It is worth pointing out that, while the transductive setting has potential liabilities in terms of applicability, it has advantages in the possibility of leveraging more information than its inductive counterparts (since it can leverage the test set distribution when propagating the labels). As we shall see, while our method is at a disadvantage here, it works quite well nonetheless.

We compare the variants ESA^{LP}+RF and ESA^{GAT}+RF to the structured graph learning with multiple kernel (SGMK) [12] and to the robust graph construction (RGC) [13]. Due to computational limitations, the experiments are performed only on a subset of the available datasets, namely: ANTIVIRUS, SONAR, PARKINSON and WINE. From the results shown in Figure 3(b), we can conclude that, within our experimental settings, ESA^{LP}+RF and ESA^{GAT}+RF are able to reach competitive performances compared to SOTA transductive methods (i.e. RGC), and, in some cases, even outperform them (i.e. SGMK).

4. Conclusion

In this paper, we have presented a new inductive semi-supervised learning framework that takes the most of two successful approaches: semi-supervised autoencoders and graph-based semi-supervised learning. While the former supports the generation of new data representations improved by labeled instances, the latter spread the label information to unlabeled instances in the new representation space. Thanks to an extensive experimental study, we have shown that a classifier trained with both labeled instances and pseudo-labeled instances achieves better prediction accuracy than its supervised counterpart trained only on labeled ones, and also outperforms state-of-the-art semi-supervised competitors.

References

[1] O. Chapelle, B. Schölkopf, A. Zien (Eds.), Semi-Supervised Learning, The MIT Press, 2006.

[2] J. E. van Engelen, H. H. Hoos, A survey on semi-supervised learning, Mach. Learn. 109 (2020) 373–440.

[3] Y. Yamaguchi, C. Faloutsos, H. Kitagawa, CAMLP: confidence-aware modulated label propagation, in: S. C. Venkatasubramanian, W. M. Jr. (Eds.), Proceedings of the International Conference on Data Mining, SIAM 2016, Miami, Florida, USA, May 5-7, 2016, SIAM, 2016, pp. 513–521.

[4] P. Velickovic, G. Cucurull, A. Casanova, A. Romero, P. Liò, Y. Bengio, Graph attention networks, in: Proceedings of the 6th International Conference on Learning Representations, ICLR 2018, Vancouver, BC, Canada, April 30 - May 3, 2018, OpenReview.net, 2018.

[5] S. Yang, D. Ienco, R. Esposito, R. G. Pensa, ESA*: A generic framework for semi-supervised inductive learning, Neurocomputing 447 (2021) 102–117.

[6] D. Ienco, R. G. Pensa, Enhancing graph-based semisupervised learning via knowledge-aware data embedding, IEEE Trans. Neural Networks Learn. Syst. 31 (2020) 5014–5020.

[7] A. L. Maas, A. Y. Hannun, A. Y. Ng, Rectifier nonlinearities improve neural network acoustic models, in: Proceedings of the International Conference on Machine Learning, ICML 2013, Atlanta, USA, June 16-21, 2013, 2013.

[8] J. J. Hull, A database for handwritten text recognition research, IEEE Transactions on pattern analysis and machine intelligence 16 (1994) 550–554.

[9] C. Peng, Q. Cheng, Discriminative ridge machine: A classifier for high-dimensional data or imbalanced data, IEEE Transactions on Neural Networks and Learning Systems (2020). Available online.

[10] V. Verma, A. Lamb, J. Kannala, Y. Bengio, D. Lopez-Paz, Interpolation consistency training for semi-supervised learning, in: S. Kraus (Ed.), Proceedings of the 28th International Joint Conference on Artificial Intelligence, IJCAI 2019, Macao, China, August 10-16, 2019, ijcai.org, 2019, pp. 3635–3641.

[11] A. Rasmus, M. Berglund, M. Honkala, H. Valpola, T. Raiko, Semi-supervised learning with ladder networks, in: C. Cortes, N. D. Lawrence, D. D. Lee, M. Sugiyama, R. Garnett (Eds.), Proceedings of the Annual Conference on Neural Information Processing Systems 2015, NIPS 2015, Montreal, Quebec, Canada, December 7-12, 2015, 2015, pp. 3546–3554.

[12] Z. Kang, C. Peng, Q. Cheng, X. Liu, X. Peng, Z. Xu, L. Tian, Structured graph learning for clustering and semi-supervised classification, Pattern Recognition 110 (2021) 107627.

[13] Z. Kang, H. Pan, S. C. Hoi, Z. Xu, Robust graph learning from noisy data, IEEE transactions on cybernetics 50 (2019) 1833–1843.

A Two-Step Method based on Embedding and Clustering to Identify Regularities in Legal Case Judgements

(Discussion Paper)

Graziella De Martino[1], Gianvito Pio[1,2] and Michelangelo Ceci[1,2,3]

[1]*Department of Computer Science - University of Bari Aldo Moro, Via Orabona, 4, 70125, Bari (Italy)*
[2]*Big Data Laboratory, National Interuniversity Consortium for Informatics, Via Ariosto, 25, 00185, Rome (Italy)*
[3]*Department of Knowledge Technologies, Jožef Stefan Institute, Jamova cesta 39, 1000 Ljubljana (Slovenia)*

Abstract

In an era characterized by fast technological signs of progress that introduce new scenarios every day, working in the law field may appear very difficult if not supported by the right tools. In this paper, we discuss a recently submitted work that proposes a novel method, called PRILJ, that identifies paragraph regularities in legal case judgments to support legal experts during the redaction of legal documents. Methodologically, PRILJ adopts a two-step approach that first groups documents into clusters, according to their semantic content, and then identifies regularities in the paragraphs for each cluster. Embedding-based methods are adopted to properly represent documents and paragraphs into a semantic numerical feature space, and an Approximated Nearest Neighbor Search method is adopted to efficiently retrieve the most similar paragraphs with respect to the paragraphs of a document under preparation. Our extensive experimental evaluation, performed on a real-world dataset, proves the effectiveness and the efficiency of the proposed method even if documents contain noisy data.

Keywords

Legal Information Retrieval, Embedding, Clustering, Approximate Nearest Neighbor Search

1. Introduction

The legal sector is generally characterized by a slow response to the new scenarios that appear every day in the modern society. In this context, Artificial Intelligence (AI) methods can support the design of advanced (also automated) solutions to improve the efficiency of the processes in this field. Among the attempts in this direction, we can mention the work presented in [1], where the authors applied AI techniques to measure the similarity among legal case documents, that can be useful to speed up the identification and analysis of judicial precedents. Another relevant example is the work in [2], where the authors consider the semi-automation of some legal tasks, such as the prediction of judicial decisions of the European Court of Human Rights.

SEBD 2021: The 29th Italian Symposium on Advanced Database Systems, September 5-9, 2021, Pizzo Calabro (VV), Italy

graziella.demartino@uniba.it (Graziella De Martino); gianvito.pio@uniba.it (Gianvito Pio); michelangelo.ceci@uniba.it (Michelangelo Ceci)
0000-0002-3492-6317 (Graziella De Martino); 0000-0003-2520-3616 (Gianvito Pio); 0000-0002-6690-7583 (Michelangelo Ceci)

CEUR Workshop Proceedings (CEUR-WS.org)

Following this line of research, in this discussion paper, we describe a novel method, called PRILJ, that identifies paragraph regularities in legal case judgements, to support legal experts during the redaction of legal documents. Methodologically, PRILJ adopts a two-step approach that first groups documents into clusters, according to their semantic content, and then identifies regularities in the paragraphs for each cluster. Embedding-based methods are adopted to properly represent documents and paragraphs into a semantic numerical feature space, and an Approximated Nearest Neighbor Search method is adopted to efficiently retrieve the most similar paragraphs. Therefore, given a (possibly incomplete or under preparation) document, henceforth called *target document*, PRILJ supports the retrieval of similar paragraphs appearing in a set of reference documents related to previous transcribed legal case judgments.

Document clustering has received a lot of attention by the research community, but together with the design of advanced algorithms [3, 4, 5, 6], the most critical aspect is in the design of a proper representation of the objects/items at hand [7, 8], as well as of similarity measures. In the literature we can find several document similarity measures implemented through *a)* network-based approaches [9, 10], *b)* text-based methods [11, 1] or *c)* hybrid approaches [11].

In this context, PRILJ has the main advantage of properly combining embedding methods, to catch the semantics, with a two-step approach, that consists in learning a different representation for each group of documents, rather than one single model. This aspect allows us to capture peculiarities of paragraphs according to the specific topic represented by each cluster of documents.

Our extensive experimental evaluation, performed on a real-world dataset, proves the effectiveness and the efficiency of the proposed method. In particular, its ability of modeling different topics of legal documents, as well as of capturing the semantics of the textual content, appear very beneficial for the considered task, and make PRILJ very robust to the possible presence of noise in the data.

2. Method

Before describing PRILJ, in the following, we provide some useful definitions:

- **Training set D_T**: a collection of legal judgments, represented as textual documents, adopted to train our models;
- **Reference set D_R**: a collection of legal judgments, represented as textual documents, from which we are interested to identify paragraph regularities;
- **Target document d**: a legal judgment (possibly under preparation) about which we are interested to identify paragraph regularities from D_R.

The training set and the reference set may fully (or partially) overlap i.e., $D_T = D_R$ (or $D_T \cap D_R \neq \emptyset$), namely, the set of documents adopted to train our models may be the same as (or overlap with) the collection from which we want to identify paragraph regularities with respect to the target document. Note that PRILJ is fully unsupervised and the target document d is never contained in either the training set or in the reference set (i.e., $d \notin (D_T \cup D_R)$).

The three phases of PRILJ are detailed in the following subsections.

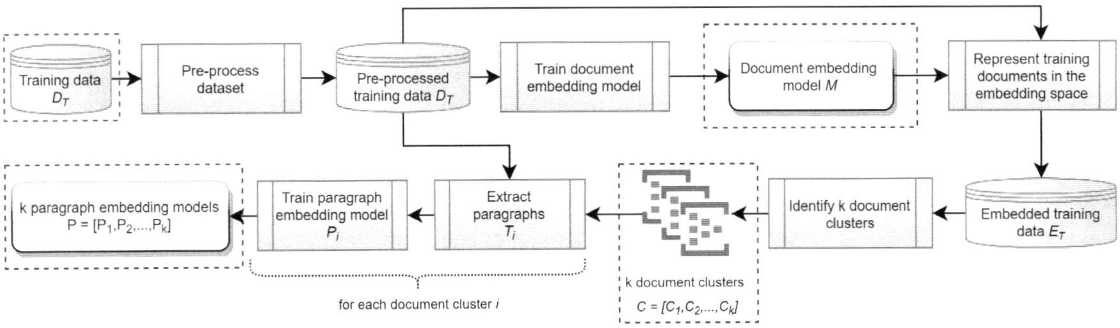

Figure 1: Graphical overview of the training phase. Green- and red-dotted rectangles represent inputs and outputs, respectively.

2.1. Training phase

As shown in Fig. 1, PRILJ starts with the application of some pre-processing steps to the documents in D_t. Specifically, the pre-processing consists of: *i)* lowercasing the text, *ii)* removing punctuation and digits, *iii)* applying lemmatization, and *iv)* removing rare words. The pre-processed documents are then used to train a document embedding model M, that is subsequently exploited to represent each document of the training set D_T in the latent feature space, obtaining the set of embedded training documents E_T. Such documents are then partitioned into k clusters $[C_1, C_2, ..., C_k]$ by adopting the k-means clustering algorithm. Each cluster of documents becomes the input for a further learning step at the paragraph level: documents falling in the same cluster will contribute to the learning of a specific paragraph embedding model. Algorithmically, for each document cluster $C_i, 1 \leq i \leq k$, we extract the paragraphs (i.e., sentences delimited by a full stop) from the documents falling into C_i and train a paragraph embedding model P_i. This approach allows us to learn more specific paragraph embedding models, according to the topic possibly represented by the identified clusters.

The embedding models, both at the document level and at the paragraph level, are learned by PRILJ through neural network architectures based on Word2Vec Continuous-Bag-of-Words (CBOW) [7] or Doc2Vec [8] distributed memory distributed memory (PV-DM). This choice is motivated by the fact that previous works demonstrated the superiority of Word2Vec and Doc2Vec over classical counting-based approaches, since they take into account both the syntax and semantics of the text [12, 1]. In addition, their ability to catch the semantics and the context of single words and paragraphs allow them to properly represent new (previously unseen) documents which features have not been explicitly observed during the training phase.

2.2. Paragraph embedding of the reference set

In Fig. 2, we show the workflow followed by PRILJ to represent the paragraphs of the documents belonging to the reference set into a latent feature space. Analogously to the training phase, we pre-process the documents of the reference set D_r. Then, each document of the reference set is embedded using the previously learned document embedding model M. The embedded representation of the document is then used to identify the closest document cluster that corresponds the optimal paragraph embedding model (i.e., P_c). We stress the fact that PRILJ

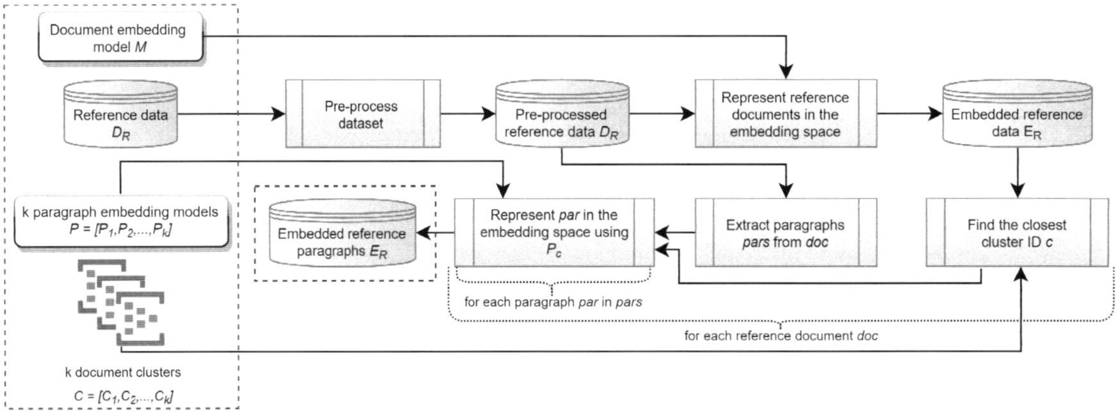

Figure 2: Graphical overview of the paragraph embedding of the reference set. Green- and red-dotted rectangles represent inputs and outputs, respectively.

performs this step to identify the most proper paragraph embedding model to represent the paragraphs of a given document.

The set of all the embedded paragraphs E_R is finally returned. Paragraph regularities for a given target document d will be identified from such set E_R.

2.3. Identification of paragraph regularities

The final phase, which workflow is represented in Fig. 3, starts by following the same steps mentioned in Sec. 2.2 to represent each paragraph of the target document d in the paragraph embedding space. Specifically, the most proper paragraph embedding model is adopted to embed its paragraphs, selected by identifying the closest document cluster with respect to d. For each embedded paragraph, we finally identify the top-n most similar paragraphs from the set of embedded paragraphs E_R belonging to the reference set.

It is noteworthy that their identification could straightforwardly be based on the computation of vector-based similarity/distance measures (e.g., cosine similarity, Euclidean distance, etc.) between the embedded paragraphs of the target document d and all the embedded paragraphs of the reference set E_r. Such a pairwise comparison would be computational intensive and would lead to inefficiencies during the adoption of the proposed system in a real-world scenario. To overcome this issue, we adopt a more advanced method for the identification of the top-n most similar paragraphs, based on random projections. In particular, we propose an approach based on Annoy [13], where the idea is to perform an approximated nearest neighbour search (ANNS), consisting in two phases: *index construction* on the paragraphs of the reference set, and *search*, that occurs when we actually need to identify the top-n most similar paragraphs with respect to a paragraph of the target document. During the index construction, we build T binary trees, where each tree is built by partitioning the input set of vectors recursively, by randomly selecting two vectors and defining a hyperplane that is equidistant from them. It is noteworthy that even if based on a random partitioning, vectors that are close to each other in the feature space are more likely to appear close to each other in the tree. During the search process, a priority queue is exploited, and each tree is recursively traversed, where the priority

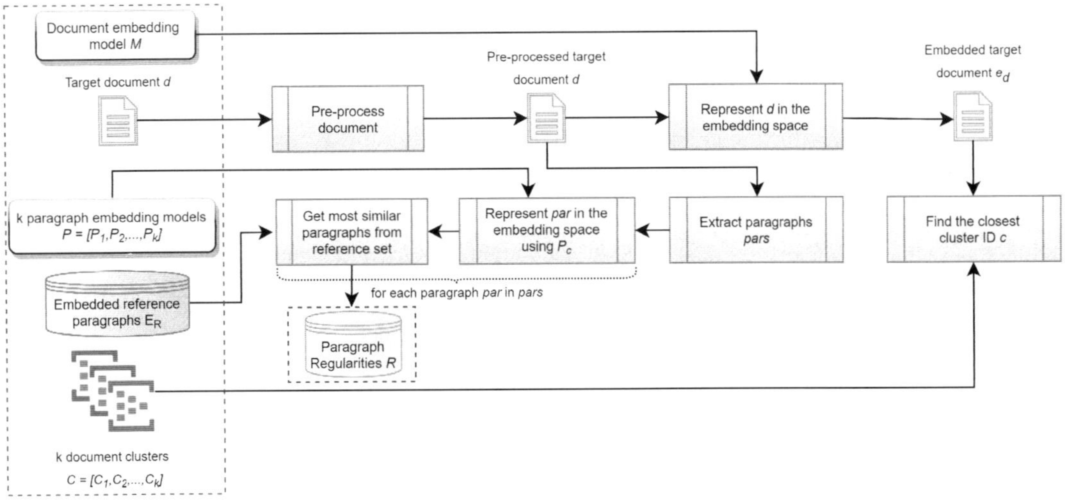

Figure 3: Graphical overview of the identification of paragraph regularities. Green- and red-dotted rectangles represent inputs and outputs, respectively.

of each split node is defined according to the distance to the query vector (that is a paragraph of the target document, in our case). This process leads to the identification of T leaf nodes, where the query vector falls into. The distance between the query vector and the set of vectors falling into the identified leaves is finally exploited to return the top-n most similar paragraphs [14].

3. Experiments

All the experiments were performed using a real-world dataset consisting of 4,181 official public EU legal documents, provided by EUR-Lex (https://eur-lex.europa.eu/homepage.html), in a 10-fold cross-validation setting. All the documents of the testing set were considered as target documents, while the reference set was built by constructing 20 replicas of each paragraph of the documents in the testing set, perturbed by introducing a controlled amount of noise. In particular, noise was introduced by replacing a given percentage of words of each paragraph by random words selected from the Oxford dictionary (raw.githubusercontent.com/cduica/Oxford-Dictionary-Json/master/dicts.json). In our experiments, we considered different levels of noise, namely, 10%, 20%, 30%, 40%, 50% and 60%, in order to evaluate the robustness of the proposed approach to different amounts of noise.

In order to assess the specific contribution of the adopted embedding strategies, we compared the results obtained through Word2Vec and Doc2Vec with those achieved using a baseline strategy, i.e., the classical TF-IDF. In all the cases, we adopted a 50-dimensional feature vector. Note that we use 50 features, since it is a commonly used dimensionality in other pre-trained embedding models. For TF-IDF, we selected the top-50 words showing the highest frequency across the set of legal judgments.

We specifically evaluated the contribution of the two-step model implemented in PRILJ with different numbers of clusters, i.e., $k \in \{\sqrt{|D_T|}/2, \sqrt{|D_T|}, \sqrt{|D_T|} \cdot 2\}$, and compared the observed performance with that obtained without grouping training documents into clusters (henceforth denoted as *one-step model*).

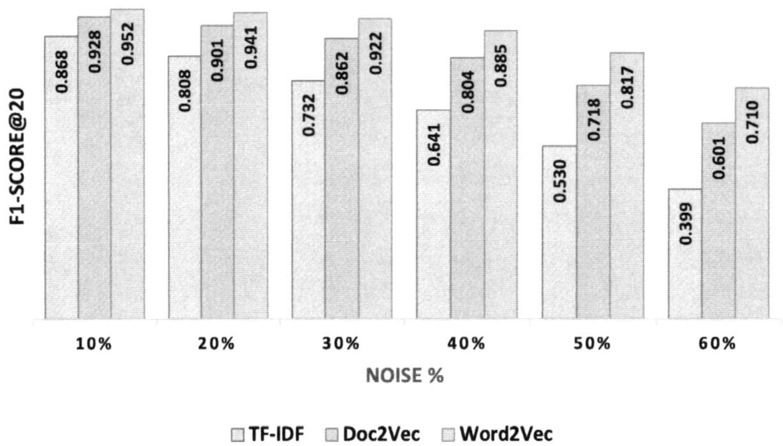

Figure 4: F1-score@20 results obtained when using TF-IDF, Doc2Vec or Word2Vec as embedding strategies, with the two-step model ($k = \sqrt{|D_T|} \cdot 2$).

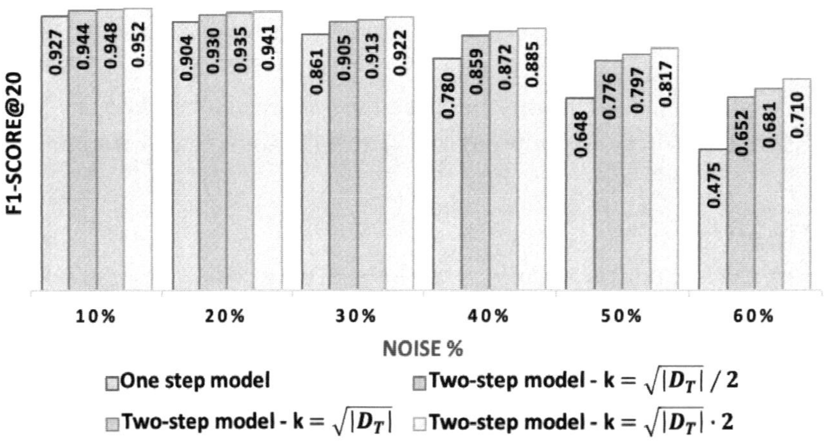

Figure 5: F1-score@20 results obtained with the two-step model (with different values of k) and with the one-step model. As embedding strategy, we considered Word2Vec.

Finally, we evaluated the effectiveness and the efficiency of the approach implemented in PRILJ for the identification of the *top*-n most similar paragraphs based on ANNS (with $T = 100$). Specifically, we performed an additional comparative analysis against a non-approximated solution based on the cosine similarity, on a subset of 100 documents randomly selected from the dataset. This analysis was performed considering the best number of clusters k, and also focused on evaluating the advantages in terms of computational efficiency.

As evaluation measures, we collected precision@n, recall@n and f1-score@n, averaged over the paragraphs of target documents and over the 10 folds, with $n \in \{5, 10, 15, 20, 50, 100\}$. Specifically, for each paragraph of a target document in the testing set, we considered as True Positives the number of correctly retrieved (perturbed) replicas from the reference set. Note that, in this discussion paper, for space constraints we only show the results in terms of f1-score@20.

	ANNS	Cosine Similarity
TF-IDF	**0.513**	407.612
Doc2Vec	**0.551**	580.842
Word2Vec	**0.610**	668.040

Table 1
Average running time (s) for the identification of the top-n most similar paragraphs, with the two-step model and $k = \sqrt{|D_T|} \cdot 2$.

3.1. Results

In Fig. 4 we can observe that, although the baseline based on TF-IDF obtained acceptable results, the adoption of the embedding methods implemented in PRILJ is significantly beneficial. Moreover, although Doc2Vec is natively able to work with word sequences, Word2Vec always obtains better results. This is possibly due to the fact that several paragraphs of different legal documents may share a similar topic, and the adoption of the unique sequence ID to associate the context with the document, as done by Doc2Vec (see [8] for details), may lead to overfitting issues.

In Fig. 5, it is possible to clearly observe the contribution of the two-step process we propose. Indeed, the results show that the proposed two-step model outperforms the one-step model, in all the situations. In particular, the two-step model is much more robust to the presence of noise: although we can still observe a decrease when the noise amount increases, its impact is much less evident. We can also observe that in general, the number of extracted cluster k seems to not significantly affect the results, even if the best results are observed with $k = \sqrt{|D_T|} \cdot 2$. This means that the documents are distributed among several topics and that learning a different (more specialized) paragraph embedding model for each of them is helpful to retrieve significant paragraph regularities.

Finally, the comparison between the adopted ANNS and the exact computation of the cosine similarity emphasized a difference of 0.6% in terms of f1-score@n, which can be considered negligible. On the other hand, the advantage in terms of efficiency is significant: the exact search required up to 1000x the time took by the ANNS implemented in PRILJ (see Table 1).

4. Conclusions

In this work, we discussed PRILJ, a novel approach to identify paragraph regularities in legal judgments. PRILJ represents documents and paragraphs thereof in a numerical feature space by exploiting embedding methods able to catch the context and the semantics. Moreover, PRILJ is based on a two-step model, that groups similar documents into clusters and, for each of them, learns a specific paragraph embedding model. This approach allows us to properly catch peculiarities exhibited by paragraphs and documents of similar topics and to handle the presence of noise in a robust manner. Finally, PRILJ is able to identify paragraph regularities very efficiently, thanks to an ANNS strategy.

Our extensive experimental evaluation has shown the accuracy and the efficiency of the developed approach on real data. This means that PRILJ can be considered a useful tool in real-world scenarios, also when large collections of legal documents have to be analyzed.

Acknowledgements

GP acknowledges the support of Ministry of Universities and Research through the project "Big Data Analytics", AIM 1852414-1 (line 1).

References

[1] A. Mandal, R. Chaki, S. Saha, K. Ghosh, A. Pal, S. Ghosh, Measuring similarity among legal court case documents, in: Proc. of the 10th Annual ACM India Compute Conference, Association for Computing Machinery, 2017, p. 1–9.

[2] M. Medvedeva, M. Vols, M. Wieling, Using machine learning to predict decisions of the european court of human rights, Artificial Intelligence and Law 28 (2020).

[3] P. Berkhin, Survey of clustering data mining techniques, A Survey of Clustering Data Mining Techniques. Grouping Multidimensional Data: Recent Advances in Clustering. 10 (2002).

[4] M. Ester, H.-P. Kriegel, J. Sander, X. Xu, A density-based algorithm for discovering clusters in large spatial databases with noise, in: Proc. of the 2nd International Conference on Knowledge Discovery and Data Mining, KDD'96, 1996, p. 226–231.

[5] G. Pio, M. Ceci, C. Loglisci, D. D'Elia, D. Malerba, Hierarchical and Overlapping Co-Clustering of mRNA: miRNA Interactions, in: ECAI 2012, volume 242 of *Frontiers in Artificial Intelligence and Applications*, IOS Press, 2012, pp. 654–659.

[6] R. Corizzo, G. Pio, M. Ceci, D. Malerba, DENCAST: distributed density-based clustering for multi-target regression, J. Big Data 6 (2019) 43.

[7] T. Mikolov, I. Sutskever, K. Chen, G. Corrado, J. Dean, Distributed representations of words and phrases and their compositionality, Advances in Neural Information Processing Systems 26 (2013).

[8] Q. Le, T. Mikolov, Distributed representations of sentences and documents, 31st International Conference on Machine Learning, ICML 2014 4 (2014).

[9] S. Kumar, P. K. Reddy, V. B. Reddy, A. Singh, Similarity analysis of legal judgments, in: Proceedings of the 4th Bangalore Annual Compute Conference, Compute 2011, Bangalore, India, March 25-26, 2011, ACM, 2011, p. 17.

[10] A. Minocha, N. Singh, A. Srivastava, Finding relevant indian judgments using dispersion of citation network, in: Proceedings of the 24th International Conference on World Wide Web, Association for Computing Machinery, 2015, p. 1085–1088.

[11] S. Kumar, P. K. Reddy, V. B. Reddy, M. Suri, Finding similar legal judgements under common law system, in: Databases in Networked Information Systems, Springer Berlin Heidelberg, 2013, pp. 103–116.

[12] K. Donghwa, D. Seo, S. Cho, P. Kang, Multi-co-training for document classification using various document representations: TF–IDF, LDA, and Doc2Vec, Information Sciences 477 (2018).

[13] E. Bernhardsson, Annoy at github, https://github.com/spotify/annoy, 2015.

[14] W. Li, Y. Zhang, Y. Sun, W. Wang, W. Zhang, X. Lin, Approximate nearest neighbor search on high dimensional data - experiments, analyses, and improvement (v1.0), CoRR (2016).

Activity Daily Living prediction with Marked Temporal Point Processes

(Discussion Paper)

Giancarlo Fortino[1], Antonella Guzzo[1], Michele Ianni[2], Francesco Leotta[3] and Massimo Mecella[3]

[1]*Università della Calabria, Italy*
[2]*Università di Verona, Italy*
[3]*Sapienza Università di Roma, Italy*

Abstract

The increasingly large availability of sensors in modern houses, due to the establishment of home assistants, allow to think in terms of smart houses where behaviours can be automatized based on user habits. Common tasks required to this aim include activity prediction, i.e., the task of forecasting what is the next activity a human is going to perform in the smart space based on past sensor logs. In this discussion paper[1], we outline a novel activity prediction method for smart houses based on the seminal probabilistic method named Marked Temporal Point Process Prediction.

Keywords

smart houses, activity prediction, human habits

1. Introduction

The establishment on the market, witnessed in the very last years, of home assistance devices (e.g., Google Home, Amazon Alexa), provided new incentives to the development of sensors and actuators based on wireless protocols (e.g., Zigbee) to be installed in private houses. These devices have the advantage, with respect to previous "domotic" technologies, of not requiring complex wiring and installation work, thus attracting the curiosity of end users who, with a limited expense, can create their own smart houses.

If, on the one hand, data coming from these devices are currently mainly employed by defining manual automation rules, on the other hand, there is now the concrete possibility of applying automatic techniques from the intelligent environment research community outside the controlled world of research laboratories.

---

[1]This paper is an extended abstract of Giancarlo Fortino, Antonella Guzzo, Michele Ianni, Francesco Leotta, and Massimo Mecella, Predicting Activities of Daily Living via Temporal Point Processes: Approaches and Experimental Results, to appear in Computers and Electrical Engineering, Elsevier, 2021.

SEBD 2021: The 29th Italian Symposium on Advanced Database Systems, September 5-9, 2021, Pizzo Calabro (VV), Italy

g.fortino@unical.it (G. Fortino); antonella.guzzo@unical.it (A. Guzzo); michele.ianni@univr.it (M. Ianni); leotta@diag.uniroma1.it (F. Leotta); mecella@diag.uniroma1.it (M. Mecella)
0000-0003-0562-7462 (M. Ianni)

Research work focused in particular on the following automated tasks: activity recognition, anomaly detection and activity prediction. As discussed in [1], prediction can be applied at the sensor level or at the activity level. The two types of prediction have different purposes. Activity level prediction is used to predict the next activity/ies the user is going to perform. Activity level prediction is usually intended for prompting expected activities to users (e.g., elderly) if they did not started at the right time [2, 3]. A survey of sensor and activity prediction is provided in [4]. Activity prediction is usually based on probabilistic models [2, 3], especially based on Markov chains, or on rules learned through classical data mining method such as rule mining [5] and clustering [6].

In this paper, we tackle the problem of *Activity Daily Living (ADL) prediction* in smart houses given past ADLs and sensor measurements, as discussed in our papers [7, 8]. We outline a prediction model for daily activities based on (Marked) Temporal Point Processes - MTPPs, that is a probabilistic method modeling random processes. In recent years, there has been an increasing number of applications to MTPPs [9, 10] in various areas including health-care analysis, finance, modeling earthquakes and aftershocks, etc. In particular, we applied MTPPs to a freely available dataset in the smart house community provided by the CASAS project. Achieved performance are evaluated against the state-of-the-art probabilistic algorithm defined in [2].

This discussion paper is organized as follows. Section 2 introduces the theoretical background behind MTPPs and their neural network implementations. Section 3 describes our approach to apply MTPPs to activities of daily living. Section 4 reports an initial evaluation of our approach based on MTPPs against the state-of-the-art technique proposed in [2]. Finally, Section 5 concludes the paper with final considerations and future works.

2. Marked Temporal Point Process Prediction

(Marked) Temporal Point Process (shortly MTPP) is a powerful mathematical tool for modeling the latent mechanisms that govern the occurrence of random events observed over time. In particular, these models can be used as predictive models, that are capable of specifying the timing of future events, based on the history of the past.

2.1. Preliminaries on MTPP

Formally, a marked temporal point process is a stochastic process modelling a list of discrete events $e_j = (t_j, a_j)$, with $t_j \in \mathcal{R}^+$, $j \in \mathcal{Z}^+$ and $a_j \in \mathcal{A}$ where the domain of $\mathcal{A}$ is application dependent [10]. Note that, with respect to the basic formulation of a TPP, the concept of event point is extended with a marked a_j, i.e. additional information associated with an event that can be of separate interest (e.g. in the prediction of an earthquake we are interested in its position and magnitude) or may simply be included to make a more realistic model of the event times (as in our case). Let the history H_t be the list of events (time and marker pairs) up to the time t, we can explicitly specify the conditional density function that the next event will occur during the interval $[t, t + \mathrm{d}t]$ with mark a by $f^*(t, a) = f(t, a|H_t)$ where the notation $*$ from [11] means that this density is conditional on the past (right up to but not including the present) rather than writing explicitly that the function depends on the history. From the density functions

$f((t_1, a_1), \ldots, (t_j, a_j))$ specifying the distributions of all events time and marker pairs, one by one, starting in the past, thus the distribution of all events is given by the joint density:

$$f(\{(t_j, a_j)\}_{j=1}^{n}) = \prod_j f(t_j, a_j | H_{t_{j-1}}) = \prod_j f^*(t_j, a_j) \tag{1}$$

A common way to model temporal point process with marker is by the conditional intensity function that could be specified by the conditional density $f(t, a|H_{t_n})$ and its corresponding cumulative distribution function $F(t, a|H_{t_n})$ for any $t > t_n$. Formally, the conditional intensity function is defined by:

$$\lambda^*(t, a) = \frac{f(t, a|H_{t_n})}{1 - F(t, a|H_{t_n})} \tag{2}$$

The conditional intensity function can be interpreted heuristically by considering an infinitesimal interval around t, say $[t, t + \mathrm{d}t]$ and the number of points falling in it N: $\lambda^*(t, a)\mathrm{d}t\mathrm{d}a = E[N(\mathrm{d}t \times \mathrm{d}a)|H_t]$ that is, the mean number of points in a small time interval dt with the mark in a small interval $\mathrm{d}t$. Based on the application domains, different forms of the conditional intensity function has been proposed aiming at capturing the phenomena of interests [9]. For example, the specific parametric could be as in Poisson process [12] when keep λ fixed over time, and to be independent of the history H_t; as non homogeneous Poisson process when keep $\lambda(t)$ as a function of only time and not the history of events you get; as Hawkes process [13], where exponential formulation of the conditional intensity simulate the fact that a point increases the chance of getting other points immediately after, and Self-correcting process [14] where as opposed to Hawkes process the chance of new points decreases immediately after a point has appeared. Beside the specific form of the conditional intensity, as those introduced above, all these different parametrizations imply specific assumptions about the functional forms of the generative processes, which may or may not reflect the reality and definitely would be unknown in the most common cases.

2.2. Recurrent Marked Temporal Point Process

Differently to the approaches where the conditional intensity has a specified parametric form, recent research on MTPP emphasizes more on the neural-network-based point process models as a promising approach that can better capture the dynamics of a complex system. In particular, two recent approaches, namely RMTPP [15] and ERPP [16], have demonstrated that Recurrent Neural Network (RNN) can be used to model and automatically learn the conditional intensity function (without any particular prior assumptions) by achieving better prediction results than simple TPP models (e.g. Point, Hawkes or Self-correcting processes).

RMTPP [15] is the seminal work that initially proposed to use RNN in the MTPP framework. Specifically, the event history is embedded into a vector h_j, and then used to define the conditional intensity as $\lambda^*(t) = \exp(w^t(t - t_j) + v^T h_j + b^t)$, where v^T is a column vector, w^t, b^t are scalars learned during the train of the network and the exponential function is used as a non-linear transformation and guarantees that the intensity is positive. Formulation of λ summarizes three contributions: (1) the first term emphasizes the influence of the current event j; (2) the second term $v^T h_j$ represents the accumulative influence from the marker and the timing information of the past events; (3) the last term gives a base intensity level for the occurrence of the next event.

By following the path traced by [15], ERPP proposed a model that automatically learns the conditional intensity function of a point process by synergically using two RNNs, one RNN with asynchronous events as input and another RNN with time series as input. The underlying rationale is that time series are more suitable to carry the synchronously and regularly updated, while the event sequence can compactly catch event driven, more abrupt information, which can affect the conditional intensity function over longer period of time. Adopting a twin RNN structure permits to deal with timeseries and event via separate RNN, and can be suitable to model point process in which the dynamics of these two source of data can be rather varying [16].

3. Prediction for Activities of Daily Living based on RMTPP and ERPP

We use (marked) Temporal Point Process (MTPP) as a mathematical framework for the modeling and learning of human's behaviors, associated with their side habit information. In fact, human activities are captured by sensors and recorded as many discrete events in continuous time.

Definition 3.1. Let the input be a set of sequence of activities performed in the time with its timestamp, i.e. $S = \{e_1 = (t_1, a_1), \ldots, e_m = (t_m, a_m)\}$ is a sequence of pairs marked by a kind of activity and its timestamp. Given two events e_i and e_j with $i > j$, we have that $t_i \geq t_j$. Considering the j-th observation, our goal is to predict the next observation (j+1), i.e. when the next activity will happen and what type of activity it will be, given the past sequence of observations.

3.1. Prediction Model Formulations

To build the model prediction based on the RMTPP's architecture, we first embed the sequence of daily activities (see Definition 3.1) into a latent space. Then, the embedded vector and the temporal features are fed into the recurrent layer. The recurrent layer learns a representation that summaries the nonlinear dependency over the previous events. Based on the learned representation h_j , it outputs the prediction for the next marker a_{j+1} and timing t_{j+1} to calculate the respective loss functions.

As evidenced in [16], based on the hidden unit of RNN, we are able to learn a unified representation of the dependency over the history. In consequence, the direct formulation 2 of the conditional intensity function $\lambda^*(t_j + 1)$ captures both of the information from past event timings and event markers. On the other hand, since the prediction for the marker also depends nonlinearly on the past timing information, this may improve the performance of the classification task as well when both of these two information are correlated with each other.

By adopting the ERPP's architecture, the model differs substantially, since time series and event sequence are predicted separately. Specifically, we fed the different timestamps into a LSTM and the sequence of activities is embedded and fed into a separate LSTM.

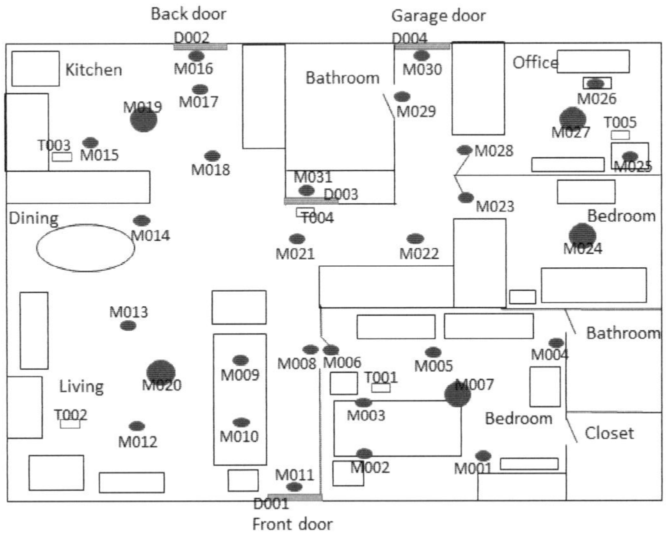

Figure 1: Aruba installation

4. An Experimental analysis

The experimental analysis has been conducted on the ARUBA dataset provided by the CASAS project [1]. The dataset has been acquired by monitoring the activities performed by an elderly during two years of daily life in the house depicted in Figure 1.

Furnitures and walls are depicted using black lines. The environment contains different category of sensors including passive infrared sensors - PIRs (denoted with ellipses and code MXXX), door-attached switch sensors (denoted with empty rectangles and code DXXX), and temperature sensors (denoted with code DXXX). In particular, the house is equipped with 31 passive infrared sensors (PIR) installed on the ceiling in correspondence of sensitive places for human activities (e.g., M002 and M003 mounted in correspondence of the bed, M009 and M010 mounted in correspondence of the sofa) and pointing at the floor. As soon as the elderly walks in the area covered by a sensor, he/she makes it trigger to the ON value. Two kinds of PIR sensors are available with two different detection area sizes: small cone sensors (denoted with small ellipses) and large cone sensors (denoted with large ellipses). The former have the goal of detecting the elderly interacting with the specific furnitures in correspondence of the sensors, whereas the latter have the goal of detecting him/her generically entering a room or an area (e.g., M019 detects the person entering the kitchen).

The dataset is labeled with the activity the elderly is performing when each sensor measurement onsets. The dataset reports 12 different activities. The dataset has been pre-processed in order to remove sensor measurements other than those coming from the PIR sensors and to remove OFF measurements for PIR sensors, which do not contain any information (PIR sensors trigger to OFF after a predetermined amount of time). The goal of the evaluation is to measure the ability of the proposed technique to predict the next activity and when this activity will

[1]cf. http://casas.wsu.edu/

be performed. Achieved performance have been compared with the state-of-the-art technique proposed in [2]. The Aruba dataset has been split in a training set (70% of the measurements) and a validation set (30% of the measurements). We evaluated the time prediction using the *Mean Absolute Error (MAE)*, *Precision* and *Recall* and *F1-score*.

4.1. Performance of chosen state-of-the-art approach

The performance of our solution have been compared with those obtained with the technique proposed by the CASAS research group in [2]. The source code of the algorithm is freely available on the project website, even though some re-coding was needed in order to compute performance envisioned in our work. In particular, performance in [2] are not computed considering all the different activities together, but with respect to a specific activity. Evaluation in the original paper [2] was conducted with a different, less recent and smaller dataset from the very same research group.

The technique proposed in [2] is based on two components. The current activity - RA, is recognized by applying Support Vector Machines - SVM, to sensor measurements. At this point the likelihood of a predicted activity - PA, is obtained by taking into account *(i)* the likelihood that activity PA occurs after activity RA, *(ii)* the confidence in the distribution of the occurrence times of PA relative to RA, and *(iii)* the mean delay between RA and PA. In addition pattern mining over sensor measurements is employed.

Performance has been computed by asking to the algorithm at each step, which is the next activity and when it is going to happen. On a total of 238 748 decisions, the next activity was correctly predicted in the 56% of the cases, which is fairly good performance considered that the number of different activities is 12. The precision obtained though was 0.19, the recall 0.18 and F1-score 0.18. The MAE with respect to the onset of a specific activity is instead of 182.1 minutes.

4.2. Performance of our approach

In order to evaluate the effectiveness of our approach, we performed the same experiments described in the section 4.1 using both RMTPP and ERPP. As introduced in section 2.2, RMTPP is a way to connect recurrent neural networks and point processes, giving us the opportunity to predict not only the marker but also the timing of the future events. It is important to notice that no prior knowledge about the hidden functional forms of the latent temporal dynamics is needed. The reference paper for the implementation of RMTPP is [15]. Using the same settings described in 4.1, we obtained the following results using RMTPP: the MAE is 4.672 with a precision of 0.648, recall of 0.907 and F1-score equals to 0.756. In order to evaluate ERPP, we used as reference the paper [16], using a single layer LSTM of size 32 with Sigmoid gate activations and tanh activation for hidden representation. The results are better than RMTPP in terms of MAE. We obtained the following values: MAE: 0.008, precision: 0.660, recall: 0.905 and F1-score: 0.763. Notably, MAE is an indication of the average deviation of the predicted values w.r.t the corresponding observed values, suggesting us that ERPP outperform RMTPP in long term model prediction.

	MAE	Precision	Recall	F1-Score
Cook [2]	182.1	0.19	0.18	0.18
RMTPP [15]	4.67	0.65	0.90	0.76
ERPP [16]	0.01	0.66	0.90	0.76

Table 1
Performance evaluation results

4.3. Discussion

Table 1 recaps the results obtained during our performance evaluation. From these preliminary tests, the proposed approaches clearly outperform the state-of-the-art algorithm proposed in [2]. The algorithm presented in [2] is essentially based on classical pattern mining and machine learning. In particular, starting from the activity currently recognized as ongoing, based on an SVM classifier, patterns are extracted on a statistical basis taking into account time relationships between activities and the value of specific sensor measurements as indicators of future activities. RMTPP [15] and ERPP [16] are instead based on recurrent neural networks, which proved themselves very effective for many different learning tasks.

5. Conclusions and Future Work

In this paper, we have proposed the application of Marked Temporal Point Process for human action analysis, which has not been explored before. We have adopted ERPP and RMTPP as methods describing the generative mechanism of event sequences. Empirical results on challenging daily life datasets demonstrate the efficacy of the proposed methods and consistent performance gain for event prediction and causality analysis w.r.t. state-of-the-art approach. In future work, we plan to enrich our test set with more references and to extend this work with a novel architecture incorporating external features in order to improve its temporal dependence modeling and to better embed the dynamics that govern the generation process of the events. We will extend validation also to other techniques.

References

[1] F. D. Casagrande, J. Tørresen, E. Zouganeli, Comparison of probabilistic models and neural networks on prediction of home sensor events, in: 2019 International Joint Conference on Neural Networks (IJCNN), IEEE, 2019, pp. 1–8.

[2] L. B. Holder, D. J. Cook, Automated activity-aware prompting for activity initiation, Gerontechnology: international journal on the fundamental aspects of technology to serve the ageing society 11 (2013) 534.

[3] B. Minor, D. J. Cook, Forecasting occurrences of activities, Pervasive and mobile computing 38 (2017) 77–91.

[4] S. Wu, J. B. Rendall, M. J. Smith, S. Zhu, J. Xu, H. Wang, Q. Yang, P. Qin, Survey on prediction algorithms in smart homes, IEEE Internet of Things Journal 4 (2017) 636–644.

[5] A. Aztiria, J. C. Augusto, R. Basagoiti, A. Izaguirre, D. J. Cook, Discovering frequent user–environment interactions in intelligent environments, Personal and Ubiquitous Computing 16 (2012) 91–103.

[6] J. Lapalu, K. Bouchard, A. Bouzouane, B. Bouchard, S. Giroux, Unsupervised mining of activities for smart home prediction, Procedia Computer Science 19 (2013) 503–510.

[7] G. Fortino, A. Guzzo, M. Ianni, F. Leotta, M. Mecella, Exploiting marked temporal point processes for predicting activities of daily living, in: IEEE International Conference on Human-Machine Systems, ICHMS 2020, 2020.

[8] G. Fortino, A. Guzzo, M. Ianni, F. Leotta, M. Mecella, Predicting activities of daily living via temporal point processes: Approaches and experimental results, Computers & Electrical Engineering (2021 - TO APPEAR).

[9] J. Yan, H. Xu, L. Li, Modeling and applications for temporal point processes, in: Proceedings of the 25th ACM SIGKDD, 2019, p. 3227–3228.

[10] Y. Zhong, B. Xu, G.-T. Zhou, L. Bornn, G. Mori, Time perception machine: Temporal point processes for the when, where and what of activity prediction, ArXiv abs/1808.04063 (2018).

[11] D. Daley, D. Vere-Jones, An Introduction to the Theory of Point Processes, Springer-Verlag, 2003.

[12] J. F. C. Kingman, Poisson processes, volume 3 of *Oxford Studies in Probability*, The Clarendon Press Oxford University Press, 1993. Oxford Science Publications.

[13] A. G. Hawkes, Spectra of some self-exciting and mutually exciting point processes, Biometrika 58 (1971) 83–90.

[14] A self-correcting point process, Stochastic Processes and their Applications 8 (1979) 335 – 347.

[15] N. Du, H. Dai, R. S. Trivedi, U. Upadhyay, M. Gomez-Rodriguez, L. Song, Recurrent marked temporal point processes: Embedding event history to vector, Proceedings of the 22nd ACM SIGKDD (2016).

[16] S. Xiao, J. Yan, X. Yang, H. Zha, S. M. Chu, Modeling the intensity function of point process via recurrent neural networkss, in: Proceedings of the Thirty-First AAAI Conference on Artificial Intelligence, AAAI Press, 2017, p. 1597–1603.

A Multiple Instance Learning Approach for the Automatic Classification of Skin Lesions

(Discussion Paper)

Eugenio Vocaturo[1,2], Ester Zumpano[1], Giovanni Giallombardo[1] and Giovanna Miglionico[1]

[1]*DIMES - University of Calabria, Rende, Italy*
[2]*CNR-NANOTEC National Research Council, Rende, Italy*

Abstract
The number of deaths linked to skin cancers has malignant melanoma as the main culprit. Early diagnosis helps manage this terrible form of cancer, but the similarity of melanoma to other skin lesions is an obstacle to effective detection. The scientific community is proposing different solutions to support the computerized analysis of skin lesions mainly focused on the dichotomous distinction of melanoma from benign lesions. The *dysplastic nevi syndrome* (DNS) correlates the number of moles present in the human body with an increased risk of melanoma development. Nowadays, the classification task concerning the differentiation of dysplastic nevi from common ones is still very little explored. In this paper, we explore the possibility of applying multiple instance learning (MIL) approaches to discriminate melanoma from dysplastic nevi and outline the even more complex challenge of discriminate between dysplastic and common nevi. The obtained results confirm that MIL techniques are useful for the automatic detection of skin lesions are promising, and give hope MIL techniques can be useful for solutions aiming at automatic detection of skin lesions.

Keywords
Dermoscopy imaging Classification, Multiple Instance Learning, Dysplastic nevi Detection

1. Introduction

The World Health Organization certifies that, in 2020, more than 57,000 people died of melanoma and that there were more than 320,000 new cases. The reported data testify that melanoma affects the populations of all geographical areas of the world and in particular those of Europe (50.1 % of total cases) and North America (27.7 % of total cases). Melanoma ranks 5th for age-standardized (World) incidence and mortality rates in 2020, for both males and females, considering all ages [1]. Despite the worrying scenario in terms of both new cases and deaths, if melanoma is identified by early diagnosis it is a treatable type of cancer. Specific clinical protocols such as the ABCDE [2] rule and the 7-PCL [3] are adopted as a guideline for identifying lesions from an early stage. The ABCDE rule, which is the most commonly adopted, suggests monitoring

SEBD 2021: The 29th Italian Symposium on Advanced Database Systems, September 5-9, 2021, Pizzo Calabro (VV), Italy
e.vocaturo@dimes.unical.it (E. Vocaturo); e.zumpano@dimes.unical.it (E. Zumpano); g.giallombardo@dimes.unical.it (G. Giallombardo); g.miglionico@dimes.unical.it (G. Miglionico)

CEUR Workshop Proceedings (CEUR-WS.org)

symmetry, irregularity of the edges, colors of the lesion, its extension and evolution over time. Our proposal was applied to skin lesion images detected through dedicated instrumentation.

In particular, the used dataset contains dermatoscopic images: this particular type is widely used in Computer Aided Diagnosis (CAD) systems to support the diagnosis.

Considering that higher risk of developing melanoma pertains to individuals with *dysplastic nevi syndrome* and/or with family history of melanoma, our research focuses on the application of DC-SMIL [4], a multiple instance learning algorithm, on the challenging tasks of classifying melanoma vs dysplastic nevi and dysplastic nevi vs common ones [19, 24].

The first task results to be difficult for the great similarity of the two types of lesions [5]. Even more complex is the classification of dysplastic nevi from common ones: this issue is completely new and has not been addressed in the literature. Our goal is to verify how the MIL approaches are of interest when applied on binary classification tasks in which the images are very similar to each other.

The paper is organized as follows. In the next section we put in evidence that the presence of dysplastic nevi and common nevi may imply risk of melanoma onset. In Section 3 we introduce the Multiple Instance Learning approach, focusing on DC-SMIL a new MIL algoritmh that adopt spherical separation surfaces [4]. In Section 4 we describe the dermoscopic dataset used to test DC-SMIL reporting some preliminary results. Finally some conclusions are given.

2. Dysplastic nevi

The *Syndrome of Dysplastic Nevus (DNS)* refers to individuals that present a high number of both benign moles and dysplastic nevi. Individuals with dysplastic nevi are more likely to develop melanoma if familiarly conditions exists. In [6], a cumulative lifetime risk of almost 100% is reported for individuals who have dysplastic nevi and are related to melanoma; about 30% of melanomas occur within atypical moles. A genetic predisposition for the formation of melanoma is present in 40-50% of cases. The correlation between the presence of dysplastic nevi and the melanoma has been also investigated in [7]. The diagnosis of a severe DNS cannot be overlooked, as it could state for a miss-diagnosed in situ melanoma [8], it may reflect the dermatopathological uncertainty related to a wrong diagnosis. Figure 1 reports a dermoscopic image of common nevi, dysplastic nevi and melanoma.

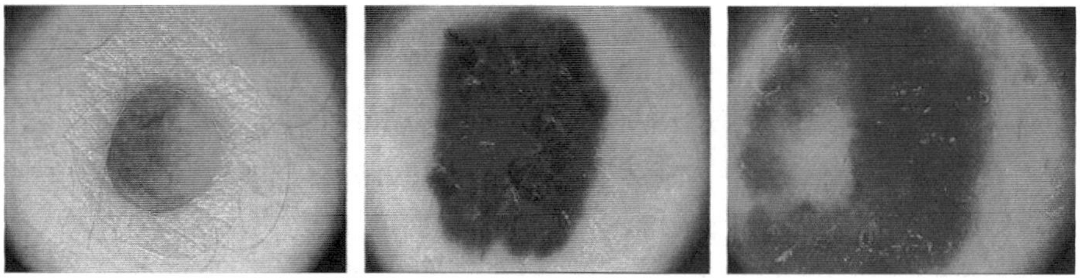

Figure 1: Dermoscopic image of common nevus, dysplastic nevus and melanoma

Basically, the risk of melanoma is related to two different objective criteria:

- An increased risk of melanoma is related to a high number of nevi [9]. Individuals with a number of nevi greater than 100 have a risk of melanoma 7 times greater than those with a count of less than 15 [10].

- An increased risk of melanoma is related to the presence of large nevi. A histological study of nevi has shown that higher is the extension of the mole, greater is the risk of turning into melanoma: the relative risk of 1 for nevi with a diameter less than 2.4 mm, while the relative risk progressively increases up to 5 if the lesion has a diameter greater than 4.4 mm [11].

Fewer attentions have been given to the discrimination of melanoma from dysplastic nevi [12]. The topic investigated in this paper is the classification task of dysplastic nevi against common nevi, which, to the best of our knowledge, has never been taken into consideration.

3. Multiple instance classification via spherical separation

Machine Learning has become very important in medical image analysis. In fact, machine learning methods are currently used in the segmentation steps, in which each pixel of an image belongs to a particular tissue and in CAD systems to assign a category label to a whole image.

Multiple Instance Learning scenario is particularly useful when disposing of local annotated labels is expensive, while global labels for whole images, such as the outcome of a diagnosis, are more readily available. MIL is an extension of supervised learning that can train classifiers using weakly labeled data. The goal is therefore to exploit the labels of the weaker bags for training. A MIL problem consists in the classification task of a set of items called *bags* and of the objects inside them called *instances*. The substantial difference compared to supervised classification consists in the fact that, in the learning phase, only the labels of the bags are known, and not those of the instances.

The MIL paradigm is particularly well suited to image classification, given that to classify an image, it is necessary to examine only some sub-regions. With MIL approaches it is therefore possible to obtain global information from local one. For general considerations on the MIL paradigm, we refer the reader to surveys [13, 14]. In [15], a detailed review is given concerning MIL applied for medical images and video analysis. MIL approaches, as far as we know, are still very rarely used for melanoma detection, and has never been used for the detection of dysplastic nevi.

In [16] we applied MIL-RL algorithm to discriminate melanoma from benign lesion. The results demonstrate the goodness of the proposed approach.

In a data driven way, we have therefore presented a new algorithm named DC-SMIL [4], which is suitable for image classification. DC-SMIL adopt spherical separation as a classification tool and come out with an optimization model which is of DC (Difference of Convex) type. In particular the adopted classification error function depend on center and radius of the sphere and we come out with an optimization model to minimize a combination of the volume of the sphere and of the classification error.

Our aim is to find a sphere $S(w, r) \subset \mathbb{R}^n$, of center $w \in \mathbb{R}^n$ and radius $r \in \mathbb{R}$, separating the two classes of bags. In order to separate the positive bags $X_1^+, \dots, X_m^+$ from the negative ones $X_1^-, \dots, X_k^-$, a sphere must have a nonempty intersection with each positive bag, while leaving outside all the instances belonging to negative bags.

A pictorial example of spherical separation is presented in Figure 2, where the sphere $S(w, r)$ separates the negative bags X_1^-, X_2^-, and X_3^- from the positive bags X_1^+ and X_2^+. In particular, we remark that while the bags depicted in Figure 2 are spherically separable, they are not separable by any hyper-plane.

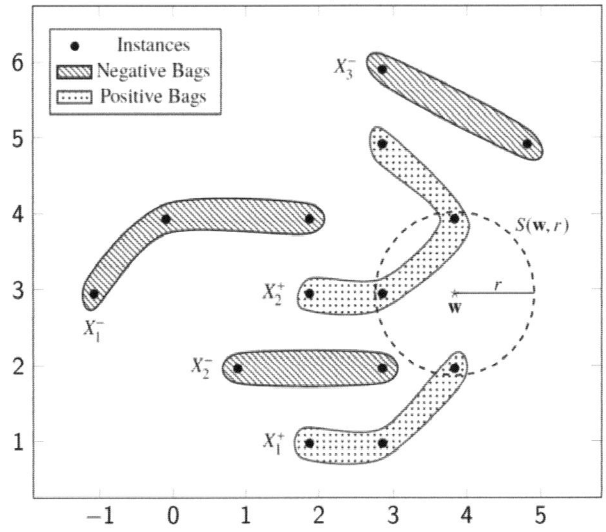

Figure 2: Spherical separation with three negative bags and two positive bags [4]

Based on the latter remark an optimization model was obtained with the aim to look for a separating sphere, if any, by minimizing a measure of all the classification errors of both the negative and the positive bags, that is

$$\min_{(w,r)\in\mathbb{R}^{n+1}} f(w,r) \tag{1}$$

where the loss function f is defined as

$$\begin{aligned} f(w,r) \;\triangleq\;& r^2 + C\sum_{i=1}^{k} \max\left\{0, \max_{j\in J_i^-}\left\{r^2 - \|x_j - w\|^2\right\}\right\} \\ & + C\sum_{i=1}^{m} \max\left\{0, \min_{j\in J_i^+}\left\{\|x_j - w\|^2 - r^2\right\}\right\} \end{aligned} \tag{2}$$

In particular, such loss function accounts for three contributions:

- the first term accounts for the volume of the sphere;
- the second one accounts for the misclassification error of the negative bags;
- the last term accounts for misclassification error of the positive bags.

Hence, the Spherical MIL program (SMIL) follows as the unconstrained optimization problem

$$\min_{(w,r)\in\mathbb{R}^{n+1}} f(w,r) \triangleq r^2 + C\mathcal{E}(w,r), \tag{3}$$

which combines, by introducing a trade-off parameter $C > 0$, the two objectives of minimizing the radius of the sphere and the classification errors of all the negative and positive bags. Here the radius minimization is aimed at reducing the false positive phenomenon when the calculated sphere is used as a classification tool.

4. Numerical results and final remarks

We have performed experiments applying DC-SMIL on various data sets to evaluate the goodness of the proposed technique and to compare the obtained results with those of other MIL methods. In particular, we applied DC-SMIL on a real dermatoscopic dataset (PH^2), with the aim of verifying that MIL spherical separation approach may be of interest in classification tasks in which the data to be classified have extreme similarity.

The entire PH^2 database contains 200 images of melanocytic lesions: 80 common nevi, 80 atypical nevi and 40 melanomas. All images were obtained using 8-bit RGB colors with a resolution of 768×560 pixels.

For the classification experiments we considered the images without taking into account the indications resulting from the manual analysis carried out by the specialists.

In [17] the authors demonstrated how, by adopting only color features, satisfactory classification performances can be obtained using dermatoscopic images. Starting from this assumptions, we used a 30-dimensional vector for the representation of each sub-regions of each image. For further details please see [16] and [4]. To avoid the problems related to the use of datasets with unbalanced classes, we have duplicated all the images of melanomas, adding to the repeated ones a Gaussian noise with zero mean with variance equal to 0.0001, as in [17]. In this way we obtained a balanced dataset containing three classes of data, Melanomas (M), Dysplastic Nevi (DN) and Common Nevi (N) each with 80 images. For each data set configuration, we performed a ten fold cross-validation. The respective results are listed in Tables 1 and 2, where we report the average of correctness, sensitivity, specificity, F score and CPU time.

In order to appreciate the MIL classification paradigm, we report in the columns MIL-RL, SVM and SVM-RBF the results obtained using MIL-RL algorithm and standard SVM approach [18] with linear and RBF kernels, respectively. The best results in Tables 1 and 2 have been underlined.

4.1. Melanomas vs Dysplastic Nevi

From numerical experiments it emerges that, in general, MIL-RL overcomes DC-SMIL and SVM technique (with both linear and RBF kernels) in terms of accuracy and sensitivity. Whenever accuracy is not 100%, low specificity values are a consequence of high sensitivity values.

In medical fields, sensitivity plays a more important role than specificity since it is a measure of the ability to identify un-healthy patients. The F-score values show the good performance of the MIL approach in classifying melanoma from dysplastic nevi against the classic SVM technique.

	10-CV			
	DC-SMIL	MIL-RL	SVM	SVM-RBF
Correctness (%)	70.00	86.25	69.38	86.25
Sensitivity (%)	69.30	91,08	69.65	87.88
Specificity (%)	71.81	82.12	69.87	85.95
F-score (%)	69.09	87.01	68.68	87.52
CPU time (secs)	0.66	1.20	2.05	0.03

Table 1
80 melanomas and 80 dysplastic nevi

4.2. Dysplastic Nevi vs Common Nevi

With regard to the experimental section on the classification of dysplastic nevi against common nevi, the performances of MIL-RL and of SVM tecniques appear totally unsatisfactory. This is obvious because the images that were separated are very similar. MIL-RL registers the worst value of F-score and sensitivity, and overall it is not effective to solve the proposed task.

	10-CV			
	DC-SMIL	MIL-RL	SVM	SVM-RBF
Correctness (%)	59.38	59.38	58.13	51.88
Sensitivity (%)	59.73	31.77	43.67	58.92
Specificity (%)	59.88	87.06	73.48	46.47
F-score (%)	57.61	42.77	48.57	53.74
CPU time (secs)	0.58	1.71	2.13	0.03

Table 2
80 dysplatic nevi and 80 common nevi

The use of spherical separating surfaces, provided by DC-SMIL algorithm, allows significant improvements in the extremely difficult task of classify dysplastic nevi from common ones.

As shown in [19, 20] better results could be obtained in case of images pre-processing aimed at eliminating the presence of possible noises, such as possible hair. Even the adoption of further useful features extracted from blob is a possibility that would allow to improve the classification performances [21, 29]. Pre-processing steps and the adoption of a more numerous set of features appear to be an obligatory step when considering non-dermatoscopic images [22, 23].

The obtained results show that in the first case MIL-RL is very promising, even in the conditions in which we performed the experiments, i.e. with only color features and without using pre-processing steps.

In the second case, MIL-RL algorithm as well as the SVM in the linear and Kernel RBF version, do not give satisfactory results. The excessive similarity of the lesions is not properly discriminated with approaches aimed at identifying linear separation surfaces. On the other hand DC-SMIL, thanks to the use of spherical separation surfaces, seems to be an interesting proposal for the development of applications in contexts in which positive and negative elements have similar characteristics.

Our proposal based on MIL approaches, among the various proposals of artificial intelligence in this specific domain, constitutes an element of novelty [26]. Our goal is to set propose a framework for supporting diagnostics both for specialists and for patient self-diagnosis examination via mobile applications. In this way, modular solution which can be incorporated into integrated diagnostic systems [27, 28] would increase the value of the proposal.

Future research could include the design of more sophisticated segmentation techniques in order to further improve classification results, as well as the application of the proposed method in other medical fields [29, 30] to identify other types of injuries.

References

[1] http://gco.iarc.fr/today.

[2] R. Sanghera and P. S. Grewal, Dermatological symptom assessment, in Patient Assessment in Clinical Pharmacy, p. 133–154, Springer, 2019.

[3] G. Argenziano et al., Epiluminescence microscopy for the diagnosis of doubtful melanocytic skin lesions: Comparison of the abcd rule of dermatoscopy and a new 7-point checklist based on pattern analysis, Archives of Dermatology, v. 134, n. 12, pp. 1563–70, 1998.

[4] M. Gaudioso, et al., Classification in the multiple instance learning framework via spherical separation, Soft Computing, v.24, n.7, pp: 5071-5077, 2020.

[5] M. Burroni, et al., Dysplastic naevus vs. in situ melanoma: digital dermoscopy analysis. Br J Dermatol, v.152(4), pp:679–84, 2005.

[6] R. Pampena, A. Kyrgidis, A meta-analysis of nevus-associated melanoma: Prevalence and practical implications, American Academy of Dermatology. v. 77, n.5, pp. 938–945, 2017.

[7] M. Arumi-Uria, NS. McNutt, B. Finnerty, Grading of atypia in nevi: correlation with melanoma risk". Mod Pathol., 16(8):764-771, 2003.

[8] KK. Reddy, et al., Atypical (dysplastic) nevi: outcomes of surgical excision and association with melanoma. JAMA Dermatol.,149(8): 928-934, 2013.

[9] E. Rieger, et al., Overall and site-specific risk of malignant melanoma associated with nevus counts at different body sites: a multicenter case-control study of the German Central Malignant-Melanoma Registry. Int J Cancer. 62(4): 393-7, 1995.

[10] S. Gandini, F. Sera, M.S.Cattaruzza , et al., "Meta-analysis of risk factors for cutaneous melanoma: I. Common and atypical nevi". Eur J Cancer.,41(1):28-44, 2005.

[11] M.Y. Xiong, M.S. Rabkin,M.W. Piepkorn, et al., Diameter of dysplastic nevi is a more robust biomarker of increased melanoma risk than degree of histologic dysplasia: a case-control study. J Am Acad Dermatol.,71(6):1257-1258, 2014.

[12] M. Rastgoo, et al., Automatic differentiation of melanoma from dysplastic nevi. Computerized Medical Imaging and Graphics, 43, 44-52, 2015.

[13] J. Amores, Multiple instance classification: review, taxonomy and comparative study. Artificial Intelligence 201:81–105, 2013.

[14] M.A. Carbonneau, et al., Multiple instance learning: a survey of problem characteristics and applications. Pattern Recogn 77:329–353, 2018.

[15] G. Quellec, G. Cazuguel, B. Cochener, M. Lamard, Multiple instance learning for medical image and video analysis, IEEE Rev Biomed Eng 10, pp:213–234, 2017.

[16] A. Astorino, et al., Melanoma Detection by Means of Multiple Instance Learning. Interdiscip Sci Comput Life Sci 12, 24–31, 2020.

[17] C. Barata, M. Ruela, M. Francisco, A.T. Mendonc, J. Marques. Two systems for the detection of melanomas in dermoscopy images using texture and color features. IEEE Syst J 8(3), pp: 965–79, 2014.

[18] V. Vapnik, The nature of the statistical learning theory, Springer, 1995.

[19] E. Vocaturo, E. Zumpano, P. Veltri, On the Usefulness of Pre-Processing Step in Melanoma Detection Using Multiple Instance Learning, International Conference on Flexible Query Answering Systems, Springer, pp. 374-382, 2019.

[20] E. Vocaturo, E. Zumpano, P. Veltri, Image preprocessing in computer vision systems for melanoma detection, 2018 IEEE International Conference on Bioinformatics and Biomedicine (BIBM), pp. 2117-24, 2018.

[21] E. Vocaturo, E. Zumpano, P. Veltri, Features for Melanoma Lesions Characterization in Computer Vision Systems, 9th International Conference on Information, Intelligence, Systems and Applications(IISA), pp. 1–8, 2018.

[22] A. Astorino, A. Fuduli, M. Gaudioso, E. Vocaturo, Multiple Instance Learning Algorithm for Medical Image Classification, Proceedings of the 27th Italian Symposium on Advanced Database (SEDB), 2019.

[23] A. Fuduli, P. Veltri, E. Vocaturo, E. Zumpano, Melanoma detection using color and texture features in computer vision systems, Advances in Science, Technology and Engineering Systems Journal, vol. 4, no. 5, pp. 16-22, 2019.

[24] E. Vocaturo, E. Zumpano, Dangerousness of dysplastic nevi: a Multiple Instance Learning Solution for Early Diagnosis, 2019 IEEE International Conference on Bioinformatics and Biomedicine (BIBM), pp. 2318-23, 2019.

[25] E. Vocaturo, E. Zumpano, G. Giallombardo, G. Miglionico: DC-SMIL: a multiple instance learning solution via spherical separation for automated detection of displastyc nevi, Proceedings of the 24th Symposium on International Database Engineering & Applications (IDEAS), pp. 4:1-4:9, 2020.

[26] Vocaturo, E., Perna D., and Zumpano E., Machine Learning Techniques for Automated Melanoma Detection, 2019 IEEE International Conference on Bioinformatics and Biomedicine (BIBM), pp. 2310-17, 2019.

[27] E. Zumpano, et al., SIMPATICO 3D: A Medical Information System for Diagnostic Procedures. 2018 IEEE International Conference on Bioinformatics and Biomedicine (BIBM), pp. 2125-2128, 2018.

[28] E. Zumpano, P. Iaquinta, F. Dattola, L. Caroprese, G. Tradigo, P. Veltri, E. Vocaturo, SIMPATICO 3D Mobile for Diagnostic Procedures,Proceedings of the 21st International Conference on Information Integration and Web-based Applications & Services (IIWAS), pp. 468-472, 2019.

[29] E. Vocaturo, E. Zumpano, P. Veltri, On discovering relevant features for tongue colored image analysis, Proceedings of the 23rd International Database Applications & Engineering Symposium, IDEAS, pp. 1-8, 2019.

[30] E. Vocaturo, E. Zumpano, The contribution of AI in the detection of the Diabetic Retinopathy, 2020 IEEE International Conference on Bioinformatics and Biomedicine (BIBM), pp. 1516-1519, 2020.

Conversational OLAP

(Discussion Paper)

Matteo Francia[1], Enrico Gallinucci[1] and Matteo Golfarelli[1]

[1]*DISI - University of Bologna, Italy*

Abstract

The democratization of data access and the adoption of OLAP in scenarios requiring hand-free interfaces push towards the creation of smart OLAP interfaces. In this paper, we describe COOL, a framework devised for COnversational OLap applications. COOL interprets and translates a natural language dialog into an OLAP session that starts with a GPSJ (Generalized Projection, Selection, and Join) query and continues with the application of OLAP operators. The interpretation relies on a formal grammar and on a repository storing metadata and values from a multidimensional cube. In case of ambiguous text description, COOL can obtain the correct query either through automatic inference or user interactions to disambiguate the text.

Keywords

Natural language processing, OLAP

1. Introduction

Following the spreading of analytic tools, a heterogeneous plethora of data scientists is accessing data. However, the gap between data scientists and analytic skills is growing since different types of data require to learn specialized metaphors and formal tools (e.g., SQL language to query relational data). Natural language interfaces are a promising bridge towards the democratization of data access [1]. Rather than demanding vertical skills in computer science and data architectures, natural language is a native "tool" to organize and provide meaningful questions/answers. Interfacing natural language processing (either written or spoken) to database systems opens to new opportunities for data exploration and querying [2].

Actually, in the area of data warehouse, OLAP (On-Line Analytical Processing) is an *"ante litteram"* smart interface, since it supports the users with a "point-and-click" metaphor to avoid writing well-formed SQL queries. Nonetheless, the possibility of having a conversation with a smart assistant to run an OLAP session (i.e., a set of related OLAP queries) opens to new scenarios and applications. It is not just a matter of further reducing the complexity of posing a query: a conversational OLAP system must also provide feedback to refine and correct wrong queries, and it must have memory to relate subsequent requests. A reference application scenario is augmented business intelligence [3], where hand-free interfaces are mandatory.

SEBD 2021: The 29th Italian Symposium on Advanced Database Systems, September 5-9, 2021, Pizzo Calabro (VV), Italy

m.francia@unibo.it (M. Francia); enrico.gallinucci@unibo.it (E. Gallinucci); matteo.golfarelli@unibo.it (M. Golfarelli)

0000-0002-0805-1051 (M. Francia); 0000-0002-0931-4255 (E. Gallinucci); 0000-0002-0437-0725 (M. Golfarelli)

CEUR Workshop Proceedings (CEUR-WS.org)

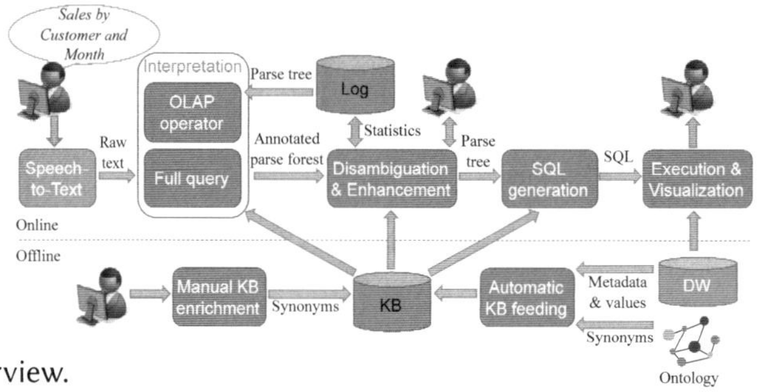

Figure 1: System overview.

In this paper, we describe COOL [4, 5] to convert natural language into *COnversational OLap* sessions composed of GPSJ queries and analytic operators. GPSJ [6] is the main class of queries used in OLAP. COOL is the first proposal addressing a full-fledged implementation for OLAP analytical sessions that is:

- *Automated and portable*: by reading metadata (e.g., hierarchy structures, measures, attributes, and aggregation operators) from a ROLAP engine, COOL automatically builds the minimal lexicon involved in the translation.
- *Robust* to user inaccuracies in syntax, OLAP terms, and attribute values, by exploiting metadata and implicit information.
- *Extendable* and easily configurable on a data warehouse (DW) without a heavy manual definition of the lexicon. The minimal lexicon is extendable by importing known ontologies in the Knowledge Base.

2. System overview

Figure 1 sketches a functional view of the architecture. Given a set of multidimensional cubes (DW), we distinguish between an offline phase (to initialize and configure the system) and an online phase (to enable the user interaction). We refer the user to [7] for an explanation of the DW terminology.

2.0.1. The offline phase

The offline phase automatically extracts the set of entities $\mathcal{E}$, i.e., the DW-specific terms used to express the queries. Such information is stored in the knowledge base (KB), which relies on the DFM expressiveness [7]. This phase runs *only* when the DW undergoes modification (e.g., cube schemas or data instances) and extracts all multidimensional metadata. A cube modeled as a *star schema* in a ROLAP engine consists of dimension tables (DTs: the cube hierarchies) and a fact table (FT: the cube). The `Automatic KB feeding` extracts measures (FT columns not in the primary key), attributes (DT columns), values (distinct instances of the DT columns), and hierarchies (either coded or inferred). These elements represent the lexicon necessary to translate natural language into conversational sessions. COOL supports lexicon extension with external synonyms that can be automatically imported from open data ontologies (e.g., Wordnet [8]) to widen the understood language. Besides the domain-specific terminology, the

KB also includes the set of standard terms that are domain independent and that do not require any feeding (e.g., group by, where, select). Further enrichment can be optionally carried out manually (e.g., when the physical names of tables/columns do not match a standard vocabulary).

2.0.2. The online phase

The online phase runs every time a natural language query is issued. In a hand-free scenario (e.g., [9]), the spoken query is initially translated to text by the `Speech-to-text` software module. Since this task is out of our research scope, we exploited a public Web Speech API. The uninterpreted text is then analyzed by the `Interpretation` step, refined in the `Disambiguation & Enhancement` step, translated by the `SQL generation` step, and finally executed and visualized by the `Execution & Visualization` step.
Interpretation consists of two alternative steps. `Full query` interprets the texts describing full queries (which happens when an analytic session starts). `OLAP operator` modifies the latest query when the user states an OLAP operator across a session (i.e., roll-up, drill-down, and slice&dice). The switch between the two steps to manage the conversation (i.e., a dialog between the user and COOL) is modeled by two states: *engage* (in which the system expects a `Full Query` to be issued) and *navigate* (in which the dialogue evolves by iteratively applying `OLAP operators` that refine the initial query). When COOL achieves a successful interpretation of a full query (i.e., it is able to run the query), it switches to the *navigate* state. Both `Full query` and `OLAP operator` follow these steps: (i) `Tokenization & Mapping`, (ii) `Parsing`, and (iii) `Checking & Annotation`.

Tokenization & mapping. A raw text T is a sequence of single words $T = \langle t_1, ..., t_z \rangle$. The goal of this step is to identify the entities in T, i.e., the only elements that will be involved in the `Parsing` step. Turning a text into a sequence of entities means finding a *mapping* between words in T and $\mathcal{E}$.

Definition 1 (Mapping & mapping function). *A mapping function $M(T)$ is a partial function that associates sub-sequences (or n-grams)*[1] *from T to entities in $\mathcal{E}$ such that: (i) sub-sequences of T have length n at most; (ii) the mapping function determines a partitioning of T; and (iii) a sub-sequence $T' = \langle t_i, ..., t_l \rangle \in T$ (with $|T'| \leq n$) is associated to an entity E if and only if $Sim(T', E) > \alpha$ (where $Sim()$ is a similarity function, later defined) and $E \in TopN(\mathcal{E}, T')$ (where $TopN(\mathcal{E}, T')$ is the set of N entities in $\mathcal{E}$ that are the most similar to T' according to $Sim(T', E)$). The output of a mapping function is a sequence $M = \langle E_1, ..., E_l \rangle$ on $\mathcal{E}$ that we call a* mapping.

The similarity function $Sim()$ is based on the Levenshtein distance and keeps token permutation into account to make similarity robust to token permutations (e.g., sub-sequences $\langle P., Edgar \rangle$ and $\langle Edgar, Allan, Poe \rangle$ must result similar).

Several mappings might exist between T and $\mathcal{E}$ since Definition 1 admits sub-sequences of variable lengths (corresponding to different partitionings of T) and associates the top similar entities to each sub-sequence. This increases the interpretation robustness since COOL chooses the best mapping through a scoring function. Given a mapping $M = \langle E_1, ..., E_m \rangle$, its score

[1] The term n-gram is used as a synonym of sub-sequence in the area of text mining.

$$
\begin{aligned}
\langle \text{GPSJ} \rangle &::= \langle \text{MC} \rangle \langle \text{GC} \rangle \langle \text{SC} \rangle \mid \langle \text{MC} \rangle \langle \text{SC} \rangle \langle \text{GC} \rangle \mid \langle \text{SC} \rangle \langle \text{GC} \rangle \langle \text{MC} \rangle \mid \langle \text{SC} \rangle \langle \text{MC} \rangle \langle \text{GC} \rangle \\
&\quad \mid \langle \text{GC} \rangle \langle \text{SC} \rangle \langle \text{MC} \rangle \mid \langle \text{GC} \rangle \langle \text{MC} \rangle \langle \text{SC} \rangle \mid \langle \text{MC} \rangle \langle \text{SC} \rangle \mid \langle \text{MC} \rangle \langle \text{GC} \rangle \mid \langle \text{SC} \rangle \langle \text{MC} \rangle \mid \langle \text{GC} \rangle \langle \text{MC} \rangle \mid \langle \text{MC} \rangle \\
\langle \text{MC} \rangle &::= (\langle \text{Agg} \rangle \langle \text{Mea} \rangle \mid \langle \text{Mea} \rangle \langle \text{Agg} \rangle \mid \langle \text{Mea} \rangle \mid \langle \text{Cnt} \rangle \langle \text{Fct} \rangle \mid \langle \text{Fct} \rangle \langle \text{Cnt} \rangle \mid \langle \text{Cnt} \rangle \langle \text{Attr} \rangle \mid \langle \text{Attr} \rangle \langle \text{Cnt} \rangle)+ \\
\langle \text{GC} \rangle &::= \text{“}\textit{group by}\text{”}\ \langle \text{Attr} \rangle + \\
\langle \text{SC} \rangle &::= \text{“}\textit{where}\text{”}\ \langle \text{SCA} \rangle \\
\langle \text{SCA} \rangle &::= \langle \text{SCN} \rangle\ \text{“}\textit{and}\text{”}\ \langle \text{SCA} \rangle \mid \langle \text{SCN} \rangle \\
\langle \text{SCN} \rangle &::= \text{“}\textit{not}\text{”}\ \langle \text{SSC} \rangle \mid \langle \text{SSC} \rangle \\
\langle \text{SSC} \rangle &::= \langle \text{Attr} \rangle \langle \text{Cop} \rangle \langle \text{Val} \rangle \mid \langle \text{Attr} \rangle \langle \text{Val} \rangle \mid \langle \text{Val} \rangle \langle \text{Cop} \rangle \langle \text{Attr} \rangle \mid \langle \text{Val} \rangle \langle \text{Attr} \rangle \mid \langle \text{Val} \rangle \\
\langle \text{Cop} \rangle &::= \text{“} = \text{”} \mid \text{“} <> \text{”} \mid \text{“} > \text{”} \mid \text{“} < \text{”} \mid \text{“} \geq \text{”} \mid \text{“} \leq \text{”} \\
\langle \text{Agg} \rangle &::= \text{“}\textit{sum}\text{”} \mid \text{“}\textit{avg}\text{”} \mid \text{“}\textit{min}\text{”} \mid \text{“}\textit{max}\text{”} \mid \text{“}\textit{stdev}\text{”} \\
\langle \text{Cnt} \rangle &::= \text{“}\textit{count}\text{”} \mid \text{“}\textit{count distinct}\text{”} \\
\langle \text{Fct} \rangle &::= \textit{Domain-specific facts} \\
\langle \text{Mea} \rangle &::= \textit{Domain-specific measures} \\
\langle \text{Attr} \rangle &::= \textit{Domain-specific attributes} \\
\langle \text{Val} \rangle &::= \textit{Domain-specific values}
\end{aligned}
$$

Figure 2: Backus-Naur representation of the `Full query` grammar. Entities from the `KB` are terminal symbols.

$Score(M)$ (i.e., the sum of entity similarities) is higher when M includes several entities with high similarity values. Intuitively, the higher the mapping score, the higher the probability to determine an optimal interpretation.

Parsing validates the syntactical structure of a mapping against a formal grammar and outputs a data structure called *parse tree* that is later used to translate a mapping into SQL.

In `Full query`, `Parsing` is responsible for the interpretation of a complete GPSJ query stated in natural language. A GPSJ query contains a measure clause (MC) and optional group-by (GC) and selection (SC) clauses. Parsing a full query means searching in a mapping the complex syntax structures (i.e., clauses) that build up the query. Given a mapping M, the output of the parser is a parse tree PT_M, i.e., an ordered tree that represents the syntactic structure of a mapping according to the grammar from Figure 2. To the aim of parsing, entities are terminal elements in the grammar.

For the sake of brevity, we omit the grammar of the `OLAP Operator` and we refer the user to [4]. Intuitively, our conversation steps are inspired by well-known OLAP visual interfaces (e.g., Tableau https://www.tableau.com/). To apply an OLAP operator, COOL must be in the state *navigate*, i.e., a full GPSJ query has been already successfully interpreted into a parse tree PT_C that acts as a context for the operator. The output of the `OLAP Operator` parser is a parse tree PT_M that is used to update PT_C.

Both GPSJ grammars are LL(1)[2] [10], not ambiguous (i.e., each mapping admits, at most, a single parse tree PT_M), and can be parsed by an LL(1) parser with linear complexity [10]. If the input mapping M is fully parsed, PT_M includes all the entities as leaves. Conversely, if only a portion of the input belongs to the grammar, an LL(1) parser produces a partial parsing, meaning that it returns a parse tree including the portion of the input mapping that belongs to the grammar (i.e., the PT rooted in ⟨GPSJ⟩). The remaining entities can be either singleton or

[2]Rules presented in Figure 2 do not satisfy LL(1) constraints for readability reasons.

complex clauses that could not be connected to the main parse tree. We will call *parse forest* PF_M the union of the parse tree with residual clauses. Obviously, if all the entities are parsed, it is $PF_M = PT_M$. Considering the whole forest rather than the simple parse tree enables ambiguities to be recovered in the `Disambiguation & Enhancement` step. Henceforth, we refer to the parser's output as a parse forest independently of the presence of residual clauses.
Disambiguation & enhancement. Due to natural language ambiguities, speech-to-text inaccuracies, and wrong query formulations, parts of the text can be misunderstood. The reasons behind the misunderstandings are manifold, including (but not limited to) a wrong usage of aggregation operators (e.g., summing non-additive measures), inconsistencies between attributes and values in selection predicates (e.g., filtering on product *"New York"*), or grouping by a descriptive attribute. Such parts of the parse forest are annotated as ambiguities. To reduce the parse forest PF_M to a single parse tree PT_M, the `Disambiguation & Enhancement` step solves ambiguities automatically whenever possible (by exploiting implicit information) or by asking appropriate questions to the user.
SQL generation translates a full-query parse tree into an executable SQL query. If an OLAP operator has been submitted, such tree must be updated accordingly. Given a full query parse tree, the generation of its corresponding SQL requires to fill in the SELECT, WHERE, GROUP BY and FROM statements. The SQL generation applies to both star and snowflake schemas [7] and is done as follows: SELECT (measures and aggregation operators from $\langle$MC$\rangle$ and attributes in the group by clause $\langle$GC$\rangle$); WHERE (predicates from the selection clause $\langle$SC$\rangle$); GROUP BY (attributes from the group by clause $\langle$GC$\rangle$); and FROM (measures, attributes, and values identify the fact and the dimension tables). The join path is identified by following the referential integrity constraints.

3. Experimental tests

Tests are carried out on a real-world benchmark of analytics queries [11]. Since queries from [11] refers to private datasets, we mapped the natural language queries to the Foodmart schema[3]. The Automatic KB feeding populated the KB with 1 fact, 39 attributes, 12337 values and 12449 synonyms. Additionally, only 50 synonyms where manually added in the KB enrichment step (e.g., *"for each"*, *"for every"*, *"per"* are synonyms of the group by statement). While mapping natural language queries to the Foodmart domain, we preserved the structure of the original queries (e.g., word order, typos, etc.). Overall, 75% of the queries in the dataset are valid GPSJ queries, confirming how general and standard GPSJ queries are. The filtered benchmark includes 110 queries. We consider token sub-sequences of maximum length $n = 4$ (i.e., the [1..4]-grams) as no entity in the KB is longer than 4 words. Each sub-sequence is associated with the top N similar entities with similarity higher than α such that at least a percentage β of the tokens in T is covered. β is fixed to 70% based on an empirical evaluation. For the sake of brevity, only the major results are reported.

Effectiveness is evaluated as the tree similarity [12] $TSim(PT, PT^*)$ between the parse tree PT produced by our system and the correct one PT^*, which is manually written by us. Although only one parse forest is involved in the disambiguation phase; for testing purposes, it

[3]A dataset of food sales (https://github.com/julianhyde/foodmart-data-mysql).

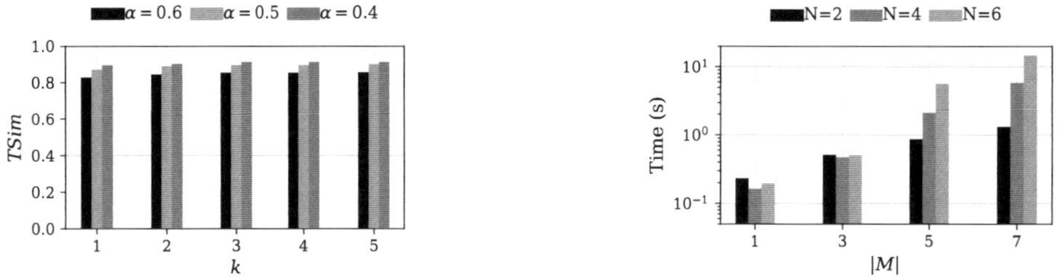

(a) Effectiveness by varying the similarity threshold α and the $Top\text{-}k$ returned queries (with $N = 6$).

(b) Efficiency by varying the number $|M|$ of entities in the optimal tree and the top similar entities N (with $\alpha = 0.4$).

Figure 3: Empirical evaluation

is interesting to see if the best parse tree belongs to the top-k ranked ones. Effectiveness is more affected by the entity/token similarity threshold α and ranges in $[0.83, 0.89]$. In all cases, the best results are obtained when more similar entities are admitted and more candidate mappings are generated. Independently of the chosen thresholds the system results very stable (i.e., the effectiveness variations are limited) and even considering only one query to be returned its effectiveness is at the state of the art [2, 13, 14]. This confirms that (1) the choice of proposing only one query to the user does not negatively impact on performances (while it positively impacts on interaction complexity and efficiency) and (2) our scoring function properly ranks parse tree similarity to the correct interpretation for the query since the best ranked is in most cases the most similar to the correct solution.

As the previous tests do not include disambiguation, only 58 queries out of 110 are not ambiguous and produce parse trees that can be fed *as-is* to the generation and execution phases. Starting from the best configuration from the previous tests (for $N = 6$ and $\alpha = 0.4$), by applying an increasing number of correcting actions the effectiveness increases from 0.89 up to 0.94. Unsolved differences are mainly due to missed entities in the mappings.

As to efficiency, we ran the tests on a machine equipped with Intel(R) Core(TM) i7-6700 CPU @ 3.40GHz CPU and 8GB RAM, with the framework implemented in Java. Figure 3b shows the average execution time by varying $|M|$ and the number of allowed top similar entities N. The execution time increases with the number of entities included in the optimal parse tree, as such also the number of top similar entities impacts the overall execution time. We recall that effectiveness remains high also for $N = 2$ corresponding to an execution time of 1 second, raising to 10 seconds in the worst case.

4. Related works

Conversational business intelligence can be classified as a *natural language interface* (NLI) to *business intelligence* systems to drive analytic sessions. Despite the plethora of contributions in each area, to the best of our knowledge, no approach lies at their intersection.

NLIs to operational databases enable users to specify complex queries without previous training on formal programming languages (such as SQL) and software; a recent and comprehensive survey is provided in [15]. Overall, NLIs are divided into two categories: question answering and dialog. To the best of our knowledge, no dialog-based system for OLAP sessions has been provided so far. SQLizer [13] generates templates over the issued query and applies a "repair" loop until it generates queries that can be obtained using at most a given number of changes from the initial template. Domain-specific approaches add semantics to the translation process through domain-specific ontologies and ontology-to-database mappings. SODA [16] uses a simple but limited keyword-based approach that generates a reasonable and executable SQL query based on the matches between the input query and the database metadata, enriched with domain-specific ontologies. ATHENA [14] maps natural language into an ontology representation and exploits mappings crafted by the relational schema designer to resolve SQL queries. Analyza [17] integrates the domain-specific ontology into a "semantic grammar"(i.e., a grammar with placeholders for the typed concepts such as measures, dimensions, etc.) to annotate and finally parse the user query. Unfortunately, by relying on the definition of domain-specific knowledge and mappings, the adoption of these approaches is not plug-and-play as an ad-hoc ontology is rarely available and burdensome to create.

5. Conclusion

In this paper, we proposed COOL, a conversational OLAP framework supporting the translation of a natural language conversation into an OLAP session. COOL supports both the interpretation of GPSJ queries and OLAP operators.

Besides proposing a technical solution and a reference architecture, the contribution of the paper lies in the discussion of specific issues related to conversational OLAP systems. Since its conception, OLAP analysis aims to allow users to analyze data without requiring technological skills. Conversational OLAP represents a step forward in this direction. We believe that conversational OLAP can be particularly useful in the context of hand-free applications such as the ones we proposed in [3]: adding conversational capabilities to an augmented OLAP solution would be highly desirable whenever the user is working in the field (e.g., a warehouse or a factory) and is not in front of a computer. To close the loop, we are working towards enabling access to OLAP results in a conversational and hand-free fashion. The idea is to create *query summaries* (e.g., [18]) that can fit augmented-reality devices or (vocal) smart assistants.

References

[1] Y. Su, Towards Democratizing Data Science with Natural Language Interfaces, Ph.D. thesis, UC Santa Barbara, 2018.

[2] F. Li, H. V. Jagadish, Understanding natural language queries over relational databases, SIGMOD Record 45 (2016) 6–13. doi:10.1145/2949741.2949744.

[3] M. Francia, M. Golfarelli, S. Rizzi, A-BI$^+$: A framework for augmented business intelligence, Information Systems 92 (2020) 101520. doi:10.1016/j.is.2020.101520.

[4] M. Francia, E. Gallinucci, M. Golfarelli, COOL: A framework for conversational OLAP, Information Systems (2021) 101752. doi:10.1016/j.is.2021.101752.

[5] M. Francia, E. Gallinucci, M. Golfarelli, Conversational OLAP in action, in: Proceedings of the 24th International Conference on Extending Database Technology, EDBT 2021, Nicosia, Cyprus, March 23 - 26, 2021, OpenProceedings.org, 2021, pp. 646–649. doi:10.5441/002/EDBT.2021.74.

[6] A. Gupta, V. Harinarayan, D. Quass, Aggregate-query processing in data warehousing environments, in: Proc. VLDB, Morgan Kaufmann, San Francisco, CA, USA, 1995, pp. 358–369.

[7] M. Golfarelli, D. Maio, S. Rizzi, The dimensional fact model: A conceptual model for data warehouses, Int. J. Cooperative Inf. Syst. 7 (1998) 215–247. doi:10.1142/s0218843098000118.

[8] G. A. Miller, Wordnet: A lexical database for English, Commun. ACM 38 (1995) 39–41. doi:10.1145/219717.219748.

[9] M. Francia, M. Golfarelli, S. Rizzi, Augmented business intelligence, in: Proceedings of the 21st International Workshop on Design, Optimization, Languages and Analytical Processing of Big Data, co-located with EDBT/ICDT Joint Conference, DOLAP@EDBT/ICDT 2019, Lisbon, Portugal, March 26, 2019, volume 2324 of *CEUR Workshop Proceedings*, CEUR-WS.org, Lisbon, Portugal, 2019, pp. 1–10.

[10] J. C. Beatty, On the relationship between LL(1) and LR(1) grammars, J. ACM 29 (1982) 1007–1022. doi:10.1145/322344.322350.

[11] K. Drushku, J. Aligon, N. Labroche, P. Marcel, V. Peralta, Interest-based recommendations for business intelligence users, Inf. Syst. 86 (2019) 79–93. doi:10.1016/j.is.2018.08.004.

[12] K. Zhang, D. E. Shasha, Simple fast algorithms for the editing distance between trees and related problems, SIAM J. Comput. 18 (1989) 1245–1262. doi:10.1137/0218082.

[13] N. Yaghmazadeh, Y. Wang, I. Dillig, T. Dillig, Sqlizer: query synthesis from natural language, PACMPL 1 (2017) 63:1–63:26. doi:10.1145/3133887.

[14] D. Saha, A. Floratou, K. Sankaranarayanan, U. F. Minhas, A. R. Mittal, F. Özcan, ATHENA: an ontology-driven system for natural language querying over relational data stores, PVLDB 9 (2016) 1209–1220. doi:10.14778/2994509.2994536.

[15] K. Affolter, K. Stockinger, A. Bernstein, A comparative survey of recent natural language interfaces for databases, VLDB J. 28 (2019) 793–819. doi:10.1007/s00778-019-00567-8.

[16] L. Blunschi, C. Jossen, D. Kossmann, M. Mori, K. Stockinger, SODA: generating SQL for business users, PVLDB 5 (2012) 932–943. doi:10.14778/2336664.2336667.

[17] K. Dhamdhere, K. S. McCurley, R. Nahmias, M. Sundararajan, Q. Yan, Analyza: Exploring data with conversation, in: Proc. IUI, ACM, New York, NY, USA, 2017, pp. 493–504. doi:10.1145/3025171.3025227.

[18] M. Francia, M. Golfarelli, S. Rizzi, Summarization and visualization of multi-level and multi-dimensional itemsets, Information Sciences 520 (2020) 63–85. doi:10.1016/j.ins.2020.02.006.

Fine-grained Provenance for High-quality Data Science

(Discussion Paper)

Adriane Chapman[1], Paolo Missier[2], Giulia Simonelli[3] and Riccardo Torlone[3]

[2]*University of Southampton*
[2]*Newcastle University*
[3]*Università Roma Tre*

Abstract
In this work we analyze the typical operations of data preparation within a machine learning process, and provide infrastructure for generating very granular provenance records from it, at the level of individual elements within a dataset. Our contributions include: (i) the formal definition of a core set of preprocessing operators, (ii) the definition of provenance patterns for each of them, and (iii) a prototype implementation of an application-level provenance capture library that works alongside Python.

1. Introduction

Data processing pipelines that are designed to clean, transform and alter data in preparation for learning predictive models, have an impact on those models' accuracy and performance, as well on other properties, such as model fairness.

However, while substantial recent research has produced techniques for model explanation that focus primarily on the model itself (e.g., [1, 2]) relatively little work has been done into trying to explain models in terms of the transformations that occur *before* the data is used for learning.

In this work, we enable the explanation on the effect of each transformation in a pre-processing pipeline on the data that is ultimately fed into a model. We consider transformations that apply to commonly used tabular or relational datasets and across application domains. These steps have been systematically enumerated in multiple reviews (see eg. [3]) and include, among others: feature selection, engineering of new features; imputation of missing values, or *listwise deletion* (excluding an entire record if data is missing on any variable for that record); downsampling or upsampling of data subsets in order to achieve better balance, typically on the class labels (for classification tasks) or on the distribution of the outcome variable (for regression tasks); outlier detection and removal; smoothing and normalisation; de-duplication, as well as steps that preserve the original information but are required by some algorithms, such as "one-hot"

SEBD 2021: The 29th Italian Symposium on Advanced Database Systems, September 5-9, 2021, Pizzo Calabro (VV), Italy
adriane.chapman@soton.ac.uk (A. Chapman); paolo.missier@ncl.ac.uk (P. Missier); giulia.simonelli@uniroma3.it (G. Simonelli); giulia.simonelli@uniroma3.it (R. Torlone)

encoding of categorical variables. A complex pipeline may include some or all of these steps, and different techniques, algorithms, and choice of algorithm-specific parameters may be available for each of them. These are often grounded in established literature but variations can be created by data scientists to suit specific needs. We consider the space of all configured pipelines that can potentially be composed out of these operators, and we focus on relational datasets, which are arguably the most common data structures in popular analytics-friendly scripting languages like R, Spark, and Python (where they are called *dataframes*).

In this framework, we propose a formalisation and categorisation of a core set of these operators. Data derivations for such operators are expressed at the level of the atomic elements in the dataset using the PROV data model [4], a standard and a widely adopted ontology. Then, with each of the core operators we associate a *provenance pattern* that describes their effect on the data at the appropriate level of detail, i.e., on individual dataset elements, columns, rows, or collections of those. Provenance patterns defined in this work for data science operators play a similar role to that of *provenance polynomials* [5], i.e., annotations that are associated to relational algebra operators to describe the fine-grained provenance of the result of relational operators. Finally, we associate a provenance function $pf_{\mathbf{o}}()$ to each operator **o**, which generates a provenance document $pf_{\mathbf{o}}(D)$ when a dataset D is processed using **o**. The document is an instance of the pattern associated with **o**. Provenance functions are implemented as part of a Python module. Collecting all the provenance documents from each operator's execution results in a seamless, end-to-end provenance document that contains the detailed history of each dataset element in the final training set, including their creation (e.g. as a new derived feature), transformation (value imputation, for example) and possibly deletion (e.g., by feature selection, removal of null values).

In the rest of this paper we illustrate the models we have adopted for describing data, operators, and provenance (Section 2) as well as the way in which provenance for a data preprocessing pipeline is captured (Section 3). Further details on the query capabilities of the resulting provenance and on the scalability of the overall approach can be found in the extended version of the paper [6].

2. Models for Data, Operators, and Provenance.

2.1. Data model

A *(dataset) schema* S is an array of distinct names called *features*: $S = [\mathbf{a}_1, \ldots, \mathbf{a}_n]$. Each feature is associated with a domain of atomic values (such as numbers, strings, and timestamps). A *dataset* D over a schema $S = [\mathbf{a}_1, \ldots, \mathbf{a}_n]$ is an ordered collection of *rows* (or *records*) of the form: $i : (d_{i1}, \ldots, d_{in})$ where i is the unique *index* of the row and each element d_{ij} (for $1 \leq j \leq n$) is either a value in the domain of the feature $\mathbf{a}_j$ or the special symbol $\perp$, denoting a missing value. Given a dataset D over a schema S we denote by $D_{i\mathbf{a}}$ the element for the feature **a** of S occurring the i-th row of D. We also denote by D_{i*} the i-th row of D, and by $D_{*\mathbf{a}}$ the column of D associated with the feature **a** of S.

Example 1. *A possible dataset D over the schema $S = [$**CId**, **Gender**, **Age**, **Zip**$]$ is as follows:*

	CId	*Gender*	*Age*	*Zip*
1	113	F	24	98567
2	241	M	28	$\perp$
3	375	C	$\perp$	32768
4	578	F	44	32768

$D_{*\mathbf{Age}}$ and D_{2*} denote the third column and the second row of D, respectively. □

2.2. Data manipulation model

The data transformation operators that are available in packages for building data preprocessing pipelines (e.g., Orange [7] and SciKit [8]) can be classified in three main classes, according to the type of manipulation done on the input dataset D over a schema S, as follows.

Data reductions. They reduce the size of D by eliminating rows (without changing S) or columns (changing S to $S' \subset S$) from D. Two basic data reduction operators are defined over datasets. They are simple extensions of two well known relational operators.

π_C: the *(conditional) projection* of D on a set of features of S that satisfy a boolean condition C over S, denoted by $\pi_C(D)$, is the dataset obtained from D by including only the columns $D_{*\mathbf{a}}$ of D such that **a** is a feature of S that satisfy C;

σ_C: the *selection* of D with respect to a boolean condition C over S, denoted by $\sigma_C(D)$, is the dataset obtained from D by including the rows D_{i*} of D satisfying C.

The condition of both the projection and the selection operators can refer to the values in D, as shown in the following example that use an intuitive syntax for the condition.

Example 2. *Consider the dataset D in Example 1. The result of the expression $\pi_{\{features\ without\ nulls\}}(\sigma_{\mathbf{Age}<30}(D))$ is the following dataset:*

	CId	*Gender*	*Age*
1	113	F	24
2	241	M	28

□

Data augmentations. They increase the size of D by adding rows (without changing S) or columns (changing S to $S' \supset S$) to D. Two basic data augmentation operators are defined over datasets. They allow the addition of columns and rows to a dataset, respectively.

$\alpha^{\rightarrow}_{f(X):Y}$: the *vertical augmentation* of D to Y using a function f over a subset of features $X = [\mathbf{a}_1 \dots \mathbf{a}_k]$ of S is obtained by adding to D a new set of features $Y = [\mathbf{a}'_1 \dots \mathbf{a}'_l]$ whose new values $d_{i\mathbf{a}'_1} \dots d_{i\mathbf{a}'_l}$ for the i-th row are obtained by applying f to $d_{i\mathbf{a}_1} \dots d_{i\mathbf{a}_k}$;

$\alpha^{\downarrow}_{X:f(Y)}$: the *horizontal augmentation* of D using an aggregative function f is obtained by adding one or more new rows to D obtained by first grouping over the features in X and then, for each group, by applying f to $\pi_Y(D)$ (extending the result to S with nulls if needed).

Example 3. *Consider again the dataset D in Example 1 and the following functions: (i) f_1, which associates the string* young *to an age less than 25 and the string* adult *otherwise, and (ii) f_2, which computes the average of a set of numbers. Then, the expression $\alpha^{\rightarrow}_{f_1(\textbf{Age}):\textbf{ageRange}}(D)$ produces the following dataset:*

	CId	*Gender*	*Age*	*Zip*	*ageRange*
1	113	F	24	98567	*young*
2	241	M	28	$\perp$	*adult*
3	375	C	$\perp$	32768	$\perp$
4	578	F	44	32768	*adult*

whereas $E_2 = \alpha^{\downarrow}_{\textbf{Gender}:f_2(\textbf{Age})}(D)$ the dataset:

	CId	*Gender*	*Age*	*Zip*
1	113	F	24	98567
2	241	M	28	$\perp$
3	375	C	$\perp$	32768
4	578	F	44	32768
5	$\perp$	F	34	$\perp$
6	$\perp$	M	28	$\perp$

□

Data transformation. The goal is to transform (some of) the elements in D without changing its size or its schema. One basic data transformation operator is defined over datasets:

$\tau_{f(X)}$: the *transformation* of a set of features X of D using a function f is obtained by replacing each value $d_{i\mathbf{a}}$ with $f(d_{*\mathbf{a}})$, for each $\mathbf{a}$ occurring in X.

Example 4. *Let D be the dataset in Example 1 and f be an imputation function that associates with the $\perp$'s occurring in a feature $\mathbf{a}$ the most frequent value occurring in $D_{*\mathbf{a}}$. Then, the result of $\tau_{f(\textbf{Zip})}(D)$ is the following dataset:*

	CId	*Gender*	*Age*	*Zip*
1	113	F	24	98567
2	241	M	28	32768
3	375	C	$\perp$	32768
4	578	F	44	32768

□

In [6] we illustrate how a large variety of pre-processing operators that are often used in data preparation workflows (including feature and instance selection, data repair, binarization, normalization, discretization, imputation, space transformation, and One-Hot encoder) can be suitably expressed as composition of the basic operators introduced in this section.

2.3. Data provenance model

The purpose of data provenance is to extract relatively simple explanations for the existence (or the absence) of some piece of data in the result of complex data manipulations. Along this line, we adopt as the provenance model a subset of the PROV model [9] from the W3C.In PROV an entity represents an element d of a dataset D and is uniquely identified by D and the coordinates of d in D (i.e., the corresponding row index and feature). An activity represents any pre-processing data manipulation that operates over datasets. For each element d in a dataset D' generated by an operation $\mathbf{o}$ over a dataset D we represent the facts that: (i) d *wasGeneratedBy* $\mathbf{o}$, and (ii) d *wasDerivedFrom* a set of elements in D. In addition, we represent: (iii) all the elements d of D such that d was *used* by $\mathbf{o}$ and (iv) all the elements d of D such that d *wasInvalidatedBy* (i.e., deleted by) $\mathbf{o}$ (if any).

Example 5. *Let E be the first expression in Example 3 and $D' = E(D)$. A fragment of the provenance generated by this operation is reported in Figure 1.* □

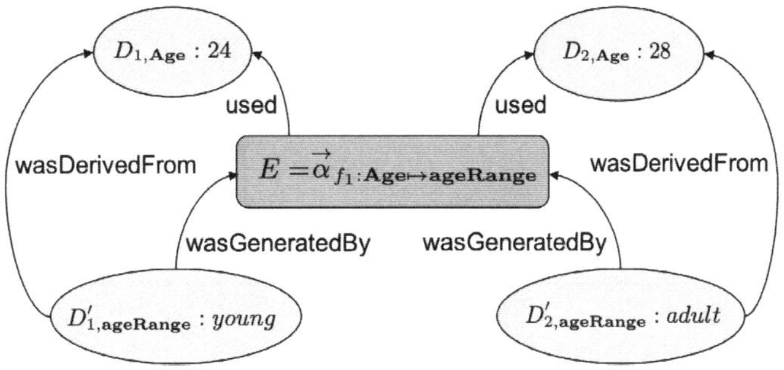

Figure 1: A fragment of provenance data for the operation in Example 5.

3. Capturing Provenance

3.1. Provenance templates

In order to capture the provenance of a pipeline p of a sequence of preprocessing operations $\mathbf{o}_1, \ldots, \mathbf{o}_n$, we associate a provenance-generating function (*p-gen*) with each operation $\mathbf{o}_k$ occurring in p. Each such function generates a collection of provenance data whenever a dataset is processed using $\mathbf{o}_k$, which describes the effect of $\mathbf{o}_k$ on the data at the appropriate level of detail. As a large variety of preprocessing operators can be defined in terms of our five core pipeline operators [6], it is enough to define a p-gen function for each of these operators.

Each p-gen function takes inputs D, D' (the inputs and outputs of their associated operator) along with a description of the operator itself, and produces a PROV document that describes the transformation produced by the operator on each element of D. The output PROV document is obtained by instantiating an appropriate provenance template [10], which is designed to capture the transformation at the most granular level, i.e., at the level of individual elements of D, or its rows or columns, as appropriate. A template is simply a PROV document where: (i) variables, indicated by the namespace **var:**, are used as placeholders for values and (ii) a set of rules is used to specify how the "used" and the "generated" sides of the template are repeatedly instantiated, by binding the variables to each of the data items involved in the transformation. We refer to each instantiated template produced by a p-gen function as a *provlet.*

Take for example the case of Vertical Augmentation (VA): $\alpha^{\rightarrow}_{f_1(\mathbf{Age}):\mathbf{ageRange}}(D)$ which we used in Example 3, where attribute **Age** is binarised into *{young, adult}* based on a pre-defined cutoff, defined as part of $f()$. The p-gen function for VA will produce a collection of small PROV documents, one for each input-output pair $\langle D_{i,\mathbf{Age}}, D'_{i,\mathbf{AgeRange}}\rangle$ as shown in the example. As these documents all share the same structure, we specify p-gen by giving two elements. First, a single PROV template for (VA) as shown in Figure 2, where we use the generic attribute names X, Y to indicate the old and new feature names, as per the operator's general definition in Section 2.2.

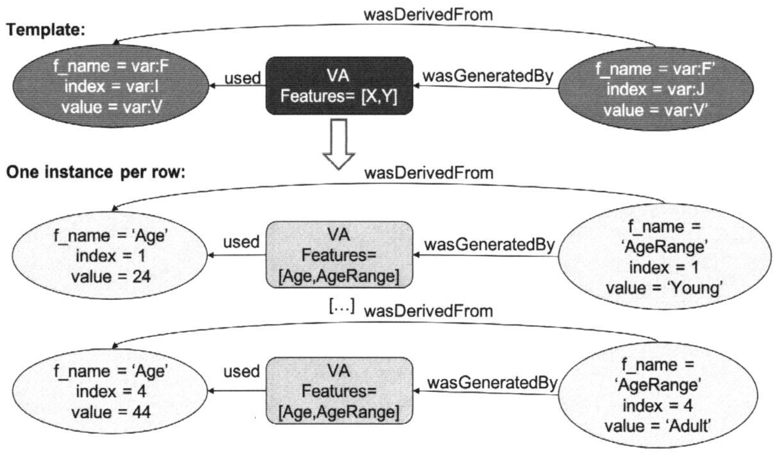

Figure 2: PROV template for Vertical Augmentation and corresponding instances.

3.2. Code instrumentation

Approaches for automated provenance capture, such as by using the python call stack fail to capture data provenance at the level of the individual element within a dataframe. To accomplish this, in our initial prototype, we opted for explicit and analyst-controlled instrumentation at the script level. We have packaged the implementation of the p-gen functions described in the previous section as a python library that analysts can add to their code where provenace capture is desired. Note also that it may be possible to automate function call injection, at least in part, by leveraging mature code annotation tools. While this does not completely eliminate the need for manual intervention, this is now a simple comment/ annotation effort (which can be driven by a smart UI) rather than requiring additional programming.

3.3. Generating provenance documents

A complete provenance document is produced by combining the collection of provlets that results from calling p-gen functions. Specifically, one provlet is generated for every transformation and every element in the dataframe that are affected by that transformation. The document is represented by such collection of provlets, where entity identifiers match across provlets, and never needs to be fully materialised, as explained shortly. To illustrate how provlets are generated, consider the following pipeline: $\sigma_C(\alpha_{\vec{f_1}(\mathbf{Age}):\mathbf{ageRange}}(D))$ where $C = \{\mathbf{AgeRange} \neq \text{'Young'}\}$ and D is the dataset of Ex. 3. The corresponding provenance document is represented in Figure 3

Applying vertical augmentation produces one provlet for each record in the input dataframe, showing the derivation from **Age** to **AgeRange**. The second step, selecting records for 'not

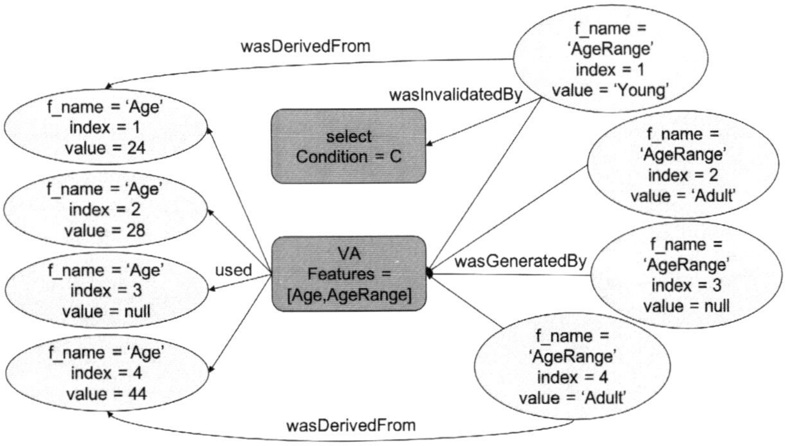

Figure 3: Provlet composition.

young' people, produces the new set of provlets on the right, to indicate invalidation of the first record. Note that the "used" side on the left refers to existing entities, which are created either into the pipeline from the input dataset, or by an upstream data generation operator.

Provlet composition requires looking up the set of entities already produced, whenever a new provlet is added to the document. For this, we have built a bespoke architecture that allows lazy provenance composition. Each p-gen function generates a set of provlets, one for each element in the dataframe (in the worst case), constructs a partial document, and stores it to a persistent MongoDB back end. This allows the provenance to be collected quickly at execution of each script, and be assembled later, minimizing execution dependencies and possible bottlenecks during the actual execution of the pipeline.

Concretely, each *p-gen* function creates, *at query time*, a provenance object containing all provlets, and an input json file representing the input dataframe. By capturing provlets from each p-gen function, it is possible to compose these provlets into a complete graph, which can be traversed as a bipartite graph for any d_{ij}. The process for composing provlets, and tracing the influence (either direct of indirect) of data and operations on d_{ij} can then support "why provenance" [11].

4. Conclusions

In this work, we have illustrated an approach for producing fine-grained data provenance in machine learning pipelines, irrespective of the pipeline tool used. Indeed, because a substantial effort goes into selecting and preparing data for use in modelling, and because changes made during preparation can affect the ultimate model, it is important to be able to trace what is happening to the data at a such level of detail. Using an implementation of this system, we have demonstrated the utility and performance of our approach over real-world ML benchmark pipelines. In order to investigate scalability issues with our design, we also used the TPC-DI generator and apply several operators over that data at scale. Our results indicate that we can collect fine-grained provenance that is both useful and performant [6].

References

[1] A. M. Alaa, M. van der Schaar, Demystifying black-box models with symbolic metamodels, in: Advances in Neural Information Processing Systems, 2019, pp. 11301–11311.

[2] M. T. Ribeiro, S. Singh, C. Guestrin, "Why should i trust you?": Explaining the predictions of any classifier, in: Proceedings of the 22nd ACM SIGKDD international conference on knowledge discovery and data mining, 2016, pp. 1135–1144.

[3] S. García, et.al., Big data preprocessing: methods and prospects, Big Data Analytics 1 (2016).

[4] L. Moreau, P. Missier, K. Belhajjame, R. B'Far, J. Cheney, S. Coppens, S. Cresswell, Y. Gil, P. Groth, G. Klyne, et al., Prov-dm: The prov data model. w3c recommendation rec-prov-dm-20130430, WWW Consortium (2013).

[5] V. Green, Todd J., Karvounarakis, G., Tannen, Provenance Semirings, in: PODS, 2007, pp. 31–40.

[6] A. Chapman, P. Missier, G. Simonelli, R. Torlone, Capturing and querying fine-grained provenance of preprocessing pipelines in data science, Proc. VLDB Endow. 14 (2020) 507–520.

[7] J. Demšar, et al., Orange: Data mining toolbox in python, Journal of Machine Learning Research 14 (2013) 2349–2353.

[8] Pedregosa, et al., Scikit-learn: Machine learning in Python 12 (2011) 2825–2830.

[9] L. Moreau, J. Cheney, P. Missier, Constraints of the prov data model, 2013. URL: http://www.w3.org/TR/2013/REC-prov-constraints-20130430/.

[10] L. Moreau, B. V. Batlajery, T. D. Huynh, D. T. Michaelides, H. S. Packer, A templating system to generate provenance, IEEE Transactions on Software Engineering 44 (2018) 103–121.

[11] P. Buneman, S. Khanna, T. Wang-Chiew, Why and where: A characterization of data provenance, in: ICDT, Springer, 2001, pp. 316–330.

An investigation on Not Safe For Work adult content in Reddit

(Discussion Paper)

Francesco Cauteruccio[1], Enrico Corradini[2], Giorgio Terracina[1], Domenico Ursino[2] and Luca Virgili[2]

[1]*DEMACS, University of Calabria, Italy*
[2]*DII, Polytechnic University of Marche, Italy*

Abstract
Reddit is one of the few social platforms that handles NSFW (Not Safe For Work) content in an explicit and well-structured way. Despite this fact, such an issue has been very neglected in the past by researchers who have studied this social network. In this paper, we aim at providing a contribution in this setting by proposing an approach to extract and analyze text patterns from NSFW content in Reddit. An important peculiarity of our approach is that patterns are extracted not only based on their frequency (as it generally happens in the past literature), but also, and especially, on one or more utility measures.

Keywords
Reddit, NSFW posts and comments, Text patterns, Pattern utility measures, Social Network Analysis

1. Introduction

The term "Not Safe For Work" (hereafter, NSFW) is used by many social media to refer to content within them that cannot be viewed in public or professional settings. The study of the phenomenon of NSFW content in social media has attracted many authors (e.g., [1]). One of the social platforms that has adopted the concept of NSFW in an explicit and well-structured way is Reddit. However, despite this, few researchers have investigated the features of NSFW content in Reddit [2, 3, 4]. In particular, in [4], the authors use Social Network Analysis to investigate NSFW posts on Reddit. They focus on the structural features of the posts without analyzing their content. In this paper, we want to continue the research efforts of [4] and, once again, we use Social Network Analysis to study NSFW posts and comments on Reddit. However, here, we shift the research focus from structure to content.

More specifically, we propose an approach for extracting and analyzing text patterns present in NSFW adult content on Reddit. In our context, we use the term "pattern" to refer to a set of words in posts or comments that satisfy certain properties. Our approach consists of three main steps, namely: *(i)* Data Cleaning and Annotation, *(ii)* Pattern Extraction and Enrichment,

SEBD 2021: The 29th Italian Symposium on Advanced Database Systems, September 5-9, 2021, Pizzo Calabro (VV), Italy
cauteruccio@mat.unical.it (F. Cauteruccio); e.corradini@pm.univpm.it (E. Corradini); terracina@mat.unical.it (G. Terracina); d.ursino@univpm.it (D. Ursino); l.virgili@pm.univpm.it (L. Virgili)
0000-0001-8400-1083 (F. Cauteruccio); 0000-0002-1140-4209 (E. Corradini); 0000-0002-3090-7223 (G. Terracina); 0000-0003-1360-8499 (D. Ursino); 0000-0003-1509-783X (L. Virgili)

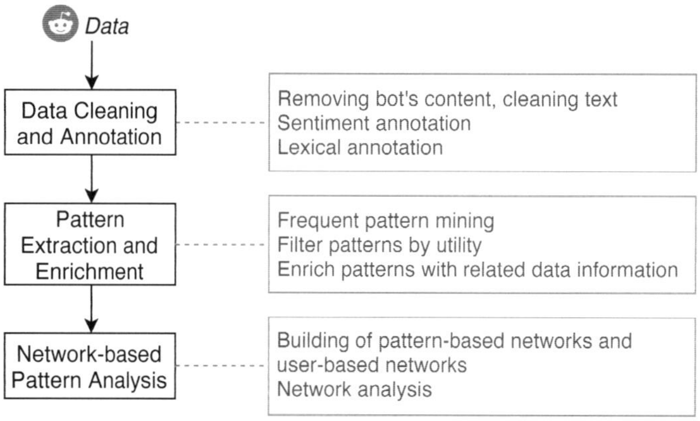

Figure 1: The general workflow of our approach

and *(iii)* Network-based Pattern Analysis. Applying our approach on Reddit allowed us to make several contributions to this research scenario. They involve: *(i)* discovering that traditional approaches to sentiment computation are unreliable in the context of NSFW adult content; *(ii)* defining and finding opinion leaders in real communities sharing NSFW adult content; *(iii)* discovering text patterns representing the building blocks of NSFW posts and comments on Reddit; *(iv)* determining new virtual communities of users sharing NSFW adult content; *(v)* identifying opinion leaders who could influence such communities.

The rest of this paper is structured as follows: Section 2 provides a general description of our approach and the dataset used for our experiments. Section 3 illustrates the Pattern Extraction and Enrichment step. Section 4 describes the Network-based Pattern Analysis step. Finally, Section 5 presents our conclusions and possible future developments of our research efforts.

2. General overview of our approach

The general workflow of our approach is shown in Figure 1, which highlights the three steps composing it (i.e., Data Cleaning and Annotation, Pattern Extraction and Enrichment, and Network-based Pattern Analysis).

The *Data Cleaning and Annotation* step removes irrelevant content and standardizes text representations. It also performs lexical (e.g., part-of-speech and named entities) and sentiment annotations. These latter highlight the polarity of sentiments expressed in the texts, represented in terms of a compound score, computed by applying Vader [5]. Due to space limitations, we do not illustrate this step in detail in this paper.

The *Pattern Extraction and Enrichment* step extracts a set of text patterns from the posts and comments identified in the previous step; they are the basis for the next Network-based Pattern Analysis step. To this end, it first extracts frequent patterns. Then, it associates each pattern with a rich set of features regarding the posts and comments it derives from, as well as the users who published them. Afterwards, it defines some utility measures and associates the corresponding values with each pattern. Finally, it selects only those patterns with high frequency and high utility. Our approach allows the definition of different concepts and utility measures and, consequently, the selection of different sets of useful patterns based on them. This allows us to analyze the available NSFW content from very different perspectives, yet adopting a uniform methodology.

The *Network-based Pattern Analysis* step applies the concepts and approaches of Social Network Analysis to the patterns obtained during the previous step with the goal of extracting information and knowledge from them. Specifically, it constructs and uses three social networks, namely: *(i) User Interaction Network*, in which a node n_i represents a user u_i, who published at least one post or comment. An arc (n_i, n_j, w_{ij}) denotes that u_i commented a post of u_j; w_{ij} indicates how many times this happened. *(ii) Pattern Network*, in which a node n_i represents a pattern p_i extracted in the previous step. An arc (n_i, n_j, w_{ij}) indicates that p_i and p_j were adopted by at least one user in common; w_{ij} indicates the number of users who adopted both p_i and p_j. *(iii) User Content Network*, in which a node n_i represents a user u_i, who published at least one post or comment. An arc (n_i, n_j, w_{ij}) indicates that there is at least one comment posted by u_i and at least one comment posted by u_j containing the same pattern; w_{ij} denotes the number of times this happened. Once these networks are built, this step proceeds by applying Social Network Analysis concepts and approaches to them for extracting information and knowledge on Reddit users publishing, commenting and reading NSFW adult posts and on the content these users exchange. Due to space limitations, in this paper, we focus only on the *User Interaction Network*.

To perform our experiments for evaluating our approach, we downloaded a dataset from the `pushshift.io` [6] website, which represents one of the main data repositories for Reddit. Specifically, we considered 449 NSFW adult subreddits listed at https://www.reddit.com/r/ListOfSubreddits/wiki/nsfw and extracted all posts and the corresponding comments published on them from January 1st, 2020 to March 31st, 2020. The number of posts on the dataset is 3,064,758, while the number of comments is 11,627,372.

3. Pattern Extraction and Enrichment

This step extracts text patterns from posts and comments in the dataset and, then, enriches them with additional information concerning their frequency and utility. Pattern mining plays a key role in this activity. It is a well known task in the literature, which extracts from a dataset some (hopefully interesting and/or unexpected) information that can be understood by humans.

Many pattern mining approaches are based on the concept of *pattern frequency* and aim at identifying the most frequent patterns in the texts received as input. They are based on the assumption that frequent patterns are interesting [7, 8]. This is true in many application contexts. However, there are cases where it does not hold. To handle these cases, the notion of *pattern utility* has been introduced. It shifts the emphasis from frequent pattern mining to High Utility Pattern Mining (hereafter, HUPM) [9, 10]. In this case, a utility function is defined; the patterns with a high value of this function are considered interesting. Recall that a utility function denotes a user preference ordering over a set of choices [9]. It is clearly a subjective measure allowing us to state the usefulness of a text pattern from different perspectives, depending on our preferences and/or needs.

After having introduced the concepts of frequency and utility of a pattern, we can illustrate our approach to pattern extraction and the model which it operates on. Let $\mathcal{C} = \{c_1, c_2, \cdots, c_n\}$ be a set of lemmatized comments, obtained at the end of the Data Cleaning and Annotation step. Each comment $c_i \in \mathcal{C}$ corresponds to a post and is written by a Reddit user. We can represent c_i as a set of lemmas $c_i = \{l_1, l_2, \cdots, l_m\}$. Therefore, if we denote by $\mathcal{L} = \{l_1, l_2, \cdots, l_q\}$ the set of all possible lemmas, then c_i is a subset of $\mathcal{L}$. From the HUPM perspective, each lemma is an item. A pattern P_j is a set of items and, therefore, $P_j \subseteq \mathcal{L}$. P_j can occur in zero, one or more comments in our dataset. We denote by $\mathcal{C}_j \subseteq \mathcal{C}$ the subset of the comments of $\mathcal{C}$ in which P_j is present, and by frequency of P_j the cardinality of $\mathcal{C}_j$. P_j inherits the set of features characterizing the comments of $\mathcal{C}_j$, and the utility of P_j can be defined as an appropriate function of all or some of these features. The choice of the features and the utility function to adopt determine the perspective one whishes to consider in the analysis of patterns.

For example, consider the features score_comm (denoting the score of a comment) and compound (indicating the sentiment value extracted from the text of a comment). Suppose that the utility function is the Pearson's correlation [11] between them, which allows us to say whether there is a form of correlation between the two features, such that a high (resp., low) score of a comment arouses a positive (resp., negative) sentiment about it. This function allows us to select those patterns whose presence in comments with high (resp., low) scores is flanked by a positive (resp., negative) sentiment. We point out that this correlation between score and sentiment is not obvious for comments because there could exist comments with high (resp., low) score and null or negative (resp., positive) sentiment. In the following, we call f_p the utility function computing the Pearson correlation. It is worth investigating both patterns having a positive value of f_p and those having a negative value of that function. Indeed, a positive (resp., negative) value of f_p indicates that there is a direct (resp., inverse) correlation between the sentiment aroused by a comment and the score it obtains. Consequently, we denote by f_p^+ (resp., f_p^-) the function that selects those patterns having a value of f_p greater (resp., lesser) than a threshold th_p^+ (resp., th_p^-).

Figure 2 shows the trend of the number of extracted patterns as th_p^- (resp., th_p^+) decreases (resp., increases). Patterns are also grouped based on their length. This figure provides us with non-obvious and extremely interesting knowledge. In fact, the number of patterns extracted by f_p^- is much greater than the one extracted by f_p^+. This allows us to say that, given a pattern, a positive (resp., negative) sentiment of it is not necessarily accompanied by a high (resp., low) score of the comments where it is present. This phenomenon is very evident for moderately positive or negative values of f_p, while it reduces strongly for extreme values. It can be explained by considering that, given the nature of the reported texts, NSFW posts and comments tend to be associated with a negative sentiment by any sentiment analysis tool. This happens even when such terms are used in goliardic comments, which are actually appreciated by this type of audience. For instance, consider the text pattern $\{hot, fuck\}$, possibly accompanied by an emoticon with two little hearts instead of eyes. Applying the sentiment analysis tools available in the literature to our dataset [5], we obtained a sentiment value of -0.1280 for this pattern. Instead, the corresponding comments have a very high score. As a consequence, the value of f_p is negative. This allows us to obtain a first important outcome of our approach, namely that traditional sentiment computation tools do not work well in presence of NSFW posts and comments. As for the choice of the values of th_p^+ and th_p^-, all the reasoning above, and the presence of a low number of extracted patterns, led us to choose low values for the two

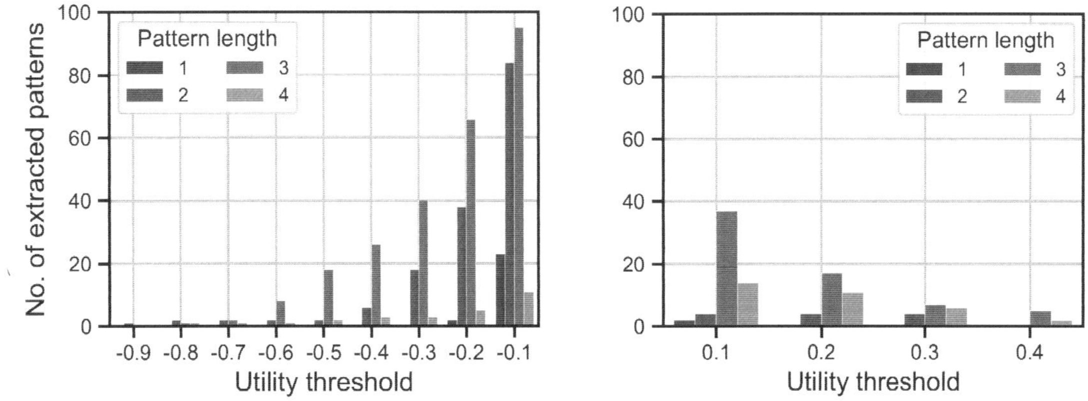

Figure 2: Number of extracted patterns against negative (at left) and positive (at right) f_p

thresholds. In particular, we set $th_p^+ = 0.1$ and $th_p^- = -0.1$.

We end this discussion by pointing out that many other utility functions could be defined on many different features concerning posts and users. This important peculiarity of our approach allows us to analyze the phenomenon of NSFW content from many different perspectives.

4. Analysis of User Interaction Networks

In this section, we formally introduce the User Interaction Network and show how information can be derived from it. Let $\mathcal{P}_f$ be the set of patterns obtained by applying the utility function f, and let $\mathcal{U}_f$ be the set of users who have written at least one comment or post containing at least one of the patterns of $\mathcal{P}_f$. A User Interaction Network $\mathcal{N}^{ui}$ can be defined as: $\mathcal{N}^{ui} = \langle N^{ui}, A^{ui} \rangle$. N^{ui} is the set of nodes of $\mathcal{N}^{ui}$. There exists a node $n_i \in N^{ui}$ for each user $u_i \in \mathcal{U}_f$. A^{ui} is the set of arcs of $\mathcal{N}^{ui}$. An arc $(n_i, n_j, w_{ij}) \in A^{ui}$ denotes that u_i made comments on a post published by u_j; w_{ij} measures how many times this task happened.

$\mathcal{N}^{ui}$ allows us to characterize the behavior of users, who interact with each other by posting and commenting NSFW adult content.

Table 1 lists some parameters of the User Interaction Networks built exploiting the dataset outlined in Section 2, the utility functions f_p^+ and f_p^-, and the thresholds th_p^+ and th_p^-. This table confirms the information derived in Section 3. For instance, $\mathcal{N}^{ui}_{f_p^-}$ contains a larger number of nodes and arcs than $\mathcal{N}^{ui}_{f_p^+}$. Note that the cardinalities of $\mathcal{P}_{f_p^-}$ and $\mathcal{P}_{f_p^+}$ follow the same trend as the number of nodes (and users) in the User Interaction Networks, even though they represent patterns instead of users. It is worth observing the high density coupled with a high clustering coefficient characterizing $\mathcal{N}^{ui}_{f_p^+}$. This tells us that, in this network, users tend to form very tight communities, whose structure resemble that of a clique. Instead, $\mathcal{N}^{ui}_{f_p^-}$ has a high density but a low clustering coefficient; this suggests the presence of very strong power users, i.e., users receiving comments from many other ones, who do not actually interact with each other. In both networks, the number of nodes composing the maximum connected component is very high, i.e., about 60%.

Table 1
Values of some parameters for User Interaction Networks

Parameter	$\mathcal{N}^{ui}_{f_p^-}$	$\mathcal{N}^{ui}_{f_p^+}$
Nodes	27,160	1,452
Arcs	60,662	7,925
Density	8.224e-05	376.15e-05
Clustering coefficient	0.004	0.129
Number of connected components	10,939	506
Size of the maximum connected component	16,030	891
Average weight of arcs	1.205	1.935
Average Indegree (weight $\geq$ 2)	16.634	14.393
Average Outdegree (weight $\geq$ 2)	6.03	7.473
Average Clustering coefficient (weight $\geq$ 2)	0.011	0.139
Average Indegree (All)	1.921	1.973
Average Outdegree (All)	1.912	1.987
Average Clustering coefficient (All)	0.003	0.039

The average number of times a user comments the content of another one is slightly higher than 1; this is confirmed by the very low average weight of arcs. In Figure 3, we investigated this aspect and found a power law distribution of the number of arcs against weights for $\mathcal{N}^{ui}_{f_p^-}$. It implies that the distribution of the number of comments of a user against the contents posted by another one follows a power law. An analogous result holds for $\mathcal{N}^{ui}_{f_p^+}$. We determined the parameters α and δ of these power law distributions; they are: $\alpha = 1.371, \delta = 0.062$ for $\mathcal{N}^{ui}_{f_p^-}$ and $\alpha = 1.507, \delta = 0.063$ for $\mathcal{N}^{ui}_{f_p^+}$. The results of these analyses show that there is a low number of pairs of users in which one of them comments a post of the other at least twice (we call them *interacting users* in the following). This can be considered a minimum condition to detect non-random relationships between pairs of users. We compared the values of the average indegree, outdegree and clustering coefficient of the interacting users, on one hand, and all the users, on the other hand. The bottom of Table 1 shows this comparison for the two considered networks. It is easy to observe that, in both networks, interacting users have indegrees and outdegrees much higher than the other users. Therefore, they can be considered power users. Also, their clustering coefficient is very high, indicating that they are able to promote the generation of communities. Therefore, it can be said that they are community leaders in the distribution of NSFW adult content in Reddit.

At this point, we found it interesting to investigate the possible existence of mutual relationship between interacting users. For this purpose, we determined the fraction of interacting users such that a user u_i comments the posts of a user u_j, and vice versa. We found that this fraction is low (i.e., 0.141) for $\mathcal{N}^{ui}_{f_p^-}$, whereas it is higher (i.e., 0.433) for $\mathcal{N}^{ui}_{f_p^+}$. Furthermore, although the number of nodes of $\mathcal{N}^{ui}_{f_p^+}$ is considerably lower than that of $\mathcal{N}^{ui}_{f_p^-}$, the two networks have similar average indegree and outdegree for both normal and interacting users. Moreover, $\mathcal{N}^{ui}_{f_p^+}$ has a much higher clustering coefficient and a much higher fraction of interacting users than $\mathcal{N}^{ui}_{f_p^-}$. Based on all these outcomes, we can state that, although the number of users of $\mathcal{N}^{ui}_{f_p^-}$ is much greater than that of $\mathcal{N}^{ui}_{f_p^+}$, these last ones have a higher attitude to be opinion leaders. Taking also the utility function underlying $\mathcal{N}^{ui}_{f_p^+}$ into account, we can deduce that the users of this network are particularly able to maintain a positive correlation between the sentiment of

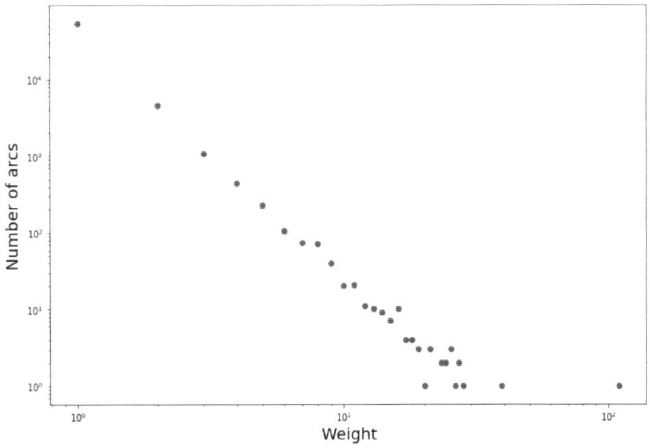

Figure 3: Distribution of arcs against weights for $\mathcal{N}^{ui}_{f_p^-}$ (log-log scale)

their comments and the associated scores. Finally, the results obtained so far allow us to state that the users of $\mathcal{N}^{ui}_{f_p^+}$ are the most dynamic ones, as they publish posts attracting interest (since they are commented by other users), and comment the posts of the other users. This feature makes them particularly important, as they are not only content producers, but also dynamic participants who contribute to maintain their communities active, and act as opinion leaders for these communities. We call them *proactive* users.

5. Conclusion

This paper presented an approach to analyze NSFW users, comments and posts on Reddit, taking into account and exploiting the knowledge extracted by investigating text patterns. The methods and results considered in this paper can represent the basis for many new applications. In fact, posts and subreddits of other target categories (e.g., vegetarian or vegan users) could be examined by means of the same methodology. Moreover, the analysis of text patterns could represent the engine of an automatic classifier aiming at tagging posts and comments containing unsuitable content. Furthermore, our approach can be adapted to other social networks managing NSFW content less explicitly than Reddit. Finally, we plan to design an automatic tool that exploits a knowledge base built by integrating utility patterns and semantic analysis tools to automatically classify new contents, and, then, suggest the most pertinent communities which they should be directed to.

References

[1] K. Tiidenberg, Boundaries and conflict in a NSFW community on tumblr: The meanings and uses of selfies, New Media & Society 18 (2016) 1563–1578. Sage Publications.

[2] J. Matias, Going dark: Social factors in collective action against platform operators in the Reddit blackout, in: Proc. of the International Conference on Human Factors in Computing Systems (ACM CHI 2016), San Jose, CA, USA, 2016, pp. 1138–1151. ACM.

[3] B. K. Narayanan, M. Nirmala, Adult content filtering: Restricting minor audience from accessing inappropriate Internet content, Education and Information Technologies 23 (2018) 2719–2735. Springer.

[4] E. Corradini, A. Nocera, D. Ursino, L. Virgili, Investigating the phenomenon of NSFW posts in Reddit, Information Sciences 566 (2021) 140–164. Elsevier.

[5] C. Hutto, E. Gilbert, Vader: A parsimonious rule-based model for sentiment analysis of social media text, in: Proc. of the International AAAI Conference on Weblogs and Social Media (ICWSM'14), Ann Arbor, MI, USA, 2014, pp. 216–225.

[6] J. Baumgartner, S. Zannettou, B. Keegan, M. Squire, J. Blackburn, The pushshift Reddit dataset, in: Proc. of the International AAAI Conference on Web and Social Media (ICWSM'20), volume 14, Atlanta, GA, USA, 2020, pp. 830–839. AAAI Press.

[7] P. Fournier-Viger, J. C.-W. Lin, B. Vo, T. Chi, J. Zhang, H. Le, A survey of itemset mining, WIREs Data Minining and Knowledge Discovery 7 (2017) e1207. doi:https://doi.org/10.1002/widm.1207, Wiley.

[8] C. Aggarwal, M. Bhuiyan, M. A. Hasan, Frequent pattern mining algorithms: A survey, in: J. H. C. Aggarwal (Ed.), Frequent Pattern Mining, 2014, pp. 19–64. doi:10.1007/978-3-319-07821-2_2, springer, Cham.

[9] P. Fournier-Viger, J.-W. Lin, R. Nkambou, B. Vo, V. Tseng, High-Utility Pattern Mining, 2019. Springer.

[10] W. Gan, C. Lin, P. Fournier-Viger, H. Chao, V. Tseng, P. Yu, A survey of utility-oriented pattern mining, IEEE Transactions on Knowledge and Data Engineering 33 (2021) 1306–1327. doi:https://doi.org/10.1109/TKDE.2019.2942594, iEEE.

[11] K. Pearson, Note on regression and inheritance in the case of two parents, Proceedings of the Royal Society of London 58 (1895) 240–242. The Royal Society.

A Multi-resolution Training for Expression Recognition in the Wild

(Discussion Paper)

Fabio Valerio Massoli[1], Donato Cafarelli[1], Giuseppe Amato[1] and Fabrizio Falchi[1]

[1]*ISTI-CNR, via G. Moruzzi 1, 56124 Pisa, Italy*

Abstract

Facial expressions play a fundamental role in human communication, and their study, which represents a multidisciplinary subject, embraces a great variety of research fields, e.g., from psychology to computer science, among others. Concerning Deep Learning, the recognition of facial expressions is a task named Facial Expression Recognition (FER). With such an objective, the goal of a learning model is to classify human emotions starting from a facial image of a given subject. Typically, face images are acquired by cameras that have, by nature, different characteristics, such as the output resolution. Moreover, other circumstances might involve cameras placed far from the observed scene, thus obtaining faces with very low resolutions. Therefore, since the FER task might involve analyzing face images that can be acquired with heterogeneous sources, it is plausible to expect that resolution plays a vital role. In such a context, we propose a multi-resolution training approach to solve the FER task. We ground our intuition on the observation that, often, face images are acquired at different resolutions. Thus, directly considering such property while training a model can help achieve higher performance on recognizing facial expressions. To our aim, we use a ResNet-like architecture, equipped with Squeeze-and-Excitation blocks, trained on the Affect-in-the-Wild 2 dataset. Not being available a test set, we conduct tests and model selection by employing the validation set only on which we achieve more than 90% accuracy on classifying the seven expressions that the dataset comprises.

Keywords

Facial Expression Recognition, Deep Convolutional Neural Networks, Multi-resolution training.

1. Introduction

Facial expressions play a fundamental role in human communication. Indeed, they typically reveal the actual emotional status of people beyond the spoken language. Moreover, the comprehension of human affect based on visual patterns is a crucial ingredient for any human-machine interaction [1] system and, for such reasons, the task of Facial Expression Recognition (FER) draws both scientific and industrial interest. In recent years, Deep Learning techniques reached very high performance on FER by exploiting different architectures and learning paradigms. In such a context, we propose a multi-resolution approach to solve the FER task.

SEBD 2021: The 29th Italian Symposium on Advanced Database Systems, September 5-9, 2021, Pizzo Calabro (VV), Italy

fabio.massolli@isti.cnr.it (F. V. Massoli); donato.caf@gmail.com (D. Cafarelli); giuseppe.amato@isti.cnr.it (G. Amato); fabrizio.falchi@isti.cnr.it (F. Falchi)

0000-0001-6447-1301 (F. V. Massoli); 0000-0002-7575-0143 (D. Cafarelli); 0000-0003-0171-4315 (G. Amato); 0000-0001-6258-5313 (F. Falchi)

CEUR Workshop Proceedings (CEUR-WS.org)

We ground our intuition on the observation that, often, face images are acquired at different resolutions. Thus, directly considering such property while training a model can help achieve higher performance on recognizing facial expressions. To our aim, we use a ResNet-like architecture, equipped with Squeeze-and-Excitation blocks, trained on the Affect-in-the-Wild 2 dataset. Not being available a test set, we conduct tests and model selection by employing the validation set only on which we achieve more than 90% accuracy on classifying the seven expressions that the dataset comprises. To let our researcher reproduce our results, we made our code publicly available on github[1]. Concerning the remaining part of the paper, we organized it as follows. In Section 2 we report several works related to the FER task, while in Section 3 and Section 4 we describe our approach and the dataset we use, respectively. Moreover, we describe the experimental campaigns we perform and the corresponding model performance in Section 5. Finally, in Section 6 we conclude our work by reporting our plans.

2. Related Works

Nowadays, the most promising approaches to the FER task are based on the use of Deep Convolutional Neural Networks (DCNN). A typical approach consists of a pre-processing phase, where the images are subject to various transformations, and a training phase where these images are iteratively given as input to a DCNN model for feature extraction and expression classification.

In [2], the authors propose a new approach for face cropping to remove useless regions in an image and a novel rotation strategy to cope with data scarcity. Furthermore, they built a simplified DCNN structure to reduce training/inference time and achieve real-time FER on devices with limited resources. Their experiments were conducted on two databases, CK+ [3] and JAFFE [4], and achieved state-of-the-art results. In [5], a novel activation function based on the ReLU function, called LS-ReLU, is presented. It exploits an adjustable log and the soft-sign functions. Neural networks based on LS–ReLU function can avoid the over-fitting problem during the training process and reduce the oscillations problem. Their experiments on JAFFE [4] and FER2013 [6] datasets showed that a DCNN based on this novel activation function has a better performance compared to most state-of-the-art activation functions. With the transition of FER datasets from laboratory-controlled to in-the-wild conditions, this task has become more challenging due to variations in pose, brightness, and background, to mention some. Therefore, in [7] the authors focus on resolving the FER task by analyzing the contribution of different face areas to different emotions, including nose, mouth, eyes, nose to mouth, nose to eyes, and mouth to eyes areas, together with the whole faces. The paper [8] addresses the problem of the class imbalance in wild FER datasets. To such an aim, the authors propose a novel Discriminant Distribution-Agnostic loss (DDA loss) to optimize the embedding space for extreme class imbalance scenarios. Specifically, DDA loss enforces inter-class separation of deep features for both majority and minority classes. In [9] the authors propose a multi-task learning framework to extract local-global and spatio-temporal information for a discriminative and robust representation of facial expressions. Their experiments achieved competitive results on the CK+ [3] and Oulu-CASIA [10] datasets. To improve the performance on the FER

[1]https://github.com/fvmassoli/affwild2-challenge.git

task, [11] proposes a novel "Masking Idea" that is implemented in a Residual Masking Network that contains several masking blocks applied across residual layers to improve the network's attention ability on relevant information. Experiments showed competitive results on the FER2013 [6] dataset.

3. Approach

Usually, face images come from heterogeneous sources [12], e.g., cameras with different resolutions or different distances from the scene. Such characteristics directly impact DL models' performance on tasks such as Face Recognition (FR) by dramatically lowering their performance [13]. Based on such an observation, we propose our approach grounded on the hypothesis that the images' resolution has a non-negligible impact on DL models' behavior when tested against the FER task. Precisely, we move our steps from [13] in which the authors explicitly take care of the multi-resolution nature of face images by designing a training technique to accommodate for such an issue adequately.

In our work, we take inspiration from the author's training procedure, and we adapted it to our case. Specifically, we experimentally notice that we do not need any Teacher-supervised signal nor curriculum learning. Thus, we simplify the training procedure by only exploiting the double random extraction to set the final image resolution. To train the models and perform model selection, we employ the Aff-Wild2 [14] dataset. We refer the reader to Section 4 for a brief description of the dataset.

Our base model is a ResNet-50 architecture [15], equipped with Squeeze-and-Excitation blocks [16], that has been pre-trained on the VGGFace2 dataset [17]. To train our models, we use the Adam [18] optimizer. We set the weight decay of $1.e^{-4}$ and the learning at $1.e^{-3}$ for the last fully connected layer and $1.e^{-4}$ for all the others. Moreover, we set the batch size to 128, and we use data augmentation techniques to avoid overfitting. Specifically, we first resize the images to have the shortest side of 256 pixels (while keeping the original aspect ratio), then we random crop a square of 224x224 pixels, and finally, we normalize the input channels. Moreover, we apply a random grayscale conversion with a probability of 0.2. We substitute the random crop with the center one, and we remove the grayscale operation to test the model on the validation set.

Concerning the random resolution extractions to train the models, we perform several experiments considering different ranges for the final image size concerning the multi-resolution training, with the minimum and maximum considered values being 8 and 256 pixels, respectively.

4. Dataset: Affect-in-the-Wild 2

The Aff-Wild2 [14] dataset is the first-ever database annotated for all three main behavior tasks: Valence Arousal (VA), Action Units (AU), and Expression (EX) classification. Concerning the last one, the dataset consists of 547 videos (collected from YouTube) that account for $\sim$2.6M of frames labeled considering seven basic expressions: neutral, anger, disgust, fear, happiness, sadness, and surprise. The annotation is made frame-by-frame by a team of seven experts. The dataset is shipped with a protocol that divides it into three non-overlapping subsets for training, validation, and test purposes. Specifically, the three partitions consist of 253, 71, and 223 videos, respectively. The cropped-aligned version of the dataset is made of images preprocessed to have a fixed resolution of 112x112 pixels. Among the ~2.6M available images, ~1.2M are available for training and validation on the FER task. We report in Figure 1 an example of training images in the Aff-Wild2 [14] dataset.

Figure 1: Example of face images from the Aff-Wild2 [14] dataset. On top of each image, we report the corresponding ground truth expression.

As we mentioned previously, the dataset comprises seven different types of expressions with a very different cardinality. In Table 1, we report the number of images for each class, both for the training and validation sets, while in Table 2, we report the classes' weight concerning the training images only.

	Expression						
	Neutral	Anger	Disgust	Fear	Happiness	Sadness	Surprise
Training	585896	23484	12497	11120	149920	100548	38564
(%)	(63.5)	(2.5)	(1.4)	(1.2)	(16.3)	(11.0)	(4.1)
Validation	181884	8003	5401	9671	52842	38534	22988
(%)	(57.0)	(2.5)	(1.7)	(3.0)	(16.5)	(12.1)	(7.2)

Table 1
Classes' cardinality for the Aff-Wild2 [14] dataset.

As one can notice from Table 1, the classes are not balanced. For that reason, we leveraged a balanced cross-entropy loss to account for the class unbalance. To such an aim we use the weights reported in Table 2.

	Neutral	Anger	Disgust	Fear	Happiness	Sadness	Surprise
Aff-Wild2 [14]	0.365	0.975	0.986	0.988	0.837	0.891	0.958

Table 2
Classes' weight. The values reported are referred to the training set only. Note that weights do not need to sum up to one. The lower the weight, the higher the cardinality of the corresponding class.

5. Experimental Results

In this section, we report the experimental results we obtained on the Aff-Wild2 [14] dataset. Since the dataset is currently employed in the Affect-in-the-Wild Challenge [19], the test set's ground truth labels are not available. For such a reason, we quote the performance of our model on the validation set. Before the training, we took a small subsample of the validation set and used it for model selection purposes to avoid bias. Subsequently, we tested the best model on the entire validation set. To quote our results, we use different metrics. First, we evaluate the F1-score on each class, then we summarize the overall performance of our best model across all the seven expressions by quoting the F1-score (macro-average) and the overall accuracy. Finally, we evaluate the same score as required by the Affect-in-the-Wild Challenge [19], which is equal to:

$$s = 0.33 \cdot \text{accuracy} + 0.67 \cdot \text{f1 score}; \tag{1}$$

where the accuracy and the f1 score are relative to the whole dataset.

We report the results in Table 3 and Table 4 concerning single classes and the whole dataset, respectively.

	Expression						
	Neutral	Anger	Disgust	Fear	Happiness	Sadness	Surprise
F1 Score	0.978	0.960	0.965	0.971	0.946	0.987	0.937

Table 3
F1 score for each class of the Aff-Wild2 [14] dataset.

Accuracy	**F1 Score (macro-average)**	**Challenge Score**
0.970	0.964	0.966

Table 4
Summary statistics on all the classes of the Aff-Wild2 [14] dataset.

From the previous tables, we can notice that our model shows promising performance on the FER task. Moreover, we acknowledge the stability of the scores among different classes even though the dataset is highly unbalanced as reported in Table 1

6. Conculsions abd Future Works

In this work, we report our first experimental campaign focused FER task. We tackle such a problem by giving more representational power to our models, assuming a multi-resolution context, and we observe promising results. As a next step, we will extend our experimental campaign to test our approach on different publicly available datasets such as FER2013 [6], RAF-DB [20], and Oulu-CASIA [10].

Acknowledgments

We gratefully acknowledge the support of NVIDIA Corporation with the donation of the Titan V GPU used for this research. This work was partially supported by WAC@Lucca funded by Fondazione Cassa di Risparmio di Lucca, AI4EU - an EC H2020 project (Contract n. 825619), and upon work from COST Action 16101 "Action MULTI-modal Imaging of FOREnsic SciEnce Evidence (MULTI-FORESEE)", supported by COST (European Cooperation in Science and Technology).

References

[1] V. Bettadapura, Face expression recognition and analysis: The state of the art, CoRR abs/1203.6722 (2012). URL: http://arxiv.org/abs/1203.6722. arXiv:1203.6722.

[2] K. Li, Y. Jin, M. W. Akram, R. Han, J. Chen, Facial expression recognition with convolutional neural networks via a new face cropping and rotation strategy, The Visual Computer 36 (2020) 391–404.

[3] P. Lucey, J. F. Cohn, T. Kanade, J. Saragih, Z. Ambadar, I. Matthews, The extended cohn-kanade dataset (ck+): A complete dataset for action unit and emotion-specified expression, in: 2010 ieee computer society CVPR-workshops, IEEE, 2010, pp. 94–101.

[4] M. Lyons, S. Akamatsu, M. Kamachi, J. Gyoba, Coding facial expressions with gabor wavelets, in: Proceedings Third IEEE international conference on automatic face and gesture recognition, IEEE, 1998, pp. 200–205.

[5] Y. Wang, Y. Li, Y. Song, X. Rong, The influence of the activation function in a convolution neural network model of facial expression recognition, Applied Sciences 10 (2020) 1897.

[6] I. J. Goodfellow, D. Erhan, P. L. Carrier, A. Courville, M. Mirza, B. Hamner, W. Cukierski, Y. Tang, D. Thaler, D.-H. Lee, et al., Challenges in representation learning: A report on three machine learning contests, in: International conference on neural information processing, Springer, 2013, pp. 117–124.

[7] Z. Lian, Y. Li, J.-H. Tao, J. Huang, M.-Y. Niu, Expression analysis based on face regions in real-world conditions, International Journal of Automation and Computing 17 (2020) 96–107.

[8] A. H. Farzaneh, X. Qi, Facial expression recognition in the wild via deep attentive center loss, in: Proceedings of the IEEE/CVF Winter Conference on Applications of Computer Vision, 2021, pp. 2402–2411.

[9] M. Yu, H. Zheng, Z. Peng, J. Dong, H. Du, Facial expression recognition based on a multi-task global-local network, Pattern Recognition Letters 131 (2020) 166–171.

[10] G. Zhao, X. Huang, M. Taini, S. Z. Li, M. PietikäInen, Facial expression recognition from near-infrared videos, Image and Vision Computing 29 (2011) 607–619.

[11] P. Luan, V. Huynh, T. Tuan Anh, Facial expression recognition using residual masking network, in: IEEE 25th International Conference on Pattern Recognition, 2020, pp. 4513–4519.

[12] F. V. Massoli, F. Falchi, C. Gennaro, G. Amato, Cross-resolution deep features based image search, in: International Conference on Similarity Search and Applications, Springer, 2020, pp. 352–360.

[13] F. V. Massoli, G. Amato, F. Falchi, Cross-resolution learning for face recognition, Image and Vision Computing 99 (2020) 103927.

[14] D. Kollias, S. Zafeiriou, Aff-wild2: Extending the aff-wild database for affect recognition, arXiv:1811.07770 (2018).

[15] K. He, X. Zhang, S. Ren, J. Sun, Deep residual learning for image recognition. corr abs/1512.03385 (2015), 2015.

[16] J. Hu, L. Shen, G. Sun, Squeeze-and-excitation networks, in: Proceedings of the IEEE CVPR, 2018, pp. 7132–7141.

[17] Q. Cao, L. Shen, W. Xie, O. M. Parkhi, A. Zisserman, Vggface2: A dataset for recognising faces across pose and age. corr abs/1710.08092 (2017), arXiv:1710.08092 (2017).

[18] D. P. Kingma, J. Ba, Adam: A method for stochastic optimization, arXiv:1412.6980 (2014).

[19] D. Kollias, S. Zafeiriou, First Affect-in-the-Wild Challenge, https://ibug.doc.ic.ac.uk/resources/first-affect-wild-challenge/, 2020.

[20] S. Li, W. Deng, J. Du, Reliable crowdsourcing and deep locality-preserving learning for expression recognition in the wild, in: Proceedings of the IEEE CVPR, 2017, pp. 2852–2861.

Applying Generative Adversarial Networks to perform gaze path prediction in websites

(Discussion Paper)

Gianluca Bonifazi[a], Enrico Corradini[a], Gianluca Porcino[b], Alessandro Scopelliti[c], Domenico Ursino[a] and Luca Virgili[a]

[a]*DII, Polytechnic University of Marche*
[b]*Data Labs, Daimler AG*
[c]*Energy Intelligence*

Abstract

In recent years, gaze path prediction has become a topic widely studied by computer scientists, who have proposed a variety of approaches to address this issue in the context of natural images. Among these approaches, the ones based on deep learning and, in particular, on Generative Adversarial Networks (GANs) have proven to be extremely accurate. When moving from natural images to websites, gaze path prediction becomes much more complex. As an evidence of this fact, no GAN-based approaches have yet been presented to solve this problem. In this paper, we aim at filling this gap by proposing two GAN-based approaches capable of predicting the gaze path of a user when looking at a website.

Keywords

Gaze path prediction, Deep learning, Generative Adversarial Networks, PathGAN, FiWI dataset

1. Introduction

With the passing of the years, more and more contents are present on the Web, leading to an increase in the difficulty of capturing the attention of a user when she visits a website. The evaluation of the attention posed by a user when visiting a website is a non-trivial problem, which depends on several factors. To cope with it, researchers have proposed a powerful tool, namely visual scanpath [1]. It represents a formal definition of the path made by a user's gaze while looking at an image. In the past, such concept was applied to natural images. However, the huge development of the web has led to an increasing interest in applying it also to websites. However, the website scenario is much more complex than the natural image one. In fact, a single web page can contain more natural images, text, logos and animations. This peculiarity makes gaze path prediction tools designed for natural images much less effective when applied

SEBD 2021: The 29th Italian Symposium on Advanced Database Systems, September 5-9, 2021, Pizzo Calabro (VV), Italy
g.bonifazi@univpm.it (G. Bonifazi); e.corradini@pm.univpm.it (E. Corradini); gianluca.porcino@daimler.com; (G. Porcino); alessandro.scopelliti@energyintelligence.it (A. Scopelliti); d.ursino@univpm.it (D. Ursino); l.virgili@pm.univpm.it (L. Virgili)
0000-0002-1947-8667 (G. Bonifazi); 0000-0002-1140-4209 (E. Corradini); 0000-0003-1360-8499 (D. Ursino); 0000-0003-1509-783X (L. Virgili)

to websites. In fact, the presence of several competing stimuli in a web page makes the accurate prediction of the eye fixation much more complex [2].

To address this problem, the past literature has proposed several approaches, belonging to different categories. Among them, deep learning represents one of the categories that recently has attracted a lot of interest. One of the first proofs of the effectiveness of deep learning in this area is reported in [3]. After this attempt, several others have been proposed, and many of them obtained important results. In particular, one architecture that is gaining increasing attention is Generative Adversarial Networks (hereafter, GANs) [4, 5, 6, 7]. It has proven to be extremely valuable in the context of gaze path prediction of natural images [8, 9, 10], where the corresponding approaches have achieved state-of-the-art results. However, as for websites, to the best of our knowledge, no GAN-based approaches have been proposed yet.

In this paper, we aim at filling this gap by proposing two GAN-based approaches specifically designed to operate on websites. We start from PathGAN [10], an approach that has been shown to be very effective for gaze path prediction of natural images, and propose two variants of it. They present a number of refinements derived from several observations we made during some experiments conducted "in the field".

The outline of this paper is as follows: Section 2 provides a technical description of our approaches. Section 3 discusses the experiments performed and the results obtained. Finally, Section 4 draws some conclusions and provides a look at possible future developments.

2. Characterization of the proposed approach

In the field of gaze path prediction, scientific research is still at an early stage. Among the few studies to address this problem, a GAN-based approach, called PathGAN [10], stands out for its results. It predicts the visual scanpath of people watching natural images in both normal and 360-degree formats. Its architecture is shown in Figure 1. The first part of the network is a generator that receives an image and returns a gaze path denoting the eye path of a potential user in observing that image. The generated path is a sequence of 63 fixations, each modeled by a tuple of 4 variables, namely an x-coordinate, a y-coordinate, a timestamp and an end of path probability. The first three variables indicate the position and the duration of each fixation. The fourth one guarantees the possibility of generating paths of variable length. To this end, a threshold is defined for this variable, which makes it possible to determine which fixations should not be included in the final prediction.

We started by applying the original PathGAN to websites; unfortunately, this task did not produce encouraging results. However, it allowed us to identify some problems to solve for improving performances.

First of all, we decided to update the weights of the generator and the discriminator with different frequencies, but the choice to make more updates on the discriminator than on the generator did not lead to performance improvements. Furthermore, assigning a very low weight to the content loss (for instance, a weight equal to 0.05) makes the discriminator much stronger than the generator. Training only the generator for the first 5 epochs was not enough to prevent this phenomenon.

The length of the gaze path to be predicted was another factor that greatly complicated the

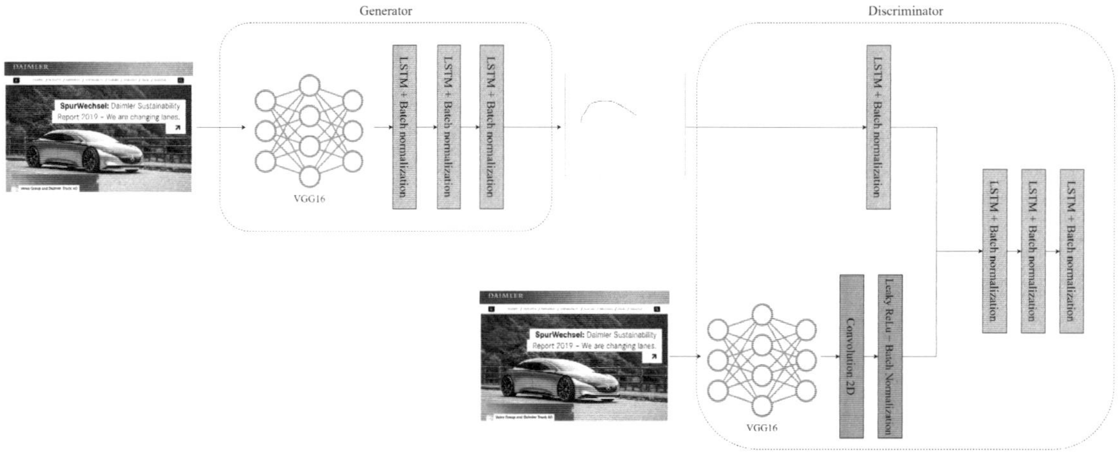

Figure 1: Original PathGAN architecture

problem. In fact, in order to handle paths of variable length, the end of path probability was included. However, the training phase proved unable to tune this variable adequately, leading to paths that were either too short or too long. Overall, we experienced completely wrong predictions that, in the long run, led to mode collapse during training. In this case, the generator tends to return gaze path predictions matching the edge of the image and completely ignoring the original ground truth.

The cause of this phenomenon was identified in the combination of several elements. The discriminator becomes too strong with respect to the generator, which can no longer make realistic predictions. The scarcity of data available does not help to solve this problem. The discriminator clearly overfits on the training data after several epochs, and this cannot be prevented by changing the update frequency of the weights of the generator and the discriminator.

The next step led us to make improvements in the way the network is trained and to change the weights assigned to content and adversarial loss. The only way to make the discriminator weaker is to update the generator weights more often. Decreasing the weight assigned to adversarial loss in the objective function produced positive effects. A higher content loss weight prevented the discriminator from taking over. The quality of the generated samples increased a lot, allowing the network training to be completed successfully. In conclusion, we decided to multiply the adversarial loss for a weight equal to 0.35 and the content loss for a weight equal to 1.

Afterwards, we tuned the correct number of updates of the weights for each part of the network. In particular, we decided to update 16 times the weights of the generator and 4 times those of the discriminator at each step. We also introduced other changes to avoid overfitting. In particular, taking inspiration from saliency prediction models, we added noise to the images passed to the discriminator.

After all these changes and updates to the original PathGAN, we obtained a new version of it called NormalGAN. It has the same architecture as PathGAN but is specifically designed to operate on websites.

In addition to this first variant of PathGAN, we designed a second one. To this end, we

Table 1
Differences between the original PathGAN, NormalGAN and WGAN

Original PathGAN	*NormalGAN*	*WGAN*
Best results with natural images	Fine-tuned for the GUI domain	Fine-tuned for the GUI domain
End of path probability	Fixed path length	Fixed path length
Content loss weight equal to 1	Content loss weight equal to 1	Content loss weight equal to 0.05
Adversarial loss equal to 0.2	Adversarial loss equal to 0.2	Adversarial loss equal to 1
Conditional GAN	Conditional GAN	Conditional Wasserstein GAN

started with the considerations that had led to NormalGAN and made additional changes. In particular, we modified the underlying architecture so that it would follow the structure of a conditional Wasserstein GAN [11] (and, for this reason, we called WGAN this new variant). We also modified the training process to comply with the characteristics of a conditional Wasserstein GAN. In particular, we updated the discriminator's weights more often than the generator's ones (i.e., 5 times compared to 1) because weight clipping was introduced. We reset the weights of the various loss terms to their original values (i.e., 0.05 for content loss and 1 for adversarial loss). These two changes allowed us to obtain a balance between the generator's and the discriminator's strength. In fact, increasing the update rate of the weights leads to a scenario where the generator and the discriminator learn too much from our dataset, causing overfitting. On the other hand, decreasing this parameter implies that the training process takes longer, or that, for the same duration, the generator and/or the discriminator cannot learn enough from the dataset.

In conclusion to these discussions, in Table 1, we provide a scheme of the differences between PathGAN, NormalGAN, and WGAN.

3. Experiments

Our approaches for gaze path prediction of users accessing websites have been implemented in a web-based tool; in the design and realization of it, we paid particular attention to user experience. We adopted Python as programming language, Keras and Tensorflow for handling GANs, and Django for managing the underlying CMS. With User Experience Design techniques in mind, we created a home page where a user can upload an image and specify the gaze path prediction technique she want to apply. Our tool returns the original image, the corresponding ground truth and the gaze path prediction. In Figure 2, we report an example of the output provided by it.

3.1. Description of the dataset

To the best of our knowledge, the only dataset available in the literature, which contains both web page layout images and gaze data is FiWI (Fixations in Webpage Images) [2]. In fact, it is used as a reference in all researches regarding gaze path prediction in the GUI domain. It was constructed by collecting data from 11 volunteers, who observed 149 websites. The limited number of volunteers makes FiWI unable to represent all the ways in which people observe websites. Also, the gender of people is not balanced in it, because 7 volunteers were female and 4 were male. All of these considerations prompted us to build a new dataset aiming at avoiding,

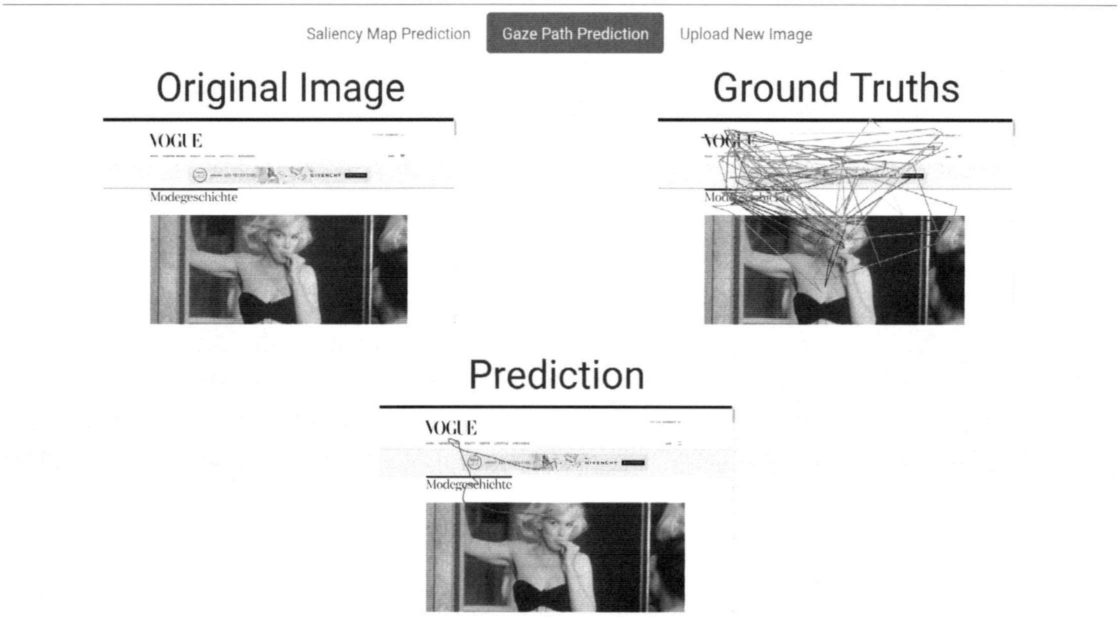

Figure 2: An example of a gaze path prediction returned by our tool

or at least mitigating, these problems.

From the beginning we thought that it was necessary to increase the number of websites present in the dataset and add new forms of layout than those considered by FiWI, because the latter did not fully represent the current variety of web. In particular, the original layouts of FiWI were three, namely *(i)* Pictorial, *(ii)* Text, and *(iii)* Mixed. First, we have extended the number of websites belonging to each layout, while keeping the corresponding fractions balanced. Furthermore, we added a fourth layout, i.e., *Business*, which presents analytical layouts (in particular, dashboards) and Daimler intranet layouts. Finally, we considered that the principles of website design have changed over time. For this reason, we decided to put our dataset both the original and the updated layout of the pages already present in FiWI. Finally, we removed from it the FiWI websites without an updated version available (for example, web pages of companies that no longer exist) to get a balanced set of old and new layouts.

Starting with this original core of 149 images, we reached a total of 262 web layouts. Finally, we felt it necessary to engage more volunteers than FiWI, to include more nuances of how different people look at images, as well as to balance their gender. For this reason, we selected 100 volunteers, 50 males and 50 females. Each of the 262 images was seen by 11 or 12 volunteers, in such a way as to collect 3000 gaze paths. Each volunteer was asked to watch 30 images. If compared with FiWI, the number of available gaze paths is more than twice. Table 2 shows several information on FiWI and our dataset.

Table 2
Characteristics comparison between FiWI and our dataset

	FiWI [2]	*Our dataset*
Number of subjects	11 (4 males, 7 females)	100 (50 males, 50 females)
Age range of subjects	21 - 25	15 - 70
Number of web pages	149	262
Time necessary to display a web page	5 seconds	5 seconds
Screen resolution	1360 × 768	1920 × 1080
Number of gaze paths	1,639	3,000

3.2. Results of the experiments

In this section, we apply PathGAN, NormalGAN and WGAN to the images of the dataset described in Section 3.1 to verify whether our two variants actually perform better. To carry out this task, we relied on Jarodzka metrics [12]. These define scanpaths as a series of geometric vectors, called saccade vectors, and compare them along the following dimensions: *(i) Vector shape*, denoting the difference in shape between saccade vectors; *(ii) Vector direction*, indicating the difference in direction (i.e., angle) between saccade vectors; *(iii) Vector length*, representing the difference in amplitude between saccade vectors; *(iv) Vector position*, denoting the distance between fixations; *(v) Fixation duration*, indicating the difference in duration between fixations. All these measures range in the real interval $[0, 1]$; the higher their value, the closer saccade vectors and the better the performance of the approach. Specifically, the first three measures are normalized against the screen diagonal, the fourth against π, and the last against the maximum value of the two durations being compared.

Since each website in our dataset was watched by 11 or 12 different users (see Section 3.1), there is no single ground truth for it, but the gaze path of each user watching it was considered as a ground truth. Therefore, the corresponding gaze path prediction returned by the approach to evaluate was compared with each ground truth and, next, the average performance for that website was computed. Finally, the performance associated with the various websites was averaged to obtain the evaluation of the approach with respect to the overall dataset. Table 3 shows the results obtained.

Table 3
Original PathGAN, NormalGAN and WGAN performances

	Shape	*Direction*	*Length*	*Position*	*Duration*
Original PathGAN	0.652	0.421	0.850	0.435	0.295
NormalGAN	0.992	0.693	0.991	0.836	0.290
WGAN	0.993	0.699	0.992	0.840	0.310

From the analysis of this table we can see that the original PathGAN returns results much lower than NormalGAN and WGAN for all the metrics adopted. As we know, this is due to the fact that it was designed for natural images and not for websites. If we compare NormalGAN and WGAN, we can observe that both of them predict vector shape and path length very well. The position of fixation is also high for both approaches. Direction similarity decreases significantly for both of them, although the values obtained still remain acceptable. Instead, both variants show a low performance in predicting the duration of each fixation. This parameter is by far the main weakness of our approaches, but also of the original PathGAN, from which they inherit this issue.

Table 3 also shows that WGAN is the best of the three approaches, because it achieves the highest score in all five metrics. NormalGAN also shows a very good performance, lower than WGAN only by a few decimal points. Finally, this table also highlights that both approaches have the same strengths and weaknesses, because they perform well and poorly on the same metrics.

As a further test, we carried out an "absolute" evaluation of WGAN (i.e., the "winner" of the previous comparison) to verify if it was adequate. In this task, we adopted the One human baseline technique [13]. Due to space limitations, we cannot illustrate this experiment here. We can only say that obtained results were extremely satisfying.

4. Conclusion

In this paper, we have proposed NormalGAN and WGAN, i.e., two variants of PathGAN conceived to predict the gaze path of a user watching a website. First, we have explained the motivations underlying our approach. Then, we have illustrated the reasons leading us to define the two variants and have described their technical features. Afterwards, we have illustrated our dataset, which represents an advance with respect to FiWI that is the dataset adopted currently in this field. Finally, we have proposed an experiment showing that our two variants outperform PathGAN when operating on websites.

Our work should not be considered as an ending point, but the starting point for further research efforts. For instance, it could be combined with an approach for saliency map prediction in such a way as that the latter guides the former in obtaining more accurate results. Furthermore, it could be interesting to apply reinforcement learning in this scenario with the ultimate goal of defining a reward function able to highlight the correct aspects of web interfaces and, therefore, to ensure an appropriate training of the model.

Acknowledgments

This work was partially funded by the Marche Region under the project "Human Digital Flexible Factory of the Future Laboratory (HDSFIab) - POR MARCHE FESR 2014-2020 - CUP B16H18000050007". The authors thank the Daimler AG for supporting them in all their testing activities by providing its laboratories and encouraging its employees to participate as volunteers.

References

[1] J. Goldberg, J. Helfman, Visual scanpath representation, in: Proc. of the Symposium on Eye-Tracking Research & Applications (ETMA'10), Austin, Texas, USA, 2010, pp. 203–210. ACM.

[2] C. Shen, Q. Zhao, Webpage saliency, in: Proc. of the European Conference on Computer Vision (ECCV'14), Zurich, Switzerland, 2014, pp. 33–46. Springer.
[3] K. Simonyan, A. Vedaldi, A. Zisserman, Deep inside convolutional networks: Visualising image classification models and saliency maps, Proc. of the International Conference on Learning Representations (ICLR'14) (2013). ICLR Press.
[4] V. Singh, H. Rashwan, S. Romani, F. Akram, N. Pandey, M. Sarker, A. Saleh, M. Arenas, M. Arquez, D. Puig, Breast tumor segmentation and shape classification in mammograms using generative adversarial and convolutional neural network, Expert Systems with Applications 139 (2020) 112855. Elsevier.
[5] R. He, X. Li, G. Chen, G. Chen, Y. Liu, Generative adversarial network-based semi-supervised learning for real-time risk warning of process industries, Expert Systems with Applications 150 (2020) 113244. Elsevier.
[6] J. Oh, J. Hong, J. Baek, Oversampling method using outlier detectable generative adversarial network, Expert Systems with Applications 133 (2019) 1–8. Elsevier.
[7] G. Douzas, F. Bacao, Effective data generation for imbalanced learning using conditional generative adversarial networks, Expert Systems with applications 91 (2018) 464–471. Elsevier.
[8] J. Pan, C. C. Ferrer, K. McGuinness, N. O'Connor, J. Torres, E. Sayrol, X. G. i Nieto, Salgan: Visual saliency prediction with generative adversarial networks, arXiv preprint arXiv:1701.01081 (2017).
[9] Y. Li, Y. Zhang, Webpage Saliency Prediction with Two-Stage Generative Adversarial Networks, arXiv preprint arXiv:1805.11374 (2018).
[10] M. Assens, X. G. i Nieto, K. McGuinness, N. O'Connor, PathGAN: visual scanpath prediction with generative adversarial networks, in: Proc. of the European Conference on Computer Vision (ECCV'18), Munich, Germany, 2018, pp. 406–422.
[11] I. Gulrajani, F. Ahmed, M. Arjovsky, V. Dumoulin, A. Courville, Improved Training of Wasserstein GANs, 2017. arXiv:1704.00028.
[12] H. Jarodzka, K. Holmqvist, M. Nyström, A vector-based, multidimensional scanpath similarity measure, in: Proc. of the Symposium on Eye Tracking Research & Applications (ETRA'10), Austin, TX, USA, 2010, pp. 211–218. ACM.
[13] A. Borji, Saliency prediction in the deep learning era: Successes and limitations, IEEE Transactions on Pattern Analysis and Machine Intelligence (2019) 679–700. IEEE.

Traffic Density Estimation via Unsupervised Domain Adaptation

(Discussion Paper)

Luca Ciampi[1], Carlos Santiago[2], Joao Paulo Costeira[2], Claudio Gennaro[1] and Giuseppe Amato[1]

[1]Institute of Information Science and Technologies - National Research Council - Pisa, Italy
[2]Instituto Superior Técnico (LARSyS/IST) - Lisbon, Portugal

Abstract

Monitoring traffic flows in cities is crucial to improve urban mobility, and images are the best sensing modality to perceive and assess the flow of vehicles in large areas. However, current machine learning-based technologies using images hinge on large quantities of annotated data, preventing their scalability to city-scale as new cameras are added to the system. We propose a new methodology to design image-based vehicle density estimators with few labeled data via an unsupervised domain adaptation technique.

Keywords

Unsupervised Domain Adaptation, Synthetic Datasets, Deep Learning, Counting Vehicles,

1. Introduction

Traffic problems are constantly increasing, and tomorrow's cities can only be smart if they enable smart mobility. This concept is becoming more critical since traffic congestion caused by the increasing number of people using different road infrastructures to travel anywhere is imposing extra costs that make all activities more expensive and put a damper on the development.

Smart mobility applications such as smart parking and road traffic management are nowadays widely employed worldwide, making our cities more livable and bringing benefits to the cities, a better quality of our life, reducing costs, and improving energy usage.

Images are probably the best sensing modality to perceive and assess the flow of vehicles in large areas. Like no other sensing mechanism, networks of city cameras can observe such large dimensions and simultaneously provide visual data to AI systems to extract relevant information from this deluge of data.

In this work, we propose a CNN-based system that can estimate traffic density and count the vehicles present in urban scenes directly on-board smart city cameras, analyzing the images captured by themselves.

SEBD 2021: The 29th Italian Symposium on Advanced Database Systems, September 5-9, 2021, Pizzo Calabro (VV), Italy
luca.ciampi@isti.cnr.it (L. Ciampi)
0000-0002-6985-0439 (L. Ciampi); 0000-0002-4737-0020 (C. Santiago); 0000-0001-6769-2935 (J. P. Costeira); 0000-0002-3715-149X (C. Gennaro); 0000-0003-0171-4315 (G. Amato)

CEUR Workshop Proceedings (CEUR-WS.org)

Figure 1: Example of an image with the bounding box annotations (left) and the corresponding density map that sums to the counting value (right).

Current systems address the counting problem as a supervised learning process. They fall into two main classes of methods: a) detection-based approaches [1][2][3] that try to identify and localize single instances of objects in the image and b) density-based techniques that rely on regression techniques to estimate a density map from the image, and where the final count is given by summing all pixel values [4]. Figure 1 illustrates the mapping of such regression. Concerning vehicle counting in urban spaces, where images are of low resolution, and most objects are partially occluded, density-based methods have a clear advantage on detection methods [5][6].

However, since this class of approaches requires pixel-level ground truth for supervised learning, they may not generalize well to unseen images, especially when there is a large *domain gap* between the training (*source*) and the test (*target*) sets, such as different camera perspectives, weather, or illumination. The direct transfer of the learned features between different domains does not work very well because the distributions are different. Thus, a model trained on the source domain usually experiences a drastic drop in performance when applied to the target domain. This problem is commonly referred to as *Domain Shift* [7], and it severely hampers the application of counting methods to very large-scale scenarios since annotating images for all the possible cases is unfeasible.

To mitigate this problem, we introduce a methodology that performs *Unsupervised Domain Adaptation* (UDA) among different scenarios. UDA techniques address the domain shift taking a source labeled dataset and a target *unlabeled* one. The challenge here is to automatically infer some knowledge from the target data to reduce the gap between the two domains. Specifically, in this work, we propose an end-to-end CNN-based UDA algorithm for traffic density estimation and counting, based on adversarial learning performed directly on the generated density maps, i.e., in the *output space*, given that in this specific case, the output space contains valuable information such as scene layout and context. We focus on vehicle counting, but the approach is suitable for counting any other types of objects.

Another contribution of this work is represented by the creation of two new per-pixel annotated datasets made available to the scientific community. One of the two novel datasets is a collection of synthetic images taken from a photo-realistic video game where the labels are automatically assigned while interacting with the API of the graphical engine. We conducted our experiments considering these two datasets and another collection of images already present in the literature, validating our approach over different types of domain shifts: i) the *Camera2Camera* domain shift, where the source images belong to some specific cameras, and the target ones are instead taken from different perspectives and context; ii) the *Day2Night* domain shift, where the source domain is represented by images taken during the day and the target domain by pictures taken at night; iii) the *Synthetic2Real* domain shift, where source images are collected using a video game and automatically annotated, while the target ones are real urban pictures. Experiments show a significant improvement compared to the performance of the model without domain adaptation.

2. The Datasets

This section describes the datasets exploited in this work, focusing mainly on the two novel datasets created on purpose in this work.

2.1. NDISPark Dataset

The *NDISPark - Night and Day Instance Segmented Park* dataset is a small, manually annotated dataset for counting cars in parking lots, consisting of about 250 images. This dataset is challenging and describes the most difficult situations that can be found in a real scenario: seven different cameras capture the images under various weather conditions and angles of view. Furthermore, it is worth noting that pictures are taken during the day and the night, showing utterly different light conditions. The images are precisely annotated with *instance* segmentation labels, and this allowed us to generate accurate ground truth density maps usable for the counting task.

2.2. GTA Dataset

The *GTA - Grand Traffic Auto* dataset is a vast collection of about 15,000 *synthetic* images of urban traffic scenes collected from the highly photo-realistic video game *GTA V - Grand Theft Auto V*. We deploy a framework that can *automatically* and precisely annotate the vehicles present in the scene with per-pixel annotations. To the best of our knowledge, it is the first *instance* segmentation synthetic dataset of city traffic scenarios. Figure 2 shows some examples of images belonging to this dataset together with the annotations.

2.2.1. WebCamT Dataset

The *WebCamT* dataset is a collection of traffic scenes recorded using city-cameras introduced by [6]. It is particularly challenging for analysis due to the low-resolution (352×240), high occlusion, and large perspective. We considered images belonging to different cameras and consequently having different views.

3. Proposed Method

Our method relies on a CNN model trained end-to-end with adversarial learning in the output space (i.e., the density maps), which contains rich information such as scene layout and context.

Figure 2: Some examples of images of our *Grand Traffic Auto* dataset, together with the *automatically* generated instance segmentation annotations.

The peculiarity of our adversarial learning scheme is that it forces the predicted density maps in the target domain to have local similarities with the ones in the source domain.

Figure 3 depicts the proposed framework consisting of two modules: 1) a CNN that predicts traffic density maps, from which we estimate the number of vehicles in the scene, and 2) a discriminator that identifies whether a density map (received by the density map estimator) was generated from an image of the source domain or the target domain.

In the training phase, the density map predictor learns to map images to densities based on annotated data from the source domain. At the same time, it learns to predict realistic density maps for the target domain by trying to fool the discriminator with an adversarial loss. The discriminator's output is a pixel-wise classification of a low-resolution map, as illustrated in Figure 3, where each pixel corresponds to a small region in the density map. Consequently, the output space is forced to be locally similar for both the source and target domains. In the inference phase, the discriminator is discarded, and only the density map predictor is used for the target images. We describe each module and how it is trained in the following subsections.

3.1. Density Estimation Network

We formulate the counting task as a density map estimation problem [4]. The density (intensity) of each pixel in the map depends on its proximity to a vehicle centroid and the size of the vehicle in the image so that each vehicle contributes with a total value of 1 to the map. Therefore, it provides statistical information about the vehicles' location and allows the counting to be estimated by summing of all density values.

This task is performed by a CNN-based model [5], whose goal is to automatically determine the vehicle density map associated with a given input image. Formally, the density map estimator, $\Psi : \mathcal{R}^{\mathcal{C}\times\mathcal{H}\times\mathcal{W}} \mapsto \mathcal{R}^{\mathcal{H}\times\mathcal{W}}$, transforms a $\mathcal{W} \times \mathcal{H}$ input image $\mathcal{I}$ with $\mathcal{C}$ channels, into a density map, $D = \Psi(\mathcal{I}) \in \mathcal{R}^{\mathcal{H}\times\mathcal{W}}$.

3.2. Discriminator Network

The discriminator network, denoted by Θ, also consists of a CNN model. It takes as input the density map, D, estimated by the network Ψ. Its output is a lower resolution probability

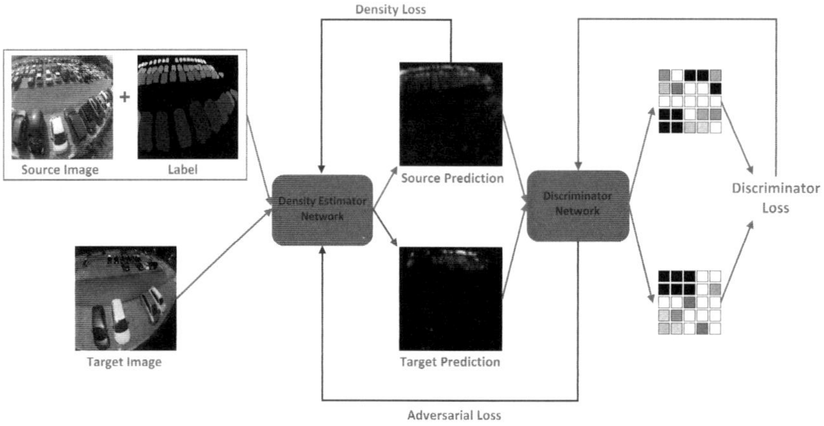

Figure 3: Algorithm overview. Given $C \times H \times W$ images from source and target domains, we pass them through the density map estimation network to obtain output predictions. A density loss is computed for source predictions based on the ground truth. In order to improve target predictions, a discriminator is used to locally classify whether a density map belongs to the source or target domain. Then, an adversarial loss is computed on the target prediction and is back-propagated to the density map estimation and counting network.

map where each pixel represents the probability that the corresponding region (from the input density map) comes either from the source or the target domain. The goal of the discriminator is to learn to distinguish between density maps belonging to source or target domains. Through an adversarial loss, this discriminator will, in turn, force the density estimator to provide density maps with similar distributions in both domains. In other words, the target domain density maps have to look realistic, even though the network Ψ was not trained with an annotated training set from that domain.

3.3. Domain Adaptation Learning

The proposed framework is trained based on an alternate optimization of the density estimation network, Ψ, and the discriminator network, Θ. Regarding the former, the training process relies on two components: 1) density estimation using pairs of images and ground truth density maps, which we assume are only available in the source domain; and 2) adversarial training, which aims to make the discriminator fail to distinguish between the source and target domains. As for the latter, images from both domains are used to train the discriminator on correctly classifying each pixel of the probability map as either source or target.

To implement the above training procedure, we use two loss functions: one is employed in the first step of the algorithm to train network Ψ, and the other is used in the second step to train the discriminator Θ. These loss functions are detailed next.

Network Ψ Training. We formulate the loss function for Ψ as the sum of two main components:

$$\mathcal{L}(\mathcal{I}^{\mathcal{S}}, \mathcal{I}^{\mathcal{T}}) = \mathcal{L}_{density}(\mathcal{I}^{\mathcal{S}}) + \lambda_{adv}\mathcal{L}_{adv}(\mathcal{I}^{\mathcal{T}}), \quad (1)$$

where $\mathcal{L}_{density}$ is the loss computed using ground truth annotations available in the source domain, while $\mathcal{L}_{adv}$ is the adversarial loss that is responsible for making the distribution of the target and the source domain closer to each other. In particular, we define the density loss $\mathcal{L}_{density}$ as the mean square error between the predicted and ground truth density maps, i.e. $\mathcal{L}_{density} = MSE(D^{\mathcal{S}}, D^{\mathcal{S}\_\mathcal{GT}})$.

To compute the adversarial loss $\mathcal{L}_{adv}$, we first forward the images belonging to the target domain through network Ψ, to generate the predicted density maps $D^{\mathcal{T}}$. Then, we forward $D^{\mathcal{T}}$ through network Θ, to generate the probability map $P = \Theta(\Psi(\mathcal{I}^{\mathcal{T}})) \in [0,1]^{H' \times W'}$, where $H' < H$ and $W' < W$. The adversarial loss is given by

$$\mathcal{L}_{adv}(\mathcal{I}^{\mathcal{T}}) = -\sum_{h,w} \log(P_{h,w}), \quad (2)$$

where the subscript h, w denotes a pixel in P. This loss makes the distribution of $D^{\mathcal{T}}$ closer to $D^{\mathcal{S}}$ by forcing Ψ to fool the discriminator, through the maximization of the probability of $D^{\mathcal{T}}$ being locally classified as belonging to the source domain.

Network Θ Training. Given an image $\mathcal{I}$ and the corresponding predicted density map D, we feed D as input to the fully-convolutional discriminator Θ to obtain the probability map P. The discriminator is trained by comparing P with the ground truth label map $Y \in \{0,1\}^{H' \times W'}$ using a pixel-wise binary cross-entropy loss

$$\mathcal{L}_{disc}(\mathcal{I}) = -\sum_{h,w} (1 - Y_{h,w}) \log(1 - P_{h,w}) + Y_{h,w} log(P_{h,w}), \quad (3)$$

where $Y_{h,w} = 0 \;\; \forall \; h, w$ if $\mathcal{I}$ is taken from the target domain and $Y_{h,w} = 1$ otherwise.

4. Experimental Results

We validate the proposed UDA method for density estimation and counting of traffic scenes under different settings. First, we employ the *NDISPark* dataset, and we test the *Day2Night* domain shift considering pictures taken during the day as the source domain, while night images for the target domain. Then, we utilize the *WebCamT* dataset to take into account the *Camera2Camera* performance gap, tackling the domain shift that takes place when we consider a camera different from the ones used during the training phase. Finally, we use the *GTA* dataset to assess the *Synthetic2Real* domain difference, training the algorithm using the synthetic images, and then test it on real data considering the *WebCamT* dataset again.

For all the experiments, we base the evaluation of the models on three metrics widely used for the counting task: (i) Mean Absolute Error (MAE) that measures the absolute count error of each image; (ii) Mean Squared Error (MSE) that instead quantifies the squared count error for each image; (iii) Average Relative Error (ARE), which measures the absolute count error divided by the true count. Note that, as a result of the squaring of each error, the MSE effectively penalizes large errors more heavily than small ones. Instead, the ARE is the only metric that

Table 1
Experimental results obtained for the four considered domain shift in terms of MAE, MSE and ARE. We achieved performance improvements for all the scenarios, considering all the three metrics.

	MAE	MSE	ARE
Day2Night Domain Shift - NDISPark Dataset			
Baseline - CSRNet [5]	3.95	27.45	0.43
Our Approach	**3.49**	**20.90**	**0.39**
Camera2Camera Domain Shift - WebCamT Dataset [6]			
Baseline - CSRNet [5]	3.24	16.83	0.21
Our Approach	**2.86**	**13.03**	**0.19**
Synthetic2Real Domain Shift - GTA Dataset			
Baseline - CSRNet [5]	4.10	25.83	0.28
Our Approach	**3.88**	**23.80**	**0.27**

considers the relation of the error and the total number of vehicles present for each image. Results are summarized in Table 1. We achieved better results compared to the basic model in all the considered scenarios and considering all the three metrics.

5. Conclusions

In this article, we tackled the problem of determining the density and the number of objects present in large sets of images. Building on a CNN-based density estimator, the proposed methodology can generalize to new data sources for which there are no annotations available. We achieved this generalization by exploiting an Unsupervised Domain Adaptation strategy, whereby a discriminator attached to the output forces similar density distribution in the target and source domains. Experiments show a significant improvement relative to the performance of the model without domain adaptation. To the best of our knowledge, we are the first to introduce a UDA scheme for counting to reduce the gap between the source and the target domain without using additional labels. Given the conventional structure of the estimator, the improvement obtained by just monitoring the output entails a great capacity to generalize learned knowledge, thus suggesting the application of similar principles to the inner layers of the network.

Another contribution is represented by the creation of two new per-pixel annotated datasets made available to the scientific community. One of the two novel datasets is a synthetic dataset created from a photo-realistic video game. Here the labels are automatically assigned while interacting with the API of the graphical engine. Using this synthetic dataset, we demonstrated that it is possible to train a model with a precisely annotated and automatically generated synthetic dataset and perform UDA toward a real-world scenario, obtaining very good performance *without* using additional manual annotations.

In our view, this work's outcome opens new perspectives to deal with the scalability of learning methods for large physical systems with scarce supervisory resources.

Acknowledgments

This work was partially supported by H2020 project AI4EU under GA 825619.

References

[1] G. Amato, L. Ciampi, F. Falchi, C. Gennaro, Counting vehicles with deep learning in onboard UAV imagery, in: 2019 IEEE Symposium on Computers and Communications, ISCC 2019, Barcelona, Spain, June 29 - July 3, 2019, IEEE, 2019, pp. 1–6. URL: https://doi.org/10.1109/ISCC47284.2019.8969620. doi:10.1109/ISCC47284.2019.8969620.

[2] L. Ciampi, G. Amato, F. Falchi, C. Gennaro, F. Rabitti, Counting vehicles with cameras, in: S. Bergamaschi, T. D. Noia, A. Maurino (Eds.), Proceedings of the 26th Italian Symposium on Advanced Database Systems, Castellaneta Marina (Taranto), Italy, June 24-27, 2018, volume 2161 of *CEUR Workshop Proceedings*, CEUR-WS.org, 2018, pp. 1–8. URL: http://ceur-ws.org/Vol-2161/paper12.pdf.

[3] G. Amato, P. Bolettieri, D. Moroni, F. Carrara, L. Ciampi, G. Pieri, C. Gennaro, G. R. Leone, C. Vairo, A wireless smart camera network for parking monitoring, in: IEEE Globecom Workshops, GC Wkshps 2018, Abu Dhabi, United Arab Emirates, December 9-13, 2018, IEEE, 2018, pp. 1–6. URL: https://doi.org/10.1109/GLOCOMW.2018.8644226. doi:10.1109/GLOCOMW.2018.8644226.

[4] V. S. Lempitsky, A. Zisserman, Learning to count objects in images, in: J. D. Lafferty, C. K. I. Williams, J. Shawe-Taylor, R. S. Zemel, A. Culotta (Eds.), Advances in Neural Information Processing Systems 23: 24th Annual Conference on Neural Information Processing Systems 2010. Proceedings of a meeting held 6-9 December 2010, Vancouver, British Columbia, Canada, Curran Associates, Inc., 2010, pp. 1324–1332. URL: https://proceedings.neurips.cc/paper/2010/hash/fe73f687e5bc5280214e0486b273a5f9-Abstract.html.

[5] Y. Li, X. Zhang, D. Chen, Csrnet: Dilated convolutional neural networks for understanding the highly congested scenes, in: 2018 IEEE Conference on Computer Vision and Pattern Recognition, CVPR 2018, Salt Lake City, UT, USA, June 18-22, 2018, IEEE Computer Society, 2018, pp. 1091–1100. URL: http://openaccess.thecvf.com/content_cvpr_2018/html/Li_CSRNet_Dilated_Convolutional_CVPR_2018_paper.html. doi:10.1109/CVPR.2018.00120.

[6] S. Zhang, G. Wu, J. P. Costeira, J. M. F. Moura, Understanding traffic density from large-scale web camera data, in: 2017 IEEE Conference on Computer Vision and Pattern Recognition, CVPR 2017, Honolulu, HI, USA, July 21-26, 2017, IEEE Computer Society, 2017, pp. 4264–4273. URL: http://doi.ieeecomputersociety.org/10.1109/CVPR.2017.454. doi:10.1109/CVPR.2017.454.

[7] A. Torralba, A. A. Efros, Unbiased look at dataset bias, in: The 24th IEEE Conference on Computer Vision and Pattern Recognition, CVPR 2011, Colorado Springs, CO, USA, 20-25 June 2011, IEEE Computer Society, 2011, pp. 1521–1528. URL: https://doi.org/10.1109/CVPR.2011.5995347. doi:10.1109/CVPR.2011.5995347.

Unbiasing Collaborative Filtering for Popularity-Aware Recommendation

(Discussion Paper)

Luciano Caroprese[1], Giuseppe Manco[1], Marco Minici[1], Francesco Sergio Pisani[1] and Ettore Ritacco[1]

[1]*ICAR-CNR, Via Bucci, 8-9c, Rende (Italy)*

Abstract

We analyze the behavior of recommender systems relative to the popularity of the items to recommend. Our findings show that most popular ranking-based recommenders are biased towards popular items, thus affecting the quality of recommendation. Based on these observations, we propose a new deep learning architecture with an improved learning strategy that significantly improves the performance of such recommenders on low-popular items. The proposed technique is based on two main aspects: resampling of negatives and ensembling of multiple instances of the algorithm. Experimental results on traditional benchmark datasets show that the proposed approach substantially improves the recommendation ability by balancing accurate contributions almost independently from the popularity of the items to recommend.

Keywords

Recommender Systems, Collaborative Filtering, Deep Learning, Big Data

1. Introduction

The massive amount of information available to users in the form of digital catalogs and online services allows users to access and consume online content, but at the same time it poses a choice paradox. Purchasing items on e-commerce sites, selecting movies on streaming platforms or connecting with other peers on social networks implies making choices among a huge amount of elements. Recommender Systems play a crucial role within this context since they provide users with a better experience through the recommendation of new content and data that users are likely to appreciate.

Recommendations can have a disruptive impact: if on one side, they assist users in their choices, on the other side they can influence the choices themselves. Indeed, Recommender systems can favor particular categories of items or particular brands over others, thus introducing a *bias* within the catalog [1]. A typical bias is intrinsic to the nature of recommendation. In systems involving interaction between significant amounts of users and items, we observe the presence of very few very popular items and many less popular others. This distribution follows the so-called *80-20 rule* that refers to the fact that 80% of users express preferences for only 20%

SEBD 2021: The 29th Italian Symposium on Advanced Database Systems, September 5-9, 2021, Pizzo Calabro (VV), Italy
luciano.caroprese@icar.cnr.it (L. Caroprese); giuseppe.manco@icar.cnr.it (G. Manco); marco.minici@icar.cnr.it (M. Minici); francescosergio.pisani@icar.cnr.it (F. S. Pisani); ettore.ritacco@icar.cnr.it (E. Ritacco)

of the available items. In practice, user preferences follow a *long tail* distribution. Recommender Systems based on collaborative filtering [2], who tend to characterize user preferences from interactions, are affected by a relevant problem: they tend to suggest very popular items and neglect less popular ones. This way, there is a reinforced effect because the most popular items will become more and more popular than the less known ones. This phenomenon is called *popularity bias*.

The quality of the recommendations is inevitably affected by the popularity bias, since most recommendations are prone to contain objects that the user will consider trivial and well known. By contrast, the capability of recommending items belonging to the long tail (i.e., less popular) can disclose new perspectives: niche items, little-known objects, hidden gems that satisfy the user's preferences can greatly improve user engagement, provided that the recommended items are consistent with user's taste.

The current literature has extensively studied the problems of fairness and bias [3, 4, 5] within recommender systems, with particular emphasis to popularity bias [6, 7, 8]. Notably, in [9], it is shown that unfair recommendations are concentrated on groups of users interested in long-tail and less popular items. In this paper we focus our attention on recommender sytems based on ranking [10, 11], which are extremely flexible and as a consequence particularly interesting to unbias. Typical approaches [12, 13] consider techniques to increase the representation of less popular items, by either post-processing techniques or constraining the recommendation score. Despite such recent efforts, unbiasing the recommendation from popular items is still an open problem.

In this paper we devise a ranking-based recommender system for implicit feedback (RVAE), based on a variational autoencoder architecture. The proposed model is a substantial extension of the MVAE model proposed in [14] and in fact it inherits its accuracy and computational efficiency. We analyze the behavior of RVAE and show that the model is characterized by the popularity bias problem. We then propose an experimental study of specific techniques to overcome it. The proposed technique is based on two main concepts: resampling/reweighting items and ensembling of multiple instances of the algorithm. Our experiments show that these simple strategies allow to unbias the algorithm and hence provide more effective recommendations.

2. Basic Framework

We start by setting the notation that we shall use throughout the paper. In the context of collaborative filtering, $u \in U = \{1, \dots, M\}$ indexes a user and $i, j \in I = \{1, \dots, N\}$ index items for which the user can express a preference. We model implicit feedback, thus assuming a preference matrix $\mathbf{X} \in \{0, 1\}^{M \times N}$, so that $x_{u,i} = 1$ whenever user u expressed a preference for item i, and $x_{u,i} = 0$ otherwise. Also, $\mathbf{x}_u$ is the (binary) row indexed at u, representing all the item preferences for user u. Given $\mathbf{x}_u$, we define $I_u = \{i \in I | x_{u,i} = 1\}$ (with $N_u = |I_u|$). The preference matrix induces a natural ordering between items: $i \prec_u j$ has the meaning that u prefers i to j, i.e. $x_{u,i} > x_{u,j}$ in the rating matrix. Our objective is to devise a model for such an ordering.

Preference Modeling. We consider a general framework where preferences are modeled as the effect of latent factors ultimately characterizing users and/or items. We shall consider two basic instantiations of this general idea, and will provide a unified framework.

The first situation we consider is the Multinomial Variational Autoencoder (MVAE) framework proposed in [14]. Within this framework, for a given user u the related $\mathbf{x}_u$ is modeled as the effect of a multinomial distribution governed by a prior $\mathbf{z}$, i.e.

$$\mathbf{x}_u \sim Discrete\,(\pi(\mathbf{z}))$$
$$\pi(\mathbf{z}) \propto \exp\left\{f_\phi(\mathbf{z})\right\}$$

Here, $f_\phi(\cdot)$ represents a neural network parameterized by ϕ. The latent variable $\mathbf{z}$ is modeled by a prior $P(\mathbf{z})$ (typically a gaussian distribution). Thus, the probability of preferences for a given user can be expressed as

$$P(\mathbf{x}_u) = \int P(\mathbf{x}_u|\mathbf{z})P(\mathbf{z})\;\mathrm{d}\mathbf{z}$$

Due to the intractability of the above integral, [15] devise a variational approach based on a proposal $Q(\mathbf{z}|\mathbf{x}_u)$ that approximates the posterior distribution. Again, Q is modeled as a gaussian distribution

$$Q(\mathbf{z}|\mathbf{x}_u) = \mathcal{N}(\mathbf{z}; \boldsymbol{\mu}_u, \boldsymbol{\sigma}_u),$$

where $\boldsymbol{\mu}_u, \boldsymbol{\sigma}_u = g_\theta(\mathbf{x}_u)$ and g_θ is a neural network parameterized by θ. By exploiting the inequality

$$\log P(\mathbf{x}_u) \geq \mathbb{E}_{\mathbf{z}\sim Q(\cdot|\mathbf{x}_u)}\left[\log P(\mathbf{x}_u|\mathbf{z}) - P(\mathbf{z})\right]$$

we can finally learn the ϕ, θ parameters by optimizing the loss

$$\ell_{MVAE}(\phi,\theta) = \sum_u \left\{\mathbb{E}_{\mathbf{z}\sim Q_\theta(\cdot|\mathbf{x}_u)}\left[\log P_\phi(\mathbf{x}_u|\mathbf{z})\right] - \mathbb{KL}[Q_\theta(\mathbf{z}|\mathbf{x}_u)\|P(\mathbf{z})]\right\}$$

The overall framework is based hence on regularized encoder-decoder scheme, where $Q_\theta(\mathbf{z}|\mathbf{x}_u)$ represents the encoder, $P_\theta(\mathbf{x}_u|\mathbf{z})$ represents the decoder and the term $\mathbb{E}_{\mathbf{z}\sim Q_\theta(\cdot|\mathbf{x}_u)}\left[P(\mathbf{z})\right]$ acts as a regularizer. In the training phase, for each u a latent variable $\mathbf{z} \sim Q_\theta(\cdot|\mathbf{x}_u)$ is devised. Next, $\mathbf{z}$ is exploited to devise the probability $P_\phi(\mathbf{x}_u|\mathbf{z})$. Users with low probability are penalized within the loss and the network parameters can be updated accordingly.

Prediction for new items is accomplished by resorting to the learned functions P_ϕ and Q_θ: given a (partial) user history $\mathbf{x}_u$, we compute $\mathbf{z} = \boldsymbol{\mu}_u$ and then devise the probabilities for the whole item set through $\pi(\mathbf{z})$. Unseen items can then be ranked according to their associated probabilities.

The second formulation we consider is inspired by the Bayesian Personalized Ranking (BPR) model introduced in [10]. The idea underlying this model is that a preference $i \prec_u j$ can be directly explained as closeness in a latent space where both items and users can be mapped. Mathematically this can be devised by computing a factorization rank $\mathbf{p}_u^T\mathbf{q}_i$ for each pair (u, i), and modeling preferences by means of a Bernoulli process:

$$i \prec_u j \sim Bernoulli(p)$$
$$p = \sigma\left(\mathbf{p}_u^T(\mathbf{q}_i - \mathbf{q}_j)\right)$$

where $\sigma(a) = (1 + e^{-a})^{-1}$ is the logistic function. The optimal embeddings **P** and **Q** can hence be obtained by opimizing the loss

$$\ell_{BPR}(\mathbf{P}, \mathbf{Q}) \approx \sum_u \sum_{\substack{i,j \\ i \prec_u j}} \log \sigma\left(\mathbf{p}_u^T(\mathbf{q}_i - \mathbf{q}_j)\right)$$

We combine the two frameworks by adapting the BPR loss to the MVAE model. In particular, instead of modeling $P(\mathbf{x}_u|\mathbf{z})$, we directly model $P(i \prec_u j|\mathbf{z})$ within a similar variational framework. In short, the current preferences are encoded within a latent variable $\mathbf{z}$ that is further exploited to decode all ranks:

$$\begin{aligned} i \prec_u j &\sim Bernoulli(p_{i,j}) \\ p_{i,j} &= \sigma(\zeta_i - \zeta_j) \\ \zeta &= f_\phi(\mathbf{z}) \end{aligned}$$

Here, ζ represents the output of a neural network parameterized by ϕ. For a given item i, the value ζ_i represents then the associated rank which can be used sort all preferences. The model can be obtained by optimizing the loss:

$$\ell_{RVAE}(\phi, \theta) = \sum_u \left\{ \mathbb{E}_{\mathbf{z} \sim Q_\theta(\cdot|\mathbf{x}_u)} \left[\sum_{\substack{i,j \\ i \prec_u j}} \log P_\phi(i \prec_u j|\mathbf{z}) \right] - \mathbb{KL}[Q_\theta(\mathbf{z}|\mathbf{x}_u) \| P(\mathbf{z})] \right\} \tag{1}$$

We call this model *Ranking Variational Autoencoder* (RVAE).

Learning by Negative Sampling. In the above formulation there are some details worth further discussion. When learning the RVAE model, optimizing the likelihood requires that all pairs of items are considered within Eq. (1). This is unrealistic with large item bases, and it is usually customary to only consider a subset $\mathscr{P}_u \subset \{(i, j)|i, j \in I; i \prec_u j\}$. The sampling of $\mathscr{D}_u$ is critical for determining the behavior of any predictive model; the most used approach in literature is to uniformly sample, for each user u and item i (called positive item), a fixed number of items $\{j_1, \dots j_n\} \subset I - I_u$ with the underlying assumption that $\forall k : i \prec_u j_k$. Thus, Eq. (1) can be rewritten as:

$$\ell_{RVAE}(\phi, \theta) = \sum_u \left\{ \mathbb{E}_{\mathbf{z} \sim Q_\theta(\cdot|\mathbf{x}_u)} \left[\sum_{(i,j) \in \mathscr{D}_u} \log P_\phi(i \prec_u j|\mathbf{z}) \right] - \mathbb{KL}[Q_\theta(\mathbf{z}|\mathbf{x}_u) \| P(\mathbf{z})] \right\} \tag{2}$$

This will be the basis loss upon which we develop our study next.

3. The Impact of Popularity

We start our analysis on the following popular benchmark datasets: i) **Movielens**, a time series dataset containing user-item ratings pairs along with the corresponding timestamp; ii) **Pinterest**, based on the social media that allows users to save or pin an image (item) to their board. The dataset denotes as 1 the pinned images for each user; iii) **CiteUlike**, a dataset obtained from the homonymous service which provides a digital catalog to save and share

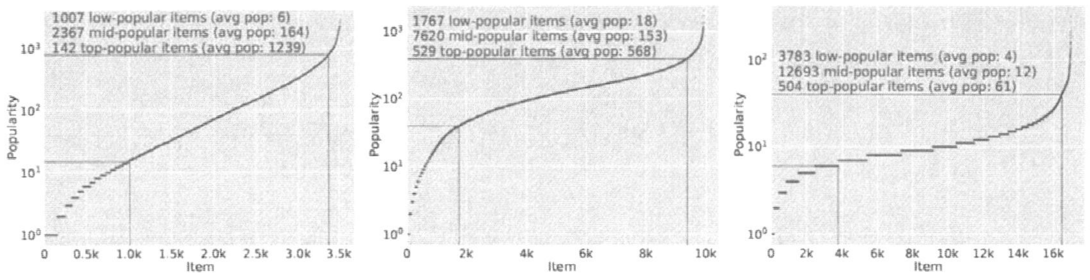

(a) ML1M (b) Pinterest (c) CiteUlike

Figure 1: Item popularity distributions.

academic papers. Within fig. 1 we plot all the items within the datasets, by increasing popularity. For each dataset we identify three classes: low, mid and high popular items.

We then study the behavior of the RVAE model with respect to the popularity classes defined. To do so, we adopt the following protocol. For each dataset, 70% of users are randomly sampled with all user's items. Each such user is associated with $\mathbf{x}_u$ and a set $\mathcal{D}_u$ of positive/negative item pairs. In particular, we consider all positive items within $\mathbf{x}_u$, and for each positive item i we sample $n = 4$ negative items. The remaining 30% users are uniformly split into validation and test. In particular, for each user u we consider a random subset $P_u \subset I_u$ representing the 30% of the positive items, and N_u represents a subset of 100 negative items sampled from $I - I_u$. The vector $\mathbf{x}_u$ is masked to remove all elements in P_u. We then feed the masked $\mathbf{x}_u$ to obtain the score vector $\boldsymbol{\zeta}_u$. Now, for a given cutoff value c, let us consider the $c - 1$ negative items for u for which RVAE gives the highest score, and, among them the item j having the minimum score. There is an hit with cutoff c, for the user u and the item $i \in P_u$, if $\zeta_{u,i} \geq \zeta_{u,j}$. Let H_u^c the number of hits for the user u with cutoff c. We define the *Hit-Rate at c* on T as $HR@c = \frac{\sum_{u \in T} H_u^c}{\sum_{u \in U} |P_u|}$. We can trivially specialize this definition for items within the low, medium and high popularity, by considering only items in P_u that belong to the specific class. The results of the evaluation are summarized in table 1a. We can see that the model suffers mainly on low-popular items. As a matter of fact, the overexposure of popular items is predominant and the model learn to predict essentially those items. The fact is that popular items are easy to predict. However, it is in the mid and especially on low popular items that the most interesting predictions can take place: niche items are difficult to discover by an end user and hence their accurate suggestions can greatly improve user engagement. The research question is hence: how can we boost the model to improve the performance on low-popular items?

4. Unbiased Recommendation

In a simple experiment, we retrain the model by only considering pairs $(i, j) \in \mathcal{D}_u$ such that i is in the low popular class. We call this model $RVAE^L$. Compared to the results in table 1a, the results for this restricted model (shown in table 1b) show that if attention is placed on low popular items, their response on prediction accuracy can be improved. Similar results can be observed for the mid popular items. Thus, in order to unbias the model we need to rebalance

Dataset	*HR@1*				*HR@5*				*HR@10*			
	Global	Low	Med	High	Global	Low	Med	High	Global	Low	Med	High
Movielens	0.2510	**0.00**	0.16	0.43	0.5853	**0.01**	0.47	0.83	0.7443	**0.05**	0.65	0.94
Pinterest	0.2731	**0.13**	0.23	0.46	0.6992	**0.46**	0.66	0.86	0.8764	**0.65**	0.86	0.95
CiteULike	0.2875	**0.07**	0.22	0.67	0.6021	**0.29**	0.57	0.90	0.7638	**0.48**	0.75	0.95

(a) RVAE

Dataset	*HR@1*		*HR@5*		*HR@10*	
	Global	Low	Global	Low	Global	Low
Movielens	0.0012	**0.15**	0.0042	**0.50**	0.0063	**0.74**
Pinterest	0.0089	**0.43**	0.0166	**0.81**	0.0192	**0.93**
CiteULike	0.0254	**0.32**	0.0561	**0.71**	0.0703	**0.89**

(b) $RVAE^L$

Table 1
Predictive accuracy.

the contribution on low (and mid) popular items with regards to the high popular ones. To achieve this goal, we study three different strategies.

The first strategy consists in weighting, for each pair $(i, j) \in \mathscr{D}_u$, the contribution to the loss with a factor inversely proportional to the popularity of the item i:

$$w_i = \frac{\gamma\left(1+e^{\alpha(f_i-\beta-1)}\right)^{-1}+1}{\gamma+1}$$

Here, f_i represents the number of occurrences of i, and α, β, γ the parameters representing the steep, center and scale of the decay of high popular items. We experiment with $\alpha = 0.01$, β representing the average frequency of mid-popular items and $\gamma = 100$ and call this variant $RVAE^W$. The above strategy has the advantage of reweighing the contributions of low and mid popular items with respect to high popular ones: the ratio between the most popular and the lowest popular is approximately $1/\gamma$. However, this weighting scheme has a main disadvantage. The weight is relative to a positive item i, but it is associated with pairs $(i, j) \in P_u$. That is, besides weighting the contribution of i, this scheme also overexposes (or dually underexposes) the contribution of the negative item j. To avoid this, an alternative strategy consists in changing the sampling scheme that produces $\mathscr{D}_u$. In practice, rather than uniformly sampling, for each positive item, a fixed number n of negatives items, we can apply an inversely stratified sampling where n_i negatives are sampled, with n_i being inversely proportional to the popularity of the item: $n_i = n \cdot \left\lceil \frac{\max(\mathbf{f})}{f_i} \right\rceil$.

The ratio with the above formula is to provide the same visibility to each positive item in the loss function. Thus, the most popular item will be associated with exactly n pairs. By contrast, low and mid popular items will be overexposed in the comparison. We call this variant $RVAE^S$.

The third strategy consists in combining the baseline *RVAE* model with $RVAE^L$. For a user u, let ζ^B the the score vector produced by *RVAE*, and ζ^L the score produced by $RVAE^L$. We define $RVAE^E$ and the model that produces the score ζ^E defined as $\zeta^E = Softmax(\zeta^B) + \delta\mathbf{m} \cdot Softmax(\zeta^L)$.

The vector $\mathbf{m}$ masks all items but the low popular. The scores are normalized (via the *Softmax* function) to make the two models comparable. Finally, δ is a weight aimed at tuning the boost for the low popular items, as devised by $RVAE^L$. We experimentally found an optimal tuning with $\delta = 0.4$.

		HR@1				HR@5				HR@10			
		Global	Low	Med	High	Global	Low	Med	High	Global	Low	Med	High
Movielens	*RVAE*	**0.2510**	0.00	**0.16**	**0.43**	**0.5853**	0.01	**0.47**	**0.83**	**0.7443**	0.05	**0.65**	**0.94**
	$RVAE^W$	0.0854	0.01	0.13	0.01	0.2958	0.07	0.40	0.10	0.4661	0.11	0.59	0.23
	$RVAE^S$	0.1245	**0.06**	0.12	0.13	0.3875	0.16	0.38	0.40	0.5825	0.28	0.57	0.61
	$RVAE^E$	0.2466	0.05	**0.16**	0.42	0.5506	**0.22**	0.43	0.80	0.6965	**0.37**	0.59	0.91
Pinterest	*RVAE*	**0.2731**	0.13	**0.23**	**0.46**	**0.6992**	0.46	**0.66**	**0.86**	**0.8764**	0.65	**0.86**	**0.95**
	$RVAE^W$	0.2196	**0.29**	**0.23**	0.18	0.6544	**0.68**	**0.66**	0.64	0.8592	**0.80**	**0.86**	0.87
	$RVAE^S$	0.2482	0.11	**0.23**	0.35	0.6770	0.45	0.65	0.80	0.8664	0.64	**0.86**	0.93
	$RVAE^E$	0.2726	0.26	0.22	**0.46**	0.6954	0.63	0.65	**0.86**	0.8620	**0.80**	0.84	0.94
CiteUlike	*RVAE*	0.2875	0.07	0.22	**0.67**	0.6021	0.29	0.57	**0.90**	0.7638	0.48	0.75	**0.95**
	$RVAE^W$	0.2711	0.09	0.25	0.46	0.6156	0.37	0.61	0.76	0.7698	0.55	0.77	0.87
	$RVAE^S$	**0.3890**	**0.32**	**0.39**	0.43	**0.7264**	**0.61**	**0.73**	0.76	**0.8399**	**0.73**	**0.84**	0.90
	$RVAE^E$	0.2805	0.16	0.21	0.66	0.5634	0.50	0.50	0.87	0.6941	0.71	0.64	0.92

Table 2
Comparative analysis.

Table 2 summarizes the results of the evaluation. We see that, in general, all the strategies considerably improve the response of the model to the low popular items. However, $RVAE^W$ has a low response on the high popular items. By contrast, $RVAE^S$ succeeds in boosting performance on both the low popular and the mid popular items. Overall, the ensemble $RVAE^E$ provides the best response, by boosting low popular items without substantially degrading over the other classes.

5. Conclusions

The approach proposed in this paper is a preliminary study: We introduce a Ranking collaborative filtering algorithm (RVAE) and study how the algorithm is affected by popularity bias. Next, we show how simple techniques based on reweighting/resampling and/or ensembling can recalibrate the recommendations. There are several aspects that are worth further investigation. First of all, both the weighting and the inverse stratified sampling schemes are based on hyperparameters that need to be carefully tuned. Also, the ensemble strategies are simple and more complex schemes that also take into account other model instantiations can be studied. We reserve the attention to these challenges in a future work.

References

[1] V. Tsintzou, E. Pitoura, P. Tsaparas, Bias disparity in recommendation systems, CoRR abs/1811.01461 (2018). URL: http://arxiv.org/abs/1811.01461.

[2] C. C. Aggarwal, Recommender Systems, Springer, 2016.

[3] B. Friedman, H. Nissenbaum, Bias in computer systems, ACM Trans. Inf. Syst. 14 (1996) 330–347.

[4] Z. Zhu, X. Hu, J. Caverlee, Fairness-aware tensor-based recommendation, in: ACM International Conference on Information and Knowledge Management, CIKM '18, 2018, p. 1153–1162.

[5] Y. Deldjoo, V. W. Anelli, H. Zamani, A. Bellogin, T. Di Noia, A flexible framework for evaluating user and item fairness in recommender systems, User Modeling and User-Adapted Interaction (2021).
[6] O. Celma, P. Cano, From hits to niches?: Or how popular artists can bias music recommendation and discovery, in: 2nd KDD Workshop on Large-Scale Recommender Systems and the Netflix Prize Competition, 2008.
[7] H. Steck, Item popularity and recommendation accuracy, in: Proceedings of the Fifth ACM Conference on Recommender Systems, RecSys '11, 2011, p. 125–132.
[8] R. Borges, K. Stefanidis, On measuring popularity bias in collaborative filtering data, in: EDBT Workshop on BigVis 2020: Big Data Visual Exploration and Analytics, 2020.
[9] H. Abdollahpouri, M. Mansoury, R. Burke, B. Mobasher, The unfairness of popularity bias in recommendation, CoRR abs/1907.13286 (2019). URL: http://arxiv.org/abs/1907.13286.
[10] S. Rendle, C. Freudenthaler, Z. Gantner, L. Schmidt-Thieme, Bpr: Bayesian personalized ranking from implicit feedback, in: Conf. on Uncertainty in Artificial Intelligence, UAI '09, 2009, pp. 452–461.
[11] T. Ebesu, B. Shen, Y. Fang, Collaborative memory network for recommendation systems, in: ACM SIGIR Conference on Research and Development in Information Retrieval, SIGIR '18, 2018.
[12] Z. Zhu, J. Wang, J. Caverlee, Measuring and mitigating item under-recommendation bias in personalized ranking systems, in: ACM SIGIR Conference on Research and Development in Information Retrieval, SIGIR '20, 2020, p. 449–458.
[13] H. Abdollahpouri, R. Burke, B. Mobasher, Managing popularity bias in recommender systems with personalized re-ranking, CoRR abs/1901.07555 (2019). URL: http://arxiv.org/abs/1901.07555.
[14] D. Liang, R. G. Krishnan, M. Hoffman, T. Jebara, Variational autoencoders for collaborative filtering, in: ACM Conf, on World Wide Web, WWW '18, 2018, pp. 689–698.
[15] D. P. Kingma, M. Welling, Auto-encoding variational bayes, in: 2nd International Conference on Learning Representations, ICLR'14, 2014. arXiv:http://arxiv.org/abs/1312.6114v10.

RECKONition: a NLP-based system for Industrial Accidents at Work Prevention

(Discussion Paper)

Patrizia Agnello[1], Silvia Maria Ansaldi[1], Emilia Lenzi[2], Alessio Mongelluzzo[2] and Manuel Roveri[2]

[1]*INAIL - Dipartimento Innovazioni Tecnologiche*

[2]*Politecnico di Milano - Dipartimento di Elettronica, Informazione e Bioingegneria*

Abstract

Extracting patterns and useful information from Natural Language datasets is a challenging task, especially when dealing with data written in a language different from English, like Italian. Machine and Deep Learning, together with Natural Language Processing (NLP) techniques have widely spread and improved lately, providing a plethora of useful methods to address both Supervised and Unsupervised problems on textual information. We propose RECKONition, a NLP-based system for Industrial Accidents at Work Prevention. RECKONition, which is meant to provide Natural Language Understanding, Clustering and Inference, is the result of a joint partnership with the Italian National Institute for Insurance against Accidents at Work (INAIL). The obtained results showed the ability to process textual data written in Italian describing industrial accidents dynamics and consequences.

Keywords

Workplace Safety, Industry 4.0, Natural Language Processing.

1. Introduction

Despite the ever-growing awareness and the advances in the technology and the procedure, the problem of accidents at work represents a relevant issue from both the social and economic point of view. In more detail, accidents at work refer to damages to the health of the worker induced by accidents correlated with the working activities. Unfortunately, such accidents can result into serious damages, such as temporary or permanent reduction or loss of working capacity, or even death. In Italy, this issue is particularly perceived as very relevant since in last few years the number of accidents at work is larger than 500.000 per year, among which more that 1000 resulted in the death of the worker. Addressing this issue in Italy is the primary goal of INAIL, which is National Insurance Institute for Industrial Accidents and Occupational Diseases. More specifically, INAIL's objectives are the reduction of injuries, the protection of workers performing hazardous jobs, and the facilitation of the return to work of people injured at workplace. To achieve these relevant and challenging objectives, INAIL explores

SEBD 2021: The 29th Italian Symposium on Advanced Database Systems, September 5-9, 2021, Pizzo Calabro (VV), Italy

p.agnello@inail.it (P. Agnello); s.ansaldi@inail.it (S. M. Ansaldi); emilia.lenzi@polimi.it (E. Lenzi); alessio.mongelluzzo@polimi.it (A. Mongelluzzo); manuel.roveri@polimi.it (M. Roveri)

novel technological and societal solutions and paradigms to provide an integrated system of protection, ranging from preventive actions at the workplace to medical services and financial assistance.

Many Natural Language Processing (NLP) applications and solutions can be found in the literature to tackle tasks like Sentiment Analysis or Text Classification, for instance [1]. However, when it comes to the Italian language, and injury prevention in particular, there are no suited solutions available. In this path, the aim of this paper is to introduce RECKONition, a novel Natural Language Processing-based system to extract knowledge from textual descriptions of accidents at work aiming at defining industrial accidents preventive actions at the workplace. The RECKONition system comprises three different modules, i.e., Association Rule Generation, Textual Description Clustering and Textual Description Inference, able to extract relationships between accident events and create groups of homogeneous accident descriptions representing the input for the definition of preventive actions. The RECKONition system has been successfully applied to a real-world database storing the textual descriptions of accidents occurring in Northern Italy from 2013-2018.

The paper is organized as follows. In Section 2 introduce RECKONition system and its three algorithmic modules. In Section 3, 4, and 5 respectively, we detail our implementation of the Association Rules Mining, Natural Language Clustering, and Natural Language Prediction modules. Section 6 summarizes our work and discuss on the possible next steps and improvements

2. The RECKONition system: extracting knowledge from textual descriptions of accidents at work

The architecture of the RECKONition system, which is described in Fig. 1, comprises three different modules: Association Rule Generator, Textual Description Clustering and Textual Description Inference. All these models receive in input a set of textual descriptions of accidents at work and provide in output *association rules* to discover relationships between terms, *clusters of textual descriptions* highlighting groups of accidents at work sharing similarities in their descriptions, and *next sentence predictions* from the textual description of the accidents. All the outputs of the RECKONition system represent valuable tools for the INAIL expert to gain knowledge about occurred accidents at work and define prevention policies. The three modules of RECKONition system are detailed in the next sections.

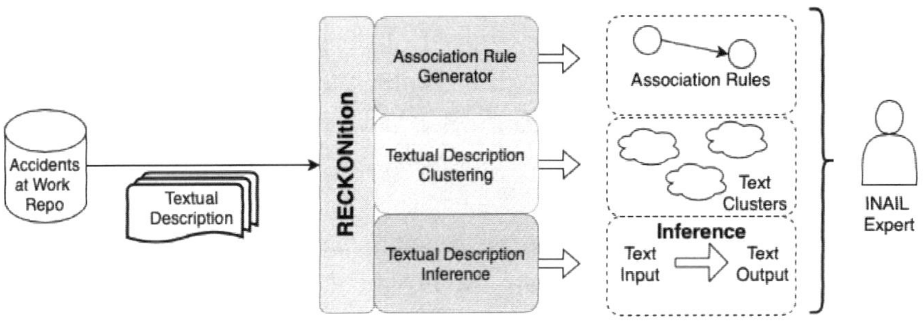

Figure 1: The Architecture of the RECKONition system.

3. Association Rules Mining

Association Rules (ARs) allow to discover relations between variables in large datasets and to graphically show such dependencies in a convenient representation which can be easily interpreted by humans [2] (we show in Figure 2 an example of an AR representation).

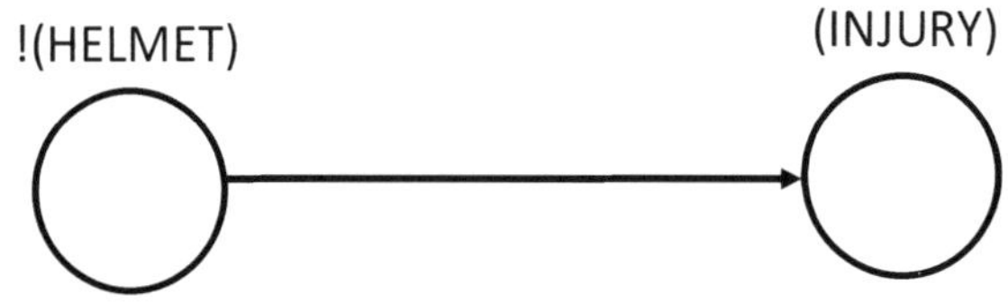

Figure 2: An example of a negative association rule graphical representation.

Let us define our *database* D as a collection of *transactions* from the transactions set T: a transaction is defined as an element of our database, i.e., a sentence containing a textual description of the work dynamics leading to an accident. Hence, for each transaction we can define a set of words or a transformation of words, called *items*, which belong to the items set I and constitute our transaction. In this scenario, an association rule $A \Rightarrow B$ indicates that the occurrence of item B is usually observed when also A is found in the transaction, for $A, B \subset I$.

Association Rules mining procedure is based on three measures, namely *Support*, *Confidence*, and *Lift*, whose values define whether a rule is meaningful or not. The support of an item A can be defined as $Supp(A) = P(A) = \frac{|\{t|\forall t \in T \wedge A \in t\}|}{|T|}$,namely, the percentage of transactions where item A is found. Support can also be defined for a rule, e.g., $Supp(A \Rightarrow B)$, to represent the percentage of transactions in the database where both A and B are found. With the confidence of a rule we model the conditional probability of observing the consequent item having observed the antecedent, so it can hence be defined as $Conf(A \Rightarrow B) = \frac{P(AB)}{P(A)}$. The third measure, i.e., the lift, is used to characterize the relationship between the antecedent and the consequent of the association rule. It is defined as $Lift(A \Rightarrow B) = \frac{P(AB)}{P(A)P(B)} = \frac{P(B|A)}{P(B)}$, a lift greater than 1 identifies a positive relationship between the items, i.e., the conditional probability of observing B given that A is found is greater than the probability of observing B in the database.

Apriori algorithm is a well-known association rules mining method in the literature, which leverages the measures we introduced to explore the itemset and build association rules from them [3]. This method only focuses on the subset of those items belonging to the Frequent Itemset (FIS), i.e, those items whose support is greater than a minimum threshold $minsupp$. However, in some settings (e.g., medical descriptions) those items whose occurrence frequency is very low can be the ones carrying more semantical importance (e.g., names of diseases or even specific injuries). Following this intuition, we provided a Python implementation[1] to the algorithm FISinFIS Apriori proposed in [4], where Positive Association Rules (PARs) and Negative Association Rules (NARs) are built from both the Frequent Itemset and the Infrequent Itemset. FISinFIS Apriori algorithm sets a minimum threshold on the Inverse Document Frequency (IDF), defined as $IDF(i) = \log \frac{|T|}{|\{t|t \in T \wedge i \in t\}|}$, to filter those items which are too frequently

[1]The code is available at https://github.com/AlessioMongelluzzo/FISinFIS_Apriori_Python

used throughout the database. Moreover, we introduced in our implementation an additional threshold to the IDF as an upper bound for too rarely used items. The rationale behind this decision is to avoid typos and missing values placeholders which constitute a non-negligible part of our dataset. The results coming from the application of the mining algorithm to our work accidents descriptions database allows RECKONition to detect those industrial properties or actions that are more likely related to an injury or, with negative rules, to their prevention, we show in Figure 3 an AR graph example from a mock experiment performed on few sentences we wrote for this purpose.

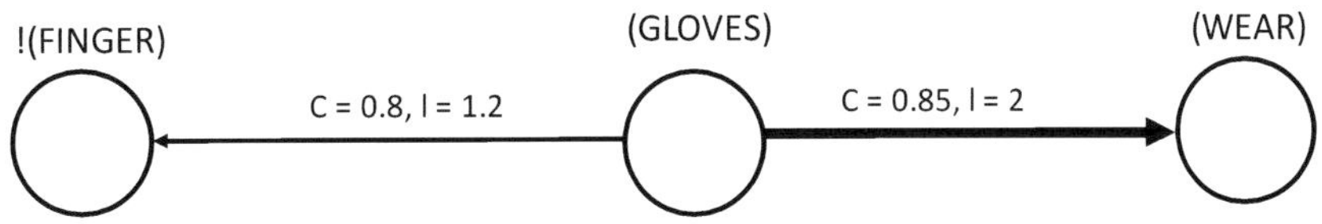

Figure 3: Example of an association rule graph from FISinFIS Apriori application.

4. Natural Language Clustering

Textual Description Clustering [5] is performed to highlight differences and similarities among accident descriptions, and to group together the similar ones in order to facilitate the identification of appropriate interventions according to the situation described. In the following sections we will show the two different approaches used by our system. We will see both of them use the *K-Medoids* algorithm [6], but differ in the operations performed on the *dataset.*

4.1. Tags Occurrence Clustering

A first approach is based on an *ontology* describing the context of interest (in the case of RECKONition, the metallurgical company) and uses TAGs representing ontological classes to integrate contextual knowledge in the clustering analysis.

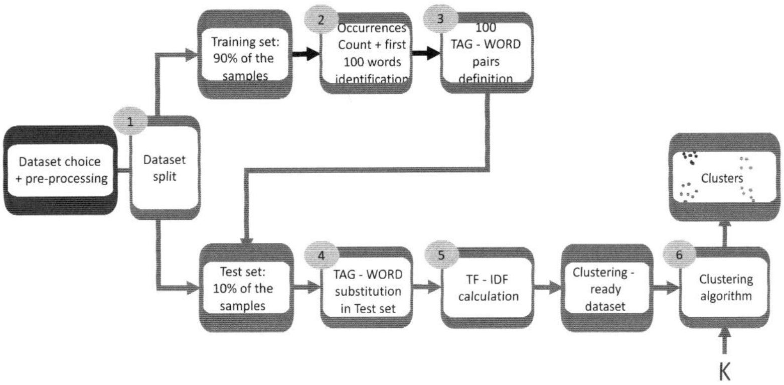

Figure 4: Tags Occurrences Clustering - The process

As you can see in Figure 4, we calculate the occurrences of each word, we identify the hundred most frequent ones, and we define TAG - WORD pairs in the training set; we then perform the hundred substitution in the test set. In this way, words representing similar concepts are read by the algorithm as the same term. As can also be seen from the diagram, before calculating the occurrences, all the necessary pre-processing operations were carried on the entire *dataset*, and in particular the stop_words were eliminated. Almost all the remaining words resulted to be descriptive of the context then, and it was possible to associate them with a TAG. In the rare case in which this did not happen, or the substitution introduced ambiguity, the terms remained unchanged. Once performed the substitution, we calculate the Time frequency - Inverse Document Frequency (TF-IDF) [5] of each term in each description. After step 5 we than have a *dataset* ready for clustering and it is composed by 6662 terms as features, whose values correspond to the calculated TF-IDF.

Once we have the *dataset*, we perform *K-Medoids*. Here we report some example of the clusters obtained by setting the $K = n\_clusters$ parameter equal to 30, and we show how we are able to separate the different situations described.

```
Cluster 12:
medoid: [USING HOSE]
elements: [USING HOSE]; [USING DRILL]; [USING HAMMER]; [USING CUTTER];...

Cluster 17:
medoid: [GOT OFF FORKLIFT]
elements: [GOT OFF FORKLIFT]; [RIDE FORKLIFT]; [MOVE TRUCK]; [RIDING TRUCK];...
```

What is important to notice is that the algorithm is not only able to group together descriptions containing the exact same words, but it is also able to identify the ones concerning similar incidents in the analysed context. In this perspective, Clusters 12 represents accidents involving working tools, while Clusters 17 represents accidents occurring on board mobile machinery.

4.2. Transformers-Based Clustering

A different clustering approach adopted by RECKONition leverages the novel Encoder-Decoder models with *Attention* and *self-Attention* mechanism to build homogenous groups of accidents descriptions [7], [8]. These techniques comprise several stacked encoder-decoder layers, which can model different syntactic structures with self-Attention modules together with feed-forward neural networks, resulting in milions of trainable parameters: the base version of the Bidirectional Encoder Representations from Transformers (BERT) [9] features 12 encoder-decoder layers, 768 hidden nodes for each layer and 12-attention-heads, resulting in 110M parameters, hence, requiring a very large amount of data to be properly trained, as well as time and computational capacity. RECKONition uses a pre-trained BERT model publicly available[2], which was trained on 13GB of Italian textual data from Wikipedia and OPUS corpora[3], and performs fine-tuning of such model on a subset of the accidents-at-work *dataset* provided by INAIL. The

[2]The pre-trained model can be found at https://huggingface.co/dbmdz/bert-base-italian-cased

[3]https://opus.nlpl.eu/

fine-tuned model is then validated on a hold-out set which is used to perform clustering on unseen textual descriptions: during the forward step of a new sentence, the hidden states of the last decoder layer in the model are extracted and used as numerical features representing the sentence. This procedure is performed for each description in the validation set, so to build a new *dataset* with shape $v \times (768 * n_t)$, being 768 the number of hidden states of a BERT layer, v the number of sentences in the validation set, and n_t the number of length of the tokenized sentences. RECKONition leverages Incremental Principal Component Analysis (IPCA) [10] to reduce the dimensionality of the representative features to a number of principal components so that at least 85% of the variability of data is explained, and performs *K-Medoids* clustering for values of the *n_clusters* k in the range $[2, 100]$. Unlike the clustering approach described in Section 4.1, this method can effectively find sentences with highly correlated syntactic structures. We show in the following two examples of clusters obtained with the Transformers-based clustering approach applied to a sample dataset.

MEDOID: "RIDING THE FORKLIFT "
["RIDING THE FORKLIFT", "RIDING THE CAR", "RIDING THE FORKLIFT ", "RIDING THE CAR", "RIDING THE CAR", "RIDING THE BIKE", "RIDING THE FORKLIFT", "REPAIRING THE FORKLIFT"]

MEDOID: "CLIMBING THE LADDER"
["CLIMBING THE LADDER", "CLIMBING THE WALL", "CLIMBING THE LADDER", "CLIMBING ON THE ROOF", "CLIMBING THE LADDER ", "CLIMBING THE LADDER ", "REMOVING HEAR DEFENDER"]

5. Natural Language Prediction

There is plenty of experimental settings where a Language Model (LM) [11], i.e., a model that is able to process textual sequences [12], can be effectively applied. These range from feature extraction (as we did with Trasformers-based clustering in Section 4.2), to text classification, question answering, next sentence prediction, natural language inference, or even text generation. RECKONinition comprises a custom LM, which was properly built and trained on the accidents *dataset* provided by INAIL, with the purpose of performing next sentence prediction from the textual description of the accidents dynamics to those of the consequences on the workers involved. The high-level architecture of the LM is shown in Figure 5. We emphasize that the tokenization step [13], which allows to move from symbolical (textual) to numerical representation, requires to define a vocabulary size to fix the number of tokens, which our model sets to 5000 items. The embedding layer is then used to project the sparse representation obtained by the tokenization step to a dense space with size 128. The sequence learning ability of the model resides in the *n* layer shown in Figure 5, which is composed of two Bidirectional Long Short-Term Memory (LSTM) with 100 units each [14], [15], a flattening layer, two dense layers with 50 neurons each and ReLU activations, and a final Dropout [16] layer with a 50% drop rate before the output dense layer with 5000 neurons (one for each item) and sigmoidal activation. This model can be trained in a supervised fashion [17] minimizing the Binary Cross Entropy loss function with Adaptive Moment Estimation (ADAM) [18]. This is achieved by providing the descriptions of the accidents dynamics as input features, together with the corresponding effects and injuries on the workers involved as input targets. For a new unseen sentence describing a working scenario, the model will output a probability vector on the items in the vocabulary defining those which better describe the consequence of the input description.

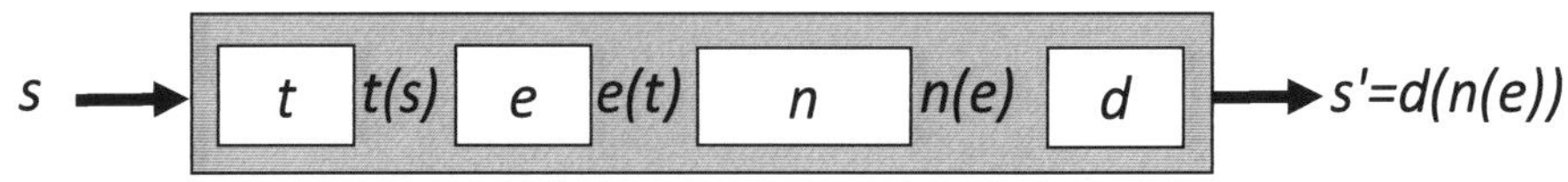

Figure 5: High-level architecture of the language model. *s* and *s'* are textual input and output, respectively. Layer *t* represents the tokenizer, *e* is an embedding layer, and *d* a decoder. The main component *n* is a recurrent neural network model.

We show in in the following two examples of textual prediction given some input descriptions, where the output sentence results in a scattered sequence of items due to the limitation on the vocabulary size.

Description: "the worker was climbing the ladder"
Prediction: ["the", "to", "its", "fall", "off", "ankle", "sprained"]

Description: "she was driving her car to go home"
Prediction: ["she", "her", "to", "the", "cervical", "trauma"]

6. Discussion and conclusion

We introduced and described RECKONition system and its application scenario on a real world dataset. The system is currently operating to understand and extract knowledge from the accidents descriptions database and support the industries towards a safer workplace. The results obtained and the continuous dialogue with INAIL's partners have highlighted the unsupervised ability of RECKONition to both cluster work activities and to identify relationship between accidents and consequences. As a next step, RECKONition will be deployed in real factories where proper sensors can produce inputs to the system, allowing real-time predictions to detect hazardous activities and at the same time improving data quality and performances of the system itself.

Acknowledgements

This work has been funded by INAIL within the BRiC/2018, ID09 framework, project RECKON. The authors wish to acknowledge all the other researchers involved in the project: Francesco Braghin (PoliMI, DMEC), Enrico Cagno (PoliMI, DIG), and their research groups. We also thank Cinzia Frascheri (IAL) and Irene Tagliaro (API-TECH).

References

[1] P. Badjatiya, S. Gupta, M. Gupta, V. Varma, Deep learning for hate speech detection in tweets, in: Proceedings of the 26th international conference on World Wide Web companion, 2017, pp. 759–760.

[2] R. Agrawal, T. Imieliński, A. Swami, Mining association rules between sets of items in large databases, in: Proceedings of the 1993 ACM SIGMOD international conference on Management of data, 1993, pp. 207–216.

[3] R. Agrawal, R. Srikant, et al., Fast algorithms for mining association rules, in: Proc. 20th int. conf. very large data bases, VLDB, volume 1215, Citeseer, 1994, pp. 487–499.

[4] S. Mahmood, M. Shahbaz, A. Guergachi, Negative and positive association rules mining from text using frequent and infrequent itemsets, The Scientific World Journal 2014 (2014).

[5] J. Leskovec, A. Rajaraman, J. Ullman, Mining of massive datasets cambridge university press, 2014.

[6] H.-S. Park, C.-H. Jun, A simple and fast algorithm for k-medoids clustering, Expert systems with applications 36 (2009) 3336–3341.

[7] K. Cho, B. Van Merriënboer, C. Gulcehre, D. Bahdanau, F. Bougares, H. Schwenk, Y. Bengio, Learning phrase representations using rnn encoder-decoder for statistical machine translation, arXiv preprint arXiv:1406.1078 (2014).

[8] A. Vaswani, N. Shazeer, N. Parmar, J. Uszkoreit, L. Jones, A. N. Gomez, L. Kaiser, I. Polosukhin, Attention is all you need, arXiv preprint arXiv:1706.03762 (2017).

[9] J. Devlin, M.-W. Chang, K. Lee, K. Toutanova, Bert: Pre-training of deep bidirectional transformers for language understanding, arXiv preprint arXiv:1810.04805 (2018).

[10] K. Cho, B. Van Merriënboer, C. Gulcehre, D. Bahdanau, F. Bougares, H. Schwenk, Y. Bengio, Learning phrase representations using rnn encoder-decoder for statistical machine translation, arXiv preprint arXiv:1406.1078 (2014).

[11] Y. Bengio, R. Ducharme, P. Vincent, C. Janvin, A neural probabilistic language model, The journal of machine learning research 3 (2003) 1137–1155.

[12] I. Sutskever, O. Vinyals, Q. V. Le, Sequence to sequence learning with neural networks, arXiv preprint arXiv:1409.3215 (2014).

[13] J. J. Webster, C. Kit, Tokenization as the initial phase in nlp, in: COLING 1992 Volume 4: The 15th International Conference on Computational Linguistics, 1992.

[14] S. Hochreiter, J. Schmidhuber, Long short-term memory, Neural computation 9 (1997) 1735–1780.

[15] A. Graves, N. Jaitly, A.-r. Mohamed, Hybrid speech recognition with deep bidirectional lstm, in: 2013 IEEE workshop on automatic speech recognition and understanding, IEEE, 2013, pp. 273–278.

[16] N. Srivastava, G. Hinton, A. Krizhevsky, I. Sutskever, R. Salakhutdinov, Dropout: a simple way to prevent neural networks from overfitting, The journal of machine learning research 15 (2014) 1929–1958.

[17] C. M. Bishop, Pattern recognition and machine learning, springer, 2006.

[18] D. P. Kingma, J. Ba, Adam: A method for stochastic optimization, arXiv preprint arXiv:1412.6980 (2014).

RECKOn: a REal-world, Context-aware KnOwledge-based lab

(Discussion Paper)

Patrizia Agnello[1], Silvia Maria Ansaldi[1], Emilia Lenzi[2], Alessio Mongelluzzo[2], Davide Piantella[2], Manuel Roveri[2], Fabio A. Schreiber[2], Alessandra Scutti[2], Mahsa Shekari[2] and Letizia Tanca[2]

[1]*INAIL - Dipartimento Innovazioni Tecnologiche*

[2]*Politecnico di Milano - Dipartimento di Elettronica, Informazione e Bioingegneria*

Abstract

The RECKON project focuses on interconnection technologies and context-aware data-analytics techniques to improve safety in workplaces, with the ultimate objective of identifying and preventing dangerous situations before accidents occur. In RECKON, prevention is interpreted through the latest monitoring, diagnostics and prognostics techniques from a safety perspective, allowing to detect and use, even in real time, a large amount of data about the entire operational context. Using sensor networks, we are able to collect information that is used in two ways: (i) when a potentially dangerous situation is detected, the system raises an alarm to prevent an accident, and (ii) whenever an accident or a near-miss (i.e., a potential accident that was narrowly averted) occurs, the related useful information is stored in a case report automatically generated and later used to update the accident-prevention politics. This work briefly describes the operational framework of RECKON, along with its modules and their interaction.

Keywords

Workplace safety, Industry 4.0, Context-awareness, Sensor data

1. Introduction

Accidents at work have been a topic of social and economic debate for a long time now. According to the data of INAIL (Istituto Nazionale per l'Assicurazione contro gli Infortuni sul Lavoro), 641,638 workplace accidents occurred in 2019, 1089 of them resulting in death [1]. Although the interest in the subject is always high, the evolution of the enterprise context, in which accidents occur, makes it necessary to continuously observe and study these phenomena and to use constantly updated systems for their prevention.

The innovative paradigm introduced by Industry 4.0 [2] has brought about structural, technological, productive and organisational changes in the world of work [3], all based on a high

SEBD 2021: The 29th Italian Symposium on Advanced Database Systems, September 5-9, 2021, Pizzo Calabro (VV), Italy

p.agnello@inail.it (P. Agnello); s.ansaldi@inail.it (S. M. Ansaldi); emilia.lenzi@polimi.it (E. Lenzi); alessio.mongelluzzo@polimi.it (A. Mongelluzzo); davide.piantella@polimi.it (D. Piantella); manuel.roveri@polimi.it (M. Roveri); fabio.schreiber@polimi.it (F. A. Schreiber); alessandra.scutti@polimi.it (A. Scutti); mahsa.shekari@polimi.it (M. Shekari); letizia.tanca@polimi.it (L. Tanca)

technological development aimed at increasing the productivity and competitiveness of companies in the market [4]. The use of innovative sensors, for example, makes it possible to analyse large amounts of data extracted directly from the production context. However, while there has been a very strong interest in the digitalization of the working environment, this has been almost entirely channelled into the dimension of machines and their interconnections with the surrounding environment, putting the equally important aspect of human presence in the background [5]. Instead, by putting the operator at the center, the introduction of innovative technological solutions may prove fundamental not only for the company's performance in terms of profits and competitiveness, but also to provide support to the operator in terms of prevention in the field of health and safety at work [6].

It is therefore clear that crucial points of the problem are an accurate and up-to-date analysis and description of the context and how the operator interacts with it, and an efficient use of the data and information derived from this analysis. This is the purpose of the RECKON system, designed to support companies in monitoring and preventing accidents in the workplace.

RECKON exploits the integration of the historical analysis with a conceptualisation and sensitisation of the working context, making it possible to highlight the correspondence between a situation that has already been identified as potentially dangerous and the current working situation. More precisely, the system can be considered as composed of three conceptual parts: (i) sensitization of the companies under consideration (in the current case study, metallurgical enterprises); (ii) integrated, context-aware sensor data stream processing and conceptualization of the context described by those data; (iii) integration of the historical data collected in the critical-events database with other datasets about accidents (both internal and external to INAIL). Thanks to the last two tasks, it will be possible to build a knowledge base for the subsequent analyses useful to improve the context-aware monitoring system.

Sec. 2 of this paper gives an overview of the system, especially focusing on the information workflow (modules two and three); Sec. 3, details module two; and finally, Sec. 4, summarizes the techniques used to perform integration in the third module.

2. System overview

As shown by Fig. 1, part of the system operates directly in the company, to minimise the latency time when a decision is to be made or an alarm is triggered, and another part works, at a higher level (the *RECKON Hub*), in the Cloud, to integrate information from different companies and other data sources.

In fact, the RECKON architecture comprises four levels. In the workplace, we find wearable devices for workers and sensorized machines, and a localisation and imaging system; these two levels allow to localize the workers and machines and to signal critical or abnormal situations via vibration or acoustic signals *(Module 1)*. In the enterprise we also find an edge-computing system to process data acquired from the second level and to generate alarms that will be sent (via second level) to the workers' wearable devices *(Module 2)*. Relevant information from specific installations of the system in the companies are collected and sent to the central Hub. At this level, it will be possible to perform wide-range analyses on alert or hazardous situations,integrate these analyses with external sources of all kinds *(Module 3)*, and visualize

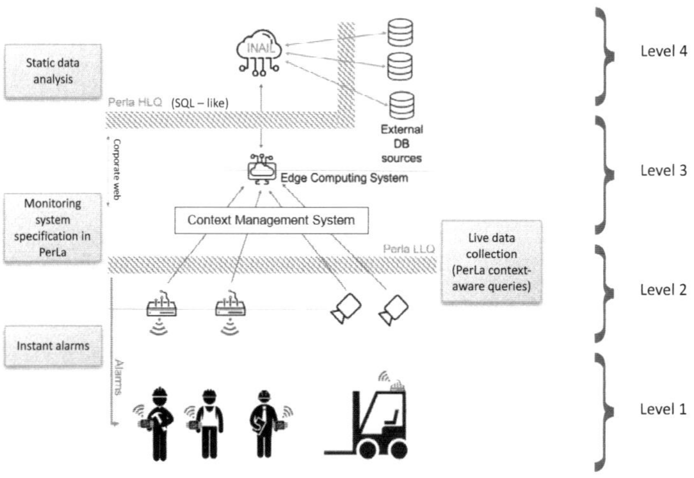

Figure 1: The architecture of RECKON.

data and results appropriately.

In all cases, when dealing with context-aware pervasive systems, two main problems arise: the integration of heterogeneous streams of data coming from distinct data sources and the problem of specifying the system behaviour at various levels, from the low-level support for hardware abstraction to the high-level support for data management, as we can see from the system overview. For this reason, we introduce the PerLa system [7], a middleware for data management and integration that uses the database abstraction for managing the pervasive system, allowing a data-centric view of the pervasive network and providing a homogeneous high-level interface to heterogeneous devices. The query language of PerLa is an SQL-like language that allows access to all the data collected by the network nodes. At the moment, PerLa has been implemented as a prototype, and using it in a real system would need proper engineering. However, being it very clear and expressive, we are using PerLa as a specification language to define the system behaviour and the application constraints. As shown in Fig. 1, there are different types of PerLa queries: the PerLa High Level Queries (HLQ) can be used for specifying the tasks for integrating different datasets; the PerLa Low Level Queries (LLQ) are interposed between level 2 and level 3 and trigger the sampling operations for the main context parameters (e.g., worker's elevation, worker's position, etc.) thus allowing correct identification of context changes; in addition, between the two levels we also find the PerLa Context-aware Queries, that are context-specific and permit to verify particular conditions within the operator-machine-environment situation.

2.1. Context-aware information workflow

In Fig. 2 we show the information workflow of RECKON, describing the context-aware behaviour of the system. Sensor data collection from the field, data processing and integration, and alarm generation, are all context-aware.

The workflow consists of eight main steps, represented in Fig. 2 and detailed below. Let

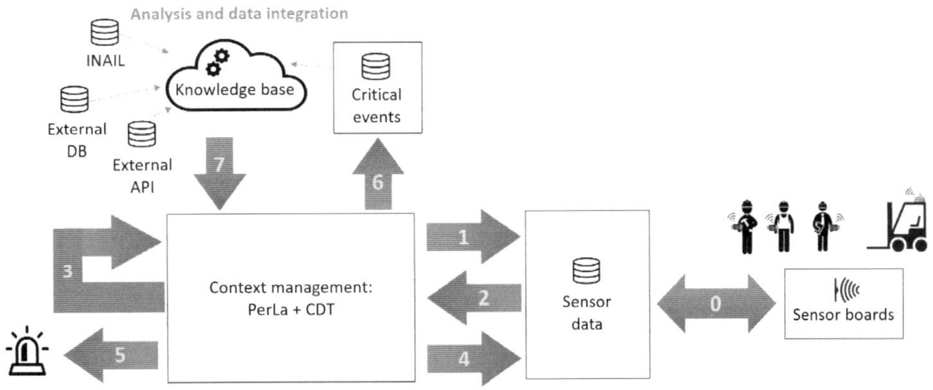

Figure 2: The information workflow in RECKON.

us consider the following use case of the system: *"A worker W enters a delimited area Y of the working facility, containing a fixed machinery X. In order to operate X, workers should use specific Personal Protective Equipment (PPE), currently not worn by W"*. We now describe how this scenario is mapped to each step of the workflow.

Step 0: Field data collection This step is responsible for collecting data from the field: without loss of generality, we assume that sensor-specific software can ensure an easy access to sensor data and measurements, in a structured format. For simplicity, we represented these data as part of a relational database.

Step 1: PerLa Continuous Query (LLQ) context monitoring is based on the continuous execution of a set of Low Level Queries on the set of available data sources. For example, to monitor the height and location of workers in real time, a continuous query will be required on all smartwatch devices; or, to update the location of mobile machines, a position parameter sampling operation will be initiated on all devices installed on the machines. In the use case, if we want to detect the usage of machine X by worker W, one continuous query could be: *"What is the distance between the worker W and the machine X?"* (List. 1).

Step 2: Context change detection We detect a context change if the result of the continuous query described in Step 1 (i.e., distance between the worker & machine X) is below the threshold.

Step 3: Critical context activation Updating context parameters may lead to the activation of contexts identified as critical, for which further checks are necessary. In the use case, the usage of machinery X requires a verification on the PPE of W.

Step 4: PerLa Context-aware Query The activation of a critical context determines the execution of Context-aware Queries, possibly generate alarm signals and finally define which are the useful data to be collected in a case report. In the use case, a context-specific query could be: *"Did the worker wear all the PPE required for using machine X?"* (List. 2).

Step 5: PerLa activates context-based alarms The alarms are triggered when critical conditions occur for the context under consideration; e.g., the worker is not wearing the PPE, thus an alarm is triggered and, possibly, some predefined security measures are activated. This closes the context-aware online phase.

Step 6: Accident and near-miss report This step is to automatically generate a case report with the details of the accident or near-miss, based on the Context Dimension Tree model described in Sec. 3. The report is stored in a database, available at both corporate and hub level,that grants the privacy of personal and sensitive information. The format of the report will be structured or semi-structured, to ease subsequent automated analysis (Step 7).

Step 7: Refinement and improvement of PerLa queries PerLa queries can be modified or added, leveraging a knowledge base generated from the integration and analysis of sensor data, reports generated in Step 6, historical datasets of accidents, and external data sources. This possibility aims at anticipating the detection of dangerous situations, reducing the number of accidents and near-misses. With reference to the use case, the system could infer that too many non-authorized workers enter area Y to operate machinery X. This new information may suggest to anticipate the control of the PPE, to the moment when workers enter area Y, without waiting for the detection of the use of X. If the PPE is not worn when entering area Y, a pre-alarm is triggered to remind workers to wear the required equipment.

```
CREATE OUTPUT STREAM MachineryLocation (id_machinery STRING, ts STRING, x FLOAT, y FLOAT, z
    FLOAT) AS:
EVERY 30 seconds
SELECT id_machinery, ts, x, y, z
SAMPLING EVERY 10 seconds
EXECUTE IF EXISTS id_machinery, x, y, z
```

Listing 1: Perla Continous Query (LLQ)

```
CREATE CONTEXT Worker_FixedMachinetry_RelativePosition
ACTIVE IF SmartwatchProfile EXISTS AND MachEquType = "Fixedmachinery" AND RelativePosition_WM <
    $mimimum_safe
ON ENABLE (Worker_FixedMachinetry_RelativePosition):
  SELECT SmartwatchProfile, Machinery_UsePermission, Workplace_Access,
      PersonalProtectiveEquipment, ProtectionBarriers, SafetyDevices
  SAMPLING EVERY 1m
  SET PARAMETER "warning message" = TRUE
  ACTIVATE ALARM
ON DISABLE:
  DROP Worker_FixedMachinetry_RelativePosition
  INSERT RECORD INTO Critical_events_db
  SET PARAMETER "warning message" = FALSE
REFRESH EVERY 5m
```

Listing 2: PerLa Context-aware Query

3. Context modelling and representation

A first step in the design of the RECKON context-aware data integration system is a conceptual modeling phase, aiming to understand and model context information. Among the methodologies for designing context-aware systems [8], we use the one based on the Context Dimension Tree (CDT) [9], because it allows to capture the context both at a *conceptual* and a *detail* level and has already been experimented for these purposes [10, 11, 12]. The CDT captures distinct situations in which the users of a system can find themselves and interact with the surrounding environments. The tree's root r represents the most general context; N is the set of nodes; nodes are either black *Dimension Nodes* N_D or white *Concept Nodes* N_C, *a.k.a*, dimension's values; N_D and N_C must alternate along the branches. White triangles are shorthands to represent

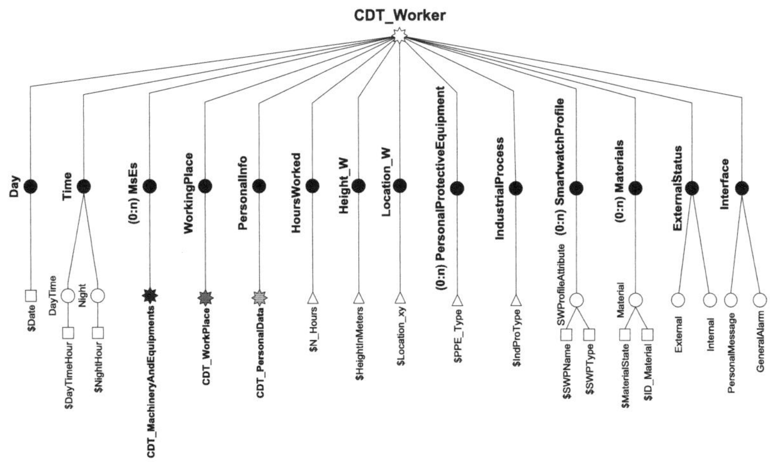

Figure 3: The Worker CDT.

a collection of N_C graphically. Also, each N_C and each leaf N_D without any children can be further detailed through *Parameters*, shown in white squares. The root's children, *a.k.a.*, *top dimensions*, specify the main dimensions of the analysis. Each N_D should have at least one N_C or parameter. Fig. 3 shows the CDT Worker, representing the most relevant dimensions for determining the accident risk exposure of each single worker in the "operator-machine-environment" context in the metallurgic Small and Medium-size Enterprises (SMEs) scenario. The context is understood both as the physical environment (e.g., the environmental parameters, the objects with which the worker interacts such as machinery and equipment) and as the set of characteristics specific to each worker (e.g., the worker's job profile, age, work experience) that help determine the most critical situation for each worker. In the CDT Worker, some N_Ds have cardinality greater than one; the cardinality was introduced to better model the context of the worker who, for example, may interact simultaneously with several machines, or, may wear several Personal Protective Equipments. Note that the dimensions "WorkingPlace", "Personal-Data" and "MachineryAndEquipments" generate sub-trees not shown here that are nested in the CDT Worker. The CDT specification allows us to model all the possible contexts and monitor them during execution, guiding system actions, data collection and interpretation. Through the PerLa Context component [13] it is possible to express formally both the context model (CDT Declaration) and the context-aware system behavior when a critical context occurs (Context Creation clause). Declaring a context also describes the conditions for its activation (ACTIVE IF clause) and defines the consequent action(s) of the system. The ACTIVE IF condition is defined on the context parameters and dimensions by considering some critical thresholds. For example, the context when: (i) a worker is in the proximity of a mobile machine, (ii) the distance between the worker and the machine is less than the critical threshold and (iii) the machine is switched on or moving, is described as: *ACTIVE IF MachEqType = 'MobileMachine' AND Velocity_M* $>$ *0 m/s AND RelativePositition_WM* $<$ *MnimumSafeDistance.* Each of the main accident categories and dangerous situations derived from the analyses defines one or more such critical contexts, that can be modified or added as the system gains "experience", i.e., based on the progressive analyses of the occurred situations.

4. Extracting knowledge from textual descriptions

A further enrichment of the description of work environments and their possible dangers is the use of ontologies. Since we could not find sufficiently rich ontologies for the Italian language, we developed a new one starting from the CDT terminology and from the analysis of the datasets at our disposal. The ultimate aim of this ontology is to integrate the context-aware knowledge with analysis techniques for Natural Language Processing (NLP), a crucial part of Module 3. To combine the semantic representation with textual data analysis, we divided the ontology into *Grammatical Categories* and *Semantic Classes*. This permits to separate the meaning of each term from its grammatical role, using these two pieces of information either independently or in a combined way, depending on the task. Currently, taking into account the methods used for NLP-based analysis, we have identified four basic *Grammatical Categories*: *Noun, Verb, Adjective and Adverb*. To identify the main *Semantic Classes*, following a bottom-up approach, we started from the most frequent terms of the CDT and the data at our disposal and then generated a hierarchy taking into account their correspondence with the dimensions of the context tree. To embed ontological classes in the textual analyses, a *TAG* is created for each class, and the most frequent terms analyzed are replaced in the datasets with these tags. Here is an example of hierarchy in the ontology with related *TAGs*: *Object(0) -> Work_Object(WO) -> Tool (WOT) -> hammer.* Regarding the combination of *Semantic Classes* and *Grammatical Categories*, at the moment we are working on the formalisation of rules that follow those of the Italian grammatical and logical analysis, being careful not to introduce redundancies. For example, to express the activity "to hammer" we chose to combine the category "Verb" with the class "Tool" in order to group all the accidents involving tools easily without creating a proper class "work activity" or "work activity involving tools".

The third and last module is RECKONition (extensively described in [14]), a NLP-based system for accidens prevention in industry that analyses Italian textual descriptions of previous accidents to build both unsupervised and supervised models. The architecture of this analysis system comprises three models: *Association Rule Generator, Textual Description Clustering* [15] – highlighting groups of accidents at work sharing similarities in their descriptions–, and *Textual Description Inference*, providing next-sentence predictions from the textual description of the accidents. Experimental results are rather satisfactory.

5. Conclusion and future works

We introduced RECKON, a context-aware pervasive system which combines different technologies to efficiently prevent accidents within metallurgical companies. In particular, we focused on describing the context of interest and its embedding within heterogeneous integration and analysis on different levels. To verify the efficiency of the proposed models, we conducted a survey campaign with many manufacturing companies, which resulted in an endorsement of our proposed framework. The next steps will be the actual installation of the sensors in situ and the analysis of the sampled data.

Acknowledgements

This work has been funded by INAIL within the BRiC/2018, ID09 framework, project RECKON. The authors wish to acknowledge all the other researchers involved in the project: Francesco Braghin (PoliMI, DMEC), Enrico Cagno (PoliMI, DIG), and their research groups. We also thank Cinzia Frascheri (IAL) and Irene Tagliaro (API-TECH).

References

[1] INAIL, Andamento degli infortuni sul lavoro e delle malattie professionali, https://www.inail.it/cs/internet/docs/alg-dati-inail-2021-gennaio-pdf.pdf, 2021.

[2] Y. Lu, Industry 4.0: A survey on technologies, applications and open research issues, J. Ind. Inf. Integr. 6 (2017) 1–10. doi:10.1016/j.jii.2017.04.005.

[3] J. Lee, B. Bagheri, H.-A. Kao, A cyber-physical systems architecture for industry 4.0-based manufacturing systems, Manufacturing Letters 3 (2015) 18–23.

[4] J. Davis, T. Edgar, J. Porter, J. Bernaden, M. Sarli, Smart manufacturing, manufacturing intelligence and demand-dynamic performance, Comput. Chem. Eng. 47 (2012) 145–156.

[5] P. Fantini, M. Pinzone, M. Taisch, Placing the operator at the centre of industry 4.0 design: Modelling and assessing human activities within cyber-physical systems, Computers & Industrial Engineering 139 (2020) 105058.

[6] V. Paelke, Augmented reality in the smart factory: Supporting workers in an industry 4.0. environment, Proc. of the 2014 IEEE ETFA (2014) 1–4.

[7] F. A. Schreiber, R. Camplani, M. Fortunato, M. Marelli, G. Rota, Perla: A language and middleware architecture for data management and integration in pervasive information systems, IEEE Trans. Softw. Eng. 38 (2011) 478–496.

[8] C. Bolchini, C. A. Curino, E. Quintarelli, F. A. Schreiber, L. Tanca, A data-oriented survey of context models, ACM Sigmod Record 36 (2007) 19–26.

[9] C. Bolchini, C. A. Curino, E. Quintarelli, F. A. Schreiber, L. Tanca, Context information for knowledge reshaping, IJWET 5 (2009) 88–103.

[10] V. Cassani, S. Gianelli, M. Matera, R. Medana, E. Quintarelli, L. Tanca, V. Zaccaria, On the role of context in the design of mobile mashups, in: RMC, 2016, pp. 108–128.

[11] A. Javadian Sabet, M. Rossi, F. A. Schreiber, L. Tanca, Towards learning travelers' preferences in a context-aware fashion, in: Ambient Intelligence – Software and Applications, Springer International Publishing, Cham, 2021, pp. 203–212.

[12] A. J. Sabet, M. Rossi, F. A. Schreiber, L. Tanca, Context awareness in the travel companion of the shift2rail initiative, in: Proc. of the 28th Italian Symposium on Advanced Database Systems, volume 2646 of *CEUR Work. Proc.*, 2020, pp. 202–209.

[13] F. A. Schreiber, E. Panigati, Context-aware self adapting systems: a ground for the cooperation of data, software, and services, IJNGC 8 (2017) 32–61.

[14] P. Agnello, S. M. Ansaldi, E. Lenzi, A. Mongelluzzo, M. Roveri, Reckonition: a nlp-based system for industrial accidents at work prevention, 2021. arXiv:2104.14150.

[15] M. J. Zaki, W. Meira, Jr, Data Mining and Analysis: Fundamental Concepts and Algorithms, Cambridge University Press, 2014.

A Deep Learning Approach for Unsupervised Failure Detection in Smart Industry

(Discussion Paper)

Angelica Liguori[1], Giuseppe Manco[2], Ettore Ritacco[2], Massimilano Ruffolo[3] and Salvatore Iiritano[3]

[1]*Department of Computer Engineering, Modeling, Electronics and, Systems University of Calabria*
[2]*Institute for High Performance Computing and Networking of Italian National Research Council*
[3]*Revelis S.r.l.*

Abstract

We propose an unsupervised anomaly detection model that is able to identify abnormal behavior by analysing streaming data coming from IoT sensors installed on critical devices. The proposed model is based on a Siamese neural network which embeds time series windows in a latent space, thus generating distance-based clusters of normal behavior. We experiment the proposed model on a case study aimed at the predictive maintenance of elevators where specific sensors measure the oscillations of the lift during its daily use. The experiments show that the proposed model successfully isolates anomalous oscillations thus correlating them to prospective malfunctions and thus preventing possible faults.

Keywords

Anomaly detection, Failure detection, Fault detection, Time-series analysis, Embeddings, Siamese networks.

1. Introduction

Maintenance is one of the most important activities in support of all industrial production systems. It represents both an opportunity and a bottleneck at the same time. In fact, if on the one hand it makes it possible to avoid the occurrence of machinery breakdowns, service interruptions and possibly monetary penalties, on the other hand it risks slowing down industrial processes, since it requires starting activities not strictly correlated with the core business, committing the production machinery and numerous resources in terms of technicians, tools, time, possible costs.

Fault detection and prevention [1] is one of the most critical part of predictive maintenance, as it aims at identifying an anomalous behavior of the system and avoid sudden interruptions and catastrophic machine failures. Typically, the focus is on developing solutions that produce warnings when an anomalous behavior is detected and fault detection methods based on machine learning aim at analyzing historical data in order to devise models of failure or malfunction, based on supervised learning. In this respect, the predictive maintenance process has largely

SEBD 2021: The 29th Italian Symposium on Advanced Database Systems, September 5-9, 2021, Pizzo Calabro (VV), Italy
angelica.liguori@dimes.unical.it (A. Liguori); giuseppe.manco@icar.cnr.it (G. Manco); ettore.ritacco@icar.cnr.it (E. Ritacco); massimiliano.ruffolo@revelis.eu (M. Ruffolo); salvatore.iiritano@revelis.eu (S. Iiritano)

benefited from the large-scale adoption of sensor devices. With the advent of the IoT technology, numerous sensors can be installed on production devices, which produce significant amounts of data based on their sampling frequency.

Despite their intrinsic predictive value, these enormous streams of data represent a challenge in several respects. First of all, sensor streams are very noisy temporal sequences, with excessive dimensionality and affected by specific issues (e.g. burst effects, seasonality). It is necessary to devise automatic methods capable of filtering out noise and produce effective representations that can be fruitfully exploited in predictive models. Moreover, often the presence of streaming data requires also the capability to meet real-time requirements. Maintenance solutions must be able to provide timely warnings to maintenance experts.

However, in a vast majority of industrial situations, there are no samples that represent the presence of failure, hence, the adoption of unsupervised methods seems better suited. The choice between supervised and unsupervised approaches does not depend only on the presence or absence of the fault indicator. There are numerous scenarios in which, despite the presence of such a flag, the classification cannot succeed in a quality prediction. Failures are rare events and are often not sufficient to define the prediction patterns that are necessary for any classification technique.

In this paper, we study a specific scenario where the above mentioned issues take place. The paper is focused on a study where the adoption of sensing technology, combined with machine learning, can effectively characterize the behavior of lifting systems and thus devise effective predictive maintenance strategies aimed at ensuring the stability and efficiency of the elevator, as well as preventing future breakdowns. The intuition is that, in their daily routine, elevators produce oscillations which can be registered and analyzed. A methodology for devising profiles of normal oscillations can hence help us detect any deviation from typical signatures and hence prospective efficiency issues.

2. Related Work

In the maintenance field, traditional unsupervised approaches use one-class classifier, e.g. One-class Support Vector Machines [2, 3] or distance-metrics, such as e.g. Isolation Forest [4, 5]. Autoencoders [6] are the core of Unsupervised Anomaly Detection methods based on Deep Learning and most recent literature on unsupervised failure detection is based on them, such as [7, 8, 9] in which the reconstruction error is used as anomaly score and, their variants, such as [10, 11] that propose an unsupervised fault detection based on a stacked autoencoder and on a sparse autoencoder, respectively. Autoencoders can also be adapted to cope with streaming data. Lindemann et al. [12] propose an anomaly detection system by combining an autoencoder with Long short-term memory (LSTM) [13]. By contrast, Jiang et al. [14] propose an unsupervised fault detection based on denoising autoencoder (DAE). Xiang et al. [15] propose a framework based on Variational Autoencoder (VAE) [16] in which the Gated Recurrent Network (GRU) [17] network unit is introduced into VAE network to replace the traditional neural unit in encoder and decoder. Alfeo et al. [18] combines an autoencoder with a heuristic-based discriminator in order to improve the interpretability of the detection. Jian and Zhiyan [19] propose an unsupervised fault detection method based on adversarial auto-encoders in which a discriminator is able to refine the reconstruction errors and hence. In [20] a one-class fault detection based on unsupervised training of Generative Adversarial Networks [21] is proposed, where the problem of distinguish real from fake data is converted in distinguish normal from anomalous data, by forcing the generator in producing normal-like generated data.

Most of the unsupervised failure detection systems in the literature exploit the reconstruction error to discriminate between normal data and anomalies. Usually, when the reconstruction error is used as measure of outlierness, a threshold is defined such that the data whose reconstruction error is above the threshold is marked as outlier. Defining a threshold is very hard, especially when there is no knowledge background.

Unlike these works, our proposal exploits the philosophy of the Siamese networks [22] to map the data into a latent space so that data that belong to the same category are located in the same area with respect that data that belong to different category. This idea mitigates the overfitting problem of the cited approaches: sequences are analyzed according to a collective approach instead of comparing any rebuilt sequence with only its original version.

3. Setting

Let $\mathscr{D}$ be a set of devices characterized by functionality, structure, purpose and/or working environment. Each device $d \in \mathscr{D}$ is equipped with a set sensors $\mathscr{M}_d$ emitting temporal sequences of events $S_d = \{e_d^{(1)}, e_d^{(2)}, e_d^{(3)}, ...\}$, where the superscript indicates the time step. Each event $e_d^{(t)}$ is a real vector of size $|\mathscr{M}_d|$ containing the values observed by the sensors. We further assume that S_d is labeled by a specific category which characterizes the process being monitored. Categories can also refer to the underlying device (i.e., each device can be seen as a distinct category); however, they can also describe the situations that the sensors are measuring, such as an elevator moving up with a load of two persons.

The objective of our research is to detect anomalous situations within a sequence S_d associated with a device. The basic approach consists in building a machine learning model which is capable of characterize the profile of each sequence, and mark anomalies whenever a given sequence does not fit that profile. However, in order to apply such a methodology, we need to face two main problems. First of all, there are several different profiles that can characterize each sequence. The categories encode different situations and we can expect that events marked with a specific category are different from events labeled with a different one. We can hence assume that the expected number of categories is high. Furthermore, we assume that $|\mathscr{M}_d|$ is large but the overall number of sequences is small compared to the number of categories. That is, we can expect that each sequence is labeled with almost a different category. This clearly poses a problem in the learning stage, since it is not possible to build specific profiles due to the lack of sufficient training data for each category.

The solution we propose is a methodology divided into two parts. The first part consists in a data transformation approach that allows the definition of a classification problem. The second part consists in the exploitation of a modular Siamese network able to map the input (sequence fragments) into data points lying on a latent space, by solving the aforementioned classification problem.

The latent space has a geometric interpretation: points that are close in the space correspond

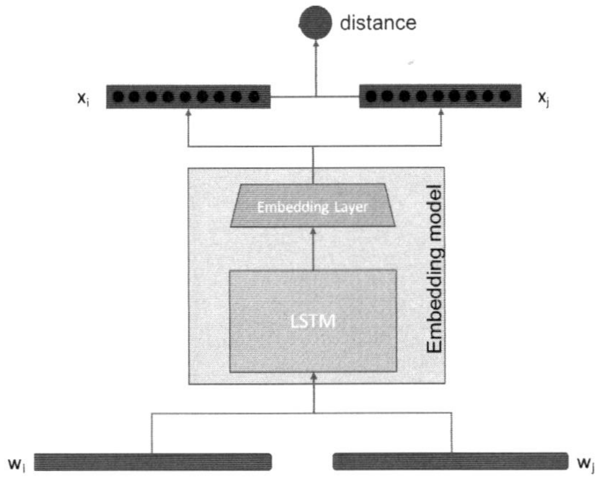

Figure 1: Network architecture.

to devices that exhibit, in some time interval of their working process, similar behavior. The core concept is that clusters of these latent data points represent the different working modes of the target devices. Any element that is on the edge of a cluster or out of all of them can be highlighted to maintenance experts for further investigation. This allows to approach situation, typical in many industrial processes, where critical anomalies (e.g. failures) are extremely rare.

4. Methodology

Since sequences may have different sizes, our methodology applies a sliding window extraction procedure to generate, for each sequence, a set of fixed-size observation windows. Notice that if the window shift is lower than the window size, contiguous windows partially overlap. Each window is a time frame that partially describes the behavior of the target devices during the interval of observation. For the rest of the paper we will name $\mathscr{W} = \{w_1, w_2, ...\}$ the set of all the time windows and we will use the function $cat(w_i)$ for denoting the category relative to the device that generated the i-th time window.

The set $\mathscr{W}$ and the function *cat* enable the definition of the following classification problem: given two arbitrary time windows w_i and w_j, the goal is to predict if they belong to the same category, i.e. whether $cat(w_i) = cat(w_j)$.

The solution we propose to address this problem is a Siamese neural network, shown in Figure 1, composed by two modules. The first one is the *Embedding model* that maps a time window into the high-dimensional latent space. The Embedding subnet is a sequential model composed by a recurrent neural network (we exploited a LSTM layer [13]), for catching the time dependencies within each window, and a feed-forward neural network (a dense embedding layer), that generates the data points in the latent space. The second module is the *Distance subnet* that outputs the euclidean distance between two embeddings.

The working flow of the whole architecture is described as follows. The input of the network is a pair of time windows, w_i and w_j, that are randomly sampled from $\mathscr{W}$. The set of all the built-up pairs, called $\mathscr{W}_s$, suitably represent each category, providing a sufficient number of

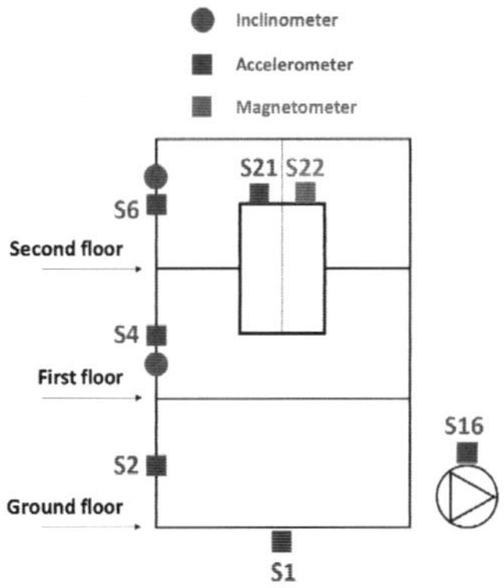

Figure 2: Graphical representation of the elevator. All sensors are set with a sampling frequency of 200Hz except S16 (4000Hz) and S22 (100Hz)

positive (windows belonging to the same category) and negative (windows belonging to different categories) comparisons. Both w_i and w_j pass through the Embedding subnet, the Siamese part of the network, that will produce two embeddings, respectively x_i and x_j, that will feed the Distance subnet that will computes and returns their euclidean distance. The loss function we chose is the following:

$$loss = \frac{1}{|\mathcal{W}_s|} \sum_{w_i, w_j \in \mathcal{W}_s} y_{i,j} \cdot f(w_i, w_j) - (1 - y_{i,j}) \cdot \log\left(1 - e^{-f(w_i w_j)}\right) \quad (1)$$

where $y_{i,j}$ is equal to 1 if $cat(w_i) = cat(w_j)$, 0 otherwise, and $f(w_i, w_j)$ is a function that computes the euclidean distance between the embeddings x_i and x_j of the time windows w_i and w_j, respectively.

The proposed loss function encourages the network to generate pairs of embeddings that are close in the latent space if $y_{i,j} = 1$; on the other hand, if the two categories are different, the network will produce pairs of embeddings that are distant.

5. Predicting Elevator Anomalous Oscillations

We applied our methodology to a real case study whose objective is to monitor the health status and the working process of an elevator in an office building. The sensor system placed in the elevator (see Figure 2 for details) records the movements in the x, y and z axes of the oscillations of the elevator guides and cabin, the inclination of the cabin and the magnetic field intensity in a relational data structure. Each record is a time-series collecting sensor emissions in a interval of time. Moreover, records provide further information about the operation status of the elevator, highlighting, for each time step its position, movement and door status.

In this case study, we applied our methodology on a limited set of similar elevators in an office building. Thus, their sequences were split into fixed size time windows that were randomly paired up to be processed by the Siamese network. The category labels we used were the operational modalities: (*i*) Stationary; (*ii*) Moving up; (*iii*) Moving down; (*iv*) Opening doors; (*v*)

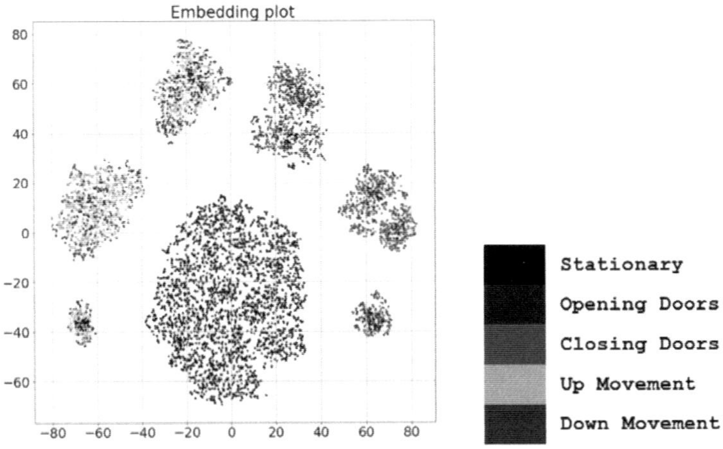

(a) Normal embeddings

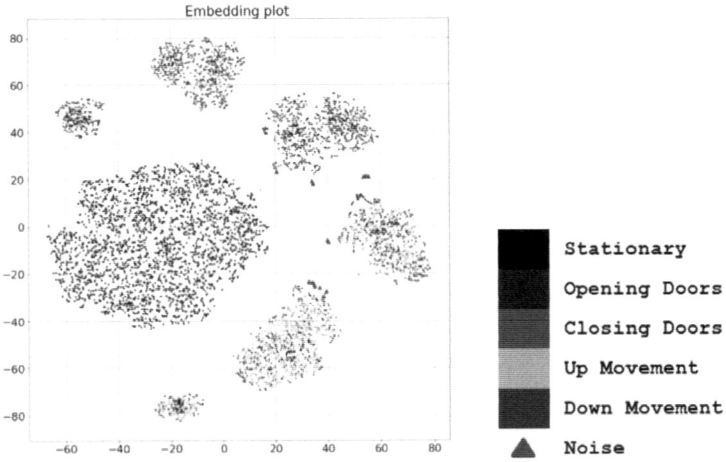

(b) Normal and anomalous embeddings

Figure 3: Embedding space

Closing doors. Each of these modalities is further labeled by contour conditions representing the load (number of people) in the lift.

The result of the training phase was that, for each elevator, the Network understood the different normal behavior models, which map into clusters of the latent space. To allow a friendly visualization of the embeddings, we used the t-distributed stochastic neighbor embedding (t-SNE) library [23]. A 2D t-SNE plot of the learnt behavior clusters is shown in Figure 3a, where each point is related to the embedding of a time window, while colors indicate the categories the windows belong to. As can be seen, the network found out 7 different behavioural clusters, in which there is a dominance of a color. The partial color overlapping is due to two factors. On one hand, category labels were noisy since they were produced by humans with external chronometers, thus, making, for each category session, the initial and final time windows imprecise. On the other hand, the sensors we used where not able to find appreciable differences in vibration when doors were opening or closing.

In order to observe the capability of the model to isolate anomalies we performed new experiments in which passengers stopped and restarted several times the elevator movements or produced (weak) unexpected vibrations. As shown in the Figure 3b, the 2d t-SNE transformation of the embeddings, provided by the network fed with these anomalous sequences, generated points, labeled as *Noise*, that are outside the clusters.

6. Conclusions

We proposed a new methodology for addressing the early detection problem of faults in critical devices that equip sensors that generate time sequences of observations. In particular, the methodology is designed to effectively work in settings where explicit information about previous failures is missing, overcoming the hindrance of the exploitation of supervised detection approaches. Assuming that failures are rare events during the life time of a device, the proposed methodology supports a maintenance expert in easily identifying them as anomalous elements that are distant from all the clusters of normal behavior.

Experiments on a real case study showed the capability of the proposal in effectively isolating anomalous time frames, suggesting that its application fields can span in many different and more complex scenarios.

Acknowledgments

This work has been partially supported by the Calabria Region (ITALY) under the project "RAISE - Revelis Artificial Intelligence Smart Environment" - POR CALABRIA FESR-FSE 2014-2020, ASSE I – PROMOZIONE DELLA RICERCA E DELL'INNOVAZIONE Obiettivo Specifico 1.4 "Aumento dell'incidenza di specializzazioni innovative in perimetri applicativi ad alta intensità di conoscenza" Azione 1.4.1 "Sostegno alla creazione e al consolidamento di startup innovative ad alta intensità di applicazione di conoscenza e alle iniziative di spin-off della ricerca".

References

[1] N. Amruthnath, T. Gupta, A research study on unsupervised machine learning algorithms for early fault detection in predictive maintenance, in: 2018 5th International Conference on Industrial Engineering and Applications (ICIEA), 2018, pp. 355–361.

[2] B. Schölkopf, R. C. Williamson, A. J. Smola, J. Shawe-Taylor, J. C. Platt, et al., Support vector method for novelty detection., in: NIPS, volume 12, Citeseer, 1999, pp. 582–588.

[3] M. Amer, M. Goldstein, S. Abdennadher, Enhancing one-class support vector machines for unsupervised anomaly detection, in: Proceedings of the ACM SIGKDD Workshop on Outlier Detection and Description, ODD '13, Association for Computing Machinery, New York, NY, USA, 2013, p. 8–15.

[4] F. T. Liu, K. M. Ting, Z.-H. Zhou, Isolation forest, in: Proceedings of the 2008 Eighth IEEE International Conference on Data Mining, ICDM '08, IEEE Computer Society, USA, 2008, p. 413–422.

[5] F. T. Liu, K. M. Ting, Z.-H. Zhou, Isolation-based anomaly detection, ACM Trans. Knowl. Discov. Data 6 (2012).

[6] D. Bank, N. Koenigstein, R. Giryes, Autoencoders, 2020. arXiv:2003.05991.

[7] D. F. Oliveira, L. F. Vismari, J. R. de Almeida, P. S. Cugnasca, J. B. Camargo, E. Marreto, D. R. Doimo, L. P. F. de Almeida, R. Gripp, M. M. Neves, Evaluating unsupervised anomaly detection models to detect faults in heavy haul railway operations, in: 2019 18th IEEE International Conference On Machine Learning And Applications (ICMLA), 2019, pp. 1016–1022.

[8] D. F. N. Oliveira, L. F. Vismari, A. M. Nascimento, J. R. de Almeida Jr au2, P. S. Cugnasca, J. B. C. J. au2, L. Almeida, R. Gripp, M. Neves, A new interpretable unsupervised anomaly detection method based on residual explanation, 2021. arXiv:2103.07953.

[9] E. Principi, D. Rossetti, S. Squartini, F. Piazza, Unsupervised electric motor fault detection by using deep autoencoders, IEEE/CAA Journal of Automatica Sinica 6 (2019) 441–451.

[10] K. H. Park, E. Park, H. K. Kim, Unsupervised fault detection on unmanned aerial vehicles: Encoding and thresholding approach, Sensors 21 (2021).

[11] X. Liang, F. Duan, I. Bennett, D. Mba, A sparse autoencoder-based unsupervised scheme for pump fault detection and isolation, Applied Sciences 10 (2020).

[12] B. Lindemann, F. Fesenmayr, N. Jazdi, M. Weyrich, Anomaly detection in discrete manufacturing using self-learning approaches, Procedia CIRP 79 (2019) 313–318.

[13] S. Hochreiter, J. Schmidhuber, Long short-term memory, Neural Comput. 9 (1997) 1735–1780.

[14] G. Jiang, P. Xie, H. He, J. Yan, Wind turbine fault detection using a denoising autoencoder with temporal information, IEEE/ASME Transactions on Mechatronics 23 (2018) 89–100.

[15] G. Xiang, R. Tao, Y. Peng, K. Tian, C. Qu, Unsupervised deep learning for fault detection on spacecraft using improved variational autoencoder, in: 2020 Chinese Automation Congress (CAC), 2020, pp. 5527–5531.

[16] D. P. Kingma, M. Welling, Auto-encoding variational bayes, 2014. arXiv:1312.6114.

[17] J. Chung, C. Gulcehre, K. Cho, Y. Bengio, Empirical evaluation of gated recurrent neural networks on sequence modeling, 2014. arXiv:1412.3555.

[18] A. L. Alfeo, M. G. Cimino, G. Manco, E. Ritacco, G. Vaglini, Using an autoencoder in the design of an anomaly detector for smart manufacturing, Pattern Recognition Letters 136 (2020) 272–278.

[19] W. Jian, H. Zhiyan, A novel fault detection method based on adversarial auto-encoder, in: 2020 39th Chinese Control Conference (CCC), 2020, pp. 4166–4170.

[20] P. Spyridon, Y. S. Boutalis, Generative adversarial networks for unsupervised fault detection, in: 2018 European Control Conference (ECC), 2018, pp. 691–696.

[21] I. J. Goodfellow, J. Pouget-Abadie, M. Mirza, B. Xu, D. Warde-Farley, S. Ozair, A. Courville, Y. Bengio, Generative adversarial nets, in: Proceedings of the 27th International Conference on Neural Information Processing Systems - Volume 2, NIPS'14, MIT Press, Cambridge, MA, USA, 2014, p. 2672–2680.

[22] G. Koch, R. Zemel, R. Salakhutdinov, Siamese neural networks for one-shot image recognition, 2015.

[23] L. van der Maaten, G. Hinton, Visualizing data using t-SNE, Journal of Machine Learning Research 9 (2008) 2579–2605.

DP-DILCA: Learning Differentially Private Context-based Distances for Categorical Data

(Discussion Paper)

Elena Battaglia[1], Ruggero G. Pensa[1]

[1]University of Turin, Italy

Abstract

Distance-based machine learning methods have limited applicability to categorical data, since they do not capture the complexity of the relationships among different values of a categorical attribute. Nonetheless, categorical attributes are common in many application scenarios, including clinical and health records, census and survey data. Although distance learning algorithms exist for categorical data, they may disclose private information about individual records if applied to a secret dataset. To address this problem, we introduce a differentially private algorithm for learning distances between any pair of values of a categorical attribute according to the way they are co-distributed with the values of other categorical attributes forming the so-called context. We show empirically that our approach consumes little privacy budget while providing accurate distances.

Keywords

differential privacy, metric learning, categorical attributes, distance-based methods

1. Introduction

Most machine learning and data analysis methods rely, directly or indirectly, on their ability to compute distances or similarities between data objects. Although different definitions of distance/similarity exist, they are relatively easy to compute, provided that data are given in form of numeric vectors. Additionally, for most of the above-mentioned distance-based methods, differentially private counterparts of them have been proposed as well. Differential privacy [1] is a computational paradigm which guarantees that the output of a statistical query applied to a secret dataset does not allow to understand whether a particular data object is present in the dataset or not. In recent years, many differentially private variants have been proposed for most distance based algorithms, including kNN [2], SVM [3] and k-means [4].

When data are described by categorical features/attributes, instead, distances can only account for the match or mismatch of the values of an attribute between two data objects, leading to poorer and less expressive proximity measures (e.g., the Jaccard similarity). And yet, intuitively, a patient whose disease is "gastritis" should be closer to a patient affected by "ulcer" than to one having "migraine". An efficient solution consists in using some distance learning algorithm

SEBD 2021: The 29th Italian Symposium on Advanced Database Systems, September 5-9, 2021, Pizzo Calabro (VV), Italy

elena.battaglia@unito.it (E. Battaglia); ruggero.pensa@unito.it (R. G. Pensa)

0000-0001-5145-3438 (R. G. Pensa)

to infer the distance between any pair of different values of the same categorical attribute from data. Among all existing methods, DILCA [5] is one of the most effective. DILCA's objective is to compute the distance between any pair of values of a categorical attribute by taking into account the way the two values are co-distributed with respect to the values of other categorical attributes forming the so-called context. According to DILCA, if two values of a categorical attribute are similarly distributed w.r.t. the values of the context attributes, then their distance is lower than that computed for two values of the same attribute that are divergently distributed w.r.t. the values of the same context attributes. DILCA has been successfully used in different scenarios including clustering [5], semi-supervised learning [6] and anomaly detection [7]. However, if applied to a secret dataset, it may disclose a lot of private information.

In this paper, we address the problem of learning meaningful distances for categorical data in a differentially private way. To this purpose, we first introduce a differentially-private extension of DILCA adopting the exponential mechanisms. We show experimentally that it provides accurate distances even with relatively small values of privacy budget ε. Additionally, we show that our algorithm (which we call DP-DILCA) is effective in two distance-based learning scenarios, including clustering and k-NN classification.

2. Background

In this section, we introduce the necessary background required to understand the theoretical foundations of our method and, contextually, we introduce its related scientific literature.

2.1. Differential Privacy

Differential privacy [1] is a privacy definition that guarantees the outcome of a calculation to be insensitive to any particular record in the data set. More formally, we report the following definition [1]:

Definition 1 (ε-differential privacy). *Let $\mathcal{M} : \Omega \longrightarrow \mathcal{R}$ be a randomized mechanism (i.e. a stochastic function with values in a generic set $\mathcal{R}$) and consider a real number $\varepsilon > 0$. We say that $\mathcal{M}$ preserves ε-differential privacy if for all pair of datasets D, D' differing for only one record and $\forall r \in \mathcal{R}$, $\frac{P(\mathcal{M}(D)=r)}{P(\mathcal{M}(D')=r)} \leq e^{\varepsilon}$.*

Differential privacy satisfies two important properties: composition and post-processing [1]. The composition property states that by combining the results of several differentially private mechanisms, the outcome will be differentially private too, and the overall level ε of privacy guaranteed will be the sum of the level of privacy of each mechanism. On the other hand, the post-processing property says that once a quantity r has been computed in a differentially private way, any following transformation of this quantity is still differentially private, with no need to spend part of the privacy budget for it.

Several mechanisms and techniques preserving differential privacy have been proposed in literature. Two of the most famous mechanisms are the Laplace and the Exponential mechanisms [1]. They both calibrate the amount of random noise they inject in the computation by looking at the sensitivity of the function (or utility function) considered:

Definition 2 (Global sensitivity). *Let* $q : \Omega \longrightarrow \mathbb{R}^d$ *be a numeric function. The global sensitivity* $GS(q)$ *is a measure of the maximal variation of function* q *when computed over two datasets differing for only one record and is defined as* $GS(q) = \max_{D \sim D'} ||q(D) - q(D')||_1$.

2.2. DILCA

Measuring similarities or distances between two data objects is a crucial step for many machine learning and data mining tasks. While the notion of similarity for continuous data is relatively well-understood and extensively studied, for categorical data the similarity computation is not straightforward. The simplest comparison measure for categorical data is *overlap* [8]: given two tuples, it counts the number of attributes whose values in the two tuples are the same. The overlap measure does not distinguish different values of attributes, hence matches and mismatches are treated equally. Among all the proposed methods for distance computation, we focus on DILCA [5], a framework to learn context-based distances between each pair of values of a categorical attribute Y. The main idea behind DILCA is that the distribution of the co-occurrences of the values of Y and the values of the other attributes in the dataset may help define a distance between the values of Y (intuitively, two values that are similarly co-distributed w.r.t. all the other values of all the other attributes are similar and so they should be close in the new distance). However, not all the other attributes in the dataset should be taken in consideration, but only those that are more relevant to Y. We call this set of relevant attributes with respect to Y the *context* of Y. DILCA distance is defined as follow

Definition 3 (DILCA distance). *Let* $y_1, \dots y_n$ *be the values of attribute* Y. *For each pair* y_i, y_j *with* $i, j = 1, \dots, n$, *the distance between* y_i *and* y_j *is computed as*

$$d(y_i, y_j) = \sqrt{\frac{\sum_{X \in context(Y)} \sum_{k=1}^{|X|} (P(y_i|x_k) - P(y_j|x_k))^2}{\sum_{X \in context(Y)} |X|}}$$

where $context(Y)$ *is the set of the attributes belonging to the context of* Y, $|X|$ *is the number of values attribute* X *can assume, and* $P(y_i|x_k)$ *is the conditional probability that* Y *takes value* y_i *given that* X *has value* x_k.

The conditional probabilities $P(y_i|x_k)$ are estimated from the data: the contingency table between attributes X and Y is constructed and this contingency table can be interpreted as the empirical joint distribution of the two variables.

3. DP-DILCA

In this section, we introduce a method whose final goal is to inject some form of randomness in DILCA in order to make the resulting distances among the values of the target attribute Y differentially private. There are two moments when DILCA algorithm accesses the original (secret) dataset: the context and the contingency tables computation phases. If the context selection is made preserving $h \cdot \varepsilon$-differential privacy (where $h \in [0, 1]$) and the computation of all the contingency tables is made preserving $(1 - h)\varepsilon$-differential privacy, then the composition

Algorithm 1: $DPContext(D, Y, h \cdot \varepsilon, k)$

Input: The original dataset D with N records and attributes $F = \{X_1, ..., X_m\}$, the target attribute $Y \in F$, the privacy budget $h\varepsilon$, the number k of attributes in the context

Result: The set $context(Y)$

```
1 gs ← (2/N) (1/ln(2) + log(N));
2 𝓕 ← {X_1, ..., X_m} \ {Y};
3 context(Y) ← ∅;
4 for t = 1 to k do
5     Select an object X ∈ 𝓕 with probability proportional to exp( hε·MI(Y,X) / (2·k·gs) );
6     context(Y) ← context(Y) ∪ {X};
7     𝓕 ← 𝓕 \ {X};
8 end
```

and the post-processing theorems guarantee that the overall algorithm preserves ε-differential privacy.

The context selection procedure used by DILCA is an application of a filter method for supervised feature selection. Indeed, some work has been done on differentially private feature selection. For instance, [9] and [10] present two alternative differentially private implementations of a feature selection method that preserves nearest-neighbor classification capability. In [11], instead, the authors study the sensitivity of several association measures used for feature selection and integrate the noised version of these measures in two differentially private classifiers. Here, we propose a differentially private selection method that measures the connection of two attributes by looking at the (distorted) Mutual Information between them and then extracts the k most relevant attributes. Mutual Information is a widely used measure of association in the supervised feature selection problem and it can be computed as $I(X, Y) = H(X) + H(Y) - H(X, Y)$ (where $H(\cdot)$ is the entropy function). Thus, finding the X which maximizes $I(X, Y)$ is equivalent to finding the X which maximizes $I'(X, Y) = H(X) - H(X, Y)$.

Theorem 3.1 (Sensitivity of $I'(X, Y)$). *Given a dataset D with N records and two attributes X and Y, an upper bound of the sensitivity of $I'(X, Y)$ is $\frac{2}{N}\left(\frac{1}{ln(2)} + log(N)\right)$.*

Algorithm 1 describes the differentially private version of context selection. It requires the specification, as input parameter, of the desired number k of attributes in the context of the target attribute. When setting the value of parameter k, one must consider that lower values of k are preferable, from a differentially private point of view. In step 5 of Algorithm 1, the exponential mechanism is applied k times, in order to extract the top k attributes: each application of the exponential mechanism requires part of the overall privacy budget; thus, the smaller k is, the higher the accuracy of the selected context. Algorithm 1 preserves $h\varepsilon$-differential privacy.

Once the context of target attribute Y has been selected, DILCA algorithm computes the contingency table $CT(X, Y)$ between Y and X, for each X in context. Instead of the exact value $CT(X, Y)$, we compute a distorted contingency table via the Laplace mechanism. This

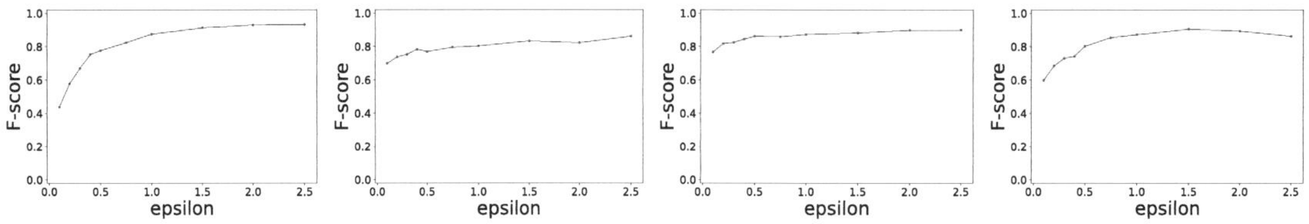

(a) NLTCS (b) IPUMS-BR (c) IPUMS-ME (d) adult

Figure 1: Average F-score of the differentially private context.

mechanism needs the specification of two parameters, the sensitivity of the function CT, that can be proved to be 2, and the privacy budget. Since the total number of needed contingency tables is $k = |context(Y)|$, the privacy budget we spend for each contingency table is $\frac{(1-h)\varepsilon}{k}$. In this way, the overall DP-DILCA algorithm preserves ε-differential privacy.

4. Experiments

In this section, we describe the experiments conducted to evaluate the performances of DP-DILCA. For this evaluation, we use four real-world datasets: adult[1], NLTCS[2], IPUMS-BR and IPUMS-ME[3].

4.1. Assessment of context selection

In the first experiment, we run DP-DILCA on the real-world datasets in order to assess the quality of the context they select. For each dataset, we consider one attribute at a time as target attribute and we compute its differentially private context for increasing levels of privacy budget ε. Then we compare the context selected by DP-DILCA with the context obtained with the corresponding non-private method. In all the experiments we set $k = 3$. To evaluate the similarity between the private and non-private context for each target attribute, we use the F-score, i.e., the harmonic mean of precision and recall. For each ε, we repeat the experiments 30 times and we compute the mean value of all scores. Figure 1 shows the results of our comparison: for each ε we report the average value of the F-score over all the attributes of each dataset. In all the datasets, the results achieved by DP-DILCA increase with respect to ε.

4.2. Assessment of the distance matrices

In this section we repeat the same experiments on the real-world data presented in Section 4.1, but we focus on the final output of DP-DILCA: the distances between the values of the target attribute. As before, for each dataset we consider one attribute at a time as target and we compute the differentially private distance matrix associated to its values, for increasing levels of privacy budget ε. Then we compare the distances obtained with DP-DILCA with those

[1]https://archive.ics.uci.edu/
[2]http://lib.stat.cmu.edu/
[3]https://international.ipums.org/

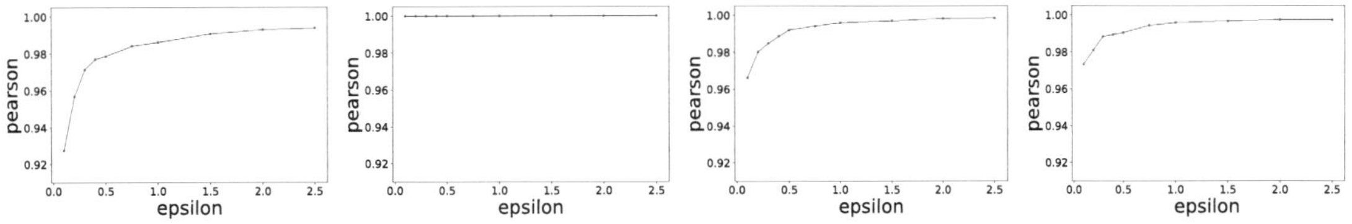

(a) adult (b) NLTCS (c) IPUMS-BR (d) IPUMS-ME

Figure 2: Average Pearson correlation between the differentially private distance matrices and the correspondent non private ones.

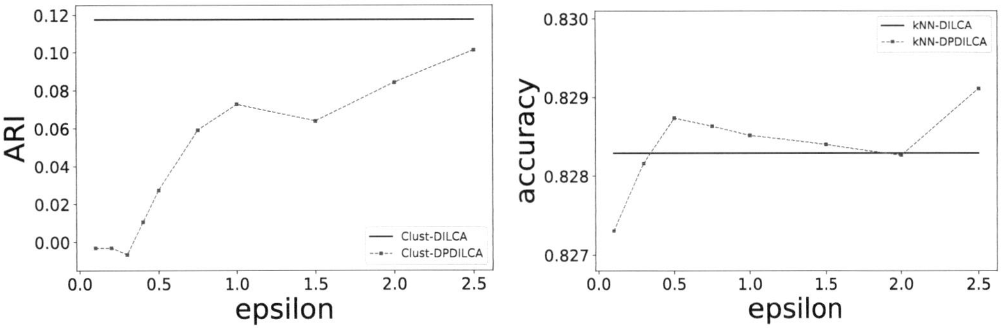

(a) Clustering (b) kNN classification

Figure 3: Results on clustering (a) and kNN classification (b).

obtained with the corresponding non-private method. In this experiment we set $k = 3$ and $h = 0.3$. We quantify the linear correlation between the private distance matrix M', with shape $n \times n$, and its non-private counterpart M through the sample Pearson's ρ correlation coefficient. The ρ coefficient takes values between -1 (perfect negative correlation) and 1 (perfect positive correlation). If the two matrices are not correlated we will have $\rho \cong 0$.

For each ε, we repeat the experiments 30 times and we compute the mean value of the sample Pearson correlation coefficient. Figure 2 shows the results of our computations: for each ε we report the average value of the measure over all the attributes of each dataset. The results show that there is positive correlation between private and non-private distances and the Pearson's coefficient increases as ε grows. Notice that the Pearson coefficient is always 1 when the target attribute has only two values. For this reason, for NLTCS (Figure 2(b)), which consists of binary attributes only, the Person's correlation is always maximum.

4.3. Experiments on clustering and classification

In this section, we assess the effectiveness and utility of the distances computed by our differentially private algorithms. To this purpose, we embed DP-DILCA into two distance-based learning algorithms: the Ward's hierarchical clustering algorithm and the kNN classifier. Both the algorithms take as input the matrix of the pairwise distances between the data objects. DP-DILCA's output is the distance between values of a categorical attribute; if it is applied to all attributes in F, then the distance between any pair of objects o_i, o_j, both described by F can be computed as $objDist(o_i, o_j) = \sqrt{\sum_{X \in F} M_X[o_i.X, o_j.X]^2}$, where M_X is the distance matrix returned by DP-DILCA for attribute X and $o_i.X$ and $o_j.X$ are the values of attribute X on objects o_i and o_j [5]. We will refer to this metric as $objDist_{DPDILCA}$. Similarly, we will call $objDist_{DILCA}$ the metric obtained by the non-private DILCA algorithm.

We run the experiment about clustering as follows: for each real-world dataset, we compute the object distance matrix using the different private and non private metrics, then we run Ward's hierarchical clustering with these matrices as input. Since the hierarchical algorithm returns a dendrogram which, at each level, contains a different number of clusters, we consider the level corresponding to the number of clusters equal to the number of classes. We call the overall clustering models $Clust_{DPDILCA}$ and $Clust_{DILCA}$, depending on the distance metric adopted. We evaluate the quality of the results through the adjusted rand index (ARI) computed w.r.t. the actual classes [12]. For this reason we run this experiment on dataset adult only. Figure 3(a) shows the mean ARI results over 30 experiments. The value of ε on the x axis of the plot is the overall privacy budget used for the learning of the metric, while the privacy budget spent for computing the distances among values of a single attribute is $\frac{\varepsilon}{m}$. The ARI values of the clustering model with private distance computation grow with respect to the privacy budget, and for high values of ε, they get results close to those of the clustering with non-private distances.

As last experiment, we run the kNN classification algorithm, with $k = 5$. We perform a 4-fold cross-validation: one fold is retained as test set, then the metrics $objDist_{DPDILCA}$, and $objDist_{DILCA}$ are learned on the remaining 3 folds and the classification model is trained on the same set. We call the overall models $kNN_{DPDILCA}$ and kNN_{DILCA}, depending on the distance learning algorithm used. For each dataset, we apply the four kNN models 30 times and compute the mean accuracy of the classification on the the test set. The process is repeated four times and the results are further averaged on the four test sets. In Figure 3(b) we report the mean accuracy of all the models for increasing levels of privacy budget ε. The results of $kNN_{DPDILCA}$ are always very close to those of kNN_{DILCA}, even for very low levels of ε.

5. Conclusion

We have introduced a new family of differentially private algorithms for the data-driven computation of meaningful and expressive distances between any two values of a categorical attribute. Our approach is built upon an effective context-based distance learning framework whose output, however, may reveal private information if applied to a secret dataset. For this reason, we have proposed a randomized algorithm, based on the Laplace and exponential mechanisms, that satisfies ε-differential privacy and returns accurate distance measures even with relatively small privacy budget consumption. Additionally, the metric learnt by our approach can be used profitably in distance-based machine learning algorithms, such as hierarchical clustering and kNN classification.

Acknowledgments

This work is supported by Fondazione CRT (grant number 2019-0450).

References

[1] C. Dwork, A. Roth, The algorithmic foundations of differential privacy, Found. Trends Theor. Comput. Sci. 9 (2014) 211–407.

[2] M. E. Gursoy, A. Inan, M. E. Nergiz, Y. Saygin, Differentially private nearest neighbor classification, Data Min. Knowl. Discov. 31 (2017) 1544–1575.

[3] K. Chaudhuri, C. Monteleoni, A. D. Sarwate, Differentially private empirical risk minimization, J. Mach. Learn. Res. 12 (2011) 1069–1109.

[4] D. Su, J. Cao, N. Li, E. Bertino, M. Lyu, H. Jin, Differentially private k-means clustering and a hybrid approach to private optimization, ACM Trans. Priv. Secur. 20 (2017) 16:1–16:33.

[5] D. Ienco, R. G. Pensa, R. Meo, From context to distance: Learning dissimilarity for categorical data clustering, ACM Trans. Knowl. Discov. Data 6 (2012) 1:1–1:25.

[6] D. Ienco, R. G. Pensa, Positive and unlabeled learning in categorical data, Neurocomputing 196 (2016) 113–124.

[7] D. Ienco, R. G. Pensa, R. Meo, A semisupervised approach to the detection and characterization of outliers in categorical data, IEEE Trans. Neural Networks Learn. Syst. 28 (2017) 1017–1029.

[8] S. Kasif, S. Salzberg, D. L. Waltz, J. Rachlin, D. W. Aha, A probabilistic framework for memory-based reasoning, Artif. Intell. 104 (1998) 287–311.

[9] J. Yang, Y. Li, Differentially private feature selection, in: Proceedings of IJCNN 2014, IEEE, 2014, pp. 4182–4189.

[10] Y. Li, J. Yang, W. Ji, Local learning-based feature weighting with privacy preservation, Neurocomputing 174 (2016) 1107–1115.

[11] B. Anandan, C. Clifton, Differentially private feature selection for data mining, in: Proceedings of ACM IWSPA@CODASPY 2018, 2018, pp. 43–53.

[12] L. Hubert, P. Arabie, Comparing partitions, Journal of Classification 2 (1985) 193–218.

Privacy Preserving Query Answering in Description Logics Through Instance Indistinguishability

(Discussion Paper)

Gianluca Cima[1], Domenico Lembo[2], Riccardo Rosati[2] and Domenico Fabio Savo[3]

[1] *University of Bordeaux, CNRS, Bordeaux INP, LaBRI*
[2] *Sapienza Università di Roma*
[3] *Università degli Studi di Bergamo*

Abstract

We study privacy-preserving query answering in Description Logics (DLs). Specifically, we consider the approach of controlled query evaluation (CQE) based on the notion of *instance indistinguishability*. We derive data complexity results for query answering over *DL-Lite*$_{\mathcal{R}}$ ontologies, through a comparison with an alternative, existing confidentiality-preserving approach to CQE. Finally, we identify a semantically well-founded notion of approximated query answering for CQE, and prove that, for *DL-Lite*$_{\mathcal{R}}$ ontologies, this form of CQE is tractable with respect to data complexity and is first-order rewritable, i.e., it is always reducible to the evaluation of a first-order query over the data instance.

1. Introduction

We consider controlled query evaluation (CQE), a declarative framework for privacy-preserving query answering investigated in the literature on knowledge representation and database theory [1, 2, 3]. The basic idea of CQE is defining a *data protection policy* through logical statements. Consider for instance an organization that wants to keep confidential the fact that it has suppliers involved in both Project A and Project B. This can be expressed over the information schema of the organization through a denial assertion of the form $\forall x.\,\mathsf{Supplier}(x) \wedge \mathsf{ProjA}(x) \wedge \mathsf{ProjB}(x) \rightarrow \bot$

In CQE, two different main approaches can be identified. The first one [4, 5, 6] models privacy preservation through the notion of *indistinguishable data instances*. In this approach, a system for CQE enforces data privacy if, for every data instance I, there exists a data instance I' that does not violate the data protection policy and is indistinguishable from I for the user, i.e., for every user query q, the system provides the same answers to q over I and over I'. We call this approach *(instance) indistinguishability-based* (IB). In continuation of the previous example,

SEBD 2021: The 29th Italian Symposium on Advanced Database Systems, September 5-9, 2021, Pizzo Calabro (VV), Italy
gianluca.cima@u-bordeaux.fr (G. Cima); lembo@diag.uniroma1.it (D. Lembo); rosati@diag.uniroma1.it (R. Rosati); domenicofabio.savo@unibg.it (D. F. Savo)
0000-0003-1783-5605 (G. Cima); 0000-0002-0628-242X (D. Lembo); 0000-0002-7697-4958 (R. Rosati); 0000-0002-8391-8049 (D. F. Savo)

in the presence of an instance $\{\mathsf{Supplier}(c), \mathsf{ProjA}(c), \mathsf{ProjB}(c)\}$, an IB system should answer user queries as if the instance were, e.g., $\{\mathsf{Supplier}(c), \mathsf{ProjA}(c)\}$ (note that other instances not violating the policy can be considered as indistinguishable, e.g., $\{\mathsf{Supplier}(c), \mathsf{ProjB}(c)\}$).

The second approach [7, 8] models privacy preservation by considering the whole (possibly infinite) set of answers to queries that the system provides to the user. In this approach, a CQE system protects the data if, for every data instance I, the logical theory corresponding to the set of answers provided by the system to all queries over I does not entail any violation of the data protection policy. According to [8], we call this approach *confidentiality-preserving (CP)*. In our ongoing example, a CP system would entail, e.g., the queries $\mathsf{Supplier}(c) \wedge \mathsf{ProjA}(c)$ and $\exists x.\mathsf{Supplier}(x) \wedge \mathsf{ProjB}(x)$, but not also the query $\mathsf{Supplier}(c) \wedge \mathsf{ProjB}(c)$.

In both approaches, the ultimate goal is to realize *optimal* CQE systems, i.e., systems maximizing the answers returned to user queries, still respecting the data protection policy. Traditionally, this aim has been pursued through the construction of a *single optimal censor*, i.e., a specific implementation of the adopted notion of privacy-preservation, either IB or CP. Since, however, in both approaches several optimal censors typically exist, this way of proceeding requires to make a choice on how to obfuscate data, which, in the absence of additional (preference) criteria, may result discretionary. To avoid this, query answering over all optimal censors has been recently studied, limited to the CP approach [7, 9], whereas query answering over all optimal IB censors has not been investigated so far. Moreover, among the complexity results obtained and the techniques defined so far for CQE, we still miss the identification of cases that are promising towards its practical usage.

In this paper, we aim at filling some of the above mentioned gaps in the context of Description Logic (DL) ontologies. We focus on the approach to CQE based on instance indistinguishability (Section 3), and study its relationship with the CP approach (Section 4). Specifically, we prove that the IB approach to CQE in DLs corresponds to a particular instance of the CP approach to CQE [9]. Based on such a correspondence, we show that, even in the lightweight DL *DL-Lite*$_\mathcal{R}$, query answering in the IB approach is intractable with respect to data complexity, unless one relies on a single optimal censor chosen non-deterministically in the lack of further meta-information about the domain of the dataset.

To overcome the above problems and provide a practical, semantically well-founded solution, we define a *quasi-optimal* notion of IB censor, which corresponds to the best sound approximation of all the optimal IB censors (Section 5). We then prove that, in the case of *DL-Lite*$_\mathcal{R}$ ontologies, query answering based on the quasi-optimal IB censor is reducible to the evaluation of a first-order query over the data instance, i.e., it is *first-order rewritable*. We believe that this result has an important practical impact. Indeed, we have identified a setting in which privacy-preserving query answering formalized in a declarative logic-based framework as CQE, for a DL (i.e., *DL-Lite*$_\mathcal{R}$) specifically designed for data management, has the same data complexity as evaluating queries over a database (i.e., in AC^0). This opens the possibility of defining algorithms for CQE of practical usage, amenable to implementation on top of traditional (relational) data management systems, as done in [10] exploiting Ontology-based Data Access engines.

This paper summarizes the results of our IJCAI-20 conference publication [11].

2. Preliminaries

We use standard notions of function-free first-order (FO) logic, and in particular we consider Description Logics (DLs), which are fragments of FO using only unary and binary predicates, called concepts and roles, respectively.We assume to have the pairwise disjoint countably infinite sets $\Sigma_C, \Sigma_R, \Sigma_I$ and $\Sigma_\mathcal{V}$ for *atomic concepts*, *atomic roles*, *constants* (a.k.a. individuals), and *variables*, respectively. A DL ontology $\mathcal{O} = \mathcal{T} \cup \mathcal{A}$ is constituted by a TBox $\mathcal{T}$ and an ABox $\mathcal{A}$, specifying intensional and extensional knowledge, respectively. The set of atomic concepts and roles occurring in $\mathcal{O}$ is the *signature* of $\mathcal{O}$. The semantics of $\mathcal{O}$ is given in terms of FO models over the signature of $\mathcal{O}$, in the standard way.In particular, we say that $\mathcal{O}$ is *consistent* if it has at least one model, *inconsistent* otherwise. $\mathcal{O}$ *entails* an FO sentence ϕ specified over the signature of $\mathcal{O}$, denoted $\mathcal{O} \models \phi$, if ϕ is true in every model of $\mathcal{O}$. In this paper, we consider ontologies expressed in *DL-Lite*$_\mathcal{R}$, the member of the *DL-Lite* family [12] which underpins OWL 2 QL, i.e., the OWL 2 profile specifically designed for efficient query answering. A TBox $\mathcal{T}$ in *DL-Lite*$_\mathcal{R}$ is a finite set of axioms of the form $B_1 \sqsubseteq B_2$ (resp., $R_1 \sqsubseteq R_2$), denoting concept (resp., role) inclusion, and $B_1 \sqsubseteq \neg B_2$ (resp., $R_1 \sqsubseteq \neg R_2$), denoting concept (resp., role) disjointness, where: R_1, R_2 are of the form P, with $P \in \Sigma_R$, or its inverse P^-, and B_1, B_2 are of the form A, with $A \in \Sigma_C$, $\exists P$, or $\exists P^-$, i.e., unqualified existential restrictions, which denote the set of objects occurring as first or second argument of P, respectively. An ABox $\mathcal{A}$ is a finite set of *ground atoms*, i.e., assertions of the form $A(a)$, $P(a, b)$, where $A \in \Sigma_C$, $P \in \Sigma_R$, and $a, b \in \Sigma_I$. As usual in query answering over DL ontologies, we focus on conjunctive queries. A Boolean conjunctive query (BCQ) q is an FO sentence of the form $\exists\vec{x}.\phi(\vec{x})$, where $\vec{x}$ are variables in $\Sigma_\mathcal{V}$, and $\phi(\vec{x})$ is a finite, non-empty conjunction of atoms of the form $\alpha(\vec{t})$, where $\alpha \in \Sigma_C \cup \Sigma_R$, and each term in $\vec{t}$ is either a constant in Σ_I or a variable in $\vec{x}$. We denote by *Eval*$(q, \mathcal{A})$ the result of the evaluation of a query q over (the model isomorphic to) an ABox $\mathcal{A}$.

A *denial assertion* (or simply a denial) is an FO sentence of the form $\forall\vec{x}.\phi(\vec{x}) \rightarrow \bot$, such that $\exists\vec{x}.\phi(\vec{x})$ is a BCQ. Given one such denial δ and an ontology $\mathcal{O}$, we say that $\mathcal{O} \cup \{\delta\}$ is consistent if $\mathcal{O} \not\models \exists\vec{x}.\phi(\vec{x})$, and is inconsistent otherwise.

In the following, with **FO**, **CQ**, and **GA**, we denote the languages of function-free FO sentences, BCQs, and ground atoms, respectively, all specified over the alphabets $\Sigma_C, \Sigma_R, \Sigma_I$, and $\Sigma_\mathcal{V}$. Given an ontology $\mathcal{O}$ and a language $\mathcal{L}$, with $\mathcal{L}(\mathcal{O})$ we refer to the subset of $\mathcal{L}$ whose sentences are built over the signature of $\mathcal{O}$ and the variables in $\Sigma_\mathcal{V}$. For a TBox $\mathcal{T}$ and a language $\mathcal{L}$, we denote by $\mathsf{cl}_\mathcal{L}^\mathcal{T}(\cdot)$ the function that, for an ABox $\mathcal{A}$, returns all the sentences $\phi \in \mathcal{L}(\mathcal{T} \cup \mathcal{A})$ such that $\mathcal{T} \cup \mathcal{A} \models \phi$.

For the sake of presentation, we will limit our technical treatment to languages containing only closed formulas, but our results hold also for open formulas. In particular, the results on entailment of BCQs can be extended to arbitrary (i.e., non-Boolean) CQs in the standard way[1]. Our complexity results are for data complexity, i.e., are w.r.t. the size of the ABox only.

[1] We also notice that, since *DL-Lite*$_\mathcal{R}$ is insensitive to the adoption of the *unique name assumption* (UNA) for CQ answering,our results hold both with and without UNA.

3. CQE through Instance Indistinguishability

A CQE framework consists of a TBox $\mathcal{T}$ and a policy $\mathcal{P}$ over $\mathcal{T}$, i.e., a finite set of denial assertions over the signature of $\mathcal{T}$. An ABox $\mathcal{A}$ for $\mathcal{T}$ is such that $\mathcal{A}$ and $\mathcal{T}$ have the same signature. In the following, when a TBox $\mathcal{T}$ is given, we always assume that the coupled policy is specified over $\mathcal{T}$, that each considered ABox $\mathcal{A}$ is for $\mathcal{T}$, and that $\mathcal{T} \cup \mathcal{A}$ and $\mathcal{T} \cup \mathcal{P}$ are consistent. A *censor* is a function that taken an ABox for $\mathcal{T}$ as input alters standard query answering over $\mathcal{T} \cup \mathcal{A}$ so that on the basis of the answers (even a possibly infinite set thereof) and the TBox, a user can never infer a BCQ $\exists \vec{x}.\phi(\vec{x})$ such that $\forall \vec{x}.\phi(\vec{x}) \rightarrow \bot$ belongs to $\mathcal{P}$.

We here propose a notion of censor which is the natural application to our framework of the analogous definitions given in [4, 5, 6, 13, 14]. The basic idea of this approach is that for every underlying instance (an ABox in our framework) and every query, a censor returns to the user the same answers it would return on another (possibly identical) instance that does not contain confidential data, so that she cannot understand which of the two instances she is querying. This is formalized as follows.

Definition 1. [Indistinguishability-based censor] Let $\mathcal{T}$ be a DL TBox and $\mathcal{P}$ be a policy. An *indistinguishability-based (IB) censor* for $\mathcal{T}$ and $\mathcal{P}$ is a function $\mathsf{cens}(\cdot)$ that, for each ABox $\mathcal{A}$, returns a set $\mathsf{cens}(\mathcal{A}) \subseteq \mathsf{cl}^{\mathcal{T}}_{\mathbf{CQ}}(\mathcal{A})$ such that there exists an ABox $\mathcal{A}'$ for which (i) $\mathsf{cens}(\mathcal{A}) = \mathsf{cl}^{\mathcal{T}}_{\mathbf{CQ}}(\mathcal{A}')$ (in this case we say that $\mathcal{A}$ and $\mathcal{A}'$ are *indistinguishable* w.r.t. cens) and (ii) $\mathcal{T} \cup \mathcal{P} \cup \mathcal{A}'$ is a consistent FO theory.

Example 1. The TBox signature consists of the atomic concepts $\mathsf{Supplier}$, ProjA, and ProjB, denoting the set of suppliers of the company, suppliers involved in Project A and those involved in Project B, respectively, and contains the axioms $\mathsf{ProjA} \sqsubseteq \mathsf{Supplier}$ and $\mathsf{ProjB} \sqsubseteq \mathsf{Supplier}$, stating that each individual instance of ProjA or ProjB is also instance of $\mathsf{Supplier}$. Data protection is specified through the policy $\mathcal{P} = \{\forall x.\mathsf{ProjA}(x) \wedge \mathsf{ProjB}(x) \rightarrow \bot\}$. The following functions are IB censors for $\mathcal{T}$ and $\mathcal{P}$:

- cens_1: given an ABox $\mathcal{A}$, $\mathsf{cens}_1(\mathcal{A})$ returns the set $\mathsf{cl}^{\mathcal{T}}_{\mathbf{CQ}}(\mathcal{A}_{P_A})$ of BCQs, where $\mathcal{A}_{P_A}$ is obtained from $\mathcal{A}$ by removing the assertion $\mathsf{ProjA}(c)$, for each individual c such that both $\mathsf{ProjA}(c)$ and $\mathsf{ProjB}(c)$ are in $\mathcal{A}$ (note that for every ABox $\mathcal{A}$, $\mathcal{A}$ and $\mathcal{A}_{P_A}$ are indistinguishable w.r.t. cens_1. Similarly in the following censors).
- cens_2: given an ABox $\mathcal{A}$, $\mathsf{cens}_2(\mathcal{A})$ returns the set $\mathsf{cl}^{\mathcal{T}}_{\mathbf{CQ}}(\mathcal{A}_{P_B})$ of BCQs, where $\mathcal{A}_{P_B}$ is obtained from $\mathcal{A}$ by removing the assertion $\mathsf{ProjB}(c)$, for each individual c such that both $\mathsf{ProjA}(c)$ and $\mathsf{ProjB}(c)$ are in $\mathcal{A}$.
- cens_3: given an ABox $\mathcal{A}$, $\mathsf{cens}_3(\mathcal{A})$ returns the set $\mathsf{cl}^{\mathcal{T}}_{\mathbf{CQ}}(\mathcal{A}_{sup})$ of BCQs, where $\mathcal{A}_{sup}$ is obtained from $\mathcal{A}$ by adding the assertion $\mathsf{Supplier}(c)$ and removing $\mathsf{ProjA}(c)$ and $\mathsf{ProjB}(c)$, for each individual c such that both $\mathsf{ProjA}(c)$ and $\mathsf{ProjB}(c)$ are in $\mathcal{A}$. □

It is easy to see that an IB censor always exists, but, as Example 1 shows, there may be many IB censors for $\mathcal{T}$ and $\mathcal{P}$, and so it is reasonable to look for censors preserving as much information as possible. Formally, given two IB censors cens and cens' for $\mathcal{T}$ and $\mathcal{P}$, we say that cens' is *more informative* than cens if: *(i)* for every ABox $\mathcal{A}$, $\mathsf{cens}(\mathcal{A}) \subseteq \mathsf{cens}'(\mathcal{A})$, and *(ii)* there exists an ABox $\mathcal{A}'$ such that $\mathsf{cens}(\mathcal{A}') \subset \mathsf{cens}'(\mathcal{A}')$. Optimal censors are then defined as follows.

Definition 2. Let $\mathcal{T}$ be a DL TBox and $\mathcal{P}$ be a policy. An IB censor cens for $\mathcal{T}$ and $\mathcal{P}$ is *optimal* if there does not exist any other IB censor for $\mathcal{T}$ and $\mathcal{P}$ that is more informative than cens. We denote by $\mathsf{OptIBCens}_{\mathcal{T},\mathcal{P}}$ the set of the optimal IB censors for $\mathcal{T}$ and $\mathcal{P}$.

Example 2. Among the censors of Example 1, $\mathsf{cens}_3 \notin \mathsf{OptIBCens}_{\mathcal{T},\mathcal{P}}$, since both cens_1 and cens_2 are more informative than cens_3. It can be then verified that cens_1 and cens_2 are the only optimal IB censors for $\mathcal{T}$ and $\mathcal{P}$. □

4. IB Censors vs. CP Censors

In [8], a different notion of censor, named *confidentiality-preserving (CP)* censor, has been proposed. Intuitively, a CP censor establishes which are the BCQs entailed by a TBox and a given ABox that can be disclosed without violating the policy. We report below the definition given in [9], which generalizes CP censors to any language $\mathcal{L} \subseteq \mathbf{FO}$, called the censor language.

Definition 3. [Confidentiality-preserving censor] Let $\mathcal{T}$ be a DL TBox, $\mathcal{P}$ be a policy, and $\mathcal{L} \subseteq \mathbf{FO}$ be a language. A *confidentiality-preserving (CP) censor* in $\mathcal{L}$ for $\mathcal{T}$ and $\mathcal{P}$ is a function $\mathsf{cens}(\cdot)$ that, for each ABox $\mathcal{A}$, returns a set $\mathsf{cens}(\mathcal{A}) \subseteq \mathsf{cl}^{\mathcal{T}}_{\mathcal{L}}(\mathcal{A})$ such that $\mathcal{T} \cup \mathcal{P} \cup \mathsf{cens}(\mathcal{A})$ is a consistent FO theory.

The notion of more informative censor previously given for IB censors can be naturally extended to CP censors, and so we can define optimal censors also in this case. We denote by $\mathcal{L}\text{-}\mathsf{OptCPCens}_{\mathcal{T},\mathcal{P}}$ the set of the optimal CP censors in $\mathcal{L}$ for $\mathcal{T}$ and $\mathcal{P}$.

Example 3. Consider $\mathcal{T}$ and $\mathcal{P}$ as defined in Example 1. An optimal CP censor cens_4 in $\mathbf{CQ}$ for $\mathcal{T}$ and $\mathcal{P}$ is defined as follows: given an ABox $\mathcal{A}$, $\mathsf{cens}_4(\mathcal{A})$ returns the set of BCQs obtained by removing from $\mathsf{cl}^{\mathcal{T}}_{\mathbf{CQ}}(\mathcal{A})$ every query containing the atom $\mathsf{ProjA}(c)$, for each individual c such that both $\mathsf{ProjA}(c)$ and $\mathsf{ProjB}(c)$ are in $\mathcal{A}$.

We notice that the CP censor cens_4 is not an IB censor. Indeed, consider the ABox $\mathcal{A} = \{\mathsf{ProjA}(c), \mathsf{ProjB}(c)\}$. We have that $\mathsf{cens}_4(\mathcal{A}) = \{\phi \mid \phi \in \mathbf{CQ} \text{ and } \mathcal{T} \cup \mathcal{S} \models \phi\}$, where $\mathcal{S} = \{\exists x.\mathsf{ProjA}(x), \mathsf{ProjB}(c)\}$. It is not hard to see that there exists no ABox $\mathcal{A}'$ such that $\mathcal{A}'$ and $\mathcal{A}$ are indistinguishable w.r.t. cens_4 and $\mathcal{T} \cup \mathcal{P} \cup \mathcal{A}'$ is consistent. □

Let $\mathcal{A}$ be an ABox and cens be either an IB or a CP censor, the set $\mathsf{cens}(\mathcal{A})$ is called *theory of the censor* cens for $\mathcal{A}$.

The following theorems explain the relation between IB censors and CP censors.

Theorem 1. *Let $\mathcal{T}$ be a DL TBox and $\mathcal{P}$ be a policy. If* cens *is an IB censor for $\mathcal{T}$ and $\mathcal{P}$, then it is a CP censor in* $\mathbf{CQ}$ *for $\mathcal{T}$ and $\mathcal{P}$. The converse does not necessarily hold.*

Theorem 2. *Let $\mathcal{T}$ be a DL TBox and $\mathcal{P}$ be a policy. Then,* $\mathsf{ib\_cens} \in \mathsf{OptIBCens}_{\mathcal{T},\mathcal{P}}$ *iff there exists a CP censor* $\mathsf{cp\_cens} \in \mathbf{GA}\text{-}\mathsf{OptCPCens}_{\mathcal{T},\mathcal{P}}$ *such that, for each ABox $\mathcal{A}$,* $\mathsf{cl}^{\mathcal{T}}_{\mathbf{CQ}}(\mathsf{cp\_cens}(\mathcal{A})) = \mathsf{ib\_cens}(\mathcal{A})$.

From Theorem 2 and the results given in [9], it follows that, given a *DL-Lite*$_{\mathcal{R}}$ TBox $\mathcal{T}$, a policy $\mathcal{P}$, an ABox $\mathcal{A}$, and a BCQ q, deciding whether $q \in \mathsf{cens}(\mathcal{A})$ for every $\mathsf{cens} \in \mathsf{OptIBCens}_{\mathcal{T},\mathcal{P}}$ is coNP-complete in data complexity.

5. Approximating Optimal IB Censors

Towards a practical approach to CQE, in this section we consider a different entailment problem that approximates entailment under *each* optimal censor, and we show that its data complexity is in AC^0 (i.e., the same complexity of evaluating FO queries over a database). The approximation we propose consists in considering a non-necessarily optimal IB censor whose theory, for every ABox, is as close as possible to the theories of all the optimal IB censors. We call such censor *quasi-optimal IB (QIB) censor.*

Definition 4. [QIB censor] Let $\mathcal{T}$ be a DL TBox, let $\mathcal{P}$ be a policy, and let cens be an IB censor for $\mathcal{T}$ and $\mathcal{P}$. We say that cens is a QIB censor if: *(i)* $\mathsf{cens}(\mathcal{A}) \subseteq \mathsf{cens}'(\mathcal{A})$, for each $\mathsf{cens}' \in \mathsf{OptIBCens}_{\mathcal{T},\mathcal{P}}$, and *(ii)* there exists no IB censor cens′ for $\mathcal{T}$ and $\mathcal{P}$ which is more informative than cens and that satisfies condition.

Example 4. The IB censor cens_3 of Example 1 is a QIB censor for $\mathcal{T}$ and $\mathcal{P}$ (but $\mathsf{cens}_3 \notin \mathsf{OptIBCens}_{\mathcal{T},\mathcal{P}}$). □

It is not hard to see that a QIB censor for a DL TBox $\mathcal{T}$ and a policy $\mathcal{P}$ always exists and it is unique. Hereinafter, we denote with $\mathsf{qib\_cens}_{\mathcal{T},\mathcal{P}}$ the QIB censor for $\mathcal{T}$ and $\mathcal{P}$.

Definition 5. Let $\mathcal{T}$ be a DL TBox, $\mathcal{P}$ be a policy, $\mathcal{A}$ be an ABox, and q be a BCQ. $\mathsf{QIB\text{-}Entailment}(\mathcal{T},\mathcal{P},\mathcal{A},q)$ is the problem of deciding whether $q \in \mathsf{qib\_cens}_{\mathcal{T},\mathcal{P}}(\mathcal{A})$.

We now focus on the case of *DL-Lite*$_\mathcal{R}$ TBoxes and prove that, in this case, entailment of BCQs under QIB censors is FO-rewritable. Formally, we say that QIB-entailment in a DL $\mathcal{L}$ is FO-rewritable, if for every TBox $\mathcal{T}$ expressed in $\mathcal{L}$, every policy $\mathcal{P}$ and every BCQ q, one can effectively compute an FO query q_r such that for every ABox $\mathcal{A}$, $\mathsf{QIB\text{-}Entailment}(\mathcal{T},\mathcal{P},\mathcal{A},q)$ is true iff $\mathcal{A} \models q_r$. We call q_r the *QIB-perfect reformulation* of q w.r.t. $\mathcal{T}$ and $\mathcal{P}$.

We prove FO-rewritability of entailment of BCQs under QIB censors in *DL-Lite*$_\mathcal{R}$ by exploiting a correspondence between this problem and entailment of BCQs under IAR-semantics for DL ontologies, which is indeed FO-rewritable for *DL-Lite*$_{\mathcal{R},den}$, i.e., *DL-Lite*$_\mathcal{R}$ enriched with denial assertions [15]. We recall that the IAR-semantics is an inconsistency-tolerant semantics that allows for meaningful entailment also when the ABox contradicts the TBox of an ontology. The entailment under IAR-semantics is defined as follows: give a DL $\mathcal{T}$, an ABox $\mathcal{A}$, and BCQ q, $\mathsf{IAR\text{-}Entailment}(\mathcal{T},\mathcal{A},q)$ is the problem of verifying whether $\mathcal{T} \cup \mathcal{R}_{iar} \models q$, where $\mathcal{R}_{iar}$ is the intersection of all the maximal subsets $\mathcal{A}_r$ of $\mathcal{A}$ such that $\mathcal{A}_r \cup \mathcal{T}$ is consistent.

Theorem 3. *Let $\mathcal{T}$ be a DL-Lite$_\mathcal{R}$ TBox, $\mathcal{P}$ be a policy, $\mathcal{A}$ be an ABox, and q be a BCQ. $\mathsf{QIB\text{-}Entailment}(\mathcal{T},\mathcal{P},\mathcal{A},q)$ is true iff $\mathsf{IAR\text{-}Entailment}(\mathcal{T} \cup \mathcal{P}, \mathsf{cl}^{\mathcal{T}}_{\mathbf{GA}}(\mathcal{A}), q)$ is true.*

Theorem 3 actually states that, to solve QIB-entailment, we can resort to the query rewriting techniques used to establish IAR-entailment given in [15], provided that we compute $\mathsf{cl}^{\mathcal{T}}_{\mathbf{GA}}(\mathcal{A})$. We recall that query entailment under IAR-semantics in a DL $\mathcal{L}$ is FO-rewritable if for every TBox $\mathcal{T}$ expressed in $\mathcal{L}$ and every BCQ q, one can effectively compute an FO query q_r such that for every ABox $\mathcal{A}$, $\mathsf{IAR\text{-}Entailment}(\mathcal{T}, \mathcal{A}, q)$ is true iff $\mathcal{A} \models q_r$. The query q_r is called the *IAR-perfect reformulation* of q w.r.t. $\mathcal{T}$.

To establish FO-rewritability of QIB-entailment in *DL-Lite*$_{\mathcal{R}}$, however, we still need to address the above mentioned computation of $\mathsf{cl}^{\mathcal{T}}_{\mathbf{GA}}(\mathcal{A})$, and turn it into an additional query reformulation step. To this aim, we can exploit the fact that, for a *DL-Lite*$_{\mathcal{R},den}$ ontology $\mathcal{T} \cup \mathcal{A}$, an FO query q evaluates to true over $\mathsf{cl}^{\mathcal{T}}_{\mathbf{GA}}(\mathcal{A})$ iff q' evaluates to true over $\mathcal{A}$, where q' is obtained by suitably rewriting each atom of q according to the positive inclusions of $\mathcal{T}$. Intuitively, in this way we cast into the query all the possible causes of the facts that are contained in the closure of the ABox w.r.t. the TBox.

To compute such a query q', we use the function $\mathsf{atomRewr}(q, \mathcal{T})$, which substitutes each atom α of q with the formula $\phi(\alpha)$ defined as follows (where A, B are atomic concepts and R, S are atomic roles):

$$\phi(A(t)) = \bigvee_{\mathcal{T} \models B \sqsubseteq A} B(t) \vee \bigvee_{\mathcal{T} \models \exists R \sqsubseteq A} (\exists x.R(t, x)) \vee \bigvee_{\mathcal{T} \models \exists R^- \sqsubseteq A} (\exists x.R(x, t))$$

$$\phi(R(t_1, t_2)) = \bigvee_{\mathcal{T} \models S \sqsubseteq R} S(t_1, t_2) \vee \bigvee_{\mathcal{T} \models S^- \sqsubseteq R} S(t_2, t_1).$$

The following lemma, whose proof can be immediately obtained from the definitions of $\mathsf{cl}^{\mathcal{T}}_{\mathbf{GA}}(\cdot)$ and $\mathsf{atomRewr}(\cdot, \cdot)$, states the property we are looking for.

Lemma 1. *Let $\mathcal{T}$ be a DL-Lite$_{\mathcal{R},den}$ TBox, $\mathcal{A}$ be an ABox, and q be an FO sentence. Then Eval$(q, \mathsf{cl}^{\mathcal{T}}_{\mathbf{GA}}(\mathcal{A}))$ = Eval$(\mathsf{atomRewr}(q, \mathcal{T}), \mathcal{A})$.*

We are now able to extablish FO-rewritability of QIB-entailment.

Theorem 4. *Let $\mathcal{T}$ be a DL-Lite$_{\mathcal{R}}$ TBox, $\mathcal{P}$ be a policy, q be a BCQ, and q_r be an FO sentence that is a IAR-perfect reformulation of q w.r.t. the DL-Lite$_{\mathcal{R},den}$ TBox $\mathcal{T} \cup \mathcal{P}$. Then, the FO sentence $\mathsf{atomRewr}(q_r, \mathcal{T})$ is a QIB-perfect reformulation of q w.r.t. $\mathcal{T}$ and $\mathcal{P}$.*

Since IAR-entailment is actually FO rewritable, as shown in [15], the above theorem proves the FO rewritability of QIB-entailment for *DL-Lite*$_{\mathcal{R}}$ TBoxes. Moreover, the above theorem identifies a technique for obtaining the QIB-perfect reformulation of a CQ, based on a simple combination of the IAR-perfect reformulation algorithm of [15] and the atomRewr reformulation defined above. Therefore:

Corollary 1. *Let $\mathcal{T}$ be a DL-Lite$_{\mathcal{R}}$ TBox, $\mathcal{P}$ be a policy, $\mathcal{A}$ be an ABox, and q be a BCQ. The problem $\mathsf{QIB\text{-}Entailment}(\mathcal{T}, \mathcal{P}, \mathcal{A}, q)$ is in AC^0 in data complexity.*

6. Conclusions

In this paper, we have studied the approach to CQE based on instance indistinguishability and identified a semantically well-founded notion of CQE that enjoys first-order rewritability in the case of *DL-Lite*$_{\mathcal{R}}$ ontologies.

An important future research direction is a deeper study of the user model. Our framework inherits from its predecessors a relatively simple model, which assumes that the user knows (at most) the TBox and all the query answers returned by the system, and considers only the *deductive* abilities of the user over such knowledge. This user model might need to be enriched to capture more realistic data protection scenarios.

Acknowledgments

This work was partly supported by the ANR AI Chair INTENDED (ANR-19-CHIA-0014), by MIUR under the PRIN 2017 project "HOPE" (prot. 2017MMJJRE), by the EU within the H2020 Programme under the grant agreement 834228 (ERC Advanced Grant WhiteMec) and the grant agreement 825333 (MOSAICrOWN), by Regione Lombardia within the Call Hub Ricerca e Innovazione under the grant agreement 1175328 (WATCHMAN), and by Sapienza Università di Roma (2019 project CQEinOBDM).

References

[1] G. L. Sicherman, W. de Jonge, R. P. van de Riet, Answering queries without revealing secrets, ACM Trans. Database Syst. 8 (1983) 41–59.

[2] P. A. Bonatti, S. Kraus, V. S. Subrahmanian, Foundations of secure deductive databases, IEEE Trans. Knowl. Data Eng. 7 (1995) 406–422.

[3] J. Biskup, For unknown secrecies refusal is better than lying, Data and Knowl. Eng. 33 (2000) 1–23.

[4] J. Biskup, P. A. Bonatti, Controlled query evaluation for known policies by combining lying and refusal, Ann. Math. Artif. Intell. 40 (2004) 37–62.

[5] J. Biskup, T. Weibert, Keeping secrets in incomplete databases, Int. J. of Information Security 7 (2008) 199–217.

[6] P. A. Bonatti, L. Sauro, A confidentiality model for ontologies, in: Proc. of ISWC, volume 8218 of *LNCS*, 2013, pp. 17–32.

[7] B. Cuenca Grau, E. Kharlamov, E. V. Kostylev, D. Zheleznyakov, Controlled query evaluation over OWL 2 RL ontologies, in: Proc. of ISWC, volume 8218, 2013, pp. 49–65.

[8] B. Cuenca Grau, E. Kharlamov, E. V. Kostylev, D. Zheleznyakov, Controlled query evaluation for datalog and OWL 2 profile ontologies, in: Proc. of IJCAI, 2015, pp. 2883–2889.

[9] D. Lembo, R. Rosati, D. F. Savo, Revisiting controlled query evaluation in description logics, in: Proc. of IJCAI, 2019, pp. 1786–1792.

[10] G. Cima, D. Lembo, L. Marconi, R. Rosati, D. F. Savo, Controlled query evaluation in ontology-based data access, in: Proc. of ISWC, volume 12506 of *LNCS*, 2020, pp. 128–146.

[11] G. Cima, D. Lembo, R. Rosati, D. F. Savo, Controlled query evaluation in description logics through instance indistinguishability, in: Proc. of IJCAI, 2020, pp. 1791–1797.

[12] D. Calvanese, G. De Giacomo, D. Lembo, M. Lenzerini, R. Rosati, Tractable reasoning and efficient query answering in description logics: The *DL-Lite* family, J. of Automated Reasoning 39 (2007) 385–429.

[13] M. Benedikt, B. Cuenca Grau, E. V. Kostylev, Logical foundations of information disclosure in ontology-based data integration, Artif. Intell. J. 262 (2018) 52–95.

[14] M. Benedikt, P. Bourhis, L. Jachiet, M. Thomazo, Reasoning about disclosure in data integration in the presence of source constraints, in: Proc. of IJCAI, 2019, pp. 1551–1557.

[15] D. Lembo, M. Lenzerini, R. Rosati, M. Ruzzi, D. F. Savo, Inconsistency-tolerant query answering in ontology-based data access, J. of Web Semantics 33 (2015) 3–29.

Improving Work Life Conditions via Portable Knowledge-Driven Recommender System

(Discussion Paper)

Maurizio Atzori[1], Alessandro Barenghi[2], Sara Comai[2], Mariagrazia Fugini[2], Diego Marcia[1], Gerardo Pelosi[2], Manuela Sanguinetti[1] and Vincenzo Scotti[2]

[1]*Dipartimento di Matematica e Informatica (DMI), Università di Cagliari, Via Ospedale 72, 09124, Cagliari (CA), Italy*
[2]*Dipartimento di Elettronica Informazione e Bioingegneria (DEIB), Politecnico di Milano, Via Ponzio 34/5 - Via Golgi 42, 20133, Milano (MI), Italy*

Abstract

WorkingAge is a EU H2020 Project (lasting 2019-2022) aiming at promoting healthy habits in working environments to improve quality of life of workers. IoT sensors are used to detect environmental and workers conditions. Raw sensors data are then transformed into interventions in the form of reminders or recommendations communicated to the user through a mobile application. This paper describes the main issues of data management in the project: the knowledge-based DSS that has been developed to infer the recommendations for the users, which is based on a set of probabilistic rules and takes into account users' preferences to promote users' well being, and the design choices to guarantee data security and privacy.

Keywords

Recommender System, Probabilistic Prolog, Privacy, Security, Risk Management, Quality of Life, Decision Support System

1. Introduction

This paper presents the overall approach and mid-term results of the WorkingAge (WA - Smart Working environments for all Ages) Project, which focuses on the use of innovative Human Computer Interaction methods, like augmented reality, virtual reality, gesture/voice recognition and gaze tracking. The purpose is to measure the user's health state at workplaces and provide recommendations about possible corrections of damaging or harmful states. The large scale introduction of social and technological innovation, such as e-health, mobile health, integrated care or independent living, can improve the efficiency of health and well being systems. Remote monitoring healthcare models, in particular those that include users actively in the design of

SEBD 2021: The 29th Italian Symposium on Advanced Database Systems, September 5-9, 2021, Pizzo Calabro (VV), Italy
atzori@unica.it (M. Atzori); alessandro.barenghi@polimi.it (A. Barenghi); sara.comai@polimi.it (S. Comai); mariagrazia.fugini@polimi.it (M. Fugini); diego.marcia@unica.it (D. Marcia); gerardo.pelosi@polimi.it (G. Pelosi); manuela.sanguinetti@unica.it (M. Sanguinetti); vincenzo.scotti@polimi.it (V. Scotti)
0000-0001-6112-7310 (M. Atzori); 0000-0003-0840-6358 (A. Barenghi); 0000-0002-9554-8815 (S. Comai); 0000-0002-0692-0153 (M. Fugini); 0000-0003-2576-8836 (D. Marcia); 0000-0002-3812-5429 (G. Pelosi); 0000-0002-0147-22080 (M. Sanguinetti); 0000-0002-8765-604X (V. Scotti)

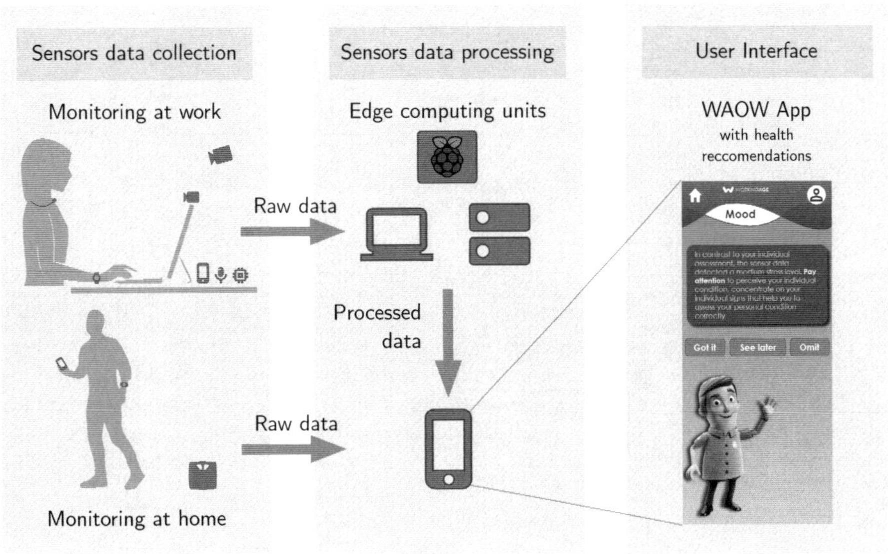

Figure 1: WA Tool concept.

health care systems, have shown clear benefits [1] and are included in recent EU actions [2]. We rely on the general concepts of the WA approach presented in [3, 4]. In particular, these papers describe the portion of the WA Tool that implements a Decision Support System (DSS) developed in the project, and discuss privacy and security aspects. The WA Project aims at creating a sustainable and scalable product that will empower users' comfort by easing work conditions and life, attenuating the impact of aging on their autonomy, health and well-being. A key point is the *adaptivity* of the WA tool to the user profile. Active user engagement is a focus, in order to ensure the match against user needs, safeguarding ethics, privacy, security and regulatory aspects of work premises. In the proposed DSS, recommendations take into account the effectiveness of previous advice on the monitored risks and the acceptance of the user of the given advice. A big issue in creating such a tool is privacy, since personal data are collected by several devices and elaborated to analyze the users features, observe wrong habits and give suggestions to improve wellness. We will show how privacy and security have been tackled in the project to face these issues.

The paper is organized as follows: Section 2 describes the issues related to data privacy and security that impacted the WA architecture. Section 3 describes the DSS we developed to infer recommendations for the users. Finally, Section 4 concludes the paper and outlines future work.

2. Data Privacy and Security

The success of the WA approach requires to collect a significant amount of personal information from different sensors both at work (through cameras, microphones, environmental sensors, etc.) and possibly also at home (through a smart band and a body scale), to provide a fitting set of suggestions to the WA tool user, as outlined in Fig.1. For example, if the camera detects a wrong posture, the worker receives an alert to change his/her position or a tip about a suggested physical exercise. In designing the solution in WA, we built on the considerable computing

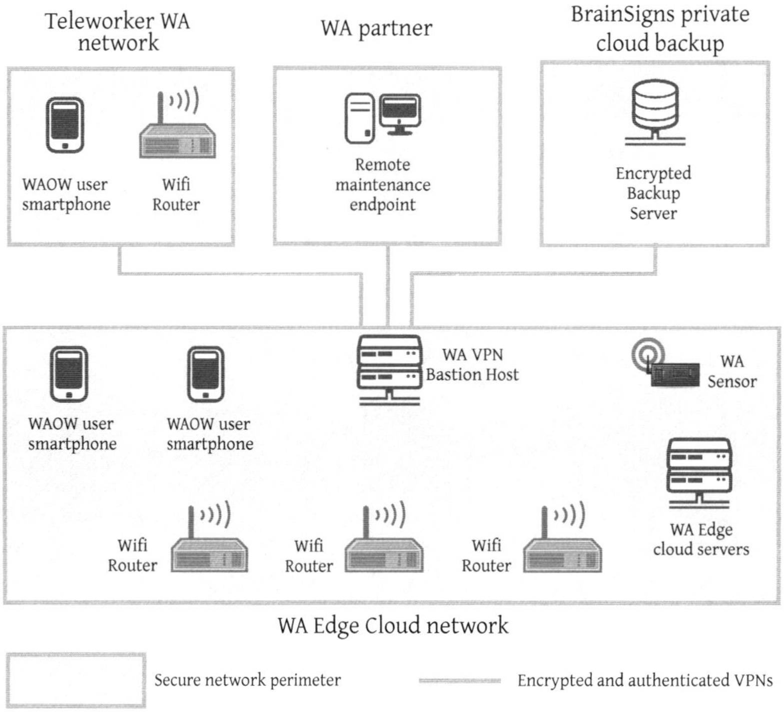

Figure 2: Logic view of the network perimeter within which data confidentiality with respect to external adversaries is provided

power available in modern mobile devices to shift the phase of data aggregation and user profiling entirely on a device which is owned by the user herself. This approach was guided by the provisions of the EU Regulation 2016/679, General Data Protection Regulation (GDPR), which states two fundamental principles: *i)* minimality of data retention and *ii)* security by design. Following the minimality of data retention approach led us to design a system where the raw data collected from the sensors, such as audio/video recordings, are processed as soon as possible by a set of dedicated machines on premise (i.e., the edge computing units in Figure 1). This early processing stage allows us to extract the relevant features from the collected data and prevent the long term storage of raw sensor datasets. Only data from the smart band and body scale that do not need preprocessing are directly sent to the mobile device. Instead, the dedicated set of processing machines supplies the DSS of the WA tool with small and highly informative pieces of data, allowing the decision support agent to be run on the mobile phone of the user. The security by design principle was embodied in the WA network and data processing infrastructure design mapping the legal basis for data treatment provided by the user consent onto cryptographically enforced access control. The first step in this sense is to provide a network infrastructure where data confidentiality is provided with respect to external adversaries. Figure 2 illustrates the WA network structure, highlighting its secure perimeter. We chose to employ well-established secure network standards for the WA edge cloud network, located on premise at the firms which host our test experiments. The network is formed by an IEEE 802.11n Wi-Fi network, employing the WPA2 key agreement and data encryption standard to provide the desired security guarantees. Extending the network to off-site locations to allow WA users to work from home, a highly desirable feature in an evolving work scenario, was performed by means of VPN tunnels relying on the standard Transport Layer Security (TLS) v1.3 secure transport protocol. The edge cloud network is thus extended via a remote VPN endpoint embedded in the WiFi router providing the teleworker WA network. The VPN endpoint connects to the WA VPN bastion host present in the WA edge cloud network placed in the hosting firm premises, allowing the sensing equipment present in the teleworker WA network to securely send the recorded data to the WA edge cloud servers. Finally the WA edge cloud network perimeter is extended, by means of VPN links, also to the WA partner workstations, which may be in need of performing maintenance on the WA edge cloud servers, and to a remote encrypted backup server, maintained by the partner BrainSigns. The latter provides off-site backups of encrypted data bundles, sent to it by both the edge cloud servers and the user smartphones. Having ensured data confidentiality and endpoint authentication for the entities connected to the WA edge cloud network, we complete the enforcement of the access control to the data by means of the standard OpenPGP hybrid encryption, combined with an appropriate certificate management. Each edge cloud server and each smartphone are endowed with a dedicated OpenPGP certificate, containing an RSA keypair and a textual identity. While the textual identity of the edge cloud servers is their common name, the identity of the smartphones is a Universally Unique IDentifier (UUID) version 4, i.e., a 128-bit wide random unique identifier. The WA sensors communicate with the WA edge cloud server which is in charge of performing the data processing to extract high level features either by means of a dedicated TLS connection, if a continuous data stream is required, or send asynchronously data bundles encrypting them with the public key corresponding to the server certificate. The WA edge cloud server in turn will send the processed data to the WA user smartphone encrypting them with the public key contained in the OpenPGP certificate bound to it. This approach effectively ensures that the consent provided by the user, which allows each specific partner to process a subset of the collected data is mapped onto the technically enforced impossibility of accessing data for which the private key required to decrypt them is not available. In addition, it is possible to provide fault resilience in terms of an off-site encrypted backup simply by storing the encrypted messages exchanged within the WA edge cloud network, with no further action. Indeed, only the entity in possession of the appropriate private key will be able to decrypt the backed-up data bundle. The WA smartphones also profit from the availability of the remote backup facility, storing on it a full backup of the DSS-derived user profile, encrypted with their own public key, and copy of the private key symmetrically encrypted under an emergency password derived key. This strategy allows the user, in case of theft or loss of the smartphone itself, to securely retrieve the backup simply providing the emergency password to a new smartphone where the WA app has been installed.

3. Decision Support System

The architecture of the system described in the previous section requires to adopt a hybrid data-driven/expert-driven approach to process the sensors data: for each type of sensor, raw data are processed with data-driven approaches based on Natural Language Processing (NLP), stochastic models, or Machine Learning (ML) to generate high-level information to be sent to the smartphone application. For example, from the video recording the posture is estimated

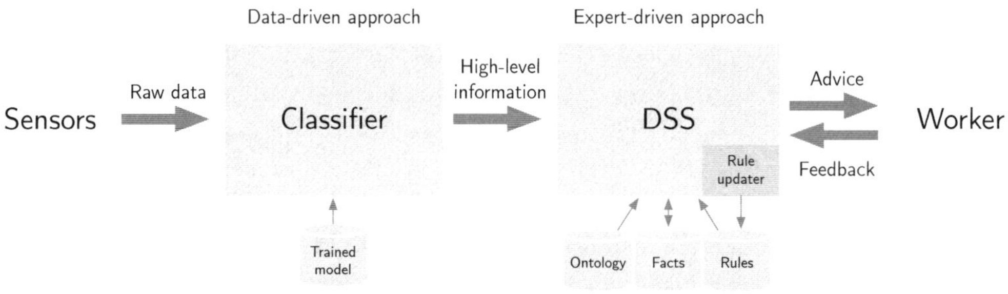

Figure 3: Overview of WA data processing approaches.

and a low/medium/high risk is computed. On the smartphone, a Decision Support System processes the high-level information to generate recommendations for the final users, based on an expert-driven approach. Figure 2 depicts the data processing flow. For coping with this "mismatch" between the data-driven classifiers and the model-driven DSS, we chose to adopt the ProbLog language [5], a probabilistic reasoning engine that allows not only inference of certainly-true facts (according to the usual declarative models), but also derives the level of confidence for the specific inferred fact.

3.1. Ontology

To determine the recommendation for the user, the DSS analyses the high-level information received from the sensors and described according to an Ontology, including eight main entities:

Worker is the core of the ontology, due to our user-centered design;

Profile holds the personal information about the worker (e.g., age, gender, etc.);

Task describes the job performed by the user (e.g., manager, clerk, etc.);

Sensor describes the High-level information collected about the worker (e.g., the sitting body posture risk can be low, medium or high; the facial expression can be positive, neutral or negative, etc.);

Smart Goal and Goal State represent what the WA tool suggests (e.g., a physical activity) and its degree of completion (goal reached or not);

Advice is the suggestion or feedback that provided to the worker (e.g., "Change pose" or "The current heartbeat is 150");

Feedback represents the attitude of the worker towards a piece of advice (e.g., the user accepts or rejects the advice).

Even though the user is the core of the Ontology, the DSS strongly depends on data coming from the sensors, classified into:

Body Sensors include wearable bio-metric devices (to gather ECG and GSR), cameras (to gather body postures, facial expressions and eye movements) and microphones (to collect voice recordings);

Environmental Sensors gather data about temperature, humidity, CO_2 concentration, noise level etc.;

Other Sensors include questionnaires that are periodically administered to understand workers current state.

3.2. Reasoning engine

The DSS developed for this project belongs to the class of knowledge-based DSSes [6] and has been implemented through an expert-driven approach. An expert defined a priori the rules we encoded in our engine. In our use case, the rules describe the *intervention strategy*, which is the set of recommendations to give to the workers. The whole DSS is based on stochastic-aware *Rules* and *Facts*. We employed fact f to state something about the worker or environment and we associated f with a truthfulness probability P_f (we see such probability value as a *reliability index* of f). In the same way, we associated rule $\mathcal{R}$ with a reliability index $P_{\mathcal{R}}$. We used a probabilistic representation to handle the uncertainty about the modelled system (including users and environment). The edge server computes the High-level information through probabilistic models and associates the predicted values with probabilities. To model this uncertainty within the DSS, we employed *ProbLog* [5]. ProbLog is a variant of ProLog, a declarative language and an inference engine, augmented with probabilistic descriptive and inference capabilities.

Hereafter we reported an example of code written with ProbLog.

```
1 1.0::time(morning).
2 0.7::state(user,stressed).
3
4 0.9::candidate_suggestion(take_a_short_pause)
5     :- time(morning), state(user, stressed).
```

Listing 1: Rules and advice example.

Lines *1* and *2* contains two facts: the former states the it is `morning` with a 100% reliability (certainty), the latter states that the `user` is `stressed` with a 70% of confidence. Lines 4 and 5 represent a rule: it suggests to `take_a_short_pause` with a 90% of reliability. The probability of displaying advice $\mathcal{A}$ is given by:

$$P_{\mathcal{A}} = P_{\mathcal{R}} \cdot \prod_{f \in F_{\mathcal{R}}} P_f \ . \tag{1}$$

while, for instance, the probability to show the advice `take_a_short_pause` is:

$$P_{\mathcal{A}} = P_{\mathcal{R}} \cdot P_{\texttt{time(morning)}} \cdot P_{\texttt{state(user,stressed)}} = 0.9 \cdot 1 \cdot 0.7 = 0.63 \ . \tag{2}$$

ProbLog is available as a Python package; as such, it can not run directly in an Android environment. To cope with this issue we adopted *Chaquopy*[1], a Python interpreter for Android, and we developed a wrapper around the whole DSS, to offer the main functionalities through Java. In this way the WA App that represents the user interface can easily interact with the DSS.

[1] https://chaquo.com/chaquopy/

3.3. Rule adaptation

For the scope of this project, we have defined two rule adaptation strategies, to adapt the probabilities of the recommendations on the basis of user preferences and system effectiveness. The former adaptation is referred to as *short-term*, the latter as *long-term* adaptation. For both long- and short-term rules adaptation, we relied on a simple, yet effective technique: the Exponentially Weighted Moving Average (EWMA) [7]. We set the initial probability of a rule $\mathcal{R}$ to a value of 1 at time $\tau = 0$; then, at a given time step $\tau \geq 1$, the chosen adaptation strategy updates the rule probability (reliability in this case), with the EWMA strategy. Short-term adaptation is achieved through user feedback on the recommendations (e.g., the user is (not) going to apply the suggested advice). We paired each $\mathcal{R}$ with a *feedback log* $\mathbf{f}_{\mathcal{R}} \in \mathbb{1}^n$. This feedback log is a sequence of Boolean values representing whether the i-th time $\mathcal{R}$ was triggered (with $i \in [1, n] \in \mathbb{N}$) the user accepted ($\mathbf{f}_{\mathcal{R},i} = 1$) or rejected ($\mathbf{f}_{\mathcal{R},i} = 0$) the advice. Each user has his own feedback log within her/his WA App. Given a feedback log $\mathbf{f}_{\mathcal{R}}$, we computed the short-term update of probability $P_{\mathcal{R}}$ as prescribed by Equation (3)

$$P_{\mathcal{R}}^{(\tau)} = \eta_s \cdot \frac{\sum_{i=1}^{n} \mathbf{f}_{\mathcal{R},i}}{n} + (1 - \eta_s) \cdot P_{\mathcal{R}}^{(\tau-1)} \ . \tag{3}$$

Long-term adaptation is achieved though the measures of effectiveness of the WA tool. In particular, we considered a subset M of such measures, so that by the end the of a time period Δt each measure $m_i \in M$ reports an improvement. In this context, we derived the effectiveness of rule $\mathcal{R}$ as the correlation (during Δt) between the number of times advice $\mathcal{A}$, generated by rule $\mathcal{R}$, collected a positive feedback and the subset of measures $M_{\mathcal{R}} \subseteq M$ such that the Pearson's correlation test between $\mathcal{R}$ and $m_i \in M_{\mathcal{R}}$ results in a p-value ≤ 0.05. On this premise, we defined with R the set of rules in the DSS and with $\rho_{\mathcal{R},M_{\mathcal{R}}}$ the average correlation between $\mathcal{R}$ and its set of measures $M_{\mathcal{R}}$. Thus, we computed the long-term update of probability $P_{\mathcal{R}}$ at time $\tau \geq 1$ as prescribed by Equation (4)

$$P_{\mathcal{R}}^{(\tau)} = \eta_l \cdot \frac{\rho_{\mathcal{R},M_{\mathcal{R}}}}{\max\limits_{\mathcal{R}' \in R} \rho_{\mathcal{R}',M_{\mathcal{R}'}}} + (1 - \eta_l) \cdot P_{\mathcal{R}}^{(\tau-1)} \tag{4}$$

In Equations (3) and (4), the parameters $\eta_s \in (0, 1]$ and $\eta_l \in (0, 1]$ are the learning factors, the parameters that control the updates. Higher values of η_s and η_l make the update system rely more on "newer" information in the update, instead of the previous one; lower values have the opposite effect.

4. Conclusion and Future Work

In this paper, we have presented the WA Tool based on the collection of sensors data and a DSS for the generation of recommendations to improve the quality of life of workers. The WA Tool is conceived to analyze the users' health and behavior at work (or, possibly, telework and smart working) and outside work, assisting with reminders and risks avoidance recommendations. Currently, we are continuing the research stream presented here by designing a platform to define safe working environments for human-robots teams (HRTs) for collaborative embodied (physical) AI. Current work has the aim of keeping people away from unsafe and unhealthy jobs in HRTs and engaging and empowering workers, regardless of their gender, age or background. This platform will enable a strong 'prevention through design' approach that integrates human factors and worker-centred design. The adaptive solutions proposed by the WA project are currently analyzing three different real working settings and living environments, by experimenting the profile of around 90 workers > 50 years old, from the one side, and the working place requirements from the other side. We are currently defining which information has to be collected and stored to improve and increase Robot capabilities and interactions with humans.

Acknowledgments

This work has been supported by the European Union's Horizon 2020 research and innovation programme under grant agreement No. 826232, project WorkingAge (Smart Working environments for all Ages)

References

[1] A. Dixon, The united nations decade of healthy ageing requires concerted global action, Nature Aging 1 (2021) 2–2.

[2] G. D. Perkins, J.-T. Graesner, F. Semeraro, T. Olasveengen, J. Soar, C. Lott, P. Van de Voorde, J. Madar, D. Zideman, S. Mentzelopoulos, et al., European resuscitation council guidelines 2021: Executive summary, Resuscitation (2021).

[3] M. Fugini, A. Barenghi, S. Comai, G. Pelosi, R. Tedesco, M. van Gasteren, C. A. Catalina, E. Arribas Leal, R. Losada Durán, R. Martins de Almeida, et al., Workingage: providing occupational safety through pervasive sensing and data driven behavior modeling, in: 30th European Safety and Reliability Conference (ESREL 2020), Research Publishing, 2020, pp. 1–8.

[4] R. M. Resende de Almeida, A. Grau Aberturas, Y. Bueno Aguado, M. Atzori, A. Barenghi, G. Borghini, C. A. Catalina Ortega, S. Comai, R. Losada Durán, M. Fugini, H. Gunes, B. Musleh Lancis, G. Pelosi, V. Ronca, L. Sbattella, R. Tedesco, T. Xu, Decision Support Systems to Promote Health and Well-Being of People During Their Working Age: The Case of the WorkingAge EU Project, in: 20th Int. Conf. on Embedded Computer Systems: Architectures, Modeling and Simulation, volume 12471 of *Lecture Notes in Computer Science*, Springer Cham, 2020, pp. 336–347.

[5] L. De Raedt, A. Kimmig, H. Toivonen, Problog: A probabilistic prolog and its application in link discovery., in: Proceedings of the 20th International Joint Conference on Artificial Intelligence, Hyderabad, India, volume 7, Hyderabad, Morgan Kaufmann Pub., 2007, pp. 2462–2467.

[6] D. J. Power, Decision support systems: concepts and resources for managers, Greenwood Publishing Group, 2002.

[7] S. Roberts, Control chart tests based on geometric moving averages, Technometrics 42 (2000) 97–101.

NanoWeb: Search, Access and Explore Life Science Nanopublications on the Web*

(Discussion Paper)

Fabio Giachelle[1], Dennis Dosso[1] and Gianmaria Silvello[1]

[1]Department of Information Engineering, University of Padua, Padua, Italy

Abstract

Nanopublications are scientific statements represented in the Resource Description Framework (RDF), a brief machine-readable form representing data. Nanopublications consist of scientific facts extracted from the literature and contextualized with provenance and attribution information.

Nanopublications are designed to enhance knowledge spreading, support the re-use of scientific facts, and provide credit to the corresponding authors. Despite these promising features, nanopublications are not widely adopted, and their use is still quite limited to experts. We believe this is partly due to the lack of services for searching, retrieving, and understanding nanopublications.

To mitigate this, we propose NanoWeb, a Web-based system designed to allow general users to search, access, explore, and re-use nanopublications publicly available on the Web. Currently, NanoWeb is tailored for the life science domain, where plenty of nanopublications are available.

Keywords

Nanopublications, Semantic Web, Data Citation

1. Introduction

In the last decades we assisted to a change of paradigm in the current world of research, more precisely towards a more data-intensive approach, following the so-called *fourth paradigm of science* [2]. As a result, data acquired a prominent role, becoming the center of scientific discovery as well as of scholarship and scholarly communication [3]. Accordingly, data science has experienced an unprecedented growth that involved also other linked research fields regarding the search [4], provenance [5], citation [6], re-use [7], and exploration [8] of data.

Despite this premises, most of the huge volume of data available in the Web, is provided in an unstructured format, which is *human-readable* but not machine-readable. Hence, the heterogeneity of data and their representations lead to issues concerning interoperability; data access, search and re-use; and domain-dependent requirements.

*This is an extended abstract of [1].

SEBD 2021: The 29th Italian Symposium on Advanced Database Systems, September 5-9, 2021, Pizzo Calabro (VV), Italy

fabio.giachelle@unipd.it (F. Giachelle); dennis.dosso@unipd.it (D. Dosso); dennis.dosso@unipd.it (G. Silvello)
http://www.dei.unipd.it/~giachell/ (F. Giachelle); http://www.dei.unipd.it/~dosso/ (D. Dosso); http://www.dei.unipd.it/~silvello/ (G. Silvello)
0000-0001-5015-5498 (F. Giachelle); 0000-0001-7307-4607 (D. Dosso); 0000-0003-4970-4554 (G. Silvello)

Semantic Web technologies, such as the *nanopublication model* [9], aim to tackle some of these issues according to the Findable, Accessible, Interoperable, Reusable (FAIR) guiding principles [10]. Nanopublications represent statements (i.e. *assertions*) leveraging on the Linked Open Data (LOD) principles [11] to convey scientific facts in an efficient, succinct, and machine-readable form. The LOD features make nanopublications suitable to handle the connections between related scientific facts, encoded in RDF. These facts are connected in a network that can be explored, so to discover connections among them.

The nanopublications model is designed to make scientific claims accessible, so that the scientific knowledge can automatically be explored by agents. Several scientific fields adopted the nanopublications model, such as the Life Science domain, where more than ten million openly available nanopublications [12] were created. There is important evidence in the biomedical domain about the benefits of using nanopublications for expanding scientific insight [13]. However, to the best of our knowledge, there is no tool to visualize nanopublications and explore their underlying network of scientific facts. BioKB [14] provides functionalities similar to NanoWeb in terms of semantic search and graph visualization. In particular, it provides access to the semantic content of biomedical articles through a SPARQL endpoint and a web interface. Thus, allowing users to search for biomedical entities and visualize their graph of relations. However, BioKB does not account for nanopublications and does not support a multi-level exploration of the graph, enabling an in-depth exploration of the entities relation network. Currently, searching for nanopublications is possible only through sparse SPARQL endpoints. NanoWeb contributes to tackle these issues by providing: (a) a unified entry-point to access all the publicly available nanopublications from the Life Science domain; (b) a user-friendly web interface that enables users without a prior knowledge of SPARQL and related technologies to search, access and explore millions of nanopublications in a human-readable form.

The paper is organized as follows: Section 2 presents some background, Section 3 provides a brief overview of NanoWeb functionalities and describes one prominent feature, and Section 4 draws some final remarks.

2. Background

A nanopublication consists of a Resource Description Framework (RDF) graph based on an assertion, that represents a scientific statement extracted, manually or automatically, from a scientific publication. Nanopublications are representated using an extended RDF syntax supporting *quads* in addition to triples, where an identifier (an IRI) is added. Hence, groups of triples may be characterized as belonging to the same subgraph, i.e. to the same *named graph* [15, 16], if they share the same extra URI. More specifically, the structure of nanopublications consists of four *named graphs*: (a) the *head*, that connects the other three sub-graphs; (b) the *assertion* graph (in blue in Figure 1) that reports the statement extracted from the scientific publications as one RDF triple (subject-predicate-object), where the the two concepts of the assertion (subject and object) are linked by a specific relationship defined by the predicate. The predicate relationship may refer to external ontologies and scientific databases storing related data. (c) The provenance graph (in orange in Figure 1) reports the assertion metadata such as the assertion's generation methods and its creators; and, (d) the publication info graph (yellow) that contains the metadata about when the nanopublication was created, its authors and the license terms for its reuse.

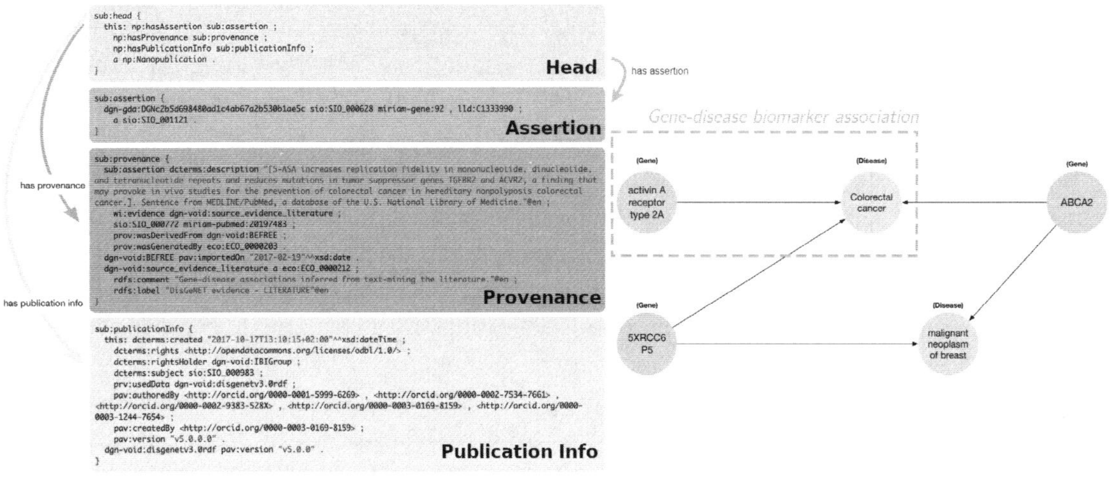

A RDF serialization of a nanopublication **B** A network of gene-disease associations

Figure 1: (A) RDF trig serialization of the nanopublication with assertion: ⟨*activin A receptor type 2A - gene-disease biomarker association - Colorectal Cancer*⟩; (B) network of gene-disease associations created by five nanopublications.

Figure 1.A shows an example of nanopublication regarding the biomedical domain. The assertion contains information about the gene-disease association ⟨*activin A receptor type 2A – gene-disease biomarker association – colorectal cancer*⟩, where *activin A receptor type 2A* is the subject, *gene-disease biomarker association* is the predicate and *colorectal cancer* is the object of the triple. The assertion is extracted from a paper [17], which states that a drug – *Mesalazine* – can reduce the mutations in a tumor suppressor gene – *activin A receptor type 2A (ACVR2)* – related to *colorectal cancer.* This assertion is represented as a RDF nanopublication with the TriG [1] serialization in Figure 1.A. TriG is a compact RDF syntax, characterized by the use of *prefixes* to avoid the repetition of IRIs. Figure 1.B illustrates an example of a five nodes network concerning gene-disease associations. If we consider for instance the *colorectal cancer* disease, it is initially connected with the gene *ACVR2,* through the gene-disease biomarker association. If we expand the *colorectal cancer* relation network, we discover two other genes *5XRCC6P5* and *ABCA2.* These genes are directly connected to the *colorectal cancer* disease and, after a further expansion, we discover that they are linked also to the *malignant neoplasm of breast* disease. These RDF triples are all inferred from five distinct papers distinguished by venue and time of publication, that also do not cite each other. The triple in Figure 1.B contained in the blue rectangle is also the one used as assertion in Figure 1.A. This shows how, by using RDF graphs, triples connected among them, the LOD principles, and nanopublications about these triples, it is possible to explore and discover new concepts and links among them not otherwise explicitly visible through the traditional scientific literature. Despite these promising features, the adoption of nanopublications by scientists is still quite limited to specific domains [18]. To

[1]https://www.w3.org/TR/trig/

date, there is no easy way to find, re-use and cite them, as well as no service that allows users to access them in a human-readable form, and search them using keywords or natural language queries. Moreover, there is no tool designed to allow the progressive exploration of the nanopublications relation network, which can be useful for the discovery of new meaningful connections between nanopublications' assertions and scientific facts.

SPARQL is a powerful but complex query language to access and interrogate RDF graphs [19]. Due to its complex syntax, SPARQL is not intuitive for end-users without a prior expertise and knowledge of the underlying schema of database, and of the IRIs used in it. To address the issues related to the use of SPARQL and enable users querying the RDF datasets via natural language queries, the *keyword search* paradigm has been introduced. Keyword-based methods are designed to ease the access to structured data [20, 21]. In contrast to SPARQL, keyword search returns a ranking of answers, ordered according to their *relevance* for the user-provided keyword query. Keyword query search systems over structured data consider both relational databases (RDB) [21] and graph-like databases such as RDF datasets [22, 20]. Keyword-based systems may be divided into three categories: (a) *schema-based* systems [23, 24] which exploit the information concerning the schema of the database to formulate structured-language queries (e.g. SQL or SPARQL queries) designed from the user-provided keyword query; (b) *graph-based* systems [25, 26] which rely on the transformation of relational databases into graphs; and (c) *virtual-document based* systems [27] which generate a *virtual document* [28] for a given graph, where the lexical content is preserved. Hence, virtual-document based systems can leverage on efficient state-of-the-art IR methods for indexing and ranking. However, there is no keyword search system for nanopublications, which are always searched via SPARQL endpoints. To allow end-users specify queries in natural language, NanoWeb exploits a very recent advancement in virtual-document based systems [29], thus enabling fast and effective keyword-search over RDF and nanopublications.

3. NanoWeb

NanoWeb[2] is a public and open-source[3] web application designed to provide intuitive search, exploration, citation [30] and re-use of nanopublications.

As of now, NanoWeb is tailored for the life science domain, and it is conceived to support life science experts in their research work. Nevertheless, NanoWeb can be applied, after domain-specific customization, to other scientific domains.

NanoWeb provides a unified access to the world of nanopublications, even to users without a specific expertise, which can search for nanopublications using natural language queries. Its main features are:

1. A crawler collecting the public nanopublications available on the web;
2. Keyword search and advanced search. The latter provides a structured guided search based on the boolean search paradigm;
3. A user-centric visual interface to search and consult nanopublications, enriched with information gathered from external authoritative ontologies;

[2] https://w3id.org/nanoweb/

[3] NanoWeb source code is available at https://github.com/giachell/nanoweb

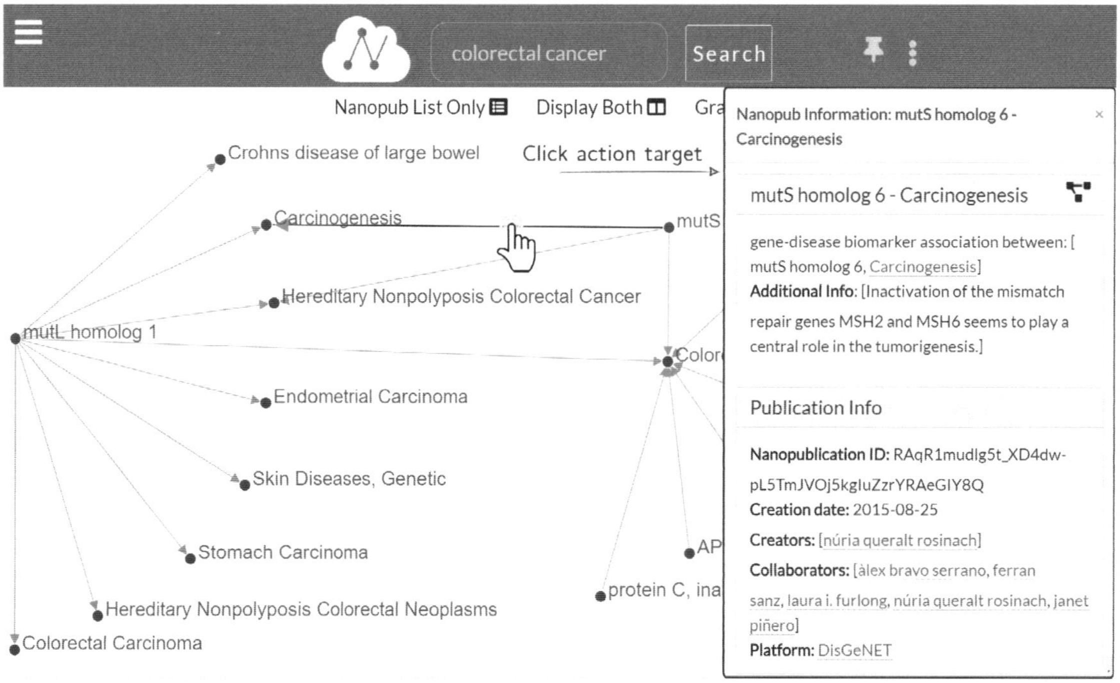

Figure 2: Graph exploration: users can inspect nanopublications and the information concerning entity connections by clicking on the edges. As a result, an information window is shown reporting the nanopublication's content, which refers to the entities linked by the edge clicked. Inside the red box (right side) is reported the information content of the nanopublication with assertion: ⟨*mutS homolog 6 - gene-disease biomarker association - Carcinogenesis*⟩.

4. A visual exploration of the nanopublications' relation network built around the scientific facts encoded in the assertions;
5. Data search capabilities providing direct connections to evidence papers and external scientific curated databases.

One of the prominent NanoWeb features is the exploration of the nanopublications relation network, i.e. the RDF graph composed by the triples extracted from the scientific evidence papers, as described above. NanoWeb represents the nanopublications relation network as a graph where the nodes are the subjects and the objects of the nanopublications' triples. The nodes are connected together with directed edges from subjects to objects.

Figure 2 shows a multi-level graph exploration of the relation network concerning the nanopublication with title *mutL homolog 1 - Colorectal Carcinoma*, which expresses a gene-disease association. The graph exploration functionality allows the user to understand the relationships between different nanopublications. The graph exploration functionality is conceived to let the user progressively expand the graph, focusing on both the nodes and connections of interest, without any limit on the depth of the exploration, i.e., to the graph's dimension visualized. Hence, the user can potentially expand the whole graph, having all the nodes of the relation network displayed. The exploration of the relation network is one of the biggest contribution, since it provides a deeper understanding of the connections between entities, such as gene-disease associations.

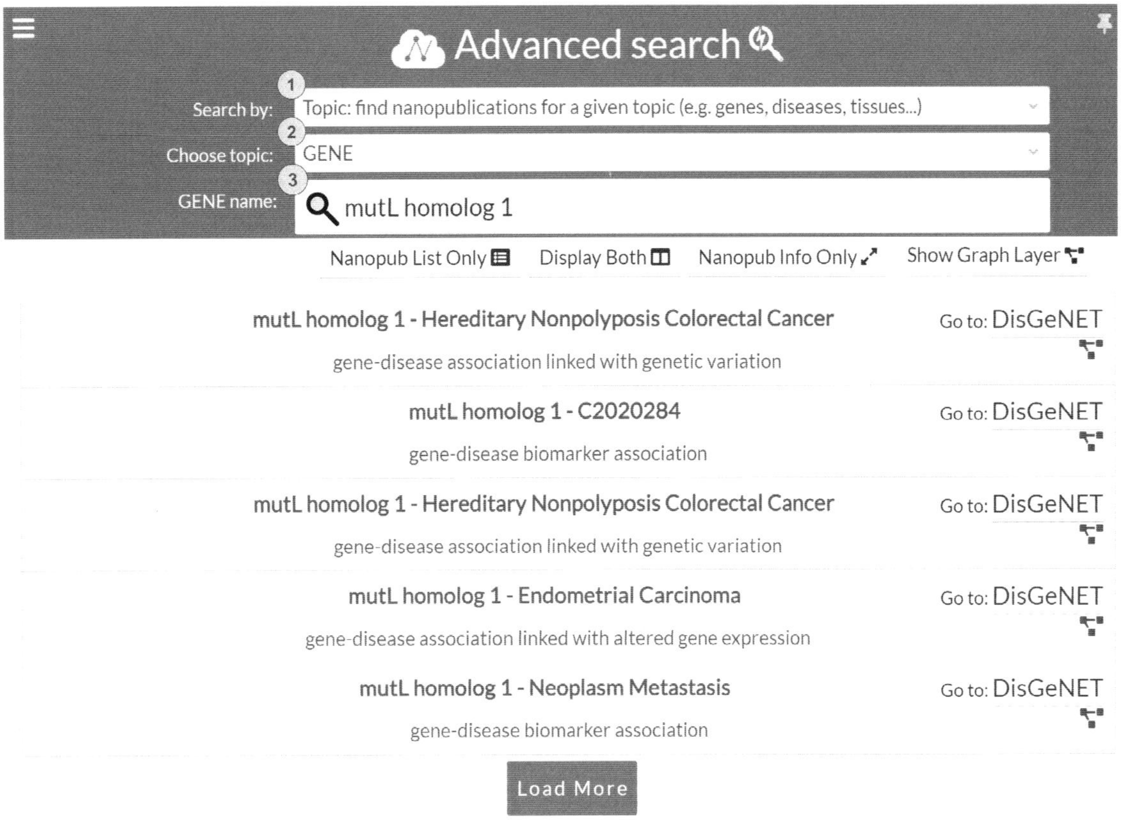

Figure 3: Advanced search: users are guided through the search process by means of sequential filters, that progressively refine the query domain and restrict the retrieval output accordingly. The figure shows an example of a topic-based search for nanopublications concerning *genes* and in particular the *mutL homolog 1* gene.

4. Conclusions

Nanopublications are concise, noise-free RDF resources designed to efficiently convey information and concepts.

The full adoption of nanopublications is held back by the lack of services to search, access, explore, and cite them. As of today, data search is possible using only SPARQL queries, that are only within the capabilities of experienced users. There is no service to search over all the publicly available nanopublications, using either keyword or natural language queries. To target these issues we designed and developed *NanoWeb*.

NanoWeb provides unified access to Life Science nanopublications so that users can search, access, explore, and re-use them on the Web. NanoWeb allows the users to (i) search for domain-specific nanopublications using keyword queries; (ii) explore their relation network to discover new nanopublications and meaningful connections; (iii) access and consult their information content; (iv) access the evidence paper information (e.g. abstract) and the entry points to related data record in external curated scientific databases; and, (v) easily cite nanopublications.

NanoWeb enables a serendipity-oriented perspective in the Life Science domain. Users can benefit from this perspective through the exploration of nanopublication graphs, which could lead to a deeper understanding of the connections between entities (e.g. genes and diseases) and enrich the domain knowledge.

Acknowledgments

This work is supported by the ExaMode project, as part of the European Union Horizon 2020 program under Grant Agreement no. 825292.

References

[1] F. Giachelle, D. Dosso, G. Silvello, Search, access, and explore life science nanopublications on the web, PeerJ Computer Science 7 (2021) e335. doi:10.7717/peerj-cs.335.

[2] T. Hey, S. Tansley, K. Tolle (Eds.), The Fourth Paradigm: Data-Intensive Scientific Discovery, Microsoft Research, USA, 2009.

[3] C. L. Borgman, Big Data, Little Data, No Data, MIT Press, 2015.

[4] A. Chapman, E. Simperl, L. Koesten, G. Konstantinidis, L. D. Ibáñez, E. Kacprzak, P. Groth, Dataset search: a survey, VLDB J. 29 (2020) 251–272. doi:10.1007/s00778-019-00564-x.

[5] J. Cheney, L. Chiticariu, W. Tan, Provenance in databases: Why, how, and where, Foundations and Trends in Databases 1 (2009) 379–474.

[6] G. Silvello, Theory and Practice of Data Citation, Journal of the American Society for Information Science and Technology (JASIST) 69 (2018) 6–20.

[7] L. A. Wynholds, J. C. Wallis, C. L. Borgman, A. Sands, S. Traweek, Data, Data Use, and Scientific Inquiry: Two Case Studies of Data Practices, 2012, pp. 19–22. doi:10.1145/2232817.2232822.

[8] P. Rahman, L. Jiang, A. Nandi, Evaluating Interactive Data Systems, VLDB J. 29 (2020) 119–146. doi:10.1007/s00778-019-00589-2.

[9] P. Groth, A. Gibson, J. Velterop, The Anatomy of a Nanopublication, Inf. Serv. Use 30 (2010) 51–56.

[10] M. D. Wilkinson, M. Dumontier, I. J. Aalbersberg, G. Appleton, M. Axton, A. Baak, N. Blomberg, J.-W. Boiten, L. B. da Silva Santos, P. E. Bourne, et al., The fair guiding principles for scientific data management and stewardship, Scientific data 3 (2016) 1–9.

[11] C. Bizer, T. Heath, T. Berners-Lee, Linked Data - The Story So Far, Int. J. Semantic Web Inf. Syst. 5 (2009) 1–22. doi:10.4018/jswis.2009081901.

[12] T. Kuhn, A. Meroño-Peñuela, A. Malic, J. H. Poelen, A. H. Hurlbert, E. C. Ortiz, L. I. Furlong, N. Queralt-Rosinach, C. Chichester, J. M. Banda, E. L. Willighagen, F. Ehrhart, C. T. A. Evelo, T. B. Malas, M. Dumontier, Nanopublications: A Growing Resource of Provenance-Centric Scientific Linked Data, in: 14th IEEE International Conference on e-Science, e-Science 2018, IEEE Computer Society, 2018, pp. 83–92. doi:10.1109/eScience.2018.00024.

[13] C. Chichester, P. Gaudet, O. Karch, P. T. Groth, L. Lane, A. Bairoch, B. Mons, A. Loizou, Querying neXtProt nanopublications and their value for insights on sequence variants

and tissue expression, J. Web Semant. 29 (2014) 3–11. doi:10.1016/j.websem.2014.05.001.

[14] M. Biryukov, V. Groues, V. Satagopam, R. Schneider, Biokb-text mining and semantic technologies for biomedical content discovery (2018).

[15] J. J. Carroll, P. Stickler, RDF triples in XML, in: Proc. of the WWW 2004 Conference (Alternate Track Papers & Posters), ACM Press, 2004, pp. 412–413.

[16] J. J. Carroll, C. Bizer, P. Hayes, P. Stickler, Named graphs, provenance and trust, in: Proceedings of the 14th international conference on World Wide Web, ACM Press, 2005, pp. 613–622.

[17] C. Campregher, C. Honeder, H. Chung, J. M. Carethers, C. Gasche, Mesalazine reduces mutations in transforming growth factor β receptor ii and activin type ii receptor by improvement of replication fidelity in mononucleotide repeats, Clin Cancer Res 16 (2010) 1950–1956.

[18] R. Page, Liberating links between datasets using lightweight data publishing: an example using plant names and the taxonomic literature, Biodiversity Data Journal 6 (2018) e27539.

[19] J. Pérez, M. Arenas, C. Gutierrez, Semantics and Complexity of SPARQL, ACM Trans. Database Syst. 34 (2009) 1–45.

[20] H. Bast, B. Buchhold, H. Haussmann, Semantic search on text and knowledge bases, Foundations and Trends in Information Retrieval (FnTIR) 10 (2016) 119–271.

[21] J. X. Yu, L. Qin, L. Chang, Keyword Search in Relational Databases: A Survey, IEEE Data Eng. Bull. 33 (2010) 67–78.

[22] H. Wang, C. C. Aggarwal, A survey of algorithms for keyword search on graph data, in: Managing and Mining Graph Data, Springer, 2010, pp. 249–273.

[23] A. Balmin, V. Hristidis, N. Koudas, Y. Papakonstantinou, D. Srivastava, T. Wang, A system for keyword proximity search on XML databases, in: Proceedings of 29th International Conference on Very Large Data Bases, VLDB, Morgan Kaufmann, 2003, pp. 1069–1072.

[24] Y. Luo, W. Wang, X. Lin, X. Zhou, J. Wang, K. Li, SPARK2: top-k keyword query in relational databases, IEEE Trans. Knowl. Data Eng. 23 (2011) 1763–1780.

[25] G. Bhalotia, A. Hulgeri, C. Nakhe, S. Chakrabarti, S. Sudarshan, Keyword searching and browsing in databases using BANKS, in: Proceedings of the 18th International Conference on Data Engineering, IEEE Computer Society, 2002, pp. 431–440.

[26] A. Simitsis, G. Koutrika, Y. E. Ioannidis, Précis: from unstructured keywords as queries to structured databases as answers, VLDB J. 17 (2008) 117–149.

[27] G. Kadilierakis, P. Fafalios, P. Papadakos, Y. Tzitzikas, Keyword Search over RDF Using Document-Centric Information Retrieval Systems, in: The Semantic Web, Springer International Publishing, Cham, 2020, pp. 121–137.

[28] J. I. Lopez-Veyna, V. J. S. Sosa, I. López-Arévalo, A Virtual Document Approach for Keyword Search in Databases, in: DATA, SciTePress, 2012, pp. 39–48.

[29] D. Dosso, G. Silvello, Search text to retrieve graphs: A scalable RDF keyword-based search system, IEEE Access 8 (2020) 14089–14111.

[30] E. Fabris, T. Kuhn, G. Silvello, A framework for citing nanopublications, in: Proc. of the 23rd International Conference on Theory and Practice of Digital Libraries, TPDL 2019, 2019, pp. 70–83. doi:10.1007/978-3-030-30760-8_6.

A Data Management and Anomaly Detection Solution for the Entertainment Industry

(Discussion Paper)

Michele Berno[1], Marco Canil[1], Nicola Chiarello[1], Luca Piazzon[1], Fabio Berti[2], Francesca Ferrari[2], Alessandro Zaupa[2], Nicola Ferro[1], Michele Rossi[1] and Gian Antonio Susto[1]

[1]*Department of Information Engineering, University of Padua, Italy*
[2]*Antonio Zamperla S.p.A., Italy*

Abstract

We present a smart monitoring system that combines a data management architecture with an unsupervised anomaly detection technique, targeting the automated equipment in the entertainment industry. Anomaly detection uses state-of-the-art univariate and multivariate algorithms, as well as recently proposed techniques in the field of explainable artificial intelligence, to achieve enhanced monitoring capabilities and optimize service operations. The monitoring system is here presented and tested on a real-world case study, i.e., an amusement park ride.

Keywords

anomaly detection, predictive maintenance, data management, entertainment industry

1. Introduction

Antonio Zamperla S.p.A.[1] designs and develops entertainment rides, continuously striving for their rides to become safer, greener and more efficient. Smart monitoring systems are expected to enrich the entertainment industry with a number of key features. For example, faults could be predicted in advance, or data analysis during the testing of the ride's prototypes could give deeper insights onto various design choices. Furthermore, maintenance operations are nowadays performed manually, following ride's manuals or government directives that are usually scheduled on a periodic basis, regardless of the actual conditions of the machines. This implies that, oftentimes, maintenance is performed without a real need, entailing a waste of time, human resources and material. This practice, although being cautious and robust, is quite inefficient. Smart monitoring systems would allow a change of paradigm from the current conservative approach to a greener and more efficient one. Lastly, automated supervision techniques would enforce the safeness of the rides by detecting subtle anomalies, which would be hardly identified by a human supervisor.

In the context of advanced monitoring of complex systems, two main Machine Learning

SEBD 2021: The 29th Italian Symposium on Advanced Database Systems, September 5-9, 2021, Pizzo Calabro (VV), Italy
gianantonio.susto@unipd.it (G. A. Susto)

CEUR Workshop Proceedings (CEUR-WS.org)

[1]https://www.zamperla.com/

(ML)-based technologies have emerged in recent years: unsupervised *anomaly detection* (AD) [1], that aims at providing enhanced diagnostic capabilities, and *predictive maintenance* [2], with the purpose of predicting failures/degradation to enable the early intervention of maintenance operators.

In this work, we present a data management architecture that combines state-of-the-art univariate and multivariate approaches for AD to reach enhanced monitoring capabilities and optimize service operation. We use a database to store the streaming data acquired by sensors, feed them to the AD algorithms, store back the features extracted by the AD algorithms, relate them to alerts and maintenance events, and support an overall Web application.

The paper is organized as follows: Section 2 briefly summarizes related work; Section 3 presents the considered use case; Section 4 describes the Entity-Relationship schema of the datastore; Section 5 introduces the proposed approach for AD; Section 6 discusses the current AD prototype and the related Web application. Finally, concluding remarks and future works are reported in Section 7.

2. Related Work

Unsupervised AD tools adopt (i) multivariate approaches based on tabular data and (ii) univariate approaches working with time-series [3]: (i) multivariate approaches [4] have the advantage of capturing multivariate anomalous behaviour that typically goes undetected by classic chart-based monitoring tools, but, when applied to time-series data, they entail the use of feature extraction procedures that are typically time-consuming for the developers and may lead to loss of information; (ii) univariate approaches typically work by predicting residuals, i.e., comparing measured and forecast time-series data, and raising an alarm as their difference exceeds a threshold. While Deep learning techniques are available for (i) and (ii), they typically need to be adapted to cope with discrete production data, where time-series are usually split into batches representing the machine cycles [5]. Another relevant issue in the monitoring field is the so-called *concept drift*, which means that the statistical proprieties of the target variables change over time in an unforeseen way [6], posing the additional challenge of tracking or estimating it.

3. Use Case

The case study is represented by a coaster (Zamperla's *DangleZ*) whose seats can freely move during the ride, independently of the underlying chassis, see Figure 1. In this case study, the coaster track is 133 meters long.

The data acquisition process provides, by means of an on-board *PLC*, a set of $q = 55$ different time series acquired with irregular sampling rate. Each time series represents a signal which can be analyzed to monitor the behavior of the machine: 9 signals are generated by the equipment sensors that report the transit of the coaster over different locations of the rail; 15 signals describe voltages, currents, frequencies and other physical quantities denoting the consumption and the movement of the machine; 5 signals are acquired by a weather station that detects the condition of the surrounding environment; the remaining signals are needed to check the

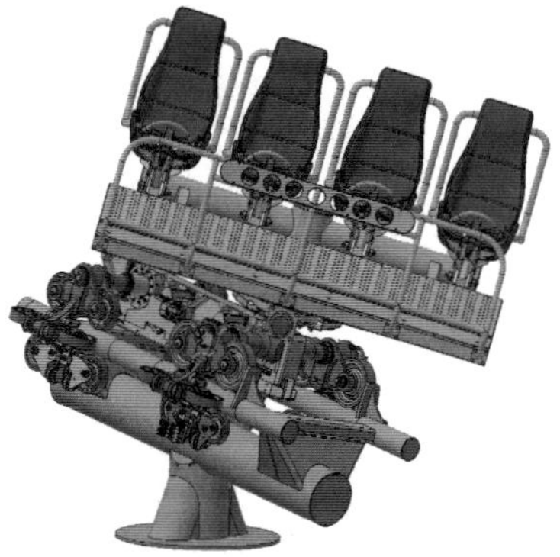

Figure 1: Case study: schema of Zamperla's *DangleZ* ride.

correct working conditions and the security of the machine (for instance, the state of the safety button).

Data are divided into *sessions* (or tests) and each session is composed of a number of *cycles*. Each cycle collects the data generated during one run of the coaster, from the moment it leaves the station to its return to the station. Each session contains data coming from an homogeneous set of measurements, typically measurements in the same day or under the same wheater conditions.

4. Conceptual Design

Figure 2 shows the Entity-Relationship schema of our database, containing four principal sets of entities:

- *parks and users* (green): park names with a reference email and Profile information of the users allows to access and insert acquisition data (Park Managers) or analysis data (Analysts);
- *ride related information* (red): each ride has a specific model and is equipped with a set of acquisition devices. All the maintenance events are stored together with their category (ordinary/extraordinary maintenance or hardware upgrade) and their type (e.g., components lubrication, replacement of gaskets). Events data are used in the AD system to identify the different feasible working conditions of the machines;
- *acquisition data* (yellow): data are organized into sessions, each of which represents a set of ride cycles under the same underlying conditions, i.e., the acquisition data related to a full morning or afternoon. These conditions are stored in the form of metatag values related to the session (e.g., weather condition, load, notes). As explained above, the acquisition is organized into cycles, each one representing a full run of the coaster. During the acquisition, each device gathers data for a set of variables, each identified by a unique TAG name. Synonymy relations between tags are stored to deal with old tag names in legacy acquisitions. Data are stored in packets, each one containing a vector of values (data_array) for a TAG coming from a device during a specific cycle;

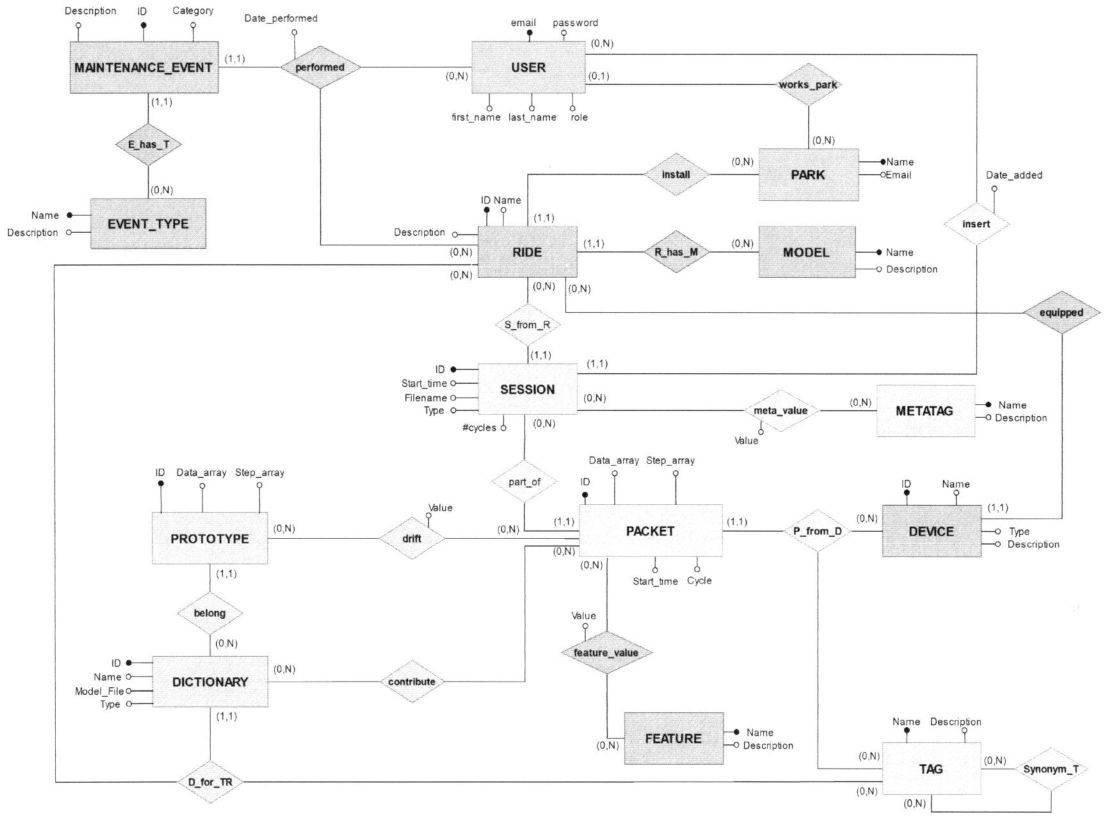

Figure 2: Entity-Relationship schema of the database.

- *analysis related data*: dictionaries (the obtained prototypes) for the univariate AD and the corresponding drift value of each packet are stored (orange entities). Features for the multivariate AD and their values for each packet are stored (purple entities).

5. Anomaly Detection

The proposed approach integrates univariate and multi-variate methods, as illustrated in Figure 3:

- at a given machine cycle, a set of raw signals $\mathcal{X} = \{X_1, \ldots, X_q\}$ coming from the equipment sensors (and additional context information) are fed to a *feature extraction* block that computes features $x_1, \ldots, x_p$, where it typically holds $p \neq q$. While signals X_j are usually time-series, features x_i are scalars. Here, we consider the case where each feature x_i is computed from a single raw signal X_j and we denote the set of features computed from X_j by $\mathcal{S}_{X_j}$;
- such features are used within a multivariate AD block having two objectives: (i) obtaining an *anomaly score* $s(\cdot)$, a quantitative indicator that summarizes the degree of "outlierness" of the machine cycle $\mathcal{X}$ under exam; (ii) using an XAI approach to obtain a *feature*

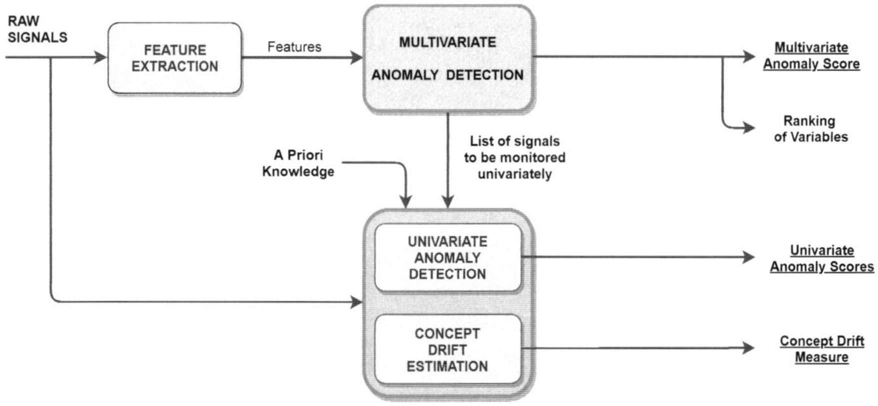

Figure 3: Functional schema of the proposed Anomaly Detection approach.

importance score $f_i(\mathcal{X}), \forall\, i \in \{1, \ldots, p\}$. $f_i(\mathcal{X})$ is a quantitative index that summarizes the impact of feature x_i in identifying machine cycle $\mathcal{X}$ as anomalous.

- raw signals that deserve to be monitored separately with a time-series based (univariate) approach are detected based on (i) expert knowledge and on (ii) the feature importance $f_i(\mathcal{X})$ coming from the AD module. The rationale is that some anomaly types are better identified by analyzing a specific time-series. To be reliably detected, the respective signal X_i should be independently assessed, thus avoiding the loss of information descending from a multi-variate feature extraction procedure. To identify such signals, all data points $\mathcal{X}$ are considered. Raw signals to be processed by a univariate approach are identified by applying the following conditions:
  1. a cycle $\mathcal{X}$ is tagged as "anomalous" if it holds
  $$s(\mathcal{X}) > \tau, \tag{1}$$
  where τ is a pre-defined threshold on the anomaly score (under the assumption that "high" values of the anomaly score indicate a high degree of outlierness). For the problem at hand, we used $\tau = 0.55$ w.r.t. the anomaly score generated by an Isolation Forest;
  2. if, for an anomalous cycle, $\mathcal{X}_a$, we detect that the features obtained from a single time-series X_i are more important than all the others in explaining the anomaly, then the corresponding time-series X_i is sent to the univariate monitoring block. Formally X_i is selected
  $$\begin{aligned} \text{if there exists} \quad & f_j(\mathcal{X}) > \delta f_k(\mathcal{X}), \\ \text{where} \quad & j, k \in \{1, \ldots, p\}, \\ \text{and} \quad & x_j \in \mathcal{S}_{X_i}, x_k \notin \mathcal{S}_{X_i}, \end{aligned} \tag{2}$$
  where $\delta > 1$ is a pre-defined quantity (for our results, we have set $\delta = 2$);
  3. if, besides the two previous steps, some expert knowledge indicates that some raw signals are particularly relevant by themselves, then, they should be monitored univariately as well.

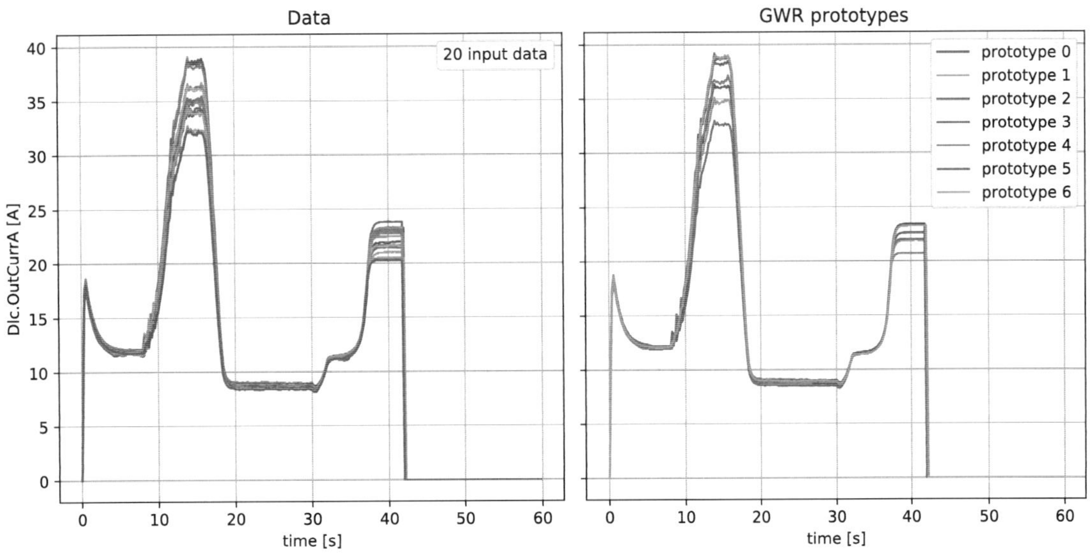

Figure 4: The left part of the figure shows the values of an engine's current consumption in a particular session. These values have been used to create the reference dictionary depicted in the right part of the figure, using GWR.

The user is finally provided with complementary information coming from the two module types, with anomaly scores, system monitoring indications, ranking of variables and concept drift estimations, allowing for a guided Root Cause Analysis.

6. Prototype

We remark that features are not only related to physical signals acquired from the machine, but also to parameters that characterize its working condition and the surrounding environment, like the machine load (number of customers carried), the lubrication, the ambient temperature and the presence of rain. To exemplify, Fig. 4 shows a particular electric current consumption during a machine cycle: this signal was processed by extracting features related to the value of the first current peak, the rising time (to rise to 90% of the peak's amplitude), the maximum current value, a standard deviation in its neighborhood, and the value of the last peak before the signal drops to zero. Once all the features were computed, a correlation analysis was performed to remove redundancy, obtaining vectors composed of $p = 23$ independent features ready to be inputted into the Isolation Forest. For the *concept drift* estimation, we focused on one specific signal, namely, the current consumption of a particular engine, since it highly correlates with the lubrication that is performed periodically on the machine. We used, as a reference, measurements collected in a day when the gears were lubricated and during which the machine was tested in all its possible load configurations (i.e., recalling that, as shown in Fig. 1, four seats are available, the possible configurations correspond to 1, 2, 3 or 4 occupied seats). The left part of Fig. 4 illustrates these data. Some of these configurations generate traces that are clearly identifiable also by visual inspection, as a higher number of occupied seats implies more

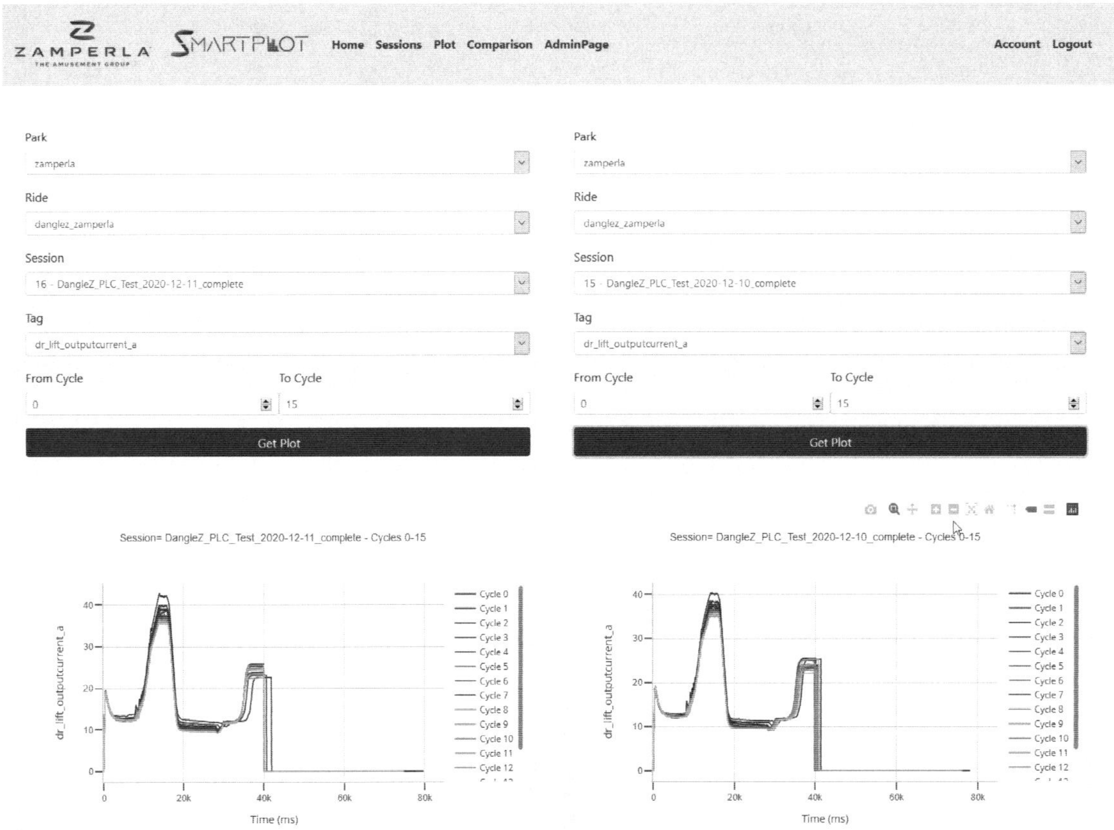

Figure 5: Example of the Web application functionalities.

weight and, therefore, a higher current consumption. However, the proposed GWR approach does this automatically, extracting and then storing the typical patterns (the prototypes) into the dictionary depicted in the right part of Fig. 4.

Data acquired from the sensors are temporarily stored into the file system where there is a folder for each Ride containing metadata about the Ride and a set of csv files corresponding to each Session for data Ride. These files are parsed by using Python scripts and stored in a relational database, namely PostgreSQL[2]. Then, a data access layer, written in Python, provides API to query the data to both the anomaly detection algorithms and to the Web application. The server-side of the Web application is implemented by using the Django REST framework[3]. On the client-side, we rely on AJAX calls implemented by using jQuery[4] and the PLOTLY[5] libraries for delivering interactive plots.

Figure 5 shows an example screenshot of the Web application we have developed. It allows designers to explore, visualize, and analyze the acquired data, according to the approaches

[2]https://www.postgresql.org/
[3]https://www.django-rest-framework.org/
[4]https://jquery.com/
[5]https://plotly.com/

described above. In particular, Figure 5 shows the side-by-side comparison of two different sessions of acquisitions and the related analysis.

7. Conclusions and Future Work

In this work, an AD system to monitor amusement rides has been presented. The system combines a database management system and a multi-faceted AD engine performing univariate and multi-variate analyses, exposed through a Web application. The approach is unsupervised, making it appealing for scenarios where tagged information is unavailable or unreliable. Also, features are ranked according to their importance in explaining an alarm, using an explainable artificial intelligence method.

Future work may concern different areas: *improvements* of the current framework by (i) using other norms (e.g., $|\cdot|_\infty$ or DTW [7]) to account for different types of anomalies, and (ii) adopting semi-supervised learning techniques, including tagged data from either manual labeling or new sensors; *extensions* of the system beyond AD, using it in the ride design phase to maximize its efficiency and the service life of wear components.

Acknowledgments

This work has been supported by the Regione Veneto POR FESR 2014-2020. Asse 1. Azione 1.1.4 (*Bando per il sostegno a progetti sviluppati da Aggregazioni di imprese*) initiative for the project "Trasformazione digitale innovativa nell'industria dell'entertainment" and by MIUR (Italian Minister for Education) under the initiative "Departments of Excellence" (Law 232/2016).

References

[1] L. Stojanovic, M. Dinic, N. Stojanovic, A. Stojadinovic, Big-data-driven anomaly detection in industry (4.0): An approach and a case study, in: 2016 IEEE International Conference on Big Data (Big Data), IEEE, 2016, pp. 1647–1652.

[2] G. A. Susto, et al., An adaptive machine learning decision system for flexible predictive maintenance, in: 2014 IEEE International Conference on Automation Science and Engineering (CASE), 2014, pp. 806–811.

[3] H. Wang, M. J. Bah, M. Hammad, Progress in outlier detection techniques: A survey, IEEE Access 7 (2019) 107964–108000.

[4] Y. Zhao, Z. Nasrullah, Z. Li, Pyod: A python toolbox for scalable outlier detection, Journal of Machine Learning Research 20 (2019) 1–7.

[5] M. Carletti, C. Masiero, A. Beghi, G. A. Susto, A deep learning approach for anomaly detection with industrial time series data: a refrigerators manufacturing case study, Procedia Manufacturing 38 (2019) 233–240.

[6] A. Tsymbal, The problem of concept drift: definitions and related work, Computer Science Department, Trinity College Dublin 106 (2004) 58.

[7] H. Sakoe, S. Chiba, Dynamic programming algorithm optimization for spoken word recognition, IEEE transactions on acoustics, speech, and signal processing 26 (1978) 43–49.

Smart Conversational User Interface for recommending Cultural Heritage Points of Interest

(Discussion Paper)

Flora Amato[1], Francesco Moscato[2], Vincenzo Moscato[3] and Giancarlo Sperlì[4]

[1]DIETI - University of Napoli Federico II, Naples, Italy
[2]DIEM. University of Salerno, Fisciano (SA), Italy
[4]DIETI - University of Napoli Federico II, via Claudio 21 - Naples, Italy
[4]DIETI - University of Napoli Federico II, via Claudio 21 - Naples, Italy

Abstract

Researchers and companies are making great efforts to create new ways of interaction with a increasing number and types of electronic devices, with particular attention to the conversational interface, whether spoken or written. The cultural heritage domain can bring many benefits from the great effort in this field, as a smart conversational system can provide both room/hotel/apartment information and information related to the area, natural or cultural points of interest, tourist routes, social events, history etc. The paper's main goal is to present a quick and effective service to the tourists visiting a city for the first time. Learning the cultural preferences of the users can enhance customer satisfaction, since a smart system can propose them customised tours in order to reach point of interests according to the expressed preferences. The interaction with the user is simplified by a conversational interface (chatbot).

1. Introduction

The Chatbot4Heritage (CB4H) project was born with the aim of integrating and centralising, on a single platform, information related to the tourism sector in Campania, generally from heterogeneous sources. In fact, the information a tourist may need during his or her stay ranges from details on local cultural sites, to upcoming cultural and entertainment events, the location of various types of services (e.g. in the catering sector), updates on the status of mobility, making it necessary to carry out numerous searches on different websites and worsening the overall user experience.

The project aims, through a service-oriented architecture, to extrapolate through a web crawler the information coming from multiple event aggregator websites, transform it into a common format and, through the mediation of an Enterprise Service Bus, store it in special databases. This information can then be made available to client applications, including a Chatbot[1, 2, 3] with which any users will be able to interact easily in natural language.

Researchers and companies are making great efforts to develop new ways of communicating with a increasing number and types of electronic devices, with particular attention to the conver-

---

flora.amato@unina.it (F. Amato); fmoscato@unisa.it (F. Moscato); vmoscato@unina.it (V. Moscato); giancarlo.sperli@unina.it (. G. Sperlì) sational interface, whether spoken or in writing. The cultural heritage domain can bring many benefits from the great effort in this field, as an intelligent conversational framework can include both room/hotel/apartment information[4] and area specific information, natural or cultural points of interest, tourist routes, social events, history etc. The main aim of the paper is to provide the tourists visiting a city for the first time with a fast and efficient service.

The system can suggest to the users most appreciated cultural sites, by analysing opinion taken from social networks[5], and specifically taking in consideration cultural heritage communities[6] or the most authoritative persons[7] in the field of cultural heritage domain. Therefore, understanding the users' cultural preferences can improve customer loyalty, as a smart system can give them personalised tours to reach the point of interest according to the preferences expressed. A conversational interface[8] (chatbot) simplifies communications with the user.

Moreover, since of Covid-19 disease spreading, many cities started to improve their mobility services, like underground, by implementing a routing service for tourists[9, 10], that offers:

- Route planning by taking as input user's first and last stop.
- number of stops from starting stop to last one.
- Number of line changes during the route.
- Detection of the nearest stop to a given tourist's attraction.

TravelBot[8] provides the aforementioned basic functions and other services like:

- Informing the user about any faults on the lines.
- Showing the metro's map.
- Informing and guiding the user to the purchase of tickets.
- Showing the order of the stops for the line selected.
- Informing the user about the working timetables of metro's services.

2. System Architecture

In order to retrieve information about locations, events or other relevant information, we have to chose a set of sources considered reliable. Then, the obtained data-set must undergo a process of processing and cleaning, removing formatting errors and non machine readable elements, so that the information contained in it can be inserted in a natural language sentence[11].

We adopted a Service Oriented Architecture because of its intrinsic modularity. In this type of architecture, in fact, each module is developed independently and can be connected and removed from the main system without compromising the others. If, conceptually, the chatbot is considered a front end module, then it is possible to delegate data extraction and cleaning operations to other back end modules, using the Service Bus as an intermediary. The chatbot, at this point, can use the received data immediately, without having to process it further at runtime.

Some example components were chosen and described in Figure 1: a scraper, whose implementation in Python is described here through the Scrapy framework, for the Napolitoday.it website; an external API, that of the Yelp website; a MySQL database, which in this field is identified as Data Service; a web application in Django for direct insertion.

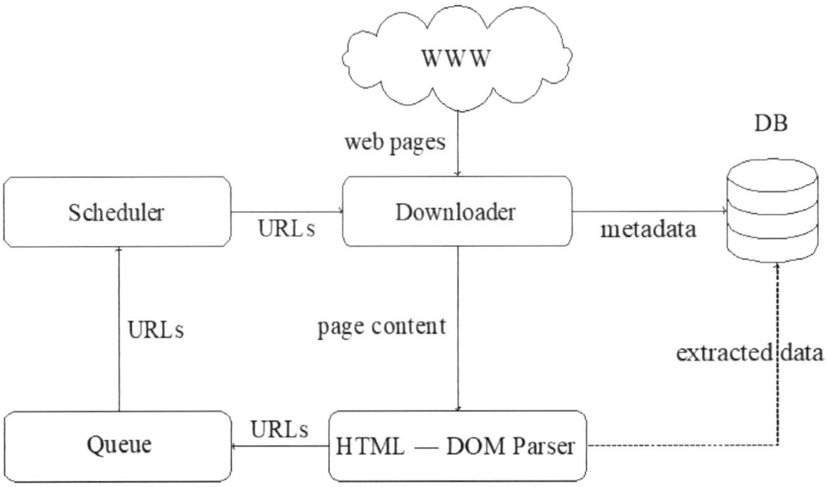

Figure 1: High level architecture of a bot. Data extraction occurs only in scraping bots.

For the implementation of the Service Bus, the choice fell on the open-source framework WSO2. WSO2 Enterprise Integrator has a graphical drag-and-drop interface for the configuration of the message flows between one component and another. One of the main features of a Service Oriented Architecture is the possibility to configure the interactions between components, instead of defining them entirely by code.

The application in Django, finally, was born as an interface for the management of CRUD (Crud-Retrieve-Update-Delete) operations by an employee or operator of a cultural entity. However, due to restrictions imposed by the framework itself, it was decided to use it for insertion only. In the section dedicated to future developments, this issue will also be dealt with[12].

3. Knowledge Base population

Information extracted from web pages sources are processed and stored in the system' Knowledge Base. The Knowledge Base was implemented in Prolog language, taking advantage of its ease of use. The code will be divided into:

- Facts: they report certain data known by the machine.
- Rules: they manipulate the facts to obtain data useful to the end user.

The "machine learning" process is used to obtain useful information for the user (e.g.) and this will help the programmer who does not need to provide too many facts to the machine.

3.1. Facts

The machine knows two types of facts:

1. Connections (conn), composed by 3 arguments:
    a) First stop;

b) Second stop;
c) Median time between that two stops, it also serves to identify which line is it.

It establishes that there is a connection between the two stops and how long the subway takes to travel from one to another.

```
conn(battistini, cornella, 2).
```

2. Locations (locate), composed by 2 arguments:
   a) List of one or more tourist attraction
   b) Nearest stop to the attraction list.

   It links a list of tourist attraction to their nearest stop.

```
locate([s_pietro,musei_vaticani],ottaviano).
```

3.2. Rules

The rules can enhance the inferential process that retrieve customised information according to user preferences. Further enhancement can be taken with the exploitation of semantic techniques[13]

Conn1 The machine can determine only a one way connection with his known fact "conn". To be able to establish a bidirectional connection between two stops, the machine uses this mathematical expression: $\exists conn(X,Y,C) if \exists conn(Y,X,C)$

The OR statement is needed to get rid off infinite recursive call that can be possible in the next set of rules.

Append The "append" rule, like his name suggest, will take care of appending one element to an existing list and it will give a new resulting list as an output.

- $[Head1|Tail1] = List$ where you want to append an element.
- List2 = Element or list of elements that you wish to append.
- $[Head1|TailResult] = Result.$

First part of the code, by using a simple fact, establishes the result of appending an element to an empty list. In the second part then we will use a rule that with a recursive call, taking advantage of backtracking, delete the head of [Head1|Tail1] and continues until the list is empty, after that it starts to rebuilt a new list starting from tail to head, using as a tail List2. This rule will come in handy when we will need to find out how many line change we have to do during end user's journey.

```
append([],X,X).
append([Head1|Tail1],List2,[Head1|TailResult]):-
    append(Tail1,List2,TailResult).
```

Change We use average time to go from one stop to the next, to check how many lines the tourist must change.

- T = Average time between two stops.
- Lc = List of changes, initially empty and used as a temporary.
- $[T|Ris] = A$ second list of changes, needed to make append rule to work and to get a result.

The rule will initially check if given T value is inside Lc by using: not(member(T,Lc)). After that if the result is true, append rule will add the given T value to [T|Ris]. Otherwise we use append with an empty list, so it will not add nothing to [T|Ris]. Result will be a list containing a maximum of three elements, that it will be then used to determine how many lines the tourist must change.

```
change(T,Lc,[T|Ris]):-
    not(member(T,Lc)),
    append([T],Lc,[T|Ris]).
change(T,Lc,[T|Ris]):-
    member(T,Lc),
    append([],Lc,[T|Ris]).
```

Len len works pretty much like append with a recursive call (backtracking) of itself and using a given fact: len([],0). goal is different, we need to evaluate the length of a given list, in our case that list will be Lc.

- $[\_HEAD|TAIL] = List.$
- N = Number of elements.

Decr This simple rule will decrement P by 1 and it will store the result in Q. decr will work with change and len to work on Lc, we will see that our main goal is to get the number of elements in Lc and decrement that number by one to get our result.

Connection connection is a rule that takes two stops as input and calculates the list of stops, line changes made and duration time of the journey. The algorithm takes care of solving the "travel salesman" problem.

Rule's arguments are:

- Fs = First stop.
- Ls = Last stop.
- Ms = Middle stop.
- Lc = List of changes.
- Pl = Prohibited list.
- T = Total time of journey.
- N1 = Number of changes.
- Result = Non decremented list of changes.
- L1c = Temporary list with last stops to do.

In the first part of code, connection will check if there is a direct connection between first stop (Fs) and last stop (Ls) by using rule conn1 and checking after if these two stops are member of Pl. Otherwise if this first part is false, the machine will search for a middle stop Ms and check if there is a direct connection to first stop (Fs). When this stop is found, the machine will check if both stops are not in the prohibited list using not(member) after that change rule will be called checking if there was a line change from one stop to another. Change rule as we saw makes a list made of average times taken only once (in this specific case), so the maximum length of this list will be three, decreasing this value by 1 will give us N1. Please note: Both Pl and Lc must be empty list while calling connection in a query, because when the tourist starts his journey he have not travelled to anywhere still. Also neither first stop and last stop can be prohibited stops. Connection is going to use a recursive call that will find a connection between Ms and Ls, using updated arguments value:

$$Fs \to s \qquad Pl \to [Fs, Pl] \qquad Lc \to Result \tag{1}$$

The recursive call has to be called until it find a direct connection between middle stop (Ms) (which is going to be updated everytime) and final stop (Fs). After the rule will find final route it will determine length of Result by using change and len, lastly to get N1 it uses decr (N,N1). Then connection will calculate T by adding each time between all the stops.

```
connection(Fs,Ls,Pl,Lc,[Fs,Ls],T,N1):-
    conn1(Fs,Ls,T),
    not(member(Fs,Pl)),
    not(member(Ls,Pl)),
    change(T,Lc,Ris),
    len(Ris,N),
    decr(N,N1).
connection(Fs,Ls,Pl,Lc,[Fs|L1c],T,M):-
    conn1(Fs,Ms,T1),
    not(member(Fs,Pl)),
    not(member(Ms,Pl)),
    change(T1,Lc,Result),
    connection(Ms,Ls,[Fs,Pl],Result,L1c,T2,M),
    T is T1+T2.
```

Visit Rule that calculate the path for the nearest stop, based on the selected attraction, it also shows the travel time, the number of changes and the stops list. Or, choose the final stop you want to reach and define the initial stop where the user is located, check if there are tourist attractions nearby. Compared to 'Connection' rule, there is an additional argument: the attraction that the user wants to visit (Att). The IM, as we already said, shows facts that associate a list of attractions with their nearest stop. Arguments:

- Att = Attraction.
- Fs = First stop.
- Ls = Last stop.
- Ms =Middle stop.
- Lc = List of changes.

- Pl = Prohibited list.
- T = Total time of travel.
- N1 = Number of changes.
- Result = List containing the number of changes not decreased.
- L1c =List that represent the remaining path.

In the first case the IM checks if there is already an attraction or a list of them X, in the Knowledge Base, that can be associated with the last stop (Ls). After the IM finds it, checks if the desired attraction belongs to the list X, if it's true the IM searches a connection between Fs and Ls. If, at the first try, the IM doesn't find a direct connection, then it recalls the OR in visit and it will repeat the initial step, but this time searching, In the facts, a connection between Fs and a middle stop Ms, with T1 as travel time, recalling the rule: conn1. For the remaining part of the code, can be checked the rule: connection.

```
visit(Att,Fs,Ls,Pl,Lc,[Fs,Ls],T,N1):-
    locate(X,Ls),
    member(Att,X),
    conn1(Fs,Ls,T),
    not(member(Fs,Pl)),
    not(member(Ls,Pl)),
    change(T,Lc,Ris),
    len(Ris,N),
    decr(N,N1).
visit(Att,Fs,Ls,Pl,Lc,[Fs|L1c],T,M):-
    locate(X,Ls),
    member(Att,X),
    conn1(Fs,Ms,T1),
    not(member(Fs,Pl)),
    not(member(Ms,Pl)),
    change(T1,Lc,Result),
    visit(Att,Ms,Ls,[Fs,Pl],Result,L1c,T2,M),
    T is T1+T2.
```

4. TravelBot

In this section we will show the main functions of the chatbot component and guidelines for correct execution. The main program uses two doc.json, these two document has been made with two different approach to test the chat bot:

1. 'doc-v1.json' had pattern made of extended question containing when/how/what/which pronouns;
2. 'doc.json' is the current document in use, and is made of keywords for each tag with no pronouns at all.

If you want to test the two different documents please make sure to delete model[8] and data files or uncomment line 46 and 123, and change the following constant to the corresponding file.

In Listing 1 we open the document 'doc.json' and download the content. With the Boolean cycle 'for' we are taking the words taken from the document and inserting them in the lists through the functions 'append' and 'extend'.

```
with open(DOC_FILE) as file: #Opens "doc.json" file and load with json libray.
  data = json.load(file)

try:
  #asfgsadf <----- uncomment this to force data parsing again
  with open("data.pickle", "rb") as f:
    words, labels, training, output = pickle.load(f)
except:
  #Empty lists
  words = [] #Words list contains all the words of our "patterns"
  labels = [] #Labels list containing all the "tag" words
  docs_x = [] #doc containing a list of all the patterns with its "tag" in the corresponding position (docs_y)
  docs_y = []

  #Start cycling through out data dictionary (doc.json)
  for intent in data["intents"]:
    for pattern in intent["patterns"]:
      #tokenize all the world in our document using nltk, after that we extend word list,

      wrds = nltk.word_tokenize(pattern)
      words.extend(wrds)
      docs_x.append(wrds)
      docs_y.append(intent["tag"])

    if intent["tag"] not in labels:
      labels.append(intent["tag"])
```

Listing 1: File open

In Listing 2 we make all the words lowercase, and remove the character "?". After that we will stem the words, in other words we find the root version of our words. This will help us to see the dimension of the whole vocabulary not counting on duplicates.

```
  words = [stemmer.stem(w.lower()) for w in words if w not in "?"]
  words = sorted(list(set(words))) #Remove duplicates and sort my list of words.

  labels = sorted(labels) #Sorts labels list.
```

Listing 2: Text Normalization

5. Conclusion

The paper main goal is to present a fast and effective service to the tourist, who is visiting for the first time a city, full of culture and connections. In this work we verified the feasibility of a centralised service-oriented system aiming to the population of a Knowledge Base to be integrated into a tourism chatbot. Further development involves the enhancement of natural language processing algorithms to perform a data extraction based on page content, using the bot only to automate navigation or to support data already extracted.

Acknowledgement. This paper has been produced with the financial support of the Project financed by Campania Region of Italy "Synergy-net: ricerca e Digital Solutions nella lotta alle patologie oncologiche" CUP B61C17000090007. "POR CAMPANIA FESR 2014/2020 – ASSE 1 – O.S. 1.2 Avviso "Manifestazione di Interesse per la Realizzazione di Technology Platform nell'Ambito della Lotta alle Patalogie Oncologiche"Dec. N 460 DEL 28/11/2018. CINI"

References

[1] E. Adamopoulou, L. Moussiades, An overview of chatbot technology, in: Proc. IFIP Int. Conf. on Artificial Intelligence Applications and Innovations, Springer, 2020, pp. 373–383.

[2] J. L. Z. Montenegro, C. A. da Costa, R. da Rosa Righi, Survey of conversational agents in health, Expert Systems with Applications 129 (2019) 56–67.

[3] J. Pereira, Ó. Díaz, Using health chatbots for behavior change: a mapping study, Journal of medical systems 43 (2019) 135.

[4] F. P. Putri, H. Meidia, D. Gunawan, Designing intelligent personalized chatbot for hotel services, in: Proc. the 2019 Int. Conf. on Algorithms, Computing and Artificial Intelligence, 2019, pp. 468–472.

[5] F. Amato, G. Cozzolino, F. Moscato, V. Moscato, A. Picariello, G. Sperli, Data mining in social network, in: Procs. Intelligent Interactive Multimedia Systems and Services, Springer, 2018, pp. 53–63.

[6] A. Castiglione, G. Cozzolino, V. Moscato, G. Sperlì, Analysis of community in social networks based on game theory, in: Proc. IEEE Int. Conf. on Dependable, Autonomic and Secure Computing, Int. Conf. on Pervasive Intelligence and Computing, Int. Conf. on Cloud and Big Data Computing, Int. Conf. on Cyber Science and Technology Congress (DASC/PiCom/CBDCom/CyberSciTech), IEEE, 2019, pp. 619–626.

[7] F. Amato, G. Cozzolino, G. Sperlì, A hypergraph data model for expert-finding in multimedia social networks, Information 10 (2019) 183.

[8] R. Canonico, G. Cozzolino, A. Ferraro, V. Moscato, A. Picariello, F. R. Sorrentino, G. Sperlì, A smart chatbot for specialist domains, in: Workshops of the Int. Conf. on Advanced Information Networking and Applications, Springer, 2020, pp. 1003–1010.

[9] V. La Gatta, V. Moscato, M. Postiglione, G. Sperli, An epidemiological neural network exploiting dynamic graph structured data applied to the covid-19 outbreak, IEEE Transactions on Big Data (2020).

[10] A. Galli, M. Gravina, V. Moscato, G. Sperli, et al., Deep learning for hdd health assessment: an application based on lstm, IEEE Transactions on Computers (2020).

[11] F. Amato, F. Moscato, V. Moscato, F. Pascale, A. Picariello, An agent-based approach for recommending cultural tours, Pattern Recognition Letters 131 (2020) 341–347.

[12] A. Amato, G. Cozzolino, C'meal! the chatbot for food information, in: Proc. Int. Conf. on Intelligent Networking and Collaborative Systems, Springer, 2020, pp. 238–244.

[13] G. Cozzolino, Using semantic tools to represent data extracted from mobile devices, in: Proc. IEEE Int. Conf. on Information Reuse and Integration (IRI), IEEE, 2018, pp. 530–536.

Panel on "Past and Future of Computer Science Theory"

(Discussion Paper)

Ronald Fagin[1], Georg Gottlob[2], Christos Papadimitriou[3], Moshe Vardi[4], Giorgio Ausiello[5], Maurizio Lenzerini[5], Luigi Palopoli[6], Domenico Saccà[6] and Francesco Scarcello[6]

[1] *IBM Research - Almaden, San Jose, CA 95120-6099, USA*
[2] *Computer Science Department, University of Oxford, OX1 3QD, UK*
[3] *Columbia University, New York, NY 10027, USA*
[4] *Computer Science Department, Rice University, Houston, TX 77005, USA*
[5] *DIAG Department, Sapienza University of Rome, 00185 Rome, Italy*
[6] *DIMES Department, University of Calabria, 87036 Rende, Italy*

Abstract

The twenty-ninth edition of the SEBD (Italian Symposium on Advanced Database Systems), held on 5-9 September 2021 in Pizzo (Calabria Region, Italy), included a joint seminar on "Reminiscence of TIDB 1981" with invited talks given by some of the participants to the Advanced Seminar on Theoretical Issues in Databases (TIDB), which took place in the same region exactly forty years earlier. The joint seminar was concluded by a Panel on "The Past and the Future of Computer Science Theory" with the participation of four distinguished computer science theorists (Ronald Fagin, Georg Gottlob, Christos Papadimitriou and Moshe Vardi), who were interviewed by Giorgio Ausiello, Maurizio Lenzerini, Luigi Palopoli, Domenico Saccà and Francesco Scarcello. This paper reports the summaries of the four interviews.

Keywords

Computer Science Theory, Database Theory

1. Introduction

Forty years ago, on September 13-19 of 1981, Grand Hotel San Michele (a fascinating resort in the Calabria's Tyrrhenian coast in Southern Italy) hosted the Advanced Seminar on Theoretical Issues in Databases (TIDB'81), organized by Giorgio Ausiello, François Bancilhon, Domenico

SEBD 2021: The 29th Italian Symposium on Advanced Database Systems, September 5-9, 2021, Pizzo Calabro (VV), Italy

fagin@us.ibm.com (R. Fagin); georg.gottlob@cs.ox.ac.uk (G. Gottlob); christos@columbia.edu (C. Papadimitriou); vardi@cs.rice.edu (M. Vardi); ausiello@diag.uniroma1.it (G. Ausiello); lenzerini@diag.uniroma1.it (M. Lenzerini); luigi.palopoli@unical.it (L. Palopoli); domenico.sacca@unical.it (D. Saccà); francesco.Scarcello@unical.it (F. Scarcello)

0000-0002-7374-0347 (R. Fagin); 0000-0002-2353-5230 (G. Gottlob); 0000-0001-8084-0445 (C. Papadimitriou); 0000-0002-0661-5773 (M. Vardi); 0000-0003-1345-5007 (G. Ausiello); 0000-0003-2875-6187 (M. Lenzerini); 0000-0003-4915-5137 (L. Palopoli); 0000-0003-3584-5372 (D. Saccà); 0000-0001-7765-1563 (F. Scarcello)

CEUR Workshop Proceedings (CEUR-WS.org)

Saccà and Nicolas Spyratos. In the early 1980s, database theory was at the early stage and TIDB'81 was one of the few pioneering initiatives organized in Europe.

TIDB'81 program included invited talks by outstanding scientists such as: Catriel Beeri, Ron Fagin, Seymour Ginsburg, Bob Kowalski, Witold Lipski, John Mylopoulos, Jean-Marie Nicolas, Christos Papadimitriou, Jan Paredaens, Yehoshua Sagiv, Mihalis Yannakakis, Carlo Zaniolo. Besides the main lectures, short talks were also given by a young (at that time) Italian scientist Carlo Batini and two promising postdocs Maurizio Lenzerini and Paolo Atzeni. More details on the seminar, including a pleasant description of the warm social atmosphere of the event, can be found in [1]. This book mentions, among other things, what Christos Papadimitriou said about TIDB'81 in the report written for the EATCS Bulletin: *There was an extensive mosaic of topics covered, reflecting the state of wild fermentation in which database theory appears to be. Relational theory, concurrency control, and logic in databases were three areas that were represented quite heavily in the list of speakers. Voices of the null value problem, schema design theory, the operational approach, conceptual modeling, and software engineering issues, were also heard.*

In 1984, a second edition of TIDB was held in Benodet (on the Brittany coast in North-Western France) and this edition too met with widespread participation and increased scientific interest. Therefore, a small group of people (Serge Abiteboul, Paolo Atzeni, Giorgio Ausiello, Catriel Beeri, Jan Paredaens, Domenico Sacca, Nicholas Spyratos) felt that there was a need to have a regular international forum for European researchers in database theory, following the format of the ACM Symposium on Principles of Database Systems (PODS), organized annually in the US starting from 1982. Then, the International Conference on Database Theory (ICDT) was set up as the successor of TIDB seminars and its first edition was held in Rome in 1986. At the 2011 celebration of the 30th anniversary of PODS, two events were remembered as progenitors of PODS and ICDT and for contributing to the birth of the field of database theory: the XP series of Workshops on Database Theory (XP1 took place at SUNY Stony Brook in 1980 and XP2 took place at Pennsylvania State University in 1981) and the TIDB Seminars.

Forty years later, on 9 September 2021, in the same Calabria's Tyrrhenian coast that hosted TIDB'81, a seminar on "Reminiscence of TIDB 1981" has been organized in connection with the twenty-ninth edition of the SEBD (the Italian Symposium on Advanced Database, the major annual event of the Italian database research community), held in Pizzo Calabro on 5-9 September 2021. The joint seminar on "Reminiscence of TIDB 1981" included invited talks given by the four organizers and two participants (Paolo Atzeni and Carlo Zaniolo) of TIDB'81 and a Panel on "The Past and the Future of Computer Science Theory". The panelists were four distinguished computer science theorists (Ronald Fagin, Georg Gottlob, Christos Papadimitriou and Moshe Vardi), who were interviewed by Giorgio Ausiello, Maurizio Lenzerini, Luigi Palopoli, Domenico Saccà and Francesco Scarcello.

The next four sections present the panel interview summaries in a question/answer format. The questions to each panelist were of three types: (1) his remembrance of database theory at the time of TIDB'81, (2) his major achievements in database and computer science theory from the late eighties on, and (3) his opinion on the future directions of database theory and, more in general, on the role that computer science theory will play in the next years.

2. Questions to Ronald Fagin

Ronald Fagin was interviewed by Luigi Palopoli and Domenico Saccà [2]. Ron Fagin is an IBM fellow at IBM Almaden research center. He is a distinguished scientist who provided fundamental contributions in several areas of theoretical computer science including database theory, logic in computer science, data exchange, reasoning about knowledge, finite model theory, information retrieval and indexing techniques. He is a member of the National Academy of Sciences, National Academy of Engineering, and American Academy of Arts and Sciences. He is an ACM Fellow and an IEEE Fellow. He obtained the Gödel Prize, the IEEE W. Wallace McDowell Award, the IEEE Technical Achievement Award, the ACM SIGMOD Edgar F. Codd Innovations Award, the Alonzo Church Award for Logic and Computation, several IBM Outstanding Innovation Awards and IBM Outstanding Technical Achievement Awards. Also, he received a Docteur Honoris Causa from the University of Paris, and a Laurea Honoris Causa from the University of Calabria.

1. *Ron, what are your reminiscence of discussions at TIDB'81 and, more in general, about the relevant topics you and other theoreticians used to investigate in the late seventies and early eighties? (By the way, we remember you working on Cetraro beach together with Marco Casanova and Christos Papadimitriou on some complexity issues of the interaction of inclusion database dependencies with functional dependencies* [3]).

   RF: When, in 1975, I moved from IBM Yorktown Heights to Almaden, I asked myself whom would be interesting to work with. And, actually, there were many interesting people around, but the one that stood out in my mind was Ted Codd. So I started to work with him on relational theory and my very first paper in this area was about data dependencies and entitled *Functional dependencies in relational databases and propositional logics* [4]. An important related topic I also addressed at TIDB was about acyclic hypergraphs and their relationships to database schemes. What is the correct notion of acyclicity for an hypergraph was not at all obvious at that time (as it was instead for ordinary graphs). I worked on this with Ullman, Vardi, Yannakakis, Maier and Mendelzon and we defined relevant notions and proved interesting properties about database schemes associated to acyclic hyergraphs [5, 6].

2. *Would you mind to tell us about the most relevant developments of your research after that pioneering period?.*

   RF: The first topic I would cite is reasoning about knowledge. I worked on that with Halpern, Moses and Vardi and, actually, the only book I wrote is about this very topic [7]. The basic questions in this context arise when trying to make sense of sentences like "*someone knows that someone else knows that a third party knows this or that*" and there are applications all over the places for this kind of reasoning and analysis: besides computer science, economics and political science and other areas where these kinds of questions naturally arise very often.
   Talking about data exchange, I would say that this topic is very fun. I worked on that with Kolaitis, Popa, Miller and Tan. There was a project called Clio on data exchange about moving data from one format to another and, after sitting for one year in meeting rooms, we decided to simply face the problem from scratch, studying it from a purely

theoretical point of view. We did that and we got some very interesting results that convinced practical people to re-implement their systems and our developments are now part of data exchange products. By the way, we won the Alonso Church award for the work on data exchange [8, 9]: this was a one time episode in which not only computer science borrows notions and results from logics, but also logics is fertilized by computer science - in this case with the notion of second-order dependency.
Another issue I would mention involved Laura Haas when she was on the Garlic project at IBM. Garlic was intended to be designed as a middleware software sitting on top of DB2 for relational data and QBIC for images in order to enable integrated querying of both sources. And Laura asked me for efficient ways to combine answers from the two domains, which clearly have very different data formats. So I developed an approach based on fuzzy logics and she seemed to be quite happy with that, but then she pointed out that straightforward ways to implement the approach would have required linear time, that was unaffordable for the huge data repositories handled by Garlic. Therefore, I developed a new algorithms that turned out to be very efficient in practice (nowadays known as the Fagin's algorithm) [10]. Few years later, together with Lotem and Naor, I developed a nice improvement of the Fagin's algorithm, known as the *threshold algorithm* [11], characterized by the so called instance optimality, which means to be optimal for every single input. This result took us to obtain the Godel Price, and that was the first database paper to win this price. Other issues I worked on producing interesting results are entity linking, differential back-ups and extensible hashing, which are very relevant in databases.

3. *Within the ample spectrum of your research contributions to database theory and, more in general, to theoretical computer science, which ones do you consider will have the most durable influence in the long run? Furthermore, which topics do you think will be relevant and hot in database theory in the years to come?.*

   RF: It is difficult to answer the first part of your question: it is like asking someone to choose among his children! Anyway, I would say that many of them are significant and retain their relevance to date, as in fact many of them are currently implemented in systems and products. As for the second part of the question, I think AI will be the big hot topic in the future also for database people. For instance, I am currently involved in working on real valued logics (a kind analogous to fuzzy logics) which is relevant in managing huge logical neural networks and optimizing them. So, again, AI is a very large area hosting relevant future research directions.

4. *What is your vision on the role of Computer Science Theory in the future?*
   RF: I am a very strong believer of the importance of theory and mathematics in computer science, to formally prove things work, to prove how long it takes for an algorithm to run or how much space it is needed. I am definitely sure that mathematics and theory will be with us forever, because we need precision, we need precise definitions, we need to prove results about how systems behave. So, I am very optimistic about the future of the role of theorists in computer science.
5. *So, can we tell the young boys and girls in the audience that they should work on theory because the future is there?*

RF: Yes, for sure!

3. Questions to Georg Gottlob

Georg Gottlob was interviewed by Francesco Scarcello and Domenico Saccà [12]. Georg Gottlob is a Professor at the Oxford University Department of Computer Science, and a Fellow of St John's College; he is Adjunct Professor at the Technische Universität in Vienna. He provided many influential contributions, by developing a common core to the underlying principles of artificial intelligence and databases, and by solving open problems in computational logic, non-monotonic reasoning and database theory. Ha was elected as a member of the Royal Society in 2010, and was recipient of many awards, such as the Wittgenstein Award, which is the highest funded Austrian award for scientific achievements, and the ECCAI fellowship. He also received a number of honorary lauree and doctorates from the University of Klagenfurt, the University of Vienna, and the University of Calabria.

1. *What about Database Theory in the 80's? You are too young at the time of TIDB '81 – how do you have later heard of it?*

   GG I knew about this pioneering workshop while I was a post-doc at Politecnico of Milano, where I also first met Mimmo Saccà, who was giving a seminar about his recent contributions on hypergraphs of functional dependencies [13, 14]. Before coming to Italy, I did joint work with Alexander Leitsch on the efficiency of *subsumption algorithms*, which find many applications in computer science and, in particular, in database theory [15]. I also studied the relationship between subsumption and implication, by identifying classes where the two notions actually coincide. I believe that very important and lively contributions in that period were about *data dependencies*, though an important scientist at PODS 1987 [16] looked at such a subject as the "last gasps of the dying swans" (which gave me quite a scare, as a young researcher just presenting a paper about covers of embedded functional dependencies! [17]) It was also the time of *deductive databases*, where logic programming was applied to databases. I enjoyed working with Stefano Ceri and Letizia Tanca at a book on Datalog covering many topics, from semantics to implementation issues and efficiency [18].

2. *Let us talk about relevant and influential theory topics and results in Database Theory and Artificial Intelligence, two fields where you played a prominent role and provided outstanding contributions.*

   GG Among the many interesting topics relating Database Theory and Artificial Intelligence, I intensively worked on the *structural properties* of problems which allow us of identify tractable classes of problems that are intractable, in general. With Francesco Scarcello and Nicola Leone, we worked on hypergraphs characterizing conjunctive queries in database and Constraint Satisfaction Problems (CSPs) in Artificial Intelligence (as well as many other problems related to homomorphisms between relational structures) [19]. We found that the complexity class LOGCFL plays an important role for such a (hyper)-tree shaped problems. In particular, it turned out that answering an acyclic query is not only feasible in polynomial-time, but also LOGCFL-complete, and hence parallelizable. The same holds

for those queries (or CSPs) having a small degree of cyclicity, more precisely, those queries having a small width *hypertree decomposition* [20].
Another interesting line of research was about the *Complexity and Expressive Power* of Logical Reasoning, where we look not only at the complexity of reasoning problems, but also on the possible ability of a given language to express all problems in a certain complexity classes. For instance, it has been shown that disjunctive Datalog is able to express all problems at the second level of the polynomial hierarchy [21], and FO logic with an oracle in NP is able to express all problems in L^{NP} [22]. Another interesting example is that Monadic Datalog over trees expresses exactly full Monadic Second Order Logic over trees, and the complexity of evaluation is $|Data| \times |Program|$ [23].
These research activities lead to concrete applications and even to the birth of spinoff companies, such as DLVsystem, Lixto, Wrapidity, and DeepReason.ai.

3. *Our last question is about future: what you see as the emerging topics in database and AI, and which role they may play in computer science theory in the next years?*

   A first interesting topic is about using database theory and techniques for Machine Learning and, in particular, for Deep Learning. Usually, in these applications everything goes into a very big flat relation, where we miss information on possible relationships among fragments of data. A second hot topic is about how we can combine reasoning with machine learning: there are human-generated rules that allow us as humans to learn and reason at an abstract and high level that deep learning systems cannot achieve, while they are instead exceptionally good at recognizing tasks and objects. Symbolic and sub-symbolic systems should work together, which needs perhaps adding some (new) form of probabilistic features to logical frameworks such as Datalog.

4. Questions to Christos Papadimitriou

Christos Papadimitriou was interviewed by Giorgio Ausiello and Domenico Saccà [24]. A Columbia University Professor, Christos is one of world's leading computer science theorists and is best known for his fundamental work in computational complexity. Using algorithmic lens, Christos has also explored other fields such as biology and the theory of evolution, economics and game theory, artificial intelligence, robotics, networks and the Internet. Recently he is attracted by the study the algorithms aspects of the brain. Christos has been the recipient of many prestigious scientific awards such as Awards: the Knuth Prize, IEEE's John von Neumann Medal, the EATCS Award, the IEEE Computer Society Charles Babbage Award, the Gödel Prize.

1. *Christos, we remember that at TIDB '81 you made a strong statement: "if you got an IT problem, look at yellow pages for CS theoreticians?" Again at Kyoto ICALP in 2015, where you gave a talk to celebrate 40 years of the journal Theoretical Computer Science, you said "In the Eighties theoreticians owned Computer Science". Did you mean that theoreticians were mastering all of CS?*

   CP This is my interpretation of history: In the Seventies and Eighties theory had a core program. Thanks to the results of Cook and Karp and others, we realized that we could study concrete CS problems and at the same time do good mathematics. I am only talking about the area of algorithms and complexity. I know that those were great decades also for track B[1], and even though for me theory is algorithms and complexity, back then you had to know about track B. For any emerging technology that was developed, we had to provide formalization and mathematical formulation. Databases was one of these areas – perhaps the most glorious. So we were not the masters of CS, we were its servants. I remember that when memories with magnetic bubbles came about, Mihalis Yannakakis and I were wandering how to treat them in theoretical terms — thankfully they went away quickly. Then in the Nineties every sub-field of CS started to develop its own theoretical framework and to have its own dedicated theoreticians, and by now there are no generalist theoreticians addressing all possible fields of CS. So, we started looking outside CS.

2. *Christos, more recently, in the Nineties you developed new very interesting fields of theoretical computer science. In particular can you tell us something about how you got interested in game theory?*

   CP In 1996 when I moved from San Diego to Berkeley, the Internet buzz was everywhere around me, and I started to think about the Internet with Prabakar Raghavan and to address issues related to it [27, 28] such as web search etc. The Internet cannot be called an artifact, it has not been created by a designer or company. The Internet has emerged from the interactions of many, thousands or millions of entities and users, each with their own incentives. This changed the rules of computation. It is in this context that I started to look at distributed mechanisms to reach a goal, involving agents who have different interests. Game theory and mechanism design and economic thinking became very important.

3. *Again in your Kyoto talk we remember that you mentioned your research work regarding evolution. You were trying to understand what evolution tries to optimize. Have you made any progress in this area?*

   CP Yes, actually we developed this subject a few years ago. When CS theoreticians start to look at new domains of science, they apply their computational lens. A lot of other areas can benefit of their ability to dissect the computational aspects implicit in natural or social systems. Together with Erick Chastain, Adi Livnat and Umesh Vazirani I wrote a paper: 'Algorithms, games and evolution' [29]. We reframed the equations of evolution in terms of convex programming and duality theory, and in terms of no-regret learning. We came to the conclusion that, from the point of view of genes, evolution optimizes a sort of convex combination of fitness and genetic diversity.

4. *Among the emerging field of theoretical computer science neural networks and deep learning have now assumed an extremely important role. What is your view of this trend?*

   CP Deep nets are an admirable advance, a fascinating chapter of computation. But my impression is that a real breakthrough happened after 2015 when deep learning started to be applied to natural language processing. Systems like Transformers or GPT3 have marked a

[1] This term comes from the Handbook on Theoretical Computer Science, which had two volumes: *A* was for algorithms and complexity [25], and *B* was for logic and semantics [26]

real revolution compared to neural networks used for image classification. Natural language is the means whereby people exchanged and recorded their thoughts while interacting with the world through their senses, over the centuries. I think it makes much more sense to train deep nets on Wikipedia or the library of Congress for the key to intelligence, rather than on images.

5. *As you certainly know we are now in a period in which Bibliometrics has become a major instrument for evaluating research activity. Nowadays many scientists are committed to write at least two papers per month as much as a war reporter! Can a theoretician prove two theorems per month? Or can a scientist conduct an experiment in 15 days? What is your view about this unpleasant situation?*

   CP Once, only biologists or physicists with big labs could write so many papers based on the results of their lab's experimental work. And in the old days a mathematician had to spend a long time trying to gather the relevant literature, and this has now become much easier. But you are right, the scientific production has become like an arms race, out of control, pushing researchers to write more and more papers. The time to produce a paper has shortened and researchers tend to write their results fresh off their brains. You can no longer read all papers that are published in some domain, you must rely on students and reviews to identify the important work in the deluge. I am at a point of my career where it only makes sense to focus on the one thing you believe is most important (and for me this is how the brain makes language), and yet I end up publishing more papers because I have students and collaborators, and of course because science is endless and problems are exciting and it is fun to indulge.

5. Questions to Moshe Vardi

Moshe Vardi was interviewed by Maurizio Lenzerini, Domenico Saccà and Francesco Scarcello [30]. Moshe Vardi, Rice University Professor and the Karen Ostrum George Distinguished Service Professor of Computational Engineering, is one of the most prominent Computer Scientists, who provided outstanding contributions in several aspects of Computer Science Theory, including Data Management, Automata Theory, Logic in Computer Science, Automated Reasoning, and Design Specification and Verification.

1. *Moshe, you did not attend TIDB'81, but you were already part of the Database community at that time. Which are the most important accomplishments of Database Theory in the 80s?*

   MV: To answer a question like that, we have to agree on the meaning of "important", "relevant", "significant", etc. These are qualitative adjectives, which are very difficult to precisely define in the context of scientific work. I recently did an exercise: I picked up a bunch of database theoreticians, namely Catriel Beeri, Jeff Ullman, Ron Fagin, Christos Papadimitriou, Mihalis Yannakakis and myself, and I checked how many publications from the 80s with more than 500 citations they have. The result was somehow surprising: not many such papers got more than 500 citations. Is it a sign that not many research results in

Database theory have had an impact? Very difficult to say!

2. *We agree that an objective answer to the question of relevance of research results is very difficult to give. So, let us switch to a different flavor of the question: what is your personal opinion about significant research results from Database Theory in the 80s?*

   MV: A first topic where foundational results have been produced in the 80s is the theory of data dependencies [31]. Dependencies are special forms of logical assertions that have several applications in the context of Data Management. Results on dependencies had an impact on various issues, such as database design, reasoning on data schemas, data quality and others. They also proved extremely important in both data exchange and, indirectly, Datalog. A second topic where fundamental research has been carried in the 80s is logic programming, which is the paradigm at the basis of the Datalog query language, as well as several rule-based formalisms, including existential rules and ontology languages. Indeed, the idea of rules seems very fundamental both from the conceptual point of view, and from the point of view of applications. For example, the impact of Datalog has been prominent in areas such as network programming, program analysis and web information extraction, maybe even more than in database systems. A third topic extensively studied in the 80s is query processing and analysis, especially the study of structural properties of queries, such as acyclicity or hypertree decomposition. Such investigations have been important for designing specialized algorithms for query answering, and singling out cases where tractability is guaranteed, taking into account the difference between data and query complexity [32].

3. *You are also recognized for your outstanding work as Editor in Chief of "Communication of the ACM". How was this experience?*

   MV: It has been a great experience, especially with respect to the goal of achieving a broad perspective of our discipline, and thinking about its potentials in addressing critical problems of our society. When you have the possibility of having a large view on the research carried out on a certain discipline, on one hand you can appreciate the variety of topics investigated by the various groups, and on the other hand you realize that sometimes the research problems addressed by the scientists do not really match with the big questions that our society is facing. I really believe that many such problems could find relevant answers with the help of Computer Science.

4. *Let us end with an eye to the future. What do you think will be the future of theory in the context of Data Management?*

   MV: I would mention two issues that I think will be prominent in the near future. The first has to do with reconciling the two aspects of Data Management that will be crucial in the data-driven society that we are experiencing, namely data analytics and data governance. Indeed, while the recent success of machine learning and data mining have stressed the role of data analysis in extracting information and knowledge from data, many observers point out the growing need of data governance, i.e. the development of effective methods for collecting and organizing data, controlling their quality and managing important properties such as completeness, consistency, fairness, and privacy. The second issue concerns Computer Science in general: while the theory of computational complexity has shown its mathematical beauty and its importance in algorithm analysis, it is now clear that it is not sufficient for explaining the behaviour of algorithms in practice. This aspect is particular important in the light of the roles played by algorithms in our society.

References

[1] G. Ausiello, *The Making of a New Science - A Personal Journey Through the Early Years of Theoretical Computer Science*, Springer, 2018. URL: https://doi.org/10.1007/978-3-319-62680-2. doi:10.1007/978-3-319-62680-2.

[2] Panel on Past and Future of Computer Science Theory, *Ronald Fagin's interview*, by Luigi Palopoli and Domenico Saccà, 2021. URL: https://drive.google.com/file/d/126EXLSpmKxV724l7LaX9qrZZmhzdG3YQ/view?usp=sharing, accessed: 2021-09-09.

[3] M. A. Casanova, R. Fagin, C. H. Papadimitriou, Inclusion dependencies and their interaction with functional dependencies, J. Comput. Syst. Sci. 28 (1984) 29–59. URL: https://doi.org/10.1016/0022-0000(84)90075-8. doi:10.1016/0022-0000(84)90075-8.

[4] R. Fagin, Functional dependencies in a relational data base and propositional logic, IBM J. Res. Dev. 21 (1977) 543–544. URL: https://doi.org/10.1147/rd.216.0534. doi:10.1147/rd.216.0534.

[5] C. Beeri, R. Fagin, D. Maier, A. O. Mendelzon, J. D. Ullman, M. Yannakakis, Properties of acyclic database schemes, in: Proceedings of the 13th Annual ACM Symposium on Theory of Computing, May 11-13, 1981, Milwaukee, Wisconsin, USA, ACM, 1981, pp. 355–362. URL: https://doi.org/10.1145/800076.802489. doi:10.1145/800076.802489.

[6] C. Beeri, R. Fagin, D. Maier, M. Yannakakis, On the desirability of acyclic database schemes, J. ACM 30 (1983) 479–513. URL: https://doi.org/10.1145/2402.322389. doi:10.1145/2402.322389.

[7] R. Fagin, J. Y. Halpern, Y. Moses, M. Y. Vardi, Reasoning About Knowledge, MIT Press, 1995. URL: https://doi.org/10.7551/mitpress/5803.001.0001. doi:10.7551/mitpress/5803.001.0001.

[8] R. Fagin, P. G. Kolaitis, R. J. Miller, L. Popa, Data exchange: Semantics and query answering, in: D. Calvanese, M. Lenzerini, R. Motwani (Eds.), Database Theory - ICDT 2003, 9th International Conference, Siena, Italy, January 8-10, 2003, Proceedings, volume 2572 of *Lecture Notes in Computer Science*, Springer, 2003, pp. 207–224. URL: https://doi.org/10.1007/3-540-36285-1_14. doi:10.1007/3-540-36285-1_14.

[9] R. Fagin, P. G. Kolaitis, L. Popa, W. C. Tan, Composing schema mappings: Second-order dependencies to the rescue, in: C. Beeri, A. Deutsch (Eds.), Proceedings of the Twenty-third ACM SIGACT-SIGMOD-SIGART Symposium on Principles of Database Systems, June 14-16, 2004, Paris, France, ACM, 2004, pp. 83–94. URL: https://doi.org/10.1145/1055558.1055572. doi:10.1145/1055558.1055572.

[10] R. J. Miller, M. A. Hernández, L. M. Haas, L. Yan, C. T. H. Ho, R. Fagin, L. Popa, The clio project: Managing heterogeneity, SIGMOD Rec. 30 (2001) 78–83. URL: https://doi.org/10.1145/373626.373713. doi:10.1145/373626.373713.

[11] R. Fagin, A. Lotem, M. Naor, Optimal aggregation algorithms for middleware, J. Comput. Syst. Sci. 66 (2003) 614–656. URL: https://doi.org/10.1016/S0022-0000(03)00026-6. doi:10.1016/S0022-0000(03)00026-6.
[12] Panel on Past and Future of Computer Science Theory, *Georg Gottlob's interview*, by Francesco Scarcello and Domenico Saccà, 2021. URL: https://drive.google.com/file/d/11llc8ou8L_12CEj7SM3bPpk_BhQBZf4_/view?usp=sharing, accessed: 2021-09-09.
[13] G. Ausiello, A. D'Atri, D. Saccà, Graph algorithms for functional dependency manipulation, J. ACM 30 (1983) 752–766. URL: https://doi.org/10.1145/2157.322404. doi:10.1145/2157.322404.
[14] D. Saccà, Closures of database hypergraphs, J. ACM 32 (1985) 774–803. URL: https://doi.org/10.1145/4221.4997. doi:10.1145/4221.4997.
[15] G. Gottlob, A. Leitsch, On the efficiency of subsumption algorithms, J. ACM 32 (1985) 280–295. URL: https://doi.org/10.1145/3149.214118. doi:10.1145/3149.214118.
[16] J. D. Ullman, Database theory: Past and future, in: M. Y. Vardi (Ed.), Proceedings of the Sixth ACM SIGACT-SIGMOD-SIGART Symposium on Principles of Database Systems, March 23-25, 1987, San Diego, California, USA, ACM, 1987, pp. 1–10. URL: https://doi.org/10.1145/28659.28660. doi:10.1145/28659.28660.
[17] G. Gottlob, Computing covers for embedded functional dependencies, in: M. Y. Vardi (Ed.), Proceedings of the Sixth ACM SIGACT-SIGMOD-SIGART Symposium on Principles of Database Systems, March 23-25, 1987, San Diego, California, USA, ACM, 1987, pp. 58–69. URL: https://doi.org/10.1145/28659.28665. doi:10.1145/28659.28665.
[18] S. Ceri, G. Gottlob, L. Tanca, Logic Programming and Databases, Surveys in computer science, Springer, 1990. URL: https://www.worldcat.org/oclc/20595273.
[19] G. Gottlob, N. Leone, F. Scarcello, The complexity of acyclic conjunctive queries, J. ACM 48 (2001) 431–498. URL: https://doi.org/10.1145/382780.382783. doi:10.1145/382780.382783.
[20] G. Gottlob, N. Leone, F. Scarcello, Hypertree decompositions and tractable queries, J. Comput. Syst. Sci. 64 (2002) 579–627. URL: https://doi.org/10.1006/jcss.2001.1809. doi:10.1006/jcss.2001.1809.
[21] T. Eiter, G. Gottlob, H. Mannila, Disjunctive datalog, ACM Trans. Database Syst. 22 (1997) 364–418. URL: https://doi.org/10.1145/261124.261126. doi:10.1145/261124.261126.
[22] G. Gottlob, Relativized logspace and generalized quantifiers over finite ordered structures, J. Symb. Log. 62 (1997) 545–574. URL: https://doi.org/10.2307/2275546. doi:10.2307/2275546.
[23] G. Gottlob, C. Koch, Monadic datalog and the expressive power of languages for web information extraction, J. ACM 51 (2004) 74–113. URL: https://doi.org/10.1145/962446.962450. doi:10.1145/962446.962450.
[24] Panel on Past and Future of Computer Science Theory, *Christos Papadimitriou's interview*, by Giorgio Ausiello and Domenico Saccà, 2021. URL: https://drive.google.com/file/d/127ufvxvGqenCGtKZuw-woeL2Gpuk10kL/view?usp=sharing, accessed: 2021-09-09.
[25] J. van Leeuwen (Ed.), Handbook of Theoretical Computer Science, Volume A: Algorithms and Complexity, Elsevier and MIT Press, 1990.
[26] J. van Leeuwen (Ed.), Handbook of Theoretical Computer Science, Volume B: Formal

Models and Semantics, Elsevier and MIT Press, 1990. URL: https://www.sciencedirect.com/book/9780444880741/formal-models-and-semantics.

[27] C. H. Papadimitriou, Theoretical problems related to the internet, in: D. Du, P. Eades, V. Estivill-Castro, X. Lin, A. Sharma (Eds.), Computing and Combinatorics, 6th Annual International Conference, COCOON 2000, Sydney, Australia, July 26-28, 2000, Proceedings, volume 1858 of *Lecture Notes in Computer Science*, Springer, 2000, pp. 1–2. URL: https://doi.org/10.1007/3-540-44968-X_1. doi:10.1007/3-540-44968-X_1.

[28] C. H. Papadimitriou, Learning the internet, in: J. Kivinen, R. H. Sloan (Eds.), Computational Learning Theory, 15th Annual Conference on Computational Learning Theory, COLT 2002, Sydney, Australia, July 8-10, 2002, Proceedings, volume 2375 of *Lecture Notes in Computer Science*, Springer, 2002, p. 396. URL: https://doi.org/10.1007/3-540-45435-7_27. doi:10.1007/3-540-45435-7_27.

[29] E. Chastain, A. Livnat, C. H. Papadimitriou, U. V. Vazirani, Algorithms, games, and evolution, Proc. Natl. Acad. Sci. USA 111 (2014) 10620–10623. URL: https://doi.org/10.1073/pnas.1406556111. doi:10.1073/pnas.1406556111.

[30] Panel on Past and Future of Computer Science Theory, *Moshe Vardi's interview*, by Maurizio Lenzerini and Domenico Saccà, 2021. URL: https://drive.google.com/file/d/124D0IV2_H-Z3n4LGH4W1RvnbCHNnqW1Q/view?usp=sharing, accessed: 2021-09-09.

[31] C. Beeri, M. Y. Vardi, A proof procedure for data dependencies, J. ACM 31 (1984) 718–741. URL: https://doi.org/10.1145/1634.1636. doi:10.1145/1634.1636.

[32] M. Y. Vardi, The complexity of relational query languages (extended abstract), in: H. R. Lewis, B. B. Simons, W. A. Burkhard, L. H. Landweber (Eds.), Proceedings of the 14th Annual ACM Symposium on Theory of Computing, May 5-7, 1982, San Francisco, California, USA, ACM, 1982, pp. 137–146. URL: https://doi.org/10.1145/800070.802186. doi:10.1145/800070.802186.

AUTHOR INDEX